ON THE ROAD AGAIN with MAN'S BEST FRIEND

A Selective Guide to the West Coast's Bed and Breakfasts, Inns, Hotels, and Resorts that Welcome You and Your Dog

Dawn and Robert Habgood

A Dawbert Press Publication

Copyright © 1997 by Dawbert Press, Inc.

All rights reserved. No part of this book may be reproduced or transmitted in any form or by any means, electronic or mechanical, including photocopying, recording, or by any information storage and retrieval system, without permission in writing from the publisher.

First Edition

ISBN: 0-933603-04-5

Library of Congress Cataloging-in-Publication
97-066169

Editors: Pamela Gerloff
Jeanne Dooley
Cover Design/Line Drawings: Glynn Brannan

Manufactured in the United States of America
10 9 8 7 6 5 4 3 2 1

Contents

Introduction
v

California
1

Oregon
186

Washington
241

British Columbia
306

The Best of the Rest
B&Bs, Inns, Motels, and Hotels
369

National Hotel/Motel Chains
Web Sites/Toll Free Numbers
419

State and National Parks/Forests
Recreation Areas
Rules and Regulations
420

Helpful Numbers
423

Index
424

Introduction

Like millions of others in this country, we cherish our dogs and their unique place within our family. Our three golden retrievers are an integral part of our lives, and we find it difficult to leave them for extended periods of time. From the earliest days of our marriage, we loved to pack our bags and hit the road in search of new, undiscovered terrain. Each of the regions in our country is so distinct from the next, we thrive on the new pleasures and discoveries around each bend in the road. However, our unwillingness to abandon our pets soon clashed with our traveling spirits.

So fourteen years ago, we started including our dogs on weekend vacations. We began compiling lists of pet-friendly accommodations. Before long, we owned virtually every regional guidebook, but had unearthed only a handful of decent lodgings. Brochures could be deceptive, and the places were not always as nice as we expected. Our dogs did not care, but we did.

Finally, we decided to solve the problem ourselves and went "on the road again" in search of a variety of accommodations that would not only appeal to us, but to other people who wanted to vacation with their dog and who were seeking quality places with character, regional flavor, and charisma.

On The Road Again With Man's Best Friend is the result — a series of regional travel guides that are both selective and comprehensive. We include listings of all accommodations that accept travelers and their dogs; however, we highlight only those that merit special attention. For well over a decade, we have traveled to, and written about, places to stay with dogs, allowing us to provide readers with our personal, first-hand impressions. If we think a place is great, we let you know, and if there are areas that could be improved, we mention them as well. We are able to do this only because we make a point of personally visiting and revisiting each entry in each of our guides.

In looking through this book, prospective guests will discover a wide range of vacation destinations that should appeal to their senses, as well as to their pocketbooks. And remember, traveling with a dog can be a delightful experience, but it is also a responsibility that, if misused, can not only completely ruin your vacation, but can deny the opportunity for others to visit that establishment in the future.

No more droopy tails or noses that are out of joint — read the book, pack a bag, grab the dog, and head out on the road again with your own best friend.

How do we Select "the Best" Accommodations?

We choose our dog friendly entries by sifting through all the accommodations that welcome dogs in a given region, looking for places that exude a warmth, charm, and quality that even dog-less vacationers would find appealing. For instance, we include cottage communities that have been around for decades and, although some are rather rustic, attract a strong following of devoted patrons. Intimate B&Bs are added for their personalized attention and ambiance, while resorts are appealing for their diversity of activities. Elegant country inns and small hotels often top our list, but equally important are the family-run farms in the countryside.

Once selected, we pay an unannounced visit to the establishment, always maintaining our anonymity. This allows us, in most cases, to provide future guests with a concise overview and detailed descriptions that are not influenced by any type of special treatment. Because we accept no money from the innkeepers or owners, we can remain objective and you can feel more comfortable with our recommendations.

How to Use the Book — General Information

Each entry begins with pertinent general information about the establishment, including the address, telephone number, owner or manager's name, acceptable methods of payment, and number, type, and cost of the various guest rooms. We also describe any pet policies, and restrictions regarding children, if any. This section tells you more about each area we cover.

Types of Accommodations:

B&Bs: These are often private homes and guests should treat this experience as though they are staying with a friend. B&Bs are usually short on amenities and on-site activities, but long on personalized attention. You can expect to find comfortable guest rooms, a common area with perhaps a television and stereo, a Continental breakfast, and a warm and friendly host who genuinely enjoys having houseguests. B&Bs generally do not serve lunch and dinner.

Inns: Inns can sometimes be confused with B&Bs. Most have the same type of intimate feeling, but with just a few more rooms. One of the biggest differences is they have either a restaurant or can serve at least breakfast and dinner. Inns are more highly regulated and must meet the various state and national health and access codes. Also, they provide more activities and creature comforts than do traditional B&Bs.

Cottages: The cottage complexes we feature vary greatly in size, amenities, and activities — but even the most rustic are very clean and well maintained. Although the cabin or cottage might offer only the bare essentials, there is always plenty to do on the premises or in the nearby area. There is almost always a main lodge with a great restaurant. In some cases, all guests eat here, and in others they have a kitchenette that gives them the option of dining in their cottage or at the main lodge. We usually choose a cottage complex because it offers a picturesque setting with plenty of open space for both owner and dog to explore.

Hotels and Resorts: Smaller hotels often label themselves inns because they feel it makes them appear more intimate. We try to warn readers of this early and explain exactly what they can expect. Hotels usually have fifty or more rooms, and are located in large towns and cities. They traditionally deliver a full range of amenities, which could include an indoor or outdoor swimming pool, concierge services, multiple restaurants, a large staff, and a health club. Resorts, on the other hand, are generally located on the outskirts of popular tourist destinations or in the countryside. They offer a wide variety of guest rooms, as well as an expansive list of amenities, activities, and on-site programs.

Motels/Motor Lodges: These vary greatly in cost and features, although guests can usually expect standard rooms, a few amenities, and perhaps a restaurant either on the premises or nearby. They do not usually warrant a description, which is why we have provided our comprehensive appendix, "The Best of the Rest," which gives readers the names, addresses, and telephone numbers of these establishments.

Rooms:

Because guest rooms vary a great deal from one establishment to the next, it is important, when making a reservation, to be very specific about your requirements. Read the descriptions carefully and decide which amenities are important, whether they are a private bathroom, a bedroom with a big closet, a firm mattress, a room on the first floor, or a separate sitting room. Do you want a room that could be out of the pages of *House Beautiful*, or modern conveniences such as televisions or Jacuzzis? Please be specific.

Rates:

The range of rates listed with each description gives you a good idea of what to expect at a particular establishment. Many of these accommodations offer special discount packages, off-season rates, weekly rates, or interesting theme weekends. Always inquire about what's offered. Almost all of the accommodations listed in our books have "shoulder" seasons too — quiet times immediately before or after the busier times of the year. In addition to saving a little money, people traveling during these months will have a better choice of rooms, be able to eat out without making reservations, and enjoy sightseeing without all the usual crowds. Guests should also be careful to check if the rates are based upon single or double occupancy and if they include local taxes, fees, and so on.

Meal Plans:

We always indicate the type of meal plan offered by a given establishment.

Bed and Breakfast (B&B) rates includes a Continental *or* full breakfast.
* European Plan (EP) does not include any meals.
* Modified American Plan (MAP) includes both breakfast and dinner
* American Plan (AP) is all-inclusive, providing breakfast, lunch, and dinner.

Method of Payment:

While most of the smaller establishments would prefer to be paid in cash or by personal check, the larger inns, hotels, and resorts accept an array of credit cards, abbreviated as follows:
* AE - American Express
* CB - Carte Blanche
* DC - Diners Club
* DSC - Discover
* ENR - EnRoute
* JCB - Japanese Credit Bank
* MC - Master Card
* VISA - Visa

More and more, small establishments do not accept credit cards for the entire balance due, but will accept them for the initial deposit and perhaps a few nights.

Children:

We provide this category to inform prospective guests about any additional rules, regulations, or benefits concerning their children. Legally, people traveling with children cannot be discriminated against; however, we have found that there are certainly places where parents with young children would be uncomfortable. When we mention appropriate ages, it is at the request of the innkeeper or manager. More often, though, there are special discounts for young children and those under the age of 12 often stay free of charge when accompanied by a parent.

Dog Policies:

This category outlines any restrictions concerning guests' canine companions. These can include size requirements, the age of the dog, and management concerns such as leaving dogs alone in the room or walking them off the property. Some establishments offer an array of doggie treats for their canine guests, which could be homemade biscuits or extra dog beds and bowls.

Opening and Closing Dates:

Seasonal openings and closings are outlined in this section. Many of the accommodations are open all year; however, during the off-season it is fairly common for B&B owners or innkeepers to shut down and go on a short vacation. Always, call ahead to make sure the establishment is open when you are planning to visit.

Planning Your Trip

In our experience, and we are sure fellow travelers agree, planning ahead of time is the best way to avoid mistakes that make for unpleasant experiences. Here are some of our time-tested guidelines.

Traveling by Car - Planning & Precautions:

If you've never traveled with your dog before, think twice about setting out on a four-day vacation together. To ease the uninitiated dog into travel mode, start with a day trip, then an overnight or weekend jaunt, then book a longer stay somewhere. If your dog has a tendency to bounce around the car, you should buy a travel crate or a car gate — something to confine him to the rear of the vehicle so that you can drive safely.

Before you set out on your trip, take your dog for a leisurely walk. This will not only give him a chance to work off a little energy, but may also coax him into sleeping during the trip. Do not feed him or give him substantial amounts of water just before leaving. Once in the car, make sure the dog's area is either well-ventilated or amply air-conditioned. Plan frequent pit stops (every two hours or so), where you can exercise your dog on a leash.

Even if the day is not hot, a car can heat up to very high temperatures in very little time. Take the following precautions to prevent heat stroke, brain damage, or even death to your dog:

* Try to park the car in the shade and leave the window open enough to provide ample ventilation.
* Do not leave your dog for long intervals of time.
* Before you leave the car, fill his bowl with cold water to ease any effects of the heat.
* *Never leave a dog in a hot car!*

Traveling by Plane - Planning & Precautions:

There are certain legal guidelines and restrictions for air travel with a dog. The United States Department of Agriculture (USDA) and the International Air Transport Association (IATA) govern air travel for pets. The airlines themselves have regulations, and they differ, so you should always contact your airline in advance to review their procedures and requirements. Regardless of your carrier, these are important guidelines to consider:

* The dog should be at least eight weeks old and fully weaned.
* The dog cannot be ill, violent, or in physical distress.
* The dog should have all the necessary health certificates and documentation.
* The travel crate must meet the airline's standards and be large enough for the dog to lie down comfortably, turn around, and stand freely in it.

Try to book a non-stop flight, and take temperature into consideration: In the summer, try to fly at night when it's cooler; in winter, fly during the day, when it's warmer.

Plan your trip well in advance and make sure you are following all the rules.

What Your Dog Needs to Enjoy the Trip:

Just as you have to pack appropriately for your vacation, your dog will need certain items to ensure he has a comfortable and enjoyable time, too. These include:
* A leash and collar with ID tags.
* A few favorite toys, chew bones, and treats.
* A container of fresh drinking water from home.
* A supply of his regular dog food.
* Food and water bowls.
* A dog "bed," whether it is a towel, mat, or pillow, or the dog's travel crate.
* Grooming aids, including extra towels for wet dogs and muddy paws.
* Any medication your veterinarian has prescribed or suggested.
* The dog's vaccination records, especially a rabies certificate or tag.

When You Arrive:

Many of the hosts and innkeepers we have met have expressed their general concerns about guests who bring their canine companions. So that your visit is an enjoyable one, we wanted to list them so you can keep them in mind.
* Tape the local address and telephone number, indicating where you are staying, onto your dog's tag.
* Dogs should not be left alone in the bedroom unless in a crate or confined to the bathroom with some favorite toys.
* Dogs should be kept leashed while on the grounds. Always clean up after the dog, and try to walk him away from the main grounds.
* Use the dog's bedding to lessen the chance of damage to the furnishings. Never let your dog sit or lie on any of the furnishings.
* Because of health codes, dogs are generally not allowed in any area where food is made or served.

Disclaimer

Please keep in mind that the hosts, managers, and innkeepers are under no obligation to accept your dog. The management of each establishment listed in our guides has indicated to us, both verbally and in writing, that they have welcomed dogs in the past, had positive experiences, and will accept them in the future provided they are very well-behaved. Prior to publication, each of the establishments was contacted again to ensure they still welcome guests traveling with dogs. We cannot, however, guarantee against last minute changes of heart. Sometimes circumstances exist that require them to decline admitting our canine friends. They may already have a few dogs there, or be hosting a special function that would make it impractical for them to have your dog stay with you. *It is imperative you notify the establishment that you will be traveling with your dog when making your reservations.*

California

Apple Lane Inn

6265 Soquel Drive
Aptos, California 95003
(800) 649-8988, (408) 475-6868

Hosts: *Douglas and Diana Groom*
Rooms: *5 doubles*
Rates: *$95-150 (B&B)*
Payment: *DSC, MC, and VISA*
Dogs: *Well-behaved dogs are welcome in the Wine Cellar with approval and a $25 fee*
Children: *Welcome (cribs and cots are available)*
Open: *All year*

The small town of Aptos is just a few miles north of Carmel and overlooks the picturesque Monterey Bay. As we turned off the coastal highway, we passed by Cabrillo College before seeing the small sign pointing us toward the Apple Lane Inn. It led us to a gravel drive that climbed a gentle hillside, past a grove of apple trees and a small red barn. The barn, we learned later, houses the inn's cows, sheep, and horses. After parking the car under the large arbor, we followed a brick walkway leading to the quaint Victorian-style farmhouse — painted a soft blue gray and cream color. The house, and some of the outbuildings, date back to the 1870s. After stepping inside, we could see the antique character had been well preserved.

The main staircase, leading to the upstairs bedrooms, dominates the foyer. We bypassed the upstairs momentarily, and instead crossed over the Oriental rug, through an archway and into the living room. Along the way, we stopped to admire the grandfather clock, just one of the many heirlooms at the inn, along with family photographs and collectibles. As we walked into the living room, we noticed a player piano and an antique globe set upon the Oriental rug that covers the hardwood floors. On cold, foggy days we would be inclined to spend some time relaxing in here before the crackling fire. Best of all, guests may select from a variety of reading material on the floor-to-ceiling shelves that flank the fireplace.

There are all sorts of nooks and crannies at the Apple Lane Inn. One of the more intriguing is the upstairs sitting room. It achieves a garden room ambiance through the use of white wicker furniture and floral accents. Guests are welcome to watch television in here, use the telephone, or sample a snack from the sideboard. A small refrigerator is also available for guests to store their perishables. Several of the attractively decorated guest rooms are located just off the sitting room. One of the more popular is the Blossom Room, with its lace-covered canopy bed set against mauve and white walls. A skylight further brightens this charming space, and the private bathroom is equipped with a unique claw-footed tub. Pineapple, an especially sunny chamber, contains a high, four-poster pine bed. A green and peach-colored shell wallpaper lines the walls in Uncle Chester's Room. In here, the most notable feature is the 17th-century, Spanish four-poster bed set under a pressed tin ceiling. Up on the third floor, guests will find the rather spacious Attic Suite. One of its two rooms contains a pair of Belgian double beds, while the other has an antique handmade quilt covering a simpler queen bed. Both have teddy bears placed on top of their pillows. The painted floors covered with dhurrie rugs — coupled with the interesting eaves and charming floral wallpapers — make these chambers delightful spaces in which to spend some time. Best of all, these guest rooms have lovely views of the meadows and orchards. As of this writing, the attic rooms can be reserved separately; but the Grooms prefer to maintain them as a suite.

While the upstairs rooms are occasionally available to people traveling with their dogs, it is the Wine Cellar that is really ideal for canine companions. This chamber is located on the garden level. As guests descend the stairs, they will find old wine bottles placed in racks along the walls. We half expected to enter into a rather dark and damp cubby, but were instead surprised by the radiance of this lovely space. Beamed ceilings and rough hewn wood walls are nicely complemented by a burgundy-and-creme color scheme and a charming stained glass window. Terracotta floors combine with walls of dusty wine bottles to provide the ambiance of a true wine cellar. Red and white decorative tiles, natural oak barrels, and an array of casks once used for wine making add to the overall experience. The ell-shaped chamber also appears substantially larger through the use of mirrored alcoves and a mirrored armoire. Guests often gather around the dining room table, or retire to the small sitting area with television. Families with a child will appreciate the daybed set across the way from the four-poster, queen bed. Even the bathroom evokes images of the wine country, with its burgundy red bath and shower combination positioned alongside yet another stained glass window. Best of all, when dogs are craving an impromptu walk, guests need only walk through the room's private entrance to the gardens and the three and a half acres of orchards and fields.

Each morning, breakfast goers gather in the upstairs parlor and dine on a hearty country repast. This usually features fresh fruit and juices, a variety of egg dishes, a selection of muffins and fruit breads, and gourmet coffee blends. In the warmer months, the brick patio beckons. Guests settle into the wrought iron furnishings, or on the swing, and let the refreshing breezes waft across the hillside to them. In season, wisteria, trailing vines, and roses are in full bloom and emit a fragrance that is difficult to forget. Others enjoy the view from the rocking chairs on the wraparound front porch. In addition to visiting the menagerie of animals down at the barn, guests may also enjoy a game of horseshoes or croquet; or they might try their hand at the dart board or the variety of board games available inside.

Dogs should be quite happy at the Apple Lane Inn. Exploring the property or walking along the quiet back roads are two of the preferred outings. Guests can venture forth to the **redwood parks** nearby, or take an equally scenic drive to the **beaches of Carmel and Monterey**. First-time visitors may wish to sample the wines from the nearby Santa Cruz Mountain wineries, walk the **picturesque streets** of Carmel, or drive along the coast highway, in hopes of finding their own unique adventures along the way.

California

The Regent Beverly Wilshire

9500 Wilshire Blvd.
Beverly Hills, California 90212
(800) 545-4000, (310) 275-5200, Fax: (310) 274-2851

General Manager: *Peter O'Colman*
Rooms: *232 doubles, 68 suites*
Rates: *Doubles $255-385 (EP), Suites $425-4,000 (EP)*
Payment: *AE, CB, DC, DSC, ENR, JCB, MC, and VISA*
Dogs: *Well-behaved dogs are welcome with approval, must be leashed*
Children: *Welcome, children under 14 years of age are free (cribs, cots, high chairs, and baby-sitters are available)*
Open: *All year*

    Beverly Hills is one of Southern California's most infamous communities. The words *elegant* and *fashionable* don't even begin to describe a place where the beautiful people (and their dogs) outnumber trendy automobiles and lavish homes. Here, the lure of Hollywood mixes with the ultra rich, or those who aspire to it, who in turn attract tourists and Beverly Hills "wannabees." To the rest of us, this is all good fun and a terrific place to people-watch. What better place to do so than from The Regent Beverly Wilshire?

    Nestled along Wilshire Boulevard, right opposite Rodeo Drive, this grand dame dates back to 1927. Walter G. McCarty, a local developer, long ago realized the potential for this area and bought a large tract of land in this then sleepy town. He subdivided it, carving out a parcel from a defunct automobile racecourse for the site of the Beverly Wilshire. McCarty spared no expense con-structing his grand hotel, even going so far as to import stone and marble from Italy. The 1940s brought the addition of an Olympic-size swimming pool and championship tennis courts, where Pancho Gonzales was the head pro. By the 1970s, the once sleepy community had grown 30 fold, prompting the owners to add the Beverly wing. A spectacular domed *porte-cochère* connects the existing Wilshire wing with the new addition. In true Beverly Hills style, 38 lanterns from Edinburgh Castle were brought over to illuminate this space. Even more recently, the Regent underwent a $65 million restoration. But what is probably the most amazing aspect of the hotel's history is the fact that it has survived three major earthquakes (in 1933, 1971, and 1994), without suffering as much as a crack to its facade.

    Arriving guests may use the entrance facing Wilshire Boulevard, but for the full effect, it's best to enter the hotel off Camino Real through the massive, *verdis gris* Louis XV wrought iron and bronze gates. Bellmen quickly attend to guests' needs, giving new arrivals some time to explore the inviting common areas. Lobbies, especially in grand old hotels, can be impressive, and this one is certainly no exception. Hand-carved marble columns support equally elaborate arches. Walking across lustrous inlaid wood floors, past huge urns filled with potted palms, we came across antique tables fashioned with lavish fresh flower arrangements. Of course, this is, after all, Beverly Hills, and spotting the famous is always fun. As we were being escorted to our room, we passed by Terry Bradshaw, who was on his way to broadcast his football television show. He is just one of countless Hollywood personalities to stay here. Warren Beatty lived at the Regent for over 11 years, before purchasing his house. Director Gary Marshall, on the other hand, thought the Regent so epitomized a luxury hotel that he used it as the set for his movie, *Pretty Woman*.

Few guests will have the opportunity to stay in the suite featured in *Pretty Woman*, but we doubt the remaining options will prove disappointing. All bedrooms exude a sense of elegance, beginning with the pastel walls and ending with the luscious fabrics covering the classic furnishings. The entire effect is perfectly coordinated, without being overdone. The array of amenities is also impressive, including those in the marble bathrooms. Guests can bathe in the deep soaking tub or in the oversized glass shower, and wrap up afterwards in thick cotton robes. Three telephones, along with a small television and full array of toiletries, complete the list of amenities. Most intriguing of all is the room's personal steward. By pushing the call button, an attendant can be summoned to assist in everything from ironing or sewing to packing suitcases. Families appreciate the Regency Executive Suites in the Beverly wing. Two spacious rooms, connected by an archway, create an expansive suite. One room holds the king bed, and the adjoining space becomes a separate sitting area. Other favorites are the ell-shaped corner bedrooms overlooking Rodeo Drive — these may be smaller than the others, but the views are hard to beat.

It isn't necessary to swim in order to enjoy the exquisite swimming pool. We recommend putting on some dark glasses and settling in under one of the yellow umbrella tables on the sun deck, or sitting among the plethora of plants and spending some time people-watching. The pool's design was copied from Sophia Loren's pool in Italy. (Ms. Loren is a regular guest at the Regent.) In addition to a full fitness center, the spa offers massages, facials, manicures, and pedicures. Beverly Hills is obviously full of fabulous eateries; however, if convenience is important, then sample the fare at the Regent's fine restaurants.

The casual café (casual by Beverly Hills standards) overlooks Rodeo Drive; yet more intimate still is the club-like bar where marquetry-paneled walls and soft leather furnishings envelop patrons. Sipping high tea in the cavernous lobby is a truly memorable experience — surrounded by enormous columns and Louis XVI furnishings set against the backdrop of floor-to-ceiling Palladian windows. It is the dining room though, known simply by the same name, that continues to attract guests and locals alike. Chef Thomas Moran is famous for developing new twists to his already fine California cuisine. Diners might start with the duck and ginger ravioli; sautéed oysters with a zesty melon relish; or the open faced lobster tortilla with a roasted corn and tomato salsa. Entrées include the potato-crusted Chilean seabass with jumbo asparagus; wood-fired filet mignon with sautéed spinach and roasted new potatoes; or the veal tenderloin with morelles and a carrot-ginger sauce. For those who have trouble choosing, we suggest the Harmony in Three, which consists of three savory mini-portions presented in a tantalizing combination.

After a delightful meal, most are interested in stretching their legs. We can think of no better place than **Rodeo Drive**. The designer showcases, extravagant boutiques, outrageous art galleries, and fashionable cafés usually extend their hospitality to welcome a visiting dog.

But before heading out to hobknob with the locals, guests may want to know which breeds of dogs are in and out of vogue. According to the Rodeo Drive Committee, the dogs that are "out" are the regal breeds, such as German shepherds and standard poodles. The current "in" dogs are the "low-key" (their words, not ours) Wheaten terriers, Chihuahuas, and Jack Russell terriers. The "in" place to walk these dogs is the **Franklin Canyon Ranch** owned by the Santa Monica Mountains Conservancy. Situated just off Franklin Canyon Drive, visitors will find trails that wend through the hills and across land once owned by the Doheny Family. Another option that is currently "out" is a visit to **Roxbury Park** near Olympic Blvd., but we don't think your dog will mind bucking the trend and playing in this pleasant place.

Hotel Nikko Beverly Hills

465 South La Cienega Blvd.
Los Angeles, California   90048
(800) NIKKO-US, (310) 247-0400, Fax: (310) 247-0315

General Manager: Manfred Moennich
Rooms: 247 doubles, 53 suites,
Rates: Doubles $270-345 (EP), Suites $270-1,800 (EP)
Payment: AE, DC, JCB, MC, and VISA
Dogs: Dogs are welcome with approval and a $50 deposit
Children: Welcome (cribs, cots, and baby-sitters are available)
Open: All year

Los Angeles, being the metropolitan melting pot that it is, offers an accommodation option to suit just about any type of traveler. The Hotel Nikko is a place long on Japanese tradition and international style. It lies within a sleek seven-story edifice in the heart of Beverly Hills. Its facade is so unobtrusive that we ended up driving in circles around it before thinking to look up to the rooftops, where we finally spied the innocuous Hotel Nikko logo. Any stress we might have been feeling soon dissipated upon entering the tranquil lobby.

Our eyes immediately focused on the light and airy atrium, naturally brightened by skylights. Massive columns frame the intricate system of streams and fountains created from marble and stone. This serene Japanese garden setting tempted us to sit and stay awhile in the sitting areas formed by supple leather chairs and couches, and surrounded by rice paper screens. But as we walked across the black marble floors, a bellman appeared and escorted us to one of the registration desks. Lucky for us — the desks are almost as unobtrusive as the outside entrance, and if it hadn't been for this helpful staff member, we might have had a little trouble locating them as well.

The same elegant simplicity found in the public areas can be found in the guest rooms. These chambers, which are equipped with an array of electronic components, maintain a decor that make them as popular with business travelers as they are with vacationers. Each of the rooms is accented with rice-paper screens fronting the windows and an assortment of naturally stained woods and black lacquered furnishings. The overall look is as inviting as it is functional. In addition to the standard amenities one would expect to find in a four-star hotel, guests will also discover large oval writing desks complete with two-line speaker phones and voicemail. There are also deep soaking tubs, terry robes, and a full array of toiletries in the black and white marble bathrooms. But what travelers are most awed by are the state-of-the-art electronics. From the bedside table, guests have the ability to control the room temperature and lighting about the room, as well as manipulate the CD player, television set, and stereo system. Many of the guest quarters are very similar to one another and are equipped with either a king or a pair of double beds. Some of the more popular standard rooms are those located on the second floor; these feature patios that overlook the interior courtyard. Guests who wish to entertain in their rooms will be pleased to know that the expansive suites are fashioned with museum-quality pieces.

This may be Beverly Hills, but the restaurants and lounge both cater to an international clientele. Hana Lounge, situated alongside the central atrium, is a tranquil spot for enjoying a drink and music. Livelier still is the contemporary Pangaea restaurant, especially with the vibrant purples, pinks, and magentas that comprise much of the room's color scheme. During the daylight hours, passive sunlight flows through a wall of windows, but in the evening, clusters of high-tech glass rods suspended from the ceiling illuminate this bi-level dining room. The exquisitely prepared and presented foods combine the best of California and Japanese cuisines. Guests might start with the broken Nori waffle with Sevruga caviar and crème fraîche, crispy Alaskan spotted prawn with soba roll and miso-tahini dressing, or more simply, oysters on the half shell. Follow-up choices include the hoisin crusted rack of lamb with an Oriental ratatouille and sweet potato cakes; the coffee-lacquered filet

California

of beef in a creamy corn risotto; or the smoked salmon on a mint-infused couscous with warm oysters in a light oyster-cream sauce. The desserts are equally appealing. Roast banana tiramisu with caramel sauce; chocolate macadamia nut butter cream torte with Kona coffee sauce; and the seared spice Maui pineapple with coconut sorbet are just a few of the standard offerings.

Those in search of some activity may wish to take a dip in the lap pool, surrounded by an intimate cobblestone courtyard. Afterwards, guests may enjoy relaxing in the sleek, black chaise lounge chairs set under dove-gray umbrellas. There is also a full fitness facility on site, offering additional exercise opportunities.

When it is time to go shopping, though, we suggest taking Bowser over to Rodeo Drive and its lavish environs. Here, an assortment of intriguing and exclusive boutiques is certain to capture the imagination (along with most of one's money). Visitors may want to pick up a "Guide to Beverly Hills" from the Visitors' Bureau and take their dogs for **an interesting walk** through this star-studded community. Few formal parks or grassy areas in Beverly Hills roll out the red carpet for dogs; however one of the fashionable places to walk a dog is the **Franklin Canyon Ranch**, where there are miles of winding trails. Others may prefer to leave the city limits and venture over to Westwood around the **UCLA campus**, where they will also find plenty of green space to enjoy.

Cozy Hollow Lodge

P.O. Box 1288
40409 Big Bear Boulevard
Big Bear Lake, California   92315
(800) 882-4480 (CA), (909) 866-9694, Fax: (909) 866-2692

Owners: Mike and Mary Kay Allen
Rooms: 13 doubles and cabins
Rates: $49-195 (EP)
Payment: AE, DC, DSC, MC, and VISA
Dogs: Welcome with manager's approval, a $50 damage deposit, and a
     daily fee of $5. Cannot be left alone in rooms and must be leashed.
Children: Welcome (cribs are available)
Open: All year

The Cozy Hollow Lodge has been featured in this book since 1985, and for good reason. Their clean and unpretentious accommodations have always been a standout in Big Bear, and they remain an ideal retreat for anyone traveling with a dog. There are a wide assortment of cabin complexes in the area, most of which are nondescript and often offer less than acceptable accommodations. Michael has worked hard to distinguish his establishment from the rest. The attractive grouping of cabins is set just off the main boulevard behind stone walls and split rail fences. The green trim and matching window boxes provide a nice accent to these charming abodes. Most of the cabins were constructed over the last 12 years and provide many modern conveniences, including recently updated bathrooms and kitchens. Since our last visit, a spacious suite has also been added in the main lodge. Even with these changes, the low-key, inviting atmosphere remains, along with spaces that are as clean as they are inviting and comfortable.

Most of the cabins are set up for between two and four people and their four-legged friends, although there is one unit that sleeps six and another that can accommodate ten. Each configuration offers slightly different amenities, but guests can count on color cable televisions, telephones, and most importantly, fieldstone or brick fireplaces in all of the units. Those who want a fully-equipped kitchen may request one, as well as a Jacuzzi spa. Some guests may prefer one of the smaller bungalows or cabins offering just a refrigerator or wet bar. The largest unit can house up to ten people using the two good-sized bedrooms and the fold-out couches in the living room. We liked the full kitchen, which was spacious enough to easily tackle meal preparation for a group of this size. The overall decor remains appealing, with multi-colored quilts on the beds and contemporary prints and posters brightening the knotty white pine walls. The overstuffed couches and chairs are perfect to settle into after a long day on the slopes or trails, but in the summer months most people gravitate to the attached porches, which are inviting with their overflowing planters and window boxes brimming with annuals.

Children thoroughly enjoy the well-planned Creek Garden play area, situated in the center of the property, where they can climb and play for hours amid the wooden tree forts, slides, and ladders. Other recreational pursuits include a Ping-pong table, a few horseshoe pits, and an outdoor Jacuzzi. The lodge also has access to racquetball courts, aerobics classes, another Jacuzzi, and weight-lifting facilities at the Big Bear Lake Athletic Club.

Big Bear is an all-season resort offering a wide variety of outdoor activities. Many of these are within a short walking or driving distance of the lodge. The cabins are also convenient to skiing in the wintertime and to hiking, fishing, and boating during the summer months. Mike is very helpful in personalizing guests' expeditions — offering suggestions on great local restaurants and shopping alternatives or intriguing outings along little known hiking trails to secret picnic spots. Bucky and Baxter thoroughly enjoy taking part in these adventures, as there are plenty of **lakes, streams, and hiking** or cross-country ski trails to explore in the area. The **San Bernardino National Forest** also allows dogs in many areas, even if they are off-leash, provided they are under voice control.

California

Shore Acres Lodge
and Vacation Rentals

P.O. Box 110410
40432 Big Bear Boulevard
Big Bear Lake, California 92315
(800) 524-6600, (909) BIG-BEAR, 866-8200, Fax: (909) 866-1580
Internet: http://www.bigbearvacations.com

Owners: *Bob and Michele MacDonald*
Rooms: *11 cottages, 50 rental cabins*
Rates: *Cottages $65-200 (EP), Cabins $75-300 (EP)*
Payment: *MC and VISA*
Dogs: *Welcome with a $5 fee ("We love 'em")*
Children: *Welcome (crib and cot are available)*
Open: *All year*

    Big Bear and its environs are a doggie's delight as there is plenty of open space to explore and relatively few rules to limit a dog's fun. Summer visitors often come to sail, fish, hike, mountain bike, and perhaps head out on the newest attraction — the Big Bear Jeep Tours. Winter travelers can downhill or cross-country ski, of course, or they may ice skate and sled. A motel room isn't always the best option for those who need a little more space and some cooking facilities, or anyone with dogs who is planning to stay for awhile. For these travelers, the Shore Acres Lodge and Vacation Rentals is especially appealing.

    Situated amid tall pine trees overlooking the sparkling waters of Fisher Cove, this low-key resort dates back to the early 1900s. Charlie Potter originally owned this hunting and fishing lodge, formerly known as Potter's Camp. Since 1907, generations of guests have made the annual trek up to Big Bear Lake and the Shore Acres Lodge. We arrived one sunny fall afternoon to find the lake brimming with people enjoying various water-oriented activities. We drove through town, and around the lake where we came across the Shore Acres Vacation Rental office. After talking with them, we continued down Lakeview Drive to the lodge office.

    As we stepped out of the car, a wonderful old Golden Retriever strolled out to greet us, and led our pair of Goldens on a tour of the grounds. Some of the cottages are nestled along the edge of the lake, and others surround the swimming pool and spa. Each of these cozy, weathered shingle cottages has knotty pine walls framing windows overlooking either the water or the forest. Wall-to-wall camel colored carpeting is topped with comfortable armchairs and sleeper sofas situated to take advantage of these picturesque vistas, as well as the warmth of a crackling fireplace. Colorful photographs and prints of the area enliven each of the walls. Although the accommodations are decidedly fine, most people spend a good portion of their time outside around the lake. Children will find plenty to do here, as there is volleyball, badminton, horseshoes, and a playground right on the premises. The lodge's dock is also a favorite spot for beginning anglers to get the feeling for the finer points of casting.

Extended families and groups of friends, might opt instead for the houses and cottages available through the Shore Acres' Vacation Rentals. They offer everything from one-bedroom cottages and studio units to two-bedroom houses with expansive living rooms and decks. Obviously, each offers different views and proximity to the lake, along with individual amenities and furnishings (ask about the decor — new, old, or retro-1950s.) In almost every case, guests can expect to find well-maintained houses though, featuring fireplaced living rooms, fully-equipped kitchens, king and queen bedded rooms, and a host of modern amenities such as televisions, stereos, and barbecues.

We especially liked the accommodations near the water, as our dogs love to swim in lake water. However, do not dismiss the more remote, hillside units. We visited a couple of new houses that were fashioned with ultra-modern appliances and a wonderful array of amenities, along with a clean and fresh decor. We know it can be confusing when trying to pick the ultimate vacation house, therefore we recommend that prospective renters decide in advance what criteria is important for their particular group and work with the rental agent until they feel completely comfortable with all aspects of the arrangement. Stay flexible — there really are a few terrific accommodations that lie a little further from the lake that offer a higher standard of decor and amenities.

Our dogs are thoroughly at home in Big Bear, especially because they can travel off leash. In addition to meandering around the old-fashioned town center, our furry friends enjoyed the expansive **San Bernardino National Forest**. Here, there are great **hiking trails**, as well as miles of **cross-country ski trails** to explore during the winter months. **The lake** is also great fun for water-oriented dogs and ours are no exception. However, as much as we tried to fish, they kept leaping from the boat thinking they were supposed to retrieve our lures.... oh, well.

Meadow Lark Country House

601-605 Petrified Forest Road
Calistoga, California 94515
(800) 942-5651, (707) 942-5651, Fax: (707) 942-5023

Host: *Kurt Stevens*
Rooms: *7 doubles*
Rates: *$100-150 (B&B)*
Payment: *AE, DSC, MC and VISA*
Dogs: *Well-behaved dogs are welcome with approval*
Children: *Most appropriate for children over 14 years of age*
Open: *All year*

Calistoga is in the midst of Napa Valley, surrounded by lush vineyards, natural mineral springs, and mud baths. Somehow, the town has managed to escape much of the commercialism that has crept into other parts of the valley, making it a lovely, low-key place to visit. For years, we have searched for a truly dog-friendly inn in Calistoga; we finally found one this time at the Meadow Lark Country House. It lies on 20 acres of sprawling lawns, pastures, and woods in an estate-like setting, yet it is only minutes from the charming town center.

As we entered the grounds, we drove across a short bridge and then followed a winding gravel driveway up to the lovely guest house. While the adjacent stables and riding ring intrigued us, an exceptionally friendly woman, with cat in tow, paused with her gardening and graciously offered to show us around. We crossed the house's expansive front deck, lined with a medley of potted plants, before stepping into the cozy foyer. We instantly liked the feeling Kurt has created here with various pieces collected during his travels. An eclectic array of country furnishings combines with more contemporary pieces to achieve an elegantly understated, yet comfortable, decor.

We proceeded from the foyer, which doubles as a reception area, past a large pine chest and umbrella rack, into the large airy living room. Overstuffed sofas, set on an Oriental carpet, occupy this inviting chamber. Groups of English hunt prints line the walls, and family photographs grace the handsome side tables. The lines are clean, with well-placed accents such as ceramic rabbits, country antiques, and baskets of potpourri.

We were interested in seeing the rooms, and headed up the central staircase to find them. Along the way, we passed another grouping of framed equine prints. The guest bedrooms are all painted a sophisticated taupe, although accents vary from carved wooden duck heads and Oriental vases to Vogue prints and pine furnishings. A Shaker-style bed rests in Room Two, while guests staying in Room Four will find a maple bed surrounded by wrought iron and rattan furnishings, inset with green cushions. Berber carpeting covers the floor in the ell-shaped Room Three. We especially like the natural light that permeates this room, due as much to the wall of windows topping a low bookshelf as to the lightly stained pine furniture. A crisp, royal blue and white striped comforter accentuates the already fresh look in here.

Some of the most spacious and luxuriously appointed rooms lie in a wing off another house, situated just 100 feet further down the driveway. These chambers seem much larger than the others, due, in part, to the abundance of glass doors and windows in them, as well as their comparatively higher ceilings. Four-poster beds are the centerpieces in here, set on Oriental rugs and surrounded by pine armoires and dressers. Hunter green rattan armchairs surround glass-topped tables to create the intimate sitting areas. We especially liked the bedroom at the far end of the house, which not only has unparalleled views of the wooded valley, but also seems to be the most private of all of the rooms. Another popular guest chamber is privy to a private deck looking out toward a lily pond and a terraced garden.

In the morning, guests wake to a hearty breakfast. This may be enjoyed in the guest house's dining room, accented with a pine hutch brimming with decorative china. If the weather permits, this hearty repast may also be taken out on the front deck. Afterwards, guests are free to swim in the pool or, if they prefer, relax in one of the chaise lounges set under white umbrellas. Most interesting, though, is that the property is really the training and breeding ground for Kurt's European Sport horses. He trains them for jumping and dressage, and those who time it right can watch some of the horses in action.

Others also enjoy taking their leashed dog for a walk amid the lovely flower gardens. The **property is perfect for dogs** as there is plenty of natural space to explore. Those who decide to venture further afield with their canine in tow will probably be somewhat disappointed in the lack of green space in the surrounding area, as there are few parks nearby that welcome dogs. Two of the more unusual options, however, are the **geyser** and **petrified forests**. Both are on the outskirts of Calistoga, have picnic areas, and welcome leashed dogs. (Small fees are charged for human visitors.)

The Pink Mansion

1415 Foothill Blvd.
Calistoga, California 94515
(800) 238-PINK, (707) 942-0558
Internet: http://www.pink mansion.com

Owners: *Mr. and Mrs Toppa Epps*
Rooms: *4 doubles, 2 suites*
Rates: *Doubles $85-140 (B&B), Suites $125-175 (B&B)*
Payment: *AE, MC, and VISA*
Dogs: *Very well-behaved dogs are welcome with notice and approval*
Children: *More appropriate for older children*
Open: *All year*

Situated at the northern end of Napa Valley is the hamlet of Calistoga, known more for its mud baths and natural hot-water geysers than for its wine making. Don't misunderstand us as there are over 150 vineyards in the picturesque Napa Valley; they just don't happen to be in Calistoga. The Pink Mansion is one of the town's more intriguing places to stay. The 1875 mansion lies on land given to William Fisher by Sam Brannon, the founder of Calistoga. Mr. Fisher was quite influential and went on to establish Calistoga's first stagecoach line connecting the town with several mining sites around Mount St. Helena. Because Mr. Fisher enjoyed playing host to various dignitaries and important personalities, he made sure his home was fashioned with lavish interior spaces and fixtures that would impress his guests. The mansion's pink facade cannot be attributed to Mr. Fisher, however, but instead to another long-term owner, Aunt Alma Simic, who painted it a pastel pink in the 1930s. Aunt Alma is also responsible for the collection of angels and cherubs, as well as an eclectic assortment of Victorian and Oriental pieces placed throughout the inn.

The Queen Anne-inspired mansion, with its turret and gables, attracts attention even though it is set up a fairly steep hillside. A pair of stone pillars delineates the lane's entrance leading to the mansion. As we ascended the hill, we passed tiered gardens accented with flagstone pathways and dotted with benches. The walkway, fashioned with a white wrought-iron railing resembling a grape arbor, led us to the large front porch. Off in the distance we could hear the faint sounding of wind chimes in the breeze. A handful of white wicker chairs is interspersed with baskets of flowers and planters. We stepped into the foyer, which of course, glows with a lovely pink hue. Crystal chandeliers hang from the 12-foot ceilings, illuminating a mural of San Francisco and a handsome grandfather clock set off along a side wall. Victorian-style sofas and chairs create an intimate sitting area around the fireplace. The inn's most interesting feature is, without question, the indoor swimming pool, located to the rear of the house. Aunt Alma is also responsible for this addition, which was installed in 1959. The current owners, after addressing a few structural problems and dealing with some cosmetic work, were just in the process of reopening the pool again.

As one might imagine in a historic mansion of this era, each room is very different — both literally and figuratively. The breezy Garden Room boasts panoramic views of Mount St. Helena and the Palisades Mountains through antique speckled windows. The bathroom has a claw-footed tub set with brass fixtures. Families can reserve this space and the adjoining Forest Room, combining them to create a suite. The Forest Room's hunter green carpeting nicely contrasts with the salmon walls and mahogany furnishings. The Angel Room, as one might surmise, contains some of Aunt Alma's angels. Sleep in the antique brass bed, or curl up in the cozy window seat for an afternoon nap. A daybed can be used as part of the sitting area, or to accommodate an extra overnight guest. The Wine Suite is the nicest chamber of all, with its handmade 'Napa Bed' and, in keeping with that theme, an array of wine collectibles and antiques. Mauve hues are the backdrop of the Oriental Suite, which is decorated with Japanese and Chinese antiques. This is also a popular space for those with dogs, as there is a private entrance, along with a private deck. For guests who have a penchant for frilly surroundings, the Rose Room Suite is a perfect choice. Roses, or rose tones, are found in everything from the comforter cover and wallpaper to the fabric that is used for the balloon shades. A brick fireplace is a charming accent, while an oversized daybed that can sleep two people, provides a little versatility.

The Pink Mansion is an eclectic oasis in the Napa Valley, where guests can completely relax amid frilly Victorian splendor. On a hot summer's day many typically read on the porch or out in the gardens. In the evening, guests can move indoors to any of the parlors, and watch television discreetly set into an unobtrusive alcove. A leisurely walk into town with Bowser is also a popular option, as there are plenty of shops and restaurants to investigate. Well-trained dogs might be more interested in a bicycle ride along one of the **quiet back roads** that crisscross the valley. Those tempted to venture further afield should visit St. Helena, where they will also find a **pair of intriguing parks** to romp through. The more distant **Lake Berryessa** is another popular destination, especially with dogs who like to follow up their invigorating hike with a refreshing swim.

Cypress Inn

P.O. Box Y
Lincoln and 7th
Carmel-by-the-Sea, California 93921
(800) 443-7443, (408) 624-3871, Fax: (408) 624-8216
Internet: http://www.places to stay.com

Manager: David Wolf
Rooms: 33 doubles
Rates: $95-175 (B&B)
Payment: AE, DSC, MC, and VISA
Dogs: Welcome with prior notification and a daily fee of $17, extra pets are $10 with a two pet maximum
Children: Welcome (baby-sitters are available with notice)
Open: All year

Since the early 1900s, hundreds of famous artists and writers have been drawn to pristine and picturesque Carmel-by-the-Sea. Many relocated from San Francisco after the 1906 earthquake, lived in shacks on the beach, and ultimately built the storybook cottages that today give Carmel-by-the-Sea its unique personality. The residents of this tiny artists' colony undoubtedly would have preferred it if civilization had passed them by; however, this was not to be the case. As with many special places, Carmel-by-the-Sea was eventually "discovered;" yet through thoughtful planning it has managed to preserve its many intrinsic charms. In order to gain a true sense of the town, we recommend visiting during the shoulder or off-season, when visitors will be more able to walk along the quiet eucalyptus-lined streets, explore the gorgeous white sand beaches, and sample the array of intriguing shops and excellent restaurants.

Of course, the off-season is also terrific because the prices of accommodations are lower and a wider array of options are available. Some people come and seek solace in the inns, while others prefer delving into every facet of this village. For either contingency, there is the Cypress Inn. This Mediterranean-style inn, with its white brick facade and Spanish tile roof, is easy to spot and has been a Carmel-by-the-Sea landmark since 1929. As with many old inns, it has also been through its share of changes, some good and some less so. Under its most recent ownership (with Doris Day as a quiet partner), the inn was extensively renovated and re-imbued with a sense of grace and elegance.

This elegance has been recaptured, not built in, and extends to all areas of the inn, including the intimate reception area found within the foyer. From here, we are always tempted to meander into the expansive living room, a restful space that is brightened by coral-colored walls and a white-beamed cathedral ceiling. It also happens to be filled with a splendid assortment of English and American antiques grouped into intimate seating areas surrounded by floor-to-ceiling windows. Those with canine cohorts in tow should take a moment to peruse the stack of photo albums on one of the coffee tables. Inside, there are hundreds of photographs sent to the inn from grateful guests — the canine variety, that is. The whimsical photos are usually accompanied by anecdotal notes and praise for the inn's hospitality to humans and dogs alike. More esoteric reading is found in the built-in bookshelves brimming with a variety of literature. Whether selecting reading material or not, most guests enjoy settling down in front of the large fireplace or near the wall of French doors that look out toward the lovely courtyard.

Equally appealing are the spacious guest rooms that fit into the intriguing nooks and crannies of the inn. Each bedroom is furnished in a traditional style and decorated with delicate floral fabrics that coordinate with the canopied beds and draperies framing the windows. The soft tones that have been selected for the walls and carpets are enlivened by the natural light pouring in through the floor-to-ceiling windows. The live ficus trees and other potted plants and flowers lend a particularly homey feeling to these spaces. The specialty rooms are our favorites, as they have the most space, in the form of separate indoor sitting areas fashioned with a sofa and armchair, or verandas set up for outdoor dining. Whether staying in the wonderful old tower room with distant ocean views, or a cavernous, deluxe room with a wet bar and separate outside entrance, guests are certain to find each space enchanting.

After a restful night's sleep, a choice of morning papers awaits. In the library a wide variety of coffees, teas, and baked goods is served by an affable hostess. Some guests enjoy taking this repast in this cozy chamber (which is accented with framed posters and memorabilia from a number of Doris Day's movies); others prefer to visit the award-winning garden courtyard where sculpted hedges, potted plants, and flowering gardens are most impressive. Tea is served every afternoon in this courtyard. Although the weather can sometimes be cool and foggy, the courtyard's fireplace and white wrought iron furniture still draw plenty of guests and their canine companions. We especially like having an early breakfast, then taking a leisurely **stroll down to the beach** to watch the waves roll in, with Baxter and Bucky romping up and down the soft white dunes.

Early morning walkers will also enjoy the calm that prevails over the village. The tourists have not yet emerged and the only folks walkers are likely to come across are the locals, who are often enjoying a cup of coffee and visiting with friends. During the day (while canine cohorts enjoy an extended siesta) there are a number of other activities available nearby, such as a visit to Cannery Row and the Monterey Bay Aquarium or playing golf at the world famous Pebble Beach Golf Club. A journey along **17-Mile Drive** is almost required viewing, and there are places along the way to stop and exercise a dog.

Highlands Inn

P.O. Box 1700
Highway 1 (4 miles south of Carmel)
Carmel, California   93921
(800) 538-9525, (408) 624-3801, Fax: (408) 626-1574
Internet: http://www.highlands-inn.com

General Manager: David Fink
Rooms: 55 doubles, 90 suites
Rates: Doubles $265-350 (EP), Suites $325-600 (EP)
Payment: AE, DC, DSC, MC, and VISA
Dogs: Small dogs are welcome with approval and a one-time $75 fee
Children: Welcome (cribs, cots, and high chairs are available)
Open: All year

Carmel is renowned, both for its intimate small-town feeling and the picturesque views of Monterey Bay. Those who are especially enamored with the latter will thoroughly appreciate the truly spectacular vistas that can be enjoyed from the Highlands Inn. Situated four miles south of Carmel, this enchanting resort is perched high above the rugged cliffs on a hillside dotted with tall Monterey pines and weathered evergreens. Originally built in 1916, the inn formerly consisted of a handful of rustic cottages and a stone lodge. During its earlier years, many an artist, including Jack London and Ansel Adams, ventured down the quiet back country road leading to this coastal oasis. Then in the early 1980s, the inn was completely overhauled and many additional rooms and suites were added, as well as exquisite common areas and restaurants. With its $41 million renovation, the Highlands Inn now boasts of luxurious facilities and panoramic views from just about every vantage point.

A chilly gust of wind practically blew us into reception area of the Highlands Inn. But after ascending the stairs to the beamed-ceiling living room, where fires blazed in the fieldstone fireplaces, we instantly began to warm up. Guests were seated in the comfortable camel and teal green leather chairs, set around marble tables. They were either talking, listening to the pianist, or simply gazing through the wall of windows to the ocean below. A brass telescope, positioned in the corner of this area, might be focused on a pod of migrating gray whales or a handful of seal lions playing in the inlet. Natural elements, replicating those appearing just outside the windows, appear in the earth-toned fabrics, bleached woods, and stonework found throughout this and other rooms in the inn. The physical decor, coupled with the dozens of fine art photographs gracing the living room's walls, was quite stunning.

Equally impressive is the Pacific Edge restaurant. In addition to winning countless awards for its food preparation and wine collection, it also hosts the world renowned *Masters of Food and Wine* events. Floor-to-ceiling windows line the walls in this expansive chamber. Although it might seem early, we recommend dining here at sunset when a rainbow of soft colors accentuates the craggy coastline below. The chef even has a special Sunset Dinner menu. Both this and the standard menu change regularly, but appetizers can include the caramelized sea scallops with English peas, white corn and crispy onion rings; the Ossetra caviar; or the grilled quail on roasted garlic croutons with mushroom potato risotto and quail jus. Other popular choices include Chilean sea bass with a white bean vinaigrette, braised leaks, and bacon potatoes; honey roasted duck served on a cake of cabbage, chestnuts, and rice with an apple rosemary jus; or the pheasant and game specials. The inn's wine cellar received the prestigious *Wine Spectator's* Grand Award for its 28,000 bottles of fine wine. For those in search of a more relaxed atmosphere, with equally tantalizing fare, there is the California Market. This fun café is ideal for impromptu breakfasts, lunches, and dinners. Not only does this eatery provide delectable meals, but it also offers an expansive deck from which to further enjoy the invigorating salt air and the magnificent views of the Pacific Ocean.

We hoped the inn's designers had saved a few of these remarkable views for the guest rooms — and they had. These lovely chambers lie in the contemporary, shingled buildings perched against the hillside. To reach them, guests follow winding, flower-lined paths. The Spa Suites, fashioned with galley kitchens (complete with a fully stocked refrigerator) and oversized bathrooms (with separate showers and hydro-massage spa tubs) lie to the rear of these spaces. The incredible views are reserved for the expansive sitting areas and master bedrooms. Guests can settle in before the corner

California

fireplace, or, if the day is warm, open the sliding glass doors to the deck and relax in one of the chaise lounges. shoji screens create privacy between the two interior rooms, where fabrics, naturally-stained woods, and granite or stone tile accents reflect many of the surrounding elements. The Sur Rooms, while smaller than the suites, also boast an array of intriguing amenities, such as wood-burning fireplaces. Thoughtful bath extras, including oversized towels, terry robes, and a full complement of toiletries are welcome touches. In the morning, guests may start the day with freshly brewed Kona coffee, while waiting for room service to deliver a more elaborate breakfast creation.

The Highland Inn may feel like an inn, but behind the facade it is a full-service resort. On one level is the free-form pool, and on another, there are hot tubs. A concierge can make reservations for tennis, golf, or horseback riding. Guests' canine companions will thoroughly enjoy the extensive **walking and jogging trails** that line the property around the inn. Guests can also head a little further afield and investigate the array of intriguing **hiking and bicycling** opportunities found in and around Carmel and Monterey.

Sunset House Bed & Breakfast

Ocean Avenue and 7th Street
Carmel-by-the-Sea, California 93921
(408) 624-4884 (telephone and fax)

Owners: *Dennis and Camille Fike*
Rooms: *4 doubles*
Rates: *$130-190 (B&B)*
Payment: *AE, DSC, MC, and VISA*
Dogs: *Welcome with approval*
Children: *Welcome*
Open: *All year*

Our book contains many long-time favorite inns and bed and breakfasts, but we recently discovered a new, intimate B&B that we wanted to highlight. The Sunset House lies in the heart of Carmel, just two blocks from the sandy beach and crashing waves. Hosts Dennis and Camille Fike have owned the B&B since 1991, but we were newcomers to their charming cream-colored stucco house.

The two-story home is tucked behind mature plantings, shade trees, and lovely gardens. The entrance sports a handsome green door flanked by overflowing window boxes. The interior spaces are just as inviting as the exterior, making it all the more appealing to come home at the end of a busy day and just collapse for a bit in the sitting room. Here, Camille generally has a wonderful selection of hors d'oeuvres and a glass of wine waiting for her guests. Time it right and you can even watch the sunset over the ocean.

There are also several guest rooms in the house offering wonderful glimpses of the sea; however, their interior spaces can be just as appealing as their views. Guests often sleep under beamed, cathedral ceilings in antique-filled bedrooms. The elongated Hideaway Room is one of the more popular chambers, with its bay window revealing only trees and the sparkling Pacific. A queen-sized bed lies in the middle of the room, while a small siting area at another end features a brick fireplace. The kitchenette helped us create both the dogs' breakfast and evening snacks for ourselves. When the day is warm, step outside and enjoy the private deck.

The Patio Room, on the other hand, is ideal for those who want to get outside easily with their dogs and enjoy the lovely gardens. Bestowed with a traditional canopy bedstead, this good-sized coffee-colored chamber also holds an array of other fine furnishings. Especially noteworthy are the highboy and a camel-backed sofa. Read one of the magazines on the coffee table, or better yet, enjoy the crackling fire in the corner fireplace. Brass sconces help illuminate this cozy space at night, while passive sunlight bathes the room through a wall of windows during the day. Best of all, guests can look forward to a rejuvenating soak in the whirlpool tub at the end of the day. The ocean views in the North Room are lovely, but the focal point is a Hans Christian Anderson king-sized bed once used at the Grand Hotel in Denmark. Today, a pretty floral comforter tops the bedstead, which is flanked by a striped loveseat, a Colonial sewing table, and a Queen-Anne dresser. The forest-green decor, warmed by rosy hues, is even richer at night when the windows are shuttered and the fireplace is glowing.

The West Room maintains a cottage ambiance with its cathedral beamed ceilings and a brick fireplace enhanced by the French country decor. Guests can relax on either the appealing chaise lounge or the wing chairs that are surrounded by French antiques. Potted plants set into a wicker stand help create the comfortable homey mood. The South Room also is decorated in green and rose tones and provides ocean glimpses. This chamber is highlighted by a hand-crafted iron bed and an equally unusual Victorian day bed. Relax in the pair of overstuffed chairs set near the corner fireplace.

The Fikes live across from the inn, which allows them to be accessible to their guests without being intrusive. Each morning finds a breakfast tray delivered to your room, stocked with freshly baked muffins, granola, juice and fruit. Guests can dine with their canine friends in the privacy of their own suite before heading out for a day in Carmel.

One of the most obvious puppy pleasures is an early morning walk down to **the beach.** This outing can take only a minute or two, but we also can spend endless hours enjoying this ever-changing space. Drive down to **Big Sur** for the day and explore the trails that follow the rugged shoreline. This section of the coast is a far more wild expanse of land than the area around Carmel, and gives visitors a rare glimpse into a well-preserved and unspoiled part of this state.

Quail Lodge

8205 Valley Greens Drive
Carmel, California 93923
(800) 538-9516, (408) 624-1581, Fax: (408) 624-3726
E-mail: qul@peninsula.com

General Manager: *Michael Hoffman*
Rooms: *84 doubles, 12 cottage suites, 4 villa rooms*
Rates: *Doubles $205-265 (EP), Cottages $295 (EP), Villas $560-930 (EP)*
Payment: *AE, DC, MC, and VISA*
Dogs: *Welcome*
Children: *Welcome (cribs, cots, and baby-sitters are available)*
Open: *All year*

The Quail Lodge lies on ten picturesque acres in the scenic Carmel Valley, just ten minutes from Carmel-by-the-Sea. This acreage was once owned by the Carmel Valley Dairy, but in the late 1960s the current owner, and 30 other residents, purchased this expansive tract of land from Dwight Morrow and Charles Lindbergh. Eventually the dairy business failed, but the new owners wanted to ensure that the land's natural beauty would be kept intact. To that end, they devised a conservative plan that called for the development of a golf course, a handful of lakes, and a small, intimate resort. Their foresight is appreciated by visitors today, who are usually struck by the tranquillity and serenity of this truly special retreat. The low-lying lodge and its assorted outbuildings are surrounded by ten small lakes, lush golf course fairways, and numerous walking paths.

Aside from these beautiful natural surroundings, the owners of the Quail Lodge have devoted equal attention to both the public and private room design and decor. One of our favorite spots remains the lodge's inviting library, where overstuffed sofas set around a stone fireplace are almost as much of a draw as the lovely vistas of the sparkling lake and verdant fairways. These views are not exclusive to the main lodge, as there are equally lovely vistas from almost all of the guest rooms. A golf cart transports guests from the lodge to their cottage rooms.

Along the way we passed Mallard Lake. Our canine cohorts were intrigued with "Cooter," the only duck who is still in residence here. Later on, when we explored the grounds, we discovered other water fowl on the resort's many lakes and ponds. Along with the resident cinnamon teals, golden eyes, widgeons and wood ducks, a large population of Canadian geese are now living on the ponds. The management, hoping to send some of the geese on their way, were told to introduce swans to the ponds. They did — and much to their surprise, the geese and the swans have become fond of one another. While the fowls' continued presence may be somewhat of a headache for the groundskeepers, the guests feel as though they have stumbled on an Audubon sanctuary.

The general configuration of the guest chambers is unique, with four bedrooms set around a central living room suite. Guests may reserve a single bedroom, the central cottage suite, with a bedroom and the fireplaced living room, or any combination of these spaces. These cavernous chambers vary in layout, although all are open and have a feeling of spaciousness, with high ceilings inset with skylights, sliding glass doors, and ample recessed lighting. The soft earth tones and rattan furnishings, coupled with brass and marble accents, further the sense of elegant simplicity. What many fine hotels consider to be additional amenities, the Quail Lodge views as standard. Four-poster and canopy beds are framed by marble-topped bedside tables. The cottage fireplace suites are the best choice for true luxury, as they are appointed with full wet bars and stereos nestled unobtrusively into the living rooms' built-in alcoves. Some of the more notable accoutrements are thick cotton terry-cloth "Quail Lodge" bath robes, along with a full complement of toiletries.

Anyone interested in the most luxurious and expansive private accommodations should consider the Executive Villa. Architecturally, the vaulted ceilings and the interesting use of brick, stone, and redwood create a unique and appealing environment. This combination, along with the black lacquered furniture, silk screens, and the Japanese standing vases all reflect a touch of the Orient. Form and function combine in the pairing of two-bedroom suites, along with a living room filled with additional sumptuous furnishings. In addition to being warmed by a fireplace, the room contains a full wet bar, a VCR, and a stereo. Best of all, there is also a private brick patio with a hot tub that is surrounded by a profusion of flowering plants.

At registration, all guests receive a club courtesy card giving them access to the two swimming pools, the four tennis courts, golf course facilities, and miles of hiking trails. The lodge now has a fitness pavilion offering everything from massages and spa facilities to herbal wraps and a juice bar.

The Covey is the hotel's premier restaurant. Although the fare changes seasonally, Beluga caviar, oysters on the half shell, and rainbow trout cured in brandy, lemon, and dill are usually on the menu. The specialties of the house include the sole with a lobster stuffing, drizzled with a spinach and shallot reduction; California king salmon in a mustard crust on bay shrimp; and the Santa Barbara abalone, dipped in a light egg coating with lemon butter.

After a dinner of this dimension, guests may be inclined to go wake up the dog and head off for a short stroll across the **wooden bridges**, on through the **lush gardens**. During the day, there are more extensive areas to explore on other **trails owned by the lodge**. The detailed maps provide legends depicting which trails are easy, medium, or more difficult. Although there are over 85 species of flora and fauna to enjoy, canine explorers will probably be more interested in the 100 or so varieties of wildlife that also appear along these hiking trails.

Vagabond's House Inn
Lincoln Green Inn

P.O. Box 2747
Fourth and Dolores Streets
Carmel-by-the-Sea, California 93921
(800) 262-1262, (408) 624-7738, Fax: (408) 624-1243

Owner: *Dennis LeVett*
Rooms: *11 doubles, 4 cottages*
Rates: *$85-185 (B&B), Cottages $145-185 (EP)*
Payment: *AE, MC, and VISA*
Dogs: *Welcome with approval and a daily fee of $10*
Children: *Vagabond's House is not appropriate for children under 12 years, but the Lincoln Green Inn does is appropriate for children*
Open: *All year*

Vagabond's House Inn and its sister property, the Lincoln Green Inn, have always been two of our favorite small inns in Carmel. Quaint Tudor-style cottages surround an intimate flagstone courtyard at the Vagabond's House Inn. Cascading waterfalls set the tone for this tranquil spot that is shaded by a massive oak tree and lined with rhododendrons, camellias, ferns, and array of flowering plants. A tiny reception area is filled with a cornucopia of objects that prove equally intriguing. Even after all these years, we are still drawn to the extensive collection of toy soldiers, antique guns, toy planes, model cars, and Big Little books. Antique clocks tick, and on cool days a fire is crackling in the corner fireplace. Guests may wish to linger a moment and take a closer look at a copy of Don Blanding's poem, *Vagabond's House*, for which the inn is named.

For all its whimsy and quaintness, the Vagabond's House Inn's guest rooms are spacious, with plenty of corners where a dog can curl up and sleep. Some rooms have inviting window seats with garden views, along with boxed-beamed ceilings and wood-burning fireplaces. Others are brightened by sunlight streaming through multiple-paned windows. The decorative themes also vary, ranging from subdued Victorian prints and country cottage florals to hunt or nautical motifs. We especially like the crisper lines and more elegant decor found in many of the most recently updated guest rooms. One of our favorites — perhaps because of the brick fireplace — has white-beamed ceilings and an appealing combination of shutters and chintz balloon shades at the windows. The same chintz is used for the quilted spread and throw pillows covering the bed.

Aside from the visual appeal, there are also the conveniences of a television, kitchenette (with microwave), and a tiled bathroom. Dennis provides decanters of sherry, coffee makers and gourmet coffee, vases of fresh flowers, bowls of fruit, and small libraries of books and magazines. Each morning, a delicious breakfast is served either *en suite* or out on the courtyard. This is a true European-style breakfast consisting of eggs, cereal, muffins, Danishes, fresh juice, and coffee or tea.

Walking is often the preferred pastime for guests, especially after a hearty morning meal, and there are plenty of areas to investigate. We suggest following the side streets down to Dennis' other property, the Lincoln Green Inn, which is located at Carmelo between 15th & 16th Streets.

"A touch of the Cotswolds" best describes the Lincoln Green Inn. These charming cottages combine the ambiance of the English countryside with Carmel's distinctive beauty. Four English-style cottages rest behind a white picket fence in a lovely residential neighborhood, Carmel Point. Well away from the center of town, these white clapboard and forest green-shuttered abodes lie amid mature plantings and bright flower gardens. Fragrant flowers also line the walkways to the cottages and overflow from the decorative window boxes.

Each cottage is named after an English storybook character: Friar Tuck, Maid Marian, Little John, and, of course, Robin Hood. Comfortable furnishings, that include white wicker, naturally stained rattan, and traditional reproductions complement the attractive decor. Floral accents illuminated by brass and wrought iron lamps, along with chandeliers, accentuate the inviting cottage ambiance.

Dennis stocks each cottage with libraries of books and magazines along with decanters of sherry. He creates decorative interest with small framed prints and paintings, potted plants, and dried wreaths. When the cool ocean breezes blow and the fog rolls in over Carmel, there is no better spot to be than in the spacious living room in front of the beachstone fireplace, sipping sherry and reading a good book.

These well designed cottages contain separate bedrooms, good-sized living rooms, and fully-equipped kitchens. Decks create additional outdoor living space amid the quiet surroundings, while supplying distant views of the Big Sur Mountains. The kitchens add a degree of self-sufficiency for cottage guests, allowing them not only to whip up a snack for their canine companion, but also to prepare a more elaborate meal for themselves. Guests may create their own breakfasts, or eat at the Vagabond's House.

During the day, we like to visit the confluence of the **Carmel River** and the beautiful **River Beach** with our dogs. This is an ideal spot for impromptu picnics or leisurely walks. Our dogs are especially fond of both the 4,500-acre **Garland Ranch Regional Park** and the **Carmel River State Beach**. Whatever excursion gets your dog's tail wagging, we are certain that everyone will thoroughly enjoy their stay at the Vagabond's House Inn or at the Lincoln Green Inn.

California

Wayside Inn

P.O. Box 1900
Mission and 7th Streets
Carmel, California 93921
(800) 433-4SEA, (408) 624-5336, Fax: (408) 626-6974
Internet: http://www.innsbythesea.com

Manager: Tony Fiano
Rooms: 22 doubles and suites
Rates: Doubles $95-125 (B&B), Suites $130-240 (B&B)
Payment: AE, DSC, MC, and VISA
Dogs: Welcome with approval
Children: Welcome (cribs, cots, and baby-sitters are available)
Open: All year

The Wayside Inn is an ideal choice for people who want to be within walking distance of Carmel's village and who do not really require all the quaintness of a traditional inn. This Williamsburg style ivy-covered brick building bears a faint resemblance to a motor lodge. However, the facade is enhanced with charming window boxes and surrounded by mature plantings. The interior spaces are equally pleasing. We were a little surprised to find them not only spacious, but also tastefully decorated and furnished. Updated since our last visit, the rooms now contain reproductions of early American antiques.

While the most sought-after chambers face the quiet side street, all have either subtle grasspaper or floral prints papered above the pine-paneled wainscoting. An informal country ambiance is achieved with the use of wicker and light pine, coupled with wing chairs and camelback sofas, set on top of Berber carpeting. All bathrooms are modern and come equipped with an additional vanity and a nice complement of fragrant soaps and thick cotton towels. The mini-suites are a great option, because they are designed with extra space to accommodate a sitting area with a sofa bed and a fully-equipped kitchen. Families with lots of children and a dog might prefer the most spacious accommodations. These not only provide many of the same features as the mini-suites, but also contain two bathrooms and a brick fireplace.

Mornings begin with a newspaper and a Continental breakfast of muffins and coffee or tea delivered to the room. More substantial offerings can be procured from several bakeries and restaurants within walking distance of the inn. The Wayside Inn is a good choice for those with dogs, as guests may park their car right in front of the room to more easily load and unload their canines and other paraphernalia. Separate outside guest room entrances also ensure easy access for owners and their dogs, who might need to take walks during the late evening or early morning hours.

Carmel is a wonderful town to **explore by foot *and* paw**. Canines and humans alike will have a terrific time walking the charming back streets or heading down to the **pristine beach**. With a leashed dog, visitors can window shop along Ocean Avenue. If your dog is content to sit outside the store while you shop for a few minutes, she will certainly receive plenty of attention from people passing by. Another point of interest that guests and their dogs should consider visiting during their stay is the **Point Lobos State Reserve**, a 1,300-acre park situated on the coastline. **Big Sur** is another favorite destination, located just a half hour south of Carmel. While your dog might not appreciate the spectacular crashing waves, she will relish the opportunity to run among the pines. For those who are visiting between October and March, look for the orange and black Monarch butterflies that take up residence in the Monterey pines. Some of the best butterfly viewing can be found on **Ridge Road**, off Lighthouse Avenue in Pacific Grove.

Valley Lodge

P.O. Box 93
Carmel Valley, California   93924-0093
(800) 641-4646, (408) 659-2261, Fax: (408) 659-4558
Internet: http://www.mry.infohut.com/valleylodge/home.htm

Hosts: *Peter and Sherry Coakley*
Rooms: *14 doubles, 5 suites, 12 cottages*
Rates: *Doubles $99-119 (B&B), Suites $139-329 (B&B),*
   Cottages $155-249 (B&B)
Payment: *AE, MC, and VISA*
Dogs: *One dog per room, with a $10 daily charge*
Children: *Welcome (cribs, cots, and baby-sitters are available with notice)*
Open: *All year*

Carmel-by-the-Sea and Carmel Valley are two distinct communities, both in appearance and in panache. Carmel-by-the-Sea remains an artists' colony with narrow shaded streets, charming shops, and picturesque ocean views. Carmel Valley is far more open — a 40-square-mile expanse of gently sloping hills dotted with oak trees. Walk to the top of any hill and the sweeping panoramas reveal expansive resorts, golf courses, and well spaced contemporary homes. For the most part, the people behind the developments have tried to keep the natural beauty and historic ambiance of the valley intact. Those who like wide open spaces and plenty of recreational options should consider the Valley Lodge. After leaving the coastal highway, visitors follow the main road some 11 miles up Carmel Valley until they reach an intimate rustic redwood complex that seemingly blends in with the lush hills.

The charming reception area, which is accented with country furnishings and lovely flower arrangements, sets the decorative tone for the rest of this resort. The room's vaulted ceiling is reinforced with rough-hewn beams and, on cooler days, a fire is often blazing in the stone fireplace. The back wall of windows reveals the gardens, although we decided to go outside and walk along the flower and ivy-lined paths to experience them first hand. We then strolled past the lily pond and over a small wooden bridge toward the two-story buildings situated further up the hillside. These well-designed abodes offer views of either the fertile, rolling hills or the swimming pool. The bedrooms were always appealing, yet they were dark. Fortunately, the Coakley's have spent a great deal of time and energy refurbishing the guest rooms. A cream-colored stain now highlights rough-hewn beamed ceilings that were once brown.

Depending upon guests' needs, there are a variety of accommodations, ranging from comfortable doubles with decks or patios to spacious suites and cottages with fireplaces, wet bars, living rooms, and private decks. Regardless of one's ultimate choice, each room is individually decorated, and has a distinct country quality to it, due in part to the pine and oak furniture. The bedsteads, which are often fitted with either floral coverlets or colorful handmade quilts, range from Murphy beds to white iron or cherry finial bedsteads. Televisions are often concealed in pine armoires or in stained cabinets, while microwaves and mini refrigerators are found amidst the wet bar alcoves. Fresh flower arrangements, picked from the lodge's gardens, are also evident in each of the bed chambers. Those traveling as a group or as a family often reserve adjoining units centrally located near the swimming pool and hot tub. We also like the inconspicuous fountain whose splashing water is the perfect backdrop for drifting off to sleep at night. Guests searching for a little more independence and space may wish to consider reserving a cottage. The one and two-bedroom cottages have more extensive "resort kitchens," good-sized living rooms with fireplaces, and private patios or decks with hibachis.

Those who do not want to prepare their own morning meal will be pleased to know there is a substantial Continental breakfast available to guests, complete with a daily newspaper. People who prefer to jump start their day with activity can work out in the 60-foot swimming pool or in the fitness center and then take a sauna or hot spa. The game room boasts less rigorous, but no less stimulating activities.

Dogs are likely to prefer the nearby **Garland Ranch Regional Park** or the **Los Padres National Forest**. Both offer miles of trails that provide a terrific morning outing for man and beast. As the afternoon sun heats up and the fog gently dissipates, guests may enjoy visiting the **sandy beaches**, both in Carmel-by-the-Sea and just to the south. **Carmel-by-the-Sea's town beach**, located at the base of Ocean Avenue, allows canine visitors to romp around without a leash, while beaches situated outside the town's limits almost always require that dogs be leashed.

Inn at Harris Ranch

Route 1, Box 777
Coalinga, California 93210
(800) 942-BEEF, (209) 935-0717, Fax: (209) 935-5061

Owners: *The Harris Family*
Rooms: *123 doubles, 28 suites*
Rates: *Doubles $86-95 (EP), Suites $98-225 (EP)*
Payment: *AE, CB, DC, DSC, MC, and VISA*
Dogs: *Welcome with a $10 cleaning fee*
Children: *Welcome (cribs, cots, and high chairs are available)*
Open: *All year*

Harris Ranch — for years, anyone traveling Interstate 5 anticipated stopping here, as they knew incredible food, especially the famous beef dishes, awaited them. This ranching family's California roots date back to well before the completion of the interstate, to the early 1900s when J.A. and Kate Harris moved to the Imperial Valley and bought a tract of land. For a number of years they operated a cotton gin here, before deciding to buy a ranch in the San Joaquin Valley. Following in his parents' footsteps, their son, Jack, and his wife started their own ranch nearby in 1937. Today, this is *the* Harris Ranch. They built a small restaurant and gas station in the 1970s to service people traveling along the interstate. Harris Ranch's reputation grew along with the increasing number of travelers who pulled in to refuel their cars, and themselves. Harris Ranch now boasts a thriving 18,000 acre ranch, an inn, numerous restaurants, a gourmet country store and yes, even its own landing strip. People no longer simply stop here on junkets between Northern and Southern California; they make a special trip to this little oasis — and these days it is worth the trip. Guests come by car and private plane to eat dinner and pick up a few choice cuts of beef to take home with them (more than a few celebrities touch down at the Harris Ranch to eat). It might not be the first place one thinks of when planning a vacation, but it is definitely the first place we think of when looking for a terrific, albeit out of the way, restaurant with equally fine lodgings.

We hadn't been to the Harris Ranch in years, and remembered it more as a gas station and small restaurant. In years past, we frequently drove from San Francisco to Los Angeles, sometimes at the height of the summer, and looked forward to stopping here so our dogs could stretch their doggie legs. In the intervening years, Jack's son John and his wife Carole "grew the business." They built an expansive and attractive Spanish hacienda-style complex, with pink adobe walls and red tile roofs. We arrived on a hot afternoon, and decided to save the restaurants for later, opting instead to investigate the guest rooms.

We drove to the inn, a sprawling building whose main entrance is flanked by French doors topped by Palladian windows. As we stepped through the doors, a cool breath of air met us (Coalinga can be HOT). Mexican tiled floors led through this space toward a small sitting area set around a carved stone fireplace. The furnishings are traditional in style — with a western flair. The couches are covered in cowhide — some are black and white spotted and others are chocolate brown. We liked the marble topped table supported by a small carved steer. This is southwest decor at its finest. Some might linger in this cool oasis, but we continued through yet another set of French doors and out to the semi-circular terrace that overlooks the Olympic-sized swimming pool.

The guest rooms are located in four matching Spanish-style buildings set around the pool amid palm trees, bushes, and brilliant flower gardens — a true oasis. The appealing rooms vary in tone with walls painted in pale hues of pink, blue, green, or yellow. Natural pine furnishings consist of two-poster beds, single drawer bedside tables, and dressers. The beautiful floral fabrics reflect the rooms colors, and are nicely coordinated with the quilted bedspreads, dust ruffles, and full length draperies framing the clear view glass doors. The entire effect is reminiscent of the country — western-style. Standard amenities include direct-dial telephones, cable television, and bathrooms fully stocked with toiletries.

Families might want to select the oversized suites with pairs of queen beds and a fold-out sofa bed. The newest rooms are in the three-story Belmont Wing that overlooks a small courtyard complete with a Jacuzzi. The best rooms are in the Del Mar or Bay Meadow wings because of their private patios or balconies. Some guests request the second floor rooms, with a balcony, so they can leave their doors open and not worry about their dog running off and perhaps taking a plunge into the pool. Even with this possible hazard, we prefer the ground floor units as it is much easier for us to walk our dogs.

The grounds are a wonderful place for a dog to explore; however, ours usually follow their noses and lead us back toward the restaurant complex. The Harris Ranch has a restaurant to match just about anyone's palate, with the most formal being the Fountain Court Dining Room and the most casual the Ranch Kitchen. While patrons wait for a table (the restaurants are usually packed), many gravitate to the circular bar where carousel horses and double-tiered wagon wheel chandelier are suspended from the vaulted ceiling. Craving a casual setting? Then try the Ranch Kitchen; where there are always hearty homemade soups, sandwiches, and Mexican offerings prepared with the famous Harris Ranch beef. If guests are planning to leave that afternoon, the staff will also pack it to go. At night, we prefer the Fountain Court with its Mexican tiled floors, and white painted tables and chairs set against a backdrop of whitewashed walls. A series of arches lined with stenciled garlands of ivy accentuates this courtyard setting.

The Harris Ranch has a terrific executive chef, Kelly Mullarney, who grew up in the area and worked at the ranch as a youngster. After cooking for some other fine restaurants, he returned and created a menu that emphasizes the local offerings. Contrary to popular belief, the Harris Ranch does not only produce great beef from their 100,000 heads of cattle, but also grows a wide variety of produce including carrots, lettuce, garlic, onions, tomatoes, melons, oranges, lemons, almonds, and walnuts. Kelly created a Farm Report to inform those dining with him what is currently in season. Their Autumn Farm Report featured hard squash, green beans, and sweet corn along with strawberries, apples, and fresh herbs from their gardens. A New York striploin might be sautéed with a Jack Daniels mushroom sauce; the filet tenderloin stuffed with garlic, spinach and mushrooms; and the top sirloin served in an enchilada with Spanish rice and black bean chili. Prime rib cuts can be as much as 20 ounces — plenty for people and their beasts.

During the day, visitors will find a number of diversions to keep them busy. One popular area is the 35-acre **Coalinga Mineral Springs park**. For the more adventurous, there are nearly 10,000-acres known as the **Coalinga Mineral Springs Trail**. The trail part is really for horses, and the rest of it an unspoiled natural setting. The Harrises also own a 450-acre horse farm, where they breed thoroughbred race horses. Stop by for a visit, and then perhaps head into the sleepy town of **Coalinga**, whose origins can be traced back to the Southern Pacific Railroad and coal mining industry. Be prepared though, because aside from Coalinga and the hamlet of Hanford, the Harris Ranch Inn is really set off by itself. For those who just want to settle in for the weekend, there is swimming, a Jacuzzi, and more than enough appetizers and entrées to keep everyone, including the dogs, busy for quite some time.

Loews Coronado Bay Resort

4000 Coronado Bay Road
Coronado, California   92118
(800) 81-LOEWS, (619) 424-4000, Fax: (619) 424-4400
Internet: http://www.loewshotels.com

General Manager: *Kathleen Cochran*
Rooms: *403 doubles 37 suites*
Rates: *Doubles $195-245 (EP), Suites $395-1,500 (EP)*
Payment: *AE, DC, DSC, MC, and VISA*
Dogs: *Smaller dogs are welcome*
Children: *Welcome (cribs, cots, high chairs, baby-sitters, and a children's program are available)*
Open: *All year*

Coronado is a lovely beach community set just across the bay from San Diego. When we were growing up, we used to take the ferry to reach the peninsula, but that was many years ago; today, the soaring San Diego-Coronado Bay Bridge shuttles people across the bay. The crossing may have lost some of its original appeal, but the expansive vistas that unfold from the bridge almost make up for it. This once sleepy town, home to mostly Navy families, now has a more diverse population. Coronado also attracts a fair number of tourists, who for years stayed at the famous Hotel del Coronado. After we drove past the grand old hotel, we came upon the Navy's practice fields, and just beyond these fields we found the new, exclusive 15-acre Crown Isle. Here, we discovered the other luxury hotel on the peninsula, the Lowes Coronado Bay Resort. An 80-slip marina, 5 tennis courts, and three free-form swimming pools surround this contemporary hotel.

We liked this place from the moment we stepped into the cavernous lobby, which is fashioned with walls of windows providing spectacular views. Muted tapestry fabrics cover the overstuffed furnishings, making this a pleasant place to pass the time. We admired the views for a bit longer and then decided to head down the gently curving hallways. Along the way, we passed aviaries filled with clutches of exotic finches; beyond, we caught a glimpse of the free-form swimming pools that are guarded by tall palms and lined with brilliant-colored flower gardens.

The guest accommodations lie in four three-story buildings, whose finger-like extensions emanate from the central recreation area. There is a freshness to these chambers, due to a combination of pale, earth tone walls and lightly bleached rattan and wood furnishings. Vibrant floral fabrics add accents of color throughout these spaces, along with the potted palms and fresh flower arrangements. Palladian windows and French doors open to the balconies. We did not find a bad view in any of the chambers we visited, as each balcony overlooks either the swimming pools, the bay, or the marina. Unless guests plan on entertaining, there isn't really a need to reserve a suite, as each standard room is quite spacious and outfitted with an array of amenities.These include a fully stocked minibar, remote controlled televisions, a pair of telephones, and oversized marble bathtubs.

For those who have come to hibernate, good luck, as there are just too many tempting recreational options to take advantage of at the hotel. Pools seem to be everywhere — actually, there are three such bodies of water nestled between the curve of the peninsula and the hotel. Most paths lead to these pools, and to the poolside bar and grill and modern fitness complex. Five bayside tennis courts await as well, with the marina lining the perimeter. The marina is the source for renting sailboats, sailboards, wave runners, and paddle boats. The fitness complex, on the other hand, has more therapeutic options that include steam rooms, masseuses, and spas. Families will love the Commodore's Kids' Club. This well thought out and comprehensive program is geared for kids from four to twelve years of age. A staff of licensed instructors offers everything from face painting, sand castle building, and nature walks to workshops, seasonal performances/events, and a variety of movies and videos.

Once we arrived here, there seemed little need to go anywhere else, especially for meals. The most informal dining option is the RRR (referencing the nautical phrase "Red, Right, Return") gourmet grocery store, where there are a variety of delectable meals available that can be taken back to one's room. This store even has some goodies the dogs might enjoy. Another informal option is the Astra Bar & Grill, which is located by the pool. The premier restaurant, though, is Azzura Point, which guests enter by following the formal curving staircase up from the lobby. The flowing movement of water is captured throughout this elongated space, where curved walls draw the eyes out through walls of windows, over the bay, and to the sparkling lights of the city. Subtle earth tones and painted hardwood floors create a garden room setting, completed by the wicker furnishings, potted palms, and decorative picket fences. First courses could include the lobster and goat cheese chile relleno with a chipotle sauce; the clams and mussels in tequila with polenta fritters; or the lobster dumplings in a green curry ginger broth. Entrées range from a grilled salmon with a summer succotash and honey cumin chipotle glaze; and the sake marinated swordfish with a potato spinach cake; to the herb crusted rack of lamb with a smoked pepper relish and socca nicoise.

After dinner, guests will want to get their dog and head out for a walk around the property and along the marina. There are **running and walking paths** just off the hotel property that are also worth investigating. During the day, we suggest borrowing a bicycle from the resort and trying the **bicycle paths** instead. Anyone who wants to head back into Coronado can visit the town beach, also known as **Sunset Park. Tidelands Park** offers even more expansive grassy areas for a leashed canine companion to stretch his legs.

Railroad Park Resort

100 Railroad Park Drive
Dunsmuir, California 96025
(800) 974-RAIL (CA), (916) 235-4440, Fax: (916) 235-4470

Managers: *William and Delberta Murphy*
Rooms: *22 cabooses, 1 box car, 4 cabins, and a campground*
Rates: *Caboose $60-75 (EP), Box Car $85 (EP), Cabins $60-65 (EP)*
Payment: *AE, DSC, MC, and VISA*
Dogs: *Welcome with approval and a $7.50 daily fee*
Children: *Welcome*
Open: *All year*

California

What a concept — spending the night on a refurbished railroad caboose that doesn't go anywhere. Perhaps it appealed to our childhood memories, when we would play with our toy trains for hours on end. Maybe it rekindled those adventurous trips we used to enjoy while riding some of the classic old trains that traversed the U.S. and Canada. Regardless of one's memories, anyone who has a penchant for trains — or who just wants to try something a little different — will find the Railroad Park Resort to be just the ticket.

Located four hours north of Sacramento in the Shasta Trinity National Forest, this resort beckons railroad buffs of all ages. As we navigated the winding road leading toward the 14,362-foot snow-capped Mount Shasta, we came upon a small valley at the base of Castle Crags State Park. After crossing over a creek (which eventually feeds into the Sacramento River), the low-key resort began to unfold. We passed by an 1893 Wells Fargo car, a gear-driven steam logging locomotive, and a restored water tower, before arriving at a massive wooden snow plow connected to three additional rail cars. The latter, as it turns out, is the resort's wonderful restaurant. Right next door is the reception area, that is filled with intriguing bits of railroad paraphernalia.

After checking in, we drove a little further down the lane to our caboose — which was set in the midst of a loose circle of rail cars surrounding a swimming pool and a lawn. Each of these cabooses once anchored the ends of some noteworthy rail lines, including the Southern Pacific, Santa Fe, and Great Northern. These are the real thing, with the original ladders, pipes, and viewing lofts still intact. The freshly painted exteriors and restored interiors are as comfortable as they are intriguing. Each caboose is unique, starting with the interior walls, which are either painted a crisp off-white or camel color, or paneled with knotty cedar. The Railroad Park Resort calls itself a motel; however, the decor and overall ambiance are decidedly more appealing. Traditional furnishings predominate, including brass beds covered in simple floral coverlets that usually coordinate with the curtains framing the original windows. Levalor blinds can be adjusted for additional privacy. These are surprisingly comfortable spaces, with intimate sitting areas created by sofas and armchairs, along with some extra space for a twin bed. Kids love to climb "the ladder," (actually a short flight of stairs) leading to the cozy viewing platforms. Adults appreciate the additional creature comforts, which include color televisions and telephones, although only one caboose has air conditioning.

Clearly, the nicest accommodation is the deluxe box car, set in the middle of the park next to the swimming pool. This expansive car is not only furnished with an array of country antiques, but also contains a king bed, a claw-footed bathtub, and a wet bar, as well as a private patio. If a caboose isn't entirely appealing, then perhaps the adjacent cabins will be more to one's liking. While we liked the names of these simply furnished abodes, B&B Gang and Train Master, we preferred the ambiance of the cabooses.

There are no cooking facilities on the cabooses, but the restaurant more than compensates for this potential shortcoming with an array of homemade and hearty American dishes. Several interconnected railroad cars comprise this elongated restaurant and bar, which are jam-packed with nostalgia and charm. The warm and inviting ambiance is due, in part, to the authenticity of the place — all we would have needed was the rhythm and sounds of a moving train for the effect to be complete.

These dining cars have original domed ceilings, walls of windows, and turn-of-the century light fixtures. Hanging from the walls, and displayed throughout each of the three cars, is an astounding array of train paraphernalia. Antique tools, carved wooden conductors, steam gauges, lanterns, model trains, and nostalgic black and white photographs — all of these set the scene for a truly enjoyable repast. We also enjoyed spending some time in the lounge, where we were able to get a closer look at the hand-built scale model of the Old Cascade — a train formerly used on the line between San Francisco and Portland. In the afternoon or after dinner, guests gravitate to the outdoor patio, where they are often privy to spectacular sunsets over the surrounding mountain tops.

After a hearty meal, visitors and their canine cohorts may enjoy meandering along the **numerous paths** that crisscross both the property and the creek that bisects the resort's grounds. The large stone fountain teeming with carp definitely intrigued our dogs; however, it was the pair of fishing ponds that ultimately held their attention. Anglers may also try their luck here, or make the short walk over to the **Sacramento River** for a slightly different sort of fishing experience. Dunsmuir lies in a fairly isolated region of Northern California, but many of the nearby recreation areas and parks welcome dogs. Hikers and their leashed dogs may traverse some of the 6,000 acres comprising the **Castle Crags State Park**. The majestic spires deserve closer inspection. Of course, the **Shasta-Trinity National Forest** is also nearby, with a mere 2,000,000 acres of outdoor opportunities. After visitors and dogs have enjoyed a nice outing, the people portion of the duo might want to play golf at one of the nearby courses. In the winter months, skiers, skaters, and sledders need drive only a short distance before finding a suitable recreational destination.

California

Greenwood Pier Inn

Box 36
5928 Highway One
Elk, California 95432
(707) 877-9997/3423, Fax: (707) 877-3439
http://www.greenwoodpierinn.com

Innkeepers: *Isabel and Kendrick Petty*
Rooms: *11 doubles, 2 suites, 2 cottages*
Rates: *Doubles $90-110 (B&B), Suites $110-165 (B&B),
    Cottages $185-195 (B&B)*
Payment: *AE, MC, and VISA*
Dogs: *Welcome with advance notice and prior approval*
Children: *Welcome*
Open: *All year*

Elk

If you happen to blink while driving along scenic Coastal Highway 1, you just might miss the small town of Elk with its charming homes and storefronts. But if you look carefully, you will certainly spy the ever expanding Greenwood Pier Inn, Café, Garden Shop, and Country Store perched on the cliffs above the crashing Pacific Ocean. These attractive yet simple structures are bedecked with whimsical signs, decorative trim, overflowing flower boxes, and stained-glass windows.

When we first visited the inn in 1984, there were only two cliffside cottages overlooking the ocean. Since that time, the inn has undergone some substantial changes. The first and most obvious is the construction of the Café and Garden Shop. The Café is a delightful open and airy chamber adorned with various shades of teal and rose, and offering nice views of the surrounding gardens through three walls of windows. The Garden Shop is sure to delight even non-gardeners with its vast array of plants, shrubs, herbs, and decorative pots, as well as gardening implements. The rest of the modifications are more subtle, and occur in the newer cottages and refurbished guest rooms.

New arrivals generally find someone to point them in the right direction at either the store or Garden Shop. Don't worry if someone is not immediately available; a series of unobtrusive signs and arrows leads people through archways and around corners, until they emerge at last in a garden setting next to the main house. The affable hosts, Isabel and Kendrick, are usually in residence and can then escort guests to their accommodations.

There are rooms in the main house, above the country store, and in a blue building off to the side; however, the cottages are the most spacious and delightful. Again, narrow paths wend around windblown trees, dense ground cover, lovely gardens, and fountains, leading ultimately to the cleverly designed wooden cottages. The most endearing cottage of the pair is Sea Castle North and South. Kendrick is responsible not only for the lovely exterior landscaping around these cottages, but also for the interior tile and marble work, as well as the airbrushed collages. Isabel, on the other hand, decorated most of the guest chambers and often displays some of her artwork in them, as well. These unusual spaces are packed with charm, that takes the form of window seats, beamed ceilings, skylights, colorful tiled mantels, and circular staircases leading up to expansive bathtubs with panoramic views. Artists, and those who appreciate locally produced works of art, will be intrigued with the pottery sinks, stained glass windows, stenciled and painted furniture, decorative wood stoves, and handmade quilts. Brass bedsteads and overstuffed sofas are inviting, especially when they are covered with an abundance of pillows.

The other cottages are more rustic and eclectically decorated with wicker chairs, painted iron furniture, and bookshelves that hold assorted knickknacks. Here, comfortable beds laden with pillows are nestled into alcoves, while fireplaces or wood stoves provide additional warmth as the ocean breeze filters through the gaps between the wallboards.

California

While the guest rooms in the blue building do not have the same sense of privacy as those found in the cottages, they do maintain a similar overall charm, intimacy, and decorative appeal. As guests open sponge-painted doors, they enter spaces accented with hand-painted tiles reflecting the name of the room — Goldfish, Whale, Bluebird, Hummingbird, etc. Brass and wood framed beds covered with handmade quilts rest upon camel-colored carpeting covered with Oriental rug runners. Japanese accent pieces are interspersed with floral sofas and marble-topped dressers. Wood stoves warm these rooms, although if the day is warm, open the doors to the private decks and enjoy the ocean breezes. In the morning, enjoy a Continental breakfast on the deck and bring along the binoculars. Very often guests will see migrating whales, frolicking seals, or graceful shorebirds from this scenic vantage point.

Before heading off on daily adventures, we recommend a stop at the Greenwood Pier Country Store, with its array of interesting collectibles, books, works of art, and other assorted sundries. Dogs may also enjoy an early morning romp on the **sandy beach** before hitting the road. In addition to investigating the Russian River area, many people opt to take their canine friends for a little tour of the **coastline just south of Elk**. There are spectacular rock formations, an array of gnarled drift wood, and wonderful coves and inlets where both guests and their dogs can kick back and relax.

After a busy day taking in the area's natural attractions, many guests return eager to sample the delicious meals served at the inn's Café. Pastas, local seafoods, and innovative salads are complemented with herbs and produce often grown right in the inn's own gardens. Some of the entrée selections include Dijon encrusted rack of lamb; duck breast with nectarine and mango chutney; and grilled salmon with garlic herbs. Diners who happen to sample the delicious breads and desserts may be interested to know that Isabel is often responsible for these creations. After a visit to the Greenwood Pier Inn, guests come away with a renewed appreciation for the simpler things in life and a yearning to return to this remote, picturesque, and most delightful place along California's coast.

Escondido

Lawrence Welk Resort

8860 Lawrence Welk Drive
Escondido, California 92026
(800) 932-9355, (619) 749-3000, Fax: (619) 749-9537

General Manager: *Mario Trejo*
Rooms: *134 doubles, 6 suites*
Rates: *Doubles $110-150 (EP), Suites $160-220 (EP)*
Payment: *AE, CB, DC, DSC, MC, and VISA*
Dogs: *Welcome with prior approval and a $50 refundable damage deposit*
Children: *Welcome (cribs, roll-away beds, and baby-sitters are available)*
Open: *All year*

There seem to be only a few resorts in the San Diego area that accept guests traveling with a dog. However, one intriguing place that offers excellent facilities and easy accessibility to San Diego, as well as La Jolla, Del Mar, and many other area attractions, is the Lawrence Welk Resort. Lawrence Welk searched long and hard to find this secluded valley for his resort village. He was looking for a property that had an abundance of space, a good climate, and was centrally located to the mountains, beaches, and deserts. He found it in the hills of Escondido. What started in 1964 as a four-room motel set alongside a nine-hole golf course has developed into a full-fledged resort that encompasses over 1,000 acres. Mr. Welk so enjoyed his new resort that, for over 20 years, he even had his television shows filmed right on the premises.

Ideally, those who have the luxury of developing a full-service resort from scratch would do so in the same manner that Lawrence Welk did: by offering guests a golf course, several swimming pools, spas, and tennis courts, as well as restaurants and guest rooms with an array of modern amenities. Guests of the Lawrence Welk Resort will probably want to spend some time investigating the Village Center, which offers a variety of shops and boutiques, as well as a dinner theater facility. Over the years, as the theater became more popular, the original resort complex needed to be expanded to accommodate the number of guests who wished to attend the shows. Today, patrons are entertained by professional casts who perform in such classic shows as 42nd Street, Camelot, Singing in the Rain, GiGi, Hello Dolly, Sweet Charity, and a special Musical Family Christmas production.

Guests will enjoy taking their meals at the rather informal resort dining room. While Mr. Welk no longer hosts dinner dances or plays his accordion for breakfast guests, it is still a great place to dine while on vacation. This elongated room boasts a wall of windows overlooking the golf course and offers a hearty yet varied fare. Entrée selections range from such standbys as

California

chicken Parmesan, filet mignon, and poached salmon fillet to dishes that are earmarked "Something Wild," featuring piña colada shrimp; Thai ribs; Kauai teriyaki ahi; and Maui macadamia nut chicken.

After a filling meal guests often retire to their spacious bedrooms. Doggie guests are welcome with their owners in the dove gray 500 building, which is one of the resort's more intimate facilities. It is set to the back of the complex, but from the private decks and patios guests can see across the golf course to the picturesque hills. Although this is a fairly large resort, care has been taken to give each room an individualized feeling. Many rooms have been recently refurbished; the overall decor is comprised of subtle earth tones and the furnishings are a combination of rattan and a Scandinavian light oak design. Standard amenities include a color cable television, a clock radio, a direct dial telephone, an intimate sitting area, and a kitchenette. The sliding glass doors in the first floor bedrooms open to patios, while those on the second floor open to covered decks with ivy climbing up their lattice work.

Canine companions will have to refrain from bounding after golf balls while staying at the Lawrence Welk Resort. Not to worry though, the grounds are expansive and great for taking dogs on extensive strolls. Guests who want to wander a bit further afield will find that the **hills** surrounding the resort are ideal for short treks. There is also the **Cleveland National Forest**, which is comprised of more than 420,000 acres of forests loaded with panoramic vistas and several hundred miles of trails to investigate.

Nearby La Jolla is a beautiful ocean-side town offering everything from cliff walks and attractive beaches to exclusive restaurants and boutiques. Unfortunately, as eager as our two dogs were to explore, they were not permitted to romp about the beaches in the **Mount Soledad Park** until the non-peak hours (from 9 p.m. until 6 a.m. or anytime during off season). The coastal beaches to the north also have various rules about bringing dogs. Some permit dogs off season while others allow them only on a restricted hourly basis. Make it up to your dog by taking her to a few parks in San Diego, including **Black Mountain, Fiesta Island, Mission Bay**, and best of all, **Ocean Beach Park**. The latter is a true doggie haven. Canine companions are sure to find dozens of buddies to romp with along this expansive beach.

The Eureka Inn

518 Seventh Street
Eureka, California 95501
(800) 862-4906, (707) 442-6441, Fax: (707) 442-0637

Manager: Stephanie Laken
Rooms: 93 doubles, 12 suites
Rates: Doubles $120-150 (EP), Suites $175-250 (EP),
   Children under 12 are free
Payment: AE, CB, DC, DSC, MC, and VISA
Dogs: Welcome with approval
Children: Welcome (cribs, cots, high chairs, and baby-sitting services
   are available)
Open: All year

The Eureka Hotel Company was created in the early 1920s. With the backing of 600 investors and $300,000, the company designed and built the Tudor-style Eureka Inn. Nearly 75 years later, it stands as a National Historic Landmark and is a centerpiece for this Northern California community. As with all date-boarded buildings, the exterior must remain true to its heritage and any renovations are carefully executed. The inn's reputation is a fine one, hosting such notables over the years as Winston Churchill, John Barrymore, Bill Cosby, Micky Mantle, J.D. Rockefeller, Truman Capote, and presidents Hoover, Ford, and Reagan.

The cavernous, high-ceilinged Grand Lobby is perhaps the inn's most impressive feature. Enormous polished redwood beams and a stately, redwood trimmed fireplace dominate the elongated room. Massive brass, English candle chandeliers cast subdued lighting throughout this space as a grandfather clock ticks quietly in the corner. Leather furniture is grouped into convenient seating areas, interspersed with leather-topped game and writing tables. Pairs of French doors lead out to the gardens and to the green umbrella tables surrounding the swimming pool. Except for its size, the lobby is reminiscent of an English manor house's drawing room. At Christmas, the inn is particularly festive as the staff prepares for its "White Christmas" celebration. During this time of the year the focal point of the lobby moves from the huge fireplace to a white fir that nearly touches the 30-foot ceiling. Each Christmas the hotel dreams up a theme. We happened to visit when twinkling lights surrounded pairs of white doves nesting in festively decorated cages. Another decorative theme included covering the tree with over 2,000 live orchids, while yet another motif focused on filling the branches with brightly painted carousel horses and glittering, wrapped packages. Guests may enjoy this seasonal extravaganza during their complimentary afternoon tea, when assorted refreshments and *hors d'oeuvres* are served in here.

The guest rooms are not nearly as grand as the lobby, although each is imbued with a sense of the inn's history. No two decors are exactly alike. Some walls are painted slate blue or burgundy, while others are fashioned with pine paneling or grasspaper with redwood accents. The Queen Anne-style tables, bureaus, and armchairs in some accommodations create a traditional setting, while other rooms, with maple furnishings, have a slightly more contemporary feeling. Regardless of the decor, each room contains a color cable television, small refrigerator, and well-equipped bathroom. The luxuriously appointed suites, on the other hand, contain fireplaces, wet bars, and Jacuzzis. Some of the more intriguing accommodations are the "salesman suites," equipped with retractable Murphy beds, and the "King's Row" rooms — a series of oversized, king-bedded rooms on the third floor. Ideally, the inn tries to encourage canine travelers and their companions to stay in the ground floor bedrooms. This arrangement makes it easier to walk dogs at odd hours of the day and night, lessening the chance that they might disturb the other guests.

For evening dining, guests may want to try the hotel's Rib Room, which offers a fine selection of Humboldt Bay seafood specialties, along with more traditional dishes. Appetizer selections range from fresh shrimp and lobster bisque to the bruschetta of hot Dungeness crab and artichoke hearts. The entrées include the pan-seared salmon with an avocado-cilantro-lime aoili; a grilled beef tenderloin with marsala-braised portabello and shiitake mushrooms; and linguine tossed with mushrooms, spinach, asparagus tips, artichoke hearts and sundried tomatoes. The wine list is especially impressive, specializing in California vintages. Afterwards, many people retire to the Palm Lounge, where darkened redwood walls, low lighting, and a crackling fire set the proper tone for quiet after-dinner conversation.

During the day we found plenty to do with our two dogs. The **Redwood National Park** is a 106,000-acre preserve with hiking trails, lakes, and ancient redwoods. Neighboring Arcata is home to **Clam Beach Park** and **Mad River Park**, where dogs have lots of room to run around. Visitors may want to drive out to the **Samoa Dunes**, a long sandy beach with hundreds of acres for dogs to romp on with their human friends. The woods and beaches may beckon, but after a long day spent exploring the forests and the shoreline, we appreciate the comforts of the heated pool, sauna, and Jacuzzi.

A Weaver's Inn

1440 B Street
Eureka, California 95501
(800) 992-8119, (707) 443-8119, Internet: humboldt1.com/~weavrinn

Hostess: *Lea Montgomery*
Rooms: *3 doubles, 1 suite*
Rates: *Doubles $65-85 (B&B), Suite $110 (B&B)*
Payment: *AE, DC, DSC, MC, and VISA*
Dogs: *Well-behaved dogs (smaller preferred) welcome with approval and a $15 fee*
Children: *Welcome with approval*
Open: *All year*

Eureka is the largest town in this relatively remote section of Northern California. Lumbering serves as the economic base up here and feeds the many industries associated with it. Equally important, though, is fishing, as Humboldt Bay is rich in crab, salmon, shrimp, and albacore. Besides lumber and fish, visitors are likely to remember areas like Old Town, where art galleries and boutiques line the streets. Just a few blocks from the heart of the city lies A Weaver's Inn — a small Bed & Breakfast we highly recommend.

The B&B is housed in a handsome, Queen Anne Colonial Revival dating back to 1883. Today, the leaded glass windows and multiple gables stand out because of the festive pink and yellow decorative shingles. Guests will have little problem finding A Weaver's Inn; as lovely arbor-lined flower gardens distinguish it from its neighbors.

As we walked up the steps to the decoratively detailed porch, we were greeted by the inn's new owner, Lea Montgomery. She was a frequent guest of the Weaver's Inn; and in 1996 when the Swendemans decided to retire, Lea bought it from them. Although she does not weave, she has decided to keep the inn's name. She feels that the warm and inviting ambiance she hopes to imbue the place with will permit her guests to "weave their own dreams." While the ownership has changed, the house remains remarkably the same.

A curved, paneled staircase highlights the front hall, although we followed Lea through a pair of pocket doors into the fireplaced parlor. This intimate space contains all sorts of collectibles, but the centerpiece is a huge loom. We found one couple nestled into the comfortable sofa and armchair in here. Another guest was playing the piano. We had to admit that although the day was warm and lovely, we could easily have settled in the overstuffed sofa, while basking in the natural light pouring through the bay windows.

Just around the corner was the charming dining room where an antique sideboard still held goodies from breakfast. Another highlight of this traditionally decorated room is the large table draped in lace. A hearty breakfast

California

is presented each morning. During our visit an apple crisp, made with apples picked from the inn's trees, accompanied a cranberry and pineapple frappe, Swedish pancakes, and crèpes filled with vegetables and herbs. Lea will continue to expand the breakfast menu; however, returning guests will be pleased to know that she also has all the Swendeman's recipes, fresh herbs from their gardens, and most importantly, a penchant to please everyone with her culinary talents.

After breakfast, many guests tend to gravitate to the parlor, where a fire is often crackling in the hearth. If the day is warm, others prefer the wicker chairs on the side porch or the comfort of the rear courtyard, which is usually ablaze in floral splendor.

The traditionally furnished and decorated upstairs bedrooms closely resemble the ambiance of the first floor common room. The queen bed in the Marcia Room is set amid an assortment of family heirlooms. Light flowing in past the window seat makes this space especially appealing. One of the room's most endearing features, though, is the Japanese soaking tub. The Cynthia Room is also lovely, boasting an extra-long king bed situated across from a fireplace. The space is not only brightened by natural light flowing in through the bay window, but also by the braided rugs and festively appointed white wicker furnishings. The bathroom, fashioned with a claw-footed Victorian tub, may be either private or shared, depending upon guests' needs.

The Amy Room is especially cozy and appointed with a double bed and a handsome collection of Victorian furnishings. The most spacious chamber of all, though, is the Pamela Suite. A pair of pocket doors divides the master bedroom from the fireplaced sitting room. A pine sweater chest, set in front of the chocolate-colored sofa bed, tops hardwood floors dotted with area rugs. A richly detailed, white lace coverlet adorns the bed, although it is the feather bed top that makes it seem especially luxurious.

After a restful night's sleep, guests are generally ready to explore Eureka and its environs with their dogs. A leashed dog and her human escort will enjoy **walking through this historic district** filled with Victorian homes. A short car ride leads to the **Samoa Dunes**, with over 125 acres of land available to visitors and their leashed dogs. This is a beautiful spot, with seemingly endless amounts of sand, surf, and sky. Upon your return, you both may wish to relax amid the lovely cottage-style gardens, the lush lawns (which are often outfitted for some impromptu croquet), and a variety of bushes and trees from which you may wish to sample their fruits. Best of all, Lea is eager to help her guests and their canine companions enjoy and explore this picturesque region.

Tenaya Lodge

P.O. Box 159
1122 Highway 41
Fish Camp, California   93623
(800) 635-5807, (209) 683-6555, Fax: (209) 683-8684
Internet: http://www.tenayalodge.com

Manager: *Paul Ratchford*
Rooms: *244 doubles, 20 suites*
Rates: *Doubles $135-199 (EP), Suites $225-375 (EP)*
Payment: *AE, CB, DC, DSC, JCB, MC, and VISA*
Dogs: *Welcome with approval and a $50 cleaning fee per visit*
Children: *Welcome — under 17 years are free when staying in parent's room (cribs, cots, and baby-sitters are available)*
Open: *All year*

There are few places more magnificent than Yosemite National Park. This diverse habitat of three-quarters-of-a-million acres supports over 80 different species of animals and 250 varieties of birds, along with some of the world's most famous waterfalls and rock formations. While dogs do have limited terrain to explore within the park's limits, visitors should still consider including them on this very special sojourn.

Accommodations on the park's valley floor are limited. Yet only two miles from the park's south entrance is a fine option — the Tenaya Lodge. This three-story mountain lodge, which officially opened in 1989, nestles on 35 acres of wooded hills and sprawling lawns at an altitude of 5,000 feet. The lodge is not just a way station for Yosemite tourists but a destination in itself, with a full complement of recreational opportunities. Guests have access to both indoor and outdoor swimming pools, along with a full-service spa that features an exercise room, sauna, whirlpool, and plenty of pampering. For the more outdoorsy crowd, there is fly fishing, mountain biking, hiking, and rock climbing, as well as golf, tennis, and horseback riding within minutes of the lodge. While contemplating all of the activities might make some a little weary, the common areas and guest rooms thankfully provide an inviting oasis to thoroughly rejuvenate.

Even though the Tenaya Lodge is relatively new, returning guests will discover some changes since their last visit. The main entrance has been rerouted to make room for more grassy areas and to incorporate hundreds of additional native trees and shrubs. The cavernous stucco lobby with its vaulted beamed ceiling and soaring stone fireplace is another noteworthy transformation. A recently completed restoration reveals a warmer, earth-tone color scheme, bentwood chairs, and an array of Native American fabrics and artifacts. Aside from appearing more at one with nature, the lodge also acts in an environmentally aware manner. This lodge is a "green" hotel that tries to have a minimal impact on its surroundings. Diffused lighting and re-filtered air, along with biodegradable products, help save the environment.

Being at one with the environment, rather than competing with it, was important to the designers of the Tenaya Lodge. Timber and stone are the hallmarks of this place. A large stone-columned port-cochere marks the entrance to the lodge, where friendly staff members greeted us and escorted us to our room.

Standard rooms are just that — standard. Each offers a pair of over-sized doubles or a king-sized bed. The Southwestern decor uses creamy off-white colors and warm earth tones highlighted by Native American-themed fabrics, pottery lamps, and pastoral prints. Sitting areas are furnished with overstuffed arm chairs and sofas that surround glass-topped tables.

In no way do guests "rough it" at the lodge. Cable televisions, complete with Nintendo are standard features, along with computer data ports, in-room safes, three telephones, and individual climate controls. Guests also have access to hair dryers, coffeemakers, irons and ironing boards, and refrigerators. Those who want to upgrade can ask for rooms with sleep sofas; separate bedrooms and sitting areas; or private balconies set with Adirondack chairs. The most lavish suites are the honeymoon, deluxe, and luxury suites, offering everything from wet bars and soaking tubs to four-poster beds and overstuffed sofas and chairs.

Most guests choose to eat at the lodge by default since there are few other dining options in the vicinity. Fortunately, the choices within the complex are good ones. The Deli is a casual eatery, festively appointed in warm earth-tone colors, checkerboard tiles, and light fixtures inspired by Native American designs. The informal ambiance, coupled with a light fare, make it a great spot for a quick bite. The Sierra dining room is far more formal, with wood paneling, brass accents, and crystal chandeliers hanging from the beamed ceilings. The varied fare begins with a long list of appetizers. Some choose to begin with the hickory-smoked venison sausage; the Tequila-marinated prawns; or the beef carpaccio. Entrées range from prime rib with an apple-horseradish sauce and rack of lamb with a mango and pumpkin-seed crust to San Francisco-style cioppino and the grilled rainbow trout.

Dogs are discouraged within the national park, as the list of doggie no-nos is extensive and severely limiting. Since dogs are allowed to walk only along paved paths and can never be left unattended, a dog companion truly limits your access to some of the park's most appealing destinations. There is a ten-stall open air kennel at the Yosemite Valley stables that will board dogs weighing 10 pounds or more (209-372-8348) for those who really want to visit Yosemite with their dogs. The area around the Tenaya Lodge, though, is wonderful for exercising a dog. There are hiking trails outside the valley as well as other areas to explore in the vicinity of the lodge. Water dogs may wish to investigate **Lake McClure** (near Coulterville) or venture into the **Sierra**, **Stanislaus**, **Inyo**, or **Toiyabe national forests**.

Isis Oasis

20889 Geyserville Avenue
Geyserville, California 95441
(707) 857-3524

Hosts: *Lora Vigne and Paul Ramses*
Rooms: *12 doubles, 2 suites, 1 cottage, 3 yurts, 1 teepee, 1 barrel room*
Rates: *Doubles and Suites $75-105 (B&B), Cottage $130 (B&B),*
Yurts, Teepee, and Barrel Room $55-65 (B&B)
Payment: *MC and VISA*
Dogs: *Welcome with advance notice and prior approval*
in the outlying buildings
Children: *Not appropriate for young children, unless "by special*
arrangement" (cots are available)
Open: *All year*

Even after all these years, the Isis Oasis remains, without question, one of the most unusual establishments we have come across in our travels. It promises and delivers an "extraordinary environment in which to relax, rejuvenate, create, perform, and expand the mind." The century-old country farmhouse is the focal point, surrounded by ten acres, a small zoo (containing Egyptian pheasants, emus, bobcats, swans, pygmy goats, doves, ocelots, and peacocks), a rustic redwood theater, a meditation temple, a pyramid, a teepee, an Egyptian shrine, and several yurts. The centerpiece, if we were to pick one, would be the giant 500-year-old Douglas Fir meditation tree.

The retreat's mystical origins stem back to the days when it was used as the Pomo Indian ceremonial grounds. Years later, it was deeded to the Bahai, who transformed it into the site for their school, in hopes of promoting oneness among all people. In 1981, Lora and Paul bought the retreat. Since then, their focus has been on building a true spiritual oasis for people to visit. Lora is a resident artist who also practices as a New Age minister and a tarot card reader; while Paul, a Gestalt therapist, concentrates on helping those who are interested in understanding their past lives. They also hold workshops, seminars, and dinner theater programs at the Isis Oasis, dealing with, as Lora and Paul describe it, "connecting ancient wisdoms with the evolving New Age."

The accommodations are as unique as is the concept behind the Isis Oasis — in fact, they border on the eclectic and offbeat. Yurts, while not commonplace, are now popping up on mountain tops as havens for back country skiers or hikers. Years ago, we stepped into our first yurt at the Isis Oasis. A modern-day yurt is a circular, canvas tent-like structure with a clear dome on top. These are decidedly rustic, with the small ones offering enough space for a double bed and an antique dresser; the largest of these can accommodate eight guests. As one would imagine, the water closet is located elsewhere — across the field in a bathhouse. For those seeking something a trifle more conventional (but only a trifle!), there is the Barrel Room. This is an enormous wine cask converted into a small bedroom, complete with a skylight and the subtle essence of Cabernet. A teepee is another option. There is also the Retreat House, which is one of the oldest homes in Geyserville. This has not only three bedrooms, making it perfect for groups of friends, but also a kitchen, dining area, and a loft. A large parlor with a fireplace and library complete the inner sanctum, while outside there is a deck with great views of the valley. To the rear of this house, on a small knoll, guests will find the Enchanted Cottage — a suite of three rooms and a private hot tub. A bottle of wine is placed in each of the bedrooms as a welcoming gift.

A 12-bedroom, chalet-style lodge is available to guests traveling without a dog. An eclectic assortment of informal American antiques surrounds beds covered with handmade quilts. Lora's artistic touches include her stained-glass windows and Egyptian-style art. Her Egyptian symbols, carvings, stained glass, and other crafts permeate the Isis Oasis — both inside and out. Breakfasts are also a part of the experience, but what most guests remember are the dinners served in the open pavilion, with its huge Scandinavian fireplace. Vegetarian dishes from the world over, along with Middle Eastern cuisine, begin the evening, with theater to follow. Other dining options exist within the Alexander Valley, but guests should definitely reserve one night for the theatrical production.

There are a number of ways for guests to unwind at the Isis Oasis. Fifteen or twenty minutes in the swimming pool, spa, or sauna are a few popular possibilities. A visit to the Isis Oasis' exotic animal menagerie is also a thought. Lora and Paul recommend taking dogs on a **leisurely walk** through the orchard and down to the pond, where there are swans and geese. Afterwards, a drive north to **Lake Sonoma** will provide an array of hiking trails, as well as refreshing lake waters for canines to cool off in. Some guests stay on the property for the duration of their visit — opting to soak in all the good vibrations that permeate this place.

Swan-Levine House

*328 South Church Street
Grass Valley, California 95945
(916) 272-1873*

Innkeepers: *Howard and Peggy Levine*
Rooms: *2 doubles, 2 suites*
Rates: *Doubles $75 (B&B), Suites $90-100 (B&B)*
Payment: *AE, DSC, MC, and VISA*
Dogs: *Welcome with approval*
Children: *Welcome (cribs and high chairs are available)*
Open: *All year*

Historic California B&Bs are not always easy to find, especially one with an intriguing past. The Swan-Levine House is one of these special places. Built by William Cambell in 1880 as a family residence, it was bought some 15 years later by Doctors John and Carl Jones, who transformed it into a small hospital and used it as the community's medical center. Peggy Swan and Howard Levine found the three-story, 8,000 square-foot house in 1975. Along with family and several friends, they embarked on a restoration process that continues even to this day. They began by replacing portions of the foundation and rebuilding the expansive front porch, before turning inside and restoring the individual rooms and kitchen. Peggy and Howard did not anticipate spending over 20 years working on this project, but with their artists' background and three children, they have a keen understanding of what a "work in progress" means. Today, the major projects have been addressed, leaving only a little fine tuning here and there.

The Victorian home reflects the Swan/Levine artistic touch. Their prints and canvases line most of the walls, filling the bookshelves, and occupying other assorted nooks and crannies. One of the more interesting heirlooms is Peggy's great-great grandmother's hand-woven paisley shawl. It is displayed against a wall in one of the parlors. These artistic expressions, both past and present, fit in well with the antique house's hardwood floors, tiled fireplaces, and decorative moldings. The collection of antique furnishings found throughout the common areas and guest rooms were Peggy's discoveries at yard sales and antique auctions.

As we made our way up the front steps, the Levine's 13-year- old dog let out a bark from his comfortable spot in the kitchen, as if to say, "I know you are here, but I'll get around to visiting with you later." Peggy and the house cats who answered the door were far more accommodating. She took us on the grand tour, pointing out the pen and ink drawings and computer-generated graphic designs set alongside hand-thrown pottery pieces. This is a feel-good place where brightly painted, life-size figures might make some jump in surprise, while electric pink walls startle the rest of one's senses. The color scheme covers a broad spectrum, including vibrant greens, deep purples, and cobalt blues, to mention just a few.

Guest bedroom furnishings mirror those in the rest of the house, with assorted antiques, reproductions, and white wicker. Peggy's handmade quilts rest upon oak beds. One of our favorite rooms is the suite where a cozy sitting room and wood burning fireplace made us want to hibernate awhile. The private porch is an extra attraction. Just across from the suite is the old operating room, resplendent with sunlight that pours in through the enormous eight-foot high windows. Only Peggy and Howard could take an operating room and create a garden room setting, with white tiled floors, decorative wainscoting, and a full complement of white wicker furniture. Peggy's oil-painted etchings line the walls, but equally attractive is the lovely candlewick bedspread Peggy's great aunt made in the 1920s. We can only imagine staying in this room in the spring, when we would be able to look through the flowering magnolia tree toward the verdant Sierra Nevada foothills. The remaining two bedrooms are the perfect choice for a family, as one has a queen bed and another a pair of bunk beds. These bedrooms contain wash basins, but share a bath off the hall. There is a claw-footed bathtub in here, as well as a triple basin sink — which dates back to the days when the house was a hospital.

After a good night's sleep, guests should arrive at the table with a hearty appetite, ready to indulge in one of Howard's creative meals. Howard still operates on the principle of "what happens to be in the house at the time" is usually what gets served for breakfast. Trust us — his larder is well stocked. Some of the more popular specialties include blintzes, huevos rancheros, and Belgian waffles topped with seasonal fruit. We recommend lingering awhile around the dining room table, where the high ceilings and original fireplace remind us of home.

Grass Valley is in the high foothills of the Sierras, which means there are also excellent hiking and cross-country ski trails within a short driving distance of the B&B. **Canoeing** and **fishing** on either the **American**, **Cuba**, or **Bear rivers** are also popular options. Check out the **790-acre Empire Mine State Historic Park**, which has 10 miles of hiking trails and over 360 miles of old mine passageways. Of course, later in the day the B&B's swimming pool awaits, as does a game of badminton.

Even those who don't profess to have an artistic bone in their body will be interested to spend a portion of their visit in the converted nurse's dorm/carriage house/artist's studio located to the rear of the property. The printing studio is fully equipped, allowing both knowledgeable students and novices an opportunity to test their artistic prowess. Guests may try anything from etching and engraving to lithography (both stone and plate).

This is an intimate B&B with two wonderful, energetic, and vivacious hosts. As Peggy is quick to point out, guests can be as active or restful as they like for "even when the house is full, you don't have to see anybody. There are lots of places to hide."

The Groveland Hotel

P.O. Box 289
18767 Main Street
Groveland, California 95321
(800) 273-3314, (209) 962-4000, Fax: (209) 962-6674
Internet: http://www.groveland.com

Innkeeper: *Peggy Mosley*
Rooms: *16 doubles, 1 suite*
Rates: *$95-175 (B&B)*
Payment: *AE, MC, and VISA*
Dogs: *Welcome in two rooms with approval for a $10 daily fee*
Children: *Welcome*
Open: *All year*

Groveland was founded in 1849, but at that time it was named Garrotte, not Groveland. Its name aptly reflected what was going on around here, as this was the Gold Rush, when the hangman's noose received a great deal of use. Two things greatly influenced this community: the Gold Rush and the Hetch Hetchy water project. The inn aptly reflects these two periods. During the peak of the rush, the Groveland Hotel was built. This adobe structure is modeled after the first American mansion, the Larkin Mansion in Monterey. In 1914, a Queen Anne-style hostelry was built next door, to accommodate the power brokers behind the Hetch Hetchy water project. More recently, these two buildings were combined to form the present Groveland Hotel. The hotel recently underwent a $1 million facelift, with extensive refurbishment of all the guest rooms and public areas; however, it remains true to its heritage.

Authenticity is the key component to Groveland's charm as well, with wooden sidewalks running in front of the historic buildings lining the streets. From the valley, a steep serpentine road climbs to an elevation of 3,000 feet before dropping into the town center. We visited Groveland on a wonderful sunny afternoon, just as the rays of the setting sun cast pastel hues upon the foothills. We entered through the rear courtyard patio, where greenery and lattice create just the right environment for passing the time. We weren't alone in thinking this, as other guests seemed well settled in around the umbrellas, enjoying a cool drink. The dogs, on the other hand, seemed especially intrigued by the wooden replica of a beagle that almost appeared to be in motion. The dog seemed to be pointing us toward the front of the creamy yellow building. As we rounded the corner, we found another clutch of guests settled into the white wicker furnishings on one of the wraparound porches. Obviously, people quickly feel right at home here.

Once inside the foyer, Peggy appeared, offering to give us the grand tour of the inn. Our first stop was in the pale yellow dining room — an airy, corner chamber highlighted with floral accents, old photographs, and interesting paintings. What captured our attention, though, were the old-fashioned dolls and teddy bears set in alcoves and along window sills. The hotel serves a Continental dinner fare that includes everything from rack of lamb and baby back ribs to poached salmon and a simple roasted breast of chicken. This is also the site for the equally hearty breakfast presented each morning.

Some guest rooms can be reached from the dining room's staircase, while a separate entrance leads to the others. We followed the dining room staircase to the Iron Door room, a sunny corner chamber brightened by yellow and blue walls and decorative stenciling. An old-fashioned, wedding ring-patterned quilt lies on the Danish bed, and an antique mirrored armoire and dresser rests off to the side. The bay window in the Sierra Nevada Phillips room also brightens this space, but the highlights are the Belgian bed, the matching armoire, and the clothes chest. The Lillie Langtry Suite is more finely appointed and contains a French oak bed, set next to an overstuffed floral fabric sofa. A fireplace warms this chamber, and the spa bathtub rejuvenates tired muscles. The Hetch Hetchy Suite is awash in Victorian flowers, whether on the wallpaper, sofa, or antique French bed. A separate sitting room, along with a fireplace and spa, makes this one of the most requested chambers. Other notable accents found throughout the guest rooms include ornately carved walnut bedsteads, marble-topped dressers, brass sconces, and ceiling fans, as well as a handsome collection of French and English antiques. And yes, there is even a resident ghost (nicknamed Lyle) who is so well liked that he has a chamber named after him. Supernatural premonitions aside, all of this country hotel's rooms are equally appealing.

During the day, guests are usually out and about. Yosemite National Park is just 25 miles away, and offers a myriad of people-oriented recreational options. Those who want to include their dog in the outing had better stick to **fishing** or **gold panning** in the local rivers, or to taking the historic walking tour of town and the outlying area — or perhaps to visiting some of the other **historic Gold Rush towns** in the vicinity. People pleasures might include river rafting, golf, or tennis. Our dogs are great rock hounds, and we were hoping they would find a gold nugget on this expedition. They didn't; so we headed out on a little shopping expedition in search of those imitation gold nuggets — a fun way to end a memorable trip to the Gold Country.

The Hotel Charlotte

P.O. Box 787
Highway 120
Groveland, California 95321
(800) 961-7799, (209) 962-6455, Fax: (209) 962-6254

Owners: *Ruth and Jim Kraenzel*
Rooms: *11 doubles*
Rates: *$50-70 (B&B)*
Payment: *AE, MC, and VISA*
Dogs: *Welcome on a limited basis; must get along with the Kraenzel's dog*
Children: *Welcome (crib and cots are available)*
Open: *All year*

The Hotel Charlotte is in Groveland — a town perched at the gateway to Yosemite Valley and only an hour's drive from the valley floor. We would like to say that Bowser is a welcome addition to this famous and majestic National Park — but sadly, it is not so. Travelers who want to visit Yosemite with their dog can do so if they camp, keep their dog off the trails, and stay with their animals at all. (Kennels are available during the high season). If that doesn't sound like much fun, then visitors may want to stay in Groveland and explore the hiking trails, lakes, and streams along the perimeter of the park and in the nearby Stanislaus forest. The town itself has an interesting history. Its roots date back to the California Gold Rush of 1849, when miners set up small camps throughout these hills. These camps eventually became known as Big Oak Flat and Garrote. (The latter was renamed Groveland.)

California

Groveland still feels a little like an old, gold mining town. When we visit, it is always fun for us to imagine what life must have been like during those spirited times.

Charlotte DeFerreri built the Hotel Charlotte in 1918. She later took over an adjacent shop and created the hotel's first restaurant. In its heyday, the hotel housed workers building the Hetch Hetchy Water Project, which carried water from the Sierras down to San Francisco. Today, visitors who climb the serpentine hills to rural Groveland will see a town reminiscent of another era. A weathered sign marks the entrance to this blue-gray stucco hotel, indicating the availability of "Rooms, Zimmers, or Pensions." Simplicity is what makes the Hotel Charlotte appealing. Visitors step into the small reception area, then into the adjacent common area where they may watch television, or even play the piano. A mural of the Gold Country graces the back walls, but before we could study it further we were distracted by the sound of Chloe's scampering feet. She is the resident dog, and over the years she has greeted many a visiting dog in the same fashion. It all makes for amicable relationships later on.

One big change since our last visit is the repainting and wallpapering of many of the bedrooms. Each cozy guest chamber lies along the hallway that runs the length of the second floor. Nothing is overdone, yet all are imbued with great character. Most of the wallpapers are either delicate florals or subtle pastel stripes. The modest, yet traditional furnishings include American antique dressers and bedside tables, along with brass and painted-iron bedsteads. Guests may choose from rooms with either double or queen beds, along with private or "western-style" bathrooms. "Western" means a sink in the room and a shared bathroom down the hall, complete with a claw-footed bathtub. In addition to the downstairs common area, there is also an upstairs living room, located to the rear of the building, with another television, a small library of books, and plenty of comfortable sofas and armchairs.

There are a few restaurants in Groveland, all within easy walking distance of the inn, but try the Hotel Charlotte's dining room. The intimate atmosphere in here is appealing, especially the beamed ceilings and the blue floral wallpaper edging the top of the wainscoting. This is not a white linen and crystal stemware sort of place, but instead, a restaurant where guests enjoy a hearty, home-cooked meal. Options range from fresh seafood to substantial portions of prime rib; the latter is usually the Saturday night special.

During the day, visitors find plenty to do in these foothills. Try panning for gold in one of the local rivers, just as they did back in the Gold Rush days, although **fishing the streams** will probably prove to be far more lucrative. In the spring, white water rafting is the sport of choice. Play golf at the Pine Mountain Lake. History buffs will want to peruse the map put out by the **Southern Tuolumne County Historical Society** and take a driving-walking tour of the antique buildings of Groveland and Big Oak Flat. Canines will enjoy the walking aspect of the tour, leaving human visitors free to check out the exteriors of the many historic buildings. Still standing, and available for exterior observation, are the Longfellow Gold Mill, the first jail, the Odd Fellows Hall, and the Gamble Block. Built for a wealthy merchant in the late 1850s, the Gamble Block is an impressive stone and block building that once housed the Express Office, the post office, and a saloon, as well as the local tinsmith, cobbler, and grocer.

The Zaballa House

324 Main Street
Half Moon Bay, California 94019
(415) 726-9123, (415) 726-4468
Internet: http://www.go-native.com/inns/0008.html

Manager: *Kerry Pendergras*
Rooms: *9 doubles, 3 suites*
Rates: *Doubles $75-170 (B&B), Suites $140-250 (B&B)*
Payment: *AE, DSC, MC, and VISA*
Dogs: *Welcome with notice for a $10 fee; one animal per room*
Children: *Appropriate for children over the age of 6 (a futon is available)*
Open: *All year*

Half Moon Bay is a small Northern California town nestled between the ocean and the San Mateo hills. Unlike many of the other towns along Highway 1, this quiet hamlet has few neon lights or fast food restaurants. In fact, it is downright sleepy. A turn onto northern Main Street leads directly to the blue-gray clapboard Zaballa House, set behind a picket fence amid flower gardens too numerous to count. Originally built in the 1850s by Estanislao Zaballa, the home is an historic landmark, and is said to be the oldest standing house in Half Moon Bay. In addition to owning a saloon, a livery stable, and a general store, Zaballa was one of the town's largest landowners and its first town planner. Over the years, Zaballa's house was used as a dentist's office, a restaurant, a newspaper, and as business offices.

Today, Simon is responsible for recreating and maintaining the home's historic integrity. In 1989, during its last renovation, the building's interior was completely refurbished. Whenever possible, Simon saved the original wainscotings, windows, and woodwork. The result of this time- and labor-intensive effort is a charming B&B, housing nine unique bedrooms. We gained a sense of this immediately upon entering the B&B, when we emerged into the intimate dusty-rose colored parlor. The corner fireplace is flanked by comfortable armchairs, a coffee table piled with magazines, and a formal grandfather clock rests off in the corner. The dining room, set off to the other side of the foyer, still held onto its morning fragrances of freshly ground coffee, homemade muffins, and baked eggs. It turns out this is an "all you can eat" buffet-style breakfast that also includes homemade granola, eggs Florentine, and banana nut bread. While guests are provided an ample breakfast, they will need to look elsewhere for lunch and dinner. A comprehensive book in the front parlor supplies menus for all of the notable eateries in the local area.

From the front common areas, new arrivals need just meander down the central hallway to find the guest chambers. Furnishings range from four-poster beds to antique pine sweater chests, and represent a collection secured by the Zaballa House's owners, the managers, and the hostesses. Some of the pieces even belonged to the Sheraton Palace Hotel in San Francisco. Guests will discover that the brass or hand-carved wood framed beds are draped in fabrics that coordinate with the balloon shades framing the windows. The lines of the vaulted ceilings flow down past the lovely floral wallpapers to the original wainscoting. Some people are tempted to spend their time sitting before the crackling fire and gazing out past the original windows to the lovely gardens and surrounding grounds. Coral-colored Room Four is a favorite — as much for the queen bed as for the double whirlpool bathtub. We thought the nooks in here, one containing a window seat and another the white wicker furnishings set around the fireplace, were especially appealing. Room Five, accented with green hues and floral wallpaper, is appropriate for families. It is somewhat larger than the other chambers, and has both a single and a queen bed. Room Six, on the other hand, is the most famous for its friendly ghost who reputedly makes an appearance from time to time. Animals usually have a sixth sense about this sort of thing, so guests can see if their canine cohort picks up on this supernatural entity. Ghost stories aside, what most impressed us was the cozy queen bed positioned before the crackling fireplace. The bathroom contains an antique tub. Anyone wondering where all the garden's flowers end up, need only look to the guest and common rooms to find vases of fresh and dried flowers.

Half Moon Bay has plenty of outdoor, canine and non-canine oriented activities. One of everyone's favorites is a **walk along the beach** (there are nine of them in the area) to investigate the wildlife and sea life in and around the tidal pools. There is also a fun hike through the **Marsh Nature Preserve**, which provides a rich environment for aquatic creatures. Other favorite pastimes include the U-pick blueberry farm, a nearby winery, and miles of terrific bicycling opportunities. If this feels like too much activity, guests may prefer to take a leisurely stroll around the intimate town center. During our visit in late September, Half Moon Bay was gearing up for its annual pumpkin festival. Everywhere we went we found pumpkins, or were enticed by the displays of Halloween paraphernalia. At the end of the day — especially a cold and foggy one — visitors will return to a B&B full of relaxed, convivial guests nestled around the fireplace. We think this is the ultimate compliment to the fine hosts and staff, who imbue this charming B&B with a warm and inviting atmosphere that makes everyone feel right at home.

Healdsburg

Madrona Manor

P.O. Box 818
1001 Westside Road
Healdsburg, California 95448
(800) 258-4003, (707) 433-4231, Fax: (707) 433-0703
Internet: http://www2.madronamanor.com/html.pages/madrona/index.html

Innkeepers: *John and Carol Muir*
Rooms: *18 doubles, 2 suites, 1 cottage*
Rates: *Doubles $140-185 (B&B), Suites $185-240 (B&B), Cottage $210 (B&B), Additional person $30*
Payment: *AE, DC, MC, and VISA*
Dogs: *Welcome in the Garden Cottage for a daily fee of $20; they must be leashed when walking the grounds*
Children: *Welcome (cribs, cots, futons, and baby-sitters are available)*
Open: *All year*

California

John A. Paxton built the Madrona Manor in 1881 as his family's summer home. Over a century later, the Muir family bought this historic Victorian landmark and started the long restoration process. Today, the three-story Manor House and outbuildings lie on eight beautifully landscaped acres. Driving through the massive main gate, we felt transported to a French chateau — without the jet lag or the language barrier.

Through the trees, we spied the gables and turrets of the main house and, as we drew closer, the inviting veranda came into view. As we stepped up to the veranda, we saw several guests reading in the comfort of its white wicker chairs. Once inside, we emerged into an open foyer dominated by a central staircase. On either side of this foyer are the Manor's two elegant sitting rooms. The centerpiece for one is the building's original rosewood piano, set on a Persian rug. This is the music room, a pleasant place to spend an inclement day, either working on a jigsaw puzzle, reading a book from the library, or perusing the notebook containing the inn's press clippings. The latter goes back years, but one of the most touching stories focuses on the Muirs' affection for stray animals. Apparently, the inn is a magnet for lost cats and dogs, some of whom find their way here; others are just left on the front doorstep. The Muirs see to it that the animals receive any necessary medical attention and then care for them until a new home is found.

After reading through this notebook, we headed over to the reception area — a cheery space highlighted by lavender lattice-patterned wallpaper dotted by bunches of grapes. We talked with a staff member, who graciously offered to reacquaint us with the inn and its grounds. Although dog guests are welcome only in the Garden Cottage, we suggest taking a look at the other bedrooms on the second floor of the Manor House. These spaces contain French *objects d'art* and antiques set on Persian carpets. Four-poster beds, and those with ornately carved headboards, are draped in antique quilts. The scale of these rooms is impressive as well, with 14-foot high ceilings and floor-to-ceiling windows framed with draperies — making each of these chambers appear all the more spacious. Fireplaces are the crowning touch.

True to its name, the nearby Carriage House formerly stored the carriages and horses. Its overall decor is more contemporary, yet there still exist wonderful built-in features such as high ceilings, porthole windows, and French doors opening onto spacious porches and decks. Guests sleep in four-poster beds set on Oriental carpets. Although five of the eight bedrooms feature fireplaces, the true standout is Suite 400. This lovely chamber has an array of sophisticated French furnishings, especially in the intimate sitting room. Doors from the master bedroom open to a private deck. The most memorable aspect of this expansive room is the marble bathroom with a Jacuzzi that looks out toward the room's fireplace. Guests staying in the Carriage House need walk only a few steps to find the billiards room, where billiards and many other board games await. The Meadow Wood Complex, offering the last set of guest rooms, was thought to be the original kitchen for the Manor House.

The Garden Suite, or honeymoon cottage, is the most private of the inn's accommodations and is the best option for guests and their dogs. This cozy cottage is set on a knoll surrounded by private gardens. In the spring, orange blossoms from the neighboring orange grove throw off a heavenly aroma. Visitors step up to the front porch and through sliding glass doors into an enchanting sitting room. White wicker and rattan furniture intermingle with decorative Japanese fans and a ceramic elephant. The marble fireplace in one corner, already set with firewood, nicely sets the mood on cool evenings. One small, windowed alcove contains a writing desk, but most people are more inclined to gaze out over the woodland setting, rather than actually tackle any work. The rear bedroom is one of our favorite spaces. Light blue walls and white wicker tables and chairs set the garden room tone, enhanced by the bed's floral coverlet and vines of ivy draped over the curtain rods. Brass lamps are conveniently placed for bedtime reading. A sunken soaking tub takes up one corner of the bathroom, with an antique pull chain commode resting at the far end. Just off the back of the cottage is an expansive deck, an inviting place to relax on sunny afternoons.

The rooms are lovely, but it is the food that draws many overnight guests and locals. Each afternoon, patrons may preview the evening's menu while enjoying complimentary wine and cheese in the sitting room. The Manor House's chef, and hosts' son, is a graduate of the California Culinary Academy. His reputation for producing creative and tantalizing meals, using the inn's freshly grown herbs and vegetables, is widespread. The inn also has an orchard that supplies a variety of fruits for making preserves, as well as a smokehouse for curing its own meats. We always enjoy reading this menu, filled with tantalizing options such as the fresh carpaccio with shallots, mustard, chives and capers; rock shrimp salsa with white corn cakes, sour cream and Tobiko caviar; or the layered Dungeness crab salad made with celery, red onions, capers, and covered in a lobster dressing. Entrées included the oven roasted squab marinated in fresh herbs, salmon marinade with saffron and garlic, or the organic beef served with a wild mushroom medley, red wine, and shallot butter. A *prix fixe* four-course menu is also available. During our visit the smoked trout fillet with a hazelnut-lemon vinaigrette and a marinated goat cheese salad were the appetizer selections. The lamb tenderloin arrived on potato lace surrounded by ratatouille and then drizzled with a sundried tomato and pesto lamb reduction sauce. A double crème brulee, white chocolate mousse Napoleon, or blueberry shortcake followed for dessert. Best of all, the culinary delights continue the next morning with locally cured meats, freshly baked breads, and eggs cooked to perfection.

Although your dog is not permitted to sit under the table and wait for a scrap from these tantalizing meals, afterwards, she can help her human friends work off their culinary indulgences. We suggest starting by exploring the **surrounding grounds**, where lavish displays of color and texture combine to form the exceptional gardens. The **hills behind the inn** are also worth investigating. **Healdsburg**, just a short drive from the Madrona Manor, provides still more scenic walks. Slightly further afield, travelers will find

California

the **Sonoma and Armstrong Redwood Forests**, as well as wild blueberries, strawberries, and raspberries in season. If the berries are ripe, guests can bring some home and the kitchen staff will create a special dessert. Another option includes a drive north to the **Lake Sonoma Recreation Area**, or south to the **Hood Mountain** and **Spring Lake Regional Park**. Both have land and water-oriented activities. A renowned section of the Northern California coast is also just a short distance away, reachable by following the winding back roads over to Jenner. Once there, the craggy coastline dotted with beaches offers panoramic vistas that are second to none. At the end of the day, while your dog takes a little afternoon nap, you might enjoy a refreshing dip in the pool.

Sorensen's

14255 Highway 88
Hope Valley, California 96120
(800) 423-9949, (916) 694-2203, Fax: (916) 423-2337
Internet: http://www.ids.net/wknd/calif/sorensen.html

Hosts: John and Patty Brissenden
Rooms: 30 cabins
Rates: $65-350 (EP)
Payment: Personal checks preferred, but MC and VISA are accepted
Dogs: Welcome in four cabins, with notice and approval
Children: Welcome (cribs, futons, cots, and baby-sitters are available)
Open: All year

Yosemite Valley and Lake Tahoe are two of California's most treasured natural resources. This area, known as Alpine County, is nestled between these two scenic wonders, deep within the Sierra Nevada mountains. Most people don't know too much about this isolated spot, which encompasses nearly 800 square miles of spectacular terrain. Majestic mountain peaks flow down to sparkling lakes, rushing rivers, and wildflower-laden meadows.

Situated in the midst of this region is the rural Hope Valley and an old-fashioned resort named Sorensen's. The Sorensen family formed this unpretentious cabin community nearly 90 years ago, to accommodate friends visiting from Carson Valley. The original guests came to camp, but as the area grew more popular, the Sorensens decided to open it to the public in the mid-1920s. The rest, as they say, is history. Today, the overall setting still feels quite remote. It is located 7,000 feet above sea level and is surrounded by over 165 acres of land that adjoins the Toiyabe National Forest. Some guests come here to escape civilization, while others love to take advantage of the array of recreational diversions offered. In addition to educational classes and theme weekends, less structured diversions include fishing, river rafting, kayaking, mountain biking, hiking, and, in the winter, cross-country skiing on over 60 miles of trails. There are also a variety of interesting courses offered by the resort, featuring subjects such as fly-fishing, painting with watercolors, bird watching, photography, and rock climbing. Theme weekends range from Historical Emigrant Walking Tours and Kokanee Salmon Kayak Tours to Yuletide Adventures and Hope Valley Wilderness Runs.

Guests stay in cabins that are situated in a large clearing amid the woodsy setting. All are within easy walking distance of the central main lodge containing the Country Café and gift shop. The Café serves three meals a day, with dinners featuring hearty soups and stews, fresh seafood, pasta specials, barbecued chicken, and steak. On inclement days and after dinner, one popular gathering spot is the common room, where guests play games, work on puzzles, read books, or simply relax in front of the fireplace. Complimentary wine, coffee, tea, or hot chocolate also draw many here in the afternoons. In addition to the countless hiking trails, there is a playground for children, with enormous toy mushrooms to climb on, a log playhouse, volleyball, and horseshoes. Other kid-friendly activities include a winter sleigh ride or fishing on the pond in the warmer months.

Of the 30 cabins, four permit guests traveling with dogs. These comparatively small cabins are lined up next to one another along the perimeter of the resort. Simply furnished (Spartan might be a better word for them), these places are exceptionally clean. They accommodate between two and four people, with Wagon Wheel being the smallest of the group. A queen bed and sitting area with a sofa bed are set alongside the full kitchen and private bathroom. The cabin known as Log has a separate bedroom containing a double bed, along with a living room containing another double bed. A wood stove adds some rustic authenticity to this abode, while the modern, full kitchen provides most of the homey creature comforts. Wa-she-shu accommodates four people. This is a two-level cabin, fashioned with a double-bedded room downstairs and a queen-bedded loft. The latter is accessed by a ladder. This cabin also contains a full kitchen and adjacent living room, with a dining room table, couch, some chairs, and a free-standing woodstove.

Most will quickly discover that the accommodations are pretty much secondary to the activities offered at Sorensen's. In addition to the array of recreational opportunities offered at the resort, there are seemingly endless hiking trails that dogs are allowed on throughout the adjacent **Toiyabe National Forest**. There is another nearby national forest, the **Eldorado**, that offers a variety of trails for canines and their human friends to explore. Given our druthers, though, we find little need to leave the scenic confines of Alpine County.

Dancing Coyote Beach

P.O. Box 98
12794 Sir Francis Drake Blvd.
Inverness, California 94937
(415) 669-7200

Hostess: *Bobbi Stumpf*
Rooms: *4 cottages*
Rates: *$95-125 (B&B), Extra person $15*
Payment: *Personal checks*
Dogs: *Welcome, with approval, in the Acacia Cottage*
Children: *Welcome*
Open: *All year*

When we lived in San Francisco, we frequently took trips to the Point Reyes National Seashore. We loved our walks along the desolate beaches and picnics on the sand dunes — usually having the place to ourselves. We know others who come here to hike, bicycle, and sometimes whale watch. Driving along the back roads leading to Point Reyes, we pass rolling hills dotted with pastures and farms, and an eclectic collection of houses perched along the water's edge. Inverness is the last small town before heading out to the beach. This is not a heavily touristed area, making it all the more appealing as an overnight destination. One of the more intriguing in-town options is the Dancing Coyote Beach.

New arrivals will need to look carefully for the entrance to Dancing Coyote Beach. (It's on the right, just outside of Inverness.) Following the dog-leg right drive to the bottom of the hill, guests will come upon four cottages, resting in a small pine and cedar grove. Although these gray, two-story vertical board cottages are connected to one another, there nonetheless exists a sense of privacy. Stepping inside, we found a vast amount of natural light flowing through skylights and floor-to-ceiling windows. These windows also happen to look out to the sparkling waters of Tomales Bay. The one cottage that allows guests with dogs is Acacia.

The living room is the cottage's natural gathering place. White wicker and hunter green rattan sofas and chairs form a half circle around the brick fireplace. We noticed the thoughtful extras, such as the seashells adorning the mantel and bookshelves loaded with books, along with an assortment of board games. Pine paneled walls provide the neutral backdrop for navy blue accents. A fully equipped galley kitchen is well-stocked with cheeses, cereals, eggs, yogurt, and other delectables, allowing guests to prepare breakfast at their leisure. The deck, where most enjoy this morning meal, may be cozy, but the bay views that unfold are expansive. Still more panoramic vistas may be enjoyed from the upstairs bedroom — right from the bed. The cathedral ceiling makes this room seem large, yet the skylighted alcove also lends a sense of intimacy. A large bathroom, tucked discreetly around the corner, has a stall shower (with yet another skylight over it) and a corner sink. A decorative coat rack holds the thick cotton towels.

There are plenty of things to do both on the property and in the vicinity. If water views and relaxation are appealing, then we recommend reclining in the hammock or in one of the comfortable chairs by the water's edge. There is also a small dock here, ideal for launching a sailboard. Our canine cohorts were most intrigued with the egrets, who were patiently searching for mid-morning snacks. The beach is another great place for sun worshipers, who might be reading or just digging their toes into the sand before testing the invigorating bay waters.

We also discovered a great spot to take our dogs to — **Kehoe Beach**. It is located at the beginning of the **Point Reyes National Seashore** and well worth the walk. There are other beaches in the area as well, further out on the peninsula, but visitors should remember to keep their dog leashed. Depending on our energy level at the end of the day, we would opt either for an impromptu barbecue back at the Dancing Coyote or a casual meal in Inverness or down the road in Point Reyes Station. Whatever the dining option, we always look forward to our nights spent at the low-key Dancing Coyote Beach.

Manka's Inverness Lodge

P.O. Box 1110
Argyle Road
Inverness, California 94937
(415) 669-1034

Hosts: *The Grade Family*
Rooms: *4 lodge rooms, 2 annex rooms, and 3 cottages*
Rates: *$115-325 (EP)*
Payment: *AE, MC, and VISA*
Dogs: *Welcome with approval in several of the rooms*
Children: *Welcome*
Open: *All year*

Naturalists — and those who are just aching to get away from it all — will thoroughly enjoy the low-key hamlet of Inverness. Surrounded by over 80,000 acres of National Seashore, this bucolic setting is also blessed with an extensive array of wildlife that includes deer, elk, fox, and hundreds of varieties of birds. After passing by the handful of buildings that comprise the intimate

California

town center of Inverness, travelers will head up a steep and winding road bringing them to the rustic-looking Manka's Inverness Lodge.

Originally founded in 1917 as the Empire Club, the lodge was supposed to be the West Coast's version of an Adirondack Great Camp. The three gentlemen and one woman who founded the club envisioned it serving two primary functions. One was as a social club and rural retreat for the well-to-do who needed an escape from the confines of their city life. They also thought it would be a perfect base for hunting and fishing expeditions throughout the region. The Empire Club succeeded on both counts until Prohibition, whereupon the heirs of the woman's family transformed the club into a gambling hall. They used a cottage on Tomales Bay, dating back to 1815, as a depot for transporting the lodge's liquor. After Prohibition, a European couple bought the lodge and operated it successfully for over 40 years. More recently, the Grade family bought it, and imbued the old place with charm equal to that found here in the early 1900s.

From the exterior, Manka's Inverness Lodge reflects its roots, with brown weathered shingles and white trim. As we walked across the gravel drive, we couldn't help noticing the window boxes overflowing with late summer flowers. The day was cool, though, and as we stepped into the parlor, our noses picked up the scent of wood smoke. One couple, obviously enjoying the fire in the stone fireplace, seemed quite comfortable nestled into the thick cushions on the log couch. Dark wood walls, lined with racks of antlers and mounted fish, reminded us of the lodge's rich heritage.

After passing an illuminated globe, we turned a corner into the equally intriguing dining room. An array of festive murals lined the walls, interspersed with noteworthy quotes. Manka's developed its reputation for fine food over the years, and still serves an inspired selection of game and fish, many of which are grilled in the original woodburning fireplace. Two of the more notable grilled choices are the quail accompanied by Chinese eggplant and a garlic cream sauce, and the venison sausage served with a creamy polenta and a spicy red and yellow pepper compote. Grilled entrées included a pork chop served with mashed potatoes and nectarine chutney, as well as the king salmon served with sautéed summer squash and local tomatoes, fingerling potatoes, and a red pepper broth. Chops of wild red deer come with a white corn sauté, wild blackberries, and Zinfandel jus. For dessert, guests should try the house specialties which range from wild berry pie to pan dowdy.

It was still too early for dinner, so we left the dining room and headed upstairs to look at some of the Lodge bedrooms. We liked these cozy chambers, especially the log-framed, four-poster beds covered with country quilts or hunting blankets. Mounted fish and woodland prints gracing the walls merely accentuate the woodsy ambiance. Red and black checked draperies frame some of the windows, while animal skins top some of the area rugs. A small sign next to the bed wishes guests "sweet dreams," but we like the one on the back of the door, casually instructing visitors that check-out time is around "noonish."

After leaving the main lodge, we discovered a pair of guest rooms in two outlying redwood buildings, constructed in the 1940s. These are especially appropriate for people traveling with their dogs because of their easy outdoor access. Mirroring the feeling of the lodge rooms, these chambers also have the added benefit of front patios. A path off to the side leads down the densely wooded hillside to Fisherman 1 and 2 — both of which were being remodeled during our visit. We were able to see that these are substantially more spacious accommodations, which will eventually boast of skylights and Berber carpeting. The feeling of a hunting lodge is unmistakable though, as old license plates, hunt prints, and assorted trophies line the paneled walls. Old-fashioned sofas and side chairs encircle the brick fireplaces, but during the nice weather most people migrate out to the porches and decks fashioned with Adirondack chairs.

Guests may pick from any of these accommodations; none will disappoint. The area around Inverness is equally interesting. Dogs will thoroughly enjoy meandering along the **quiet back roads** that encircle the surrounding hills. **Heart's Desire beach**, located just outside of Inverness, allows dogs in its remote areas. Any of the nearby towns, including Inverness, Point Reyes Station, and the more distant Stinson Beach, are enchanting communities that are not only worth investigating, but are also quite dog-friendly.

Point Reyes Cottages

P.O.. Box 273
Inverness, California 94937
(800) 808-9338, (415) 663-9338,
Internet: http://www.nbn.com/people/rosemary

Hostess: *Suzanne Storch*
Rooms: *3 cottages*
Rates: *$130-180 (B&B)*
Payment: *Personal checks*
Dogs: *Welcome with approval (and a flea bath) for a $10 fee*
Children: *Welcome*
Open: *All year*

Even with Northern California's rapid development, the Point Reyes Peninsula remains a wonderful oasis. As the crow flies, it is only 30 miles from San Francisco, but the back roads leading here make the area seem far more isolated. Naturalists come for the abundant wildlife and protected seaside setting. We came to unwind. Hilly, provincial countryside (some of it blackened by a recent wildfire) surrounds Inverness. The land, unprotected by the government, is privately owned and supports dairy farms and ranches. In addition to the beaver, raccoons, deer, and moose who live in the area, there are also Tule elk and over 400 species of birds that call this sanctuary home. An appealing combination of hillside cottages here should intrigue anyone traveling with their dog.

Two of the three cottages rest at the end of a steep, winding road surrounded by 200-foot fir trees and fragrant herb gardens. When we arrived, Suzanne was unloading a variety of gardening implements from her vintage Volvo station wagon. She directed us up the tiered gravel path leading to the Fir Tree Cottage. This abode was a little deceptive, appearing somewhat smaller from the exterior. Once inside, a cathedral ceiling (built with timbers reclaimed from an old San Francisco pier) spans the living room, which is furnished with a futon and a leather couch set on an Oriental rug. Interspersed throughout are antiques and Japanese prints; however, we thought the window seat, flanked by walls of bookshelves, to be especially inviting. A central wood stove is the main source of heat. The full kitchen is as well equipped as it is visually appealing, with painted cupboards and decorative tiles splashing color throughout this space. A curved central staircase leads to the upstairs quarters, where guests may choose from a king bedded room or another containing a queen and a twin bed. Quilts and dhurrie rugs set the pleasant country tone for these spaces. Two built-in features of note are the oversized windows that let in plenty of natural light, along with built-in bookshelves. If the day is clear, guests spend their time on the deck, either sunning, picnicking, or just delighting in the woodland setting.

Rosemary Cottage lies down the hill from the Fir Tree Cottage, surrounded by an intimate spa and herb garden. We walked along a gravel path, lined with tiny light posts, and passed under a canopy of bushes and trees before reaching this second cottage. While it is decidedly smaller than Fir Tree, with its entire living space set on one level, the decor is similar to the others. We walked into the large sitting room where high ceilings are inset with a skylight. Next to this is a full kitchen, whose focal points are the handmade cabinetry and beautiful painted tiles. A wood stove occupies a far corner of the room, resting on a Spanish tiled floor accented with colorful rugs and royal blue wicker furniture. A separate master bedroom contains a queen bed covered with a red down comforter. Even with this inviting interior, we preferred sitting on the deck shaded by a massive oak tree. Birds seemed to be everywhere, whether flitting through the trees or hopping through the garden. Suzanne provides her guests with binoculars should they wish to get a closer look.

The third cottage, referred to as the Ark, is located a mile or two from the others. A steep set of switch backs leads new arrivals closer to their hillside destination. The creative house numbering offers little help when looking for the Ark, but eventually guests will find this humble dwelling. This cottage lies in a woodsy setting, protected by shade trees laden with moss. Originally built in 1971 by Berkeley architecture students, the design concept revolved around creating structures that melded with the surroundings. The class salvaged wood from an old chicken coop, glass from a nearby dump, and other assorted materials to create this rustic treasure. The entire project is documented in an array of photographs and scrapbooks placed in the cottage's back bedroom. If this all sounds too avante garde, trust us, it isn't.

This place is well built, with an interior space that is creative, fun, and reminiscent of the quintessential garden cottage. We entered through the living room, and rather than roaming through the place as we usually do, we settled instead into the dove gray sofa nestled in front of a picture window. Diffused light from the skylight brightened the space, and as our eyes adjusted, the many paintings and crafts created by local artisans began to take shape. This cozy common room is warmed by a wood stove and doubles as the primary sleeping area, as there is a queen bed off to the side covered with an attractive paisley quilt. We finally did manage to get up from the sofa, then followed the path created by woven rugs, past a small dining area, to the corner kitchen. Although the mood in here is distinctly 1950s, with orange Formica countertops and an old-fashioned stove, we loved the woodland views through the expanse of windows.

From the kitchen, we stepped down into the long library, which is fashioned with twin beds and walls of windows. A stereo, some board games, and plenty of books are stacked on top of the many shelves in here. A desk resides in one of this room's alcoves. One other sleeping area is reached by climbing a narrow ladder to the low-ceilinged loft. A futon is set on the soft gray Berber carpeting up here, and Japanese artwork lines the walls. Windows allow guests to feel as though they are sleeping up in the trees. The array of amenities may not mirror those of the other two cottages, but we think the place is very endearing — in an off beat sort of way.

Dogs love it here and have free reign investigating the area around these cottages. We got plenty of exercise just **walking** up and down the hills. The **Point Reyes National Seashore** is only a short drive from the cottages, and offers various access points that allow dogs. One of our favorite off-season pastimes is to visit the picturesque **lighthouse**, where it is possible to view pods of the migrating 50-foot long gray whales.

The National Hotel

P.O. Box 502
77 Main Street
Jamestown, California 95327
(800) 894-3446 (CA), (209) 984-3446, Fax: (209) 984-5620
Internet: http://www.sonnet.com/dancers/bandb/national/#historic

Hosts: *Stephen and Pamela Willey*
Rooms: *11 doubles*
Rates: *$65-80 (B&B)*
Payment: *AE, CB, DC, DSC, MC, and VISA*
Dogs: *Well behaved dogs are welcome with approval and a $50 refundable deposit. They merely ask that dogs be "smaller than a pony"*
Children: *Over ten years of age are preferred (one high chair is available)*
Open: *All year*

The historic National Hotel has catered to overnight guests since 1859. Of course, the history of Jamestown goes back to 1848, with the discovery of a 75 pound gold "nugget" in nearby Woods Creek. This event started the famous California Gold Rush and with the ensuing rush of prospectors, The National Hotel was born. The building survived a potentially devastating fire in the 1920s and was quickly refurbished. When Michael Willey and Don Hazelwood bought it in 1974, neglect had inflicted a toll on the foundation, plumbing, and wiring. Michael hired his brother Stephen who, as acting manager, undertook the hotel's final restoration. Working with limited funds, he carefully refurbished the old bar and guest rooms, taking particular care to preserve the historic integrity of the building. With the complete restoration of the front porch and facade, the hotel now better reflects its 19th-century roots and stands as one of the ten oldest hotels in California.

Stephen's priorities were to ensure that the restaurant and bar were operational before turning his attention to the 11 second floor bedrooms. We always like wandering around the old hotel, as it is a bit like a museum. The guest room doors are left open, with a simple brass chain across the threshold, which keeps visitors from entering. This allows guests, and the curious, to peruse most of the chambers at will. What they will find are spaces decorated simply, with brass beds draped in patchwork quilts. Period wallpapers combine with wainscoting and country antique furnishings to add authenticity. The more noteworthy pieces include antique radios, sewing machine tables, and mirror-top dressers. Dried floral and herbal wreaths enliven the walls, fresh flower arrangements rest on bedside tables, and lace curtains frame the windows. Although some bedrooms share bathrooms, they all contain antique wash basins and woven baskets brimming with towels and soaps. Both the private and shared bathrooms have pull-chain commodes and stall showers.

Those who prefer a little less authenticity and a few more creature comforts, amid this 'Mother Lode-style' ambiance, will appreciate the air conditioning and electric heat found in each of the rooms. Televisions are available upon request. We always love ghost stories, and learned that the National Hotel has its own resident ghost, Flo. Her origins are unclear, but she often plays pranks on guests and staff members. She frequents only one or two rooms; therefore, a good ghost avoidance technique would be to request a 'Flo-less' bed chamber. Bedtime reading is quite amusing, however, because many of her highjinks are recorded in the notebooks found in each guest room.

Flo is an interesting aspect; yet, for us, the hotel's highlight is still the old-fashioned saloon with its original wood wainscoting, stained glass windows, antique cash register, and massive redwood bar. Even those who limit their drinking to wine and beer will be strongly tempted to sidle up to the bar and order a shot of whiskey. Wooden trains and model cars lined up on the shelves above the front window are reminders of the area's historic past. The recently restored restaurant has earned accolades from both near and far. The *Wine Spectator Magazine* awarded The National Hotel an "award of excellence" for its wine list. The wine list is almost surpassed by the vast array of California micro-brewery beers. Guests may enjoy drinks and dinner either inside or out around an umbrella table, on a patio surrounded by decorative lattice walls. The house specialties include the trout almondine, brandy apple pork, and prime rib. With over 20 entrée items to select from, including veal marsala, sherried scallops and bay shrimp, and brandied medallions of tenderloin, the choice is not an easy one to make.

We like staying at The National Hotel for many reasons. One is its proximity to such destinations as **Chinese Camp, Angel's Camp**, and **Murphy's**. While Chinese Camp is an unrestored ghost town, the **Columbia State Historic Park** is often buzzing with activity. The scoop on dogs: Visitors may bring them for a little gold panning, but they are not allowed inside the buildings. Another dog-along option is the **Railtown 1897 State Historic Park**, with some 26 acres and all sorts of railroad paraphernalia that train buffs will enjoy. Those who are looking for hiking, mountain biking, or picnicking might try the **Red Hills** just west of Chinese Camp. Visitors can even talk to one of the local shopkeepers about gold panning expeditions. There may not be much gold left in these waters, but this area is certainly a wonderful outing option for vacationeers traveling with dogs.

It is tough to visit a town like Jamestown and not become immersed in its history. We happen to think The National Hotel is the perfect complement to a day spent delving into this region's intriguing past.

Jenner Inn & Cottages

P.O. Box 69
Coast Highway 1
Jenner, California 95450
(800) 732-2377, (707) 865-2377, Fax: (707) 865-0829
Internet: http://www.jennerinn.com

Manager: Jenny Carroll
Rooms: 7 doubles, 2 suites, 4 cottages, 6 private homes
Rates: Doubles $85-175 (B&B), Suites $130-160 (B&B),
  Cottages $120-175 (B&B), Private Homes $175-245 (B&B)
Payment: AE, MC, and VISA
Dogs: Welcome, with approval, in several accommodations, with a $15 fee
Children: Welcome in most of the accommodations
Open: All year

Jenner is just one of many picturesque hamlets dotting this spectacular coastline north of San Francisco. It lies at the confluence of the Russian River and the Pacific Ocean, on land dating back to the Spanish land grants. The grants' recipients ultimately divided them into sprawling ranches. John Rule owned a ranch, but his name never became associated with this region because of another man, Charles Jenner. In 1868, Charles Jenner, an aspiring author, traveled to this portion of the coast and fell in love with its beauty and solitude. He asked for, and received, permission to build a small cottage on Mr. Rule's land, in the canyon above the mouth of the Russian River. Before long the locals referred to this area as Jenner Gulch. Mr. Jenner's cottage was the only structure here until the 1900s, when A.B. Davis built a lumber mill. The mill thrived for a period of time, due to the huge demand for lumber needed to rebuild San Francisco after the devastating earthquake of 1906. The mill went out of business in ten years, but the remaining buildings were the framework for a new town and the Jenner Inn. When the town was finally established, it seemed to make the most sense to name it after someone who truly loved this oasis by the sea — Charles Jenner.

The topography hasn't changed much since Jenner's time, and neither has the sense of isolation. As we drove along the cliffside, serpentine roads, enjoying the sweeping vistas, we went past a collection of buildings and cottages. Another five minutes up the road, we realized this tiny populated section was the *town* of Jenner — so we turned around and drove back. The town, and the inn, are a pleasant surprise. The Jenner Inn is roughly 15 years old, and bears little resemblance to a traditional inn. Instead, it consists of a handful of cottages and small houses nestled into a hillside. The most modern element is the long, single-story main building covered in weathered, blue-gray shingles. Lined with windows, this is a bright space where guests gather for meals and afternoon tea. A sitting area, created with several burgundy couches, lies at one end of the cathedral-ceiling parlor. In the morning, a Continental breakfast of fresh fruits, muffins, pastries, and granola is laid out on the enormous sideboard in here. After guests gather their breakfast, they may enjoy it at one of the small tables surrounding the central wood stove. Stained glass windows add interest to the walls, as does the array of framed black and white photographs. The restaurant is located on the opposite end of this building. The chef, Ron Klaus — who purchased the restaurant from the innkeepers nearly six years ago — mixes California cuisine with a few specialties from his native Switzerland.

Just as the chef combines a variety of culinary styles, guests may expect variety in the accommodations that are scattered among the buildings on the property. Brambleberry contains an antique double bed set across from an intimate sunroom. A pair of French doors opens to reveal a deck set over a creek. The Heron and Gull rooms are notable for their river and ocean views, as well as for the shared deck with a hot tub. A Victorian motif prevails in the fireplaced Pelican Suite, and guests in this room have access to exceptional ocean and hillside views, either through the oversized bay windows or from the private deck. The kitchenette is also a welcome convenience.

The most appropriate accommodations for those traveling with dogs are the Tree House Cottage and the Hillside Cottage. To reach the Tree House Cottage (which is shaded by a massive pine tree), guests ascend 14 steps up the hill. (Yes, we counted them.) We liked the feeling of this cozy adobe, where flowers are predominant, both on the wallpapered walls and on the fabrics covering the cushions in the white wicker furnishings. The queen bed, topped by a country quilt, faces the French doors that open to a private deck and views of the river. A fireplace adds a touch of romance to this studio space. The Hillside Cottage is more rustic, and may be reached by climbing some two dozen steps. High ceilings, in the redwood-paneled living room, span hardwood floors covered in Oriental rugs and topped by traditional furnishings and antique collectibles. We like the idea of lighting a fire and

California

curling up against the thick, soft, burgundy pillows on the window seat. French doors lead out to terraced gardens and the hot tub. The open country kitchen is also reminiscent of another era, with its marble basin and blue tiled countertops.

The area around Jenner is still very dog-friendly, which is part of the reason we enjoy coming here. Guests should bring binoculars for watching the wildlife, while their dogs explore the more than 15 miles of **sandy beaches** that surround Jenner. Those interested in canoeing or kayaking will discover that the river's estuary is ideal for viewing seals, otters, and a variety of other wildlife. Some suggested day trips with dogs lead visitors to the charming fishing village of **Bodega Bay**, or to the equally impressive, historic **Fort Ross**.

Stillwater Cove Ranch

22555 Highway 1
Jenner, California 95450
(707) 847-3227

Owner: Linda Rudy
Rooms: 6 doubles, 2 cottages, 1 bunkhouse
Rates: Doubles $55-80 (EP)
Payment: Personal checks
Dogs: Welcome with prior approval and a $4 nightly fee — must be leashed at all times
Children: Welcome (cribs, cots, and baby-sitters are available)
Open: All year except the week around Christmas

Coastal Highway 1, near Jenner, is not for the squeamish. Hairpin turns and few guard rails make for some spine tingling driving, as much of this winding road is several hundred feet above the pounding Pacific surf. Anyone who conquers their fears, however, or who likes heights, will marvel at the magnificent ocean views and lush, rugged coastline. We won't tell readers what category we fall into, but we will say that the dogs love this drive and the ocean breezes. Just when we think, "We should have come upon the Stillwater Cover Ranch by now," all of a sudden it appears around a bend in the road.

The 150-acre ranch dates back to 1931, when Paul P. Rudy opened it as a small boys' boarding school, complete with a full complement of farm animals. Three decades later the school closed, but the property passed on to Mr. Rudy's sons and a daughter. They subsequently decided to turn it into a low-key guest ranch, although they decreased the size by giving approximately

100 acres to the state for use as a park. The ranch still has plenty of wide open spaces for people and their dogs to roam, accompanied occasionally by one or two of the resident peacocks. After turning onto the ranch's dirt drive, visitors come across several low-lying buildings set upon rocky knolls, reminiscent of an old summer camp. Many of these buildings are original to the property; for instance, the stone-fronted reception hall once served as the dining room for the boys' school. Today, it is imbued with even greater character, as an ancient wood stove pumps heat into the room, and collectibles, gathered from the ranch and coast, line the shelves. If no one is there to greet you, just pick up the reception desk telephone and the hostess, or one of her assistants, will come down the hill to escort you to your room.

The matching East and West Rooms are most appropriate for people and their dogs. These are situated on a knoll overlooking the distant Stillwater Cove. An elongated porch, set under mature eucalyptus and pine trees, fronts these spacious chambers. Linoleum floors covered with throw rugs lead through the simply furnished and decorated rooms. The living room has the most character, highlighted by a beachstone fireplace. Shells, gnarled wood, interesting rocks, and other collectibles from the ocean pack the shelves flanking the fireplace. We prefer the comfort of the log-framed window seats, but are always willing to recline in the well-worn chairs fronting the fireplace. A full kitchen, circa 1950, provides the basics for meal preparation. A pair of double beds, covered with calico coverlets, completes the rustic country decor. A step into the bathroom reveals a dose of north country whimsy. We liked the cow motif shower curtains, but what made us chuckle was the amusing tale, posted next to the sink, about gremlins who become exceedingly grumpy when improper things end up in the septic system.

Guests and their dogs are welcome as well in the Teacher's Cottage, set further up the hill. This charming little abode has a decor similar to that of the East and West Rooms, including a pair of double beds and a fireplace. Its large windows overlook the grounds and woods, rather than the ocean — an important distinction for those valuing water views. The Dairy Barn has the most basic amenities. Located near the top of the hill, this cinder block building is really a bunkhouse with eight bunks, two showers, a wood stove, and a kitchen. While the facilities are rustic (guests should bring towels and linens), it is a bargain. A group of eight people spend about $15 per person, per night.

In addition to drives along the scenic country roads, there are also numerous **beaches for swimming** (an option for dogs, not people), for collecting shells, fishing, or just catching a glimpse of the migrating whales. The **Salt Point State Park** consists of nearly 6,000 acres, although the beach is what interests most people. (The beach is north of Jenner on Route 1.) The **Stillwater Cove Park** is another good option for beach combing with a dog. The Kruse Rhododendron State Reserve is another popular option, as well; however, dogs must stay in the car. We find, though, that once we've arrived at the Stillwater Cove Ranch, it is just as nice to explore the grounds around the ranch, and relax amid this low-key cottage retreat.

La Valencia Hotel

1132 Prospect Street
La Jolla, California 92037
(800) 451-0772, (619) 454-0771, Fax: (619) 456-3921
Internet: http://www.preferredhotels.com/preferred.html

General Manager: Michael Ullman
Rooms: 75 doubles, 15 suites, 5 cottages
Rates: Doubles $160-350 (EP), Suites $375-625 (EP),
   Cottages $350 (EP), Children under 12 are free of charge
Payment: AE, MC, and VISA
Dogs: Welcome in the cottages with approval
Children: Welcome (cribs, cots, and high chairs available)
Open: All year

La Jolla is a mecca for anyone who loves exquisite restaurants, intriguing art galleries, extraordinary clothing boutiques — in short, the finer things in life. First-time visitors might have a little trouble navigating the meandering roads that lead to the town center, but once they arrive they will be hard pressed to find a reason to leave. Best of all, the coral pink Mediterranean-style La Valencia Hotel is situated in the heart of town and has commanding views of the water.

Upon our arrival, an enthusiastic staff member seemingly materialized and acquainted us with the hotel's many enchanting aspects. We followed him through the Tropical Patio, where palm trees and flowering plants intermingled with wrought iron tables and chairs. A decorative fountain nicely complemented the relaxed environment. Once inside, we emerged into one of the more inspiring rooms at the hotel, a cavernous Mediterranean-tiled living room. Rising high overhead were the massive hand carved beams supporting the ceiling. Across the room is a garden alcove, inlaid with blue and yellow Spanish tiles. Throughout the space, overstuffed couches and armchairs create intimate sitting areas; guests may sit cozily next to the grand piano or near the wall of windows and French doors overlooking the tiered gardens and beyond to the picturesque La Jolla Cove. When the sun is not shining through these windows, the rose colored adobe walls lend a sense of warmth to this inviting chamber.

Although ready to relax, we were instead led to the seventh floor for check-in. We then proceeded out to the cottage suites, which are nestled upon the rather steep hillside to the right of the hotel. We quickly learned that the cottages' decor and layout are as unique as the view. The traditional furnishings, accented by grasspapered walls and royal blue carpeting, sets the decorative tone for one cottage. Guests may lounge in the king bed, relax in the spacious sitting area, or open the pair of French doors to the private porch and ocean breezes. The suite's bathroom is also lovely, lined with patterned, royal blue wallpaper and set with fixtures made of Corian with brass accents. Another popular suite easily accommodates four in the queen- and king-bedded rooms. Pale Berber carpeting and dove gray walls lighten this space. This particular chamber does not have a patio, but it does contain a deep alcove closet that kids often transform into a secret hideout. A third cottage contains a spacious bedroom and sitting room combination, and the whole effect is brightened by the festive fabrics found on the sofas and armchairs.

One of our favorite cottages lies right behind the hotel. Lattice, framing the entrance, is virtually dripping with bougainvillea. Once inside, a European ambiance unfolds, as Pierre Deux fabrics cover the love seats and simple armchairs. A queen bed, tucked under the eaves, lies at one end of the L-shaped room, and a pair of French doors opens onto the intimate patio. We especially appreciated the spacious bathroom, mostly due to the step-up Jacuzzi, which was surrounded by large, decorative tiles. These are luxurious accommodations, which also happen to be very appropriate for guests and their dogs. The full array of amenities is impressive, including minibars and refrigerators, as well as in-room coffee makers. Blow dryers, thick cotton bathrobes, and an assortment of toiletries top off the list of amenities found in the marble clad bathrooms. Guests will soon discover, however, that while the cottages may vary in layout, each exudes a sense of privacy and fresh decor that makes them universally appealing.

A leashed dog is welcome to accompany guests on tours of the gardens and grounds. The pool is off limits to canines, but guests are free to leave their furry friend napping in the cottage, while they head off for a swim. Umbrella tables and chaise lounges ring the pool, each privy to lovely ocean views. The Ping-pong table, found at the far end of the pool, is a welcome diversion. Those looking for a more rigorous workout will be pleased with the mini-gym found inside.

Those who prefer the outdoors may want to meander along the **paths that wend along the coast.** Early risers and their dogs may visit the picturesque beaches before 9:00 am. The **beaches** are also canine friendly after 6:00 p.m. While the limited hours might bother some, we feel these hours are really the best time to bring a dog to the beach — not only are there fewer people, but the morning and evening sunlight casts colorful accents upon the shoreline. Another dog-oriented activity involves taking the self-guided walking tour of **La Jolla's coastal district.** However, once the dogs are tuckered out, then their human friends may enjoy visiting either the Scripps Institute or the Stephen Birch Aquarium. Besides hosting the annual USGA tournament, La Jolla is also the site for the National Senior's tennis tournament.

After an eventful day, guests may return and enjoy a delightful meal at any of the hotel's three restaurants. The Mediterranean Room and Whaling Bar & Grill are decidedly casual, both in style and food. The hotel's premier

California

restaurant is the intimate Sky Room. When we say intimate we mean it; there are only a dozen tables found in this elegant restaurant. In addition to the lovely setting and exquisite menu, this dining room is also privy to unparalleled ocean views from its tenth floor location.

Guests may wish to start with the open face stone crab meat ravioli with asparagus tips and a saffron onion compote; the Beluga caviar (at last count, $55 an ounce); or the assiette of singing scallops and sautéed prawns. This may be followed by the blackened swordfish covered with sun-dried tomatoes, shiitake mushrooms, and a roasted bell pepper sauce or the roast tenderloin of beef with sage potatoes, fresh forest mushrooms, and a Pinot Noir sauce. Two notable specials were the grilled gray pheasant stuffed with wild rice and exotic mushrooms and the combination of veal tenderloin and boneless quail seasoned with Pinot Noir, thyme, and pear ginger. Afterwards, it is only a short trip in the elevator before guests find themselves just steps from their cottages. Best of all, as we returned home each night we found that the refreshing ocean breezes not only cooled off our rooms, but the fresh salt air helped us quickly drift off to sleep.

La Quinta Resort and Club

P.O. Box 69
49-499 Eisenhower Drive
La Quinta, California   92253
(800) 598-3828, (619) 564-4111, Fax: (619) 564-7656
Internet: http://www.desertresorts.com/laquinta/index.html

La Quinta

General Manager: *Scott Dalecio*
Rooms: *613 doubles, 27 suites*
Rates: *Doubles $160-365 (EP), Suites $220-2,600 (EP)*
Payment: *AE, DC, DSC, MC, and VISA*
Dogs: *Welcome with approval and a one-time $25 fee*
Children: *Welcome (cribs, cots, baby-sitters, and children's programs are available)*
Open: *All year*

The Spanish phrase "la quinta," translates as "the fifth day." As the story goes, the fifth day of a journey used to be special for travelers, as they were known to ride only a short distance before stopping to enjoy great drink, music, food, and dance. The La Quinta Resort and Club dates back to 1926, when six red-tile roofed casitas harbored wealthy and famous people seeking the ultimate in privacy. It was, and continues to be, an ideal location for many of Hollywood's more notable stars who use it as their own secluded oasis. Over the years a myriad of personalities have stayed here, ranging from Bette Davis, Greta Garbo, Errol Flynn, and Katherine Hepburn to Clark Gable, Charlie Chaplin, and (more recently) Johnny Carson. Frank Capra even created nine of his movie scripts at La Quinta, including the famous *Lost Horizon*.

CRI, Inc. bought the hotel in 1984 and completed its $45 million expansion and restoration project in four short years. Not only did CRI double the number of accommodations, but it also added a few more restaurants and created the beautiful multi-level central plaza. Although the complex expanded and grew well beyond the original design, the overall layout still emphasizes privacy. We had not seen the resort since the the newest owner, KSL Recreation Corporation, took over, but were pleased to discover that it is still as enchanting as ever.

The cypress-lined lane leading into the resort ends at the central plaza. This lovely addition to the original configuration contains shops and restaurants encircling a tiered hillside of multi-colored gardens, flowing fountains, and meandering streams. We wanted to save the shopping for later, so we instead walked over to the intimate lobby and immediately felt transported back through California's history. Whitewashed walls and Spanish tile floors, accented by wrought-iron railings and colorful Mexican collectibles, set the decorative tone here and in most of the other common areas. One of the more popular chambers at the resort is still the adjacent Santa Rosa Lounge, where overstuffed sofas are placed alongside the huge fireplaces. The hand-blown glass in the windows reveals lovely views of the outdoor courtyard and beautifully landscaped grounds.

The charming guest rooms and cottages situated amidst 45 acres of towering palms, orange, lemon, and grapefruit groves, are linked by paths lined with flower gardens. All of the accommodations — from the original casitas erected in 1926 and the deluxe casitas constructed between 1968 and

1984, to the superior casitas built in 1981 — are spacious and stylish. Most of the casitas, housing between three and eight bedrooms each, surround an intimate courtyard and swimming pool. The traditional cottages are fashioned with red tile roofs and white stucco exteriors with blue shutters. Inside, the darkly stained furnishings look even richer when contrasted with the royal blue or rust carpeting. As in the common areas, the whitewashed walls and vaulted beamed ceilings reveal a bit of the resort's heritage. Windows framed by thick, wooden shutters overlook the flower gardens. Comfortable armchairs with ottomans flank the fireplaces, and televisions are concealed in the armoires. Writing desks are as convenient for working as they are for jotting a few postcards. In a hot climate such as this, the refrigerators tucked under the tiled counters are welcome additions, as are the ice makers.

The older casitas are ideal for most guests' needs, although some do prefer a few additional amenities. We especially liked the 600 and 700 series of rooms, not only because of their extra space, but also because they have private patios. Two-poster, king beds are positioned to provide unobstructed views of the fireplaces. Fully-stocked honor bars overflow with tasty treats to be enjoyed in either the whirlpool tubs or on the private lanais. Bathrooms are modern, luxuriously appointed, and boast a complete array of toiletries. Pairs of telephones, individual climate controls, and twice daily maid service are also standard features. If the dogs could have walked themselves, it would have been easy for us to hole up here for a day or two and rejuvenate.

A swimming pool is especially convenient to the rooms in this part of the complex, although an even larger pool, as well as 22 others, are scattered about the grounds. It is always fun to explore the most luxurious rooms on the property, and at La Quinta these include the spacious suites or the Hacienda Grand Suite. The latter is especially exquisite, with a private pool, a dining room that can accommodate 20, and an array of unique collectibles. However, it isn't imperative to reserve the most expensive or expansive room at La Quinta to appreciate the lush surroundings or the picturesque pastel sunsets framing the Santa Rosa Mountains.

The resort is also a sports person's dream, with 30 tennis courts (including six grass and three clay), 72 championship holes of golf (KSL recently acquired PGA West), 24 swimming pools and 38 outdoor spas. La Quinta continues to win accolades for its golf and tennis facilities, and each ranks among the top ten in the country. Sports aside, dogs are also equally enthralled with the facilities at La Quinta.

Of the **45 acres**, most are available to dogs and their human friends. The area just outside the resort also offers a whole other realm for exploration, and the **foothills** are especially appealing to hikers and nature lovers looking for the region's wildlife. This is the land of coyotes, coyotes, and still more coyotes — as well as lizards, snakes, and various other desert dwelling creatures. Travelers can escape the heat by driving into Idyllwild and visiting their local park. Heading deeper into the **San Bernardino National Forest**, there is an array of hiking trails.

After a long day enjoying this picturesque region, guests may return to dine in any of the four restaurants at the resort. The hotel's most authentic restaurant is Montanas, whose constantly changing menu and comprehensive wine list will satisfy even the most discriminating palates. During our visit the entrées included a crispy duck, a rollatine of veal, and a scallion crusted lamb Provencale. Architecturally appealing as well, the restaurant has a warm and inviting Spanish feeling, with beamed ceilings, columned whitewashed archways, and tiled murals complementing the earth tone decor. A profusion of live plants and flowers freshen this tranquil setting. There are also several other options, including La Cantina, the Adobe Grill, and Morgans. During the day, we prefer the casual atmosphere and delicious food at the tennis clubhouse or at the La Quinta golf course. Those who prefer to dine out on the town usually head over to Palm Desert for an even wider variety of restaurants and shopping alternatives. Guests may want to bring Bowser, who will certainly enjoy the window shopping (and occasionally, a merchant may invite both shoppers and their dog inside). Those familiar with Florida laws regarding dogs left in cars should understand that the same rules apply on the desert — *never* leave a dog inside the car. Air conditioning is practically a necessity just about any time of year.

The Carriage House

1322 Catalina Street
Laguna Beach, California   92651
(714) 494-8945

Innkeepers: Thom and Dee Taylor
Rooms: 6 suites
Rates: Suites $95-150 (B&B)
Payment: Personal checks
Dogs: Very well-behaved dogs are welcome with approval and a $20 fee
Children: Welcome, but must be very well behaved (cribs are available)
Open: All year

The Carriage House is a delightful B&B that we discovered years ago. It was, and still is, reminiscent of something out of New Orleans' French Quarter. The charming brick courtyard, accented by black wrought iron gates, contains a fountain and an array of lush plantings. Built in the 1920s and designated as an historic landmark, the Carriage House Inn is located in a quiet residential neighborhood just a few blocks from town and its popular sandy beach. The Taylors bought this American Colonial saltbox nearly 25 years ago and started creating their little piece of paradise. They painted the clapboards a slate blue, designed the interior spaces, and planted an interesting and exotic assortment of plants, flowers, and trees. The trees, now covered with moss, shade the lovely courtyard whose centerpiece is a tiered fountain. We find, however, that we always gravitate to the charming aviary occupied by several canaries and finches.

The day we arrived, we found Dee putting together for her guests a list of the area's attractions. Her able assistant gave us the grand tour and we soon discovered that little had changed since our last visit. Guests may choose from either first or second floor suites, all of them overlooking the courtyard. Each chamber is unique, filled with antiques and other interesting furnishings left to the Taylors by their Grandma Bean. The suites' names, which include Mockingbird Hill, Primrose Lane, or Home Sweet Home, reflect their decorative theme.

Green Palms, for instance, has deep green walls, highlighted by white shutters edging the windows. Cushioned white wicker furnishings and a rocking chair encircle the fireplace. As the ceiling fan turns overhead, guests may rest in the inviting window seat and catch up on some reading. This suite also has a well-equipped kitchen, complete with china, flatware, and glassware — along with a refrigerator, stove, and a television (to entertain the cook). The bedroom is just a continuation of the tropical theme, where mosquito netting covering the bed is the main focal point. A down comforter is the only indication that we are in Laguna Beach, not the Caribbean. A full bath and dressing room complete this spacious suite. The Mandalay chamber explodes in tropical hues of coral and pink accented by a Japanese screen, decorative bird cage, and rattan furnishings. The cranberry and lavender-colored Lilac Time suite offers a mix of traditional Sheraton-style antiques combined with Japanese screens. A brass bed overflows with pillows. The step-down sitting room is a lovely extension of this abode, and here guests will find the suite's fireplace. Opening the pair of French doors, guests enter the courtyard, which extends the living area of the suite even more. The bathroom contains one of the suite's most charming features: a pint-sized, claw-footed bathtub. The Home Sweet Home room is the most reminiscent of Grandma Bean, as calico and gingham combine with lovely antiques and personal momentos to create an inviting and homey chamber. Whichever guest room most tickles one's fancy, all new arrivals are greeted with a bottle of California wine, fresh fruit, fragrant baskets of potpourri, and vases of flowers.

The dining room is often the site of the morning breakfast. The dove-gray wainscoting lined by fresh floral wallpaper is nearly as appealing as the mound of teddy bears occupying one corner of this intimate chamber. The centerpiece is a large table covered in white linen, although there are two more tables nestled off to the side. Oversized mahogany antiques, lit by brass sconces and chandeliers and accented by decorative dishes and hand-painted tiles, complete the effect. The family-style full breakfast starts with fresh fruit and homemade coffee cake, followed by a heartier entrée. When the weather is particularly pleasant, many guests choose to take this meal out on the brick courtyard. Afterwards, some venture the few blocks into town for window shopping or walks along the **beach paths**. During the summer months, dogs are welcome on **Laguna Beach** on a time-limited basis, but in the off-season the visiting hours expand dramatically. Another option Dee told us about is the **Laguna Beach Park** (a few miles north of Route 1). This is a favorite destination for dogs who want space from romping or chasing balls. Afterwards, a sleepy canine can return for a nap, while human guests sip sherry and relax in the courtyard.

Casa Laguna Inn

2510 South Coast Highway
Laguna Beach, California 92651
(800) 233-0449, (714) 494-2996, Fax: (714) 494-5009

Manager: *Kathlyn Flint*
Rooms: *15 doubles, 4 suites, 2 cottages*
Rates: *Doubles $70-125 (B&B), Suites $90-155 (B&B),*
    Cottages $155-225 (B&B)
Payment: *AE, CB, DC, DSC, MC, and VISA*
Dogs: *Welcome with a $5 daily fee; "one neutered pet welcome in larger*
    accommodations"
Children: *Welcome (cribs and high chairs are available)*
Open: *All year*

Laguna Beach is a Mecca for artists, writers, naturalists, and even a surfer or two — not to mention our dogs. This lovely coastal community, nestled against steep hillsides and abutting the Pacific Ocean, highlights the arts each July and August with its famous Festival of Arts and Pageant of the Masters. Even the not-so-artistically-inclined will be inspired by this hamlet by the sea that somehow manages to maintain its character, through fires, earthquakes, and modernization. Dogs and Laguna Beach mix quite well together, and for years we have been trying to find additional places that welcome overnight guests and their canine companions. We finally came across the Casa Laguna Inn.

This Mission-style inn, topped by red Spanish tile roofs and lined by adobe walls, lies just off the Pacific Coast Highway (locals refer to it as PCH), partly obscured by lovely landscaping. The complex is expansive, but is interspersed with several levels of patios and courtyards linking the main buildings and a host of rooms and cottages. We walked up some stairs and down a tiled path to an intriguing subterranean library, whose coral pink walls and festive decor make it especially appealing. Guests tend to congregate here, both for breakfast and afternoon tea, wine, and *hors d'oeuvres*. Further up the hillside, we came across a well-concealed aviary patio, lined by planters overflowing with flowers and accented with white wrought iron garden furniture. A large cage filled with morning doves drew our attention. From the aviary patio we then climbed a path through more tiered gardens filled with tropical plants and flowers, all of which were shaded by queen palms, banana, and avocado trees. We ultimately reached a heated swimming pool encircled by another expansive courtyard, where picturesque ocean views unfolded. Still better vistas appear from the observation deck in the adjacent Bell Tower; and on a clear evening, it is possible to see the sun set over Catalina Island.

We must admit, the exquisite gardens and lush tropical setting appealed to us, but we also liked the many different room styles — especially in the cottages which appeared to be a perfect choice for guests and their dogs. Known simply as the Cottage and Green House, these two charming, one-bedroom abodes offer plenty of living space. In addition to a master bedroom, each also has a full kitchen, a combination living and dining room, and a sitting room with a fireplace. Earth tones are used throughout, accented by stained glass windows and mosaic tiles. Furniture combinations include antique, rattan, and traditional pieces to create a sophisticated beach house ambiance. The modern bathrooms contain showers built for two. Guests typically find themselves on the patios, though, with their distant ocean views. The most spacious cottage, at 1,340 square feet, is the Mission House, which is situated to the rear of the pool. Formerly the owner's residence, this expansive building was recently refurbished. The circular floor plan allows guests to flow easily through the two bedrooms, living room, and full kitchen. Ease of movement aside, the beamed ceilings and two fireplaces appealed to our romantic side. The only drawback is that the Mission House overlooks the PCH and can be noisy at times.

Bringing a dog to the Casa Laguna can also mean reserving some of the larger rooms. The other chambers of interest are the suites that occupy two larger buildings, which are set around yet another courtyard. We prefer the two corner suites, with unobstructed ocean views from both their interior spaces and their private balconies. It would be easy to spend a week's vacation in these expansive chambers (and many people do), which contain a living room, a dining area, and a full kitchen. One suite has a living room large enough to easily accommodate a pair of sleeper sofas, while another has two bedrooms and sleeps six guests. A third suite, situated above the reception area, also boasts ocean views, and a fourth suite overlooks the aviary patio. Those with teeny tiny dogs might be able to persuade the management to let them reserve one of the smaller guest rooms situated to the rear of the main courtyard. These spaces may not have as impressive a view of the ocean, but they do overlook lush gardens filled with blooming hibiscus, bougainvillea, and impatiens.

It is easy to settle in at the Casa Laguna, but as we all know, dogs need their exercise. When we were growing up, Laguna Beach was always our favorite beach community and we spent much time **meandering around here**; however, we hadn't been back since the fires swept through the area. The hillside vegetation is still recovering, but the village seems relatively unscathed. There are almost as many intriguing shops and boutiques worth investigating as there are art galleries and outdoor cafés. The **beach** always beckons, although dogs are limited to early morning and late evening hours.

Trinity Alps Resort

Star Route Box 490
1750 Trinity Alps Road
Lewiston, California 96052
Telephone and Fax: (916) 286-2205
Internet: http://www.trinityalps.com

Hosts: *Morgan and Margo Langan*
Rooms: *43 cabins*
Rates: *$455-865 per week*
Payment: *Personal checks*
Dogs: *Welcome — dogs are part of the family*
Children: *Welcome (cribs, high chairs, and cots are available)*
Open: *Mid-May to October 1st*

A sense of tradition permeates the Trinity Alps Resort. Built in 1923, it is situated some 13 miles north of Weaverville and is comprised of over 90 acres of land. A serpentine road cuts across high ridges and through 500,000 acres of wilderness, before arriving at a narrow metal and wooden bridge. Those tempted to cross the bridge should resist the urge and instead continue down the dirt road a few hundred more feet to the resort's reception area. Here, we discovered a grouping of tin-roofed buildings edged by flower gardens. To one side of this complex are the one- and two-bedroom cabins that blend into the dense forest canopy. Each cabin overlooks the rushing waters of Stuart Forks, a river teeming with rainbow and native brown trout. Getting reacquainted with nature is easy — majestic mountain peaks, curious wildlife, and the strong scent of pine often envelop guests. This informal family resort is a wonderful find, especially because dogs are considered to be such an integral component of this vacation experience.

Three and four generations of families make the yearly pilgrimage to the Trinity Alps Resort. After seeing it, we can understand why people come once and return for "the rest of their lives" (as Morgan and Margo like to put it). Little has changed at the resort over the last 70 years, except for the owners, who are relative newcomers. The Langans, unlike some who acquire vacation properties, found that with an amazing 95% guest return rate there was really no need to change anything at all.

The unpretentious cabins, built with wood originally lumbered from the property, look much the way they did decades ago. The antique ice boxes, sleeping porches lined with metal beds, and camp-style bathrooms complement the well-worn furnishings. Uneven floorboards add their own bit of character. The crisp report of a slamming porch door might even rekindle memories of overnight camp for a few visitors. The cabins, named after various California towns, can accommodate between four and ten people. The largest of these contain two bedrooms, two bathrooms, and two sleeping porches. What guests may wish to consider, in addition to the cabin's size, is its location on the grounds. We prefer the cabins directly on the river's edge, but there are others set closer to the community center, livery stables, and beach. Linens are another option; guest may use the resort's or bring their own supply. Regardless of which linen choice guests eventually decide upon, it is advisable to bring plenty of extra towels. It isn't often we can recommend a family resort that makes the entire family happy, but at the Trinity Alps, adults, children, and dogs will find plenty to do and inevitably make many new friends. During our visit, it seemed most cabins had a dog or two in residence.

This place is special, and it isn't just because of the casual atmosphere and natural surroundings — it is also because of the abundant recreational diversions. Guests can look to the central bulletin board for a list of the day's activities and a copy of the dinner menu. Days may be spent swimming, tubing, panning for gold, batting the birdie in badminton, or playing shuffleboard, volleyball, basketball, tennis, or horseshoes. One of the more amusing adventures, especially for a dog, is crossing the **swinging bridge**. Although it is very safe, it does tend to bounce around quite a bit, sending dogs and photographers (trying to capture the essence of the resort) all over the place. Anyone who prefers bouncing on a horse can take the "dependable trail horses" on a one- or two-hour ride. The breakfast ride is the most popular, and guests should sign up for it shortly after they arrive.

There are also great **hiking trails** nearby, leading into the **Trinity Alps Wilderness Area** and to **Trinity Lake**. Guests can either have lunch packed for them before they leave or return to have lunch at the General Store. If the weather becomes inclement, we suggest heading over to the General Store or the other outlying buildings for Ping-pong, darts, pool, and assorted arcade games. For those who may have forgotten something, the General Store, true to its name, has a variety of sundries (no meat or vegetables). Here, guests will also find a charming, old-fashioned soda fountain that delights visitors of all ages. Daytime activities can often extend into the evening hours, allowing guests time to relax and chat, read a favorite novel, or play pool or Foosball. The evening also brings square dances, talent shows, movies, bingo or perhaps a sing-along around the campfire.

Although guests usually prepare their own meals, they may also eat at the resort's riverside restaurant. This is a wonderful old building that lacks nothing — including character. A good-sized, carved wooden bear resides on its the front porch, while an assortment of old farm tools and collectibles hangs from the interior walls. We especially liked the variety of cowboy boots lined up on top of the piano lid. The full menu (with a separate children's menu) offers everything from hamburgers to prime rib. Most enjoy taking this meal out to the porch and dining under the colorful umbrellas, while the breeze blows through the shade trees and the river rushes below. We can think of no better way to end yet another terrific day at the Trinity Alps Resort.

S.S. Seafoam Lodge

6751 North Highway 1
Little River, California 95456
Mailing Address: P.O. Box 68
Mendocino, California 95460
(800) 606-1827, (707) 937-1827, (707) 937-1022
Internet: http://www.touristguide.com/b&b/ca/seafoam

Manager: *Jackey Perry*
Rooms: *19 doubles, 4 suites, 1 cottage*
Rates: *Doubles $95-150 (B&B), Suites $135-150 (B&B),*
  Cottage $150-200 (B&B)
Payment: *AE, DSC, MC and VISA*
Dogs: *Welcome with a $10 daily fee*
Children: *Welcome (cribs, cots, and baby-sitters available)*
Open: *All year*

California

Mendocino is a favorite getaway for vacationers seeking a peaceful and relatively remote oceanside destination. With the dense surrounding forests it is not too surprising that the town's roots were centered around the lumber industry. However, when the lumber boom was over, the once bustling hamlet became a virtual ghost town. Fortunately, artisans rediscovered this picturesque region some 70 years ago and began to infuse some life into the community. Many of the artisans also discovered that they relished the solitude and tranquillity of this region, and that the magnificent rocky coastline seemed to enhance their creativity. Like so many who came before us, we were instantly enamored with Mendocino, as much for the magnificent ocean views and pine covered mountains as for the charming New England village atmosphere.

There are plenty of accommodations to choose from, both in town and in the surrounding area. However, one of the best values is the reasonably priced S. S. Seafoam Lodge. Set off the winding rural coastal highway, the lodge's one- and two-story brown buildings resemble a rustic motor lodge. Upon closer inspection, though, visitors will discover a place that not only has character, but also has quaint guest rooms boasting ocean views. A winding gravel driveway lined with rhododendrons and small shrubs leads up a hill to the main building. Along the way, guests pass a cottage that is a favorite of many. Known as Captain's Quarters, it is set apart from the other accommodations. The remaining lodge rooms line the ridge, with a dense forest serving as the harmonious backdrop.

The lodge's simple, rustic exteriors give way to cheery bedrooms, decorated around a strong nautical theme. The painted beamed ceilings, walls dotted with woodland or seaside prints, and pairs of sliding glass doors make these good-sized chambers seem all the more open and airy. Floral bedspreads, draped over the queen and king beds, set the color scheme. From either the beds or the comfortable russet-colored sofas and armchairs, guests have nice views of the sloping front lawn and distant water. Each state room or suite also offers many standard amenities, such as clock radios, televisions, and coffee makers. Baskets filled with pot-pourri are placed on bedside tables, while jars brimming with salt-water taffy are set atop bookshelves.

In the morning, a basket of breakfast goodies arrives at the door, allowing for a leisurely start to the day. Each guest chamber also shares a porch that runs the length of the building. The second floor porches have the advantage of better water views, while the suites provide additional creature comforts, and are often reserved by long-term guests. Guests may request suites with a living room and kitchenette, a wood stove or fireplace, and a private deck — or all of the above. A perennial favorite is Room 21, an expansive chamber at the end of the Promenade building. This spacious corner suite is filled with an array of additional amenities and offers easy access to the surrounding grounds.

Guest rooms aside, the main attraction is still Mendocino. While golf and tennis are easily accessible, doggie companions would probably prefer something a little less people oriented. Some of our favorite options are bicycle rides along the scenic back roads, walks along the **picturesque beaches,** or canoe trips down the many rivers. Lodge guests also have access **Buckhorn Beach,** which is ideal for beach combing or birding. The paths lining the bluffs are fun to explore as well, and certain to be enjoyed by canine companions.

A short drive from the lodge will bring visitors and their dogs to **Mendocino's village,** where there are a number of fun walks to be enjoyed along the charming back streets. There are many intriguing galleries, boutiques, and restaurants worth closer inspection. Afterwards, a jaunt down to the park along **the headlands** will surely appeal to patient canine friends.

Checkers Hotel

535 South Grand Avenue
Los Angeles, California 90071
(800) WYNDHAM, (213) 624-0000, Fax: (213) 626-9906
Internet: http://www.travelweb.com

General Manager: *Jim Chin*
Rooms: *173 doubles, 15 suites*
Rates: *Doubles $145-285 (EP), Suites $450-1,000 (EP)*
Payment: *AE, DC, DSC, JCB, MC, and VISA*
Dogs: *Welcome with notice and a one-time fee of $25*
Children: *Welcome (cribs, cots, and baby-sitters are available)*
Open: *All year*

In 1927, the million dollar Mayflower Hotel opened its doors, to much fanfare. It drew rave reviews at the time, as much for its Spanish Renaissance facade, complete with gargoyles and intricate plaster work, as for its interior spaces, which combined a Colonial and Spanish motif. For years it catered to the privileged, offering fine accommodations and an excellent restaurant. As with most luxury hotels of that era, the Depression brought about financial instability. For many years thereafter, the famous Mayflower Hotel floundered under various owners.

It wasn't until 1985 that the 535 South Grand Associates purchased the hotel and closed it down. Leaving only the shell intact, they spent $49 million to overhaul the interior and bring the structure up to California's stringent earthquake codes. The 348 tiny guest rooms were reconfigured into 190 more spacious chambers, and the interiors were imbued with a sophisticated decor. The designers combined Oriental with English and French and Art Deco to create an international feeling. They then coupled subtle pastel colors and delicate accent pieces to create an effect that even seasoned travelers will find unusual. Finally, they named the hotel Checkers, after Richard Nixon's dog. The hotel has been featured in our book over the years, yet we were a little concerned to learn that there is another new owner — Wyndham Hotels. We soon discovered, though, that Checkers is still appealing as ever.

First impressions of the hotel are soothing, as much for the color schemes as for the furnishings. Intimate sitting areas, created from delicately carved armchairs and overstuffed peach sofas, intermingle with Oriental antiques. As guests pass through the marble foyer, they will see that a clever use of mirrors accentuates the intimate alcoves. We found several new arrivals chatting in the living room-style lobby, which adjoins an even more intimate bar. Noteworthy treasures displayed here and throughout the hotel consist of 19th-century mother of pearl elephants and Song-style urns, as well as Chinese lacquered boxes and Japanese screens. Mirrors framed in hand carved guilded woods are placed above unusual Art Deco stands topped by brass bowls. The overall effect is alluring.

This design theme carries through into the guest bedrooms. The detailed moldings and tasteful furnishings nicely contrast with the neutral color schemes, creating an understated elegance. Esthetics aside, the rooms are well-equipped with all the necessities. Desks are large enough to accommodate computers and other work paraphernalia, while small side tables are ideal for a light breakfast. Handsome armoires conceal remote controlled televisions and well-stocked minibars. Even with the room reconfigurations, some of the bedrooms remain diminutive, but the mirrored alcoves and oversized windows make them appear more substantial. This extends into the marble bathrooms, which are fully appointed with custom toiletries, terry robes, oversized towels, hair dryers, bathroom scales, and one of three telephones. The king bedrooms (or the "08" chambers), are probably the most luxurious and occupy the hotel's north corners. These bedroom and sitting room combinations are privy to abundant natural light and of course, additional space. Along with the aforementioned amenities, the hotel staff provides a long list of additional services, including valets who will pack and unpack for the guests.

As we mentioned, the designers who restored Checkers not only met the state's rigid earthquake standards, but they also created some new surprises along the way. Two of the more notable are the ever-popular rooftop spa and swimming pool. Set amid planters of trees and flowers and surrounded by wrought iron chairs and tables are a gorgeous outdoor Jacuzzi and a lap pool. For those who are so inclined, there is also a state-of-the-art gym, as well as men's and women's saunas. Many enjoy dining up here in the outdoor café, which offers a more casual dining atmosphere than that of the renowned Checkers Restaurant.

The hotel's first floor restaurant is comprised of columns and half walls topped with marble and lovely floral arrangements, all of which create three distinct dining areas. The color scheme is reminiscent of the hotel's other common areas, with cream-colored walls accented by celadon green and peach. The cuisine is light, with an emphasis on quality rather than quantity. Unusual flavors combine to create the innovative and savory entrées. Two of the most requested appetizers are the rum smoked salmon with a celery, apple, and cucumber-dill salad, and the maple wood smoked duck breast carpaccio with a gnocchi and artichoke salad. Diners may then be tempted by such selections as the roast pheasant with duxelles of chanterelles and apples; the veal medallions with spinach and forest mushroom ragoût; or the salmon with corn and leek fondu, semolina crème fraîche rounds, and a roasted red chili sauce. The ever-changing menu is creatively prepared and artfully presented — delighting even the most discriminating palates.

While the Checkers location — right in the heart of Los Angeles' financial district — is not ideal for long, picturesque walks, Southern California's more notable attractions are nearby. **Griffith Park** (4,000 acres) and **Elysian Park** (a 585-acre park that is also home of the Dodgers baseball team) are close to the hotel. We can also recommend a trip to **Descanso Gardens** in nearby La Cañada as another outdoor adventure. Within a short drive of the hotel are Chinatown, the Los Angeles Zoo, and Will Rogers State Park. Be prepared to drive though, after all, this is Southern California and cars are the preferred mode of transportation.

Four Seasons Hotel

300 South Doheny Drive
Los Angeles, California   90048
(800) 332-3442, (310) 273-2222, Fax: (310) 859-3824
Internet: http://www.fshr.com

General Manager: *William MacKay*
Rooms: *169 doubles, 106 suites*
Rates: *Doubles $295-355 (EP), Suites $450-3,000 (EP)*
Payment: *AE, DC, DSC, MC, and VISA*
Dogs: *Welcome with approval*
Children: *Welcome (cribs, cots, high chairs, and children's programs are available)*
Open: *All year*

The Four Seasons and Regent hotels merged a few years ago, combining their collection of high end accommodations around the world. Southern California has plenty of luxury hotels — certainly enough to take care of the well-heeled business and leisure travelers who frequent these destinations. Very few, though, offer the high level of service, exquisite accommodations, and well-designed facility provided by the Four Seasons Hotel, Los Angeles. Situated just five minutes from the heart of Beverly Hills and the renowned Rodeo Drive, this relatively new hotel lies in a quiet residential neighborhood.

After driving down the grand, palm-lined avenue leading to the hotel, we got out of the car and instantly fell in with a festive group of people. They were part of a huge wedding reception; although we were tempted to join them, an attentive staff member instead whisked us past the group and through the front door. Along the way, we did take a moment to look at the two bronze statues by Seward Johnson. In true Johnson fashion, he captured his subjects' qualities so well that these lifelike figures appear totally immersed in a very real and animated conversation.

The lobby is awash with pale peach and ivory hues, especially across the variegated marble floors and tables. Recessed and diffused light emanating from tray ceilings enhances the light and airy effect. Potted palms and magnificent flower arrangements seem to be everywhere, and are especially prevalent in the formal sitting rooms. In here, overstuffed sofas and armchairs, set upon floral hand-woven carpets, are placed around the central fireplaces. A wall of windows and French doors, overlooking the fountain and lushly landscaped courtyard, seems to bring that garden setting inside.

After exploring the first floor, we were eager to see the bedrooms. There is, of course, a myriad of room configurations and views available, but we were thankful to be in a room offering a little of both. Rooms on floors two through nine are "deluxe," with "superior" rooms on the floors above these. The suites are scattered throughout the hotel. Our "deluxe" room was perfect, as it was slightly larger than a standard room and seemed downright enormous because of the high ceilings. The ivory walls serve as a backdrop for the pale blue and peach fabrics covering the traditional furnishings. Walls of French doors open to the private patios and reveal views of the palm-lined streets surrounding Beverly Hills. Tailored spreads and dust ruffles cover the beds, including the four-poster king versions. The distinct residential feeling is achieved through contemporary artwork, intriguing *objets d'art*, and vases of fresh flowers. Unlike at our own house, though, we had an attentive and courteous staff attending to our every need. Maids visit twice a day and valet and laundry service are available on a 24-hour basis, as is room service. Bathrooms are awash with marble and brass accents, and stocked with a complete array of toiletries and terry robes. Of course, the Four Seasons trademark doggie tray is awaiting Bowser's arrival. Guests do not even have to bring their canine's bowl, as the hotel supplies it along with bottled water and dog biscuits. The hotel staff will even walk the dog for guests who would like a little time to themselves.

This is the land of well-toned physiques and the Four Seasons has just the place to inspire anyone. Up on the fourth floor we found the turquoise waters of the rooftop swimming pool. Set around it are palm trees and lush plant life reminiscent of the tropics, not downtown Los Angeles. After swimming and sunning some in the chaise lounges, we noticed some guests getting up and disappearing into a tent. The fitness center is located in there, complete with televisions tuned to intriguing sports events. It isn't necessary to work out in order to visit the juice bar, where an array of fruity concoctions awaits.

Of course, more extensive gourmet offerings are available at Gardens, the hotel's premier restaurant. As we walked through the salon to get there, we spied another pair of Seward Johnson bronze statues just outside the bay window. They appeared to be tending to the landscaping duties of the day. Sitting in the restaurant, surrounded by wood paneling and ivory walls interspersed with half walls overflowing with fragrant flowers, we perused the menu. Appetizer selections included the grilled Hudson Valley *foie gras* with a salad of mache, kohlrabi, and mangoes; the carrot and ginger soup with roasted squab; or the Russian Beluga caviar (for those who want to splurge at $75 for 30 grams). Entrées are not as pricey as the caviar, and are even more inspired. One choice is the roast magret duck with late summer figs and pears, blossom honey and tarragon jus; red snapper Mediterranean style with a potato purée, zucchini, eggplant, and a tomato saffron bouillon; or the violet mustard crusted rack of lamb with a salad of forest mushrooms, ratatouille, and tarragon jus.

After a lovely dinner, most people walk their dog around the block and go to bed. During the day, though, this is *the* place to walk, to see, and to be seen. We thought it would be fun to walk all the way over to Beverly Hills — the Beverly Hills city limit is just across the street from the hotel. We like the hotel because it is surrounded by a **residential neighborhood**, where dogs and people should feel comfortable walking most times of the day and evening. Those who prefer to shop will surely want to pay a visit to the world-renowned Rodeo Drive. Others may want to investigate some of the more low-key parks in the area, such as **Franklin Canyon Ranch** or **Roxbury Park**. Locals and their pampered pooches frequent both of these spots.

Hotel Bel-Air

701 Stone Canyon Road
Los Angeles, California 90077
(800) 648-4097, (310) 472-1211, Fax: (310) 476-5890

General Manager: *Frank Bowling*
Rooms: *52 doubles, 40 suites*
Rates: *Doubles $285-435 (EP), Suites $495-2,500 (EP)*
Payment: *AE, CB, DC, DSC, MC, and VISA*
Dogs: *Welcome with approval and a $250 cleaning fee*
Children: *Welcome (cribs, roll-away beds, and baby-sitters are available)*
Open: *All year*

The Hotel Bel-Air's main building, constructed in 1922 by oil millionaire Alfonzo E. Bell, once housed the planning and sales offices for the exclusive Bel-Air subdivision. Within this edifice, Bell's architects and designers drafted the plans for the winding roads and lavish estates that would one day occupy the neighboring hills and canyons. Reasoning that no estate would be complete without equestrian trails, Bell also established the Bel-Air stables. The 60 miles of trails enabled residents to ride within the boundaries of their exclusive enclave. Then in the early 1940s, Joseph Brown bought the land, offices, and stables and converted them into a luxury hotel. Keeping the 1920s mission-style charm of the buildings, Mr. Brown added beautiful gardens, Swan Lake, the Pavilion Room, and the swimming pool and cabañas. Since that time, the exquisite Hotel Bel-Air has long been a favorite destination for the famous and wealthy, accommodating stars such as Gary Cooper, Grace Kelley, Gregory Peck, Howard Hughes, and Marilyn Monroe, along with the Kennedy and Rockefeller families. The secluded and magnificently appointed grounds are unequaled. All this, coupled with the elegant guest rooms and first-class service, combine to create one of this country's premier hotels.

One of two gates leads into Bel-Air, which still maintains its private, totally residential feeling. Tucked into 12 acres of flowering trees, shrubs, and lush gardens is the intimate hotel. Azaleas, tulips, gardenia, jasmine, camellias, bougainvillea's, and hyacinths create a harmonious sensory experience. The sounds of falling water are everywhere, emanating from courtyard fountains, Swan Lake's waterfall, and from the gently flowing stream. We followed the gracefully arching footbridge to the hotel's entrance, where the sight of the red-flowering trumpet vines covering the Mediterranean-style building always causes us to pause. From here, a variety of narrow, winding paths lead past lovely courtyards to the guest quarters.

Guest rooms give the distinct impression of being individually decorated. The lavish yet traditionally tasteful furnishings and decor are the work of five different designers. We must admit, the backdrop for their creative efforts could be the source of this inspiration. High-beamed ceilings flow down to walls lined with wood-burning fireplaces, bay-windowed alcoves, and French doors. The decorators hand-stenciled the vaulted ceilings and then brightened the spaces with perfectly coordinated floral fabrics, needlepoint rugs, and one-of-a-kind chairs and tables. Some bedrooms reflect a cool, French country ambiance, a few are swathed in English chintz, and still others are reminiscent of the American Southwest. Each bedroom is refined, yet tranquil. Fresh flower arrangements, along with potted plants and trees, create the feeling of being in the midst of botanical gardens, right in the bedroom. The preferred guest chambers lie in the older building, but those in the newer section are generally more spacious. The suites provide small kitchens, along with private landscaped patios and Jacuzzis. A full array of five-star services includes a nightly turndown, 24-hour room service, and a valet.

Fortunately, the hotel's restaurant is as noteworthy as are its accommodations. Subtle tones of peach and moss green seem reflective of the garden views that may be enjoyed through the paned doors and windows. Flowers also adorn the dining room, adding interest to the intimate table arrangements. The chef is renowned for his use of fresh ingredients and unusual herbs to prepare his California-style haute cuisine. Interested patrons may visit the chef's herb garden and examine his extensive array of plants, or just let the magic unfold as aromatic fragrances tantalize the senses. Appetizers often include a fricassee of scallops, asparagus, and morels in a light Riesling-tarragon sauce; a ginger-cured salmon with shiitake mushroom chopsticks; and a tempura quail. Breast of squab on a compote of wild rice; rack of lamb with a sun-dried tomato and black olive risotto; or a grilled seabass and a shellfish-fennel roulade top the long list of entrées. The exquisite dessert selections are too tantalizing to resist. Options include the bittersweet chocolate cake with a Black Forest ice cream and sun-dried cherry sauce; the apple-pumpkin cobbler with maple sauce; or mango, blood orange, and avocado sorbets in a cinnamon-dusted tortilla shell with berry salsa. Afterwards, guests may want to settle in for a bit in the Bar, which is still the place to see, and be seen by, the city's famous.

While at the hotel, guests and their dogs may walk along the **winding residential roads** that encircle the grounds. Later in the day, vistors might try a swim in the heated, oval swimming pool. This oasis is so peaceful that guests will be equally comfortable relaxing on the chaise lounges or under the white umbrellas. The new, fully equipped Fitness Center lies in what *was* known as the Marilyn Monroe Cottage. There is also tennis and golf, available off the property, as well as some of the best (and probably most expensive) shopping in the country. Dogs are welcome to explore **Rodeo Drive** and, if very well behaved, may be invited into the stores and perhaps given a biscotti while his owners shop. Less formal — and far more fun — is the **UCLA campus**. Here, there are large grassy areas to play on and plenty of young collegiates who would be willing to share their Frisbees or balls with an eager retriever.

California

The Stanford Inn by the Sea

P.O. Box 487
Comptche-Ukiah Road & Coast Highway 1
Mendocino, California 95460
(800) 331-8884, (707) 937-5615, Fax: (707) 937-0305
E-mail: stanford@stanfordinn.com   Internet: http://www.stanfordinn.com

Innkeepers: *Joan and Jeff Stanford*
Rooms: *22 doubles, 3 suites*
Rates: *Doubles $190-235 (B&B), Suites $225-325 (B&B)*
Payment: *AE, DC, DSC, JCB, MC, and VISA*
Dogs: *Welcome with a $25 one-time fee ($7.50 for each additional dog); must be kept leashed*
Children: *Welcome (cribs, cots, high chairs, and baby-sitters are available)*
Open: *All year*

The Pomo Indian tribe once inhabited the magnificent coast where Mendocino now lies. By the mid-19th century, lumbermen from New England also settled in this region. Despite a mill and housing for the workers, established by the logging companies, the area was soon abandoned. Many years later, the artisans arrived, and were eventually followed by others drawn to the solitude and unspoiled beauty that surrounds Mendocino. The Stanfords are one of these families, who came here in 1981 with their young children and decided to stay. Their tradition of exceptional hospitality is renowned.

Their inn, The Stanford Inn by the Sea, is set on a hillside where the village's townspeople and loggers once grew their own fruits and vegetables.

Since our last visit, the Stanfords have been busy — refurbishing guest rooms, expanding their Big River Nurseries (a wonderful California-certified organic farm), and tending to their Big River Llamas. While we welcome these grand additions to an already superb inn, there are many aspects that, fortunately, have not changed over the years. These include the exquisite ocean views from the private decks and balconies, the gently swaying, towering pine trees, and the beautifully maintained grounds.

As we followed the gravel driveway up the hill, the familiar two-story redwood inn, nestled into a grove of trees, came into view. Over the years, the tiered gardens have become even more magnificent, with elaborate flower displays and mature plantings fronting the building. Window boxes, overflowing with geraniums, line the other side. We always enjoy walking into the intimate reception area, where nooks contain all sorts of collectibles and gifts, including an assortment of teddy bears. An equally charming common area accommodates guests who want to stay awhile and soak up the atmosphere.

After seeing a rustic exterior overgrown with ivy, some may find it tough to imagine what the guest rooms look like. There are certain places that stand out in any traveler's mind, and even the most jaded of voyagers is likely to remember the rooms at the Stanford Inn. These pine-paneled spaces are long on comfort and amenities. Sleigh or four-poster beds are surrounded by local artwork, crafts, and country antiques. Guests may select a favorite novel from the small library of books and settle into the overstuffed sofa or armchair that are set before a wood burning fireplace or Waterford stove. French doors open onto the balcony for panoramic views of the gardens, the pond teeming with waterfowl, and the llama farm. We look forward to the foggy days or cool nights when we can light the fire, play some music, and enjoy a bottle of local wine and chocolate truffles left by our hosts. On these days, our canine cohorts enjoy curling up before the fire for their afternoon naps, while we watch a videotape or settle in with a good mystery. Bathrooms, while not overly spacious, are well appointed with Waterpick shower heads, thick towels, terry robes, and fragrant soaps and lotions.

These bedrooms are ideal for couples; however, families might wish to consider staying in the suites or barn apartment. Our favorite is the quaint cottage, located near the gardens and pond. There are two options in this building — one is a good sized, first floor suite and the other is actually located on two different floors. The latter offers a master bedroom downstairs and a kitchen and living room upstairs under the eaves. The amenities and decor here are basically the same as those found in the standard rooms — there is just more space. Dogs are very welcome additions to the Stanford Inn, and are invited to explore the property. Most end up visiting the llamas, who are curious creatures that welcome your — and your canine companion's — attention.

Each morning guests are invited to enjoy a hearty Continental breakfast served in the parlor, off the reception area. Fresh fruit, granola, hot cereals, and yogurt are complemented by hot muffins, quiche, croissants, and pastries. Freshly ground coffee, tea, and hot chocolate are not unusual, but the champagne is. While enjoying breakfast, we recommend sifting through the inn's plethora of information detailing the area's numerous activities and diversions. Catch A Canoe & Bicycles Too, also operated by the Stanfords, is a canoe and bicycle rental service — renting canoes for trips up the tidal river and bicycles for exploring the picturesque back roads. **Big River Beach** is just a few minutes from the inn and is a great place for dogs to romp, swim, or just dig for clams. The nearby parks offer wonderful hiking trails, as well as the unique and impressive **Redwood** and **Pygmy** forests. At the end of the day, though, we thoroughly enjoy returning to the inn and heading over to the greenhouse — one of Joan and Jeff's newer and most elaborate projects. Surrounded by botanical splendor, guests can take a dip in the heated pool, lounge amid the warmth of the greenhouse, or rejuvenate in the sauna or spa.

Mendocino Village Cottages

P.O. Box 1295
45320 Little Lake Street
Mendocino, California 95460
(707) 937-0866

Hostess: *Gisela Linder*
Rooms: *2 cottages, 1 cabin*
Rates: *$60-110 (EP)*
Payment: *MC and VISA*
Dogs: *Welcome with a $10 fee*
Children: *Welcome*
Open: *All year*

Reminiscent of the towns that hug Maine's craggy coastline, Mendocino Village Cottages evoke a similar feeling, except they lie near the majestic headlands overlooking the Pacific. In order to gain a real sense of the community, some visitors like to stay in the charming village of Mendocino. Those traveling with dogs; however, have always been out of luck — until now. Finally, on our fourth visit in a decade, we found two excellent options at the Mendocino Village Cottages. To find the cottages, guests drive through town toward the more remote headlands. Here, they will come across three cottages, albeit eclectic ones, with nice views of the ocean.

Set a few hundred yards from the headlands, the Mendocino Village Cottages are located along a quiet dirt road, across from what appears to have once been an old lighthouse. Guests enter through a side gate into a small grassy yard lined with flower and herb gardens. Nestled in among the greenery are three simple cottages. Off to the right of the courtyard is the Green House, which is not appropriate for those traveling with dogs; however, both the New House and Garden Cabin welcome canine companions. We passed under a canopy of climbing flowers and honeysuckle before reaching the French door leading into the weathered New House. Open-beamed ceilings, inset with skylights, add interest to this charming abode. We expected the natural wood walls to darken this space, however; the sizable windows allow a good deal of sunlight to permeate all levels of the cottage. The centerpiece of the intimate sitting and dining area is a free-standing wood stove, which is fashioned with a pair of rocking chairs and handmade furnishings set on an Oriental carpet. Occupying another corner of the room is the old-fashioned kitchen with its butcher block countertops. Guests can sleep in the platform bed, lined with thick pillows so that it doubles as a couch, or in the queen bed situated up in the cozy loft. While there is only five feet of clearance at the peak of the loft's roof, the westward facing skylights and six-foot long window enhance the sense of space and light. Most memorable, though, are views of the headlands gained from this chamber (as well as from the downstairs' bathroom). While the views are most enticing, we found we spent most of our time out on the deck amid refreshing ocean breezes and the halcyon splendor of the gardens.

The Garden Cabin is substantially smaller and even more rustic than the New House, although we liked its weathered walls, interesting woodworking, and wood slat ceilings. This cozy dwelling is just 12 by 14 feet. It may not offer a fully-equipped kitchen like the New House, but it does have water views from its high platform bed. It also contains a freestanding stove, with just enough space left over for a pair of armchairs, a breakfast table, and a bookcase. The modest bathroom contains a shower, commode, and a small sink. While the overall feeling of this cabin is a little unpolished, we can highly recommend its bucolic surroundings. We found that the comfortable accommodations, low-key atmosphere, and proximity to the town center make both of these accommodations delightful places to spend some time. Moreover, while there are a number of fine inns and B&Bs in Mendocino's village, few can boast of such incredible views of the setting sun as it disappears behind the headlands and ocean.

Best of all, guests will find the **Headlands State Park** just across the way from the cottages. Dogs are not only welcome in this park, but they can also happily romp along the paths without being disturbed. We also love meandering along the **quiet back roads**, through **open fields**, and across the area's **sandy beaches**. Another one of our favorite walks is back into town, where there are all sorts of shops and cafés frequented by both people and their dogs.

California

The Homestead

P.O. Box 13
Midpines, California 95345
(209) 966-2820

Hosts: Blair and Helen Fowler
Rooms: 1 house
Rates: $95-120 for first couple, plus $25 for each additional person
Payment: Personal checks
Dogs: Welcome with notice and approval
Children: "Well-supervised" children are welcome (baby-sitters can be arranged for with notice)
Open: All year

The Homestead is approximately 40 minutes from Yosemite Valley and is set in the town of Midpines. This refurbished, rustic ranch-style house lies on 23 acres of woods and meadows, surrounded by a virtually endless amount of natural beauty. One of the B&Bs' best features are that guests, whether couples, families, or groups of friends, have the whole house to themselves for the entire length of their visit. The Fowlers live in a separate home across the meadow from the ranch.

In many ways, The Homestead is like having a second home, but better. The house is well stocked with linens, board games, and plenty of food in the kitchen for all the meals. Guests will find the spacious living room to be a favorite gathering place. The ceilings are beamed and the walls finished with knotty pine boards. A large fieldstone fireplace, complete with a stag's head mounted above it, is an interesting contrast to the family antiques and more traditional American country furnishings.

Three bedrooms, two upstairs with single beds, and one downstairs with a queen bed, sleep six comfortably. Festive, quilted calico spreads cover these beds. The honey-colored knotty pine walls provide a nice backdrop to an antique trunk, a pair of bedside tables, and framed prints. The bathroom situation is a bit sparse for groups, but most people will be more than content with the first-floor full bath and the half-bath upstairs. When decorating, Blair and Helen were wise to keep things simple and uncluttered. This makes it easy for guests, their children, and any dogs to completely relax without navigating around knickknacks, collectibles, or family heirlooms.

Evenings at The Homestead are often spent outside, on the fieldstone patio with outdoor fireplace. We can think of nothing easier when vacationing than barbecuing meals and eating outdoors. There are plenty of large shade trees to nap under, while letting the refreshing valley breezes waft overhead. Guests are engaged by the visiting ducks waddling by the house and by the horses grazing in the adjacent field. The Homestead is particularly appealing to those who want an easy, stress-free vacation without the distractions of the outside world. Besides the fact that The Homestead is a real bargain, guests tend to return year after year because of the B&B's lack of pretense, the friendly hosts, and its isolated, cabin-like setting.

When looking for other things to do off the property, guests might consider the neighboring **Sierra National Forest,** whose several large lakes, an array of excellent hiking trails, and plenty of fishing opportunities offer a nice assortment of dog-friendly diversions A short drive out of Midpines leads visitors to the famous Highway 49. Follow this rural route north a bit to **Lake McClure,** where there are a number of areas that allow leashed dogs.

San Ysidro Ranch

900 San Ysidro Lane
Montecito, California 93108
(800) 368-6788, (805) 969-5046, Fax: (805) 565-1995
Internet: http://www.sanysidroranch.com

Innkeepers: *Bob Harmon and Claude Rouas*
Rooms: *45 bedrooms and suites in 22 cottages*
Rates: *$325-2,500 (EP)*
Payment: *AE, DC, MC, and VISA*
Dogs: *Welcome in freestanding cottages with a $45 cleaning fee (pet menus are available)*
Children: *Welcome (summer camp program, children's menus, cribs, cots, and high chairs available)*
Open: *All year*

California

The San Ysidro Ranch, located in the Santa Ynez foothills, has a long and colorful history. Its origins can be traced back to the Santa Barbara Padres, who used to raise cattle on this land. By 1893, the property was better known as a citrus farm and guest ranch. In 1935, actor Ronald Coleman discovered the property, and with the aid of Senator Alvin Weingand, transformed the ranch into one of Hollywood's favorite retreats. Notable guests included Sinclair Lewis, Sir Laurence Olivier, William Powell, Winston Churchill, Bing Crosby, Jack Benny, and finally John and Jacquelyn Kennedy who spent their honeymoon here. Susie and Jim Lavenson (the former President of the Plaza Hotel in New York City) bought the ranch in 1976 and totally overhauled the property. Their restoration included rebuilding the ranch's already outstanding reputation, both for its exquisite accommodations and for its fine foods. More recently, Bob Harmon and Claude Rouas, who also own several other prestigious inns in California, took over ownership. Returning guests should feel comfortable knowing they, too, have maintained the ranch's historic charm and appeal, deciding only to enhance the restaurant and its wine cellar.

New arrivals will drive through the exclusive residential community of Montecito before heading into the hills leading towards the San Ysidro Ranch. Once guests enter the property, they will find that high hedges and groves of eucalyptus, sycamore, and oak trees provide walls of privacy. Before too long, the combined scent of jasmine, rose, honeysuckle, and orange blossoms will waft through the air, creating an aroma that new arrivals will long remember and returning guests will immediately recognize. There are an array of exquisite gardens that surround the lavishly appointed, "elegant but rustic" one-story cottages. This lovely inn has always pampered people, but it now deserves a few accolades from the pampered pet contingency, as well. Our two canines were quite happy to be back, eyeing the gum-ball machine filled with doggie treats, while we signed them into the guest pet book. Next to the reception area lies the inviting Hacienda Lounge. Here, guests can write postcards at the oversized desk or perhaps play the piano. In the evening, people gravitate to the billiards table, or draw a chair up to yet another table for a game of cards, backgammon, or chess. Others prefer to make their favorite libation at the honor bar and simply relax in the comfortable sofas set by the fieldstone fireplace.

The atmosphere at the San Ysidro Ranch is convivial, but always with an eye toward respecting guests' privacy. The name branded on a wooden plaque hanging from a cottage's front door may be recognizable, but no one would consider disturbing another guest's solitude. Just as each guest is unique, so is each individual cottage. Some traditional cottages, which usually house between one and three guest chambers, feature French doors and Palladian windows, while others highlight contemporary beamed cathedral ceilings with paddle fans and skylights. In one room, a chintz comforter covers the four-poster bed backed by a hanging quilt, while in another, the bed rests in front of a wood burning stove or brick fireplace. More formal spaces contain bold floral chintzes on the overstuffed sofas and armchairs. Standing brass lamps cast their light over plush carpeting or Oriental rugs. Dried wreaths placed amidst botanical or waterfowl prints grace many of the walls, while shuttered windows allow just the right amount of light into these spacious abodes. Some cottages have full kitchens, wet bars, coffee makers, and expansive porches, often inset with hot tubs. All the bathrooms are good-sized and equipped with Corian sinks set in antique bureaus or chests and accented with brass fixtures. Fragrant soaps and lotions, thick towels, and soft cotton bathrobes (folded at the end of the bed) are just a few of the additional luxuries. The Lilac Two cottage is a favorite for many guests, with its Palladian windows and brass bed tucked into a windowed alcove. Others prefer the Creek cottage for its festive blue and white pinstriped couches fronting a brick fireplace that is flanked by walls of bookshelves.

Some people might want to sequester themselves in the cottages, but if their canine companion can't entice them out, then the abundant recreational diversions should provide enough of a reason. Many people come here to ride on the seemingly endless **equestrian trails**. (The ranch has extra stable space for those who want to bring their own horse.) We enjoy hiking across portions of the **ranch's 540 acres** with the dogs, or playing a little catch in between games on one of the two tennis courts. We also like the idea of peaceful strolls through the **fragrant gardens** or a refreshing dip in the swimming pool (always comfortably heated). Those who have children in tow may be interested in the complimentary Camp SYR, which runs from 9 a.m. to 3 p.m. daily. A full complement of massages and body treatments are also available at the inn's spa — Bodyworks. Further afield, Dogs are welcome to explore the trails in the **Los Padres National Forest**. We do recommend saving enough energy for one final extravaganza at the end of the day: dinner in the Stonehouse Restaurant.

Dinner at the ranch has always been memorable, but now it is exceptional. An unusual chandelier, formed from deer antlers, still illuminates the camel-colored adobe walls and beamed ceilings. The noteworthy copper doors still provide the same backdrop to the simply elegant table settings and arrangements of fresh flowers. It is the food that is different from before, culled from a constantly changing menu. Guests may order à la carte or they may order off the Ranch Classic or Chef's Tasting menus. During our visit patrons could choose from eight delectable appetizers, including the lobster and sweet corn tamale with chipolte chile and citrus cream and *foie gras* on Parmesan cheese grits with shaved ham and 100-year-old balsamic vinegar. Entrées included salmon roasted on an oak barrel plank with garlic mashed potatoes and chive sauce; the ancho pepper-honey glazed lamb shank with an herbed cornmeal Johnnycake, five roasted peppers and onions; and the artichoke and mushroom tart with roasted garlic red pepper sauce. The food — in any combination — will certainly serve as the perfect complement to the lovely accommodations, exquisite surroundings, and abundance of diversions available both at the ranch and in the nearby area.

Victorian Inn

487 Foam Street
Monterey, California 93940
(800) 232-4141, (408) 373-8000, Fax: (408) 373-4815
Internet: http://www.placestostay.com/mont-victorianinn/

General Manager: *Randy Venard*
Rooms: *68 doubles, 2 suites*
Rates: *Doubles $99-189 (B&B), Suites $190-300 (B&B)*
Payment: *AE, CB, DC, DSC, JCB, MC, and VISA*
Dogs: *Welcome with a one-time fee of $25 and a $100 refundable deposit*
Children: *Welcome (cribs and cots available)*
Open: *All year*

The Monterey Peninsula offers a wide variety of great vacation opportunities for people traveling with a dog. Located within proximity of Fisherman's Wharf, Cannery Row, the Aquarium, and the area's picturesque beaches is the Victorian Inn. There is some "Victorian" left in the inn, as the century-old home has now been transformed into an inviting reception area, breakfast room, and gathering spot. The guest rooms, while appealing, fill the more contemporary gray clapboard buildings set around the main inn.

What we found especially unique about the Victorian Inn (apart from its in-town location) is that the guest rooms incorporate many traditional features, even though the rooms themselves are relatively new. We liked the sunny window seats set near the marble-rimmed fireplaces and sitting areas. Victorian reproduction furnishings often include writing desks and wing chairs. The matching duvets and pillow shams on the carved oak beds coordinate with the balloon shades at the windows. Subtle earth tones warm the walls, while potted plants and dried wreaths combine with brass accents and colorful lithographs to enliven these spaces. Private patios and balconies overlook the attractively landscaped courtyard, which always seems to be in bloom. Rooms on the third floor not only command the best views, but also have beamed cathedral ceilings and oversized window seat alcoves. The well appointed, modern bathrooms have double sinks, thick cotton towels, and a full array of toiletries. For guests' convenience, the bathrooms not only have a second telephone, but also a second sink and vanity set just outside.

Each morning, breakfast is served in the elegant parlor just off the reception area. This long, narrow chamber contains a crimson carpet set over the tiled floor. Brass chandeliers illuminate the ornate Victorian collectibles placed around the room and the lovely impressionist paintings over the fireplace. An expanded Continental breakfast awaits on the handsome sideboard, featuring freshly squeezed orange juice, eggs, croissants, pastries, and coffee or tea. This is a good time to read the local newspaper or peruse the pamphlets and brochures featuring the more notable activities in the Monterey area. In the afternoon, the inn offers wine and cheese in the parlor between 4 p.m. and 6 p.m. While this sounded appealing, we preferred to head over to the courtyard's Jacuzzi and later relax around the umbrella tables.

During the day, we liked walking with the dogs on paths wending along the bay and through the scenic parks. One of our favorites is the walking trail that follows the coastline between Cannery Row and Pacific Grove. There are also excellent running or walking trails in the **Don Davee Park** (off Munras Avenue) that meander through the pine and oak groves. The Chamber of Commerce provides the **Monterey Walking Path of History** map. If the day is hot, the sandy **Monterey Bay Beach** is a fun place to play with your dog or to perhaps try some sailboarding. Unfortunately, canines are not welcome at Cannery Row or the Monterey Aquarium. If visitors should find a little time — when their dogs are just too tuckered out to enjoy any more sights and attractions — then we suggest taking the opportunity to visit these two famous landmarks.

Newport Beach Marriott
Hotel and Tennis Club

900 Newport Center Drive
Newport Beach, California 92660
(800) 228-9290, (714) 640-4000, Fax: (714) 640-5055
Internet: http://www.marriott.com/marriott/ca-017.htm

General Manager: Michelle Strieck
Rooms: 570 doubles, 15 suites
Rates: Doubles $145-175 (EP), Suites $178-750 (EP)
Payment: AE, CB, DC, DSC, ENR, JCB, MC, and VISA
Dogs: Small dogs are welcome with approval
Children: Welcome (cribs, cots, and baby-sitters are available with notice)
Open: All year

Occupying one of the more enviable hillside locations in Newport Beach, the Marriott Hotel & Tennis Club has lovely views of the adjacent golf course, distant harbor, and the Pacific Ocean. Mirroring its California locale, the hotel's interior spaces exude a warm tropical feeling. Carefully cultivated, the lush foliage and fragrant flowers permeate all the common rooms as well as the open, airy pathways connecting the hotel's wings. The botanical gardens alone are noteworthy; however, when they are combined with the sound and spray of water cascading from the massive 125-year-old brass fountain

California

(weighing a mere 30 tons), guests will find the overall effect to be positively inspiring.

A number of years ago, the management spent a great deal of time and money renovating both the guest rooms and common areas, and constructing the new North Tower. By combining the relatively older guest rooms with the newer units, the hotel is now able to offer a wide range of accommodation configurations. Guests should keep in mind, though, that this is a huge hotel, and although the rooms are well appointed, the decor is fairly neutral. Striped or grass wallpapers, accented by floral fabrics on the beds and rattan furnishings, set the predominant tone. Armoires conceal color cable televisions, and clock radios and telephones are placed atop the bedside tables. An array of toiletries is placed in each of the good-sized bathrooms. While the individual climate controls allow for optimum temperature fine-tuning, most will find that the overall temperature around Newport Beach is quite favorable.

The Concierge levels offer more personalized service, along with some additional amenities. Surprisingly, the rates on these rooms are frequently discounted, and the views are often exceptional. Unless fear of heights is a problem, we highly recommend the guest rooms on these and other upper floors of the hotel's towers. South Tower rooms might appeal to those who prefer easier accessibility to the swimming pools and terraced gardens. We liked walking to this section of the hotel, as we passed through an ivy-laden open atrium, where the lulling sounds of the massive cascading fountain resonated from below. The bedrooms in the middle section of the South Tower (10, 11, 12, and 14) are known especially for their terrific views of the golf course, swimming pool, and gazebo. North Tower rooms, on the other hand, face the tennis courts, golf course fairways, and the distant Newport Beach harbor.

We especially like the Marriott because it is a full service resort, offering a diversified array of recreational facilities. In addition to the eight lighted tennis courts and two swimming pools (one with underwater music), the hotel is also fashioned with a hydrotherapy spa, sauna, health club, and masseuse. During the summer months there is a "Kids' Club," offering an assortment of organized activities for children, thereby giving mom and dad a little time to themselves. There are also **jogging paths**, golf courses, and a terrific variety of stores, galleries, and restaurants within a short walk and/or drive of the hotel. Even though the Marriott is situated in a fairly commercial area, canines will be able to enjoy plenty of access to open space during their walks. We thoroughly enjoyed our excursion down to **Balboa Island**, where we strolled along the narrow streets and ate frozen bananas. Those who want to feel the sand between their toes should head over to **Corona Del Mar State Beach** and **Newport Beach**, where dog access is available at different times of the day, seasonally. Visitors may also want to take their dog on the Balboa Ferry over to the Newport Peninsula, where they will be able to catch a glimpse of the Southern California lifestyle as they meander along the **boardwalk**.

Four Seasons Hotel

690 Newport Center Drive
Newport Beach, California 92660
(800) 332-3442, (714) 759-0808, Fax: (714) 759-0568
Internet: http://www.fshr.com

Manager: *Mehdi Efpekari*
Rooms: *192 doubles, 93 suites*
Rates: *Doubles $145-300 (EP), Suites $350-2,175 (EP)*
Payment: *AE, CB, DC, ENR, MC, and VISA*
Dogs: *Small leashed dogs are welcome (larger welcome with manager's approval)*
Children: *Welcome (cribs, cots, baby-sitters, and a children's program are available)*
Open: *All year*

Every aspect of the Four Seasons Hotel, Newport Beach exudes a remarkable sense of elegance and sophistication. As we approached the entrance, we came across two of J. Seward Johnson's remarkably lifelike bronze sculptures in the courtyard of this impressive hotel. The sculptures fit right in with their surroundings; one is of a businessman reading a newspaper, the other features a twosome playing Frisbee — very Southern California. Once inside the sumptuous reception area, we were surrounded by a profusion of soothing earth tones accented with an array of marble, brass, and glass. Enormous earthenware pots containing trees are set alongside massive columns. Pale pink and green hand-woven carpets are the basis for the Louis XV furniture that is placed in intimate seating arrangements.

The standard bedrooms are mirror images of the exquisitely appointed public areas. The intimate seating arrangements in here are often situated alongside floor-to-ceiling windows and doors that open to private terraces. Some of our favorite rooms are those located on the upper floors, where there are terrific views of both the Pacific Ocean and the gently rolling hills. Another room configuration we found especially appealing was the executive suite, where a pair of French doors separates the master bedroom from the living room. Regardless of the layout, the standard decor is formal French. Chairs and armoires, reproduced from the Louis XV period, nicely complement the more contemporary *objets d'art* placed upon the brass and glass coffee and side tables. Exquisite earth tone fabrics and wall treatments look marvelous against the potted trees and fragrant fresh flower arrangements. The array of amenities is impressive, although they are just what we have come to expect from the Four Seasons. In the evenings, the triple-sheeted and goose down-pillowed beds are turned down. Late night tidbits await in the fully stocked minibars, and in the morning, complimentary newspapers are waiting outside the doors. The bathrooms are distinctive, spacious, and well equipped. Hair dryers, plush terry robes, illuminated makeup and shaving mirrors, an array of toiletries, and televisions are just a few of the standard features. The VIP treatment even extends to dogs. At the Four Seasons, they dine on Bonkers doggie treats and drink Evian water — delivered by room service on silver trays, of course.

Best of all, this lovely hotel even has an extensive array of diversions and recreational options available, either right on the premises or in the nearby area. Guests can play tennis on the hotel's lighted courts or try their hand at croquet amid a garden setting. Others may enjoy table tennis or volleyball, or possibly a more strenuous workout in the fully equipped Fitness Center. Those who are feeling a little adventurous may wish to borrow a bicycle and take their canine companion for a little tour of the area. Neighboring Fashion Island offers everything from fine boutiques and shops to elaborate food halls and restaurants. Our two dogs found plenty of intriguing shops and an assortment of treats (What a surprise!) that appealed to them. Upon returning, guests can take a refreshing dip in the 3,000 square foot swimming pool that is accented with beautiful landscaping. Those with a penchant for hitting the links will be pleased to learn about the two courses at the Pelican Hill Golf Club. Other people-pleasures include hot air balloon rides, wine tasting tours, horseback riding, and a variety of sail and motor charters available nearby. For those traveling with smaller children, the Four Seasons also provides a comprehensive children's program during the summer months. Parents may or may not wish to take advantage of this program, yet every child will be delighted to discover balloons, juice, candy, and cookies awaiting their arrival in the room. Should parents or guardians require any additional assistance, the hotel has a long list of helpful items ranging from diapers, baby bathtubs, and strollers to pacifiers, thermometers, and baby wipes.

Those who don't want to leave their dog alone in the room can enjoy a wonderful meal off the room service menu; however, there are also some excellent restaurants just an elevator ride away. The Pavilion is the most elegant option, serving exquisitely prepared California-style Nouvelle cuisine. Chef Mark Kropczynski offers patrons a wide array of options. Some of the more popular appetizers include the lightly spiced corn chowder with smoked shrimp and the lobster medallions with crushed new potatoes and citrus vinaigrette. Seafood entrées feature the Pacific seabass broiled under a fresh herb crust and finished with a Chardonnay wine sauce; and the roasted swordfish with Provencale herbs, artichokes, and fennel. The meat and fowl selections range from the grilled filet of beef with morels, garlic mashed potatoes, and sherry sauce to the pepper crusted lamb with a port wine reduction. The Cabaña Café, while a little less formal, is quite popular. Its rattan furnishings and exposed beam ceilings provide an attractive complement to its pool-side location. The intimate Conservatory Lounge is appealing just about any time of day, whether for afternoon tea or an early evening cocktail.

Dogs will thoroughly enjoy **Newport Beach**, even though most of the nearby beaches are out of bounds during the prime time hours of the day. We recommend that visitors check the signs. Access is limited, depending on the season; however, we found that, in general, early morning and evening hours are fine for dogs to be on the beach. Those who are determined to take their dogs for a mid-day jaunt should head south to **Laguna Beach**, where there are a variety of intriguing parks worth investigating. There are also **trails that wend along the cliffs**, where the views are always spectacular.

California

Holiday Harbor

P.O. Box 112
O'Brien, California 96070
(800) 776-2628, (916) 238-2383
E-mail: holidayharbor@lakeshasta.com
Internet: http://www.lakeshasta.com

Owners: *The Barry Family*
Rooms: *70 houseboats*
Rates: *$270-1,340 for 2-4 nights, $745-3,150 weekly, with a 2-night minimum, year round, except during high season, when there is a 1-week minimum*
Payment: *MC and VISA*
Dogs: *Welcome*
Children: *Welcome*
Open: *All year*

Houseboating is a unique vacation idea and one that easily accommodates a dog. One of the most popular places for houseboat vacations is on Lake Shasta, California's largest manmade lake. While there are many companies in the houseboat rental business, Holiday Harbor appeals to us because it is a full-service resort. To find the resort, we headed toward O'Brien and followed the signs for Holiday Harbor, which led us down a meandering back road to the marina store and restaurant. After parking the car, we met a veteran houseboat family and their Golden Retriever, Rusty, who was anxiously trying to pull his human friends down the hill toward the dock. We waved good-bye to Rusty and company, before walking up to the store and small restaurant. When we arrived, a small group of guests, seated on the back deck, were chuckling as they watched someone painfully attempt to back his boat trailer down the steep 100-foot ramp. We smiled too (actually it was more of a wince), as we envisioned ourselves trying to navigate a trailer down the same ramp.

For those unfamiliar with Lake Shasta, ourselves included, we learned it is approximately 400-feet deep and boasts more than 370 miles of shoreline, along with plenty of intriguing diversions. These include the Lake Shasta Caverns, the Shasta Dam, and always, in the distance, picturesque vistas of snow-capped Mount Shasta. In the summer months, the level of the lake drops about one foot per day. Those who visit in September will find hillsides, normally underwater, lying exposed. As we meandered down the hill to the docks, we found several groups loading their gear into push carts and pulling them out to the houseboats. Supplies vary, depending upon the group, but guests may expect to provide their own food, as well as blankets, linens, towels, a first-aid kit, and cassette tapes for the stereos on board. Holiday Harbor's beautifully maintained houseboats lie tied to the dock and contain all of the amenities most would want for a week on the water.

These are not Hinckley yachts, but are very functional and well designed for maximum comfort and minimal upkeep. For the most part, they resemble floating RVs, and navigating one is similar to driving a large car. Paneled walls and linoleum floors are the backdrop to the plastic captain's chairs and the cushioned gaucho benches that double as beds. Fully-equipped kitchens are quite spacious, especially for a boat. Those in the luxury houseboats will find such extras as trash compactors and microwave ovens, although most people prefer to cook on the gas barbecues (which are available on all the boats). The heads, or bathrooms, are not typical of most boats, in that they are relatively spacious, and the showers have a good supply of hot water.

The smallest model is the Diplomat, 37 feet by 14 feet, with a pair of gaucho beds (wide sofa-like berths) off the bow and a private bedroom in the stern, which is equipped with another gaucho bed, walk-in closet, and dressing table. We liked the roof deck for private sunbathing. This is the most reasonably priced houseboat, especially because it easily accommodates a family or two couples. The Monarch, Premier, and Ambassador houseboats are 12 to 15 feet longer, more spacious, and have double and full-size bunks in the stern. The more luxurious houseboats are the Marquis and Emperor, which sleep 12 and 16 people, respectively. The Marquis is ideal for a group of friends, with its six gaucho beds and bunks, while the Emperor offers two staterooms, a second floor penthouse, and a flying bridge. We especially like the swimming platforms available on all boats, except for the Monarch and Premiere, that allowed us and our canine cohorts easy access to the water.

Additional water "toys" may be rented through the "Toy Box," also operated by Holiday Harbor. If guests call in advance the Toy Box will stock the boat with everything from rowing sculls, kayaks, and sailboards to sailboats, jet skis, and water-skiing boats. Bowser may want to try out some of these toys with his human friends; or, more likely, explore the trails around Lake Shasta when the boat pulls up along the shore. Fishing for bass, catfish, trout, and salmon is what lures most people to the picturesque lake. Fishing isn't exactly the most popular pastime for dogs, especially when summertime temperatures hover in the 90s. But for those who are in search of a different kind of vacation experience with a wide range of water-oriented recreational options at their disposal, we highly recommend considering Holiday Harbor.

Ojai Valley Inn

*Country Club Road
Ojai, California 93023
(800) 422-OJAI, (805) 646-5511, Fax: (805) 646-7969
Internet: http://www.ojairesort.com*

General Manager: Thadius Hyland
Rooms: 200 doubles, 15 suites
Rates: Doubles $195-260 (EP), Suites $345-395 (EP), Children are free
Payment: AE, CB, DC, DSC, ENR, MC, and VISA
Dogs: Welcome with notice and approval; a one-time fee of $25 is required
Children: Welcome (cribs, cots, and baby-sitters are available)
Open: All year

Ojai remains an oasis — not quite undiscovered, but still seemingly overlooked by most of the tourists who are passing through into Southern California. Situated 30 miles southeast of Santa Barbara, the Ojai Valley is nestled in the hills some 1,000 feet above sea level. Thousands of years ago, the Chumash Indians came over the Topa Mountains and dropped down into this picturesque valley. So inspired by its abundant natural beauty, they named it Ojai or "the nest." The mountains still cradle this valley, yet within it lies a quiet rural town. Stretching away from it are miles of trails, beautiful rolling hills, and of course the expansive grounds of the Ojai Valley Inn.

Ojai was "rediscovered" in 1870, when a journalist named Charles Nordhoff described in his travel essays the tiny town of ranchers and citrus growers. Years later, in 1923, Edward D. Libby, a millionaire glass manufacturer, conceived of the Ojai Valley Inn. With the assistance of architect Wallace Neff, Libby built a clubhouse reflecting the influences of southern Spain. The adobe haciendas, with their terra-cotta roofs and flagstone terraces, were the next additions to the property. Neff could not have known this at the time, but these buildings would later exemplify what we know today as Southern California architecture. Over the years, the resort was quite popular with Hollywood notables such as Walt Disney, Clark Gable, and Lana Turner. Frank Capra also stayed here while filming *Lost Horizon* in 1937.

More recently, a division of Hilton International took over the reigns of the resort. During its tenure Hilton infused over $35 million into the grounds and facilities. The company refurbished worn guest rooms and common areas and added over 100 new bedrooms and the expansive Topa Conference Center. Today, the well-planned landscaping, having reached maturity, nicely complements the Spanish-style architecture.

The property is so expansive that golf carts usually transport guests to their rooms. To help maintain the bucolic setting, new arrivals often park their cars in lots along the perimeter of the property. When guests first step into their bedrooms, they will find a strong Southwestern influence exerting itself in the earth tone colors, Navajo printed fabrics, and original artwork. Rattan furniture and brass accents enhance the decor. The attention to detail is evident in both the standard doubles and spacious cottage suites. Cable televisions, complete with in-room movies, well-stocked minibars, and coffee makers are just a few of the extras. Refurbished bathrooms offer the additional conveniences of hair dryers and terry robes. Guests may also request fireplaces, along with private patios or balconies. The designers were careful to ensure that all chambers have panoramic views of either the mountains, golf course, or rock gardens. Dogs are always welcome at the Ojai Valley Inn, but when it is especially busy, they are often placed in rooms in the newer Arbolada South and North Buildings. Set apart from the resort center, these buildings overlook the emerald green golf course. Except for their more private location, the amenities and decor of these accommodations mirror those rooms closer to the inn.

Recreational opportunities abound at the Ojai Valley Inn. In addition to the 18-hole golf course (which was just infused with a 3 million dollar upgrade), there are eight newly resurfaced tennis courts, two year-round swimming pools, croquet courses, putting greens, and bicycle trails (useable with the inn's complimentary bicycles). The bicycle trails wend across the inn's 220 acres. Equestrians may opt for Western or English riding, take private lessons, or learn how to drive a team of Belgian draft horses. Hay rides are great fun for younger guests, while adventurous adults may wish to try the Outward Bound course, available through the inn. The latter is run by a well-trained Outward Bound staff. Participants can test their mettle on the 30-foot alpine tower, ropes course, slack wire walking, a high Burma bridge, the wall, and much, much more. Parents should also consider the Camp Ojai children's program.

We enjoy walking our dogs on the grounds, where there is a plethora of flora and fauna, as well as intriguing wildlife. The central aviary, teeming with cockatiels, love birds, and parrots is also a favorite destination for canines and humans alike. The **extensive bicycle paths and trails** found throughout the valley are also good choices for longer outings. Finally, a ten-minute **walk to town** reveals additional shops, restaurants, and galleries worth investigating.

The Ojai Valley Inn offers several excellent dining options, ranging from a casual outdoor terraced café to the more formal Vista dining room. We like the café's outdoor arbor setting, with wrought iron tables set upon the fieldstone patio, while a fountain cascades in the background. On warm evenings, guests tend to linger around the tables, sipping their cool drinks. For those who need a more elegant dining experience, there is the intimate Vista dining room. Walls created by hundreds of wine bottles lead into this elongated chamber overlooking the gardens and fairways. The chef, classically trained in France, offers an alternating array of tantalizing dishes. Diners

California

might select between the local vegetable fritters with cilantro ginger chutney; the ceviché of lobster and scallops, or the *foie gras* with kumquat chutney. Some of the more outstanding entrées include the breast of crispy duck with an orange chipotle sauce and red wild rice; the filet mignon with a roasted garlic sauce and crumbled Navajo blue cheese; and the Pacific prawns with fusilli pasta covered in a sundried tomato and garlic sauce.

While the Ojai Valley Inn has grown considerably in recent years, its simple origins still shine through. The familiar adobe cottages are still here, as is the high level of personalized service. Guests and their dogs can do a little or a lot and have an equally memorable vacation amid the picturesque valley setting.

Ojai Manor Hotel

210 East Matilija
Ojai, California 93023
(805) 646-0961

Owner: *Mary Nelson*
Rooms: *6 doubles*
Rates: *$90-100 (B&B)*
Payment: *MC and VISA*
Dogs: *Very well-behaved dogs welcome with notice and approval; they must be kept on leash*
Children: *Not appropriate for children under 12 years of age*
Open: *All year*

The Ojai Manor Hotel is reputed to be the oldest building in Ojai. It dates back to 1874, when it was first used as a schoolhouse. Today, it has been transformed into an intimate Bed and Breakfast, but when Mary Nelson's family bought it in the 1950s, it was as their private home. Set just one block off the town's historic main street, the Ojai Manor Hotel is truly one of the more intriguing homesteads in this intimate community. It isn't easy to see though, as its dove gray exterior is muted by the huge shade trees that surround the home.

We gravitated, as always, to the wraparound porch festooned with flowering plants. Some guests appeared to be dozing off in the Adirondack chairs, perhaps taking their cue from the house cats slumbering in the sun along the wide banister rail. Not wanting to interrupt their reverie, we ventured inside the house. The front parlor, like most of the house, has hardwood floors covered with Oriental rugs. Set around the fireplace are comfortable sofas and armchairs, while above the mantel hangs an enormous dried floral wreath.

We passed through a pair of pocket doors, to the rear of this chamber, and into the dining room. This intimate space, warmed by a wood stove, also contains an eclectic array of collectibles — including a guitar set on a stand and a saddle placed whimsically over a sawhorse. The array of lovely flower arrangements, intriguing contemporary paintings, and vibrant *objets d'art* (the latter, designed by Mary's friend, Boyd Wright), always draw our attention. During this particular visit, we had to smile at the six pairs of forearms artfully arranged on the coffee table.

On our way up the front stairs, we literally ran into Mary's two rambunctious Chihuahuas. They were having a fine time, wrestling playfully and then chasing each other through the house. Leaving them to their antics, we ventured into one of the bedrooms — each is individually decorated with turn-of-the century furnishings. The only twist to the traditional decor of these uncluttered spaces is the small contemporary prints hanging from the walls. Guests might find a rocking chair and lace-covered end tables in one room, or a brass and white iron bed topped by a lace coverlet in another. Oriental or rag rugs cover the hardwood floors. Other bedrooms, including Room Six, might not have great views, but they more than compensate for it with outdoor porches appointed with Adirondack chairs. We are also fond of Room Five, where corner windows overlook the back of the property. A colorful handmade quilt covers the bedstead in this good-sized chamber. The only potential drawback for some guests is the shared bathrooms; but all three of these are well stocked with toiletries.

After a restful sleep, guests arrive in the dining room to a bountiful Continental breakfast. Choices include the locally grown fresh-squeezed orange juice, assorted cereals, fruit scones, and homemade coffee cakes, muffins, and breads. We liked taking this meal out on the front porch, while other guests sometimes enjoy gravitating to the backyard terrace with its comfortable bentwood chairs. After breakfast, we headed off with our dogs for a walk through the town center, where shops, bookstores, galleries, and cafés abound. The extensive bicycle paths, and nearby **Libby Park**, are popular doggie destinations, as are the 1.7 million acres of the **Los Padres National Forest**. Guests will be happy to return at the end of the day to the comfort and personalized attention of the Ojai Manor Hotel. We think it offers just the right mix of an inviting atmosphere and a low-key setting, sure to make guests' stay in Ojai a most enjoyable one.

Andril Fireplace Cottages

569 Asilomar Blvd.
Pacific Grove, California 93950
(408) 375-0994

Owners: *Kevin and Linda Smith*
Rooms: *16 cottages*
Rates: *$70-165 (EP)*
Payment: *AE, MC and VISA*
Dogs: *Welcome with approval and a nightly fee of $8*
Children: *Welcome (cribs, cots, and baby-sitters are available)*
Open: *All year*

Pacific Grove lies between Monterey and the world renowned Pebble Beach. Founded as a Methodist summer camp in the late 1800s, the community has grown well beyond its religious heritage, although the stately Victorian homes do serve as reminders of its noble past. While not a part of the original community, the Andril Fireplace Cottages are a veritable institution in their own right, dating back to the 1950s.

This intimate cottage complex, owned by the same family since the 1960s, lies along a coastal road amid tall pines. Even though the old-fashioned signboard reads "motel," and the Smith's refer to it as such, what lies within the cottage walls offers far more character and charm than most motel accommodations. In-season, the cottages are usually rented on a weekly basis. The resort is not trendy, nor is it fancy, but those who know about it usually book their cottages well in advance. We suggest our readers do the same.

These simple tan structures, accented with yellow trim, edge a semi-circular drive. The layouts differ, as do the decor and furnishings. Individuals or couples will be perfectly comfortable in single-room cottages. The combination of double or queen beds varies; however, there is always a fireplace and kitchen. Families, on the other hand, will appreciate the suite cottages, with either one or two separate bedrooms containing queen or double bed combinations. Separate fireplaced sitting rooms offer extra living space, as do the small backyards and private redwood decks. As we noted earlier, the decor may be homey and unpretentious, but it is appealing. Beamed ceilings, inset with skylights, nicely complement the knotty pine walls that are lined with windows framed by simple, tab curtains. Contemporary sofas and wing chairs flank the fireplaces, interspersed with eclectic groupings of painted and naturally-stained pine furnishings. Dried flower arrangements provide colorful accents, while small libraries of books and color cable televisions with VCRs help fill voids in the day. A variety of restaurants is convenient to the cottages; however, guests usually opt to create their own meals in the fully-equipped kitchens or barbecue on their outdoor decks.

One of the many appealing things about the Andril Fireplace Cottages is that they are set off the beaten track, which gives guests a sense of solitude. Guests and their dogs often spend a great deal of time outside enjoying the bucolic setting — hoping the resident raccoons, opossum, and deer might make an appearance. Others prefer relaxing in the shaded courtyard among the calla lilies, where they may have the chance to delve into a good book. This place is not long on formalized activities, but it does provide a Ping-pong table and a spa. Dogs love it here, as they are only a short walk from the beach, where they are allowed to explore on leash. Dogs are also allowed in other open space areas throughout **Pacific Grove** — just as long as there aren't signs posted to the contrary. **Washington Park** is one such option, as is **Burwick Park**. Also within a short driving distance are several not-to-be-missed, people-oriented attractions — such as the Monterey Bay Aquarium and Fisherman's Wharf.

Casa Cody

175 South Cahuilla Road
Palm Springs, California 92262
(800) 231-CODY, (619) 320-9346, Fax: (619) 325-8610

Owners: *Therese Hayes and Frank Tysen*
Rooms: *10 doubles, 6 suites, 1 cottage*
Rates: *Doubles $65-115 (B&B), Suites/Cottage $125-185 (B&B)*
Payment: *AE, DC, DSC, MC, and VISA*
Dogs: *Welcome with a $10 fee*
Children: *Well-behaved children are welcome (cribs and cots available)*
Open: *All year*

Years ago, Palm Springs was a discreet hideaway for many of Hollywood's more notable stars. Here, they could unwind in the desert sun, and play golf and tennis without being disturbed by the paparazzi. Places like Casa Cody were built in the 1920s to accommodate many of these visitors. Harriet Cody (niece of Wild Bill Cody), was the original owner of the inn, and over the years hosted many renowned actors. General Patton's officers also stayed here while training for their North Africa campaign. Unfortunately, Palm Springs has been very much "discovered," and many of the famous now prefer the more remote areas further south. We still like the feeling of old Palm Springs, and encourage first-time visitors to look a little harder to find these quainter areas. We think Casa Cody offers just the right combination of tradition and hidden charm.

California

Casa Cody still feels like a private enclave, yet it is within easy walking distance of town and the beautiful San Jacinto mountains. Bougainvillea climbs over stucco walls surrounding the small complex. Shade trees overhang the flowering plants, lovely gardens, and mature bushes that meld to create a tropical paradise. Most of the bedrooms and suites surround one of the two swimming pools.

The day we visited, the gardens were in full bloom, especially the bougainvillea whose fuschia flowers blanketed the stucco walls and climbed the posts to the porch roofs. As we walked up a path in search of Therese, a family of boisterous kittens greeted us (we later learned two of the more friendly kittens' names — Calamity Jane and Wild Bill). Therese emerged from the office, apologizing for its disarray, and at the same time telling us that this space would soon be converted into a library suite. The office would eventually be moved into another building they recently bought, just down the street. Our focus, for the time being, was on the original rooms.

As we walked with Therese past the sparkling swimming pool surrounded by teal-colored umbrellas, we learned that all the bedrooms and suites had been recently updated. The new Southwest decor is reminiscent of Santa Fe, New Mexico with an emphasis on soothing earth tones. Navajo patterns predominate, whether on the throw rugs covering the terra-cotta floors or the fabric cushions on the comfortable rattan sofas and chairs. Contemporary artwork and festive murals line the walls, coupled with terra-cotta pottery, pottery lamps, and other colorful knickknacks. French doors open to private patios, and ceiling fans suspended from the eaves help circulate the cool night air. Air conditioning permits guests to forget about the desert heat, although most look forward to the cool evenings when they might be able to light a fire or take a dip in the Jacuzzi. The well-equipped, tiled kitchens allow those who are so inclined to prepare their own meals, or to simply store snacks and drinks. In the morning, the expanded Continental breakfast may be enjoyed by one of the pools, at an intimate garden-side table, or back in one's room.

As we noted, it is easy to **walk dogs downtown** or **into the hills** when staying at Casa Cody. Within minutes visitors can also hike along some very **scenic trails**, which are as spectacular under the pink early morning skies as they are during the late afternoon glow of the setting sun. Unfortunately, Palm Springs does not look kindly upon dogs frequenting its parks — so do not even bother trying to visit these green oasises. People-friendly diversions are plentiful, though, with golf, tennis, and riding opportunities all close to the inn.

The Lodge at Pebble Beach

P.O. Box 1128
17-Mile Drive
Pebble Beach, California 93953
(800) 654-9300, (408) 624-3811, Fax: (408) 625-8598
Internet: http://www.pebble-beach.com

Manager: Gary Davis
Rooms: 155 doubles, 6 suites
Rates: Doubles $350-575 (EP), Suites $900-1,850 (EP)
Payment: AE, CB, DC, JCB, MC, and VISA
Dogs: Small well-behaved dogs are welcome with approval
Children: Welcome (cribs, cots, and baby-sitters are available)
Open: All year

The Lodge at Pebble Beach lies within the Del Monte Forest on a magnificent piece of property just off 17-Mile Drive. Here, the spray from the crashing Pacific Ocean and majestic beauty of the rugged coastline combine to provide a spectacular setting for the famous Pebble Beach Golf Links. Originally built in 1919 as Charles Crocker's Old Hotel Del Monte, the Lodge still exudes a strong sense of history. After nearly three-quarters of a century, its understated elegance is upstaged only by the breathtaking natural beauty surrounding it. Even though it has undergone some changes in ownership in recent years, the Lodge is still one of this country's premier resorts.

Some stay at The Lodge at Pebble Beach because of its tranquil setting combined with unparalleled golf and tennis facilities. Others know the Lodge by reputation, and come because of its attentive staff and fine accommodations. Picturesque grounds, comprised of six acres of tall pines and twisted cypress trees, surround the guest rooms set in both the main lodge and in the two- and three-story outer buildings. Stepping inside, guests feel enveloped by the sophisticated use of soft earth tones and muted floral fabrics. These colors cover wing chairs and welted sofas, with accents of brass and glass adding to the traditional living and sitting rooms. Full view French doors open to the private patios or balconies that overlook the lovely gardens, the undulating fairways, or the pounding surf. The preferred bedrooms offer ocean views and beachstone or marble fireplaces laid with oak logs. Enhanced views and additional amenities often translate into less space; therefore, those who are willing to upgrade may want to reserve a suite.

The suites lie in the Alvarado and Portola buildings lining the 18th fairway, and feature impressive water views. Avid golfers would most likely reserve a suite in the Sloat or Vizcaino buildings, where vistas extend along the full

California

length of the famed 18th fairway situated alongside the ocean. These suites, along with the standard doubles, contain well-stocked honor bars and concealed remote-controlled televisions. The modern bathrooms offer second telephones, terry robes, oversized cotton towels, and fragrant soaps and shampoos. Families, or friends who want to stay together, can reserve Fairway One, a private home with multiple bedrooms, a formal living room and dining room, and a kitchen. This is the ultimate in style and space — all contained in a low-level building overlooking the first tee.

The charming town of Carmel, offering an array of shops and eateries, is just a short drive from the Lodge. But if guests are searching for impressive *and* convenient dining choices, they need not look any further than the confines of the Lodge. Depending upon one's mood, guests may reserve a table at The Gallery, the Cypress Room, offering grilled seafood, Club XIX, featuring French cuisine, or the more informal Tap Room. Verdant vistas are revealed to patrons who dine in the Cypress Room. Each item among its extensive selection of fresh shellfish and fish is cooked in one of seven ways. Abalone may be pan fried with a lemon caper sauce, and then served with red creamer potatoes and a vegetable medley. Swordfish may be seared in a cast iron skillet and then accompanied by a corn and black bean relish, ancho chile marmalade, and fried cactus leaves. Also available are the ahi tuna served with a coconut and red curry sauce; the snapper baked in an herb crust; or the grilled lobster. The grilled fillet of beef, with a vegetable medley and horseradish potatoes, or the veal medallions covered with wild mushrooms, are other options. Club XIX features a more traditional French menu with rack of lamb encrusted with ground pistachios or roasted sea bass with a red pepper and clam coulis topping the menu. One of our favorite spots is The Tap Room, as much for its collection of golf memorabilia as for its informal fare. Here, diners may enjoy everything from prime rib to crabcakes with a jalapeño hollandaise. In the afternoons, a popular gathering spot is the Terrace Lounge, with its high ceilings and garden-like setting. Here, guests may settle into any of the intimate seating areas, which are set up to take advantage of the magnificent views of the 18th fairway and the Pacific, through a wall of Palladian windows.

For active guests, dogs included, there are plenty of outlets available at the Lodge. These include a hike through the 5,328-acre **Del Monte Forest**, or along the various **par courses** and **jogging trails** that wend through the area. Leashed dogs are allowed to explore most facets of the property, golf courses excluded; or they might enjoy walking through the **residential neighborhoods** that surround the resort.

The four championship golf courses (guests have preferential tee times) and 14 tennis courts (with a pro who organizes an array of clinics and tournaments for guests) should keep even the most active people busy. Traditional tennis is complemented by two Eastern-style platform tennis courts. Some will want to work out in the heated swimming pool or exercise studio, then relax in one of the private steam rooms or saunas. A day on the water can be arranged through the concierge, with fishing and sailing charters available. Horseback riders may wish to take advantage of the 34 miles of equestrian trails that surround the Lodge. Finally, vacationers may want to pick up some supplies or goodies in any of the boutiques that line the charming shopping area across from the main Lodge. We realize the Lodge at Pebble Beach is not for the budget conscious, but the experience is well worth the tariff, especially for golfers.

Thirty-Nine Cypress

P.O. Box 176
39 Cypress Road
Point Reyes Station, California   94956
(415) 663-1709

Hostess: *Julia Bartlett*
Rooms: *1 cottage*
Rates: *$100-125 (B&B)*
Payment: *MC and VISA*
Dogs: *Very well-behaved dogs are welcome with notice and approval*
Children: *Welcome*
Open: *All year*

Point Reyes Station is always a delight to return to, especially after negotiating the early morning traffic out of San Francisco. Our leisurely drive over the mountain took us past golden hills dotted with stands of trees and deer who magically appeared, then just as quickly disappeared behind the large boulders. Wisps of morning fog reminded us the coast was close by. Point Reyes Station was just waking up. Some people, coffee in hand and dogs by their sides, were chatting, while others readied their stores for the day ahead. Our trip took us further north, along a winding back road, until we reached Thirty-Nine Cypress.

This is an unusual spot, where guests don't feel like guests — they feel as if they are visiting friends. To reach Thirty-Nine Cypress, travelers follow a dirt drive, past a house in the midst of construction, to a small picket fence. On the fence a tiny sign indicates that this is the parking area. We parked the car, then followed the path through a gate, under a rose-covered arch, and into a lovely garden setting. A few more steps and we were at the stairs leading down into the low-lying, redwood cottage.

Our first impressions of the interior were of a colorful handmade quilt hanging from a rough-hewn redwood wall. Stepping from here into the inviting living room, we found a comfortable, worn sofa and armchairs set in front of the fireplace. This place is packed with personality; walls lined with bookshelves leave just enough space for the original artwork. Through the windows we spotted all sorts of wild birds, using the binoculars conveniently placed on the antique pine hutch. As we surveyed the pastures, our gaze fell on the herd of Holsteins peacefully munching the dewy grasses. To the right of the wall of windows is the full kitchen with its cathedral-ceilings, skylights, and a complete array of cooking utensils placed on the open shelves. Each morning a hearty breakfast is delivered to the cottage. It usually consists of fresh juices and fruits, along with an egg dish or casserole, homemade muffins and breads, and tea or freshly roasted coffees. This meal can be taken indoors or out on the back patio overlooking the flora and fauna. Afterwards, many enjoy cuddling up in the large, windowed alcove topped with a futon, situated along the back wall of the living room.

Bedrooms lie on either side of the central living area. As with the living room, the bedrooms also have tiny-pebbled, composite floors, covered by worn Oriental rugs. An oversized wooden headboard backs the master bedroom's queen bed. This minimally furnished space has accent pieces that include a rocking chair and a dressing table topped with decorative shells. In addition to the pleasant views, skylights provide additional natural lighting. An intimate bathroom doesn't offer views, but reflected in the black and white photographs are plenty of bucolic scenes. The second bedroom is somewhat smaller, highlighted by the bent wood headboard framing the queen bed. As with the rest of the cottage, there is plenty of artwork and other collectibles hanging from the walls. A small sink tucked into one corner of the bedroom frees up space in the small bathroom — housed in what appears to be an old closet. A third double-bedded chamber, occupies the other end of the house. This is the smallest guest room, but it appears all the more spacious because of the sliding glass doors. This cozy chamber is also enlivened with bright, colorful photographs of exotic bird heads.

Thirty-Nine Cypress appeals to most people because of its private location and comfortable charm. Most memorable, though, are the lovely views of the cattle ranch, Tomales Bay, and distant Point Reyes Peninsula. Whether cooking, bathing in the outdoor shower, or just relaxing on the patio, our glance was always out toward the tranquil setting surrounding the cottage. Visitors who explore a bit further, down the bluff, will find the outdoor spa, where there are even better views of the cattle and waterfowl. Dogs are free to explore the **property around the cottage**. We also enjoyed taking our canines for a walk on the trails wending through the **Point Reyes National Seashore**. Bicycles are another popular way to tour the region. Anyone looking for more intriguing ideas should speak with Julia, who knows of some unusual places for guests and their dogs to visit.

Berry Patch Cottage

P.O. Box 712
68 Messa Road
Point Reyes Station, California 94956
(800) 663-1942, (415) 663-1942, Internet:http://www.coastalgetaways.com

Host: *Jeri Jacobson and Herb Goldberg*
Room: *1 cottage*
Rates: *$100-120 (B&B)*
Payment: *Personal checks*
Dogs: *Well-behaved dogs are welcome with notice and a $5 nightly fee*
Children: *Welcome (a futon and sofa bed are available)*
Open: *All year*

The Point Reyes National Seashore is a favorite destination for those interested in an unspoiled setting teeming with wildlife. This is where the seashore and gently rolling hills converge, creating a virtual paradise for visitors who come to bicycle on the winding back roads or to just dig their toes into the pristine sandy beaches. Not only is Point Reyes Station surrounded by all of these components, but it is also a charming, unpretentious hamlet offering an interesting selection of stores, restaurants, and Bed and Breakfasts. One of the more low-key accommodations is the Berry Patch B&B.

A winding lane leads to the Berry Patch Cottage, tucked unobtrusively behind shrubs, hedges, and a split rail fence. The dove gray main house and guest cottage rest on just over an acre of land, protected by groves of pine and crabapple trees. A welcoming committee of curious cats are usually on hand to greet us; friendly little creatures who disappear just as quickly after seeing the dogs. If nobody answers the door at the main house, guests should check around the side, where someone is usually gardening or puttering about. On our most recent visit, our hostess was spreading wood chips on the cottage's flower beds.

We always enjoy coming back to this airy cottage. Its simple furnishings enhance the interior's crisp, smooth lines. A spacious living room has a sofa bed flanked by a pair of comfortable chairs. In here, guests can listen to the stereo or watch television or one of the tapes from the extensive video library. The adjoining master bedroom is accented with a free-standing wood stove that makes the room quite cozy on a cool evening night. The colorful bird-patterned quilt placed across the queen bed nicely complements the floral pattern draperies. Gray-flecked carpeting provides a neutral base for the corner hutch and decorative dried flowers. Ambiance aside, the modern amenities are also well conceived, especially in the white-tiled kitchen with its assortment of appliances and well-stocked cupboards. Each day a variety of foods, including eggs, yogurts, cheeses, coffees, and cereals, seems to magically appear in the refrigerator. This convenient supply of food allows guests to leisurely prepare their own breakfast the following morning. This meal may be eaten inside, of course, or taken out to the sizable redwood deck. The deck is also a delightful place to barbecue as the sun begins to set. This is usually the time of day that deer begin to appear around the crabapple trees, searching for their evening snack.

We cannot visit the area without making at least one trip out to the seashore to see either the **Point Reyes Lighthouse** or, in season, to watch the magnificent migrating Gray Whales. Others prefer the rugged coastline and pristine wilderness along the **Point Reyes National Seashore**, home to an array of birds, elk, and mountain lions. If heading back to San Francisco, we recommend stopping at either **Stinson** or **Muir** beaches with your dog, or perhaps **Mount Tamalpais**. Bodega Bay, immortalized by Hitchcock's movie, *The Birds,* is another popular destination. Whether visitors come to Point Reyes Station for a day, or for a few, they should consider staying at the Berry Patch Cottage; it is a natural base for exploring all parts of this exquisite region.

Jasmine Cottage & Gray's Retreat

P.O. Box 56
Point Reyes Station, California   94956
(415) 663-1166, Fax: (415) 663-1390

Hostess: Karen Gray
Rooms: 2 cottages
Rates: $145 (B&B with Jasmine only)
Payment: MC and VISA
Dogs: Welcome with notice, but they cannot be left alone and must be leashed ($15 one-time fee)
Children: Welcome (cribs, cots, high chairs, and baby-sitters available)
Open: All year

An hour's drive north of San Francisco lies our favorite refuge from civilization: the Point Reyes Peninsula. National and state parks permeate the area. Depending upon the route taken, visitors will pass through the Muir Woods, Stinson Beach, Bodega Bay, and beyond to the Point Reyes National Seashore. We especially like the casual approach to life of the area's residents, who seem more focused on life's quality rather than its quantity.

Karen Gray is one woman willing to share her piece of paradise with visitors — whether they be guests in the Jasmine Cottage or in Gray's Retreat.

Both cottages overlook rolling pastures, the charming Point Reyes Station, and the more distant Inverness Ridge. Jasmine Cottage is the original carriage house to the 1879 schoolhouse, also on the property. The latter is now Karen's home. The newer Gray's Retreat is a barn-style abode built to accommodate Karen's parents when they visit. Fruit trees, along with incredible herb, vegetable, and flower gardens, surround the first two houses. Gray's Retreat is more private, set further down the gravel drive.

Jasmine Cottage is the ultimate romantic hideaway for two, with the capacity to accommodate four (plus a baby in the crib). To get there, guests follow the narrow, winding stone path to the gray stained cottage. We fondly reminisce about this place, especially the cozy sitting room where we can curl up on the window seats, read a book, and feel the warmth of the sunlight as it filters through the lace curtains. Everything about the cottage is diminutive, yet not at all claustrophobic, due to a skylight, plenty of windows, and very few interior walls. An arch separates this chamber from the rest of the cottage, including the fully-equipped kitchen. The kitchen's hand-painted tiles, forming the back splash, make this an especially cheery space. Ivy-painted walls form the alcove containing a queen bed. Endearing caricatures of a cow, rabbit, duck, and egret are painted on another wall around a wood stove. Life's modern distractions, such as a telephone and television, are blessedly absent. While most like to relax on the patio, the recent addition of a garden spa is also quite appealing.

Gray's Retreat is substantially larger than Jasmine Cottage and overlooks pastures used for centuries by the area's dairy farmers. This newer, cedar-sided barn is fronted by a small, enclosed patio dotted with potted plants and lined by perennial beds. The white picnic table, set in the midst of all this, is as perfect for outdoor dining as it is for chipping away at the Sunday morning paper's crossword puzzle. Karen obviously focused on the spectacular views when designing Gray's Retreat. A wall of windows fronts the house, letting in an abundance of natural light. Guests may rest on the floral couch, fire up the Franklin stove, and enjoy the bucolic setting from the living room. The mustard yellow walls are a delightful backdrop for the milk-painted desk, bureau, and sweater chest. Rattan furnishings rest on the colorful throw rugs scattered over tiled floors. A four-poster bed is tucked into an alcove, surrounded by still more milk-painted furnishings and dried flowers. We wondered where all the wonderful restored antiques came from, and Karen told us they were bequeathed to her by her grandmother. Decorative touches abound in here, just as they do at the Jasmine Cottage — with dried wreaths, floral balloon curtains, and baskets of flowers setting the country cottage motif. The open kitchen, set behind a half wall, allows guests to converse easily and still enjoy the views. A dining area near the kitchen is slightly more formal, with six Chippendale-style chairs set around a double-pedestal table. Guests may eat in here or on one of the two outdoor patios. We like the informal brick patio, where flower gardens and large eucalyptus trees supply all the necessary ambiance. The resident donkey, Radar, is usually

California

grazing in the neighboring pasture and welcomes visits by other friendly creatures.

Each morning, guests in Jasmine Cottage enjoy a full breakfast. Egg dishes created with fresh eggs from Karen's chickens, pastries and muffins, fresh fruit, and locally-made cheeses are just some of the offerings. An early-morning snack can be created from the selection of cereals, and coffee or tea stored in the kitchen cupboard.

Without their dogs, many might be tempted to just relax and do nothing at all, but our dogs are quite good at motivating us to get up and take them for a walk. They lead us up the softly sloping **hills**, or out to the **beaches** edged by shimmering water and teeming with wildlife. Some people might want to take their dogs over to **Heart's Desire Beach** or **Indian Beach**, then out to the **Point Reyes National Seashore**. Others may enjoy taking a five-minute walk into town, where a handful of intriguing shops and eateries awaits.

Rancho Las Palmas Resort

41000 Bob Hope Drive
Rancho Mirage, California 92270-4416
(800) I-LUV-SUN, (619) 568-2727, Fax (619) 568-5845
Internet: http://www.marriot.com

General Manager: *Ron Franklin*
Rooms: *428 doubles, 22 suites*
Rates: *Doubles $135-245 (EP), Suites $450-1,275 (EP)*
Payment: *AE, DC, DSC, MC, and VISA*
Dogs: *Welcome, but they cannot be in the room when the maid cleans and guests must sign a damage waiver*
Children: *Welcome (cribs, cots, baby-sitters, and children's day camp are available)*
Open: *All year*

The Rancho Las Palmas Resort may be a part of the Marriott chain, but its atmosphere and array of amenities sets this Marriott apart from the rest. Reflected throughout the resort is a sense of elegant simplicity. Physically, the hotel resembles an expansive Spanish hacienda — a theme carried into the lobby and extending through many of the other public areas. Arriving guests walk across Mexican tiles and through wide arches to the three-story beamed-ceilinged lobby lined with adobe walls. Triple-tiered, black iron chandeliers softly illuminate this cavernous area, with accents provided by a series of massive flower arrangements. Pairs of doors open onto the expansive outdoor patio. The free-form swimming pool looked tempting; however, we opted, instead to sit under one of the white umbrellas in the fountain courtyard and order a cool drink from the adjacent kiosk. While waiting for our libations, a fine mist drifted down from the kiosk's rooftop, cooling us off considerably. Just beyond this area is the multi-fingered Lake Rancho reaching out toward the resort's many casitas.

Updated since our last visit, the guest rooms now contain earth tone fabrics and a decor reflecting a combined Spanish/Southwest motif. These rooms are long on creature comforts as well, with minibars, individual climate controls, remote-controlled televisions, and clock radios comprising just a few of the many standard features. The two dozen suites are even more spacious, with their combination dining and living rooms. They also offer a few additional amenities, such as wet bars and refrigerators. For a better view of the grounds guests need only slide open the glass doors to their private terraces or balconies. Unlike some resorts that relegate those who travel with their dogs to the least desirable rooms, the dog-friendly casitas contain some of the resorts' best accommodations. Guests stay in first-floor chambers that are not only in the heart of the complex but also overlook the golf course. They are also equidistant from all restaurants and recreational facilities.

Some come to Rancho Las Palmas for the slow-paced, "hang out by the pool" desert lifestyle, while others prefer to participate in some of the many activities offered by the resort. Guests may test their prowess on the 27-holes of championship golf, and then sample any of the 25 tennis courts on the premises. More organized group activities include weekend aerobics classes and a small fitness center. There is even a Kactus Kids camp, for children ages five through twelve. In the morning, children can participate in games, arts and crafts, and lunch. During the holidays the programs are all the more extensive.

Those with a dog will enjoy walking along the paths that wend through Rancho las Palmas. The grounds are as quiet and tranquil as they are pleasing to the eye. There are lovely gardens, **footbridges** crossing portions of the lake, and **paths** that are ideal for extensive walks with a canine companion. Some may want to **rent a bicycle** and take their dog for a brisk ride further afield. Within the landscape of the desert there are many other diversions as well. These range from hot air balloon tours and horseback rides to a trip to the Living Desert museum.

As we mentioned, Rancho Las Palmas is an all-inclusive resort with a variety of shops and restaurants. Cabrillo is its premier restaurant, offering a delightful array of California and Mexican-style cuisine amid a relaxed and comfortable environment. Most people like to start the day at the Sunrise Terrace, which specializes in breakfasts, delicious brunches, and luncheon buffets. The Sunrise Terrace overlooks the pool, golf course, and mountains, which makes it an ideal place to meet with friends after a long day in the sun. Rancho Las Palmas bills itself as a desert oasis. After staying here, most would thoroughly agree — and add that it is also an oasis in a companionable country club setting.

California

Rancho Valencia Resort

P.O. Box 9126
5921 Valencia Circle
Rancho Santa Fe, California 92067-4126
(800) 548-3664, (619) 756-1123, Fax: (619) 756-0165
Internet: http://www.integra.fr/relaischateaux

General Manager: *Michael Ullman*
Rooms: *43 suites*
Rates: *$315-2,000 (EP)*
Payment: *AE, DC, MC, and VISA*
Dogs: *Welcome with a $75 daily fee (unbelievable, but true)*
Children: *Welcome (cribs and cots are available)*
Open: *All year*

We know, we know, Rancho Valencia isn't for everyone, but those who can afford it (including the steep doggie stipend) will find it worth every penny. Nestled within the exclusive community of Rancho Santa Fe, just over the hills from Del Mar and La Jolla, travelers will discover an exquisite resort that offers not only sensational accommodations and amenities, but also an array of recreational diversions. Built by developer Harry Collins in 1989, the resort was initially billed as an elegant tennis camp. Before too long, Collins realized the formula was wrong and sought the advice of Claude Rouas and Bob Harmon. These two also manage the equally popular and exclusive San Ysidro Ranch and Auberge du Soleil. Collectively, they turned the resort around and transformed it into an fabulous and exclusive hideaway.

We found it by meandering along a scenic back road, past the Rancho Santa Fe Polo Fields, where a lively match happened to be underway. Further up the valley, we came upon the serpentine drive, adhered to the unusual speed limit of 19 mph, and slowly made our way through the resort. The expansive property is comprised of 21 red tile-roofed casitas set on a plateau amid 40 acres of lovely citrus orchards, terraced gardens, and sprawling lawns. New arrivals and their dogs are escorted through a charming, tiled courtyard accented by a lovely central fountain, festive green umbrella tables, and an array of potted plants and exquisite flower gardens.

After dispensing with check-in at the adjacent reception area, guests are led along the wide paths to their sumptuous suites. There are two suite configurations available at the Rancho Valencia. The standard chamber, referred to as the Del Mar Suite, features a master bedroom, which steps down to a living room, where French doors then open to the private terrace. Equally spacious is the dressing room, with a walk-in closet and a luxurious bathroom set just off the entry. The substantially larger Rancho Santa Fe Suite has a slightly less elaborate master bedroom, but the other spaces and amenities are considerably more spacious and deluxe than those found in the Del Mar Suite.

Guests will find luxurious appointments in both configurations. Their bleached-wood, beamed ceilings, Berber carpets, paver tiled floors and countertops, and subtle earth tones set the overall tone. Bright, festive fabrics cover both the overstuffed couches and rattan armchairs, as well as the beds and chairs — all are beautifully coordinated. The decor is decidedly Southwestern, accented by pottery lamps, hand-painted tiles framing the fireplace, and vases of fresh and dried flowers. Other standard features include wet bars, color televisions with VCRs, private safes, and baskets brimming with an array of edibles set on the minibars.

The bathrooms contain a full complement of toiletries, along with terry cloth bathrobes and hair dryers. After taking in the details of the suites, our eyes were drawn to the valley, viewed through the French doors and shuttered windows. The terraced grounds planted with lush landscaping make each suite seem all the more private.

Small groups or extended families may wish to reserve the Hacienda Suite. This is a separate, free-flowing building encircling a central courtyard. Three good-sized bedrooms provide ample sleeping space, although groups tend to gather in the suite's many other rooms — whether it be the kitchen, card room, or living room. A pair of enclosed patios, along with a private pool, completes the list of additional amenities this enchanting suite offers its guests.

Rancho Valencia's accommodations are so lovely that some people never feel the need to leave their suite, although a little exploration reveals an array of intriguing diversions. Visit the Clubhouse, highlighted by the cascading fountain and botanical splendor of the central courtyard. At La Sala, open-beamed ceilings and pairs of French doors lead to a huge terrace. Picture windows reveal exceptional views of the grounds, making it especially delightful on sunny mornings. The day of our visit a huge tent filled much of the English-style croquet lawn, ready to accommodate the 125 polo players who would soon arrive for dinner. In addition to croquet, guests may play golf on any of the four neighboring courses, sample the expansive spa program, or take advantage of the extensive tennis facilities.

The tennis program is so good that it has been ranked by *Tennis Magazine* as one of the top ten tennis resorts in the country. Whether benefiting from the lessons taught by the top-notch staff or cooling off afterwards with pitchers of lemon water, guests will find the facilities are first rate. A swim in the pool or a soak in any of the Jacuzzis are ideal ways to rejuvenate tired muscles. Guests may also venture into the sky on a hot-air ballooning trip, watch the horses race at Del Mar, or charter a sail or deep-sea fishing boat.

Dogs, on the other hand, should be game for an entirely different set of adventures. Guests with dogs may want to walk or **jog along the rancho's trails**; borrow a bicycle for a leisurely ride through the San Dieguito Valley; or take the complimentary shuttle over to Del Mar's picturesque beaches.

California

The **beaches in Del Mar** allow dogs in the off-peak hours and discourage them during the summer months.

After a busy day, most can hardly wait to return to the tranquil confines of the resort. The La Sala Terrace is a favorite spot for enjoying a refreshing libation as the sunset casts a warm glow over the grounds and hills. If the views don't set the mood, then the combination of open-beamed ceilings, Spanish tiled floors, and first class service certainly will. Guests may start their meal with the martini cocktail of Alaskan king crab and Mexican prawns; Sonoma duck *foie gras* sautéed with apples, calvados, and wildflower honey; or the Prince Edward Island black mussels and saffron bisque. Any of these dishes may be followed with the peppered sea scallops on a bed of roasted fennel and tomato coulis; the grilled Long Island duckling and confit with gaufrette potatoes and sundried blueberry essence; or the rack of lamb with lemon scented orzo and a Cabernet rosemary sauce. After a delightful meal, most fall happily into bed in an attempt to re-energize for the following day.

The Inn at Rancho Santa Fe

P.O. Box 869
5951 Linea Del Cielo
Rancho Santa Fe, California   92067
(800) 654-2928, (619) 756-1131, Fax: (619) 759-1604

Rancho Santa Fe

Owner: *Duncan Royce Hadden*
Rooms: *76 doubles, 8 suites, 6 cottages*
Rates: *Doubles $85-185 (EP), Suites $265-500 (EP), Cottages $275-500 (EP)*
Payment: *AE, CB, DC, MC, and VISA*
Dogs: *Welcome, with notice, in cottage rooms with patios or porches*
Children: *Welcome (cribs, cots, high chairs, and baby-sitters are available)*
Open: *All year*

The land around Rancho Santa Fe was first deeded to a Spanish soldier of fortune in 1845. His name was Juan Maria Osuna and he later named the area San Dieguito. The land lay in relative obscurity until 1923, when the Santa Fe Railroad bought it and planted some 3,000,000 eucalyptus tree seedlings. These were to be used for making railroad ties, but the wood was too soft, and the trees were left to grow. Then came prospective land buyers, who often stayed at the 12-room guest house built amid these eucalyptus groves. Nearly two decades later, George Richardson bought the property and developed it as a private resort, adding extensive landscaping, a library, and additional cottages. Steve Royce — who pitched for the New York Giants and later owned and managed the Fairmont Hotel in San Francisco and the Huntington Hotel in Pasadena — bought the inn in 1958. The Royce family has been here ever since. Unlike many other developers of the time, the Royces worked to preserve the inn's integrity. Today, it is still a lovely retreat, set on 20 acres of rolling hills, citrus groves, and eucalyptus trees.

We always look forward to visiting the Inn at Rancho Santa Fe, and on this day the views along the serpentine road leading to the inn were especially magnificent. A handful of colorful hot air balloons suddenly appeared over the hilltops, ingraining the already perfect scene into our memories. The dogs, who had just woken up, found the balloons mildly intriguing, but they didn't get really excited until we reached the inn. For all of us, it was like coming home again and we happily noted that little had changed since our last visit. The original inn is adobe and topped by a Spanish tile roof. All of the cottages created since then, while not necessarily made of adobe, do adhere in style to their predecessor.

As we walked up the path to the main inn, we noticed two couples having a fine old time playing croquet. We stepped inside to our favorite room by far — the beamed-ceiling living room, with its array of family antiques, numerous models, and shadow boxes displaying ships' models. Two chintz-covered sofas rest before the enormous fireplace, providing the perfect environment for relaxing, reading a book, or conversing. The intimate library contains a number of books, as well as backgammon and chess tables. Relaxation would have to wait a bit, though, as we wanted to see the cottages.

These vary in size and contain between two and ten bedrooms. Individually decorated, they offer a wide range of amenities that can include wet bars, separate sitting rooms, and even full kitchens. Pastels or more muted color combinations are typical, whether on the wicker, cushioned chairs or chintz-covered sofas and matching armchairs. These spaces open to private sun terraces, complete with chaise lounges, tables shaded by umbrellas, and privacy hedges. These accommodations are ideal for those traveling with a dog, as they not only provide easy access to the out of doors, but also offer a little more privacy. There is little to report in the way of change — that thrills some guests while others might be happier with a few more high-tech features. Although not appropriate for people traveling with a dog, there are also guest rooms in the main inn. These bedrooms are not as spacious as those in the cottages, but the decor and furnishings are similar. A separate sitting room may be requested. Lastly, there are some private homes near the inn, which become available when their owners are out of town. Guests staying in these houses may use all of the inn's services and amenities.

There are a number of fine restaurants in the area, but the inn itself has a few interesting options. The Garden Room is one of our favorite spots for breakfast. Pastoral murals, a lattice-work ceiling, and walls of windows overlooking the garden and swimming pool accentuate the light and airy feeling in here. The Vintage Room serves cocktails, lunch, and dinner. On the weekends, the adjacent Patio Terrace is a favorite spot for dancing. For a truly romantic dinner, the Library is our preferred choice.

Beamed ceilings, walls of books, and a crackling fire set the tone for a fine meal. To start, diners might select the giant crab claws served with aoili and lemon, or the vichyssoise with avocado. Entrées range from a fresh red snapper and a grilled Pacific salmon with a caper sauce to fillet mignon and veal medallions topped with avocado and hollandaise. Men must wear a jacket and tie to dinner, but aside from this tradition, the atmosphere remains relaxed and relatively informal.

During the day, there are many ways to entertain both humans and dogs. **Del Mar Beach** is one of the most popular destinations. It is only a fifteen minute drive from the inn. Here, the inn maintains a cottage where guests may shower and change. If the thought of sitting on a sandy beach does not sound appealing, then relax under the white umbrella tables set around the swimming pool. Later in the day, some people walk their dogs along the **trails and paths surrounding the inn**, or perhaps **into the village** for some window shopping.

There are three tennis courts on site, as well as an English croquet course. For a more invigorating workout, guests might head over to the workout room. In addition to the five championship golf courses in the area, there are an assortment of shopping alternatives in the neighboring towns. Finally, after having tired out their dogs, guests may wish to drive over to Del Mar Racetrack. The inn maintains box seats there, along with some Turf Club passes, which it makes available to its guests. Those who want even more suggestions need only ask the staff. Staff members are always extremely helpful, without being intrusive. Their friendly manner ensures that each guest's stay at the Inn at Rancho Santa Fe is all the more enjoyable.

The Horton Grand Hotel

311 Island Avenue
San Diego, California 92101
(800) 542-1886, (619) 544-1886, Fax: (619) 239-3823
Internet: http://www.gothere.com/horton/grad.htm

Manager: *John Schmidt*
Rooms: *128 doubles, 24 suites*
Rates: *Doubles $139-199 (EP), Suites $218-329 (EP)*
Payment: *AE, MC, DC, and VISA*
Dogs: *Welcome with approval in the ground floor rooms with a $25 fee (dogs under 18 pounds are preferred)*
Children: *Welcome (cribs, cots, high chairs, and baby-sitting services are available)*
Open: *All year*

With the recent restoration of San Diego's Old Town historic district, the city is now able to draw additional business and pleasure travelers who used to opt for waterside accommodations. One of the more notable sections is known as the Gaslight Quarter, which covers nearly 16 blocks south of Broadway. In its early days, this section was commonly known as the Stringaree district, due to its high concentration of saloons, gambling halls, opium dens, and brothels.

Despite numerous clean-up raids, the area flourished. Two hotels were built during this era to accommodate the thousands of visitors who would arrive via the transcontinental train. These hotels were known as The Horton Grand Hotel and the Brooklyn Kahle Saddlery Hotel. The former was an elegant building, inspired by the Innsbruck Hotel in Vienna. The Brooklyn Kahle Saddlery Hotel, on the other hand, combined a wild west and Victorian motif into one hostelry. The first floor was dedicated to a saddle and harness shop, which is perhaps what attracted Wyatt Earp who reputedly stayed in the hotel for seven years.

Years later, when the city planners finally decided to renovate this seedy waterfront district, they needed some help. They offered to let people buy the old buildings for the modest sum of $1, if they agreed to renovate them. Dan Pearson purchased both hotels, dismantled them, and moved them to their current location. These historic landmarks are now joined by a lovely atrium, and today, attract a new breed of guest.

We thought the Horton Grand Hotel to be a delightful combination of the past and present, with a whimsical twist. A large *papier maché* horse named Sunshine was our first indication of the whimsy. She resides in the sun-drenched lobby and serves as a reminder of the days when the building was a saddle and harness shop. We walked past a large cage of chirping finches before emerging into the central, cavernous brick courtyard. This festive spot is dotted with white umbrella tables and wrought iron garden furniture set amid large potted palms and ficus trees. Ivy grows over the white balcony railings, while the sound of cascading water can be traced to a fountain boasting the image of a lion.

If someone wrote a book on neat old hotel bars and restaurants, the Palace Bar and the Ida Bailey restaurant would certainly be included. The former is especially elegant, with richly hued wood-paneled walls. It rises two floors in some sections, and guests can see various historic pictures lining the uppermost coral pink walls. Victorian-era murals, more reminiscent of the great masters, depict well rounded, scantily clad women in bucolic settings. On that note, we move to Ida Bailey's restaurant, named after a famous madam who operated the Canary Cottage brothel on the same site. Traditional entrées are served in here and include Pacific red snapper, chicken picatta, veal marsala, and filet mignon. We also liked the idea of high tea, which guests can enjoy in the Tea Room. The formal decor is intriguing; however, most guests are more enamored with the abundance of sunlight pouring through the two-story floor-to-ceiling windows.

The guest chambers are equally unique in both decor and furnishings. Some are small, but they more than compensate for this shortcoming with extras such as gas fireplaces and intriguing architectural details. These details include paddle fans suspended from the high ceilings, arches leading to intimate sitting rooms and alcoves, and Palladian windows. The period decor and hand-crafted antiques nicely complement the half-canopied beds. Well-coordinated fabrics cover the wing and armchairs, while sheer lace curtains frame the windows. Anyone who has a big dog, or who wants a little more space, should reserve a mini-suite. These provide guests with a separate sitting area and a dining room table, along with kitchenettes. Regardless of the room size, we suggest that guests do make a point of requesting a chamber overlooking the lovely courtyard.

Those with a penchant for ghosts and things that go bump in the night, will be interested to learn about the friendly poltergeist, named Roger Whitaker. For a number of months a mysterious presence was felt by guests and staff alike. It wasn't too long before the beds began to shake and the lights would inadvertently turn on and off. The management decided to enlist the aid of two psychics, who spent the night in Room 309. After a while, old Roger appeared before the psychics. He turned out to be a gambler, who lived in the 1800s and was shot and killed by an associate, at the ripe old age of 37. Although Roger was murdered elsewhere, he thought the Horton Grand would be a lovely home in his afterlife. It is all right to remain skeptical; however, those who might be a bit unnerved by the whole thing can rest a little easier, as one of the psychics found Roger to be "really very nice and very warm." The other psychic added, though, "He is also a bit naughty." With all the notoriety surrounding Room 309, it is important for those who wish to stay there to book it well in advance, as there are plenty of other hopeful guests waiting to meet Mr. Whitaker.

All that aside, dogs (and their human friends) should thoroughly enjoy these historic accommodations, as well as leisurely walks through the nicely restored **Gaslamp Quarter**, which is now a National Historic District. Other options include meandering over to the **Horton Plaza**, **Seaport Village**, the Children's' Museum, Santa Fe Depot and Railroad Museum, or the Palladian Shopping Center. The **Embarcadero Marina Park** is also a short walk from the hotel and is a nice outlet for people and their dogs.

San Diego Princess Resort

1404 West Vacation Road
San Diego, California 92109
(800) 344-2626, (619) 274-4630, Fax: (619) 581-5929
Internet: http://www.princessresort.com/princess/

Manager: *Thomas C. Vincent*
Rooms: *359 doubles, 103 suites*
Rates: *Doubles $150-220 (EP), Suites $260-365 (EP)*
Payment: *AE, DSC, MC, and VISA*
Dogs: *Welcome; a damage deposit may be requested at check-in*
Children: *Welcome, children under 12 years of age are free (cribs, cots, baby-sitters, and "Kids' Kamp" are available)*
Open: *All year*

The San Diego Princess lies on a 44-acre manmade island just north of downtown San Diego. In 1962, movie producer Jack Skirball (who is responsible for productions such as *Cleopatra* and *El Camino Real*) developed these marshlands into the Vacation Village Resort. In its prime, it was one of the more popular family resorts in California, offering an array of recreational options and great accommodations. Unfortunately, the Vacation Village concept went bust and the resort floundered for years until Princess Cruise Resorts and Hotels finally purchased it in 1983. Today, the San Diego Princess Resort is once again an attractive facility, offering terrific accommodations for all types of travelers, including those with dogs.

The extensive resort is best navigated by golf cart or by car. The circuitous roads meander around tropical gardens, waterfalls, palm and banana trees, and footbridges crossing small lagoons teeming with water lilies and an assortment of waterfowl. Each of the single-story, stucco bungalows, houses between two and six bedrooms, with views of the lush gardens, lagoons, or sparkling bay. Accommodations range from a cozy lanai room, with pairs of queen beds, a table and chairs, and a private patio to the larger, pie-shaped studio suite. The latter offers a king-bedded room separated by a short wall from the cozy living room and kitchenette. A pair of dressing rooms, each with a bureau, borders the central bathroom. The one-bedroom suite is a good choice for families, with a large, separate living room and dining area, along with a kitchen. Guests sleeping in the sofa beds may use the private dressing room for storing their belongings and changing. Updated since our last visit, most of the guest rooms are now in wonderful shape. The overall decor is pretty basic, but more memorable is the clever use of space, especially in the smaller units.

Visitors should be clear about where they want to stay on the property. We recommend asking for the hotel's map before making reservations. Some guests prefer to be closer to the tennis courts, putting greens, or marina, while others are strictly water-view people, looking for something overlooking the lagoons or Mission Bay. We preferred the rooms facing the bay. Rooms 104 through 133 are privy to the best prevailing winds. Guests with small children might forgo the refreshing breezes for direct access to a sandy cove. We also recommend the mid-500 rooms that are set near both the lagoons and the cove. Anyone sleeping in a cove-side room should know the entire area around the resort is a "Low-wake Zone" — therefore motor boats, which are required to stay away from the swimming area, are relatively quiet here.

As we mentioned earlier, most people come to the San Diego Princess Resort for the abundance of recreational opportunities. Guests may play tennis, volleyball, shuffleboard, or Ping-pong, as well as golf, swim in one of the five pools, or exercise on the par course. Water-oriented guests can charter a boat and sail or motor around Mission Bay. Others may want to head out on a bicycle and travel the relatively flat roads around the island with their dog. An observation tower, set in the middle of the complex, allows guests to view the surrounding area. Children will undoubtedly gravitate to the "Kids Kamp," where an array of activities awaits. These range from beach volleyball, sand castle building, and kite building/flying to monster bubble making, model boat races, and scavenger hunts.

After a busy day, the resorts' three restaurants are all available: the Dockside Restaurant, the Bay Lounge — with a South Sea Islands motif — and the less expensive, informal Barefoot Bar & Grill. After dinner, there are even more activities available, including treasure hunts, family movies, beach campfires, storytelling, and an array of the theme nights.

Canine hot spots include **Balboa Park**, **Mission Bay Park**, **Ocean Beach Park**, and **Coronado City Beach** — all supremely dog friendly places. For guests who need even more open space, a visit to the expansive **Cleveland National Forest** is a beautiful and relaxing option.

Rancho Bernardo Inn

17550 Bernardo Oaks Drive
San Diego, California 92128
(800) 854-1065, (760) 487-1611, Fax: (760) 675-8401

General Manager: *Rick Mansur*
Rooms: *229 doubles, 58 suites*
Rates: *Doubles $165-220 (EP), Suites $290-425 (EP)*
Payment: *AE, DC, MC, and VISA*
Dogs: *Welcome with approval and a $50 deposit*
Children: *Welcome (cribs and baby-sitters are available)*
Open: *All year*

Although officially located within the boundaries of San Diego, the Rancho Bernardo Inn lies at the foothills of the San Pasqual Mountains. Set in a quiet residential area, the inn is a sprawling complex consisting of the low-lying resort and the surrounding golf course. Stepping inside the intimate reception area, guests will find beamed ceilings and white adobe walls, creating a sense of tranquillity. Numerous alcoves, intimate sitting areas, and assorted shelves filled with Californian and Mexican collectibles give this area an overall charm. A favorite gathering place is the Music Room, where an assortment of antique musical instruments is displayed. Visitors may settle into one of the overstuffed sofas that is set on Oriental rugs, or, in the afternoon, listen to the pianist play the concert Steinway. Many enjoy gathering around the central fireplace, flanked by bookshelves. Others can be found bent over the inlaid game and puzzle tables set about the perimeter of this room. Those who are interested may enjoy afternoon high tea amid these charming surroundings.

Eight red-tile roof haciendas, housing the guest rooms, are well spaced and are primarily accessed by covered walkways. Lush landscaping, antique fountains, and lovely views of the surrounding golf course and mountains make the walk to these accommodations very pleasant. The guest rooms vary not only in size and amenities, but also in the views they offer and in their proximity to one another. Some of our favorite chambers are the Castillo and Palacio suites, which overlook the tennis courts and first tee of the golf course. These, and the guest rooms in the 700 building, are relatively new units and are the most private of the resort's accommodations. The decor here is similar to that of the other guest rooms, utilizing an array of earth tones and a subtle Southwestern theme. Furnishings are a combination of rattan and more traditional pieces, and fill the beamed-ceiling sitting rooms and bedrooms. Fireplaces take the chill off a cool night, while the walls of sliding glass or French doors, opening onto the private brick terraces, keep the overall feeling open and airy. Original artwork and creative plant arrangements add to the residential quality of these spaces. Modern conveniences include an honor bar, refrigerator, a remote controlled television, and a wall safe. Double vanities are a thoughtful luxury in the bathroom, as are the hair dryers, secondary telephones, terry cloth robes, and occasionally, a whirlpool bath.

Meals may of course be enjoyed in the privacy of one's room, or guests may investigate either of the hotel's two excellent restaurants — The Veranda or El Bizcocho. The Veranda is the more casual of the two, offering lovely views of the putting green and 18th fairway. This is the busiest during breakfast and lunch. El Bizcocho, on the other hand, is an elegant spot for evening meals. The dining room consists of two seating areas. The warm and intimate La Taberna lounge has beamed ceilings and a low wall of bookshelves, which effectively divides the lounge from the larger restaurant below. The lower level is substantially more open and overlooks the patio and emerald green golf course. A few of the more notable appetizer selections include the lobster salad, dressed in walnut oil, basil, and truffles; the escargot with garlic and butter in a puff pastry; and the lobster bisque with Armagnac. Seasonal entrée specialties feature such selections as the grilled quail with wild mushrooms; the sea bass with a black olive and herb crust; and the roasted duckling served with apples and Calvados Bigarade sauce.

The meals may be sumptuous, but this *is* Southern California, and there are a vast array of recreational options for guests to take advantage of, should they wish to expend a few calories. The golf and tennis facilities are some of the finest in the area, offering clinics, private instruction, and videotaped sessions. There are two swimming pools, along with an immense 5,000-square-foot fitness center. The latter offers a full complement of workout equipment, along with steam and sauna rooms and a choice of massages — shiatsu, sports, or Swedish. Families are not overlooked, and children may participate in a wide variety of programs through Camp RBI. These start at 9:00 a.m. and end at 9:00 p.m. The carefully designed sessions, staffed by experienced counselors, offer an array of activities and well thought-out projects. Camp RBI is available during most school holidays.

Those who choose to leave the confines of the resort will find many other diversions in nearby San Diego, including such attractions as Sea World, the San Diego Zoo, and the Wild Animal Park. Dogs are not overlooked; they may run freely along the many **jogging trails at the inn**, or blend in with the other local dogs who can be found walking around the surrounding **residential neighborhood**. Another popular excursion entails heading over to San Diego's **Mission Trails Park**, where leashed dogs are welcome to explore the 5,000 acres. Hikes lead visitors and their dogs to a dam, a lake, and other scenic areas in the park. This place is definitely worth considering when looking for a day-long adventure with your dog.

U.S. Grant

6 Broadway
San Diego, California 92101
(800) 237-5029, (619) 232-3121, Fax: (619) 232-3626
Internet: http://www.grandheritage.com/htmlcode/hus_usgrant.html

Managing Director: *Joe Duncalfe*
Rooms: *220 doubles, 60 suites*
Rates: *Doubles $135-185 (EP), Suites $255-1,000 (EP)*
Payment: *AE, CB, DC, DSC, MC, and VISA*
Dogs: *Their "Pampered Pet" program is the ultimate doggie indulgence*
Children: *Welcome (cribs, cots, high chairs, and baby-sitters are available)*
Open: *All year*

Considered the birthplace of California, San Diego's beaches and its Mediterranean climate have long attracted vacationers, along with its fair share of permanent residents. As with most major cities, though, San Diego also went through a period of decline. Many factors contributed to its resurgence, including, in more recent years, playing host to yachting's most prestigious competition — the America's Cup.

San Diego's historic downtown was in need of the most attention, and fortunately received plenty of it. This area now attracts a steady stream of visitors, and one of their preferred accommodation options is the U.S. Grant. Originally constructed in 1910 by Ulysses S. Grant, as a tribute to his father, the hotel comprises one entire block in the center of San Diego. Renowned as the jewel of the city, the hotel's stature and reputation for fine service attracted celebrities such as Albert Einstein, Charles Lindbergh, and a dozen U.S. Presidents. The hotel remained solvent until the 1970s, after which a quick succession of owners failed to make a go of it. The U.S. Grant finally received an $80 million face lift in 1985, which restored its grand common areas and revitalized the lovely guest chambers.

Today, visitors still have a strong sense of the hotel's history, especially in the expansive lobby, which is highlighted by massive Palladian columns supporting hand-carved ceilings painted with gold leaf and inset with crystal chandeliers. Walls covered with tapestries and damask are adorned with Dutch and Venetian oil paintings, while Chinese porcelains, imported marbles, and impressive flower arrangements round out the decorative motif. Traditional 18th-century mahogany reproductions line the inviting chamber; however, it is the grand marble staircase that beckons travelers to explore the depths of this landmark property.

The bedrooms exude a feeling similar to that of the public areas, although clearly, many of the rooms were not designed to meet today's more demanding standards. We feel that the many fine appointments and the handsome furnishings more than make up for these minor limitations. Wing chairs, armoires, and good-sized writing desks surround the mahogany Queen-Anne, two-poster beds. The rich combination of woods nicely complements the earth tone walls lined with botanical prints. Spacious bathrooms combine travertine marble and ceramic tile (150 tons of marble was imported for the hotel's renovation) with an array of amenities that include terry robes, hand-milled soaps, and other luxurious toiletries.

Business travelers may opt for the rooms on the Presidential Club Levels — located on the tenth and eleventh floors. These spaces not only offer better downtown vistas, but are also equipped with computers, printers, and fax machines. A concierge staffs just these two floors, and guests staying here receive complimentary shoeshine service, newspapers, cocktails and *hors d'oeuvres*, nightly turndown, and breakfast. The suites, of course, are our favorites. Guests and their dogs are treated to fireplaces in the parlors, Jacuzzis in the bathrooms, and fully stocked bars. The suites, too, are located on the upper floors and have the most impressive views. The townhouse suites go a step further by providing a pair of bedrooms, a spacious living room, and several balconies from which to enjoy the picturesque vistas. Dogs are welcome in all rooms and receive (by our rating) the five-star treatment as part of the hotel's Pampered Pet program. Dogs are provided with a soft sleeping pillow, and at night a rawhide chewy toy and a biscuit are left on this pillow — all part of the pet-friendly evening turndown service. Dogs are also treated to special doggie meals prepared by the hotel's chef. Canines will be in doggie heaven while at the U.S. Grant, especially if their human counterparts adhere to a few simple rules. Dogs must be leashed in all public areas, and they must be left in a crate or carrier when guests are out of the room. The hotel even provides a special card, to be placed over the doorknob,

San Diego

letting the staff know that a dog is in the room.

This full-service hotel also has some inviting common areas to congregate in, whether guests want to meet friends for a drink or enjoy an intimate dinner for two. If the former is what people have in mind, then they should try the Lounge set off the main reception area. We walked past a wall of wine bottles (the rest of the hotel's million-dollar wine cellar resides elsewhere) before emerging into the formal club-like setting. Immense, paneled white birch walls surround a large fireplace and small grouping of tables. A billiards table is located in front of the floor-to-ceiling windows overlooking the downtown area. The equally clubby Grant Grill is situated just next door. This intimate restaurant also has paneled wood walls, but its wood is imported from West Africa. Brass sconces and equestrian oil paintings fill the walls above the burgundy-colored booths.

Winning numerous accolades from around the country, the grill's new chef, Gunther Emathinger, presents a varied menu of diverse proportions. Appetizer selections include such dishes as tiger prawns with snow peas, mint and a ginger timbale with Belgian endive and lobster mayonnaise; the chilled venison roast served on a Kohlrabi-potato salad with saffron tartar sauce; or the famous Grant Grill's mock turtle soup or lobster bisque with truffle crêpe vermicelli. Main courses feature grilled sea scallops wrapped in smoked salmon with grappa-flambéed crêpes, fennel, and grapes in a light saffron-thyme sauce; or the roast venison served with brioche pudding baked with pears, rose hips, juniper berries, and woodruff herb. More traditional fare includes the New York steak, filet mignon, roasted free range chicken, and grilled salmon.

The U.S. Grant is in the center of it all. The six square block Horton Plaza shopping complex is situated just across the street, while Seaport Village, the Gaslamp Quarter, Balboa Park (home of the San Diego Zoo), Sea World, and the Wild Animal Park are all just a short car ride away. As the hotel is nestled right in the heart of the city, most people can take their dogs with them and **explore the area by foot and paw**. While there are a number of intriguing parks nearby, many of them restrict dog access to early morning or late evening hours. Thus, instead of waiting around, we would recommend investigating either **Ocean Beach** or the **Fiesta Island** section of Mission Bay Park, where dogs can run, swim in the water, and even romp without their leashes — provided they are under voice control.

California

Campton Place Hotel

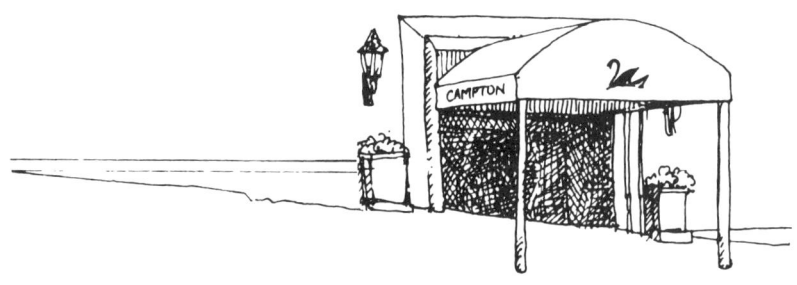

340 Stockton Street
San Francisco, California 94108
(800) 235-4300, (415) 781-5555, Fax: (415) 955-5536

General Manager: *Paul Zuest*
Rooms: *119 doubles, 8 suites*
Rates: *Doubles $230-345 (EP), Suites $450-1,000 (EP)*
Payment: *AE, CB, DC, JCB, MC, and VISA*
Dogs: *Welcome with a $25 fee per stay*
Children: *Welcome (cribs, cots, and baby-sitters are available)*
Open: *All year*

Years ago, the Campton Place was known as the Drake-Wiltshire hotel, but in 1981 Ayala International bought the deteriorating building, gutted it, and completely redesigned its interior spaces. Two years and $18 million later, the hotel reopened as one of the first new intimate luxury hotels in San Francisco. We were very impressed not only with the exquisitely decorated guest rooms and intimate surroundings, but also with the highly personalized service. The hotel also happened to contain an exquisite restaurant, which quickly became one of the finest in the city. On our recent return, we learned the hotel just went through another extensive restoration and the facilities are more outstanding than ever.

Located just off Union Square, the Campton Place is ideally sited for easy access to the city's best shopping and sightseeing. The reception area is intimate, but its lavish use of marble accents and exquisite furnishings sets the opulent tone for the rest of the hotel. Oriental *objets d' art*, including antique urns and Japanese screens, are softly illuminated. Overstuffed chairs and couches, covered in sumptuous muted fabrics, occupy recessed sections of the lobby. One design feature we always admired was still intact — hallways encircling the center open-air atrium, allowing natural light to filter through the interior of the building. This not only ensures a good deal of natural lighting, but also imbues these spaces, which often have just four guest chambers on each floor, with an additional sense of intimacy.

All of the relatively spacious bedrooms are elegantly appointed with oversized beds, Henredon and McGuire furnishings, Louis XVI writing desks, and limited-edition contemporary artwork. Televisions, concealed in the armoires, and the sophisticated lighting systems are both remote controlled. The rooms' sliding windows open, allowing the cool salt air to filter in; yet they are also double-glazed so that when closed, any street noise from below will not disturb the guests. Brass is used quite liberally throughout the rooms, from the trim on the coffee tables to the fixtures in the modern bathrooms. The large bathrooms are fashioned with thick cotton robes, French milled soaps, large fluffy towels, baths with thermometers, hair dryers, scales, and even telephones. The residential quality is enhanced with freshly cut flowers and potted plants. The Campton Place Hotel has always been a place "where high expectations are quietly met." Their extensive list of complimentary services includes daily newspaper delivery, and a valet to draw a bath or unpack and repack the luggage (with tissue paper, of course). While any of the guest accommodations would receive our highest recommendation, we especially like the "01" series. These light and airy corner chambers are privy to copious amounts of afternoon sun, and directly overlook Union Square.

It is rare that a hotel of this size will have a restaurant to match its exquisitely appointed guest rooms; however, the Campton Place is unique in this respect. Passing the curved glass partition etched with graceful swans, we entered the elegantly appointed restaurant, accented with warm peach tones. We had heard rave reviews about the executive chef, Todd Humphries, and were anxious to sample his latest presentations. Dinner appetizers featured such selections as the soft-shelled crab with corn relish, and the seared buffalo carpaccio with pumpkin and spiced cranberries. Entrées ranged from steamed Thai snapper with crispy shallots, sautéed pea sprouts and a ver jus sauce; and a squab and *foie gras* with grilled figs, chanterelles, and tender greens to a rack of lamb with eggplant, tomatoes, pine nuts, and saffron. The menu may change regularly, but the inspiration behind it ensures an intriguing outcome. One of our favorite places to go after dinner is the cozy bar, followed by a walk over to Nob Hill, or window shopping around Union Square.

Dogs will be thrilled with their Campton Place digs. As we mentioned,

California

the walks around here are stimulating, both visually and cardiovascularly. Travelers who want to get out of the city with their dogs can hop on the **ferry to Sausalito** and investigate the shops and parks there. Landlubbers might opt for a trip across the Golden Gate Bridge instead, where the spectacular vistas unfold. In addition to visiting such picturesque communities as Mill Valley, Tiburon, and Sausalito, we also highly recommend heading out along the winding coastal route leading toward **Point Reyes** and **Inverness**. The abundance of nearby **city parks**, coupled with the array of sightseeing options just a short drive away, will thoroughly appeal to any canine — almost as much as the overall atmosphere and ambiance will appeal to the human guests of the Campton Place Hotel.

The Clift

495 Geary Street
San Francisco, California 94102
(800) 65-CLIFT, (415) 775-4700, Fax: (415) 441-4621

General Manager: *Sileshi Mengiste*
Rooms: *298 doubles, 31 suites*
Rates: *Doubles $145-295 (EP), Suites $350-750 (EP)*
Payment: *AE, DC, ENR, JCB, MC, and VISA*
Dogs: *Welcome with approval and a $40 nightly fee (pet treats are available)*
Children: *Welcome (cribs, cots, high chairs, baby-sitters, and Young Travelers Program are available)*
Open: *All year*

One of the most striking things about The Clift is its rich history, which spans over 80 years. This landmark lies just a few blocks from San Francisco's famous Union Square, and is ideally situated for anyone who wants to be within walking distance of the downtown shopping and business districts. There are few hills to negotiate (unusual in this seemingly mountainous city) because the hotel lies on the edge of the city's flatlands. The site was perfect for the hotel, but even more inspirational was the design.

The Clift, built in 1915, incorporated many eras into its interior plan. During its heyday, it hosted such personalities as Judy Garland, Ethel Merman, George Raft, Rosemary Clooney, and David Rockefeller. Unfortunately, in the late 1960s, with the declining health of its maverick owner Robert Odell, the hotel slowly began to loose some of its allure and appeal with its longstanding patrons. The Four Seasons purchased the hotel in the early 1970s and pumped vast amounts of money into refurbishing the restaurant, common areas, and guest rooms. Although the Four Seasons is no longer associated with the hotel, The Clift reflects the same charm and appeal that made her popular and fashionable decades ago.

We entered the handsome wood-paneled reception area to find traditional furnishings and a decor that is reminiscent of the turn-of-the-century. Delicate cut-glass chandeliers hang from the carved-wood ceiling and Oriental works of art are interspersed with pale, Italian marble and brass accents. In contrast, the adjacent Redwood Room is a sophisticated bar reflecting the Art Deco era, and is a favorite haunt of local residents and tourists alike. Warm hues from the redwood paneling are highlighted by the frosted Art Deco sconces and chandeliers. Gustav Klimt prints line the walls. The old-fashioned redwood burl bar is inlaid with exotic woods and trimmed with a brass rail. The adjoining French Room is the ultimate combination of classic architecture and fine food. This exquisitely appointed space still attracts a strong following. Patrons might begin their meal with the cognac seared scallops; Sonoma *foie gras* with a crisp potato terrine and a raspberry-beet reduction; or the salmon soup with sweet corn, watercress, and fresh herbs. Lobster cioppino tops our entrée list, along with the lamb loin cooked with citrus and fresh herbs and served with a summer vegetable galette. Other perennial favorites include the Petaluma duck with confit, black cherry compôte, and potato gratin; and the tenderloin of beef with fresh asparagus, morels, and *foie gras* potatoes.

This pursuit of excellence is also extended into guest rooms. These spacious chambers are reminiscent of another era, especially with their high ceilings and oversized windows (that actually open). Some of the executive suites have bedrooms and sitting rooms separated by French doors; however, even the standard chambers are still large and luxuriously appointed. The sophisticated decor highlights pastel pinks, blues, and rose colors on the painted walls, the floral wallpapers, and in the matching draperies. The Georgian-style furnishings look appropriate with the more contemporary glass and brass-trimmed coffee tables, mahogany desks, and overstuffed sofas and armchairs. Marble bathrooms have fragrant soaps and shampoos, along with terry robes for guests and their children (if they are in attendance). In the evenings, the beds are turned down and gold-wrapped mints are placed upon the pillows. The staff, on call 24 hours a day, attends to guests' needs quickly, efficiently, and without pretense.

The staff is also well-equipped to accommodate the smaller travelers, whether these be children or dogs. We were impressed, as most families will be, with the Young Travelers Program. Guests may select from a staggering selection of services that includes everything from supplying a baby bottle, crib, or stroller to baseball cards, video games, and books. The hotel also likes to know the names and ages of the children so it can have an adequate supply of age-appropriate items on hand.

Not to be outdone, dogs also receive the royal treatment. The Clift's expansive list of doggie amenities includes doggie beds, bathrobes, bowls, and snacks. There is also a complimentary dog walker available, a vet on call, and traveling crates/cages. The concierge is well versed in doggie-oriented

California

attractions, amenities, and intriguing dog-friendly sights and attractions near the hotel. Without exception, The Clift will surely meet, and possibly surpass, every human and pet expectation.

San Francisco is a delightful city to explore by automobile, cable car, or on foot. There are almost as many picturesque parks and intriguing areas to walk as there are interesting shops, boutiques, and restaurants. Most of the parks are dog-friendly, especially the expansive **Golden Gate Park** or the smaller **Julius Kahn** and **Moscone Parks**. Lovely coastal beaches and terrific hiking trails are just a short drive from the hotel. Those who want to venture further afield can take day trips to Napa Valley, Half Moon Bay, Point Reyes National Seashore, and Carmel-by-the-Sea — all of which are within an hour and a half of the city.

The Inn San Francisco

943 South Van Ness Avenue
San Francisco, California 94110
(800) 359-0913, (415) 641-0188, Fax: (415) 641-1701

Owners: *Marty Neely*
Rooms: *15 doubles, 6 suites, 1 cottage*
Rates: *Doubles $85-135 (B&B), Suites $175-225 (B&B), Cottage $185 (B&B)*
Payment: *AE, DC, DSC, MC, and VISA*
Dogs: *Well-behaved dogs are selectively welcome with notice and approval, but cannot be left alone*
Children: *Welcome (crib available)*
Open: *All year*

San Francisco's vibrant nature is partly due to its diverse neighborhoods, combined with interesting topography and a mild climate. Visitors may want to follow the winding streets to hilltops where spectacular views unfold, or take some time to discover one of the many lovely parks set in the city's residential neighborhoods. Anyone can book themselves into the larger hotels in the city, but finding a smaller inn offering individual attention, coziness, and Victorian charm is not as easily accomplished. We were therefore very pleased to discover The Inn San Francisco, set in one of San Francisco's more historic neighborhoods. This 27-room, Italianate Victorian home was built in 1872 for a San Francisco City Commissioner, John English. It is a part of the once famous "Mansion Row," and although this is not toney Pacific Heights, the area maintains a lovely residential quality. Best of all, the inn was completely restored in 1979 by Joel Daily and Anthony Kramedas.

We followed the steps leading from the street to the massive wooden front doors where we marveled at the intricately carved moldings, columns, and pilasters comprising the facade. We eventually went inside, found the tiny reception area nestled under the pair of staircases, and then stepped into the high-ceilinged double parlor. The hunter green walls nicely complement the intricately detailed mahogany woodwork and etched parlor doors. An elaborately carved, gilt-framed mirror is fashioned above one marble fireplace. Victorian antiques, set on Oriental carpets, accentuate the effect. Contrary to what one might imagine, the dark hues of the room are enlivened with a good deal of natural light emanating from the sunny alcoves.

The main mansion contains most of the guest rooms, although some are also found in the Garden Cottage. All are equally appealing — as the Victorian decor, period wallpapers, and antiques pervade these spaces and make each chamber distinctive. The room sizes vary, ranging from small, cozy bedrooms with double beds and shared bathrooms, to more deluxe spaces with four-poster feather beds and private bathrooms containing two-person spas. There are also suites with fireplaces and a chamber with a redwood hot tub. Accents, including the brass fixtures, are also antique. These elements look especially appropriate set against the exposed brick and white vertical board walls, or the warm burgundy or slate blue walls.

While Marty has maintained the Victorian mood, he has not forgotten such amenities as color televisions, clock radios, small refrigerators, and telephones. Fresh flowers are visually appealing, while the Joseph Schmidt chocolate truffles and fruit bowls are certain to please most palates. For the ultimate in privacy, we recommend reserving the Garden Cottage Suite, which accommodates up to six people. This offers a fireplaced living room, a kitchen, and a master bedroom with a brass bed. Just outside, in the English garden, is the redwood hot tub that all guests are welcome to utilize.

Each morning, a delicious breakfast buffet awaits on the massive sideboard, set in the rear parlor. The fruit muffins and breads, including Irish soda bread, are homemade. French roasted coffee, freshly squeezed orange juice, and fruit are also available. Some guests select cereals, cold cuts, or a hot egg dish to accompany this, and then take their meal out to the rear garden. This is one of our favorite places for breakfast, sitting on the white wrought iron furniture and listening to the splashing fountain. In the afternoon, we like to visit the gazebo and enjoy a complimentary glass of sherry, cider, or tea.

After breakfast, some enjoy heading up to the roof deck, where there is a 360-degree view of the city. There are, of course, plenty of options for the day ahead. Within walking distance of the inn are two parks that dogs might enjoy. The first is the **Mission Dolores Park**, and the other, while not really a park, is **McKinley Square**. **The Presidio**, on the bay near the Golden Gate Bridge, has plenty of places to run a dog. We also like **Allyne Park** on Green Street. We used to take our puppies to this tiny verdant spot, because it was fenced in and they could have the run of the place. There are a variety of parks just up the hill, or for those who want wide open spaces, there is always the ultimate park — **Golden Gate Park**.

The Mansions Hotel

2220 Sacramento Street
San Francisco, California 94115
(800) 826-9398, (415) 929-9444, Fax: (415) 567-9391
Internet: http://themansions.com

Innkeeper: *Robert C. Pritikin*
Rooms: *13 doubles, 8 suites*
Rates: *Doubles $129-179 (B&B), Suites $189-350 (B&B)*
Payment: *AE, CB, DC, DSC, MC, and VISA*
Dogs: *Welcome*
Children: *Welcome (cots and baby-sitters are available)*
Open: *All year*

"Not your ordinary room," may be how the Mansions Hotel describes itself, but anyplace where guests rub elbows with ghosts is yet another reason it belongs in the not-so-ordinary-hotel category. Unique — yes. Magical — without a doubt. This wonderful Queen Anne Victorian mansion and its impressive gardens occupy a portion of one of San Francisco's most prestigious neighborhoods. This also happens to be the center for the Bufano Society of the Arts, housing the largest collection of Bufano's sculptures anywhere. Besides the sculptures, inside the mansion is a variety of other original art housed in four "museums" — the Museum of Art and Antiques, the Museum of Magic, the Museum of Historic Documents, and last but not least, the Museum of International Pigs. Paintings by Joseph Mallard Turner and Joshua Reynolds are interspersed with murals depicting the history of the hotel. Artistic treasures abound. One particular standout is an awe-inspiring, stained glass window mural in the dining room — reportedly the largest in the world. The list of collectibles is extraordinary, highlighted by the eclectic array of antiques.

Stepping over the threshold and into the grand foyer, we heard faint melodies from Bach and Mozart echoing from further within the mansion — interspersed with shrill comments from the resident macaw. The crystal chandelier casts a soft glow across the gumwood walls and the ruby red carpeting. The freshly cut flowers, exploding from an enormous Oriental vase, send off a delicious aroma. Lingering is never a problem for us, but after all, a Victorian-garbed staff member was waiting. He escorted us past the celebrity wall, filled with signatures of the mansion's more famous guests. A few more steps and we arrived in the sitting room, whose focal point is a glass case filled with rare documents from John Hancock, Eleanor Roosevelt, Abraham Lincoln, Thomas Edison, and Jack London. Ascending the stairs, the elegantly dressed mannequins and abundant collection of pig memorabilia caught our eye. The life-size cross section of a human, dating back to 1886, made us do a double take, while an enormous stuffed pig merely amused us. The numerous wood, porcelain, brass, and ceramic pigs are a distinctive theme, used as a bribe to appease the resident ghost, Claudia. Evidently, she used to keep pigs as pets when she owned the mansion.

Each of the bedrooms is equally impressive, furnished through the efforts of Bob, his staff, and, of course, Claudia. Names of historic personalities are engraved on each bronze door plaque. Inside, classical music resonates through the room, softened by the Oriental carpets. Interesting ceiling angles provide an intriguing visual backdrop to the fine antiques, museum-quality paintings, and Victorian lamps. Candies and a vase of fresh flowers decorate the bedside tables. The chambers vary in both configuration and decor, yet guests most often request rooms with a fireplace or a private terrace overlooking the gardens. West wing bedrooms are most traditional, with Laura Ashley fabrics and formal furnishings. From the Lillie Coit Room, there are distant views of the Golden Gate Bridge, while the Tom Thumb Room boasts (not too surprisingly) of being the smallest chamber. It is the third floor Presidential Suite we find most appealing, with its hunter green walls highlighted by built-in bookshelves and a pair of fireplaces flanking the canopy bed.

Guests are likely to awake refreshed (unless Claudia has graced them with a midnight visit), to the smells of French roasted coffee wafting up from the dining room. Downstairs, a full breakfast awaits, which may be enjoyed in the West Wing Dining Room or *en suite*. Modeled after a true English breakfast, this one begins with freshly squeezed orange juice, cereal, fruit, and English crumpets. Eggs, prepared in any manner guests' choose, are accompanied by bangers, au gratin potatoes, and of course, a local newspaper.

The Mansion Hotel's true calling, though, is the evening meal, winning accolades from critics everywhere — including those at the *San Francisco Examiner* and New York's *Fine Dining Magazine*. Dinner starts with the famous sourdough bread and salad. This is often followed by shrimp in a garlic salsa, salmon roasted in parchment, and the steak topped with pepper paté, spiked with cognac and baked in a puff pastry. Most look forward to the meal, but an even more highly anticipated event is the Cabaret Theater afterwards. As the lights dim, Bob makes his appearance, while the applause light flashes and tinsel drops down from the ceiling — casting an eerie sparkle about the room. What follows is a wonderful show featuring magic, theatrical numbers, and several melodies performed by Bob on his classical hardware-store saw. Claudia is on the grand piano. (Claudia, by the way, not only wanders the halls late at night, but will challenge late-night merrymakers to a game of billiards.)

Dogs and ghosts are always an interesting combination, and hopefully, your dog will enjoy the experience. More mainstream experiences are found just outside the door, with several parks within easy walking distance of the mansion. Guests can walk up the hill to the **Alta Plaza Park**, which is one of our favorite haunts with the dogs. Or they might head south to the **Alamo Square Park**, where there is plenty of grass and lots of doggie activity. Filmore Street is also teeming with intriguing eateries, boutiques, and fun stores that visitors and their dogs will thoroughly enjoy. Water dogs can head over to the **St. Francis Yacht Club**, where there is a terrific path leading along the sandy beach. Our dogs like swimming in the bay, and occasionally encounter a playful seal who literally swims circles around them. On the weekends, this park is also filled with kite flyers and Rollerbladers, who play against the backdrop of sailboats racing across the bay.

The Pan Pacific Hotel

500 Post Street
San Francisco, California 94102
(800) 327-8585, (415) 732-7747, Fax: (415) 398-0267

General Manager: *Volker Ulrich*
Rooms: *311 doubles, 19 suites*
Rates: *Doubles $250-340 (EP), Suites $390-1,700 (EP)*
Payment: *AE, DC, DSC, ENR, JCB, MC, and VISA*
Dogs: *Welcome under 30 pounds welcome with a $25 fee*
Children: *Welcome (cribs, cots, high chairs, and baby-sitters available)*
Open: *All year*

San Francisco

We can remember the San Francisco hotel scene before the building of the Portman Hotel; we can also recall the excitement the residents felt when they learned the famous architect, John Portman, would be designing it. That was in 1987, well before the Pan Pacific hotel chain took over. The hotel is visually appealing, especially the 21-story marble-faced edifice where Portman used a series of graduated arches to make it seem more intimate. In a hotel of this size, a sense of intimacy is important. We especially liked the fact that all ballroom and conference facilities are grouped on the first two floors. Thus, individual travelers bypass all the corporate hubbub and emerge right into the cavernous third-floor lobby atrium.

This inspiring open space reaches up to the 17th floor, with staggered beams, large marble columns, and an array of stately trees and floral accents cleverly breaking up this vertical space. The focal point for this handsome lobby is the circular marble fountain topped with an Edward Weiberg bronze sculpture entitled *Joie de vivre*, positioned directly under the atrium's skylight. Off to one side, a combination of leather sofas and mahogany colored rattan chairs set on Oriental rugs are grouped near a marble fireplace. Across from this inviting sitting area is the reception desk, nestled under a glass canopy ribbed with twinkling lights. After dispensing with check-in guests are whisked up to their floor by way of the sleek brass and glass elevators. To reach their bedrooms, guests follow the gentle curves of the brass and wrought iron railing that line the atrium's perimeter.

Anyone who is feeling a little harried will delight at the sense of calm that pervades these understated guest chambers. Subtle gray, rose, and cream colors combine with black lacquered accents to provide a sophisticated, high-tech ambiance. Reminiscent of the arch theme found in the other common areas, semi-circular window casings create an appealing frame for city views. Accents include plenty of brass and glass, along with Oriental vases, flower arrangements, and contemporary paintings. The list of luxurious appointments is bountiful, with televisions in both the bedroom and bathroom, fully stocked refrigerators, and three telephones. Portuguese Breccia marble and etched glass make the bathrooms feel exceptionally sumptuous. In addition to the French milled soaps, terry cloth robes, and array of exquisite toiletries, there is a glass-enclosed shower and a large Jacuzzi bathtub. Personal valets assigned to each floor are well equipped to handle any special requests — even if these concern a dog. These assistants not only clean the room each time a guest departs, but they will also help guests with their dry cleaning, unpack their suitcases, or just ensure that the rooms' refrigerators are continually restocked. There are various gourmet treats in the room; however, far more elaborate offerings are available downstairs in the hotel's restaurant.

This restaurant, The Pacific, has a new chef, Takayoshi Kawai, who brings with him an innovative cooking style and plenty of accolades. Patrons dine in an open and inviting space awash in rose marble. A crackling fire is usually blazing at night, which patrons can enjoy through the array of potted plants and flowers. Guests may want to start with the marinated salmon with

California

caviar and *crème fraîche*; the Sonoma *foie gras* sauté with caramelized peach and sauternes sauce; or the lobster salad. Entrées include the breast of duck with corn crêpes, spinach, and a wild berry sauce; grilled salmon with an aromatic ragoût; or the filet mignon with truffle mashed potatoes, fava beans, and baby carrots. The *prix fixe* menu is not only a great value, but also offers a terrific combination of intriguing dishes. Afterwards, some people gravitate to the cozy bar. This is one of the more popular late-evening public areas in the hotel. Passing under an arch illuminated by hundreds of small white lights, guests will enter an intimate chamber lined with variegated marble. Brass lamps illuminate the rattan furniture, contemporary artworks, and abundance of plant life.

In the evening, our canine cohorts usually enjoy one last walk before bedtime. **Union Square** is just a short stroll from the hotel. Those who are so inclined may use the hotel's chauffeur-driven Rolls Royce; when requested it will whisk guests to nearby parks for a more verdant experience. We favor two parks with dogs: **the Presidio**, and the park down by the **St. Francis Yacht Club**. Those who choose the latter can walk along the adjacent beach path or let their dogs swim in the bay. **Golden Gate Park** is, of course, the most expansive option, with an assortment of green spaces available to dogs.

Pension San Francisco

1668 Market Street
San Francisco, California 94102
(415) 864-1271, Fax: (415) 861-8116

Owner: Andy Sik
Rooms: 8 singles, 28 doubles
Rates: Singles $45 (B&B), Doubles $55-60 (B&B)
Payment: AE, CB, MC, and VISA
Dogs: Very well behaved dogs are welcome with approval, "credit card deposit required"
Children: More appropriate for older children
Open: All year

San Francisco on a budget, especially with a dog, might seem almost impossible. With the average room night running well over $150, there should certainly be some room for alternative accommodations. Europeans are renowned for their inexpensive, clean, and comfortable *pensions* — the operative word being *inexpensive*. Located on San Francisco's bustling Market Street, the Pension San Francisco brings a touch of Europe to this city by the bay. Set in an attractive five-story brick building, this 1900s-era Edwardian-style structure once housed earthquake refugees. Today, it is situated alongside an intimate café; if we close our eyes for just a moment, we can almost envision a Parisian café — a dozen tables, surrounded by flowers, are set alongside windows overlooking the street.

Stepping through the interior door linking the café to the pension, our eyes fell on the sign stating, "Never mind the dog, beware of the owner." Smiling at the thought, we caught the old-fashioned elevator to the upper floors. We like the pension's design; on each floor there is an intimate sitting area decorated around a different creative theme. One of the more interesting is the wilderness motif, offering as decorative highlights an antique toboggan, a pair of old wooden skis, a mounted deer's head, and an oar. Another area features historic black and white photos of San Francisco set alongside 1940s' movie stock photographs. Throw rugs generally cover the hardwood floors, wicker and rattan are the furniture of choice, and there is always a television set off in the corner. A fireplace in the third-floor sitting room makes that room a little cozier than the rest. Woven baskets and wicker collectibles line the hallways leading to the bedrooms.

The bedrooms are as unique as the rest of the place. We prefer those on the upper floors, since they are a little more removed from any potential street noise. The guest rooms at the front of the building tend to be a little noisier than those at the back, but they also offer a good deal more sunlight throughout the day. Although the rooms toward the rear of the building are lacking in natural lighting, they do compensate for it with their innovative furnishings, decor, and interesting built-in features — such as window wells containing lovely botanical gardens. One room has splatter-painted bureaus and dressers accented by sponge-painted end tables. Another reflects the Orient, with Japanese screens and paper lanterns hanging from the walls and ceiling. Still others utilize toboggans, sleds, and skis for their decorative motif. Double or twin beds are common, as are pedestal sinks. The vanities and small refrigerators generally recess into alcoves.

As in traditional European pensions, a simple Continental breakfast starts the morning. Heartier fare is available at numerous other restaurants within easy walking distance. Dogs familiar with the hubbub of city life will be most comfortable at the Pension San Francisco, as the closest park is a 5-minute drive or 20-minute walk from the inn. We prefer the energizing walk to **Lafayette Park** in Pacific Heights or to **Nob Hill. Golden Gate Park**, the **Marina Esplanade**, or perhaps even the **Presidio**, are also good options for extended jaunts. This may all seem a little inconvenient, but it can easily be overlooked when taking into account the reasonable room price.

Guests should reserve space early, though; this pension is usually booked several weeks in advance, making it difficult to make last-minute reservations. A final note: the management tells us that the Pension San Francisco tends to attract an international crowd, along with a good number of gays and lesbians. During our visits, we always found a broad mix of guests, making for a congenial environment.

California

Inn at the Opera

333 Fulton Street
San Francisco, California   94102
(800) 325-2708, (415) 863-8400, Fax: (415) 861-0821

Manager: Thomas R. Noonan
Rooms: 30 doubles, 18 suites
Rates: Doubles $140-190 (EP), Suites $215-265 (EP)
Payment: AE, DC, MC, and VISA
Dogs: Very well-behaved small dogs are welcome on a case by case basis with a $25 fee
Children: Most appropriate for older children
Open: All year

Travelers don't have to use opera as an excuse to stay at the Inn at the Opera, but it certainly doesn't hurt. Built in 1927, this lovely inn has long been used as a home away from home by musicians and artists, as well as those who come to listen to their music and view their works. Today, after extensive renovations, it is less a hostelry than it is a quiet, elegant European-style inn. Music permeates this place — and well it should, as it is in the heart of San Francisco's cultural district. The Opera House, Louise Davies Hall, San Francisco Ballet, Herbst Auditorium, and the San Francisco Museum of Modern Art are all within walking distance of the inn. Given its central location, one would surmise that a cacophony of traffic sounds would reverberate through the inn, but as we stepped through the front doors, we heard only music — Bach, to be precise.

The melodies soothed us, but more soothing still was the front parlor, decorated around a sage and rose color scheme. A lovely Aubisson Rug, a French floral and ribbon paneled screen, and a handful of damask upholstered chairs all reflect these soft hues. As we waited to go upstairs, we had the opportunity to look around, and were entranced by the wall of Paul Renouard etchings of the Paris Opera. Immense flower arrangements and Oriental vases, resting off to the side, add to the elegant ambiance.

A similar sense of subdued luxury is prevalent on the upper floors, with hallways lined by French mahogany sideboards and set with Oriental bowls filled with pot-pourri. Crystal sconces cast their subdued light over the pastel walls. Pale peach and sage green are the colors of choice for the guest rooms. Quarter canopies overhang beds invitingly covered with tailored, quilted bedspreads and oversized pillows. Antique armoires conceal remote-controlled televisions, and refrigerators are filled with gourmet delicacies ranging from champagne to paté. Baskets of other delicate edibles are set out near arrangements of fresh flowers. Suites are slightly more luxurious than the other rooms; the major difference is the French doors that separate the master bedroom from the expansive sitting area, allowing guests to entertain their friends after a late-night performance.

While some guests may want to entertain privately in their suites, most prefer a table at the famous Act IV restaurant. Brass sconces illuminate this dark, wood-paneled chamber highlighted by hand-carved columns, Belgian tapestries, and lovely flower arrangements. The tapestries aren't confined to the walls, though; tapestry-covered pillows comfort guests who opt for the velvet sofas, instead of the straight-back leather chairs. After the opera, patrons may be found grouped around the lustrous mahogany bar or near the green marble fireplace. Those who arrive before a performance will find many sipping champagne, nibbling *hors d'oeuvres*, or enjoying a gourmet dinner. A selection of delectable appetizers and entrées awaits, with diners feasting on crab and celery root ravioli; lobster toast with a corn juice and truffle vinaigrette; and tuna tartare with soy sauce, wasabi, and mustard greens. Entrée selections might include roasted squab on a bed of frisée; chicken with baby artichokes, sun-dried tomatoes, and potato galette; and the seared salmon and oysters with a lemon mirin sauce. More intriguing still is the opportunity dining patrons may have to meet the performers who frequently stay at the inn.

Over the years, the Inn at the Opera has hosted an array of celebrities, including Mikhail Baryshnikov, Luciano Pavorotti, Herbie Hancock, Dizzie Gillespie, and Bobby McFerrin. Potential guests should know that the Inn at the Opera buys huge blocks of the best symphony, ballet, and opera tickets and then sells them to guests. Anyone who wants to mix tradition with more trendy, night-time entertainment will be happy to note that the inn is also just a short jaunt from SOMA (south of Market Street) area, which is renowned for its alternative music clubs and funky eateries, like Hamburger Mary's.

After a culture-filled evening, your dog will certainly be ready to get going the next morning. A drive up to **Coit Tower** is especially pleasant early in the morning before the tourists arrive. There are nice paths around it for exploring with a canine, as well as paths down the hill and through the surrounding neighborhoods. In addition to the variety of parks around **Pacific Heights, Cow Hollow**, and the **Marina** areas, another spot worth visiting is the Buena Vista Park situated over in Haight-Ashbury. Later, visitors may want to head over to **Union Square** for a little shopping, or perhaps down to **Ghiradelli Square** and **Fisherman's Wharf**. There are plenty of sidewalks and open areas on the waterfront. We like listening to the street musicians down here — they may not be Pavorotti, but their music is fine nonetheless.

The Westin St. Francis

335 Powell Street, Union Square
San Francisco, California 94102
(800) 228-3000, (415) 397-7000, Fax: (415) 774-0124
Internet: http://www.cdiguide.com/415/a_hot/westin.html

Managing Director: *Ray Jacobi*
Rooms: *1,117 doubles, 83 suites*
Rates: *Doubles $195-315 (EP), Suites $300-1,700 (EP)*
Payment: *AE, DC, DSC, JCB, OPT, MC, and VISA*
Dogs: *Small dogs welcome with notice*
Children: *Welcome (cribs, cots, high chairs, baby-sitter referrals, and kids' club are available)*
Open: *All year*

Guarding its coveted Union Square location since 1904, the Westin St. Francis is a firmly established San Francisco landmark, one that even managed to survive the devastating San Francisco fire of 1906. It is a grand hotel, built by skilled craftsmen, whose fine workmanship is still in evidence. Such notables as Queen Elizabeth II, General Douglas MacArthur, John

Barrymore, Charlie Chaplin, and just about every U.S. president since Taft have stayed at this wonderful old hotel. Many of these dignitaries' and celebrities' photographs are now displayed in the hallways throughout the hotel. The wood-paneled reception area — with its immense columns, ornately carved ceilings, and collection of French and Victorian antiques — offers a taste of grandeur and formality rarely found in hotels today. All this might sound overwhelming — but it isn't. Moreover, after a $50 million "non-intrusive" renovation, which is slated to be completed sometime in 1996, the essence of the entire hotel should match that of the magnificent lobby.

The number of rooms at the St. Francis is mind boggling; however, if asked to choose our favorites we would opt for those chambers in the original building. These evoke the strongest sense of tradition, with formal English furnishings, intricate moldings, and floor-to-ceiling double hung windows. Rich burgundy or emerald green-colored walls frame some bedrooms, while others take on more subtle earth tones. Chintz fabrics cover the tailored armchairs, sofas, and bedspreads. Brass fixtures illuminate these spaces, casting a soft glow across the inlaid woods. The most stunning spaces are the "09" chambers; corner bedrooms that not only provide substantially more space than the others, but also better views and a good deal more natural light. Special occasions might be worthy of a suite, and guests have the option of choosing from among 16 different types of suites at the St. Francis. Finally, there are the tower rooms, built in 1972, which are elegantly appointed, but lack the overall character of the chambers in the original building.

Concerns about service are always valid at a hotel this large; however, the high staff-to-guest ratio here will quickly alleviate such concerns. While most guests' requests are mundane, over the years the staff here have been asked to provide some rather unusual services. For instance, Anna Held, a famous opera star, insisted on bathing in milk each day — 30 gallons of it. Ethel Barrymore's chimpanzee accompanied her to the hotel, and rumor has it that the staff ended up with the baby-sitting duties. (Our canine should be so lucky!) This hotel is so steeped in tradition that it even continues to launder its money, a custom dating back 60 years to when silver dollars were the coin of the day. The hotel would collect all the coins each day, then wash, dry, and recirculate them to the front desk. While these anecdotes are fun to recount, most guests are more likely to remember the hotel's picture postcard views of Union Square — a center of activity for locals and tourists alike, as well as for its resident pigeons.

Contained within the walls of the St. Francis hotel is also an array of dining and entertainment options. Of the seven eating and drinking establishments, one of our favorites is the intimate Compass Rose with its massive fluted oak columns, Palladian mirrors, and rich oak-paneled ceilings and walls. Here, guests may enjoy high tea, evening jazz, or just an informal cocktail. Surprisingly enough, the most popular aspect of this room seems to be the champagne, as guests consume over 3,000 glasses of bubbly each month. Club Oz, atop the tower, is another late-night option for those interested in a little dancing. Victor's, an award-wining restaurant, is located on the 32nd floor of the tower, affording panoramic views and even more memorable food. It is named for the hotel's flamboyant chef, Victor Hirtzler, who reigned over the kitchen from 1906 to 1925. Hirtzler was a man ahead of his time, developing an early version of the now popular California cuisine. Those in the kitchen today follow right in his footsteps. Appetizers might include quail braised in a Madeira cream sauce, Santa Cruz abalone, or duck paté of Sonoma *foie gras*. The menu is ever-changing; however, some of the entrée choices included a gratin of scampi with shiitake mushrooms; oven roasted Sonoma rack of lamb in an herb crust; Muscovey duck with Chinese mushrooms; or the roast tenderloin with a Vermont maple syrup glaze.

Working out afterwards (or better yet, in the morning) is easily accomplished in the fitness center. Others opt instead for a stroll with their dogs around **Union Square** and up the hill to the park on the top of **Nob Hill**. Virtually endless entertainment possibilities exist, all within walking or cable car distance of the hotel. Cable cars scoot visitors over the hills to Ghiradelli Square, North Beach, Union Street, and Fisherman's Wharf. Guests can jump in the car with their dogs and head over to the **St. Francis Yacht Club** and the **Esplanade**, where there are plenty of waterside walks. Here, the infamous San Francisco Bay winds kick up to challenge everyone from sailboarders and sailors to kite flyers. Other interesting park-like settings can be found at the **Presidio** and **Baker Beach**.

Heritage Inn Bed & Breakfast

978 Olive Street
San Luis Obispo, California   93405
(805) 544-7440, Internet: http://www.slo-online.com/heritageinn/

Hosts: Kathy and Rob Strong
Rooms: 9 doubles
Rates: $85-120 (B&B)
Payment: AE, MC, and VISA
Dogs: Well-behaved dogs are welcome with approval, preferably during less busy times
Children: Most appropriate for children over the age of 10
Open: All year

In 1772, San Luis Obispo was merely one of the many missions lining the Pacific coast. Some 120 years later, the Southern Pacific Railroad laid tracks to this quiet hamlet, thereby providing easier access to this area. With the arrival of Highway 101 and the California Polytechnic State University, the community expanded a bit more and, to this day, continues to grow. The Heritage Inn has an interesting history as well. Built in the 1900s, it survived three moves and multiple uses. Originally owned by a local constable, the home has also served as a gas station, a YMCA, town offices, and a boarding house. In 1981 Kathy and Rob bought the home at a county auction. Following what we all hope was its final move, the home now resides on Olive Street.

Decorative blue shingles line the lower section of this beautifully restored house. As we walked across the cobblestone driveway toward the inn, a bleary-eyed cat checked us out from on top of an old milk can set near the porch swing. He obviously did not feel threatened, and settled back into slumber before we even entered the inn. Kathy greeted us, then gave us the grand tour of the place. Along the way, she told us an amusing story about how their original "No Dogs" policy had been changed by the inadvertent actions of one guest. A French woman with a rather heavy accent telephoned and inquired whether the inn accepted "donations." The assistant innkeeper paused, thinking it an odd request, but graciously said they would of course be pleased to accept any and all donations. The French woman reserved a room for a night, arrived, and the next morning came downstairs with her "Dalmatian." The obvious misunderstanding amused everyone, but what is more important, the well-behaved dog got along so well with the Strongs' cat, they reconsidered their dog policy and now allow well-mannered canines to visit.

By the time Kathy finished the story, we were in the midst of the parlor. The room's bow window, framed by shutters, makes it feel all the more spacious. As we talked, one guest was reading on the comfortable couch, while another couple had settled into the armchairs. They looked especially content, sipping sherry from cut crystal glasses and sampling a few of the *hors d'oeuvres*. A decanter of sherry, with glasses, is always set out on the fireplace mantel. The shelves in here are also well stocked with books and board games. We found the breakfast rooms through a pair of pocket doors. It happened to be late in the day, but in the morning, sunlight floods through walls of windows into these charming spaces, which are further enhanced by a corner fireplace. Creamy colored walls and dusty rose carpeting set the decorative tone for the lace covered tables and country collectibles in these rooms. Each morning guests receive a hearty Continental repast consisting of quiche, fruits, croissants, and freshly baked muffins and breads.

We returned to the central hallway and headed upstairs to find the bedrooms. These are the rooms of choice for those traveling with a dog, as there is less chance here that guests' dogs and the resident cat will have a close encounter — of any kind. Pastels enliven these spaces, enriching the walls and providing subtle accents of color. Several bedrooms feature a fireplace, some a cozy window seat, and still others a walk-out balcony. The warm blue and white rose motif on the walls of Auntie's Room is enhanced at night by the glow from the fireplace. Guests may enjoy this from the love seat, or from the comfort of their queen-size bed. John & Amelia's Room, with cerise accents, contains an antique brass and white iron bedstead and yet another fireplace. This is one of the more private rooms because it lies to the rear of the house. Mountain View is another airy chamber, fashioned with creamy yellow walls and sunflower accents. Best of all, it is also privy to French doors leading to a small balcony overlooking the creek and Bishop's Peak. Three of the bedrooms have private bathrooms, while the other six share three bathrooms among them. The latter bathrooms contain claw-footed tubs and terry cloth robes as a convenience for guests traveling to and from their bedrooms. Each bedroom sharing a bathroom does have a pedestal sink conveniently set within its confines.

During the day, guests will find plenty of noteworthy adventures to enjoy with their dogs. Kathy tells us that most guests visit the creek with their dogs, before heading downtown to the array of shops and eateries. (There are a list of menus back at the B&B.) She also informed us that San Luis Obispo is very dog-friendly, and although she and Rob don't have a dog, she always sees them hanging out at coffee shops and at outdoor cafés. As if to stress the point, we then saw an elderly man on a scooter buzzing past the inn with a little dog sitting on his lap — its paws resting on the handlebars. All of the parks in San Luis Obispo welcome leashed dogs. Some options might include the **El Chorro** or **Laguna** parks. There is, of course, the famous San Luis Obispo mission to visit without a dog, but while there, pick up a map for the self-guided **"Path of History" tour** of the town. Leashed dogs may accompany visitors on this latter adventure, providing both humans and canines with an intriguing way to stretch their legs.

The Mary May Inn

111 West Valerio Street
Santa Barbara, California   93101
(805) 682-3199, Internet: http://www.silcom.com/~ricky/mary.htm

Owner: *Kathleen Pohring*
Rooms: *8 doubles*
Rates: *$85-160 (B&B)*
Payment: *AE, MC, and VISA*
Dogs: *Small "house dogs" are welcome with notice, approval, and a $10 nightly fee*
Children: *Not appropriate for small children*
Open: *All year, except Christmas*

Santa Barbara has long been a favorite getaway for Southern Californians, whether they choose to spend just a few days or several weeks. The dramatic coastal location, coupled with its mountainous backdrop and mild climate, create a distinct Mediterranean feeling. Combine this with abundant

California

recreational and culinary diversions and it is easy to see why Santa Barbara tops many people's lists for a vacation destination. Those who shy away from the large resort atmosphere offered by many oceanside accommodations, will be interested to learn more about the intimate Mary May Inn.

Set in the heart of old Santa Barbara, and partially obscured by a thick hedge, lies the Mary May Inn, which was formerly the Bayberry Inn. A couple of years ago Kathleen, who owned the Mary May B&B across the street, decided to purchase the Bayberry. While she has updated a few things, the overall ambience is much the same. As we passed by the stately, white lattice fence covered with climbing roses, we could more easily see the traditional, blue-gray shingled home that houses the inn. Built in 1886 as a summer home for a French diplomat, this Federal-style house is now part of a quiet residential neighborhood. Upon entering the foyer, after passing a decorative fountain, we were finally able to view this exquisitely furnished post-Victorian home. The decor surpasses that of most traditional inns, with its highly selective group of furnishings, collectibles, and decorative items. The dining room is just one example of this. The 16-foot, coral pink, silk-covered ceilings are accentuated by a crown of beveled mirrors and a grand crystal chandelier. Italianate high-back chairs, covered with tapestry fabric, encircle the dining room table. We then proceeded into the equally impressive teal-toned living room, filled with elaborately carved wing chairs and sofas covered in lavish fabrics. Nestled in-between were small tables topped by collectibles, along with fresh and silk flower arrangements. (Flagrant tail wagging is strictly forbidden in here.) A baby grand piano occupies a space near one wall of windows. Our favorite spot, though, continues to be the sun porch, where a pair of zebra finches chirp merrily from their cage set alongside the oversized sideboard. The latter conceals a small refrigerator and an ice maker. Just beyond the sun porch is a good-sized backyard, ideal for croquet, badminton, or quiet contemplation amid the lovely plantings.

The bedrooms at the Mary May Inn expand upon the elegance found in the common rooms. Each is named for, and decorated around, the colors of berries. A central staircase, lined by fabric padded walls, leads to the bedrooms. A large statue of a distinguished-looking dog guards the second floor landing, pointing the way to the bed chambers. Delicate raspberry-colored wallpaper imbues the Raspberry Room with character, while fragrant gooseberry potpourri permeates the Gooseberry Room. Canopy beds covered in fine linens and down comforters are almost secondary to the antiques and original artwork filling these spaces. Guests may ask for a fireplace or perhaps a whirlpool or Victorian claw-footed bathtub as an extra amenity. The larger bedrooms contain separate sitting areas, although most appear spacious because of their use of skylights, mirrored walls, or extra windows. If we had to pick a favorite room it would be Thimbleberry. This secluded space lies to the rear of the house and is accessed through the garden. French doors lead from the small porch into the room. As if to match its garden setting, floral fabrics line the interior spaces, including the coverlet on the bed. Guests can bask in the sunlight as it pours through the skylights above the soaking tub.

Breakfast is served in the dining room each morning, and in the afternoon, guests return to find soft drinks, cider, coffee, tea, or even hot chocolate waiting. There is no doubt that guests will find much more to occupy their time than just eating, relaxing, and sleeping (although that doesn't sound too bad). Some borrow the inn's bicycles, located in an old garage/artist's studio. The **surrounding neighborhoods** are fun to explore by bicycle, or if the dogs are in tow, on foot. A lengthier excursion leads visitors and their furry friends to the **wide sidewalks lining the ocean**, where there is always plenty of action. For guests looking for more expansive acreage, how does a million and a half acres sound? — all of which are conveniently located in the **Los Padres National Forest**. Afterwards, some may enjoy a visit to the local polo grounds, where there is frequently a match in progress. Diversions abound, and we have only touched the surface; however, we think The Mary May Inn alone is reason enough for planning a visit to Santa Barbara.

Casa Del Mar Inn

18 Bath Street
Santa Barbara, California 93101
(800) 433-3097, (805) 963-4418, Fax: (805) 966-4240
Internet: http://www.casadelmar.com

Owner: *Michael and Becky Montgomery*
Rooms: *15 doubles, 6 suites*
Rates: *Doubles $69-109 (B&B), Suites $119-209 (B&B)*
Payment: *AE, DC, DSC, MC, and VISA*
Dogs: *One small dog is welcome with a $10 daily fee, provided they are not left alone in the room*
Children: *Welcome (cribs are available)*
Open: *All year*

There are not many inns that allow dogs set within walking distance of Santa Barbara's picturesque coastline; but we found one excellent option in the Casa Del Mar Inn. Situated less than a block from West Beach, and a short bicycle ride from the heart of Santa Barbara's downtown shopping area, this intimate Mediterranean-style inn offers an array of pleasing amenities. Built in 1929, and fashioned with stucco walls and red tile roofs, this expansive structure was formerly a series of beach bungalows. That was well before Michael took over, and he has subsequently transformed it into the wonderful, low-key beachside inn that guests see today.

California

When we arrived, Michael was offering two guests some suggestions for romantic picnic places in and around Santa Barbara. After they left, Michael showed us around. He escorted us to the front of the inn, where we saw several different guest room configurations. As we entered one, we completely startled an assistant who was immersed in repainting the interior. These chambers are very nice, but as it turns out, our favorites are those surrounding the rear courtyard. We headed down the path lined by lush plantings and flowers, where we found Izzy, the resident cat, sunning on a step leading to a second floor suite. She graciously allowed us to pass, and we entered the traditionally furnished suite.

This particular space is composed of two distinctive sections, with a large sitting area on one end, and a king bedded alcove set off on another. A separate bedroom offers an attractive finial bed. In all the rooms, cream-colored walls and earth toned carpets provide neutral backdrops to the festive lithographs, pottery lamps, vases of fresh flowers, and oversized wicker baskets overflowing with either ivy or inset with ficus trees. Floral bedspreads further accentuate the conservative decor. In some rooms, comfortable armchairs and sofas are set in front of terra-cotta tiled fireplaces. Others offer a series of paned windows and doors opening to private patios and porches. Many of these spaces are light and airy, with pleasant views of the well landscaped courtyards.

Before heading out for the day, guests gather in the breakfast room, just off the reception area. A substantial Continental buffet may be enjoyed in these cheerful surroundings, back in one's room, or out on one of the courtyards.

Activities abound throughout the area that should intrigue everyone in the family. Some take their dogs for walks along the wide, palm-lined sidewalks that run alongside **West** and **East beaches**. Others prefer to jog, bicycle, or skate along this stretch. The older part of Santa Barbara is also only a few minutes away and filled with intriguing shops, galleries, boutiques and cafés for man and beast to investigate. Those who are enamored with flora and fauna, may wish to drive over to the **Santa Barbara Botanical Gardens**. In the afternoon, guests return to find wine and cheese, along with other edibles, waiting for them. But one of the most popular of the inn's attributes is the whirlpool spa, which provides the perfect complement to an enjoyable day exploring this wonderful town by the sea.

Four Seasons Biltmore

1260 Channel Drive
Santa Barbara, California   93108
(800) 332-3442, (805) 969-2261, Fax: (805) 969-5715
Internet: http://www.FSHR.com

General Manager: *John Indrieri*
Rooms: *212 doubles, 22 suites*
Rates: *Doubles $199-475 (EP), Suites $475-1,700 (EP), Children are free*
Payment: *AE, CB, DC, ENR, MC, and VISA*
Dogs: *Well-behaved dogs are welcome in the cottages*
Children: *Welcome (cribs, cots, baby-sitters, and children's program are available)*
Open: *All year*

In the mid-1920s, the Bowman-Biltmore Company had the foresight to buy an exquisite 20-acre piece of property nestled between the Pacific Ocean and the Santa Ynez Mountains. It subsequently hired the architect, Reginald D. Johnson, to conceptualize and create a first-class luxury hotel. What the company could not have known at the time was that Johnson would conceive an award-winning design by drawing on the region's rich Spanish heritage — which extended well beyond traditional adobe walls and red-tiled roofs. Johnson designed three main buildings, with curving exterior staircases, cozy balconies, and massive archways flanking the intimate patios. Cottages were later built around the perimeter of the remaining land. His plans for the Biltmore garnered the Medal of Excellence from the Architectural League of

New York and continue to stand the test of time.

In December of 1927, the Biltmore officially opened its doors to the public. Ever since then, it has been winning accolades for its impeccable service, luxurious accommodations, and striking views. It is no wonder that it has played host to personalities such as Herbert Hoover, Calvin Coolidge, Mary Pickford, Charles Lindbergh, and the Prince of Wales. A number of years ago, the Biltmore came under the watchful eye of the Four Seasons Hotels. Fortunately, little about the hotel changed during this transition, except that the grounds, accommodations, and service are once again in first-class shape.

Returning guests will notice one slight modification: they can no longer enter the complex from Cabrillo Blvd. We prefer the new entrance off Olive Mill Road, though, as it brings guests in through the lovely hamlet of Montecito. What hasn't changed are the exquisite cottages scattered about the perimeter of the complex — truly some of the finest dog-friendly accommodations in all of California. Each cottage contains between three and six bedrooms, as well as a one-bedroom suite. Guests may reserve one or more of these chambers, depending upon their needs. These elegant spaces are enhanced by vaulted, beamed ceilings and French doors leading to private patios. Ceiling fans slowly turn overhead, gently recirculating the cool ocean breezes flowing in through the shuttered windows. Elegant chintz fabrics still cover the overstuffed sofas and chairs in many cottages; however, newly redecorated rooms offer an equally sophisticated, but slightly more muted color scheme. We prefer the fireplace cottage suites, with inviting window seats and separate sitting rooms. Standard amenities in all the cottages include remote-controlled televisions and refrigerators inconspicuously concealed in armoires; private bars topped by baskets of snacks; and in-room safes. Bathrooms contain one of three telephones, terry robes and bath towels, along with a full complement of cotton balls, pot-pourri, soap, and other toiletries. Evening turndown service is a part of the twice daily housekeeping. Dogs, of course, are catered to, as well. Upon arrival, a bowl of dog food, chew toy and even a little "pooper scooper" await canine guests. Additional doggie treats may be secured by calling room service.

For those seeking the ultimate cottage experience, there is the Odell Cottage, which is approximately four times the size of a standard cottage. Formerly the hotel owner's residence, this enchanting abode contains a spectacular 35-foot beamed ceiling salon filled with handsome furnishings placed upon pickled hardwood floors. Built-in features include window seats and a wood burning fireplace. Fireplaces in the master and guest bedrooms are also appealing, although the third bedroom offers a patio overlooking a garden setting.

The estate-like gardens and grounds surrounding the Four Seasons Biltmore are also quite spectacular, and exploring them is always a treat. Equally intriguing are the recreational outlets, including tennis courts, putting greens, croquet lawns, shuffleboard, and a whirlpool/spa. Dogs aren't the only family members being catered to, as children between the ages of five and twelve may participate in the *Kids for all Seasons* program. Guests of any age may use the Coral Casino Club. This beachfront oasis, situated across the street, boasts a 50-meter Olympic-size pool overlooking the ocean, a fully-equipped cardiovascular fitness room (with whirlpool, saunas, steam and massage rooms), and informal patio dining. Guests may also access facilities off the premises, including sport fishing, sailing, golf, and polo.

Toward the end of the day, a visit to the La Sala Lounge may be in order, where traditional British high tea is served. In the evening, patrons can select from two excellent restaurants — the formal La Marina or the more casual Patio. The Biltmore defines La Marina's menu as continental American cuisine. Some of the more notable appetizers during our visit were the smoked salmon torte and lemon chive blinis served with a wasabi crème fraîche; or the *foie gras* and griddled pear, accompanied by duck and Napa cabbage streudel and huckleberry preserves. These were followed by such entrée selections as roast pheasant and green herb risotto served with a ragoût of sweetbreads and yellowfoot chanterelles; poached lobster with cilantro, and a corn and bell pepper Charlotte; or lavender roasted veal served with a toasted vermicelli cake and a Sonoma escargot ragoût.

Dogs will undoubtedly want to romp across the scenic beach in front of the Biltmore, where he will undoubtedly meet up with other furry friends. **Palm Park**, a long expanse of grass set alongside the ocean, is a great place for playing Frisbee or throwing the ball with a dog. Guests may borrow one of the hotel's complimentary bicycles and ride along the quiet residential roads around the resort. **Hiking trails** are also abundant in the local **Santa Ynez mountains**. We recommend asking the concierge for a detailed map of the area before embarking on any excursions. There are a myriad of entertaining diversions available in this beautiful oceanside community. Anyone who is familiar with our books knows that we are always impressed with the Four Seasons hotels — both for their style of service and amenities and for their ability to cater to their doggie patrons.

California

Fess Parker's Red Lion Resort

633 East Cabrillo Boulevard
Santa Barbara, California 93103
(800) 879-2929, (805) 564-4333, Fax: (805) 465-4964
Internet: http://www.doubletreehotels.com

General Manager: *Tim Bridwell*
Rooms: *335 doubles, 25 suites*
Rates: *Doubles $189-289 (EP), Suites $355-700 (EP)*
Payment: *AE, DC, DSC, MC, and VISA*
Dogs: *Welcome in first floor rooms with approval and a $50 refundable deposit*
Children: *Welcome (cribs, cots, and baby-sitters are available)*
Open: *All year*

It is difficult to miss seeing the sprawling Red Lion Resort, although the distant Santa Ynez Mountains on one side, and the white, sandy beach on the other, can be quite distracting. As we drove past the vast expanses of white stucco walls and red tiled roofs that comprise the resort's buildings, we came across numerous signs warning us of "Lion Crossings." We smiled, thinking how surprised the dogs would be if the signs proved to be true. Without a lion in sight, we made our way past the doormen and into the cavernous lobby; just one of the many cleverly designed spaces at the resort. A series of massive, open and leaded-glass archways filters natural light into the Spanish-tiled courtyards and foyers. Here, groupings of rattan furniture form intimate sitting areas, made all the more private by immense ceramic pots containing trees, plants, and flowers. Walls accented with carved wood and tiled murals complete the motif. Little time is spent in the lobby, though, as most guests are eager to get settled in their rooms.

On the way to see some of the guest rooms, we met up with the lion to which the sign might have been referring — a playful Keeshond who was missing her owner and having a fine time greeting several of the new arrivals. The Red Lion Resort continues to do all things well, which includes maintaining the spacious bedrooms and their separate sitting areas filled with overstuffed armchairs and settees. Earth tones predominate, whether on the quilted spreads, draperies, or carpets. Reproductions of English mahogany armoires, dressing tables, and writing desks create a sense of refinement. Of course, the usual four-star amenities are also present, including color televisions, minibars, baskets of toiletries, and a pair of vanities. Suites are substantially larger and more lavish than the other guest rooms. In them, walls of glass doors open to private patios or balconies that face either the mountains, the pool, the garden, or the ocean (the latter is most desirable and therefore more expensive). We especially liked the 700 and 800 series of rooms, as they offer the best views of the Pacific Ocean.

The guest rooms are not the only thing that initially attracted us to the Red Lion Resort; the resort also has a pair of fine restaurants — Maxi's and Café Los Arcos. Maxi's is the most formal of the resort's two restaurants, offering an excellent menu. Entrées range from the Channel Island paella and peppered Muscovey duck breast with grilled radicchio, red onions, and port to the herb-crusted prime rib with garlic mashed potatoes, and garlic fettuccine with grilled prawns, spring vegetables, and herbs. The French bread is plentiful and baked on the premises in an authentic French oven. The dinner setting is tranquil, as soft colors and a combination of natural and recessed lighting create an atmosphere as conducive to quiet conversation as it is to fine dining. Café Los Arcos provides a less formal atmosphere, both indoor and outdoor seating, and a less expensive menu selection. We can think of nothing better than enjoying a casual dinner on their patio, and then taking a late evening walk along the water or across the grounds.

As guests explore the expansive grounds with their dogs, they will discover such diversions as tennis, shuffleboard, basketball, volleyball, and putting greens. For those wanting a more strenuous outing, we suggest heading off on the **22 miles** of walking, bicycling, and running trails along the **Cabrillo Path**. Wide, picturesque oceanside paths can also be enjoyed with a dog. Bicycles and in-line skates may be rented from the hotel. Those who are craving a bit of tropical splendor should drive over to **Santa Barbara's Botanical Gardens** where 60 acres of nature trails are certain to tire dogs and their human friends. Afterwards, let the dog nap and head over to the pool for a refreshing swim — a fine way to end the day at the Red Lion Resort.

Ocean View House

P.O. Box 20065
312 Salida del Sol
Santa Barbara, California   93109
(805) 966-6659

Hostess: *Carolyn Canfield*
Rooms: *2 doubles*
Rates: *$70-80 (B&B)*
Payment: *Personal checks*
Dogs: *Welcome with approval; must follow Carolyn's "Pet Rules"*
Children: *Welcome (cribs and cots are available)*
Open: *All year*

California

Dogs and their human companions sometimes require different things when traveling. Some like the informality of a motel; others prefer the full services of a resort. Still others want the personalized attention they get at a Bed and Breakfast. B&Bs that welcome dogs can be difficult to find, especially in Santa Barbara. One excellent option is the Ocean View House, set in a quiet residential neighborhood and, perhaps most importantly, on a hillside overlooking the ocean.

We always look forward to our greeting from Carolyn's friendly dog, Jesse, and know that Carolyn can't be far away. She and Jesse escort their newest arrivals through a gate fitted with a tinkling bell, into the private backyard. Guests cross a patio, open the sliding glass door, and step into the suite's wood-paneled den. Carolyn created a homey atmosphere when designing this space. We can imagine settling into the comfortable sofa bed to watch television in the evenings, and then, during the T.V. breaks, raiding the small refrigerator hidden in the closet. We did discover, however, that the collection of books also provides an intriguing source of pre-bedtime entertainment. A private bathroom with a shower separates the den from the bright and cheery master bedroom. The highlight in here is an antique finial bed covered by a floral spread. Pink striped wallpaper further enlivens this space, which, like the den, contains many of the family's heirlooms and collectibles. There is another television in here, for those who prefer to watch from the comfort of their bed.

Carolyn enjoys having dogs as house guests. In fact, the number of people traveling here with their pets increases each year. She recently put together a short list of rules for visiting dogs. These are basic rules that involve cleaning up after the dog, feeding the dog outside, and ensuring that the dog sleeps on his bedding. Carolyn rarely has problems, but she told us that well-behaved dogs earn big points with her. She laughingly followed this up with a story about two perfectly behaved German Shepherds, and one not-so-perfect brother. One sunny morning, her brother took his dogs on a shopping expedition to Sears. He walked the dogs up to the entrance, told them to sit and stay, and then went inside. He came out with an armful of goodies, deposited them in his car, and drove off. Halfway home, he realized (OOPS!) the dogs were still at the store. He dashed back, finding them patiently waiting for his not-so-imminent return. Staying at the Ocean View House does not mean it's time to enroll the family dog in obedience school, but we suggest that guests be considerate.

Each morning, Carolyn serves breakfast on the patio. The birds frolic among the fruit trees, while sailboats cruise past the distant Channel Islands and the morning sunshine provides just enough warmth for guests to relax and read the morning paper. Dogs seem to like these surroundings, where walkways meander through the **quiet neighborhood** and eventually lead down to the bluffs overlooking the ocean. Guests can explore locally on foot, or, for a real workout, walk down the hill and visit the **1,000 Steps, Shoreline,** or **Leadbetter parks.** The trek to the ocean is much easier than the ascent home, but it is well worth the effort. Anyone searching for other activities can visit **Santa Barbara's Botanical Gardens**, where over five miles of trails wend through 60 acres of aromatic gardens. Santa Barbara is a casual, dog-friendly place, making it an excellent choice for a hassle-free vacation with a canine companion.

Harvest Inn

P.O. Box 65
One Main Street
St. Helena, California 94574
(800) 950-8466, (707) 963-WINE, Fax: (707) 963-4402
Internet: http://www.harvestinn.com

Manager: *Jeff Perry*
Rooms: *55 cottage rooms*
Rates: *$100-366 (B&B)*
Payment: *AE, DC, DSC, MC, and VISA*
Dogs: *Welcome with a daily fee of $30 in the ground floor cottages*
Children: *Welcome (cribs, cots, and baby-sitters are available with notice)*
Open: *All year*

California

The charming town of St. Helena, which is host to an array of intriguing restaurants, boutiques, and accommodations, is surrounded by verdant vineyards and hillsides. The idyllic wine country ambiance is a combination that often draws an overabundance of tourists. Thus, we recommend visiting during the off-season, when the pace is less hectic and visitors can more leisurely explore the town and valley. While there are plenty of places to stay, few accept dogs. One spot that has long mixed lovely accommodations with a dog-friendly attitude is the Harvest Inn.

The English Tudor-style inn occupies over 14 acres — acreage once dedicated to vineyards. With the inn's success came a need for more rooms, forcing the owners to convert some of this land in order to build new cottages. But even with the expansion, the management has made a concerted effort to preserve its estate-like setting. With each visit, we notice that the meticulously maintained gardens are even more mature and beautiful than the last time.

As we meandered up the front walk to the inn's reception area, we came across Blackie (the resident cat who "thinks he owns the place"), sprawled across a bale of hay. The cat and our dogs pretended to ignore one another, and we then proceeded inside. The cavernous lobby is one of those places that continually delights us, with its beamed ceilings and inviting leather couches and armchairs set upon hardwood floors. Several large glass jars brim with peanuts, bubble gum, and M&Ms, with still more tempting edibles filling the antique popcorn maker and gumball machine. The adult equivalent to this veritable candy store lies in an even larger chamber situated off to the rear, where there is a wine bar. After a long day in the wine country, we like to return here and cozy up in front of the fieldstone fireplace, listen to melodies emanating from the piano, and sample a few of the local vintages.

Those who prefer the privacy of their guest room may wish to rejuvenate there. Whimsically named after English storybook characters, varieties of wine, flowers, or birds, each room is delightful. Each room's design is as unique as its name, with some containing separate sitting areas, others enhanced by beamed or vaulted ceilings. Floral wallpapers, along with brightly patterned area rugs covering the pegged, mahogany-stained floors, complete the English country cottage motif. King beds are standard (all but four guest rooms have them), while fine antique and reproduction furnishings occupy various nooks and crannies. The focal point for our favorite rooms is an enormous brick fireplace, complete with a variety of regional wine bottles placed upon its mantel. Additional amenities include wet bars, refrigerators, and color televisions. Sliding glass doors generally open to brick patios or decks. Fresh flower arrangements, taken from the inn's gardens, are a festive touch. The bathrooms are all spacious, modern, and equipped with brass fixtures, double sinks, telephones, and, often, Jacuzzi bath tubs.

A delicious complimentary breakfast of freshly baked muffins, rolls, pastries, fresh fruit, juice, and coffee or tea can be enjoyed in the "breakfast building," overlooking the vineyards. Flanking the entrance to this building are stained glass windows inset with depictions of pheasants, quail, partridge, and a cornucopia of fruits and vegetables. Guests dine under beamed ceilings, in front of the brick fireplace. We were so busy looking at the brass pots and assorted antique collectibles inside that we almost missed the two well-behaved yellow labs who were napping outside on the stone wall encircling the patio.

After breakfast, we like to walk the dogs through the inn's vineyards and fruit orchards and then down into town. The **Lyman Park** in St. Helena is a good option for dogs, as well, although on hot days, the **Napa River** is a canine favorite. Some people enjoy a leisurely picnic in **Stonebridge Park**, while their furry friend goes in for a dip. There are also a vast assortment of people-oriented diversions, including glider and hot air balloon rides — and, of course, wine tasting. After a busy day investigating this picturesque region, we were happy to return for a refreshing swim in one of the inn pools, followed by a rejuvenating soak in the Jacuzzi.

Wine Country Victorian
Inn and Cottage

400 Meadowood Lane
St. Helena, California 94574
(707) 963-0852, Fax: (707) 963-2111, Internet: (web site pending)

Hostess: Jan Strong
Rooms: 2 doubles, 1 cottage
Rates: Doubles $115-150 (B&B), Cottage $150 (B&B)
Payment: MC and VISA
Dogs: Welcome with notice, approval, and a daily fee of $10
Children: Welcome
Open: All year

Years ago, people would venture up the Napa Valley to "get away from it all." There were miles and miles of open land and narrow country roads. Today, that feeling has changed considerably. During the height of tourist season, lines of cars make their way up the serpentine back roads, wineries burst with visitors, and there is inevitably no space at the inn — so to speak. This is why we are always happy to return to the Wine Country Victorian Inn.

From the main road leading into St. Helena, we headed off down a back country road, flanked with vineyards and dense woodlands, to a hidden lane. The main house (a neat old Victorian) and cottage are set on a one-hundred year-old estate amid a few acres of towering elms, pines, and oaks. The semicircular gravel driveway wraps around the main house, which is nestled

California

on an ivy-covered knoll and surrounded by lush gardens. We liked the privacy though of the cottage, set just a short distance away near a red barn adorned with a Pennsylvania Dutch hex.

Each of the B&B's rooms is intriguing; prospective guests need only decide how much privacy they really want during their sojourn. Two bedrooms occupy the main house and a third rests in the charming cottage. The accommodations in the main house are brimming with a lovely collection of antiques. In the White Lace Room, the centerpiece is an old-fashioned white iron and brass double bed draped in a pink velvet coverlet. Complementing this is an array of pink and white lace accents. The spacious Queen Anne Room lies in a turret, with a California king-size bed set near a five paned bay window that overlooks the front gardens and beyond to the vineyards. Laura Ashley fabrics lend a delicacy to these spaces. The shared bathroom has a tub and shower combination, and is always well-stocked with thick towels, soaps, and other toiletries. For those who are traveling as a family, these two bedrooms and the Redwood Library, set to the rear of the house, may all be reserved as an expansive suite.

The cottage, on the other hand, offers the most privacy and is the best choice for those traveling with dogs. There is a quaint, rustic country feeling to this intimate abode, accented by white clapboards and a green roof. Stepping inside, natural board walls frame rooms filled with antiques, collectibles, and Ralph Lauren accents. A king-size bed, covered with a country quilt and accented with a dust ruffle, along with a wonderful old bureau, occupy this chamber. An adjacent sitting area contains comfortable overstuffed furniture; the living space extends outdoors too, to the private garden patio. (A bear occasionally makes appearances on the property, but we have yet to see it.) Cottage guests feel especially self-sufficient, as their kitchen is well equipped, making it easy to create meals and impromptu snacks. The bathroom is also well appointed, and the closet large enough to hold a week's supply of clothes.

A generous breakfast arrives each morning, consisting of crêpes or cheese puffs, fresh fruit, and coffee or tea. Jan often brings a portion of the breakfast out to the cottage the night before, so that early risers will have something to nibble on before the main meal arrives. For an additional $25, a bountiful champagne brunch can also be arranged. This is a delightful treat and one well worth considering. Jan has put together a scrapbook on restaurants in the area, complete with short reviews; this is quite helpful when trying to decide between the many available options. She will also make reservations for her guests.

We thoroughly enjoy walking the dogs around the grounds and along the quiet country roads surrounding the inn; however, if the dogs need more action, they can visit any of St. Helena's many parks. All of these parks welcome leashed dogs, with some offering more room to roam than others. Options include **Stonebridge, Lyman, Crane, and Baldwin parks.** A newer park, known as the **Mary Friar park**, is an especially good choice for people traveling with their canine companions.

After guests' furry friends are sufficiently tuckered out, they may wish to investigate some of the popular people-oriented diversions in the area. These include visits to the local wineries or the Calistoga mud baths, or possibly heading up, up, and away on a glider or a hot air balloon ride. Afterwards, guests can return to the tranquillity of the inn — a place so appealing that the Lipton Tea Company once used this bucolic setting for an iced tea commercial.

Norfolk Woods Inn

P.O. Box 262
6941 West Lake Blvd.
Tahoma, California 96142
(916) 525-5000, Fax: (916) 525-5266
Internet: www.tahoecountry.com/wslodging/nw.html **or** norfwds@sierra.net

Owners: Allen and Patty Multon
Rooms: 7 doubles, 2 suites, and 5 cottages
Rates: Doubles $75-100 B&B), Suites $110-125 (B&B),
    Cottages $130-155 (EP)
Payment: AE, MC, and VISA
Dogs: Welcome in the cottages with a $10 fee
Children: Welcome (cots, high chairs, and baby-sitters are available)
Open: All year

Lake Tahoe is exceptionally beautiful, and as it turns out, exceptionally deep. The bottom lies some 1,600 feet below the surface, making it the third deepest lake in North America. That fact alone is impressive, but even more inspiring are the majestic Sierra Nevada mountains ringing its perimeter. We love visiting the area with our dogs, because of the great number of recreational options available to all of us; however, finding a nice place (quite frankly, anyplace) to stay with our canine cohorts has been virtually impossible — until now.

The Norfolk Woods Inn is well located, equidistant from north and south Lake Tahoe. This rural hamlet is substantially less developed than many of the towns that line the other side of the lake, and for us, the accommodations are the nicest ones that allow dogs. It took awhile to traverse the winding roads leading to Norfolk Woods, but the sparkling lake views were worth every twist and turn. Upon arrival, we wandered into the inviting reception area. Apparently we weren't the only ones, as we startled a little chipmunk who was cavorting around this spacious knotty pine-paneled chamber. We all had a good chuckle as he took one look at the dogs and scampered right back out the front door.

It is easy to make oneself at home here, whether in the comfortable sofas and side chairs set around the stone fireplace or up at the old-fashioned bar. Country collectibles fill out the corners, as do paintings depicting various rural settings. The adjacent restaurant (open all year except in November and May) serves a hearty fare — perfect for those who have spent the day delving into strenuous recreational pursuits. The menu choices can include Aussie lamb, prime rib, roasted chicken, and plenty of pasta.

We visited in the late summer, when verdant lawns and tiered gardens were still in full color. We knew a blanket of snow would soon cover the foliage, but we hoped not the rock walls. Four of the five cottages are quite similar; the exception being Amy's Cottage. This 100-year-old log cabin is set down the hill from the rest of the cottages, near the heated swimming pool and spa. Recently refurbished, it now contains many luxurious amenities. The first floor's highlight is the expansive living room and fieldstone fireplace. Basic necessities include a fully-equipped kitchen, laundry area, and a full bathroom. The upstairs is all master bedroom; a bedroom so enormous that it easily dwarfs the king bed. A cable television and VCR are thoughtfully provided for those who enjoy the luxury of watching television from their bed. If this all sounds good, then reserve early because Amy's Cottage is the most requested cottage at Norfolk Woods.

Boasting names like Granite Chief, Rubicon, Ellis, and Tallac, the more rustic log cabins lie up the hill from the main inn. Green porch railings and window trim accent the simple cabins' exteriors. The interiors are similar to those in the main lodge where knotty pine walls and beamed ceilings give these spaces character. Comfortable sofas and armchairs are drawn up around the stone fireplaces whose mantels overflow with pine cones, wooden clogs, and assorted knickknacks. The homey feeling is completed with the array of country collectibles scattered about the cottage. A full kitchen and dining area lie to the rear of the chamber, alongside a separate bathroom. Cottage guests can either eat at the restaurant or prepare their own meals in their fully-equipped kitchens. A steep flight of stairs lead to the two cozy bedrooms. These spaces are quite versatile, as one room contains a double or queen bed and the other a similar configuration combined with a twin bed. Steep eaves and gabled ends give a good deal of additional character to these chambers.

As we indicated, Lake Tahoe is an outdoor person's dream. Depending upon how far one is willing to travel and the season in which one is visiting, visitors can mountain bike, fly fish, and rock climb or snowmobile, ice skate, and cross-country ski. Dogs can frolic across the area's expansive national forests, which include the **Eldorado National Forest** and, more locally, the **Tahoe National Forest**, the latter encompassing some 800,000 acres. For those who wish to venture a little further afield, the **D.L. Bliss Park** offers over 1,000 acres for people and their dogs to explore.

Ripple Creek Cabins

Box 4020, Star Route 2
Eagle Creek Loop of Highway 3
Trinity Center, California 96091
(916) 266-3505, (510) 531-5315
Internet: http://www.travelsphere.com/cdi/916/a_res/ripplec.html

Owners: Jim and Michele Coleman
Rooms: 7 cabins
Rates: Daily $74-115 (EP), Weekly $465-700 (EP)
Payment: Personal checks
Children: Welcome (cribs, cots, high chairs, and baby-sitters are available)
Dogs: Welcome with a one-time fee of $10, just as long as "the dogs and their owners are well mannered." Please bring the pet's bed.
Open: All year

The Ripple Creek Cabins are located on the site of the original Eagle Creek Ranch, which not only supplied the meat for the workers at the Bonanza King Mine, but also served as the stagecoach stop for a line that ran from California into Oregon. The barn and three of the cabins have been here since the 1800s. This complex housed the packers and their teams of horses who grazed at Sunny Flat. In this part of the country, cattle often graze in the mountain foothills during the winter and spend their summers in the high country. A woman named Gussie Lee ran cattle from Ripple Creek into the Trinity Alps until age 86. Gussie's friend, Ethel Steel, also shuttled cattle between the ranch and the high country every year until well into her 70s.

Guests who visit today will gain a strong sense of this rich tradition. The ranch and the cabins occupy opposite sides of Ripple Creek. Although the cattle continue to be an integral part of the ranch, most guests come to hike, fish, and ride horses through this picturesque region. Mountain meadows, dense forests, granite peaks, and sparkling alpine lakes create innumerable opportunities for picnics and day hikes. A portion of the Trinity River, alive with Rainbow and German Brown trout, runs by the cabins, although some anglers prefer fishing on nearby Trinity Lake. This combination of clear mountain waters, high peaks, and rustic cabins are all most people are looking for when they think of vacationing in this region.

The cabins at Ripple Creek are uncluttered, rustic, and meticulously kept. The decor won't win any awards, but then again, it isn't supposed to. We think the homey charm allows guests to focus less on cleaning and more on vacationing. Knotty pine wallboards, beamed ceilings, and old-fashioned linoleum floors set the overall tone. Guests can relax on comfortable, vintage furnishings set before wood stoves. The eat-in kitchens are equally well outfitted, down to the garlic presses. In most places, kitchens in efficiency cabins are ill-equipped, forcing us to lug half our personal kitchen ware with us on vacation — but it is not necessary this time. The bedrooms contain queen beds and the adjacent bathrooms are well stocked with towels. Just outside each cabin are a picnic table and a Weber grill for impromptu barbecues. On cool summer nights, the wood stove supplies an even heat, supplementing what is provided for electrically.

Friends or extended families may be interested in the newest four-bedroom and two-bath cabin. Compared to the other cabins, this one is luxurious. The kitchen is state-of-the-art and includes a microwave and dishwasher. (Yes — all other guests get to clean dishes the old-fashioned way.) The cozy parlor is a beautiful accent to the cabin, especially because it contains an antique wood stove lined with shiny brass fittings. Best of all, for those staying for longer periods of time, there is a washer and dryer.

While dogs should have a great time exploring the **local streams**, nosing around after a cow or two, or circumnavigating **the forest**, it is the children who are likely to most enjoy this rural oasis. Here, children and adults together can walk along trails cut through deep forest glens, picturesque meadows of wild flowers, and impressive granite outcroppings. Children can also spend hours on the playground, riding ponies or bicycles and playing volleyball, horseshoes, or badminton. If it happens to rain, there are also plenty of board games and a Ping-pong table to help while away the hours. The main reason most people and their dogs come to the Trinity Alps, though, is to enjoy the spectacular scenery and sense of solitude in what is truly one of the last unspoiled regions in the state.

Howard Creek Ranch

P.O. Box 121
40501 North Highway 1
Westport, California 95488
(707) 964-6725, Internet: http://www2.howardcreekranch.com

Hosts: Charles and Sally Grigg
Rooms: 4 doubles, 3 suites, 3 cottages
Rates: Doubles $55-100 (B&B), Suites/Cottages $55-155 (B&B)
Payment: AE, MC, and VISA
Dogs: Welcome with approval
Children: Accepted by arrangement only
Open: All year

The Howard Creek Ranch dates back to the year 1867. It was always more than just a sheep and cattle ranch; it also served as a dairy, a sawmill, and a blacksmith shop. In 1871, Alfred Howard bought the 1,000-acre ranch from his father. Over the next four decades he married, had seven children, and eventually died in this old farm house.

Today, the Howard Creek Ranch is as vital as ever, but rather than bursting with children, it is overflowing with guests. It lies on 40 acres, just three miles from the tranquil village of Westport. Visitors come to this rugged and isolated part of California because of its abundant natural beauty and virtually deserted black sand beaches pounded by Pacific surf. The Howard Creek Ranch is situated in a small valley surrounded by pastures, yet it is also just a short walk from the ocean. On the day we returned, fog rolled in across the

California

upper meadow, where we could just make out the cows, horses, and deer grazing. As we drove down to the farmhouse, we found the Griggs rebuilding portions of the barn.

Steep, pitched roofs connect the two original redwood farmhouses, creating one long main building. This restored farmhouse contains dozens of American antiques, collectibles, and family heirlooms, including a piano and organ. Cherished black and white photographs line the wall near the immense sideboard, whose cubby holes are loaded with board games. The original fireplace, topped by a bow and arrow, still heats the parlor. Upon arriving, we walked under the six-foot loggers' rip saw, set over one door, and entered the intimate dining room. This space is also full of the Griggs' American antiques, whether they be carved oak chairs or hutches filled with glassware. In the morning, guests gather here for a hearty, ranch-style breakfast cooked over old-fashioned wood stoves. Fresh flowers from the gardens grace the table, along with edible flowers that top some of the foods. Guests might be served baked apples with granola and French whipped cream, raisins, or yogurt. During our visit the strawberry banana hotcakes, drenched with real maple syrup, topped the menu. The omelet is also appealing, with tomatoes, green onions, cheeses, sour cream, and avocado. Fried potatoes, thickly sliced bacon, fresh biscuits, and fruit salad with candied blackberries and violas are other house specialties. Later in the day, guests often return here to enjoy the wine and beer tastings, coupled with scrumptious edibles.

One of our favorite bedrooms is the Garden Room, which lies just beyond the dining room. This also happens to be the one farmhouse guest room appropriate for guests traveling with dogs. A king-size, canopy bed, topped by a colorful handmade quilt, dominates this cheery yellow-hued corner suite, which also contains a small sitting room. Opening the French door to the porch, the award-winning perennial garden unfolds, leading to an expanse of lawn.

A short walk across the lawn brings guests to Howard Creek Ranch's more eclectic and varied accommodations. One might offer a private balcony, while another has a kitchen or a skylit loft. Some accommodations are rustic, but that makes them all the more appealing because they also exude a strong sense of history. Two especially noteworthy rooms are in the Boat House and Beach House, heated by electricity and wood stoves. Interestingly enough, the Boat House is a separate redwood cabin lovingly built around the hull of an abandoned boat, complete with a galley kitchen. With headroom at a premium in some places, visitors quickly learn to duck when making their way through this abode. This space also has creek views (illuminated at night) through a picture window framed with sailboat-patterned tab curtains. Guests can watch the starry skies through skylights positioned above the double bed tucked into a tiny alcove. From here, the good-sized head is just three stairsteps up.

Another interesting spot is the Beach House, set just beyond the old barn. To get to this part of the property, some people might have to coax (or carry) their dogs over the 75-foot long swinging bridge that crosses Howard Creek. Once over, guests will need to look for the enchanting redwood dwelling set at the meadow's edge. One piece of this long, narrow building contains a king bed, skylights, and a partial water view. Set opposite the entry way is another space, divided into a kitchenette, a bathroom with a Jacuzzi, and a double-bedded loft. The Willow room is also intriguing, because it occupies the first floor of the old barn. Guests generally enter through the master bedroom, where they will see how the room earned its name — a photograph of a willow tree grove is wallpapered across one entire wall. From here, guests can follow the terra-cotta tiled floor into a sitting room and settle into the comfortable armchairs set on an Oriental rug. Another set of French doors leads outside, which is where most people spend their time exploring the property.

Some love the gardens; others come for the bird watching. The Griggs have a list of 65 bird species sited here over the years. These include the usual hummingbirds, sparrows, and finches, along with more noteworthy red-tailed hawks, pygmy owls, and ruby-crowned kinglets. Guests may want to walk out to the **beach** with their dogs, which is two miles long at low tide. Here, dogs can romp and play, and people can explore the tidal pools. Dogs and ocean swimming seem to be a nice complement; however, people often prefer the relative warmth of the swimming pool back at the ranch. Travelers who bring bicycles can take their canines along the **10-mile paved lane** that wends through the sand dunes. At the end of the day, we recommend having a therapeutic German massage, given in a mountain top cabin, and then heading back to the ranch for a hot tub and sauna. After a full day, a massage, and a sauna, sleep will descend as quickly as the fog rolling in off the coast.

Sheep Dung Estates

P.O. Box 49
(off of Highway 128)
Yorkville, California 95494
(707) 894-5322, Internet: www.traveldog.com

Hosts: *Anne Bennett and Aaron Weintraub*
Rooms: *3 cottages (with a fourth on the way)*
Rates: *$85-120 (B&B)*
Payment: *Personal checks*
Dogs: *Very welcome, with only a couple of simple rules*
Children: *Welcome (a futon is available)*
Open: *All year*

We love this place, but we must say up front, there are two factors that might cause prospective guests to think twice about staying here. The name alone — Sheep Dung Estates — might disturb those with a sensitive proboscis. The second factor is the inn's remoteness — two hours from San Francisco, but seemingly thousands of miles from anywhere. While we can't do much about the former (except chuckle), the latter is worth overcoming to experience this truly enchanting retreat. Telling anyone how to get here is futile (Anne gives great directions), except we might mention that there is a steep, winding 2 1/2 mile ascent over a dirt and gravel road. At the end of the road, we came upon the main house and the three cottages. Max, our hosts' friendly Golden Retriever and German Shepherd mix, came out and greeted us. Anne was close behind, and although it had been a few years since our last visit, her vivacity made it easy to pick up right where we had left off.

The name may have stayed the same, but the Sheep Dung Estates are not where we left them. Anne and Aaron sold the original property and moved two miles closer to Yorkville. Wearing various hats, most notably those of general contractor and B&B host, they have accomplished what few would ever have the gumption to try. After seeing their accomplishment, we could only marvel at their foresight and tenacity. They graded a steep mountain road, carved a few buildings into an isolated ridge, and dug a pond — somehow knowing that B&B guests would find them. "Just a hunch," Anne might say; but as guests learn a little more about Anne and Aaron's past, the success of the Sheep Dung Estates seems to have been almost inevitable.

These two once spent their free time refurbishing old Victorian homes. Although they lived in one themselves, they found it was too big for them. They used just three rooms: the kitchen, bedroom, and parlor. This realization, coupled with a need to abandon their urban life, led them to first buy a 40-acre parcel of land between Yorkville and Mendocino. Anne spent months scouring magazines, construction books, and restoration periodicals in search of the ultimate design for their weekend retreat. She and Aaron finally settled on something so unusual that *Home Magazine* featured it in one of their issues. Anne tells readers that "the key to our big little house is that nowhere does one feel closed in. Our walls, our decor, and our television are the outdoors. We didn't need a separate bedroom, living room, and dining room, so the living area became flexible. With the easily moved furniture it can be a dining room for a seated dinner for eight, a casual living room, or our master bedroom." A guest cottage followed the completion of their dream house and shared many of these same features; however, shortly thereafter, Anne and Aaron found an even more impressive piece of property, where they could expand upon this theme.

While the new location boasts more awe-inspiring valley views, it is the undefiled setting that continues to attract guests. The main house lies near the 25-foot-deep pond, which guests (and canines) can use as their own private swimming hole on hot days. We arrived in the early evening, just in time to see the sun disappear behind the ridge, and made our way up to our cottage.

Accentuating the spacious studio's crisp interior lines are off-white walls and natural pine-board cathedral ceilings. The furnishings are minimalist, with Scandinavian-style chairs placed on colorful throw rugs resting upon maple floors. An enameled wood stove occupies one corner, and a platform bed, topped by a fluffy down comforter, fills another. A shelf, set alongside the bed, holds a portable stereo and a selection of tapes, while a full bookshelf occupying the wall behind the bed contains everything from a variety of intriguing books to fun games for guests to enjoy. On this night, we needed little entertainment, as we spent our time simply watching the shower of shooting stars whizzing through the sky. In the morning, it was still cool, so we opted to eat breakfast at the table in the windowed alcove. Everything guests might need for a hearty Continental repast, including juices, breads, and cheeses, have already been placed in the apartment-size refrigerator. A basket of fresh fruit, crackers, and wine, resting on the kitchen counter, provides a nice basis for an impromptu picnic lunch or evening *hors d'oeuvres*. Our hosts have even gone so far as to stock the cupboards with cans of tomato juice to be used "in case Rover encounters a skunk."

We were up at dawn and discovered we had visitors: resident deer and jack rabbits lounging in front of the cottage. Fog then began to fill the valley, creating the illusion that we were on a mystical island. Excited at the thought of an early-morning swim in the pond, our dogs patiently accompanied us on a walk over the hill to see the other cottage. The design is similar to our cottages, but the floors in here are terra-cotta tiles instead of hardwood. An entire wall of windows and doors provides incredible, virtually unobstructed vistas of the surrounding hillsides. A well-placed bed maximizes the views, broken up only slightly by the central chimney of a freestanding wood stove. A third cottage was in the process of being built during our visit, and is probably just being completed at the time of this writing. We were able to view the site for it, though; a lovely spot set on a plateau carved out of an adjacent ridge. Anne also mentioned that she was drawing up plans for another cottage that would be completed in 1998. Anne and Aaron have become so enamoured with this region, that they have purchased a couple additional tracts of lands bringing their total acreage to 320.

Your hosts know how to make guests supremely comfortable, but for those who expect a variety of recreational diversions, this probably is not the B&B of choice. Here, most people just relish the solitude and picturesque views, as well as the chance to relax without telephones, televisions, and other distractions cluttering up their vacation. Because this is such a remote hillside location, the hosts rely on solar panels, a series of 12-volt batteries, and a standby generator to supply the electricity for the cottages (and the main house). Thus, when not using an electrical fixture, guests are asked to turn it off to conserve electricity. If this sounds just a little too woodsy and primitive, travelers may rest assured, it is not. While the setting is unadulterated, the furnishings, appliances, modern bathroom, and overall ambiance of the cottages are first rate.

California

Sheep Dung Estates is the sort of place where dogs can just relax and be themselves. Leisurely **walks through these hills** are one of our favorite pastimes. Guests can visit the adjacent Lazy Creek Vineyards or head down the hill to Boonville and its charming **Faulkner Park**. From here, it is also easy to take day trips north to Mendocino, where there are plenty of beaches and trails for dogs. Heading west to Ukiah and the **Cow Mountain Recreation Area**, visitors will find streams, lakes, and trails lying on acreage numbering in the tens of thousands. We decided to simply relax and enjoy the solitude. Lying in a chair on the deck, as the sun filters through the trees, visitors here can listen to the symphony of sound that only nature can produce.

Vintage Inn

P.O. Box 2536
6541 Washington Street
Yountville, California 94599
(800) 351-1133, (707) 944-1112, Fax: (707) 944-1617
Internet://www.vintageinn.com/

General Manager: *Patty Larson*
Rooms: *62 doubles, 18 mini-suites*
Rates: *Doubles $175-225 (B&B), Suites $250-275 (B&B)*
Payment: *AE, DSC, CB, DC, MC, and VISA*
Dogs: *Welcome with a one-time fee of $25*
Children: *Welcome (cribs, cots, and baby-sitters are available)*
Open: *All year*

The Vintage Inn occupies land that was formerly a portion of the old Vintage Estate (also known as the Groezinger winery), back in the 1870s. In the mid-1980s, Kipp Stewart (designer of the exquisite Ventana Inn in Big Sur) received the commission to conceptualize an equally captivating resort in the Napa Valley. The grand plan included restoring the winery's existing buildings and turning them into a collection of boutiques, galleries, and fine restaurants. Interwoven among the newly built villas, he placed lovely courtyards, fountains, streams, and fragrant gardens.

The cavernous reception area creates the strongest first impressions of the inn. Light flows in past thick, louvered shutters and across the hardwood floors to the massive, exposed brick fireplace. The ambiance is enlivened by the pickled woods in the beamed, cathedral ceilings and light oak furniture. Earth tone fabrics cover the overstuffed sofas and armchairs. A similar look prevails within both the brick and clapboard-sided French country villas.

The guest rooms are very similar to one another, imbued with a strong sense of sophistication and the predominant color schemes of Napa — lavender, burgundy, mauve, and plum. Windowed corner alcoves contain breakfast tables, fashioned with cushioned window seats. Most memorable, though, are the wood burning fireplaces and large bedsteads, perfectly positioned for guests to enjoy the warmth emanating from them. Furnishings are a combination of rattan and lightly stained oak; many of the pieces are custom made and have hand-painted fabrics covering them. French doors open to private verandas, where striking views of the vineyards, gardens, and surrounding hills unfold. Bathrooms are equally well thought out, with whirlpool tubs, terry robes, and luxurious toiletries. Guests can dip into the well-stocked refrigerators or sample some of the complimentary Vintage Estate Sauvignon Blanc provided for each visitor.

Our favorite bedrooms are the second floor chambers, with their beamed, cathedral ceilings fashioned with fans that pull cool air through the plantation-style shuttered windows. These may be our favorites, but we also recognize how much more easily guests and their dogs can access the property from the ground floor rooms. The especially charming villa 101 has a private and enclosed grassy yard — something dogs definitely appreciate. Our Goldens easily made themselves comfortable by the fireplace, but we knew what they truly looked forward to: their early morning walk, when they could more freely investigate the decorative rivers and fountains on the property.

Early risers can make their own coffee in the morning, although soon to follow is a hearty, champagne breakfast buffet, served in the reception area. Guests may enjoy this at the tables surrounding the baby grand piano and fireplace, or outside on the patio, where the morning sun falls invitingly across the verdant valley. For those in search of other meals, we suggest asking one of the gourmet grocery stores to pack a picnic lunch or dinner, or perhaps investigating one of the valley's fabulous restaurants. Compadres, the restaurant next to the inn, also offers a varied menu selection, and permits guests to charge meals to their inn room.

During the day, guests frequently play tennis on the inn's courts or swim in its 60-foot lap pool. Visitors can either bring a bicycle or borrow one, but in any case, they should exercise their dogs only during the cooler times of the day, as Napa can become quite hot around mid-afternoon in the summer time. There is also an assortment of interesting shops and restaurants, as well as a number of walking paths to explore, both in Yountville and in some of the nearby towns.

With so much beauty available to both dogs and their owners, it doesn't seem necessary to wander much further afield. But eventually, most people can hardly resist a visit to one of the wineries. One of the more popular and closest is the Domaine Chandon winery, located just a few minute's drive from the Vintage Inn. The grounds are fabulous; but then, so is the sparkling wine.

For those who wish to explore some of the nearby parks, we were

California

informed by the Napa County Parks staff that leashed dogs are allowed along all river and creek trails in the county parks, as well as in the **Allston Park, Shurtleff Park, Kennedy Park**, and in the lower part of **Allston Park**.

The Webber Place

P.O. Box 2873
6610 Webber Street
Yountville, California   94599
(800) 647-7177, (707) 944-8384

Hostess: *Diane Bartholomew*
Rooms: *4 doubles*
Rates: *$120-185 (B&B)*
Payment: *AE, MC, and VISA*
Dogs: *Welcome in the Veranda Suite, with a $20 fee and approval*
Children: *Most appropriate for children over 12 years of age*
Open: *All year*

Yountville is a charming hamlet set along the scenic route stretching from Napa to Calistoga. Most come to sample wine and explore the surrounding vineyards, but in doing so they might miss the essence of the area that draws the full-time residents. This essence is easily found at an old-fashioned, homey Bed & Breakfast known as the Webber Place. This red clapboard home, looking festive with its hunter green trim, lies on a quiet side street just outside of town.

A picket fence surrounds the property, but we found an opening through the lattice arbor entwined with roses. We soon discovered Diane's animal menagerie lounging on the wraparound porches and cavorting across the grass. An adorable bunny hopped amid the clover, while a one-eyed cat sunned himself on the porch's hunter green rocker. An old dog rested on the kitchen's back stoop, hoping for a delectable handout. The source of his interest lay inside this warm and inviting abode, where we found Diane just finishing her morning baking. She gave us a tour of her intriguing farmhouse, which dates back to the 1850s.

Thoughtfully restored 35 years ago, the house maintains a strong sense of history. Diane has been in residence for over ten years, after having spent a good portion of her life in Southern California. Rather than overdoing it with the decor and furnishings, she tried to keep things simple by using her artistic talents to create a warm and cozy country motif. The country accents include a selection of folk art paintings displayed throughout the B&B, along with bunches of dried flowers and herbs. As we walked down the center hall, past the staircase and towards the large country kitchen, we saw a roll-top desk topped with seaweed soaps, herbal lotions, and bathing accoutrements. These are available for purchase. We then headed toward the foyer and staircase lined by original redwood paneling and harvest red walls.

The three upstairs bedrooms are quite spacious. The Sun Room and Redwood Room share a bathroom with an extra large old-fashioned tub highlighted with brass fittings. While the East Room contains its own tub occupying a secluded alcove in the room, all three of the guest chambers have pedestal sinks. The decor features brass and white iron beds draped in festive quilts; country furnishings with Oriental or braided rugs set across hardwood floors; and rose colored eyelet curtains framing the paned windows. The most notable of the three is the Sun Room, where tongue and groove paneled walls climb to the vaulted ceilings. True to its name, this spacious chamber receives plenty of sunshine that filters through the branches of a large oak tree just outside the windows.

The guest room that is most appropriate for those traveling with a dog is the Veranda Suite. The double doors to this chamber form a separate outside entrance, accessed off a lattice-trimmed veranda. As we meandered past the white wicker chairs, we looked longingly at the hammock that seemed to beckon us. This suite is substantially larger than the other three bedrooms, but offers a similar country decor. Even those with allergies to feathers will be tempted to jump into the feather bed topped by a down comforter. Climbing roses highlight the papered walls. As with the East Room, this suite has a private clawfooted bathtub set off in one corner.

In the morning, guests often stop in the intimate living room to warm themselves in front of the wood stove before heading in for breakfast. Diane cooks a full country repast. Some of the wonderful baked goods, whose aroma we enjoyed upon arrival, showed up on the breakfast table the next morning. Eggs, bacon, biscuits and fresh coffee accompanied these homemade creations. In the afternoon, Diane likes to serve sun tea or lemonade and cookies out on the front porch, weather permitting. Some people might try to take a little afternoon nap in the hammock, but more likely than not, it will be hard to doze off with a wet nose nudging through the spaces between the ropes.

Anyone who wants to stretch their legs, generally heads to town where intriguing shops and eateries keep humans and canines alike quite entertained. The small town center is usually quiet, except for the occasional tour bus. For park visits, it is best to head south to **Napa's Allston Park** or east to **Lake Berryessa**. The latter is a favorite with our two dogs, who love to just hang out under the trees while we take turns Windsurfing.

Just before we went to press, we learned that Diane was in the midst of some fairly extensive renovations. She was not only going to add private bathrooms to a couple of the inn rooms, but also build four additional garden guest rooms. Prospective visitors should not dismay though, as the overall character of the B&B is slated to remain much the same.

Oregon

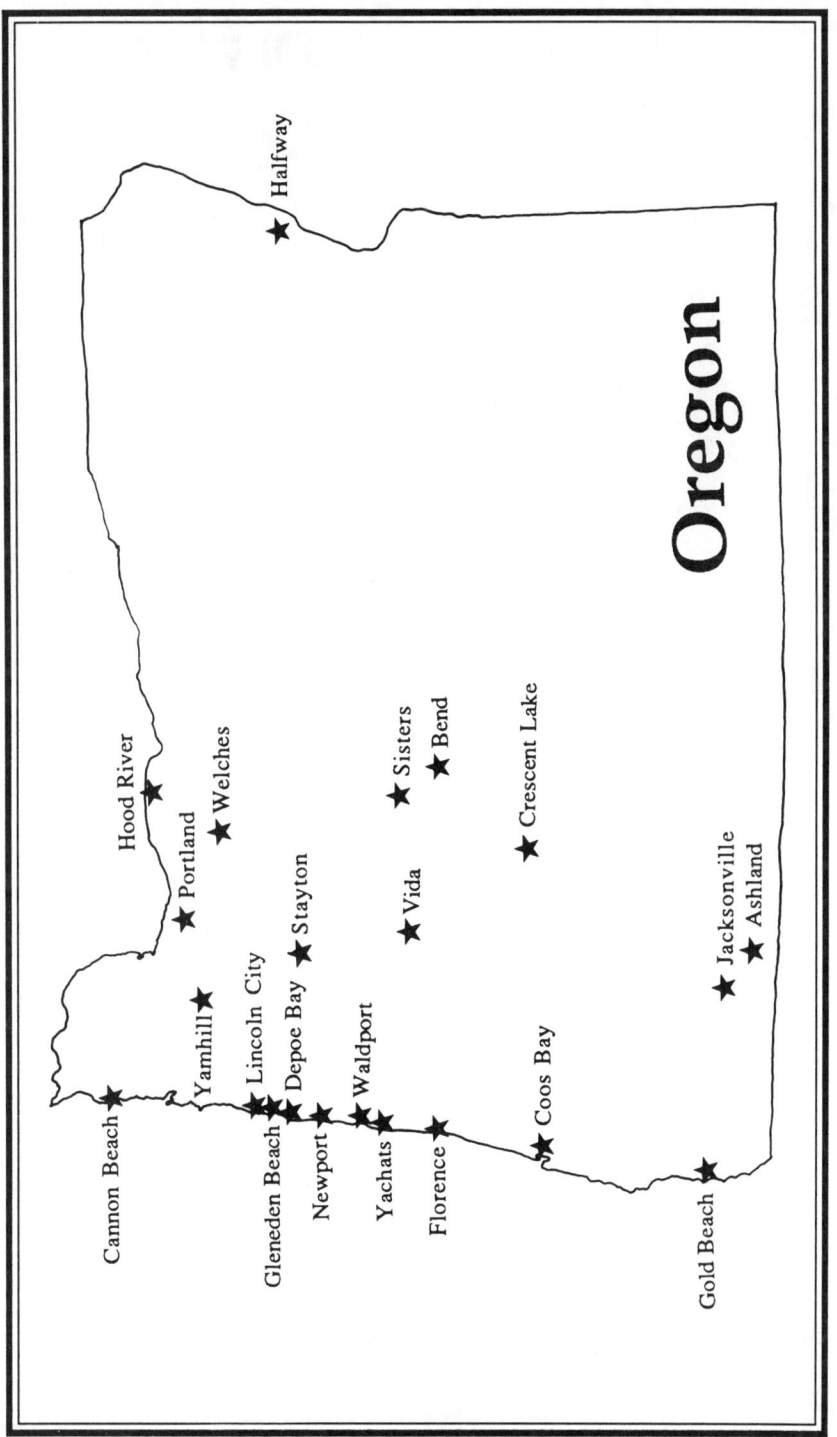

The Green Springs Box R Ranch

16799 Highway 66
Ashland, Oregon 97520
(541) 482-1873

Hosts: *Don and Jean Rowlett*
Rooms: *4 houses*
Rates: *$110-150 (EP), weekly rates are available*
Payment: *Personal checks*
Dogs: *Welcome in the houses*
Children: *Welcome*
Open: *April through December*

Any place that offers the coordinates for private planes to land seems as if it would be exceptionally exclusive and remote. Sure enough, the Green Springs Box R Ranch lies in southern Oregon's Cascades; however, it is also only a 30-minute drive from Ashland, home to the Oregon Shakespearean Festival and the Pacific Northwest Museum of Natural History. While some choose to fly in, most drive, as it is an easy jog off Interstate 5 to Route 66 and the ranch.

The Green Springs Box R Ranch has an interesting history, dating back to the turn of the century, when the main ranch house served as a stage coach stop along the Applegate Trail — a trail established in 1846 that ran from the Klamath Basin to Jacksonville. Taking the ranch's history into account, the Rowletts are in the process of putting together their own small museum and an authentic Old Western town. A few historic buildings from around Oregon now rest on this land, including the oldest building in Jackson County, a hand-hewn smokehouse, and a blacksmith's shop. Guests might also want to visit the historic Boot Hill graveyard or investigate the collection of authentic covered wagons, also on the property. History aside, the Green Springs Box R Ranch is also an authentic 1,000-acre working cattle ranch.

The old-fashioned ranch house and modern log cabins overlook lush green meadows and ponds surrounded by pines. The Aspen and Shasta houses are the smallest of the four, accommodating eight people each, while the Landing and Lakeview cabins can house 12 and 16 people, respectively. A single family might reserve one of the smaller cabins, but these are also ideal for groups of friends or extended families. Each cabin configuration is slightly different, but all are fully carpeted and well equipped with all the necessities for a week-long vacation. The largest of these houses contains two bedrooms; however, what the children find especially appealing are the carpeted loft spaces. In these, the hosts supply the foam pads — guests just need to bring their sleeping bags. Many children find the idea of "roughing it" appealing.

(Bed linens are supplied for the lucky ones who get beds.) Each cabin's central gathering place is in the living room, where comfortable sofas and chairs surround the natural rock fireplaces. An unlimited supply of wood inspires many guests to have a fire nearly every night. The kitchens are fully equipped and modern, although guests should plan on stocking up on groceries before they arrive. There is also a small store in the area for buying perishables and assorted wares, or guests can head over to the Green Springs Inn and Jenny Creek Café for a casual, hearty meal.

There are no organized activities at the ranch designed especially for children or dogs, although there are ranch tours by wagon or sleigh available. Belgian draft horses — Willy and Waylon — will take guests along portions of the old Applegate Trail. This is a really fun way to get to know the lay of the land. Guests may volunteer to help with some of the chores on the ranch, including feeding the animals or gathering eggs. Most come to relax, though — perhaps **fish** a bit, or just explore this vast open country with their dog. There are trails right on the property, and the **Pacific Crest Trail** is also close by. Anyone spending a week here might take the day and drive up the Dead Indian Road. One particularly popular trail begins at the **Daley Creek Campground** and parallels **Beaver Dam Creek**. In this typically dry country, many enjoy spending a few hours exploring the creek and the old growth forest throughout this region. But that's not all — there are plenty of other intriguing hikes throughout the area that would also be appropriate for guests and their canine companions.

The Riverhouse

3075 North Highway 97
Bend, Oregon 97701
(800) 547-3928, (541) 389-3111
E-mail: riverhouse@emp.net.com

General Manager: *Wayne Purcell*
Rooms: *220 doubles and suites*
Rates: *Doubles and Suites $65-86 (EP)*
Payment: *AE, DC, MC, and VISA*
Dogs: *Welcome, provided they are not left alone in the room*
Children: *Welcome (cribs, cots, and high chairs are available)*
Open: *All year*

Bend lies in Oregon's high desert, with nothing around it but spectacular scenery. It has grown remarkably over the years; what started out as a small ranching town has developed into a virtual metropolis. In the winter months,

Mount Bachelor is the primary draw, but in the summertime visitors flock here for the assortment of outdoor diversions and for the mountain biking in the nearby foothills. While there are plenty of roadside motels in Bend that welcome dogs, one of the standouts is The Riverhouse.

Yes — it is technically a motel; it does lie next to busy Highway 97; and it does have more than 200 rooms. Even more unusual, though, is that the Deschutes River runs right through the middle of the complex, adding an intriguing dimension to this mini-resort. When making a reservation, we suggest that guests request a room overlooking the river, as far away from the main road and restaurant as possible. Our favorite rooms are those in the 150-163 block on the first floor of the two-story riverside building. Almost as appealing are Rooms 122-149. Although these occupy the building next door, they are also a little closer to the restaurant and lounge. A footbridge leads guests across the river to another building. While these rooms are furthest from the main road, they are not quite as private and they look back towards the dining room. We definitely recommend staying away from the rooms situated over the lobby, as they are quite close to the highway and can be very noisy at times.

Keeping all this in mind, once new arrivals drop down into the complex they will discover that the guest rooms are basically oversized, upscale motel rooms. Contemporary oak headboards back pairs of queen beds covered with attractive floral spreads and edged by dust ruffles. Cream-colored walls are devoid of decoration, with the exception of a few framed bird prints. The bathrooms are quite modern, with separate vanities and a full complement of toiletries. A long, low bureau is topped by a television equipped with movie channels (VCRs may be rented). The direct-dial telephones feature voicemail, and clock radios supply pleasing background music. These are the most basic standard rooms. There are also chambers with an in-room Jacuzzi, a fireplace, or a kitchenette. We recommend the riverside guest rooms, though, as they have sliding glass doors that open to private patios. From here, guests and their dogs can walk right out past pine trees and shrubs to the river's edge. When the water is low, many enjoy hopping from one flat rock to the next and exploring further up or down the river bed.

The Riverhouse Restaurant offers an extensive Continental menu. Those who don't get to stay in the riverside rooms can enjoy the same river views from the restaurant. The restaurant's specialties are beef, and include such favorites as filet mignon, prime rib, and tenderloin. We also suggest trying the fresh rainbow trout or the filet of salmon. The portions are enormous, so there is usually plenty left over to share with your dog. Another feature that is unusual for a traditional motel is that guests may order from the room-service menu and enjoy a quiet meal in the privacy of their room. Afterwards, many enjoy heading to The Fireside Lounge, which, most nights, offers live entertainment, as well as a big screen television.

During the day, there is plenty to keep everyone happy — right on site. As we mentioned, dogs can explore the river, or perhaps follow the road up to the golf course. There is also a jogging path that wends along the golf course and the canal. Children and their parents will undoubtedly gravitate to one of the two swimming pools. If it is warm, most choose the outdoor pool and the adjacent whirlpool that is surrounded by attractive landscaping. For inclement days, there is a covered pool and spa, with an adjacent deck. A separate exercise room and spa are located across the river in another building.

Just south of Bend, hikers can pick up the **Deschutes River Trail**, which leads them over fairly easy terrain to **Benham Falls**. Dogs will love dipping their paws in the river, or occasionally stopping for a drink. Also south of Bend, are a series of caves. These are more interesting for people than for dogs, although canines might enjoy the cool interiors on hot days. These caverns are known as the **Boyd**, the **Wind**, and the **Skeleton Caves** and each has a short trail leading to it from the road. One other option is **Shevlin Park**, just west of Bend, where a leisurely five-mile trail follows **Tumalo Creek**.

Hallmark Resort

P.O. Box 547
1400 South Hemlock
Cannon Beach, Oregon 97110
(800) 345-5676, (503) 436-1566, Fax: (503) 436-0324
Internet: http://www.hallmarkinns.com

General Manger: Liz Kee
Rooms: 132 doubles and suites, 4 houses
Rates: Doubles $59-425 (EP)
Payment: AE, MC, and VISA
Dogs: Welcome with an $8 fee per pet per day
Children: Welcome (cribs are available)
Open: All year

Cannon Beach is named, appropriately enough, after a cannon that washed up on its shores in the 1800s. Modern-day visitors know it for something else entirely: its 235-foot-high Haystack Rock, the third largest freestanding monolith in the world. Equally memorable is The Hallmark Resort, which is dramatically perched on the cliffs overlooking this natural wonder and surrounding sandy beach.

The resort sits unto itself on the hill, in a cluster of attractive shake buildings. It has all the trappings of a larger hotel, with a concierge, an array of amenities, and restaurants just footsteps away. Our top choice for room selection should come as no surprise — the Oceanfront Rooms. These range from a standard bedroom with a queen bed to a studio with a Murphy bed to the one- and two-bedroom suites with a Murphy bed and a separate bedroom. The premise behind the Murphy beds is a good one. During the day they are tucked out of sight, thereby creating a good-sized living room; at night they fold down to form a bedroom — complete with a fireplace and nice ocean views. Families like the suite arrangement, because the children can sleep in the rear bedroom, while the adults can enjoy the sounds of the waves and the warmth from the fireplace in their living room/bedroom. The decor is typical of many upscale motels, utilizing Scandinavian-style oak furnishings.

Rooms that don't come equipped with kitchenettes do have small refrigerators, ideal for storing all sorts of goodies. Packages of Starbucks gourmet coffee are left next to the coffee makers, so that guests can make their own coffee in the morning before heading into town for a more substantial repast. One interesting item that was provided in the rooms made us chuckle: earplugs. They are left for guests to use during Sou'westers, when the wind is blowing so hard that some find it difficult to sleep. Those concerned about the storms can keep abreast of the weather in the *Oregonian*, which is delivered to one's door each morning. Other amenities available for guests to use include irons, ironing boards, hair dryers, popcorn poppers, and laundry facilities.

Those who want to save a bit of money can reserve one of the rooms in Hallmark Square, just behind Dooger's restaurant. Guests staying here pay substantially less — and they should, since the rooms overlook a parking lot. While these rooms do not offer exceptional water vistas, they do have access to all other amenities at the hotel.

The ocean water may be a bit chilly for the average person, although not for the average dog. But not to worry, the hotel has a really nice indoor pool. Everyone will enjoy spending time in and around it. Sloping ceilings lined with skylights provide plenty of natural light for this space, which is surrounded by a plethora of plants. Bright blue and white tiles provide a fresh, clean feeling to this good-sized area. Guests may swim in the pool; they also have a choice of two whirlpool spas, a wading pool for the little ones, and even an exercise room. Those who want a private spa may wish to reserve an oceanfront room, outfitted with a Jacuzzi tub large enough for two.

The management feels strongly that doggie guests need to leave the beach as clean as they found it. To that end, the management has placed a supply of disposable pooper scoopers at the top of every staircase descending to the beach. In addition, they ask that dogs not be left alone in the rooms or on the patios, as they might disturb the other guests. This should not be a problem, though, as there are plenty of things to do in the area.

Obviously, long beach walks are a wonderful way to spend time with your dog. Other options include a hike up **Neahkannie Mountain** or along the **Oswald West State Park's beaches and trails**, both of which are close to the resort. The village of Cannon Beach is another great place for taking a stroll with your dog, especially along the **road paralleling the beach**, as it is lined with small restaurants, art galleries, and kite shops.

Quiet Cannon Lodgings

P.O. Box 174
372 North Spruce Street
Cannon Beach, Oregon 97110
(503) 436-1405 or 436-1805

Hosts: Don and Joan Holden, Al and Charlotte Hovey
Rooms: *2 condominium units*
Rates: *$85-95 (EP)*
Payment: *Personal checks*
Dogs: *Welcome with a one-time fee of $5*
Children: *Not appropriate for children*
Open: *All year*

Each traveler has a different concept of what the ideal vacation should entail. For those who prefer vacations where they can settle into their own apartment, prepare meals at their leisure, and live autonomously, the Quiet Cannon Lodgings are a delightful option.

The Quiet Cannon Lodgings consist of two apartments located in a contemporary, weathered-shingle building at the end of a cul-de-sac on Cannon Beach. They are surrounded by a grove of pine trees, flower beds, and mature plantings. The units are spacious, with large kitchens (loaded with modern conveniences), separate bedrooms with queen beds, and living rooms with fireplaces. Those who enjoy cooking out-of-doors will appreciate the barbecue. The interior decor is contemporary, yet very simple — perhaps this is best, as it does not detract from the views through the walls of picture windows. Best of all, the apartments overlook Ecola (meaning big fish or whale) Creek, which flows into the Pacific just beyond. The larger and more expensive of the two units faces the creek and ocean, while the somewhat smaller one has views of the creek and sand dunes. They both share a long patio, offering yet another way to enjoy this lovely setting.

The apartments' location is what especially endears guests to the Quiet Cannon Lodgings. They can step out the door and immediately sink their toes into the soft sand and explore in any direction. (A small sign attached to the house reminds guests to clean the sand off their dogs before heading back inside). Many guests and their dogs like to take a swim in the fresh waters of the creek or go off in search of ocean life harbored in the tidal pools. One of the more popular excursions is to follow the beach down to the town center and walk back along the quiet side streets. Others are content to relax by the ocean and try their hand at flying a kite — which seems to be a popular pastime in these parts.

While the Hoveys and Holdens greatly respect their guests' privacy, they are also very willing to recommend a favorite restaurant or activity. Al even

Oregon

compiled a 6-page brochure on some of the nearby sights and attractions. Some suggestions include **the Les Shirley Park (a Lewis & Clark campsite),** and **Tillamook Head.** The latter choice is part of the **Ecola State Park,** just two miles north of Cannon Beach. The views that lie along this section of the **Oregon Coast Trail** are memorable, but dogs will probably be more interested in sniffing out the little critters that sometimes poke their heads up from behind the craggy rocks.

Coos Bay Manor

955 South Fifth Street
Coos Bay, Oregon 97420
(800) 269-1224, (541) 269-1224
Internet: http://www.virtualcity.com/ons/or/c/orc360/.htm

Innkeeper: *Patricia Williams*
Rooms: *5 doubles*
Rates: *$65-75 (B&B)*
Payment: *DSC, MC and VISA*
Dogs: *Well-mannered dogs are welcome, but they must get along with the resident cat. There is an outdoor dog run for dogs who prefer sleeping outside.*
Children: *Welcome; not appropriate for children under the age of 4*
Open: *All year*

We have driven *through* Coos Bay a number of times over the years, but we never thought to stop and spend the night, as we were always heading further north along the coast. It turns out that Coos Bay is an interesting place. It dates back to 1854 and is best known for having the largest deep-water port along the Oregon coast. As a result of its size and its central location, the port is also the largest shipper of timber and timber-related products anywhere in the country. While there is always plenty of activity in port, and huge trucks rumbling along the main roads, there are also lovely neighborhoods in this bustling town. Just before leaving the southern end of Coos Bay, visitors can make a turn west and head up the hill into a quiet, residential neighborhood lined with gracious homes and cottages. Many of the largest and most historic of these buildings were commissioned by wealthy lumber barons at the turn of the century. The Coos Bay Manor is one such home.

There is no sign announcing the Coos Bay Manor, but armed with the address and a good description, it was not hard to find it. Set on a knoll, this gracious manor house is bedecked with wisteria and surrounded by beautiful gardens. This historic Colonial-style house was built in 1912 by two Finnish brothers, the Nerdrums, who worked for one of the local lumber companies. Today, guests will discover it has been nicely restored and is now listed on the National Register of Historic Places. Patricia showed us the black and white picture of the original house. Her initial thought after purchasing the house was to keep it basically the way she had found it. Then she discovered the old photograph and realized all of the work that really should be done to bring it back to its former stature.

She was just the woman to do it too — a friendly and vivacious redhead who seems to have unlimited amounts of energy. We met her in the grand foyer. As we looked around, it was clear to us that her restoration has been a total success. The highlight in here is the central staircase that rises to an open-air banister edging the entire second floor. Patricia, accompanied by her friendly black cat, gave us the grand tour. We started in the living room, where guests were relaxing on the couch in front of the fireplace. Behind it was a long table set with a huge vase of roses picked from the garden. A baby grand piano occupies one end of this formal space, while at the other end an archway leads into the dining room. As with all the other rooms in the house, high ceilings and hand-carved paneling add architectural interest. Many B&Bs have a large communal table set up for meals, which is fine if the mix of guests is a good one. We like the individual tables in here, as they afford breakfast eaters a little more privacy. The expanded Continental meal might include such options as Belgian waffles, pancakes topped with berries, an omelet, and an assortment of breads and muffins. Fresh huckleberries are often available, depending on whether or not the hostess has had time to go out and pick them.

After our tour of the first floor, we climbed the staircase to the bedrooms. Our first stop was in the yellow-hued Country Room that occupies the front corner of the house. The brass bed looked especially appealing with its thick featherbed and handmade quilt. When we stopped to admire the delicate embroidered flowers edging the pillow cases and sheets, Patricia modestly told us she had done the handwork. Off in a corner rests a spinning wheel. The Country Room and Garden Room next door are the only two bedrooms to share a bathroom. This bathroom is a large converted closet that is now fashioned with French blue marbled walls that match the room next door.

The Garden Room overlooks the rhododendrons in the back yard and is favored, for some reason, by women traveling alone. We can understand the appeal, as a crisp white handkerchief-patterned duvet covers this featherbed and a white gauze quarter-canopy frames it — the effect is serene. White wicker furniture forms a small sitting area under the windows. Our next stop was the Cattle Baron's Room, a totally masculine space with a bear skin stretched across one entire wall (it must have been some bear) and a coyote skin along another. There are all sorts of books in here, along with Native American portraits and artifacts. The good-sized bathroom is private and also has attractive marbleized accents.

A favorite room for romantics is the Victorian Room, with its canopied bed and plenty of lace and frills. A sitting area, set near the window, overlooks the front yard. The bathroom in here is virtually the same as it was back in the early 1900s. This large space was opulent for the time, and still has the original wallpaper, oversized bathtub, and fixtures. The rose theme in the wallpaper is carried through to the antique dressing table, which contains a small dish of soaps, shampoos, and lotions that are all accented in various hues of pink. The Colonial Room is perfect for people who need two beds. This room has a pair of four-poster bedsteads covered with simple white spreads. Guests look out these windows onto a pair of huge redwood trees. The small bathroom is situated just outside the door. Its brass basin and marble countertop were salvaged from a friend's house that, unfortunately, burned down. Patricia appreciates details and even showed us where the basin has been worn down from years of use.

French doors from the second-floor landing open to a roof deck, where guests are welcome to sit and take their breakfast, or perhaps, on a clear evening, watch the stars. After a hearty morning repast, most people are ready to head out for the day. Extensive exist in some of the local state parks. Our first choice is the **Sunset Bay State Park**. Here, dogs are welcome to visit the sandy beach, or perhaps set out along the three-mile trail leading to the **Shore Acres State Park**. This was once owned by a gentleman who planted the area with exotic plants from all over the world. There is another path that leads from here down to **Simpson Beach**. Another popular option is to head north to the **Oregon Dune National Recreation Area**, where mountainous sand dunes provide a wonderful outlet for romping dogs and frolicking children.

Odell Lake Lodge

P.O. Box 72
Crescent Lake, Oregon 97425
(541) 433-2540

Hosts: *John, Janet, and Kelly Milandin*
Rooms: *8 doubles, 17 cabins*
Rates: *Doubles $38-52 (EP), Cabins $55-200 (EP)*
Payment: *MC and VISA*
Dogs: *Welcome in the cabins only. Limit of one pet per cabin at $5 per night. Dogs must be leashed at all times and are not allowed on the cross-country ski trails.*
Children: *Welcome*
Open: *All year*

Odell Lake is one of the largest natural lakes in Oregon. Formed by a glacier thousands of years ago, today it encompasses 3,800 acres and is over 280 feet deep. Mackinaw and native rainbow trout thrive along with Kokanee salmon in these cold waters. Anyone who happens to fall in while fishing will just as quickly hop right out again. We followed a one-lane road along the lake for a short distance before reaching the lodge. Alhough it was late October and there was not another diversion in the area for miles, the Odell Lake Lodge was bustling with adults, children, and a few dogs — all enjoying the warm fall weather. Children were riding their bicycles along the quiet back road, while others could be seen walking the path that skirts along the shoreline. The faint smell of wood smoke was everywhere.

The main lodge is a neat, old-fashioned place, with a dark wood exterior and inviting front porch. This is the centerpiece for the small community, as guests and visitors come here both to enjoy one another's company and to purchase everything from fishing licenses and tackle to drinks and candy. We especially liked the great room, with its light pine walls and big beams. The focal point, though, is the huge stone fireplace that comprises most of the far wall, except for the small windows revealing views of the lake. A lending library of books, games, and puzzles fills two other walls of built-in shelves. Comfortable overstuffed couches and chairs are set everywhere. When we arrived, many of the guests were either reading, working on a puzzle, or sorting through the fishing books while New Age music played softly in the background.

Off in another wing of the lodge, there is a small restaurant. It is equally light and airy, and is privy to some of the best lake views, through a long wall of windows. The meals are all home cooked. The dinner menu has a little something for everyone, with steak and shrimp, pork chops, chicken and mushroom Alfredo, and shrimp scampi topping the list of entrées. A well thought out children's menu is just as reasonably priced. Among the most popular aspects of this hearty affair are the fresh fruit pies that are offered for dessert.

We liked the option of using the restaurant, but the cabins also contain fully-equipped kitchens. We suggest planning ahead and bringing enough supplies for the duration of one's stay — remembering, though, that great food is always available at the lodge. The cabins can be rustic, although there are a few exceptions. The most desirable accommodations line the bluff overlooking the lake (#6-8, 10, 12, 16, and 17); the second tier of cabins backs up to the children's play area, which might appeal to some parents. The cabins can sleep anywhere from 2-16 people. The most common configuration consists of a double bed with bunk beds in either one or two separate rooms, and sleep sofas in the living rooms (when there are living rooms).

Cabins #1-4 are the smallest, and are capable of housing four people — a very close foursome. One small bedroom has a double bed and a bunk bed, while the kitchen/sitting room contains just enough space for a wood stove, table, and a few chairs. Couples traveling with a dog would find any of these smaller cabins to be just fine. If we were to pick one of the cabins as our favorite, it would be #10, as it is newer than the rest and is probably the best designed. Two bedrooms contain queen beds, while the living room is outfitted with a pair of sofa beds. What we like most, though, is the bay window overlooking the lake, and its private lakeside deck. Cabin #12 is huge, and rambles all over the place. This would be a good choice for extended families who would like to stay together. Regardless of one's final choice, all guest cabins have fully-equipped kitchens, private bathrooms, linens, and plenty of firewood for the wood stoves or fireplaces. Barbecues are also available for outdoor cooking.

Not too surprisingly, we found that people and their dogs weren't spending all that much time in their cabins. As we mentioned, they were riding bikes, playing down by the stream, and heading off into the forest for leisurely hikes. The small children's play area down by the lake was very popular, especially the slide and swing sets made out of old logs. Those who may have forgotten something can probably rent it here. Water-oriented rentals range from canoes and row boats to 18-foot motor boats. Mountain bikes are also available. In the winter months, people come here to cross-country ski.

While dogs are not allowed on the groomed, cross-country ski trails, they are welcome on the back-country trails. There are snow shoes and skis available to rent, as well as affable instructors. Guests soon discover that the lodge lends itself to days of relaxation interspersed with explorations of this incredibly beautiful mountainous terrain. There is plenty of space for canines to roam once they get away from the cottages.

Throughout the **Deschutes National Forest** and **Diamond Peaks Wilderness Area,** there are countless trails that allow dogs. One popular option, beginning right at the lake, leads hikers to a pair of beautiful, high mountain lakes — **Yoran** or **Diamond View** lakes. The **Pacific Coast Trail** also wends through this region. Those who are interested can pick up a portion of it near Odell Lake and hike up to any of the **Rosary Lakes**.

Inn at Arch Rock

P.O. Box 251
70 Northwest Sunset Street
Depoe Bay, Oregon 97341
(541) 765-2560

Innkeepers: Greg and Susan Lyons
Rooms: 11 doubles, 1 house
Rates: $78-98 (B&B), House $130 (B&B)
Payment: DSC, MC, and VISA
Dogs: Welcome in rooms 5-8 with a $10 fee
Children: Welcome; children under 12 years of age are free of charge
Open: All year

    Set on the cliffs looking back toward Depoe Bay, the Inn at Arch Rock is part inn and part unconventional motel. The main inn is a traditional dormered Cape, set on a quiet side street, well off busy Highway 101. After walking into the small reception area and seeing the steep narrow staircase leading to the inn's guest rooms, we suspected that guests traveling with dogs would probably not be prime candidates for these compact spaces. We were instead directed out to either the cottage or the three-room "motel." We thought we would give the motel rooms a chance — after all, we had been pleasantly surprised on plenty of other occasions.
    This time was no exception. From the exterior, this is an attractive building bedecked with white shingles and a farmer's porch. The interiors are even more attractive, with hardwood floors and wood-paneled walls that imbue them with some character. A chintz valance above the window or an ivy-patterned wallpaper help enhance the overall decor. What might once have been one large bedroom, is now neatly broken up into a sleeping area, sitting room, and breakfast nook. A queen beds lies under a window toward the rear of the room. A sofa bed and rattan chairs form an intimate sitting area facing the ocean; in another there is a small breakfast table flanked by two ladder back chairs. A series of windows not only allows the sun to permeate these spaces, but also reveals spectacular water views. A tiny kitchenette is surprisingly well stocked, including a large basket filled with microwave popcorn and coffee and tea. Drinks and other perishables may be stored in the small refrigerator. Each morning, guests are offered a simple Continental repast of homemade muffins and cinnamon rolls.

Oregon

Our favorite room of the three is Room 8, which is decorated around an English country theme. The decor in Rooms 6 and 7 is not as sophisticated, but it is attractive nonetheless. Guests with dogs can also stay in the quaint one-bedroom cottage, which can accommodate four people by utilizing both the queen bed and sofa bed. It is set apart from all the other units, which might make it even more appealing to families with dogs — they don't need to worry as much about an inadvertent peep late at night.

What most people remember about the Inn at Arch Rock are the views and the sounds of the crashing surf. Just in front of the inn is a small lawn — a nice place for relaxing when the surf isn't too wild. The cliffs are also quite famous for their spouting horns. This occurs when the water rushes into small vertical crevices and sprays up to 50 feet in the air. People come to Depoe Bay just to watch this natural phenomenon. When near the cliffs, we recommend that dogs be leashed. It is fun to take them for a walk along these cliffs into town; but visitors need to be careful about the sporadic spouts, as they can unnerve and completely soak both human and beast.

Two miles north of Depoe Bay is **Fogarty Creek State Park**, that has more than 150 oceanside acres. The park offers some nice picnic sites and walking trails, but many come here to watch the sea lions. The **Beverly Beach State Park** also welcomes dogs and has easy nature walks through the forest, as well as an expansive beach with intriguing tide pools. Further south, visitors and their dogs are welcome to investigate the 400 acres around **South Beach** or the 230 acres around **Ona Beach**.

Salishan Lodge

P.O. Box 118
Highway 101
Gleneden Beach, Oregon 97388
(800) 452-2300, (541) 764-3600, Fax: (541) 764-3510
Internet: http://www.travelweb.com

General Manager: *Stuart Hurst*
Rooms: *205 doubles*
Rates: *Doubles $119-269 (EP)*
Payment: *AE, DSC, MC, and VISA*
Dogs: *Welcome with a $15 daily fee*
Children: *Welcome (cribs, cots, and baby-sitters are available)*
Open: *All year*

The Salishan Lodge is the one of the most luxurious resorts along the Oregon coast — it also happens to welcome dogs. Its dramatic oceanside setting, overlooking Siletz Bay, amid 700 acres of landscaped and natural surroundings, puts this resort on our short list of highly recommended places to stay in the Northwest. Although the resort is expansive, a distinct feeling of privacy pervades. Guest rooms lie in villas set into hillsides, and are mostly linked by covered footbridges and paths that are reminiscent of ancient Japanese palace gardens. A wending drive leads guests past rivers and waterfalls, through fir, spruce, hemlock, and cedar groves, until they reach their villa. (There are eight guest chambers per villa.) Contemporary lines, coupled with weathered-wood siding, cause the villas to blend with the surrounding landscape.

This feeling of seclusion continues inside, as each room is not only well designed, but also soundproofed. Many guests will be thoroughly impressed with the magnificent views revealed through the walls of sliding-glass doors. Not all windows overlook the bay; some pan out over dense forests or the verdant golf course. Many of these rooms contain hemlock-beamed cathedral ceilings and walls painted in subtle earth tones that produce an atmosphere of understated elegance and character. Lithographs by artists of the Northwest are limited to two per room. Although we would have enjoyed seeing more, they deftly capture the unique rugged beauty of this idyllic place.

The newer Siletz Bay rooms are the most distinctive guest chambers, offering exceptional bay views, separate sitting areas, and stone fireplaces. The Salishan Chieftain rooms contain slightly less formal furnishings, but similar views. Those who are more interested in spending their money on their recreational pursuits, rather than on their room, may request the simplest and least expensive Salishan rooms. These spaces do not contain separate sitting areas, but in all other respects are well appointed and furnished. The decor is very attractive but not especially noteworthy, except in the Siletz Bay rooms, where everything is upgraded to create a more luxurious setting. In all cases, though, every effort has been made to maximize the views; so whether guests are lying in bed or sitting on the couch in front of the fire, they can enjoy the lovely vistas. The extra large bathrooms received special attention, with their Corian sinks, whirlpool tubs, baskets of toiletries, and separate showers.

The resort's amenities are bountiful. Golfers will appreciate the challenging, 18-hole, par 72 golf links (built in the Scottish tradition on land reclaimed from the ocean). The three indoor and one outdoor tennis court will appeal to some, while others may prefer working out using the exercise equipment in the Fitness Center. This complex also houses an indoor swimming pool, hydrotherapy pool, saunas, and circuit weight training. Children will enjoy the game room and expansive playground.

Dogs, on the other hand, will thoroughly relish exploring the **three-mile long beach**. **Digging for clams and mussels**, searching for seashells, and watching migrating whales are favorite activities for human counterparts. The resort even furnishes comprehensive maps of the area's **nature trails** and **running loops** for guests to investigate with their canine cohorts.

Oregon

It is easy to work up an appetite, and even easier to satisfy it in one of the resort's five restaurants. One of the most popular meals is the famous Sunday brunch, which is presented in the Cedar Tree restaurant. Guests may select from a seemingly endless list of items, which can including Eggs Benedict; Belgian waffles; apple smoked salmon hash; sourdough, buckwheat or buttermilk pancakes; and authentic English bangers (sausages). The Dining Room, situated on three levels, is the most formal of the restaurants, and serves an extensive array of seasonal native seafoods and game. We munched on the crispy sourdough bread while perusing the extensive menu. Our choices included the double lamb chops topped with roasted garlic and peppers; veal loin with a ragoût of woodland mushrooms; the Tillamook cheddar cheese fondue with sourdough bread; and the Oregon seafood soup with oysters, baby shrimp, smoked salmon, and Dungeness crab. Subtle burgundy and mauve tones, coupled with the picturesque views of Siletz Bay and the surrounding forest, set the mood for a memorable dining experience. For simpler fare, there is the informal Sun Room, which is an especially sunny spot in the morning.

It is difficult to sum up this terrific resort in just a few paragraphs, except to say that prospective guests truly need more than a day or two to fully appreciate the beauty and overall peacefulness of the Salishan Lodge.

Jot's Resort

P.O. Box J
Highway 101 at the Rogue River
Gold Beach, Oregon 97444
(800) FOR-JOTS, (541) 247-6676, Fax: (541) 247-6716
Internet: http://www.jotsresort.com

Owner: *Virginia McKinney*
Rooms: *98 doubles, 3 suites, 20 cottages*
Rates: *Doubles $90 (EP), Suites and cottages $120-300 (EP)*
Payment: *AE, DC, DSC, MC, and VISA*
Dogs: *Welcome in the ground floor units with a daily fee of $10*
Children: *Welcome (cribs and cots are available)*
Open: *All year*

Jot's Resort has been around for over 20 years, and with good reason. It not only occupies a portion of the Rogue River's northern banks but is also a great base for fine fishing further upstream. Jot's is easy to find — just before crossing the expansive bridge into Gold Beach, look for the sign and a rather steep driveway leading down to a small complex of one- and two-story buildings. The reception area and tackle shop are situated in the middle of this compound, opposite an outdoor swimming pool and an indoor spa and pool. As we arrived, we found an enthusiastic group of guests preparing to head up the Rogue River by way of jet boat.

The accommodations at Jot's Resort are basically glorified motor lodge rooms. Located in several buildings at the mouth of the river, all guest rooms overlook the water as well as the town of Gold Beach. The decor in each room is comprised of Danish-style furnishings and neutral color schemes. Each guest chamber is outfitted with a cable television, a direct-dial telephone, and a large bathroom. In each bedroom, an additional vanity sits just outside the bathroom. Sliding glass doors open to porches or decks.

A separate, two-story building offers more modern accommodations with an enhanced list of amenities. These are especially suitable for families, as they contain living rooms with cathedral ceilings and fireplaces, kitchens for preparing meals (perhaps the catch of fish from the day), and skylit lofts that afford additional sleeping space. The newer rooms also have private decks and equally fine water views. Some of the best features, however, are found outside, where the distant sounds of the crashing waves combine with the sight of shore birds, sounds of sea lions, and the pulsing lighthouse beacon.

For us, the accommodations are almost secondary to the numerous diversions available in and around Jot's. In addition to fishing, there is beach combing, digging for clams, Windsurfing, whale watching, or crabbing. Anglers come prepared to catch the fish of the season, which includes salmon from May to November, cutthroat trout during the summer, and giant sturgeon and steelhead year round. The resort's extensive sport shop is brimming with everything one might require. The folks running the marina have plenty of rental boats, but they can also arrange for guided river expeditions and deep sea fishing charters. Another favorite pastime is riding the jet boats along the Rogue River.

Dogs who grow weary of pacing the banks looking for waterfowl and aquatic life will be entertained with some of the local day hikes. The neighboring **Siskiyou National Forest** is just south of Gold Beach. Within this park is the **Chetco Gorge Trail**, which leads hikers and their canines along the Chetco River to Eagle Creek. There are even places along the way for swimming, which will certainly appeal to furry friends. The **Samuel H. Boardman State Park**, also south of Gold Beach, has 1,400 acres of hiking trails that allow leashed dogs. When guests return at the end of the day, they should probably park their dogs for a nap and then take a swim in either the outdoor heated pool or the indoor pool and spa.

Whatever the day's diversions, guests need look no further for their evening meal than the Rod 'n' Reel, a favorite eatery among visitors and locals alike. The restaurant provides an intimate setting and an extensive menu. Salmon, jumbo prawns, and the Admirals' Delight, top the seafood menu, while prime rib and filet mignon highlight other portions. After dinner, we enjoy heading back to the room, opening the sliding glass doors, and letting in the sounds and the smells of the sea while we drift off to sleep.

Clear Creek Farm

P.O. Box 737
Halfway, Oregon 97834
(541) 742-2238, Fax: (541) 742-5175
E-mail: baphillips@igc.org
Internet: http://www.triax.com/granthbb/GH_html/home.html

Hosts: *Barbara Phillips, Mike and Rose Curless*
Rooms: *4 doubles, 2 cottages*
Rates: *Doubles/Cottages $60 (B&B), $10 per child, $16-19 per teenager*
Payment: *MC and VISA*
Dogs: *Welcome*
Children: *Welcome*
Open: *All year*

Anyone unfamiliar with northeastern Oregon may be surprised to find a climate very different from that of its western counterpart. While western Oregon gets an abundance of rain and cool ocean winds, the eastern region is much hotter and drier, because the Cascades obstruct the path of the ocean storms. Clear Creek Farm is in the far reaches of northeastern Oregon, just a short distance from Idaho. The closet town is a hamlet known as Halfway — an appropriate name for a town that used to be the halfway point for the stagecoach that ran between Pine Town and Carson. Today's visitors will more likely view it a bit differently, as the farm and town lie halfway between Upper Hell's Canyon and the Eagle Cap Wilderness, two spectacular natural recreation areas.

Clear Creek Farm is a real working ranch, and has been for well over 100 years. Bison roam across its 160 acres, which are also planted with orchards and gardens fed by ponds and a year-round stream. In the spring, the acreage is dotted with colorful wildflowers. This is a rustic place, which tries to reacquaint people with a simpler lifestyle and the beauty of nature. As with most ranches, Clear Creek Farm consists of an old-fashioned farmhouse and various other rustic outbuildings. While guests traveling with a dog may stay in any of the accommodations, we prefer the two outbuildings because of their additional privacy.

One of these is really a modified, open-space barn. This not only sounds unique, it is unique. The artist who built the barn designed it to be rustic and intimate, and in keeping with its surroundings. One of the two bedrooms contains both a king and a queen bed, while another offers a pair of bunks. Guests who stay here also have views of the ponds and mountains from their covered porch. Barbara said guests *think* they will rock on the porch to enjoy these views, but the *reality* is there are so many other pleasant diversions that few return to their room until after nightfall. Another popular guest chamber lies just behind the barn, in a second converted building containing a queen bedstead and two bunks. A modern bathhouse is immaculate, supplying guests with plenty of hot, running water.

These outbuildings are closed in the winter months, so those who venture out this way between October and April will stay in the cozy farmhouse. It contains four guest bedrooms, which are named after their predominant color — blue, pink, etc. Guests with children might be interested in the extra bedroom, which contains both a pair of bunk beds and a crib and is often used as a nursery. The early American antiques are simple and attractive, as are the other collectibles and furnishings. The bathroom is shared and is always clean and tidy.

Everyone looks forward to the full country breakfast, which Barbara laughingly describes as "one hell of a breakfast." In the summer, it is cooked in the unusual, open-air summer kitchen just off the back of the farmhouse. It includes homemade breads, such as sourdough and cinnamon, eggs, bacon, and buffalo sausage. Dutch babies, delicious puffed pancakes baked in a casserole, are the house specialty. Fresh fruits, berries, and vegetables from the farm and its orchards are always featured. (The farm is especially famous for its delicious peaches.) In the afternoons, freshly squeezed lemonade and other refreshing libations are made available to guests returning from their day's adventures. The morning meal is so good, we asked about lunches and dinners. Barbara told us they now offer a *Guests of the Ranch* package that includes a lunch and dinner, served at guests' convenience, for an extra charge of $20. (The *Guests of the Ranch* package also entitles participants to take advantage of all aspects of ranch life, if they are so inclined. This might encompass everything from a simple chore like feeding the chickens to something a little more complicated, such as vaccinating the buffalo.) Barbara also mentioned that there are several good restaurants in town, and one exceptional eatery that is well worth splurging on at least once during a visit.

With acres to explore and so much to do, guests who opt for a week-long vacation at the farm rarely run out of things to do. There is a **creek for fishing** and a pond for swimming. Of course, **long walks** and hikes are always a highly recommended activity. The resident dogs like to accompany hikers on these adventures, as well. Children love helping milk the goat, pick berries, or visiting with the other farm animals.

Those interested in venturing further afield will discover that the famous **Hell's Canyon** is just a short distance away. There are also white-water rafting and jet boat trips, an abundance of steelhead, sturgeon, and trout to be caught, interesting auto tours, backpacking, and extensive horseback riding trails available throughout the region. The climate ranges from desert-like conditions on the canyon floor to cool alpine air with crystal blue lakes at the higher elevations. At the end of a busy day, it is always nice to return to the Clear Creek Farm's low-key, homey atmosphere, either to watch the setting sun or to relax in the rejuvenating hot tub.

Pine Valley Lodge
Halfway Supper Club

P.O. Box 712
1563 North Main Street
Halfway, Oregon 97834
(541) 742-2027

Innkeepers: *Dale Beatty and Babette Russell*
Rooms: *6 doubles*
Rates: *$55-65 (B&B)*
Payment: *Personal checks*
Dogs: *Welcome with notice and approval*
Children: *Welcome (a crib is available)*
Open: *All year*

If the *Hells Canyon Journal* could give the Halfway Supper Club a "four forks up" rating, then we felt it was worth investigating too. Actually, our curiosity was initially sparked by the Clear Creek Farm's recommendation, when Barbara Phillips told us it serves some of the finest food around. Little did we know it also has six extraordinarily unusual guest rooms.

From the exterior, the Pine Valley Lodge looks like many of those western lodges lining the highways — plenty of natural wood, wraparound porches, and steep roofs. We thought the array of antlers displayed over the front door made the place look especially authentic. New arrivals can just step inside, put their Stetson on the hat rack, and turn around to an unusual place filled with an eclectic, yet sophisticated, mix of furniture, collectibles, and art. Hardwood floors and naturally finished wood walls support the beamed ceilings in the great room. This chamber is filled with a wonderful assortment of antiques, ranging from classic armchairs to rustic sofas, all covered with bright fabrics reflecting Native American and western-style prints. It is difficult to know where to look — there is almost too much to take in visually. A mounted fish hangs on one wall next to a rip saw blade, while on another are a pair of fishing rods. A milk painted hutch is nestled against another wall, alongside a lightly stained oak table topped by a lamp. The lamp's base is also a little unusual, as it is formed by figurines of a man and woman entwined in dance. Games abound, including backgammon, Mah-Jong, and cards, as well as stacks of books covering a myriad of subjects.

Keeping all this in mind, it is the use of color that galvanizes this place. The ceilings in the great room are a cranberry red, as is one wall in the intimate dining room. The other pine-paneled wall in here is painted a deep teal reminiscent of the tropics. Draped dining room tables and chairs don't always match, but neither do the candle holders, which range from crystal to silver.

It doesn't matter — it all somehow works beautifully. Guests should note that even they must make reservations for dinner, as there is limited seating, and limited hours — the dining room is open from 6 to 8 p.m. The appetizers might include a French onion soup made with sweet onions, white wine, and brandy, or Babette's tomato and basil brochette. There are also plenty of meat dishes on the menu. The hefty New York strip steak comes in either 14- or 16-ounce portions, or guests may try the more diminutive filet mignon. Both arrive grilled and served with twice-baked potatoes and fresh vegetables. Lamb chops are marinated in lemon and rosemary and then grilled, as well. There is also a fish of the day, and if guests catch their own, Babette will be happy to prepare it for them. Diners should take care not to be fooled by the whiskey cake; it is actually loaded with chocolate. Others might prefer the more delicate crème caramel — Cuban style.

After a meal of this magnitude, the short walk to the bedroom is a welcome relief. Guests should ignore for a moment that they share a single bathroom, because the unique bed chambers more than compensate for this. One of our favorites is the Bayou Room. The highlight is a massive four-poster bed with carved-wood, snowy egrets seemingly poised for flight from the tops of the finials. Royal blue, emerald green, and dusty rose all combine — on a lampshade, on a rustic armoire, and in the fabrics covering the pillows. The Western Room features one wall painted a pale green, while the eaves are an eye-catching hue of yellow. A day bed, covered with a Hudson Bay blanket and intricately patterned pillows, rests under one of these steep eaves. Native American patterned blankets cover both the oak framed bed and an old armchair. Each room is a fascinating study of color and artistic presentation, especially in one bedroom, whose walls and ceilings are painted a turquoise blue and stenciled with flowering hibiscus. Light and dark woods combine to create the unusual antique bureaus. Down comforters grace every bed, except in the summer, when white chenille spreads are substituted.

In the morning, Babette cooks an extensive breakfast that includes her fresh breads and preserves. This will give guests enough energy to take their canine cohorts out to explore the surrounding territory. Halfway is located at the gateway to the famous **Hell's Canyon**. From here, it is easy to access the nearly three quarters of a million acres of trails, scenery, and isolation. Deciding which part to investigate first is up to guests and their dogs, but wherever they end up, there will undoubtedly be some bighorn sheep, elk, bear, and even bobcats and cougars. Rattlesnakes and other reptiles also inhabit the area — so we advise treading carefully. Visitors and their dogs can head on up to Cornucopia and take hikes through the two million-acre **Wallowa-Whitman National Forest**. This is relatively undisturbed and wild countryside that appeals to most anyone who has a sense of adventure... and we have to say, the Pine Valley Lodge provides the perfect base from which to explore it.

Columbia Gorge Hotel

4000 Westcliff Drive
Hood River, Oregon 97031
(800) 345-1921, (541) 386-5566, Fax: (541) 387-5414
E-mail: cghotel@gorge.net, Internet: http://www.gorge.net/lodging/cghotel/

Owner: *Boyd Graves*
Rooms: *42 doubles, 4 suites*
Rates: *Doubles $150-270 (B&B), Suites $295-365 (B&B)*
Payment: *AE, DSC, MC, and VISA*
Dogs: *Well behaved dogs are welcome; must be leashed in the public areas*
Children: *Welcome (cribs, high chairs, and babysitters are available)*
Open: *All year*

Simon Benson, a Portland lumber baron, built the Columbia Gorge Hotel in 1921. He thought it would be the perfect destination for those traveling along the Columbia Gorge Scenic Highway. He wasn't the first person to be enamored by these cliffs or the gorge, though. Robert Rand had discovered this picturesque region some 17 years prior to Benson's arrival, and had constructed a summer resort. Moreover, Rand decided to give the hotel a name in keeping with its Native American meeting ground status — the Wah Swin Gwin Hotel. When Benson purchased the property from Rand, he tore down the existing structure, but left the grounds, trails, and landscaping intact. We like to think of the Columbia Gorge Hotel as an amalgamation of both these men's visions. The majestic hotel is all Benson, while the estate-like setting is vintage Rand.

This combination of internal and external features attracted a renowned patronage for many years, with such notables as Presidents Roosevelt and Coolidge staying here, as well as actresses Myrna Loy, Jane Powell, and Clara Bow. Rudolph Valentino also became such a frequent guest that the management eventually named a room after him. In keeping with Benson's vision, this Spanish-style structure did become a landmark property. Unfortunately, even with all its notoriety, the Columbia Gorge Hotel eventually fell on hard times. After being sold some years later, it was converted into a nursing home. Finally, in the 1980s, Boyd Graves purchased the hotel and began a re-restoration process that continues to this day.

Through Graves' extensive efforts, the hotel once again achieved landmark status and is listed in the National Register of Historic Places. The open lobby is impressive, with high ceilings, lavish draperies framing the windows, and vintage 1920s' furnishings. Gilt-edged mirrors rest above long tables set with fresh flower arrangements. Sofas and chairs are grouped for private conver-sations in the Valentino Lounge, where the marble fireplace is kept well-stoked during the cold winter months. The most popular tables are those near the floor-to-ceiling windows that overlook the gorge. Once settled in here, most guests are quite content to wait awhile for their table in the adjacent dining room.

The Columbia River Court dining room is an equally elegant space — especially at night, when brass chandeliers and candles illuminate these inviting chambers. One of our favorite sections is the elongated enclosed porch, which is graced with walls of windows. The most desirable tables are those set under these windows, or just across from them. The largest of the dining areas is also lovely, but patrons would have to strain their necks to achieve the same views. Fortunately, everyone, regardless of their table, receives the same fine service and delectable food. This seasonally- changing menu offered appetizers that included a shrimp and cilantro tart; a crèpinette of pheasant made with wild mushrooms and served with a walnut and sage crème fraîche; or the house smoked salmon risotto. Entrées ranged from the scallops in a huckleberry and lavender vinaigrette and loin of venison encrusted with pistachios to the Pacific spot prawns sautéed in lobster oil with cilantro, tomatoes, and lemon zest. The dessert specialty is the apple tart — Columbia Gorge style. Local apples are blended with a rich caramel and then baked in a sweet puff pastry. It is then flambéed at the table with orange licquer— a fitting end to a most memorable meal.

After dinner it is easy to linger awhile, but eventually it is time to head upstairs for bed. We could have walked or taken the modern elevator, but we preferred using the old-fashioned elevator that must be operated by a hotel staff person. A walk down these historic halls reveals little change from the days of Benson, and after opening the bedroom doors, we were pleased to discover that this feeling also permeated the guest chambers. Each bedroom is fashioned with formal combinations of deep greens, blues, and maroons reflected in the floral fabrics that cover the traditional furniture. Hand-carved canopy beds and fireplaces highlight the specialty rooms, but generally, guests find simpler brass or two-poster bedsteads, a simple chest of drawers, an armoire, and little else in the way of decoration. Modern amenities are also quite minimal — color televisions and telephones. The spacious tiled bathrooms are a bit old-fashioned but they are also spotless, and the baskets of toiletries are thoughtful extras. We especially appreciated the rose and handmade chocolates laid on the pillow each night. Moreover, we found that the strong historic appeal, coupled with the unparalleled views, provide an ambiance that is hard to match. Each of the rooms overlooking the gorge is blessed with a slightly different perspective of the river. Some of our favorite chambers are in the west wing near the waterfall. Guests can open the window at night and feel the breezes, while listening to water cascade over the falls to the river below. Families may reserve the suites (two bedrooms connected by a bathroom) that overlook the mature gardens situated on the opposite side of the hotel.

In the morning, guests can gather the newspaper resting outside their door and head downstairs to enjoy the hotel's "World Famous Farm Breakfast" — one that is so unique its name has been trademarked. The breakfast originated at the Snoqualmie Falls Lodge over 25 years ago, but has expanded since then. As the hosts like to remind their patrons, "It's not a choice, you'll get it all." You may wish to begin with fresh fruit, and possibly an apple fritter with sugar and spice. This may be followed by oatmeal served with brown sugar and sweet cream, or possibly three farm fresh eggs. Fresh grilled trout may be substituted for the bacon, smoked pork chop, or the apple and maple-flavored sausage. We suggest taking a short break before sampling the hashed brown potatoes, baking powder biscuits with apple blossom honey, and the stack of buttermilk pancakes. Coffee or champagne are often the preferred complement to this expansive offering. Best of all, a patient canine cohort will thoroughly enjoy any leftovers.

After everyone has enjoyed breakfast, guests may wish to gather up their dogs and explore the **ten acres of lush gardens** that surround the hotel. It is a park-like setting, with wonderfully landscaped grounds, footbridges, and trails. A creek meanders through the property, eventually reaching the edge of the cliffs and dropping over 200 feet to the river below. The spectacular **Wah-Gwin-Gwin Falls** are, in themselves, reason enough to visit the hotel.

For active guests, there are a variety of things to do in the nearby area.

Windsurfing has become "the" activity of choice among the residents; but only for experts, as the winds are strong and tricky, making the board sailing rigorous and exciting. Hiking is another wonderful option for human and beast and there are plenty of trails just off Interstate 84. Down the road, west of the Hood River, is a particularly easy climb along **Tanner Creek** to the **Wahclella** Falls. Another popular option is found just south of the Bonneville Dam. This trail leads hikers a short distance to the **Wauna Point** overlooking the dam, and then on to the scenic Dublin Lake.

Hood River Hotel

102 Oak Avenue
Hood River, Oregon 97031
(800) 386-1859, (541) 386-1900, Fax: (541) 386-6090
E-mail: hrhotel@gorge.net, Internet: http://www.gorge.net/lodging/HRH

Owners: *Pasquale and Jacquie Barone*
Rooms: *32 doubles, 9 suites*
Rates: *Doubles $49-99 (EP), Suites $89-145 (EP)*
Payment: *AE, DC, DSC, MC, and VISA*
Dogs: *Welcome with a $15 daily fee*
Children: *Welcome (cribs, cots, high chairs, and baby-sitters are available)*
Open: *All year*

The Columbia River, referred to as "the Gorge," serves as a natural boundary between Oregon and Washington. This region is a haven for Windsurfing enthusiasts who flock here from across the country to challenge the high winds and squirrelly currents. Windsurfing is what initially drew Pasquale down from Canada on vacation some years ago. Once he arrived, he could think of little else but Windsurfing the Gorge. But his instincts as a developer prompted him to look past the river to the low-key town of Hood River. There he discovered the dilapidated, turn-of-the-century Mount Hood Hotel. He decided to purchase and completely restore it. In 1989, the revitalized four-story brick hotel once again opened its doors to the public.

As new arrivals walk into the reception area of the Hood River Hotel, with its original hardwood floors, detailed moldings, and Victorian antiques, they will feel a strong sense of the building's history. This light and airy chamber is blessed with an abundance of sunlight, which streams in from all over: through the French doors, through a wall of floor-to-ceiling paned windows, and through a pair of 20-foot high windows flanking the fireplace. It would seem difficult to create a sense of intimacy in such a cavernous space as this; yet an intimate effect is cleverly achieved by providing guests with cozy sitting areas broken up by a plethora of potted floor and hanging plants. The brass lamps and chandeliers cast a soft glow throughout this inviting chamber; at night, this lovely effect accentuates the teal and coral color schemes.

We checked in at the small reception area set toward the rear of this space. Since it was off season, we had our pick of guest rooms. As most visitors will quickly discover, the guest rooms vary considerably, in both size and furnishings. Turn-of-the-century reproductions are standard, whether they consist of canopy, brass, and four-poster beds, or cherry bureaus, mirrors, or dressing tables. Oriental patterned rugs accent the fir floors. Calico or chintz curtains frame the windows, which coordinate with the comforters and dust ruffles on the beds. We thought the dried flowers, whether shaped into a wreath over a bed or arranged in a vase, provided soothing accents of color, as did the rose or green painted trim. When the wind isn't blowing off the river (which is fairly rare), ceiling fans circulate the air. Heat is provided by wonderful, old fashioned radiators. The most requested rooms are those that overlook the river, but the rooms with views of the interior courtyard are also appealing. Some guests, especially families, may require more space than is found in the standard rooms; they may wish to consider the spacious suites, with their sitting areas and full kitchens. Not too surprisingly, many of the hotel's bathrooms have been created from spaces that were formerly closets.

In the evening, guests need not venture far for their meal, as fine Northern Italian cooking is as close as the hotel's lobby. We were pleased to find that Pasquale's Ristorante is as popular with the locals as it is with guests of the hotel. The casual, European atmosphere in the café revolves around the enormous mahogany bar, which is backed by glass and brass. We had difficulty choosing between the calamari sautéed in garlic, olive oil and white wine; the Pacific oysters on the half shell; or the cream cheese and pesto torta. The pasta dishes are fairly typical, ranging from the fettuccine Alfredo and spaghetti vongole to tortellini with basil, and angel hair pasta with pesto and garlic shrimp. Veal Marsala, pork and beef tenderloin, and filets of salmon or halibut, with either garlic dill or lemon dill butter tops off the main menu. In the morning, after savoring a frothy cup of cappucino, guests may sample such dishes as the eggs Florentine, a frittata, Belgian waffle, or the crêpes stuffed with Hood River spiced apples.

There are enough hills to climb in Hood River to work off any culinary indulgences. The historic Hood River train is just down the hill. A bit further, guests will spy the Windsurfers testing their prowess on the Gorge. A short drive from the hotel, there is also golf, horseback riding, and, in the wintertime, downhill skiing.

Along the road leading from Portland to Hood River are various hiking options — for both people and dogs. The closest option is the **Wygant Peak Trail**, where climbers are treated to terrific views of the surrounding area and the Gorge far below. A far more difficult climb is the trail leading up

Mount Defiance, beginning at the **Starvation Creek State Park**. The falls along the **Eagle Creek Trail** continue to lure enthusiasts of all hiking abilities (and their eager canines), as much for their spectacular chain of waterfalls as for their abundance of natural beauty. Among the more popular hiking trails are the **Deschutes River Canyon, Dog River, Old Dalles Road**, and **Buck Creek**. Each offers a different perspective of this spectacular region.

At the end of the day, return to the Hood River Hotel; let your dog take a nap; and head downstairs to the health club for a soak in the Jacuzzi or a steam in the sauna.

Jacksonville Inn

175 East California Street
Jacksonville, Oregon 97530
(800) 321-9344, (541) 899-1373,
E-mail: jvin@mind.net, Internet: http://www.mind.net/jvinn

Oregon

Hosts: *Jerry and Linda Evans*
Rooms: *8 doubles, 3 cottages*
Rates: *Doubles $80-135 (B&B), Cottages $185-225 (B&B)*
Payment: *AE, CB, DC, DSC, MC and VISA*
Dogs: *Welcome with approval in all but two cottages; owners must bring dog bed; dog must be housebroken*
Children: *Welcome (air mattresses and cribs are available)*
Open: *All year*

Jacksonville is a beautifully preserved historic town, nestled into the mountains of southern Oregon. It was founded in 1852, when the promise of gold in the surrounding hills seemed to guarantee prosperity for its residents. Fortunes were made, grand estates were constructed, wealthy merchants built stores, and government buildings were erected. Prosperity appeared to have no end. However, the veins of gold eventually dried up and many residents moved on, leaving behind their rich heritage. Today, Jacksonville has nearly 100 buildings that are a part of the National Register of Historic Places. The main street, and those immediately surrounding it, are still historically intact, giving visitors a good feeling for life as it might have been back in the 1800s. The Jacksonville Inn is no exception. It was built in 1863 by two merchants who operated it as a general store. The original two-story brick structure now houses guest rooms, a restaurant, and an excellent wine store.

We first visited the inn about six years ago. While it was attractive then, it is even more so now. One reason the Jacksonville Inn is so ideal for people traveling with dogs is that guests access the bedroom wing through a separate outside entrance. Each guest room is named after either a local or famous personality. For instance, the Peter Britt room is named after the renowned photographer who took award-winning pictures of Crater Lake. Vance Colvia was the first Bozo the Clown, and the voice behind many of the Disney cartoon caricatures. Madame Jeanne de Reboan was the operator of the town's "boarding" house.

The unique personalities and sense of history behind these names carry through into the bedrooms. Early American oak antique beds, tables, and chairs are usually featured, although our room contained a scrolled iron bed and another room down the way was outfitted with a canopy bedstead. This feeling of authentic Americana fits in well with the exposed brick walls and beamed ceilings. The decor is sophisticated, with coordinated, floral Waverly prints that are used on everything from wall treatments and comforters to the fabrics covering the armchairs and sofas. The Gin Linn room is one of our favorites, especially in the morning when the sun streams through the lace curtains into the yellow floral bedroom. Across the hall is a more masculine room, with an enormous square oak headboard and a couch covered in a sophisticated black and white print. Our bedroom was like a garden room with a green and white trellis wallpaper. The tiled bathrooms are totally modernized, and have baskets of toiletries — the Peter Britt room even offers a Jacuzzi. Extras not usually associated with historic inns include individual climate controls, direct dial telephones, and televisions tucked away in oak armoires. We also appreciated the glass ice buckets for chilling our wine, the small refrigerators for storing snacks, and the tray of fruits, cookies, and candies.

Anyone looking for a little more privacy may reserve the historic cottage set just a few blocks from the inn. Guests staying here are treated to luxurious accommodations. The lovely pencil-post canopy bed is positioned so that guests can lie in bed and still enjoy the crackling fireplace. Some may enjoy setting a peaceful mood by lighting a fire and listening to music on the stereo, while others might prefer to rent a movie and settle in for a leisurely evening in their room. The cottage's kitchenette is well stocked with supplies, and the bathroom is appointed with both a Jacuzzi and a steam shower. The Evans recently renovated two more cottages. As of this writing, even the most well-behaved canine guests were not allowed to place a paw on either of these properties. We can understand how the Evans' feel, but hope that they will welcome dogs in these luxurious abodes in the future.

Cottage guests need walk only a short distance for the delicious morning meal, served by the inn exclusively to its guests. We started with fresh fruit and coffee, with our main course options including Belgian waffles, French toast, and omelets. We finally decided upon a delicious egg, spinach, and mushroom gâteau in a puff pastry with a sherried cream sauce. A popular champagne brunch is featured on Sunday. The Jacksonville Inn's restaurant is always highly rated, and most patrons enjoy the cozy ambiance found in the basement. The gold-flecked mortar in the sandstone and brick walls creates an intimate atmosphere, which is enhanced by a roaring fireplace and candlelight flickering from the elegantly set tables. The multi-course meal may be accompanied by any of the 700 wines from the expansive cellar. The menu is primarily Continental and quite extensive, featuring a good selection of vegetarian and heart-healthy foods, along with more tantalizing offerings such as filet mignon with a bernaise sauce (the house specialty), prime rib, and veal marsala.

Jacksonville is a great town for leisurely walks, and dogs will feel right at home. (We even saw a couple of canines hanging out inside one of the old-fashioned bars.) The famed Britt Music and Art Festival is held here each year in July. Day hikes are another popular option, especially for those willing to drive south a short distance to **Applegate Lake**, which is situated in the Rogue River National Forest. Hikers and their dogs can follow the **Grouse Creek Trail** or take a different route along the trail that edges Applegate Lake. One final option is the **Little Squaw Trail**, which wends around both Little and Big Squaw Lakes. Whether people and their dogs decide to investigate the sights and attractions around town or explore the assorted hiking opportunities available nearby, they will thoroughly enjoy the warm and convivial atmosphere found at the Jacksonville Inn.

The Hideaway Motel

810 Southwest 10th
Lincoln City, Oregon 97367
(541) 994-8874

Owner: *Sharon Odenthal*
Rooms: *6 doubles*
Rates: *$70-125 (B&B)*
Payment: *MC and VISA*
Dogs: *Welcome for a daily fee of $5 with a limit of two dogs per room*
Children: *Welcome (cribs available)*
Open: *All year*

We were a little skeptical that a nice, quiet lodging could be situated in a busy seaside town like Lincoln City. But sure enough, nestled just a short distance from the fast food restaurants, the non-descript seaside motels, and the general hubbub is the Hideaway Motel. The private residences in this neighborhood are an attractive blend of three-story houses, cottages, and even a few nice trailers. In the midst of this is the Hideaway Motel, which frankly is a complete misnomer — this is a charming, light blue shake cottage with white shutters that bears no resemblance to a motel. It is set on a cliff, with the blue Pacific and sandy beach providing a lovely vista. During our visit, a crane was attempting to rebuild an eroding path that leads guests to and from the beach. The cottage, on the other hand, is in no danger of going anywhere.

This is a low-key place; most guests enjoy it for its casual, beach-side setting. Of the six suites available, the largest and most requested is the Master Suite. This is the one unit that doesn't have stairs. Guests just open the door, make a jog to the right, and enter a cozy two-bedroom suite. We were drawn to the living room's bay window and its expansive views. Best of all, families or a group of friends will discover that six guests can easily be accommodated in this suite, between the two bedrooms and the sofa bed. The full-kitchen is well equipped, and includes a dishwasher. We could imagine almost looking forward to a Sou'wester blowing in, as an excuse to light a fire and relax amid the cozy surroundings. Just upstairs from the Master Suite is the intimate Crow's Nest. Aptly named, it is tucked under the eaves of the house's mansard roof. The window up here is also built into the end eave and provides dizzying views out to the ocean. The Sunset, Honeymoon, and Royal suites have equally lovely water views, while the Canyon Suite, true to its name, overlooks the wooded canyon, which is often lush with colorful wildflowers. Guests requiring a little extra space may wish to reserve either the Canyon or Sunset suite, as both offer living rooms and private decks.

Regardless of room choice, guests are certain to enjoy the casual ambiance at the Hideaway. The pine-paneled walls nicely complement the mix of maple and oak furnishings. With the exception of the Honeymoon Suite and Crow's Nest, each suite does have a fireplace supplied with unlimited amounts of wood. Kitchens are outfitted with most everything one would require to make an impromptu meal. Equipped with microwaves, coffee makers, and popcorn poppers, they're great places for preparing light snacks and *hors d'oeuvres*. Guests who return to the Hideaway year after year do so for its proximity to the water and beach, coupled with the lulling effects of the crashing waves and fresh salt air.

One of the best routes for walks with dogs is along the road that circles back down the hill to the beach. There is also a small grassy area near the beach's entrance, where visiting dogs can romp with other local canines. Once out on the sand, it is easy to be gone for hours, as it is possible to walk for awhile before turning around and heading home. Lincoln City is also centrally located for pleasant day trips. The **Cascade Head Trail**, just off Highway 101, is comprised of waterside forests that provide all sorts of options for hikers and their dogs. Another alternative, for those who are interested in boating or fishing expeditions, is the **Devil's Lake State Park** in Lincoln. There is also a trail up **Mount Hebo** that many hikers enjoy investigating; it begins in the Mount Hebo Campground. Our dogs very much enjoyed this pleasant hike, as it offers plenty of meadows, forests, and streams.

Starfish Point

140 Northwest 48th Street
Newport, Oregon 97365
(541) 265-3751, Fax: (541) 265-3040
Internet: pending

Owners: *Neil and Kathleen Atkinson*
Rooms: *6 suites*
Rates: *$150-170 (EP)*
Payment: *AE, DSC, MC, and VISA*
Dogs: *Welcome with a $5 daily fee and a limit of 2 pets on the property at any time. Must be leashed, cannot be left alone in the room.*
Children: *Welcome (a crib and high chair are available)*
Open: *All year*

Starfish Point is a wonderfully evocative name, but it contains even more fabulous accommodations, nestled into a wooded hillside overlooking the ocean. These attractive, contemporary condominium suites were originally built as luxury time-share units — but unfortunately, the project went bankrupt. Thankfully, the Atkinsons bought the place, imbued it with additional charm, and opened it to the overnight guests. We couldn't be more pleased at discovering this tempting retreat along the Oregon coast.

The small complex is set on the edge of Newport, but is well concealed from Route 101 by mature trees and bushes. As we entered the complex, it was hard to imagine what lay inside the dove gray wood-sided buildings. Perhaps this was best, because once we saw the interiors it was as if we had stumbled upon a hidden treasure. The architect who designed these spaces created intimate spaces. Each room is set on a different level and privy to spectacular hillside and ocean views, through walls of glass. We had the impression of being situated alone on a hillside with only the green forest surrounding us with the blue Pacific below.

These interior spaces flow nicely together, with few wasted corners. Guests step in through a small tiled foyer and down into the central living room, complete with color television and a stereo. Each unit is fully carpeted and fashioned with good-quality rattan furniture and bright cotton floral fabrics. This common area opens onto two more glass-walled rooms — the formal dining room and the octagonal captain's study. Guests who sit in either of these spaces will find their eyes continually drawn out to the natural world just beyond the expanses of glass. Depending on the suite, guests walk either up or down from the captain's study to the equally lovely master bedroom with its private bathroom. In one suite, tiny cobalt blue tiles surround the two-person Jacuzzi. We think the candles in here are a nice addition for those wanting to set a particularly romantic mood.

We feel the most desirable units are those situated on the end of the building, with unobstructed views of the ocean. The master bedroom in these particular buildings offers a window with wonderful views of the water and beach. Because these were built as time-share units, very little expense was spared when it came to quality. Therefore, guests can expect to find modern kitchens equipped with an array of state-of-the-art appliances, such as Jenn-Aire ranges. Starfish Point is as ideal for families as it is for a pair of couples (although the two couples would have to flip a coin for the upstairs master suite). Each suite also has a private deck allowing guests to venture outside and soak up some Oregon sun.

Dogs are definitely welcome additions at Starfish Point. Although they don't have acres of grounds to romp on, they need only persuade their owners to take them down a path leading through dense pines to **Agate Cove**. Once at the shore, human and canine can walk for hours together, either up toward **Yaquina Head** or down toward Newport. There are also three state parks south of Newport — **South Beach, Lost Creek,** and **Ona Beach**. All allow dogs to explore their paths, beaches, and tide pools. Another option is the **Beverly Beach State Park**, where there are even more spectacular hillside and oceanside walks to be enjoyed with a beloved canine companion.

The Benson

309 Southwest Broadway
Portland, Oregon 97205
(800) 426-0670, (503) 228-2000, Fax: (503) 226-4603
Internet: http://www.placestostay.com

General Manager: *Robert Parsons*
Rooms: *232 doubles, 55 suites*
Rates: *Doubles $145-190 (EP), Suites $210-600 (EP)*
Payment: *AE, CB, DC, JCB, MC, and VISA*
Dogs: *House-broken dogs are welcome*
Children: *Welcome (cribs and cots are available)*
Open: *All year*

Built at the turn of the century, The Benson Hotel remains a French baroque architectural classic, set among the more contemporary high-rise buildings dotting Portland's skyline. Simon Benson commissioned this building, and others, after making his fortune in Oregon timber. He went to great lengths to secure the finest materials and craftsmen to build his hotel, even going so far as to import Circassian walnut from Russia. Some years ago, when we first wrote about The Benson, the physical structure was in need of repair and restoration. We are pleased to report that after a thorough restoration process, it is once again a showplace. Besides refurbishing the public areas and revamping the two restaurants, the management has pumped over $16 million into the renovation of the guest rooms.

The elegant lobby was, and continues to be, the hotel's showpiece. Its walls are paneled in dark red walnut, while huge, cut-glass chandeliers hang from the ornately-carved, coffered ceilings. Massive columns break up what would otherwise be a cavernous space, providing a number of intimate sitting areas. One of our favorites spots is over by the marble fireplace, especially during afternoon high tea. Oriental rugs cover the Italian marble floors, while an impressive collection of antiques and fine furnishings are placed about this handsome chamber. Immense flower arrangements provide fragrant aromas and colorful accents.

While each guest chamber has been thoughtfully updated, it still adheres to the historic integrity of the hotel. We noticed (especially when walking along the upstairs hallways) that even the original guest room doors, complete with inlaid wood, had a rich patina to them. The finialed headboards contain inlaid woods in the same hues as the doors, while the classic furnishings (such as writing tables, sofas, and chairs with ottomans) fill out the rest of the guest chambers. Taupe and cream color schemes, combined with subtle black accents lend a certain opulence to these rooms. In addition to gilt-edged mirrors and lovely botanical prints, many of the walls are graced with hand-colored architectural prints.

The Benson Rooms are perhaps the most popular chambers, as they offer intimate sitting areas in the bedrooms. The once rather small, antiquated bathrooms have been enlarged and modernized, and now boast of shower/tub combinations, hairdryers, baskets of toiletries, and terry robes. Guests who reserve the most deluxe suites will discover Jacuzzis in the bathrooms and wet bars in the spacious living rooms. Regardless of room choice, guests will find big baskets of gourmet goodies placed on the honor bar and televisions concealed in the armoires. The Grand Suite is the most opulent accommodation at the hotel, with a four-poster, king-size bed resting in one huge alcove, and a black lacquered dining room table set on the edge of the living room. (President Clinton stayed here in 1993.) Its corner location makes it an especially light and airy chamber. While few guests will be interested in paying the hefty sum for this luxurious suite, they will be happy to learn that many of the other corner guest rooms offer similar views.

The London Grill, with its light wood paneling and arched ceilings, is a favorite among visitors and locals alike. This contemporary motif is reflected in the nouvelle menu as well. Dinner patrons might start with the Japanese lobster tails served in a rich garlic butter, the smoked salmon and caviar, or the lobster bisque. Our entrée selections included an intriguing Northwest hunter's plate consisting of stuffed quail, a venison chop and wild mushrooms, although guests could also dine on the rack of lamb laced with garlic mustard and herbs, the Dover sole with an herb lemon butter sauce, or the yellow fin tuna, sautéed with garlic and ginger and served with a lemon Szechwan sauce.

We especially recommend The Benson Hotel to travelers whose dogs are used to the city. We would recommend the RiverPlace Hotel (which is situated alongside two parks) to those with canines who require a lot of exercise. The area around the Benson Hotel consists mostly of sidewalks and stores, offering very little nearby green grass or open space on which to burn off a little energy. The **Esplanade** is a short distance away and will give your dog more than enough room to run and play. It is also fairly easy to jump in the car and head to a few of the more dog-oriented destinations just outside the city. One option includes the **Powell Butte Trail**, that offers a three-mile hiking trail and terrific views of the more distant mountains, as well as some fine local scenery. Another popular destination is situated some 30 minutes outside Portland, just off Interstate 84. There, a rather easy trail leads up to and around the picturesque **Latourell Falls**.

Mallory Hotel

729 SW 15th Avenue
Portland, Oregon 97205
(800) 228-8657, (503) 223-6311, Fax: (503) 223-0522
Internet: http://www.malloryhotel.com

Manager: *Linda Anderson*
Rooms: *124 doubles, 18 suites*
Rates: *Doubles $70-90 (EP), Suites $80-120 (EP)*
Payment: *AE, DC, DSC, MC, and VISA*
Dogs: *Welcome with a $10 fee, provided they are not left alone in the room*
Children: *Welcome (cribs are available)*
Open: *All year*

    Situated just a short walk from the city's more popular shopping areas, the Mallory Hotel is a tall, tawny building offering guests comfortable accommodations at a very affordable price. Originally built in 1912, the hotel underwent a substantial face lift in the late 1980s. Despite the extensive nature of the work done here, we feel there are still a few details that could use a little more attention — but because the price is right, we're willing to overlook a couple of well-worn aspects. Although the Mallory Hotel may not be one of the city's premier luxury hotels, it remains a favorite destination for many visitors, as it still retains much of its old world charm and unpretentious atmosphere.
    We climbed the long, wide staircase to reach the expansive lobby. The wall of mirrors here makes the space appear all the more cavernous. Comfortable couches, flanked by green wing chairs, form the various sitting areas, while glass chandeliers, suspended from gilded, boxed-beamed ceilings, make the room seem to twinkle. We actually sat here awhile looking up at the ceilings — they were that intriguing. The lobby and its adjacent restaurant are the two most resplendent spaces in the hotel. The dining room is a favorite for Sunday brunch, and is as formal as the lobby; but in the dining room, balloon shades frame the floor-to-ceiling windows. We happened to be visiting on a Sunday, when the hotel was packed with locals and guests alike enjoying the Mallory's famous brunch.
    The staff is quirky, but lovable — sort of like the characters in the television show *Seinfeld*. The front desk assistants, for instance, are all very friendly and genuine — not like the ultra-polished types we sometimes encounter whose frequent refrain is "My pleasure" (but who clearly aren't taking much, if any, pleasure in what they are doing for their guests). When we checked in with the front desk, the staff couldn't supply us with a brochure, but they had plenty of stories to tell us about the hotel. One of these was

about the resident ghost — Mr. Mallory. He is not an ordinary ghost, but one who reputedly pounds on the wall with what sounds like a hammer. Some patrons think this is really neat (in theory), but after the first "tap, tap, tap" most scamper down to the front desk asking to be moved to another room. We didn't get to see Mr. Mallory's room, but did check out many of the others.

Physically, the Mallory's guest rooms look much the same as they probably did in the 1930s. Some of the double rooms are still in need of a little attention, while others are very attractively, albeit eclectically, furnished, with some of the chairs and sofas appearing as though they were carryover's from the hotel's earlier years. Most of the bedrooms have either a king bed or a pair of twin beds covered with simple, white cotton spreads. The rather Spartan decor is complemented by standard amenities such as color televisions and refrigerators. The private bathrooms have colorful tiles reminiscent of the Art Deco period (they probably are originals from that period), and, in many cases, guests must step up to reach them. Without exception, though, everything is extremely neat and clean. Some of our favorite bedrooms are the corner rooms on the upper floors. These are substantially larger than the other chambers, and some boast expansive views of the city and Mount Hood.

As we've noted, while the Mallory Hotel might be a bit dated, it still offers good value and a lot more pizzazz than some of the larger chain hotels in the region. Guests who stay here are not only close to the opera and theater district, but are also just a short car ride from the **city parks** and the **riverfront** area. In addition to investigating these areas, we also suggest driving south to the **Tryon Creek State Park**. Here, hikers and their leashed dogs can follow some of the short nature trails or the longer hiking trails, through beautiful forests and alongside picturesque creeks. Maps are supplied, so bring a picnic lunch and spend the day exploring the more than 600 acres available to visitors.

RiverPlace Hotel

1510 Southwest Harbor Way
Portland, Oregon 97201
(800) 227-1333, (503) 228-3233, Fax: (503) 295-6161

General Manager: *James Jones*
Rooms: *27 doubles, 35 suites, 10 condominiums*
Rates: *Doubles $220-285 (B&B), Suites $220-700 (B&B),*
   Condominiums $360-450 (B&B)
Payment: *AE, MC, and VISA*
Dogs: *Welcome with a $100 non-refundable deposit*
Children: *Welcome (cribs, cots, high chairs, and baby-sitters are available)*
Open: *All year*

Portland

The RiverPlace Hotel has always been one of our favorite city hotels in the Northwest. When we first reviewed it, the prestigious Alexis group was managing its overall operations. Today, it is a part of the Westcoast Hotels group and we are pleased to report that it is just as appealing as ever, perhaps even more so. The RiverPlace lies on the northern banks of the Willamette River in a section of Portland known as the Esplanade. On one side of the hotel are six-story condominiums, shops, restaurants, and boutiques; on the other, vast expanses of grass leading down to a marina. Long ago the area was seedy; however, with the arrival of the hotel in 1985, this section of the city has become a very desirable destination for travelers and local residents alike.

Architecturally, the hotel gracefully combines the old with the new. Its turrets and rotunda roof, crafted with bleached wood and brick, make it reminiscent of the massive, turn-of the-century great cottages. Oversized windows draw in ample amounts of natural sunlight and provide good views of the river, marina, and adjacent park. The interior is a little more contemporary, though, with an abundance of light oak and marble, forming clean lines. Bright colors seem to permeate the interior spaces — on the chintz-covered sofas and chairs grouped into intimate sitting areas, in the fresh flower arrangements set on antique tables, and in the abundance of ornamental potted palms and ficus trees. All these combine to create the residential feeling that guests find so appealing.

The bedrooms are as elegant as the common areas. The hotel just completed a "soft" rennovation and replaced all the carpets, bedspreads, and draperies. The furniture that was not recovered was replaced. The new look features lightly stained woods reminiscent of the inns on Nantucket. In some spaces, blues tones predominate, while in others, pale yellows and greens are featured. Fine reproduction antiques are still mixed in with the newer furnishings and include wing chairs with ottomans, overstuffed sofas, and expansive writing desks. Brass sconces and framed botanical prints grace the walls. Our favorite rooms are those with woodburning fireplaces, wet bars, and whirlpool bathtubs, although all guest bathrooms feature marble sinks and tiled floors, baskets of European toiletries, and thick terry cloth robes. Anyone planning an extended stay may wish to reserve one of the hotel-managed condominiums. These provide substantially more space and a varied assortment of amenities — especially ideal for families staying here with their dogs. In the evenings, complimentary sherry is served before dinner, and guests returning to their rooms afterwards will find that their beds have been turned down and gourmet chocolates rest on their down pillows. In the morning, a gourmet Continental breakfast and a newspaper are delivered to the room.

The hotel's former no-tipping policy disappeared with the Alexis management group; however, there are still a few complimentary services, such as shoe shines, valet, and concierge. One of the most impressive features is the fact that the hotel has three restaurants overlooking the water, each of which offers a different atmosphere and river view. The Esplanade restaurant is the most formal, specializing in local cuisine, with an emphasis on fresh seafood. The veteran chef, John Zenger, has recently begun to make some exciting menu changes. When we visited, three dishes seemed especially noteworthy: the wild mushrooms, mountain cheeses, Fino sherry, and garlic, baked in an herbed filo; Dungeness crab and bay shrimp cakes; and Manila clams steamed in a chipotle broth. Entrées included the grilled marlin with Kona crab hash and lime mustard sauce; the red pepper linguini with mesquite-seasoned chicken; and the salmon with a pistachio pesto crust and a fresh tomato coulis. But it is not only the dinner menu that is bringing rave reviews; it is also the popular brunches. Not surpris-ingly, Eggs Benedict is on the menu, although an even more interesting version, with a Thai twist, is what most patrons are talking about. In this concoction, poached eggs are set on Dungeness crab and bay shrimp crab cakes, then covered with a light, red curry hollandaise. At The Esplanade, there is also an emphasis on healthy, light dishes such as the ten-grain flapjacks served with a lemony berry compôte, and the egg-white omelets filled with items such as wild mushrooms, scallions, chopped fresh herbs, or a tomatillo salsa. The Bar offers a more casual and intimate dining setting, with its woodburning fireplace and jazz pianist setting the overall mood. In the summer months, most people gravitate to the outdoor Patio for their meals.

The RiverPlace Athletic Club, situated just a half block from the hotel, is outfitted with tennis, squash, and racquetball courts, as well as three swimming pools, aerobic classes, a massage therapist, and a weight room. The hotel's steam room is private, and may be reserved for an hour at a time. Those who prefer outdoor exercise (your dog perhaps), will appreciate the ease of access to the landscaped walkways around the **Esplanade**. Some might shop or eat their way along this waterfront park; however, the wide expanses of grass are far more extensive than the shopping and are certainly more intriguing for dogs. Just a short drive away is the **Hoyt Arboretum** which offers pleasant walks through the stretches of forest and metropolitan areas. At the arboretum, visitors and their dogs will find the **Wildwood Trail** along with some other trails that walkers and their dogs can follow for either short or long distances. Wending alongside lush lawns, a thriving marina, and winding river is sure to keep both canines and their human counterparts well occupied.

Lake Creek Lodge

Star Route
Sisters, Oregon 97759
(800) 797-6331, (503) 595-6331
Internet: pending

Hostess: *Roblay McMullin*
Rooms: *16 houses and cottages*
Rates: *$60-150 (MAP), $70-170 (EP), Additional person $35-50 (MAP)*
Payment: *Personal checks*
Dogs: *Welcome with an $8 daily fee. Dogs must always be leashed when on the property and walked in dog-walk areas.*
Children: *Welcome (cots are available)*
Open: *All year*

The Lake Creek Lodge, set in the heart of the Deschutes National Forest, is surrounded by spectacular mountain peaks and alpine valleys. The nucleus of the resort consists of a small complex of cottages and houses that are encircled by 60 acres of pine forests, emerald lawns, well-tended flower gardens, and the Lake Creek Pond. We arrived on a quiet fall afternoon. Although few people were out and about, there was still a sense of vitality about the place. Bright flowers bloomed along the walkways; a dozen or so guests were relaxing in the Adirondack chairs; and parents were fishing with their children at the pond.

The resort, we later learned, dates back to 1935, and the original owner lives in a small cottage on the property. She is 88 years old, and still tends to her extensive flower gardens. We also suspect she has had a lot of influence in creating the array of flower gardens scattered about the rest of the property. Some of the small, brown clapboard cottages also date back to the resort's beginnings; however, there are newer and larger knotty-pine houses that offer modern amenities as well. The older cottages generally accommodate up to four people in their one- and two-bedrooms. While these are fashioned with a bathroom, they do not have a living room or kitchen. A refrigerator is set out on the small porch, allowing guests who stay here to store their drinks and perishable snacks. These rather sparsely furnished cottages are often reserved as "grandparent" units. The children and grandchildren, on the other hand, generally stay in the newer houses. This gives the extended family a central gathering place, but allows the grandparents to slip off and enjoy a little quiet time.

The houses are decidedly more expansive and are outfitted with a large central living room and a variety of bedroom configurations. The light pine walls and large windows brighten these spaces, while the fireplaces add a bit of warmth and character. The attractive furnishings are comfortable, and a few knickknacks add a homey touch to the expansive chambers. Colorful handmade quilts cover the pine bedsteads and cotton curtains frame the paned windows. Although the overall ambiance is a little on the Spartan side, everything is very neat and clean.

The low-key setting, along with the abundance of diversions and the affable nature of the staff, are some of the reasons many visitors have been coming here for generations. All guests, and especially children, love the warm, fuzzy feeling of the Lake Creek Lodge. Children are not only permitted to be first in line at dinner, but are also invited to enjoy their meal with their peers in a separate dining room. This is a very relaxed set-up for both the children and their parents. The weekly "wiener roast" is always fun for the kids, while the adult contingency can enjoy the varied entrée selections in the main dining room. These range from salmon and prime rib to lamb and fried chicken. Guests will quickly discover, however, that the meals are merely a small component of a vacation at the Lake Creek Lodge.

Toddlers like having their own small, shallow pool, while older "water-safe" children may use the full-size swimming pool. The pond is stocked each year with trout, and is reserved for children under the age of twelve. Adults are not disregarded, though, as the clear, spring fed Metolius River runs right through the property. Fly-fishing is the only type of fishing permitted on this river, and it has certainly tested the skills of many an angler. In addition to the swimming and fishing, guests can play basketball, paddle or standard tennis, shuffleboard, horseshoes, and volleyball. While dogs cannot freely romp about the grounds, we found the **trails** that edge the forest to be ideal for burning off a little steam.

Day hikes are also quite popular. One of our favorite routes begins at the **Canyon Creek Campground** and follows the Metolius River Trail through canyons and past many natural springs. Hikers and their dogs are certain to encounter plenty of wildlife along the way, especially if they are quiet. Another option is the **Black Butte Trail**, which leads to a spot with panoramic views of the valleys and of the Mount Washington, Mount Jefferson, and Three Fingered Jack. In the winter, many bring their cross-country skis and take their canines on excursions along some of the aforementioned trails.

Bird and Hat Bed & Breakfast

717 North Third
Stayton, Oregon 97383
(503) 769-7817

Hostess: *Jacqulin Kirby*
Rooms: *3 doubles*
Rates: *$55-65 (B&B)*
Payment: *Personal checks*
Dogs: *Welcome*
Children: *Welcome for a $5 additional nightly fee*
Open: *All year*

    The Willamette Valley is fast becoming a wine aficionado's Mecca. Its rich soil and moist climate causes the grapes to develop slowly, which allows wine makers to create some fairly complex vintages. These wines are beginning to win accolades at some of the country's most prestigious festivals. Before all this notoriety, though, this was traditional farm country with the land dedicated to dairy production and crops more basic than grapes. While this region has not quite reached the status of Napa Valley, in many ways this makes it all the more appealing for visitors who are in search of an up-and-coming wine producing region. We like it because it lies at the edge of some spectacular national forests, near scenic covered bridges, and amid plenty of natural lakes.

Within this small community is a quaint B&B called the Bird and Hat. Longtime residents probably would refer to it as the old Brewer House, as it was built in 1907 by Dr. Charles Brewer. Over the years, this humble abode has served many purposes — part private residence and part commercial enterprise. Dr. Brewer practiced medicine here for many years; at one time it was a beauty shop, at another time, a gift shop; and a little more recently, it was a small restaurant. Today, the residential quality has been restored under Jacqulin's tutelage.

We found this charming house to be especially appealing from the street, with its gambrel roof flowing down to an inviting farmer's porch. The house is situated on a corner, but is surrounded by small, flowering fruit trees, rose gardens, and mature shrubs. One side of the house is also shaded by an enormous old tulip magnolia. We followed a stone path around the side of the house where we discovered Jacqulin's extensive organic vegetable garden. Since we were visiting in the fall everything was still quite lush; we cannot even begin to imagine how beautiful it would be in the spring and summer.

Guests are treated like members of the family, and as we arrived another couple was wistfully departing. It is easy to feel comfortable here. The first floor is an inviting open space, with hardwood floors, walls of windows, and plenty of places in which to curl up with a good book. The highlight is the living room, with its white brick fireplace. A couch is set in front of the fireplace, and guests often sit here and enjoy the fire, listen to music, or watch a movie on the television or VCR. A wide archway leads from this inviting chamber into the dining room — another sunny space. A lace-covered table is the site for the morning repast. Jacqulin is more than happy to prepare just about any dish for her guests, and she often tries to incorporate fresh fruit or vegetables from her gardens. Eggs Benedict can be served just as easily as an overstuffed omelet or a stack of pancakes covered with fresh fruit. Whatever the meal, it is always substantial.

Upstairs there are three bedrooms. The largest of these is situated in the front of the house, with a small private porch. Light pours in through the windows, although it seems even brighter because of the pale peach and green color schemes that are used throughout this space. This is a good room for families because of the additional sleeping areas. A virtual mountain of pillows covers one day bed tucked into a corner; behind another wall is another tiny room, which looks as if it were converted from a former walk-in closet. When Jacqulin's grandchildren were babies, this was their crib room. It still works well for those staying here with children. Darker colors prevail next door, especially on the bed, which is backed by a dark oak, hand-carved headboard. Navy blue is the predominant color tone, but it is balanced with just enough creamy colors to give it some life. A little balcony opens to views of the tulip tree. The separate sink in here is convenient, as the shared bathroom is situated across the hallway. We especially like the bedroom towards the rear of the house. The four-poster mahogany beds are covered with navy floral comforters, and an antique armoire is placed against one wall. Especially appealing is the adjacent wall of double hung windows that make the room feel like an old-fashioned sleeping porch. As we looked out through the windows, we spied a little rock-lined pond that appeared natural amid all the greenery. It is built with old cattle feeding troughs — we thought it was a clever way to recycle something.

It is rarely a problem finding something to do around Stayton; the difficulty is deciding what to do first. One of the simplest and most pleasant activities is just walking around this unassuming rural town. As we mentioned, a few trendy establishments, such as the gourmet restaurants, are beginning to creep into town and this is starting to change the flavor of this farming community.

Naturalists, however, will be impressed that this region is renowned for having the largest concentration of waterfalls anywhere in the country. Some of the highlights include the **Silver Creek Falls** and **Salmon Falls**. The 8,000-acre **Silver Falls State Park** is the largest in Oregon and welcomes human visitors and their dogs. Another popular destination is the **Willamette National Forest**, where there are ample hiking opportunities. **Phantom Bridge** is one of our favorite hiking destinations in the area. The trail leads people and their dogs past **Dog Rock** (how appropriate) and on to the Phantom Bridge, which is a naturally created rock bridge. People can either marvel at it or walk right out on it. **Coffin Mountain** is another great day hike, easily accessible from the town of Marion Forks. One last option is situated outside of Quartzville and is called **Chimney Peak**. Hikers can reach the top of the peak by following the **McQuade Creek Trail**.

The Wayfarer Resort

46725 Goodpasture Road
Vida, Oregon   97488
(541) 896-3613

Hosts: Karen and Mike Rogers
Rooms: 13 cottages
Rates: $70-195 (EP),Weekly rates are available
Payment: MC and VISA
Dogs: Welcome with a one-time fee of $10, provided they are leashed
Children: Welcome (cribs and baby-sitters are available)
Open: All year

The Wayfarer Resort is located just 25 miles east of Eugene, yet guests feel very removed from the urban world. It lies in a dense forest on the banks of the McKenzie River and the glacier-fed Marten Creek — a region that traditionally lures those who love fly fishing. After crossing the 50-year-old covered bridge that spans the McKenzie River, visitors meander along a country road, where sunlight filters through the cedars, birches, and spruces, casting a soft glow upon the forest floor.

We arrived at the Wayfarer Resort late one afternoon to find a few guests quietly casting their flies into the creek. This is a low-key, storybook kind of place, where most of the red cottages are clustered along the river's edge, overlooking the forest on the opposite banks. These guest quarters are simply constructed, with open-beamed ceilings and natural knotty pine walls. The furnishings are comfortable; big sofas and deep chairs are perfect for curling up and watching the crackling fire or reading a favorite book. Picture windows in many of the cottages frame views of the river and forest, as do the sliding glass doors that lead out to good-sized decks. Each cottage also has an outdoor barbecue and a fully-equipped kitchen. Handmade quilts adorn the beds, which vary from twin to king-size.

The cottages range from an intimate studio to the spacious Octagon cottage with two bedrooms and two bathrooms. The semi-circular central stone fireplace is the centerpiece for the Octagon Cottage's large common room, which also is outfitted with a piano, television, and wet bar. The kitchen is fashioned with a variety of modern amenities including a Jennair stove. While the interior is quite comfortable and impressive, guests will undoubtedly spend much of their time on the expansive wraparound deck overlooking the rushing river. If we could make only one suggestion, it would be to try to reserve one of the cottages directly on the creek — it is well worth the additional stipend.

In addition to the excellent fly fishing, guests can play badminton, volleyball, horseshoes, or tennis. The swing set and a stocked pond are geared for young children, while adults can take advantage of the golf opportunities at the Tokatee links. Rafting trips and hiking trails are also conveniently located nearby. Just west of Vida and north of Blue River is one popular hiking option — the **Tidbits Mountain Trail**, set in the heart of the Willamette National Forest. This is a pleasant hike through a forest that eventually leads to an area offering a lovely view of the valley below, and of some of the surrounding mountains. **Castle Rock**, also situated just west of Vida, is another great hiking opportunity for those looking for a more leisurely outing with their canine. As with all good hikes, there is always a reward at the end — usually a fabulous view. This one is no exception.

Most guests do not come to The Wayfarer Resort to be pampered and catered to; they prefer the self-sufficiency it offers, enjoying its natural surroundings and relaxing amid the uncomplicated and unpretentious ambiance.

Edgewater Cottages

3978 S.W. Pacific Coast Highway
Waldport, Oregon 97394
(541) 563-2240

Innkeepers: *Cathy Sorenson and Chuck Turpin*
Rooms: *9 cottages*
Rates: *$60-355 (EP)*
Payment: *Personal checks*
Dogs: *Welcome, providing they are housebroken, stay off the furniture, and are not left unattended. Daily fee of $5-7.*
Children: *Welcome (a crib is available)*
Open: *All year*

The Edgewater Cottages have been operated by the same family for the past 30 years. Set along the dunes overlooking a sandy beach, most of these cottages are privy to beautiful views of the water. There are no cliffs around here, just ocean, sand, and surf — making this an ideal vacation spot for guests with older children or dogs, since there is little need to worry about anyone getting into much trouble.

As we drove down the coastal road, we almost passed right by the complex. A weathered sign, partially obscured by a line of pine trees that fronts the complex, pointed to the entrance. These are not cookie cutter cottages set in a row; instead, we discovered a hodgepodge of gray-shingled cottages — some nestled into a knoll and others along the beach. Mixed in with these rentals are private residences, providing a combination of locals and guests. When we visited, we noticed that some of the older cottages were being re-shingled, but in general, they offer the kind of charm that many have come to associate with a low-key beach vacation.

Our first stop was the Crow's Nest, an intimate space that sleeps two. It does not have direct water views, but that didn't matter — we could smell and hear the ocean. Although the walls are knotty pine and the floors hardwood, red highlights give it a more contemporary look. We stepped across the hemp rug to warm ourselves in front of the red enameled wood stove. As we looked back into the room, we spied the tiny kitchen fashioned with red countertops. Off to the side was a queen bed with a red quilt, and over to one corner a white flag was festooned with a red crab on it. A sliding glass door leads out to a very private sun deck.

The Chart House is one of the most reasonably priced rooms at just $45. It is a studio apartment set into a knoll, with views of the sandy beach through the sliding glass doors and plate glass windows. We like the effect of the thick rope that frames the entrance to this space, as well as the dark, knotty pine walls that collectively give these quarters a nautical feeling. The Chart

Room consists of a queen-bedded room and a small living room with a freestanding fireplace. Guests may also reserve the Chart Room's Crew Quarters, which adds a second bedroom to this configuration. The double bed and a pair of twin day beds look quite spiffy under their red, white, and blue sailboat cotton spreads.

Just upstairs there are two even sunnier spaces, the Wheel House and the Commodore's Cabin. Though these, too, have knotty pine interiors, the expanse of glass found in the sliding doors and windows makes these chambers bright. The tiny Wheel House is a cozy studio; but it is well equipped with a complement of amenities. Whether guests are lying in their bed or sitting at the breakfast table, they may enjoy good views of the ocean. The raised-hearth brick fireplace keeps things toasty. The modified kitchenette has a small refrigerator, two burners, a microwave oven, and a coffee maker. The Wheel House can connect to the Commodore's Cabin, just next door. This latter space has two bedrooms and a living room with a rock fireplace — but what makes it truly noteworthy is the sliding glass door that opens onto a sheltered sun deck.

There are individual cottages available as well. These include West Wind, Rustic, Pine Rest, and the granddaddy of them all: Beachcomber. The latter can accommodate eleven guests, while the smallest, Pine Rest, sleeps just two. Beachcomber can also be split up into a wide array of sleeping and living combinations. With the exception of Chart House, all the units have some cooking capabilities. No matter which configuration best suits guests' needs, they will find each kitchen stocked with at least the bare minimum of what we consider to be the essentials for a beach vacation: nutcrackers for crab, cork screws, wine glasses, and coffee makers.

Guests will need to purchase their groceries before arriving at the Edgewater Cottages, as there are not any large supermarkets within easy driving distance of the complex. Each of the cottages is outfitted with televisions, and VCRs and video tapes can be rented at a store just down the road. The telephone is located up in the office and guests are welcome to use it for making local calls. Every unit is also equipped with some sort of fireplace, and there is an unlimited supply of firewood. Since these units are basically housekeeping units, the innkeepers ask that guests leave them in the same condition as they found them. Fresh linens can be exchanged during the stay, along with toiletries, towels, etc.

The beach is so beautiful here that we could walk for miles with our dogs and never get bored — tired maybe, but not bored. It is just as pleasant to sit in one's room in the mornings and evenings and just watch the ocean crash onto the shore. To the east of Waldport, guests will find the **Drift Creek Wilderness**, which many hikers and their dogs love exploring. It is unusual to find any old growth forests in this region that have been left untouched by the lumber industry; however, this is one of them. The **Horse Creek Trail** is another popular option for hikers. Those who prefer to stay close to the ocean can also spend the day investigating the state parks that line the coastline.

The **Governor Patterson Memorial State Park**, in Waldport, offers just over 10 acres to explore with dogs. The **Ona Beach** or **Lost Creek State Parks** are often preferred options, with hundreds of acres to investigate. The inn's hosts are also happy to suggest intriguing outings that guests and their canine companions may enjoy.

Old Welches Inn

26401 East Welches Rd.
Welches, Oregon   97067
(503) 622-3754

Innkeepers: *Judi and Ted Mondun*
Rooms: *3 doubles, 1 cottage*
Rates: *Doubles $75-95 (B&B), Cottage $150 (EP)*
Payment: *MC and VISA*
Dogs: *Welcome "if they are fully house trained and very friendly." They must get along with Judi's dog Sadie.*
Children: *Most appropriate for children over age 12*
Open: *All year*

The Old Welches Inn was built in 1890 by Samuel Welch, and was one of Mount Hood's earliest resorts. The hotel didn't survive, but the house did — and stayed within the Welch family for the next 80 years before the Monduns bought it. Judi told us that even though the house was in a total state of disrepair, the Welches were hesitant to sell it, fearing that whoever bought it would tear it down and build a monstrosity — realizing the inherent value of this riverside property. Fortunately, Judi and her husband also feel strongly about preserving the past. So after they purchased the old place, they shored up the foundation and renovated every inch of the house. Today, guests will find a charming old farmhouse, painted white and highlighted with bright blue trim and shutters. The house still overlooks the river, as well as the golf course, and beyond to the mountains that rise steeply from the valley floor.

We arrived one morning to find Sadie, an Akita Shepherd mix, and Judi out tending to the gardens. As we passed through the white picket fence, we meandered about the yard, which is fashioned with shade trees and free-flowing flower gardens. Sadie bounded up to greet us and then escorted us to the farmhouse. While the guest rooms in the main house are fine for those traveling with a dog, the cottage is perhaps the best choice. Built in 1901, this cottage — like many of the other cottages around the valley — were rented to people for the summer. By the 1930s all the cottages except for this one were owned by individuals. Today, this cottage has the same white and blue color treatments that are found on the main house. Once inside, we emerged into a living room filled with well-worn furniture set around a river rock fireplace. This cozy chamber is well stocked with games and books, as well as a television. Oddly enough, though, the best river views are reserved for the cook, through the small windows over the sink. The kitchen is outfitted with a few condiments, which include such items as popcorn, snacks, herbs, and coffee and tea. Some guests enjoy preparing their own breakfasts, while others might be able to persuade Judi to make them breakfast on a slow day. Of the two bedrooms, the largest has a queen bed while the other is furnished with a pair of twin bedsteads. The master bedroom has an old-fashioned radio that provides a little entertainment; the other guest chamber has the best views of the river, through a pair of small windows. We love the sloping hardwood floors in the cottage — so off-kilter that the doors have been shaved, so they can open and close across the floors. The fairly rustic ambiance is nicely complemented by a faint scent of wood smoke.

Guests staying in the cottage may come and spend as much time as they would like in the main house. The first floor of this antique home flows beautifully, and seems especially light and airy because of the walls of windows and the cream-colored Berber carpeting. The living room is the natural place to congregate, especially on the overstuffed sofas in front of the fireplace. The sun porch is just as popular, with its three walls of windows, comfortable furnishings, and lovely views. During the day, some come in to just soak up the sun; while at night, guests gather here to watch a movie on the big screen television. The hosts have more than 60 videos that guests may choose from.

The three bedrooms are found upstairs. Judi tells us that men generally prefer Columbine, which overlooks the river. In the fall, she puts the hunter green and burgundy flannel sheets on the cannon ball-style bed. Duck decoys and hunt prints add to the masculine feeling in here. The Sweet Briar room, on the other hand, is somewhat more feminine, with its brass and white iron bed covered in a pale pink, green, and white comforter. This guest room also overlooks the river. The only drawback, for some, is the double bed. The largest chamber is called Trillium, and it overlooks the the golf course. In here, English chintzes predominate, whether on the bed or the overstuffed chairs. Judi sets chocolate out on little china plates in each of the guest rooms. Cotton towels are laid out for guests to use in the two shared bathrooms, which happen to be fully stocked with soaps and shampoos. In the morning, guests staying in the main house enjoy breakfast in the dining room, where plants thrive and there are views of the rock-walled porch and river.

While the house is beautifully restored, it is the property that guests and their canine are most likely to enjoy. When the Monduns bought the house, the grounds were covered with thorn bushes and dense foliage. As they cleared it, they discovered all sorts of old bottles and other bits of rubbish down by the water. They cleaned up all the debris, planted gardens, built rock walls, and even came across an old set of stone steps that hadn't been used in years. They built a river rock patio and a wonderful gazebo, along with an outdoor fireplace. We thoroughly enjoyed sitting out here at the end of the day, while listening to the soothing sound of the river and the smaller stream feeding into it.

It is always pleasant to walk the dogs along the country road the runs past the golf course and continues into the hills. **Mount Hood** is only a fifteen minute drive from the inn, and the **Salmon-Huckleberry Wilderness Area** is even closer, with almost as many trails to access. Just outside of Zigzag, hikers and their dogs will find the **Salmon River Trail**; the **Salmon Butte Trail**; or they can climb with their dog to the **Devil's Peak Lookout** — which reveals exceptional views of Mount Hood. Dogs are welcome throughout this wilderness area and in the neighboring **Mount Hood Wilderness Area**.

The See Vue

95590 Highway 101
Yachats, Oregon   97498
(503) 547-3227

Manager: Robert Barzler
Rooms: 9 doubles, 1 suite, 1 cottage
Rates: Doubles $43-57 (EP), Suite $58-70 (EP), Cottage $43-50 (EP)
Payment: MC and VISA
Dogs: Welcome with a $5 per pet nightly charge. Maximum of two dogs per room.
Children: Welcome
Open: All year

We were some six miles south of Yachats when we spotted The See Vue. From the road, it looks very much like any other motel found along the Oregon coast — but there was something subtly different about this place, something that caused us to pull off the highway and take a closer look. We were glad we did. This may have been an ordinary motel when it was first constructed, but ten years ago it was transformed into the eclectic, kitschy spot that it is today. New owners bought it a year or so ago, but the longtime manager has stayed on to maintain the feeling that has made The See Vue so popular with returning guests. The building's exterior is fashioned with naturally-weathered shakes, a plethora of planters filled with blooming flowers, and other mature shrubs, giving The See Vue plenty of visual appeal.

Though the rooms may be lined up in typical motel style, the unusual names on the doors hint at out-of-the-ordinary interior decor. Stepping inside

The Sea Rose Suite, The Salish, The Princess and the Pea, The Santa Fe, and Granny's Rooms, preconceived impressions of a traditional motel disappear. These places have character — whether they're filled with granny's antiques, Southwest memorabilia, or original works of art. We like the natural board walls in some, the beamed ceilings in others, and, in some cases, the beachstone fireplaces. The Far Out West Room is found at the end of the building; when we stepped inside, we were somewhat taken aback by the animal skin stretched on the wall over the bed — but it does fit in well with the old west theme, which includes western wool blankets, authentic pictures, and country antiques. Around the corner is a 1950s-style kitchen with plenty of windows revealing ocean views. We also loved Granny's Room, with its hand-carved mahogany double bed backed by a collection of decorative china hanging on the wall — all of which are illuminated by old-fashioned fringed lamps. The white-washed board walls in the kitchen also feature a few pieces of china, along with a collection of woven baskets. Of course, all the culinary necessities are also provided. The Salish, too, captured our attention with its original Northwest Native American mural painted on its walls. The Princess and the Pea would appeal to those with a penchant for the whimsical, as wicker collectibles and assorted knickknacks abound, including an array of old-fashioned musical instruments. The Princess theme might have been derived from the brass rubbings of a knight and his lady. This is the sort of chamber where most find it easy to relax — a crackling fire, a good book, and a picturesque sunset over the Pacific.

Families traveling with their dog will be most comfortable in the Sea Rose Suite, which consists of a double-bedded room, along with a separate alcove that can accommodate a single bed. The loft space and family room with a sofa bed make this suite even more versatile. A full kitchen allows guests to prepare simple snacks and meals that may be enjoyed in the adjoining dining room. With the exception of the Sea Rose Suite, most of the rooms are generally quite cozy. Guests requiring a little more privacy may wish to reserve the cottage. While it is situated closer to the highway, it is nonetheless set off by itself. Stained glass windows enliven one wall of this small abode, while another offers nice vistas of the ocean.

The See Vue lies on a bluff near the edge of the ocean, but there is a large grassy area that dogs are welcome to explore; it is slightly protected by low bushes and a split rail fence. (Visitors must be vigilant about poop patrol). As not all the units offer kitchens, some guests will be happy to learn about the Sea Perch, located just next door, which serves an excellent homemade breakfast. Locals and visitors alike come here for their buckwheat pancakes, Belgian waffles covered in berries, fresh baking powder biscuits and gravy — and endless refills of coffee. We also ordered deli sandwiches to go before we headed out for the day.

Visitors and their dogs need not travel far to find great hiking opportunities or intriguing beach walks. The **Carl G. Washburne State Park** is probably the closest option. Some trails meander through the coastal mountains, while the **Hobbit Trail** leads back down to the beach. Anyone who wants to stay near the water can also drive to the **Sutton Creek Sand Dunes**, where people and their dogs can meander along the sand dunes and observe the array of wildlife. Finally, there is **Devil's Elbow State Park**. The park has a trail leading up to **Heceta Head**, where there are terrific views to be enjoyed by both humans and their beasts.

Shamrock Lodgettes

P.O. Box 346
Yachats, Oregon 97498
(800) 845-5028, (503) 547-3312, Fax: (503) 547-3843

Hosts: *Mary and Bob Oxley*
Rooms: *12 doubles, 7 cabins, 1 apartment*
Rates: *Doubles $71-95 (EP), Cottages $91-99 (EP), Apartment $65 (EP), Children $5-7 (EP)*
Payment: *AE, DC, CB, MC, and VISA*
Dogs: *Welcome in the cabins and the apartment with a $3 daily fee*
Children: *Welcome (cribs and baby-sitters are available)*
Open: *All year*

Yachats is a quiet community set directly on a low-lying section of the Oregon coast. There is plenty to do here: long walks with dogs on sandy beaches, fishing, or searching for bloodstones, petrified wood, and agates along the shoreline. The Shamrock Lodgettes are some of the more interesting accommodation options in the area, especially because of the four acres of park-like land that buffers guests from any noise emanating from Highway 101.

A meandering drive wends past stands of pines, clusters of azaleas and rhododendrons, and a sprawling, emerald green lawn until it reaches the cozy log cabins. Although there are a few different types of accommodations at the Shamrock Lodgettes, those who bring a dog will be asked to stay in the cabins. (We feel these are preferable to the motel units.) Self-sufficiency is the key here, as each cabin is considered a housekeeping unit and is outfitted with an efficiency kitchen ("efficiency" denoting no ovens), towel and linen exchange upon request, daily garbage pickup, and firewood drop off. While not as pampered as one would be at a traditional inn, guests are well-taken care of. The Oxleys deliver a daily paper to guest room doors, offer color cable television (with in-room movies) and direct-dial telephones, and are always available to assist with any special requests.

The four oldest cabins, constructed in the early 1950s, are named after various rivers in Oregon. Alsea, Siuslaw, and Umpqua have two double beds in the master bedroom and a sofabed in the living room — enabling them to easily accommodate five guests. Siletz, on the other hand, is one of the largest of the cabins, with two good-sized bedrooms, a sofabed in the living room, and a panoramic ocean view. Yaquina is another two-bedroom cabin that can sleep up to seven people. Osage and Apartment #7 are suitable one-bedroom accommodations. But enough about the basics, because what truly impressed us about this cottage resort was the character we found inside.

Natural wood pervades these spaces, with authentic log walls and pine boards lining the ceilings and floors. The color schemes vary from natural hues of gold to a deep red. While all the living rooms are fashioned with either a stone fireplace or a freestanding wood stove, we especially enjoyed the homey quality of the stone fireplaces. The furnishings are almost secondary, but guests should expect to find camp furnishings such as Adirondack chairs, pine tables, leather chairs, and comfortable sofas — perfect for afternoon naps. Not all the cabins have direct views of the water, but it is worth requesting one that does.

We like this area because there is plenty to do with a dog. The most popular option is to walk about the grounds and down along the shore. Should dogs tire of this routine, guests might bring them over to **Tillicum Beach**, **Yachats State Park**, or **Neptune State Park**. The latter is a 300-acre park with an abundance of wildlife and natural wonders. One of the more notable natural wonders is the famous **Cook's Chasm**, a spectacular gorge that has been carved out by the ocean over the centuries. Hiking trails also dot this area. **Cape Perpetua** is probably the best spot for day hikes with a dog.

There is an abundance of information in the reception area, covering vacationer's options ranging from scenic sights and attractions to nearby restaurants and shopping areas. When deciding to explore this region, visitors should keep in mind that it gets more than 100 inches of rain a year. We suggest bringing a raincoat, and perhaps an extra towel or two for drying off your dog after a day spent outside. At the end of the day, most human guests look forward to visiting the small spa on the property, featuring a hot tub, a sauna, and the services of a licensed massage therapist.

One final note: the Oxleys have owned the Shamrock Lodgettes for over 25 years and their guests usually book a year in advance for the following summer. Thus, for those who are interested in visiting, we highly recommend making reservations well in advance.

Flying M Ranch

23029 N.W. Flying M Road
Yamhill, Oregon 97148
(503) 662-3222

Hosts: *Bryce and Barbara Mitchell*
Rooms: *4 singles, 24 doubles, 7 cabins*
Rates: *Singles $60 (EP), Doubles $65-75 (EP), Cabins $75-200 (EP)*
Payment: *AE, DC, DSC, MC, and VISA*
Dogs: *Welcome, but must be leashed when exploring the grounds*
Children: *Welcome (cots are available), children are free of charge*
Open: *All year, except Christmas*

Anyone who loves the west's vast expanses of open land, but who doesn't want to travel too far to get it, will be intrigued with the Flying M Ranch. Surrounded by more than 600 hundred acres of land (this is where the vast part comes in), the Flying M Ranch is situated at the end of a bumpy and winding five-mile-long road that was once the old stagecoach route. With every bump we gained a greater appreciation for what stagecoach travelers must have experienced along this road more than 120 years ago. The ranch is set in the Oregon Coast Range near the base of Trask Mountain. Those with small planes can fly in and land on the ranch's 2,200-feet grass runaway, disembarking directly in front of the main lodge.

This place has plenty of things to recommend it, especially for those who like horseback riding. Anyone ten years of age or older can choose between the short, day-long or overnight trail rides. Those choosing the latter will likely end up spending a night at the log cabin on Trask Mountain. Along the trail, riders will enjoy some spectacular scenery, as well as fine fishing in the many streams. Guests return to the ranch's wonderful home-cooked meals and comfortable accommodations — along with some country and western dancing for those who are still able to muster enough energy after a long day in the saddle.

Most of the ranch's activity revolves around the massive timber lodge, which guests enter by way of the large double doors, that are outfitted with axes as door handles. This cavernous space is dominated by bleached log walls adorned with bear and moose heads set alongside animal skins, rip saws, apple presses, antlers, saddles, and other assorted collectibles. The equally enormous restaurant, effectively divided in half by a massive stone fireplace, offers an array of western-style entrées (buffalo, venison, and elk) and is especially known for its barbecue. Towards the rear, guests will find the Sawtooth Lounge, which serves up live music, along with terrific views of the river from its bar — a six-ton log.

The accommodations vary, and lie just across the river from the lodge. Guests may choose from rooms in either the Bunkhouse Motel or the cabins, or really "rough it" and reserve one of the 100 or so campsites for a nominal fee. The Bunkhouse Motel is a large single-story building with a wraparound porch, offering 24 simply decorated and furnished guest quarters. While these rooms don't have televisions or air conditioning, each does contain a pair of queen beds, wall-to-wall carpeting, and modern bathrooms with stall showers. The rooms facing the river are our first choice, primarily because of their river views and large shade trees lining the banks. The cabins, on the other hand, range from the single-bedroom Wrangler's and Rustler's Roost cabins to the more expansive two-bedroom Royal Hideout and Dement cabins. Most have a living room with a sofa bed, a wood stove or fireplace, and a kitchen. Anyone requiring additional amenities should consider the Honeymoon Cabin, where they can bask in the luxury of a Jacuzzi tub, a color television, and a true country decor.

When not on horseback, guests will find numerous activities available, ranging from swimming in the huge pond to more organized events such as tennis, basketball, horseshoes, volleyball, and softball.

Dogs are rarely allowed to visit guest ranches, even though they seem like natural spots for these four-legged critters. We feel all the more fortunate then that the Flying M allows canine visitors to explore their **600 acres,** sniff out the wildlife, and even cool off in the **refreshing river**. It truly is a "dog's life."

Washington

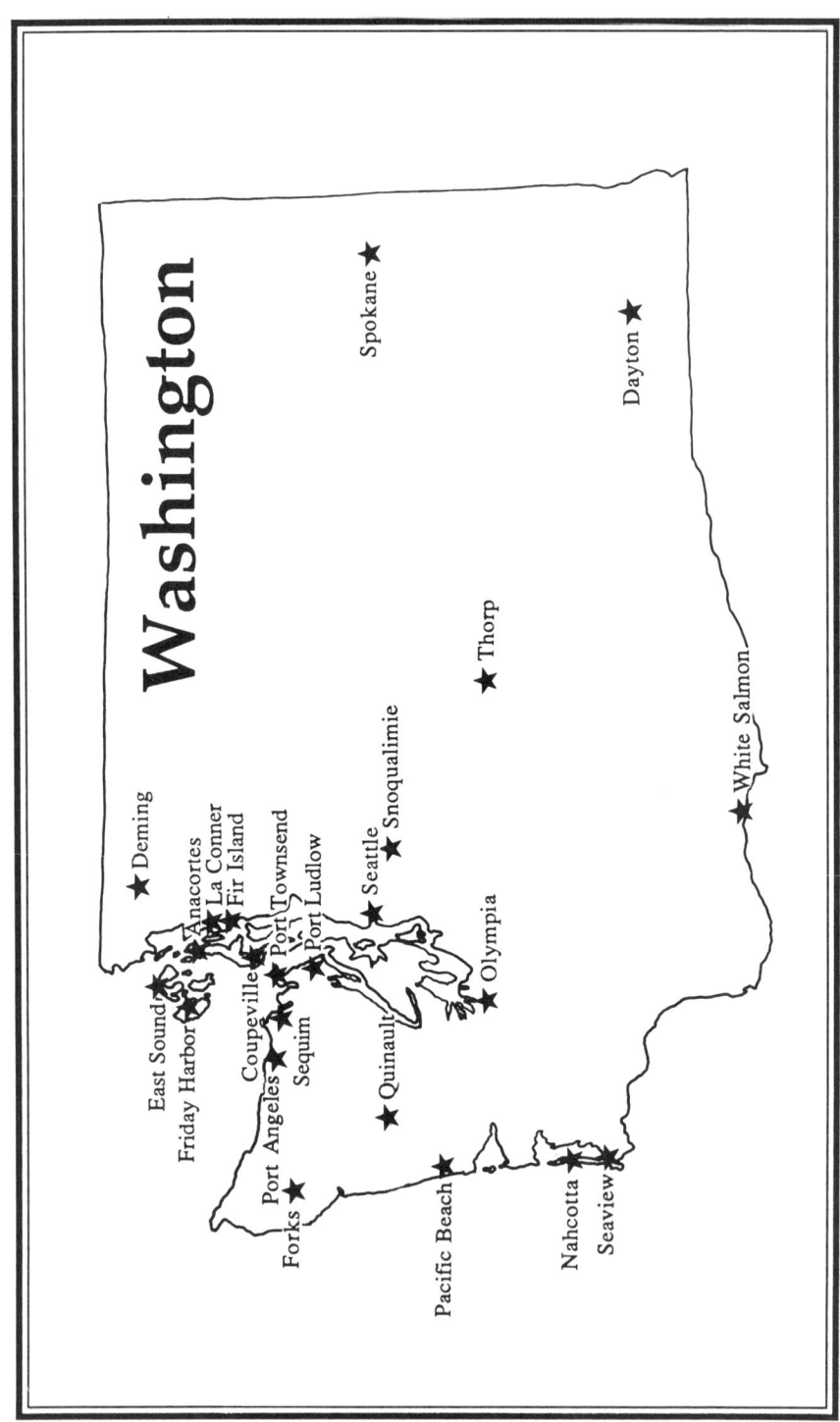

Albatross Bed and Breakfast

5708 Kingsway West
Anacortes, Washington 98221
(800) 484-9507 ext. 5840, (360) 293-0677

Hosts: *Barbie Guay and Ken Arasim*
Rooms: *4 doubles*
Rates: *$75-85 (B&B)*
Payment: *MC and VISA*
Dogs: *Welcome in the off season, but please bring dog's bedding*
Children: *Welcome, but most appropriate for children over the age of 4*
Open: *All year*

The morning ferry from Anacortes to Vancouver Island and the San Juan Islands leaves early — a bit too early for those coming from any distance. We have long thought it would be nice to have a place to stay in Anacortes, so that rolling out of bed to catch the ferry could actually be a pleasant, if not leisurely, experience. We finally found just the spot at the Albatross Bed and Breakfast.

The Albatross B&B is located at the edge of a residential neighborhood, overlooking a marina, various out buildings, and the more distant water. The Cape Cod-style house and the couple who own it are equally fascinating; however, we will begin with the house. In 1927, the E.K. Wood Mill Company built this cedar house for its mill manager. From about that time until 1943, the company operated one of the largest lumber mills in the state. Unfortunately, all that remains of that facility is a 600-foot-long planing mill. The rest of the buildings were torn down to make room for private homes, which, today, line the hills sloping down toward the water.

The Albatross rests on a street corner in a residential neighborhood. We initially had trouble finding the B&B, as there wasn't a sign with its name on it. Then we spied a bright blue building with white trim that was partially obscured by mature plantings. Ken, who is exceptionally friendly, greeted us and gave us a tour of his home. We half expected to be surrounded by the fragrant smell of cedar, but instead discovered that the exposed cedar was only in the guest wing and that its aroma was faint. Although the scent of cedar had diminished with the years, the deep red hues of the wood had only grown more beautiful. Two unusual features, beaded ceilings and extra thick doors — double the normal width — were especially noteworthy. Our first stop was in the Scarlett O'Hara room. Ken explained that friends of theirs bought an antique bedroom set out of an old Southern mansion. The friends later moved, didn't have room for it, and offered it to Ken and Barbie. This appealing addition to the B&B dates back to the 1850s; its focal point is the half-tester bed with its original velvet canopy, headboard, and footboard. Also present are a matching Lincoln rocker and a marble-topped commode. The commode holds a Victorian lamp with a cranberry-fluted shade of a thousand eyes. Ken and Barbie even have an old-fashioned "necessary chair," although guests won't need it, since a private, modern bathroom is only steps away. The other most popular bedroom lies at the opposite end of the hall. Known as the Monet room, it, too, contains some antiques, but it is named for the florals and lovely color schemes for which Monet is renowned. The Captain's Room is another intriguing space, which contains plenty of nautical paraphernalia sure to delight seafarers and landlubbers alike.

Guests are encouraged to use the living room as their sitting room. Most people are initially drawn to the two walls of plate glass windows offering distant water views. Later in the evening, when the sun has set, guests' attention shifts inward to the fireplace and the comfortable sofa. As we walked from one room to the next, we began to have a better understanding of Barbie and Ken — they are collectors. They collect all sorts of things, notably, fine art, bears, and clocks. More importantly, they know the history behind most pieces in their collections and can give guests a little story on just about everything in the house. But the two most extensive collections are Ken's antique cars and Barbie's — surprise, surprise — Barbie dolls. She displays these in the living and dining rooms, including some wearing Bob Mackie-designed gowns. One Erté doll gown called *Stardust* has over 7,000 decorative beads sewn into the fabric. The curious may wish to inquire about some of the B&B's original paintings. We learned that one actually shimmers — because of the gold dust mixed into the paint. With all these collectibles, guests will feel right at home — and they'll have a myriad of intriguing things to browse through during their stay.

In the morning, guest (even those trying to catch an early ferry) are treated to a hearty meal at the lace-covered dining room table. Barbie can make just about anything, and is happy to adjust her meal to fit guests' special needs. She usually begins breakfast with a fruit plate, which is then followed by homemade pancakes, Belgian waffles, or perhaps a baked-egg dish. Bacon and sausage are also available. Afterwards, guests may catch their ferry, just relax, or perhaps walk down to the water with your dog. There are grassy areas along the shore that are great fun for running a dog.

Ken told us about one great spot where people can walk with their dogs — **Washington Park**. This is a great seaside park that has plenty of places for picnicking or exploring with a canine. (There are more than 200 acres of grass, forest, and trails that lie on **Fidalgo Head**.) Other good hikes include the trail around **Cranberry** and **Heart Lakes** and the **Mount Eerie Trail**. Longer day trips can take visitors to **Deception Pass**, where there are even more hiking options available. Guests should keep in mind, though, that all of these areas are easily accessible from Seattle, so they tend to be crowded during the summer months. After a busy day, guests will probably want to return to the Albatross B&B for a little tea and more homemade baked goodies.

The Victorian B&B

P.O. Box 761
602 North Main
Coupeville, Washington 98239
(360) 678-5305, Internet: http://www.whidbey.net~asasso/

Innkeepers: *Al and Marion Sasso*
Rooms: *2 doubles, 1 cottage*
Rates: *Doubles $80 (B&B), Cottage $100 (B&B)*
Payment: *AE, MC, and VISA*
Dogs: *Welcome in the cottage only*
Children: *Welcome in the cottage only*
Open: *All year*

    Whidbey Island lay hidden from most navigators until 1792, when Joseph Whidbey discovered it quite by chance. One day, while sailing through the area, he observed an uncharted river that seemed to flow in the wrong direction. Whidbey secured a small boat and set out to explore the strange passageway, discovering, in the process, an intriguing island. The waterway leading to the island was ultimately called Deception Pass and the island named after Joseph Whidbey. Coupeville was the first settlement on the island. It was established in the 1850s — which makes it the second oldest town in Washington state.
    The Victorian Bed and Breakfast is equally historic. This Italianate Victorian home was built over 100 years ago by Jacob Jenne. It is one of a group of homes, all of similar architectural style, that comprise a portion of the town's historic district. Guests may not have water views, but they do feel a strong sense of history when staying at the inn. The Victorian Inn occupies a corner location, and is surrounded by mature shade trees. Its rich shade of blue, with rose highlights inset into the decorative trim, causes The Victorian to stand out from its neighbors. Bay windows seem to add definition to every ell, but the interior remains hidden from view by lace curtains. Guests step across the little half-porch and through the front door into a Victorian parlor, where Marion displays all sorts of handmade items available for purchase. Upstairs are two guest rooms decorated around a causal country theme — one in blues, the other in pinks; both are quite feminine in decor.
    The cottage is separate from the main house, but connected to it by a small courtyard framed with white lattice. It actually lies behind the house, on a side street, making it feel all the more private. This cottage, too, is historic, and, from the exterior, it looks like something out of a storybook. The cottage is difficult to see from the road, especially in the spring, when the pink and white wisteria cascade over the porch roof and down to the lavish display of pink lilacs. The aroma produced by this combination of flowers is thoroughly intoxicating. During the rest of the year, the pink hues are maintained with

climbing roses entwined on the white trellis. The four-room cottage's interior spaces are quite cozy, but ideal for anyone traveling with a dog. A separate bedroom contains a queen bed, a bureau, and the convenience of a television and VCR. There is a small sitting room with a trundle bed that sleeps two and also doubles as a sofa. As with the rooms in the main house, there is a low-key country feeling to the interior, with draped tables, small flowered prints, and muted color schemes. The convenience of a kitchen is helpful, especially when preparing an impromptu snack or a hearty breakfast for your dog. Humans are treated to their morning meal either at the inn or out on the courtyard. The menu varies, but guests may expect the usual selection of coffee, teas, and juices, along with, perhaps, the broiled grapefruit, homemade muffins, and the house specialty, a Dutch Baby pancake filled with strawberries or baked apples. Bacon may also be requested.

One of the many appealing things about staying here is that guests and their dogs can easily walk around Coupeville's waterfront. We like to avoid the main road when heading downtown, instead turning right out of the cottage and following a back road to the main street, which runs parallel to the harbor. The closest recreational outlet is the 200-acre **Fort Ebey State Park**, which is within a few minutes' drive of Coupeville. It was built in 1942 to offer some defense to Seattle, should the city be attacked via the Strait of Juan de Fuca. Today, visitors and their leashed dogs can visit the armaments or walk on the trails that wend through the park. One of the obvious, and more popular, choices is a trail that wends along the edge of the water. Another doggie option lies at **Fort Casey**, just south of town. Here, there are over 400 acres of fields, picnic sites, and trails to investigate.

The Purple House

415 East Clay Street
Dayton, Washington 99328
(800) 486-2574, (509) 382-3159

Innkeeper: *D. Christine Williscroft*
Rooms: *4 doubles, 2 suites, 1 cottage*
Rates: *Doubles $85 (B&B), Suites $125 (B&B), Cottage $125 (B&B)*
Payment: *MC and VISA*
Dogs: *Welcome*
Children: *Welcome*
Open: *All year*

Dayton is not necessarily the first town people think of for a weekend getaway, but it is a surprisingly good choice for those who enjoy hiking, fishing, or cross-country skiing with their dog, as the Umatilla National Forest is just minutes away. Although visitors might equate Dayton with the mountains, it is primarily a farming community. Its roots date back to the 1860s when gold lured prospectors to this region. Those who decided to stay built the Victorian homes we see here today. In the 1880s, the railroad, too, came to town, connecting Dayton with the rest of the west for nearly 100 years. Unfortunately, the train is gone, but the depot remains as a reminder of the town's history. Many of the Victorian homes, as well as the various civic buildings, have been beautifully preserved and form the town's two historic districts.

The Purple House shares in the town's rich history as well. It was built in 1882 by a Dr. Pietrzycki, who was both a physician and a philanthropist. This Queen-Anne Victorian is impressive, though it is a smaller version of the more expansive examples found in other parts of the country. Resting on a quiet side street, it is partially obscured by shade trees and other mature plantings. When Christine bought the house about ten years ago, it was in need of renovation. She spent many years working on her home and furnishing it with her many antiques and collectibles.

Christine left Germany more than 30 years ago, yet she has preserved her rich heritage and shares it with her guests. Here in Washington's countryside, guests are treated to an authentic European B&B. When new arrivals walk in the door, they are generally greeted by Christine's two Shih Tzus, Molley and Melley, who will no doubt want to show guests and their canines around the place. The front parlor is one of the more interesting areas in the house, with one wall of eight-foot-high windows overshadowed by the 18-foot ceilings. As one might imagine, this was not an easy room to fill, but Christine has done a wonderful job with her collection of Oriental antiques, assorted carvings, and a lovely silk screen. In most rooms a grand piano would be the highlight, but in this spacious chamber it barely fills one corner.

Couples traveling together usually reserve the two upstairs bedrooms that share a marble bathroom. Christine thinks this is especially suitable, as there is also an expansive library up here, and deep comfortable chairs ideal for sitting in and reading. One bedroom contains an antique sleigh bed that was covered with black paint when Christine first bought it. She spent hours taking the paint off to reveal the rich grain of the wood underneath. She likes to put feather comforters and pillows on the beds; however, for guests who are allergic; the other room's bed has a lovely Nettlecreek blanket on it.

Those who want a private entrance may choose between the first-floor bedroom or the carriage-house bedroom. The former is fashioned in rose tones, highlighted by a floral comforter on the queen bed. This already-bright space is lightened further by French doors that open directly onto the deck around the swimming pool. The bathroom in here is private, and is outfitted with a sunken bathtub. One final accommodation lies out in the carriage house. This offers the most flexibility of all the guest rooms, as it is separate from the main house. While it may lack some of the sunlight of the other bedrooms, the queen bed does face a glowing fireplace. Guests may prepare snacks in the kitchenette, although most people leave the food preparation up to Christine. She creates delicious European breakfasts, and, with a little notice, can produce delightful dinners.

In the morning, guests awake to the smell of freshly-baked breads. Christine says, almost apologetically, that she isn't really fond of American bread. We thought that just fine, as she creates the most fabulous and memorable breads using recipes brought from her homeland. Some are hearty breads; others are more reminiscent of rich pastries. The meal generally starts with a plate of bread and fresh fruit, followed by quiche or an overstuffed omelet. Christine is very flexible, and will prepare meals to order as well. Among her favorite food items are raspberries grown locally, specifically for her. Guests who may have missed her baked goods at breakfast may sample her pastries during afternoon tea.

After breakfast, some guests might want to take their canines for a leisurely walk along the quiet streets. The Chamber of Commerce supplies a map of the historic districts, making the outing all the more interesting. The **Blue Mountains** are within a short driving distance of The Purple House. In the wintertime, many come here to downhill and cross-country ski. (Your dog would probably prefer the latter.) Great day hikes and plenty of overnight hiking opportunities are also available in these mountains. The **Panjab Trailhead** is about an hour's drive from the inn. While the trail can keep hikers busy for days, it is also a good option for shorter outings. Another popular option can be found along the Eckler Mountain Road at the **Teepee Trailhead**. Hikers may head up or down, depending upon their mood. Those who follow the trail into the valley will end up at the East Butte Creek. Another popular hike off Eckler Mountain Road is the **Meadow Creek Trail**.

Christine is a flexible, gregarious hostess. We especially like her pet policy, which shows her true affinity for dogs. It reads as follows: *You and your well-behaved owners are welcome. The Purple House's resident Shih Tzus, Molley and Melley, love making friends of all sizes. Owners should inquire about providing for your comfort when making their reservations.*

The Logs Resort

9002 Mount Baker Highway
Deming, Washington 98244
(360) 599-2711

Hostess: *Hazel Ohlsen*
Rooms: *5 cottages*
Rates: *$75 (EP), $10 for each additional person, $6 per child*
Payment: *Personal checks*
Dogs: *Welcome, with approval, for a $4 daily fee*
Children: *Welcome (playpen available)*
Open: *All year*

Anyone who is looking for a rustic retreat, offering an assortment of outdoor activities and an abundance of natural beauty, should think about spending a week at The Logs Resort. A meandering country road lined by dense forests and a scenic river eventually leads to a dirt drive and the sign for the resort. Guests follow this driveway under a canopy of trees laden with hanging moss to a good-sized main house, resting upon the banks of Canyon Creek and the Nooksack River. Initially it may not look like much, but this house and cabins are The Logs Resort. With the change of seasons come copious amounts of rain, and occasionally the river crests; on some occasions the rain has flooded not only the riverside swimming pool but every other low-lying area as well. The rise in water level also carves deep grooves in the rocky river bed. Fortunately, the long-term damage is minimal, and those familiar with this low-key, unpretentious resort return each year to find the same handful of rustic cabins set amidst the forest, river, and more than 70 acres of grounds.

Each of the log cabins offers a different perspective of the surrounding forest and picturesque valley, but all provide the same basic amenities and general room configurations. The natural wood walls and timber-beamed ceilings nicely complement the simple decor and furnishings. All of these abodes contain two bedrooms, each with a pair of bunk beds and a private bathroom. The cozy living room, whose focal point is a stone fireplace, is also simply decorated and appointed. The foldout sofa bed gives guests the potential of transforming the living room into a third bedroom. Besides supplying linens and towels, Hazel stocks the kitchen with utensils, china, and pots and pans. There is always a substantial supply of wood stacked just outside the front door. While most guests enjoy the rustic ambiance of their accommodations, the primary draw to this spot is the pull of Mother Nature.

The surrounding valley, its array of recreational activities, and the scenic river area (complete with its associated wildlife) create the perfect environment for visitors and their canine companions to enjoy. We especially like the solar heated swimming pool perched on the banks of the river, although guests can also play horseshoes, badminton, and volleyball. Various swings are suspended from tall evergreens. Anglers will appreciate the excellent trout and salmon fishing, while dogs might prefer striking out with their human friends on the hiking trails that cut through the **Mount Baker National Forest**. Others may be interested in taking a short drive to the town of Glacier, where a series of hiking trails can be found — all of which allow dogs. The trails in this area offer spectacular natural beauty for all types of hikers. Some combine hiking with blueberry picking, especially along the **Excelsior Pass Trail** that leads to the Damfino Lakes. The equally pleasant **Skyline Divide** hike offers incredible vistas, along with spring wildflowers. This exceptionally easy trail leads hikers up to three lakes — **Hildebrand, Elbow,** and **Doreen**. Some visitors may prefer to confine their adventures to the resort, where they might choose to pick blueberries or follow the riverbed in search of fossils.

Those who visit during the winter months will find cross-country and downhill skiing at the Mount Baker Ski area (only 20 miles from the resort). The Logs Resort is a great destination just about any time of year, particularly for those who are looking for a low-key cabin experience they can share with their dog.

North Beach Inn

P.O. Box 80
Eastsound, Washington 98245
(360) 376-2660

Owners: *The Gibson Family*
Rooms: *11 cabins*
Rates: *Daily $95-170 (EP), Weekly $550-1,025 (EP)*
Payment: *Personal checks*
Dogs: *Welcome with a $10 daily fee*
Children: *Welcome (cribs and high chairs are available)*
Open: *March - November*

Orcas Island is a paradise for people who love exploring the outdoors with their dog. The highlights, of course, are Moran State Park and Mount Constitution. The island is more than just a state park, though; at nearly 60 miles, it is also the largest of all the San Juan Islands. Visitors are dropped off by ferry at the southern side of this horseshoe-shaped island; from there they need to drive north to Eastsound. Along the way, first-time visitors will get a good feeling for the island, with its pine forests, rolling green hills, and dramatic craggy shoreline.

Eastsound is the largest town on this lightly populated island, and it still exudes an old-world feeling. Just outside of town is a low-key retreat that is equally old-fashioned — and it should be; it has been here since the 1930s. Time seems to stand still at the North Beach Inn, and its owners, the Gibson family, don't see any need to speed up the clock. Their weathered cottages line a beautiful strip of stony beach and are surrounded by nearly 100 acres of upland — making this a most private retreat. When guests need a place to hide from the modern world and all its technology, this is the place to do it — there are no telephones, televisions, beepers, or fax machines. Guests just need to bring enough supplies to stock the cabin (there is a one-week minimum in July and August) and then just settle into the slow-paced rhythm of the place. Those who come to the North Beach Inn should come prepared to be charmed by the simplicity of this place.

The cottages are all similar to one another; but guests should keep in mind that they are just a few notches above camping. While this might appeal to dogs and children, adults need to know how to plan for such a vacation. Guests can expect a full kitchen and a barbecue for cooking, separate sleeping areas, and a fireplace. The furnishings are an eclectic mix of what appears to be hand-me-downs from well meaning friends. Linens are supplied, or guests may bring their own. But with the surrounding beach, ocean, and forests in the area, guests spend most of their time outside.

People like to have bonfires on the shore at night, run their dogs along the beach, and take long walks through the forest. Most will discover, much to their delight, that it is easy to reconnect with the natural world after just a few days. Guests may want to bring a kayak, or rent one locally, and explore these calm waters and fjord-like bays. When it rains, which is rare, it's time to head inside, build a fire, and read or play games. There are some good restaurants on the island, but they are a bit of a drive from the resort. Once guests arrive, most tend to settle in for the duration.

If they do leave, it is generally to make the short drive over to the 4,600-acre **Moran State Park**. Here, visitors will more than 31 miles of hiking trails traversing the park, all of which welcome dogs. The varied scenery is truly spectacular. Some like to hike to the top of **Mount Constitution**, which, at over 2,400 feet, rises dramatically from sea level. A shorter hike leads to **Twin Lakes**, or people and their canines may prefer to spend the day at **Mountain Lake**. Visitors can always get around the island by car, but it is often more fun — and more interesting — to tour by bicycle. They may either rent or bring their own mountain bikes, which can easily navigate the dirt roads and sandy trails that lead to the some of the more isolated portions of Orcas Island.

South Fork Moorage

Box 633
2187 Mann Road
Fir Island, Washington 98238
(360) 445-4803
Internet: http://www.virtualcities.com/ons/wa/f/waf3501.htm

Houseboat Captain: *Jessy Demick*
Rooms: *2 houseboats*
Rates: *$80-115 (EP)*
Payment: *Personal checks*
Dogs: *Welcome with approval*
Children: *Welcome — but call first; they should be swimmers*
Open: *All year*

The South Fork Moorage is another one of our unique finds — two unusually fine houseboats nestled on the serene Skagit River. Jessy tells a wonderful story about how it all started. During the Depression, one of the houseboats, the Karma, floated on Lake Union. It was one of forty dwellings used as inexpensive housing for those who could afford little else at the time. Jessy and Karma crossed paths some 25 years ago, when he discovered the partially submerged houseboat slowly making its way into the murky waters of Lake Union. He recovered it, began an extensive restoration process, and over the next quarter century, moved it from harbor to harbor looking for an ideal home. He finally found a permanent place to keep it on Fir Island, and just six years ago purchased the property that adjoins the moorage. Jessy recently added another houseboat — the equally appealing Teahouse.

Now there are houseboats, and then there are *houseboats* — these are *houseboats*. They aren't visible from the country lane where visitors enter, as there is a mounded earthen dike, and plenty of trees and bushes creating a natural barrier between the lane and water. We parked in a small dirt parking area, then followed a raised wooden walkway that leads to the river. First in line is the Teahouse, aptly named because it does resemble an authentic Japanese teahouse. Its exterior walls of pale gray wood flow up to the gentle peaks of the shingled roof, inset with subtle skylights. We thoroughly enjoyed the porches off either end, fashioned with benches and assorted pots overflowing with flowers. These decks nicely expand the amount of sitting areas the vessel can offer, while providing a pleasant sanctuary from which guests can enjoy their surroundings. The Teahouse is also graced with many paned windows, the largest of these facing the river. The living room, with its wide window seats and breakfast table, is outfitted with one wall of glass doors that open directly to the porch. Privacy is created, when needed, by drawing the pretty cotton floral curtains. Beyond the sitting room is a tiny galley, a head, and a cozy bedroom that is just right for two.

The Karma is the granddaddy of them all, though. Its redwood shingles and deep green trim accentuate a boat outfitted with an array of nooks, crannies, and levels. One side is fashioned with Palladian windows, while on another, there are tiny paned windows interspersed with exquisite stained-glass windows. The varying hues of color that fall across the lustrous woods in the interior are soothing to the eye and mind. To come aboard the Karma, guests must navigate through a miniature door. As we stepped down into the living room, we entered what would eventually be one of our favorite congregating spots. This inviting chamber is fashioned with one wall of plate-glass windows, a fireplace, and plenty of thickly-cushioned seats. On one side of the room, there is a lovely Palladian-shaped, stained-glass window. The galley kitchen opens up into the living room, so the cook never feels isolated. At the other end of the Karma lies the first-floor bedroom, but it was the sleeping loft, with its wall of stained glass, that proved most intriguing. Skylights provide guests with more than enough natural light during the day. The deep green background of the floral cotton fabrics used on the Karma look all the more handsome against the varnished teak. The head in both these boats is, of course, of the marine variety — so guests should be careful of their usage. Although Jessy does not supply breakfast, he does stock the kitchen with two welcome amenities: champagne upon arrival and coffee for the next morning. Barbecues are available for outdoor cooking. Those who may be concerned about their privacy, need not be, as a small sign is posted at the beginning of the boardwalk indicating "Guests on Board."

Though Jessy obviously has a love for the water, he now lives in a little farmhouse that overlooks the river. We visited late in the season, but his extensive gardens were still in various stages of bloom. During our wanderings, we encountered a few cats cruising the property — which is probably the biggest reason why visitors should heed the sign about keeping their dogs on a leash.

There are plenty of places that are lots of fun for taking long walks with a dog. The **lane running alongside the houseboats** is generally quiet and parallels the dike on one side and farms on the other. In the summer months, Jessy will take guests and their dogs up river to Mt. Vernon or Burlington and let them **canoe or kayak** back down the river. Some of the more popular off-river options include a visit to the **Padilla Bay Estuary**, where there are various nature trails to follow that welcome leashed dogs. Another possibility includes heading over to Whidbey Island, where the **Deception Pass State Park** is located. It, too, welcomes hikers and their canines. While the park can get a little crowded at times, it is easy to find a little solitude on the miles of trails that wend through the dense forests, along the cliffs, and down near the water.

Kalaloch Lodge

H.C. 80, Box 1100
Forks, Washington 98331
(206) 962-2271
Internet: http://www.travel-in-wa.com/ADS/hadley.html

Manager: ARA Leisure Services
Rooms: 18 doubles, 40 cabins
Rates: Doubles $48-89 (EP), Cabins $70-187 (EP)
Payment: AE, MC, and VISA
Dogs: Welcome in the cabins ($10 fee)
Children: Welcome (cribs and cots are available)
Open: All year

The Kalaloch Lodge occupies one of the most scenic locations in the Olympic National Park. From its cliff-top position, visitors enjoy spectacular panoramic ocean views. At this juncture along the coastline, the sandy beaches stretch almost endlessly, linked during low tide, isolated from one another when the tide rolls in. It is for these reasons — beautiful beaches and incredible views — that the lodge is usually booked well in advance on both weekends and holidays, year round.

Many guests consider the accommodations secondary to the beautiful surroundings. The lodge consists of a weathered, gray-shingled and blue-trimmed main building (built in 1952) with eight guest rooms, a motel, and either the bluff or traditional log cabins. Guests traveling with dogs are allowed in the cabins, so we will focus on these accommodations. The cabins contain brass beds, kitchenettes, and Franklin-style fireplaces. (The staff supplies ample amounts of wood.) In 1997, a group of cabins were refurbished with new siding, but aside from this improvement, these places remain rustic and simple. In lieu of amenities guests and their dogs get *plenty* of character.

One cabin has the luxury of a whirlpool tub; however, this is the exception — the other bathrooms are equipped with the basics: a toilet, sink, and stall shower. The kitchenettes are not, we repeat, not equipped. So those planning on preparing their own meals should bring everything they need from home. The cabins serve as clean and comfortable quarters; it is really the view and the surrounding environs that bring guests back year after year.

Although there are basic kitchen facilities, many want to feel as if they are truly vacationing, so they opt to take their meals in the hexagonal restaurant. The Galley restaurant is decorated in a nautical motif and boasts ocean views. Here, dining patrons may sample the lodge's numerous seafood entrées, which are freshly caught and well prepared. Guests may choose from such standards as salmon, prawns, oysters, cod, and scallops, as well as a few beef and chicken dishes. A coffee shop sits apart from the main dining room, offering the same food without the ocean view and at a less leisurely pace. (It is ideal for those with children.) Meals can be expensive, and guests should consider themselves a captive audience — there are no other restaurant options (or anything else, for that matter) in the nearby area.

There is much to do in and around the lodge. In many respects, this region is like a huge wildlife refuge, with water fowl and animals living comfortably alongside humans. The **local beach** is sandy, flat, and inviting — for everything except swimming. Guests may rent clam shovels at the lodge's grocery store and dig for razor clams (in season). Some enjoy collecting seashells, **hiking along the waterside trails**, or just watching the migrating gray whales each season. Of course, the area is also famous for its flora and fauna, found amid the lush rain forests. The Hoh and Queets rain forests are within a short driving distance of the lodge. Guests should keep in mind, though, that the entire Olympic National Forest and Park are off-limits to dogs. So people staying at the Kalaloch Lodge need to feel content keeping their dog within the confines of this seaside domain.

Kalaloch means "lots of clams," "easy living," or "land of plenty," depending on one's interpretation. Just as the word holds different meanings for each individual, so will the breadth of one's vacation here. Many come to relax and contemplate, some to explore every nook and cranny, and still others to enjoy the fishing and clamming. Guests who visit during the winter months might find a little more rainfall, but we have to say, the off-season is perfect for those who are looking for total peace and quiet.

Westwinds and Harmony Cottage

4904 H. Hannah Road
Friday Harbor, Washington   98250
(360) 378-5283, Internet: http://www.karuna.com/westwinds/

Owner: Christine Durbin
Rooms: 1 house, 1 cottage
Rates: House $165-245 (B&B), Cottage $150-195 (B&B)
Payment: MC and VISA
Dogs: Welcome
Children: Welcome
Open: All year

    The address for Westwinds and Harmony Cottage indicates they are in Friday Harbor, but they really are not. They are actually situated well off the beaten path on the western side of San Juan Island. We figuratively traveled over hill and dale to find this B&B, passing rolling hills dotted with farms and livestock. Our inland adventure, gradually led us to the ocean, where we rounded one corner to discover breathtaking views of the Juan de Fuca Strait and beyond, to the snow-covered Olympic Mountains. Even though we could see snow on the distant mountains, the blackberries along the side of the road were bountiful, causing us to stop for a moment to sample a few handfuls while enjoying the wonderful views. We headed off half wondering if we were not extremely lost, when around another corner we found Hannah Road. This led us up a steep hill to a dirt road and a small sign pointing the way to Westwinds.

    Flanked on one side by pines, and on the other by ponds and pastures, we followed the dirt lane a short distance to a corral, where we came across Chris's miniature ponies. We couldn't resist stopping a moment to visit with these endearing creatures, and it was from this vantage point that we were able to get a better feeling for Westwinds. Red-hued woods, windows, and skylights dominated this one-story house tucked into a conifer grove on the hillside above us.

    We made one last short trip up the steep incline to reach the house and found Chris outside gardening with her Golden Retriever, Brandy. Actually, Brandy was lying in the sun and Chris was gardening. After getting to know Chris, we can understand why people (and their dogs) generally feel so comfortable around her. Chris is relaxed and friendly, but recognizes that guests often enjoy their privacy. She offers two choices — Westwinds and Harmony House. Westwinds is a large two bedroom retreat that is perfect for two couples or a family, while Harmony House is best just for two (and your dog of course).

Our first stop was Westwinds, and once inside it was easy to see the effect of all this glass, as the same incredible ocean and mountain views we delighted in from the road, were even more dramatic from this vantage point. As we walked through the entry and emerged into the central cathedral ceiling living room, a pair of soft modern couches and chairs created a most inviting gathering space. We would have been content to relax in this room, with a crackling fire and a stereo setting the tone, while we just soaked in the views. However, the two bedrooms are equally appealing, although only one, the master bedroom, has water views. These vistas can be enjoyed from the bed, or from the patio that is accessible through the glass doors. Each bedroom does have a private bathroom, which is a pleasant convenience. Guests can cook all their meals in the fully-equipped kitchen, and enjoy them in the good-sized dining room.

Harmony House in a one bedroom cottage that is even more private and intimate than Westwinds. It lies on four forested hillside acres, and is just a few minutes from Westwinds. The cottage seems to be made entirely of windows, with ruddy hardwoods merely serving as the framework. Wherever one looks there are bucolic views, whether of the distant ocean or more immediate forests. Guests can open the French doors to the refreshing breezes, or when the day turns cool, light a fire and settle into the deep sofa with a good book. As with Westwinds, there is a fully equipped kitchen for cooking dinner, but when it comes to breakfast, let Chris deliver one of her bountiful baskets of healthy gourmet goodies.

She brings this basket the night before, so that guests can dip into it at their leisure. Chris laughingly told us, though, that most guests often sample many of the breakfast wares the night before because they just cannot wait until morning. She is a vegetarian and believes strongly in animal rights. Therefore, do not expect to find any meat dishes, although she does use eggs in some of her baked goods. This substantial affair usually features fresh muffins, banana breads, fresh berries and other island fruits, homemade granola, and her special apple crisp. (It is made with a secret ingredient — butterscotch pudding.) Chris will also create exotic fruit smoothies, with a splash of protein powder — and many other intriguing libations.

Exploring the property around Westwinds and Harmony House is always a delightful way to spend one's time. At Westwinds, take your dog down to visit the miniature horses or to **investigate the pond**. There are **woods** just beyond this, and a little path that provides even more dramatic views. There isn't much car traffic in these parts which makes it pleasant to explore the **back country roads** on foot with your dog. For those who may wish to explore a little further afield, Westside Road leads to the **Lime Kiln State Park**, where dogs and their human friends are welcome to explore. Best of all, guests will quickly learn that Westwinds is the kind of B&B where people feel free to do their own thing. One word of advice, Westwinds is often booked well in advance, so we recommend making reservations as far in the future as possible — to be guaranteed of sharing this little bit of paradise.

Friday Harbor House

P.O. Box 1385
130 West Street
Friday Harbor, Washington 98250
(360) 378-8455, Fax: (360) 378-8453
Internet: http://www.specialplaces.com

Manager: *Jim Skoog*
Rooms: *19 doubles, 1 suite*
Rates: *Doubles $185 (B&B), Suite $325 (B&B)*
Payment: *AE, MC, and VISA*
Dogs: *Welcome in dog-friendly rooms with a $100 refundable deposit*
Children: *Welcome*
Open: *All year*

The Friday Harbor House is just one of a small group of boutique inns in this region. Its sister properties, the Inn at Langley and the BoatYard Inn, lie on Whidbey Island, while the third establishment, the Inn at Ludlow Bay, is situated on the Olympic Peninsula. All of these share one especially pleasing characteristic — idyllic waterside settings. The Friday Harbor House is perched on a bluff overlooking Friday Harbor, with fabulous water views from just about every vantage point. It was completed just over a year ago — a rather contemporary, shingled building, designed as a retreat that would complement its native environment. We thought its wood-shingled exterior blended very well, but weren't terribly impressed with the contemporary lines of the facade. However, as we stepped inside, a far more inspired setting unfolded.

The tiny lobby is fashioned with natural woods and glass, and still exudes the aroma of freshly-milled timber. We were warmly greeted by a staff member, and while waiting to see the guest rooms, sampled some of the fruit set out in a basket on a side table. Guest rooms occupy two buildings, with the most desirable of these situated in the main inn looking out toward the water. All of these well-designed chambers are spacious and bright, especially when the sun streams through the floor-to-ceiling windows and glass doors. The latter open onto tiny porches, most of which are ideal places from which to take in the views. A distinct Asian theme permeates throughout, set against a backdrop of subtle luxury. Slate blue, cream, and chestnut complement the fabrics and highlight some of the moldings. The beds rest on boxed platforms, which, in the winter months, are topped with extra thick European mattresses and duvets. Instead of headboards, the beds are backed by a creative arrangement of decorative tiles. Guests can settle into the soft cushions on the cherry wood-framed chairs and gaze into the fireplace or out across the water. Books are provided in the room, just in case guests have forgotten theirs. These chambers are also well appointed, with small refrigerators stocked with mineral water; coffee makers and all the necessities for preparing tea or coffee; and corkscrews for opening a bottle of wine. Equally well thought out are the tiled bathrooms, complete with Jacuzzi bathtubs, baskets of Lord and Mayfair toiletries, hair dryers, and thick cotton bathrobes. Each room at the Friday Harbor House is lovely; however, given a choice, we would reserve a corner room, as much for the two walls of windows as for the additional privacy.

In the morning, a Continental breakfast of scones, pastries, fresh fruit, and coffee or tea is available downstairs. We love the intimate restaurant for dinner. It feels almost subterranean, as it is tucked against the lower terrace, providing guests with lovely views of the San Juans over the adjacent rock wall. Bleached and naturally-stained woods brighten this intimate space. The management of the inn has worked hard to bring in a fine culinary talent — Greg Atkinson. While the menu is short, it does emphasize the freshest island produce, fruits, and game. Guests may wish to sample such appetizers as the Westcott Bay oysters baked with sweet red pepper butter, the thin crust pizza loaded with fresh island vegetables, or the Dungeness crab cakes with a remouláde. Entrées include a filet of wild king salmon with a sun-dried tomato butter, filet of beef with artichoke hearts, and the island seafood stew.

After dinner, we enjoy walking with our dogs, especially down the quiet back streets, which are rarely busy at night, even during the height of tourist season. Just next to the hotel is a **tiny public park**, which consists of no more than a couple of benches set amid a little grass and shrubbery. Many visitors and locals alike enjoy coming up here with their dogs to look out over the harbor, read, or just visit. Others like to **rent a canoe** and take their dogs for a trip along the protected waters leading out to some of the neighboring islands. Another popular option is to visit **Jackson Beach**, where furry friends are welcome to explore, while their humans, perhaps, fly a kite.

Wharfside Bed and Breakfast

P.O. Box 1212, Slip K
Friday Harbor, Washington 98250
(360) 378-5661, Fax: (360) 378-4271
Internet: http://www.rockisland.com/~pcshop/wharfside.htm

Hosts: *Clyde and Bette Rice*
Rooms: *2 doubles*
Rates: *$80-85 (B&B)*
Payment: *MC and VISA*
Dogs: *Welcome, with a small fee*
Children: *Welcome (cribs and high chairs are available)*
Open: *All year*

A stay aboard the *Jacquelyn* is such a wonderful experience that even those who profess no affinity with the sea could be tempted to come aboard for a night or two. This is a 60-foot, ketch-rigged, motorized sailing vessel owned by Bette and Clyde Rice. For 12 years, these amiable hosts have provided landlubbers and seafarers alike with a truly extraordinary B&B experience.

We always enjoy the walk to the *Jacquelyn* because we feel as though we are about to set off on a grand, sea-going adventure, even though we know we will remain at the dock for the duration of our stay. Sada, the Rice's frisky canine welcomed us aboard. (His full name is Hosada, but according to Clyde, "Ho" sounded too much like "no," so they simply call him Sada.) On this day, we found Clyde fixing something in the galley, but he gladly left this duty to reacquaint us with his floating B&B.

Very little ever changes aboard the *Jacquelyn*, and for that we are grateful. The Rices' was the first floating B&B on the West Coast, and while there are now more houseboat B&Bs on the waters around Washington state, few are as intriguing as this one. Clyde led us down to the Victorian parlor that serves as the nucleus of the ship, particularly during the cooler months. This is not a dark space, being lit naturally, with skylights and numerous portholes. This salon features plenty of comfortable, built-in spots for reading, listening to music, or even watching a video. The lustrous woodwork is the backdrop to the pair of settees, a carved wooden desk, a television, a small bar, and an abundance of knickknacks and collectibles that the Rices gathered during their world travels. A wonderful combination of Oriental rugs, Victorian antiques, nautical paraphernalia and other unusual collectibles creates an intriguing atmosphere.

There are two good-sized accommodations from which guests may choose. The more popular Aft Stateroom's white walls and ceiling highlight the gentle curves and strapping of the boat; these flowing lines are interspersed with portholes and small prints depicting seaside scenes. Guests settle into the large, cradle-like bed topped by a rich burgundy, paisley-patterned comforter and matching sheets. Guests can turn on a little music, sample one or two of the gold wrapped chocolates, and let the refreshing salt air help them drift off to sleep. Two of the reasons for this stateroom's popularity are the private head and separate entrance. Bette reminds us, though, that although the Forward Cabin does not have a private head, the adjacent parlor is rarely used by anyone except the guests staying in the Forward Cabin — which really makes the setup seem more like a suite. The Forward Cabin contains a large double berth and two seaman-size bunks that make for a cozy sleeping experience if the children are along. All the berths are covered with patchwork quilts; as with the Aft Stateroom, electric mattress pads keep seafarers warm and cozy. The tiled shower is shared, with far more elbow room and hot water than most people equate with a boat. Robes are thoughtful additions, making trips to and from the shower more pleasant.

Breakfast is a full-blown affair, with guests sitting around the semicircular table in the galley or, weather permitting, up on deck. Bette is the head chef, and produces excellent breakfasts from her efficiently appointed galley. Her specialties still include quiche or a spiced apple strudel-like dish she calls Captain's Crunch. Our breakfast started with a hollowed pineapple filled with exotic fruits, and was followed by spicy baked eggs, shell-shaped parmesan potatoes, bacon, blueberry muffins, and coffee. Guests should be sure to ask Bette how she makes this rich coffee. (Her answer surprised us.) This happened to be a wonderful and warm fall morning, and we enjoyed this splendid repast on the upper deck.

The Wharfside is appealing not only because it offers a unique B&B experience, but also because of Bette and Clyde. They go out of their way to answer questions, point out interesting sights, and provide a variety of suggestions on what to do in the area. Clyde is also a seasoned skipper, who has sailed almost around the world with the Scripps Institute in La Jolla, California. He and Bette have wonderful stories of their extensive adventures and travels. At guests' disposal is an Eddon Gig rowboat for exploring the harbor, as well as a skippered Boston Whaler. Numerous forms of wildlife, ranging from otters and seals to whales and eagles, are often spotted during a visit. In season, many a fisherperson has caught shrimp and crabs right from the dock. We can think of no better way to enjoy an island vacation than on the water. There are times, though, when your dog will want to get her paws on a little grass or sand. The walk from the boat up the hill is an adventure unto itself. Just after hitting dry land, there is a **small, shaded park** where dogs are frequently found cavorting. **Leisurely walks through town** with a dog are also lots of fun, especially along the quieter side streets. South of Friday Harbor is a small strip of sand that dogs can run on called **Jackson Beach**. Another popular outing is the **San Juan County Park**, a waterfront campground located on the west side of the island, which dogs are also welcome to explore.

Tucker House

260 B Street
Friday Harbor, Washington 98250
(800) 965-0123, (360) 378-2783, (360) 378-6437
Internet: http://www.virtualcities.com/ons/wa/j/waj6601.htm

Owners: Skip and Annette Metzger
Rooms: 2 doubles, 3 cottages
Rates: Doubles $85 (B&B), Cottages $105-195 (B&B)
Payment: AE, DSC, MC, and VISA
Children: Welcome (high chairs, cots, and portable cribs are available)
Dogs: Welcome in the cottages, with notice and approval, for a $15 daily
    fee. They must be under 40 pounds and there is a maximum of two
    dogs per cottage
Open: All year

    The Tucker House, built in 1898 by Clarin Tucker, lies in the heart of Friday Harbor on San Juan Island. The main Victorian residence is as close to a human-sized doll house as most people will probably ever find. (This tiny house includes a front porch bedecked with potted and hanging flowering plants.) A white picket fence encircles the entire property. Hidden within are tiered flower gardens and patches of grass interspersed with mature fruit trees. This serene setting is as ideal for reading or relaxing as it is for providing a safe setting for frolicking dogs and children.
    Repeat guests will be pleased to know that life at the Tucker House remains much the same as always, as the Metzgers' share the theory that "if

it ain't broke, don't fix it." Thus, the overall decor, furnishings, and atmosphere remain very much intact from visit to visit. Since our last visit, though, the main house's two guest rooms have again been made available to guests, and the three cottages have been slightly updated. The cottages nestle into the garden terraces set behind the house, thus providing private enclaves that are perfect for those traveling with dogs.

One of these, the Rose Cottage, has a bedroom and a separate sitting room. The trellis lining the lower interior walls, coupled with the flowered comforter resting upon the bed, accentuate the garden cottage motif. A tiny, separate sitting room contains a sofa bed and has a wall of sliding glass doors that open to a private deck. Guests looking for a refreshing breeze need only open the glass doors and the top of the Dutch door to let the invigorating sea breezes flow through the cottage.

Just down the knoll is the Willow Cottage, the accommodation most often requested by couples. We passed through yet another Dutch door and into the kitchenette of this cottage. The high-ceilinged bedroom, complete with a wood stove, lies to the rear of this abode. The walls are bare, except for a few prints, but the king bed's fluffy comforter and oversized pillows add plenty of interest to this space. Upholstered armchairs create an inviting sitting area off to the side. Another entrance, off the bedroom, leads out to a deck.

The most private cottage of all, though, is the Lilac Cottage, which is where the Metzgers lived when they renovated the main house. It lies across from the other two cottages and is reached by passing through various decks. We entered the cottage through the double French doors, passed beyond the kitchen and bathroom, into the wonderful bedroom with loft space. (The loft is not accessible.) This dark, cozy chamber is lined with walls of bookshelves, including some within easy reach of the queen bed. There are all sorts of quirky things about this place, but what we liked most was the unusually small door, situated up another step, that opens onto a private deck behind the cottage. A pass-through window is one link between the bedroom and the kitchen. Each cottage, with or without a kitchen, does have a table that is usually pre-set for the next morning's breakfast.

When new arrivals do venture out of their cottage, they might go for a dip in the hot tub, wander about the gardens, or head over to the main house. When we poked our heads inside, we met up with Chloe and Sophie, the resident Poodle and Cocker Spaniel who padded through the house with us. There is a crispness to the interior, yet the historic Victorian details are also evident, especially in the hand-carved window and door moldings. The front parlor is where guests often gather at the beginning or the end of the day. Here, they may recline in the white wicker chairs and either enjoy a good book or watch a little television. Sunlight pours through the room's bow window during the day, while at night this inviting chamber becomes all the more cozy when the blinds are drawn.

Skip's breakfast is the highlight of each morning. Guests may eat in the solarium or take their meal back to their cottage. We especially like dining in the solarium, as it overlooks the garden and is generally quite warm, even when the outside temperature is cool. Fresh fruit bowls may be complemented with a cheese soufflé, muffins, and Skip's famous cinnamon bread. Juice, tea, and excellent coffee also accompany the meal. The Metzgers are always eager to share the recipes to their more popular dishes, even going so far as to printing the recipes on small cards and sending them home with interested guests. The most requested recipes are for their cinnamon bread and baked eggs.

Guests can work off breakfast by walking their dogs **two short blocks** into town where they will find art galleries, shops, restaurants, and the ferry. Just around the corner from the Tucker House is a great place to rent a moped — or to stop and let their dogs play with the owner's dog who is usually lying in the sun in front of the place. This is a doggie haven, with the local dogs leading a casual, carefree kind of life. It is easy to meet some of the local pooches in the **sunken park** just across from the Tucker House. This is a wonderful spot to run a dog, as there are plenty of informal grassy areas, wildflowers, and even a few shade trees. For those who want to travel further afield, the **San Juan Island National Historical Park** is great for picnicking — and for exploring some of the restored barracks and outbuildings used by the British and American troops during their occupation of San Juan Island in the mid-1800s. There are two sections to this park, one on the northwest side of the island, the other on the southeast end — neither one will dissapoint. At the end of the day, return for tea in the garden at the Tucker House.

La Conner Country Inn

107 South Second Street
La Conner, Washington 98257
(360) 466-3101, Fax: (360) 466-5902

General Manager: *Gary Tachiyama*
Rooms: *26 doubles, 2 suites*
Rates: *Doubles $89-102 (B&B), Suites $130 (B&B)*
Payment: *AE, DC, DSC, MC, and VISA*
Dogs: *Welcome, with notice, in two rooms on the ground floor with a one-time $25 cleaning fee.*
Children: *Welcome (cribs, cots, and baby-sitters are available)*
Open: *All year*

Once best known as a farming and fishing village, La Conner's brilliant springtime show of tulips and daffodils is what now draws visitors to Skagit Valley. This region is somewhat reminiscent of Holland, with dikes holding back the encroaching sea — and, when successful, leaving exceptionally fertile farmland. Those who don't happen to visit in springtime will still find quaint shops lining the Swinomish Channel. These offer everything from antiques to trendy clothes. The centrally located La Conner Country Inn is set just a block off the channel. While it is a relatively new building, the rough-hewn board and weathered-shingle facade allows it to easily blend in with the town's other historic homes.

Guests driving in under the *porte cochère* to the rear of the building will find that the overall ambiance changes markedly to that of a traditional motor inn style: two floors of accommodations, all with separate outside entrances. This is actually a bonus for anyone traveling with a dog, as it makes it easy to get in and out of the room without disturbing the other guests. We are unhappy to report, though, that since our last visit there has been some abuse of the dog privileges. Guests traveling with dogs were once allowed a full range of room choices, but now they are limited to just two ground-floor units. We checked out these two chambers and discovered they were comparable to the other accommodations offered at the inn.

The La Conner Country Inn's Victorian decor has always appealed to us because it isn't too ornate. Brass beds fill only a portion of the room, leaving plenty of floor space for guests and their dog. One of the designated canine rooms has both a queen and a twin brass bed, and both are covered with floral spreads reflecting the room's subdued burgundy and slate blue hues. The well-positioned beds face the crackling fire, which is flanked by a pair of black leather wing chairs. Off to the side is a small breakfast table that lies under a paned window. The room's decorative treatments are minimal, as loosely woven baskets are the only accents against the crisp white walls. A color television, a direct dial telephone, and a clock radio set on the oak bedside table are just a few of the additional amenities. The large bathroom has the added convenience of a second separate sink. We liked the touch of the Caswell Massey shampoos, conditioners, and soaps.

When not relaxing in their rooms, guests have a couple of options — the library and Palmers restaurant. The former is an inviting space, where a mix of traditional furnishings, including overstuffed sofas and wing chairs, all rest on an Oriental carpet covering the hardwood floor. Guests may select from a variety of newspapers and magazines set out on the coffee table, or simply put their feet up and enjoy the warmth emanating from the beachstone fireplace. Dried and fresh flowers provide some decorative interest to this cozy chamber. In the morning, a substantial Continental breakfast is also served here. Guests may choose from cinnamon buns and scones, granola, and other cold cereals, along with juice, coffee, tea, and hot chocolate.

Dinner is an entirely different experience. The intimate Palmers restaurant is not operated by the Thompsons, but by Thomas and Danielle Palmer. This cozy, multi-level eatery is housed in a cottage nestled into the hillside behind the inn. Guests may step into the English-style pub, specializing in micro brewery beers, and sip one of these libations. We love the character of this intimate chamber, as there are only four seats at the bar and just two additional tables. Up a flight of stairs, we found the equally charming restaurant with its beamed, cathedral ceilings, stained glass windows, and a fireplace. Some patrons choose to start with the pan fried oysters in a lemon caper aioli; the steamed mussels with white wine, shallots, garlic and butter; or the wilted spinach salad with smoked duck. The pasta menu is extensive, with the spinach fettuccine topped by smoked king salmon, artichokes, hearts of palm, sundried tomatoes, and roasted pistachios; or the penne with prawns, shiitake mushrooms, leeks, spinach and a pernod cream setting the tone. Entrée specialties run the gamut as well, featuring a hazelnut crusted halibut with an sherry beurre blanc; the roast duckling with fried polenta and a wild raspberry demi-glacé; or the grilled medallions of beef tenderloin with a bordelaise sauce and roasted garlic cream.

After dinner, we took the dogs for a **walk into the village** for a little window shopping. We always enjoy strolling along these narrow streets, up and down the hills, viewing the Victorian homes and the intimate canalfront area. Another jaunt worth investigating is the **Padilla Bay National Marine Estuary**. This is a series of interpretive trails that are open to hikers and their leashed dogs. There are **three trails** worth exploring: one forested route, another hugging the shoreline, and a third that follows a dike. All of these walks are under three miles. However visitors choose to spend their time in and around La Conner, we recommend a visit during the quiet seasons when the town is peaceful and the pace is leisurely.

Moby Dick Hotel and Oyster Farm

Box 82, Sandridge Rd.
Nahcotta, Washington   98673
(360) 665-4543, Fax: (360) 665-6887
E-mail: mobydick@aone.com, Internet: http://www.aone.com/~mobydick/

Owners: *Fritzi and Edward Cohen*
Rooms: *10 doubles*
Rates: *Doubles $75-85 (B&B)*
Payment: *MC and VISA*
Dogs: *Welcome for a $10 nightly fee; dogs may not be left alone in the room and it is preferred they spend the day outdoors*
Children: *Welcome with a $10 nightly fee when sharing a room with parents*
Open: *All year*

Nahcotta. The name originated from a Chinook chieftain, but today, people are more likely to know this village for something else entirely — its oysters. Unlike the towns on the southern shore of Long Beach Peninsula, this tiny northern community is based more on oystering than on tourism. Oystering in Nahcotta dates back to well before the 1800s, and it is what still drives most of the business in this hamlet. So, along with the abundance of natural beauty in and around Nahcotta, visitors will also find plenty of oyster processing companies lining its shoreline. Two people who discovered this low-key place and decided to make it a part of their lives are Fritzi and Edward Cohen. Although they also own the Hotel Tabard Inn in Washington D.C. and a small organic farm in Virginia, they call the Nahcotta and Moby Dick Hotel their home.

We were cautioned to overlook the hotel's less than appealing exterior, and to focus instead on the interior spaces. After seeing the yellow stucco rectangular building, devoid of ornamentation, we heeded the warning, crossed our fingers, and ventured inside. What we found is a surprisingly expansive space that is long on character. Though it was originally built as a hotel in 1929, during World War II it housed the Coast Guard Horse Patrol. Everyone we spoke with credits the Cohens for having the patience and foresight needed to create the distinctive 1930s decor. It is the interior decor that endears guests and locals alike to this low-key hotel, nestled upon the forested shores of Willapa Bay.

The building's overall scale is small, with the exception of the first floor, which contains two living rooms and a dining room. Guests frequently spend a good deal of time nestling into the chairs and couches set around the fireplace, after having picked out something interesting to read from the Cohen's collection of books. (By the way, the hosts own over 20 copies of *Moby Dick*, any of which guests are welcome to borrow.) Others might be more inclined to play the piano, watch television, or perhaps try to identify a distant shore bird by using the telescope. Given enough notice, there is little need to leave the hotel, as gourmet dinners can be arranged for and enjoyed in the adjacent dining room. These meals always feature fresh produce from the hotel's garden, along with a choice of fresh seafoods that might include everything from salmon and Dungeness crab to shrimp and oysters (of course). The oysters grow in beds just off shore from the hotel, raised exclusively with non-chemical methods.

After dinner, we headed upstairs to one of the small and simply furnished bedrooms. Nature, art, and literature play a big role at the hotel, and it is especially evident in these spaces. The furnishings may reflect the Art Deco period, but in each room a motif is developed — centering on, for example, the ocean, its wildlife, or a piece of literature. Most of the guest rooms contain double beds and share a bathroom. Room 11 is the only one with a private bath. Families usually need to reserve a pair of bedrooms — or request Room 8 which is outfitted with both a double and a twin bed. A downstairs bedroom is the most desirable for those traveling with a dog, as it has a separate outside entrance. Though the bedrooms are a little on the small side, we found the upstairs sitting area, naturally lit by a skylight, to be a delightful place to gather, as it was rarely used by any of the other guests.

In the morning, guests are treated to a full breakfast in the dining room. This is an ample meal that ranges from standard American fare to something a little more intriguing. Some choose to start with the homemade granola and juice, and follow it with eggs, bacon or sausage, and toast. Guests seeking something a little out of the ordinary are generally asked what they would like for their breakfast special. Oysters are usually an integral component of breakfast, whether served raw, on the half shell, or baked into an omelet. Buttermilk, banana, or berry pancakes are other options. The Cohens are advocates of garlic, and it grows abundantly in their garden. They, like many others, feel that it holds some medicinal value, so they include it in most of their recipes. (The pancakes are perhaps the only exception.)

The Cohens welcome dogs; however, they prefer that during the day dogs remain outside touring the area with their owners. This is usually not much of an imposition, as there is plenty to do nearby. The hotel rests on plenty of acreage and it is a pleasant **stroll down to the water** from the hotel. Nahcotta is also easy to explore on foot, whether checking out the oyster fleet or observing one of the canning operations. We recommend that guests make time, at some point, to have dinner at The Ark — a fine restaurant within walking distance of the hotel. The Ark serves oysters every which way, along with other native seafood. Kite flying, a favorite pastime here, isn't the only thing to do on the peninsula. Just up the road apiece, visitors will discover **Leadbetter Point**, a veritable natural preserve, with trails crossing the dunes, following the ocean, and winding around to the bay. Dogs must be leashed when they are visiting, but this helps protect the waterfowl and other wildlife who make their homes within this sanctuary. At the end of the day, guests will want to return to the hotel and head out to the sauna in the woods, where any aching muscles will be thoroughly rejuvenated.

Puget View Guest House

7924 61st Avenue N.E.
Olympia, Washington 98506
(360) 459-1676

Hosts: *Barb and Dick Yunker*
Rooms: *1 cottage*
Rates: *$89 (B&B)*
Payment: *MC and VISA*
Dogs: *Welcome, with notice and approval*
Children: *Welcome*
Open: *All year*

We can understand why people love Washington state — especially along the coast, where the confluence of mountains and ocean is inspiring, particularly on a clear day when the sparkling blue waters and surrounding evergreens meld into a rich backdrop of color. It is on these days that the scenic inlets are meant to be explored, whether in search of a heron, bald eagle, or perhaps a frolicking sea lion. There are plenty of private homes tucked along these inlets, but few accept guests and their canine companions. So we felt fortunate to discover the Puget View Guest House, where guests have a private cottage and virtually unlimited opportunities to explore their natural surroundings.

This was our third visit to the cottage, and we followed the familiar road meandering through the forest to the Guest House. As we drew closer, the forest seemed to envelop us, but not in a claustrophobic sense — rather, in a protective way. We pulled into the Yunkers' driveway, where we found their house and cottage nestled on a bluff. Barb was puttering about, enjoying her few free moments by tending to her garden. She brought us inside her house into an inviting, beamed-ceiling room warmed by a wood stove and filled with traditional furnishings. The simple, uncluttered lines form a backdrop to the expansive views of the water through the picture window. We lingered in here for a bit before Barb, who is as energetic as she is gracious, escorted us out to the cottage.

The two-room cottage, which is surrounded by gardens of rhododendrons and lilacs set beneath a canopy of trees, is separated from the main house by a short path. With the onset of spring, the magnolias and other flowering plants create an awesome display of color across the property. The interior has not changed much since our last visit, with a master bedroom to the back of the cottage and a sitting room set toward the front. The bedroom's white spread dotted with pink flowers stands out against dove gray walls. Some framed prints and posters adorn these walls, but a look beyond them through the small windows reveals lovely views of the woods. The best views of the sound — albeit not as dramatic as those garnered from the Yunkers' living room — are through the windows in the sitting room. Braided rugs cover the bleached hardwood floors in here, and off to one end, a sofa bed and chair create a small sitting area. A small table, equally appropriate for meals or for working on a puzzle, is set up in the opposite corner. There are no formal cooking facilities, except that guests can create simple *hors d' oeuvres* with the microwave and store drinks in the small refrigerator. A barbecue on the back porch is ideal for those who wish to create their own dinners. Barb arrives at the cottage each morning with a generous Continental breakfast consisting of fruit and juice, coffee or tea, and a variety of homemade breads and pastries. The Yunkers also offer a variety of theme picnics that may be of interest to some guests.

The idea of offering picnic lunches and dinners developed because the Yunkers felt as though their guests were arriving and then "immediately jumping back into the car for dinner." Unfortunately, in doing so, they were missing the quiet summer evenings and beautiful sunsets. The Yunkers now offer different types of picnics, which they refer to as their summer cookouts. One of these allows guests to stay at the cottage and cook their own meal. The Yunkers will furnish briquettes and all the "fixings," including hamburgers, buns, a deli salad, and potato chips and relishes. Those who prefer to dine at the beach will want to try the old-fashioned "wiener roast," where guests cook hot dogs over a campfire. These are accompanied by a deli salad, a beverage, and a dessert. Finally, there are also boat outings, where the Yunkers take guests on their boat for oystering, or simply exploring the picturesque waterways. Barb suggests that guests bring their own canoe or kayak, which may be launched from the Yunkers' beach.

A switch back trail leads down the steep hillside to this **beach**. It is as fun to walk along it with your dog as it is to search for agates and sand dollars on it. Some 500 feet away is the 100-acre **Tolmie State Park**, which is teeming with wildlife and nature trails. This park is rarely crowded, perhaps because it is set well off the beaten path. Dogs and their human friends are welcome to explore the trails or picnic along the beach. Those with scuba equipment may wish to investigate the underwater park just offshore. A good day trip is an expedition into the **Olympic National Forest** for day hikes with dogs.

The Sandpiper Beach Resort

P.O. Box A
Pacific Beach, Washington 98571
(800) 567-4737, (360) 276-4580

Manager: Betty Stensrud
Room: 30 condominium suites
Rates: $55-165 (EP), children between the ages of 2 and 14 are $5
Payment: MC and VISA
Dogs: Welcome with a $10 daily fee, but they must be on a leash when on the property and properly curbed.
Children: Welcome (cribs and high chairs are available)
Open: All year

Out on the Olympic Peninsula, near the southwestern edge of the Quinault Indian Reservation, lies Pacific Beach. One of the northernmost beach towns, it begins in the heavily-touristed town of Ocean Shores and extends to the quieter hamlet of Moclips. While plenty of people flock to the easily accessible southern section of the coast, we prefer pushing further north to Pacific Beach and The Sandpiper Beach Resort.

We've received many rave reviews about the Sandpiper Beach Resort, especially from families who like to bring their dogs along on vacation. This place gives guests that warm, fuzzy feeling, and even extends it to their kids and dogs — the staff genuinely seems to like having them here. The Sandpiper is the sort of spot that can easily become a family tradition, and many guests book their accommodations a year in advance. A pair of gray-shingled buildings (known as Beach Houses I and II) comprise the bulk of the guest rooms, although a few individual cottages also dot these well-tended grounds overlooking the Pacific Ocean.

Each suite can accommodate from two to six people. In general, the largest suites occupy the top floors of the four-story Beach Houses, where cathedral ceilings add dimension to the well-designed spaces. Guests may choose from between one, two, and three-bedroom units. The kitchens may not be overly spacious, but they are well stocked for preparing just about any type of meal — from snack to gourmet. The sliding glass doors in the fireplaced living rooms open to small porches and provide lovely views of the ocean. Telephones and televisions are absent, so guests will have to resort to the old-fashioned way of entertaining themselves — conversation, puzzles, and an array of board games. Guests are generally left to themselves during their stay, unless they require more firewood, or perhaps an additional towel or extra bar of soap. We liked the extra touch in the bathrooms — electric towel warmers similar to those commonly found in England.

Most visitors don't feel too compelled to do very much here, other than take their dogs for long walks on the **sandy beach,** fly kites with their children, or just dig their toes into the sand. Guests may use the barbecue area in front of the Beach Houses for impromptu barbecues. A children's playground is also on the beach. Our dogs love to dig holes in the sand, so we thought it would be fun to enlist them in a clamming expedition. Afterwards, it's easy to clean off any shells or clams in a little shack at the resort. Unless guests plan to have clams as their primary staple, we advise bringing enough food and drink to last for the length of the stay; however, a few forgotten items can be picked up in the well-stocked gift shop. The shop is also well outfitted with buckets, zorries, and kites, and they also serve a pretty good cup of cappucino.

Dogs must be leashed on the property, although they have a little more freedom down on the beach. There are plenty of state parks that line these shores, beginning with **Pacific Beach State Park** and continuing south to **Griffith's Friday State Park** and **Ocean City State Park.** Pacific Beach encompasses nearly nine acres; as we mentioned, it's a great beach for clamming. Ocean City State Park, on the other hand, covers more than 100 acres and is a favorite among scuba divers. Guests and their canine companions will love roaming the sandy shores and, perhaps, even venturing into the water in the warmer summer months.

Lake Crescent Lodge

National Park Concessions, Inc.
HC 62, Box 11
416 Lake Crescent Road
Port Angeles, Washington   98362-9798
(360) 928-3211

General Manager: *Garner B. Hanson*
Rooms: *25 doubles, 33 cottages*
Rates: *Doubles $75-96 (EP), Cottages $101-140 (EP)*
Payment: *AE, DC, CB, MC, and VISA*
Dogs: *Welcome with a daily fee of $10*
Children: *Welcome (cribs and cots are available)*
Open: *April through October*

Travelers searching for simple accommodations amid spectacular natural surroundings will find the Lake Crescent Lodge to be an ideal destination. The lodge is nestled among giant fir, spruce, and hemlock trees along the shores of Lake Crescent. The renowned rain forest is further inland, while the Juan de Fuca Strait are just a short distance away. It used to be that small ferries would steam back and forth along the lake, bringing visitors to this isolated spot. Today, Highway 101 loops past the lodge, allowing easier access without encroaching too much upon this natural setting.

The main lodge was built in 1916 and was formerly known as Singer's Tavern. It remains much the same today as it was 80 years ago. New arrivals enter the rustic great hall, where the impressive stone fireplace is usually crackling and popping. Any time of day, a few guests are comfortably settled into the cushioned mission-style chairs and sofas or enjoying the warmth of the solarium. The solarium is one of our favorite places on a sunny day, as its walls of paned windows overlook the deep blue waters of Lake Crescent. Planters filled with red geraniums, placed amid a sea of wicker chairs and tables, thrive in this tropical environment. As guests step back inside, they will see an extensive collection of Northwest Native American artifacts that are displayed on the mantel, in glass cases flanking the fireplace, and along the eaves. We were especially drawn to the miniature totem poles placed on the beams.

Interested guests can then go directly from the great hall into the dining room, where they will a find beamed ceiling and whitewashed walls, with a contemporary ambiance. The dining room is situated on the same side of the lodge as the solarium, and its plate glass windows offer equally inviting views of the lake. We visited late in the season, just a few weeks before the lodge was due to close. Even then the menu offered an array of hearty and enticing meals. Ample breakfasts start the day, with stacks of pancakes, French toast, and overstuffed omelets topping the menu. Dinner patrons may select from an array of entrées including the shrimp piquant, scallops florentine, king salmon filet, and chicken Dijonaise. Oysters and crab, when in season, are always a favorite option with the lodge's clientele. We suggest ending the meal with one of the specialties — a freshly baked piece of pie. After dinner, most head back to their cottages to give their canine companions an evening walk.

There are a number of cottage choices, although our favorites are the Roosevelt Fireplace Cottages and the Singer Tavern Cottages. The bleached wood shingles and eaves make the exterior of the Singer Tavern Cottages very appealing. These are set closest to the main lodge; although an expanse of lawn and shade trees separate them from the lakefront, their water views are largely unobstructed. The narrow porches that run the length of the cottages are bedecked with rocking chairs. The interiors are reminiscent of a motel room, with attractive peach colored walls and pairs of double beds. There is no need to worry about the children or the dogs breaking any knickknacks — there are none. Most families appreciate the preponderance of outdoor activities, without the distractions of televisions or telephones. We quickly discovered that most guests come to this resort for the assortment of recreational diversions and not for the functional accommodations.

While the Singer Tavern cottages are appealing, and probably easiest to reserve, our first choice is the four Roosevelt Fireplace Cottages. Situated directly on the lake, these cozy abodes were constructed in 1937, when Franklin Roosevelt was exploring the region to consider designating it as a national park. The bleached shingle exterior walls are interspersed with expanses of paned windows, while the interior knotty pine walls and hardwood floors set the overall homey ambiance. Simple sofas and chairs form inviting sitting areas around the beachstone fireplaces, while queen or king beds covered in white cotton spreads abut the opposite walls. Coffee makers and small refrigerators are welcome amenities, especially in these otherwise rustic surroundings. Anyone interested in making a reservation for the Roosevelt Fireplace Cottages should note that they are often booked months in advance and it is critical that guests reserve early. We were happy to learn that even though most of the resort shuts down in October, the Roosevelt Fireplace Cottages remain open year round. Guests who choose to stay here in the off season receive a Continental breakfast delivered to their cottage.

The final dog-friendly accommodation option is the Marymere Motor Lodge, whose rooms lie along the shore. From the exterior there seems little to recommend these rooms; however, the interior spaces are actually quite appealing and are similar in decor and furnishings to those in the Singer Tavern Cottages — simple, clean, and uncluttered. Most people who select the motor lodge rooms do so for their totally unobstructed lake views.

There is plenty to do at the Lake Crescent Lodge, although we are always disappointed when we remember that dogs are not allowed to set paw in the Olympic National Park (with the exception of the parking lots, the Kalaloch beach, and the **Shady Lane Trail** at Staircase). Guests and their leashed dogs are free to wander the **expansive property**, though, and the open grassy areas surrounding the lodge. Water-oriented canines can accompany their human friends on **fishing expeditions** for salmon, steelhead, or the crafty Beardslee trout. Those who don't want to fish can always explore the miles of lake shore, perhaps stopping for a picnic. (The lodge staff will pack box lunches).

After a busy morning, some might leave their canine companion to nap on his own while they take the short hike to scenic Marymere Falls. A trip to the Lake Crescent Lodge may not be an appropriate vacation for people who want to spend their days hiking with their dogs, yet it is worthwhile for anyone willing to compromise a bit and mix a bit of dog-less hiking with all the other activities at the lodge.

Inn at Ludlow Bay

P.O. Box 65460
One Heron Road
Port Ludlow, Washington 98365
(360) 437-0411, (360) 437-0310

Manager: *David Hott*
Rooms: *35 doubles, 2 suites*
Rates: *Doubles $135-200 (B&B), Suites $300-450 (B&B)*
Payment: *AE, MC, and VISA*
Dogs: *Welcome in 3 rooms*
Children: *Welcome (cribs, cots, and high chairs are available)*
Open: *All year*

The Inn at Ludlow Bay rests at the end of a small peninsula within the lovely resort community of Ludlow Bay. It is near, but should not be confused with, the Port Ludlow Resort. Though the inn is new, it has been built in a style reminiscent of the expansive shingled cottages lining Maine's coast. Porches add definition to the first floor, while the lines of the upper levels form interesting eaves and turrets. Equally intriguing are the expansive interior spaces lined with walls of windows overlooking beach grass and gardens, offering views that extend beyond this point of land to the water. Guests staying here usually have the sensation of being on an island.

Each of the guest rooms is well designed, and we can vouch for the fact that the dog-designated rooms are as lovely and gracious as all the other bedrooms. The guest chambers are furnished with natural cherry, Mission-style furnishings — with writing tables filling alcoves and cushioned chairs set in front of fireplaces tiled in a black and white Art Deco style. With the exception of taupe highlights, all the walls and trim are white. The down comforter, too, is covered in a white duvet and is complemented by black-and-white-checked accent pillows resting against the oversized bed pillows. The extra high king or queen bedsteads allow guests to lie in bed while enjoying the water views. Another place guests enjoy relaxing (and, surprisingly, are still able to take in the views) is in the Jacuzzi soaking tub. Though the tub is located in the bathroom, its frosted glass windows slide open in the direction of the bedroom windows. A separate and oversized, glassed-in shower is also available. After a refreshing shower or bath, guests can wrap up in the supple terry cloth robes provided. Lord and Mayfair chamomile soaps, shampoos, creams, and bath crystals, are placed in baskets set upon marble and cream colored tiles lining the tub and counters. Modern conveniences, such as a television and VCR, are concealed in the cherry armoires, while a small refrigerator, coffee maker, and basket of gourmet coffee with Stash teas are set in an unobtrusive alcove. A wine opener is included in this potpourri of goodies, as is an extensive list of wines available for purchase.

The Inn at Ludlow Bay is the sort of place where guests can make themselves comfortable in a number of areas. During a cool day, the sun room is just the place to be, while on inclement days we prefer the fireplace bar. We thoroughly enjoy settling into one of the deep couches in front of the fireplace and sampling one of the inn's many microbrews or wines. Another area popular for reclining is out on the porch, where rattan tables are positioned to take advantage of the water views and the activity at the marina. When the sun sets, though, most guests gravitate to the dining room, whose three walls of windows can be opened to allow in the breezes. We visited when the fall menu was in place. Appetizers included the mussels steamed in lemon grass, coconut milk and a cilantro broth; the roasted garlic pumpkin bisque; and the tea-smoked Guinea fowl set on a couscous salad with a walnut sherry vinaigrette. Entrées included the rack of lamb with a pomegranate lamb reduction, the free range chicken with a pecan honey mustard sauce, and the roasted pear and cherry stuffed rabbit with a rosemary cream sauce. We rarely run across a menu with so many appealing options.

After dinner, some guests might want to walk their dogs to the end of the peninsula. Out here, there are a few shade trees, but the highlight is the enormous Port Ludlow totem pole — carved out of a 720 year-old western red cedar tree that blew down in a big storm. It was erected in 1993, after being carved by local artisans. There are a few picnic tables here, but mainly, it is just a peaceful spot for an early-morning or late-evening stroll. Guests are also free to walk along the lane leading to the Port Ludlow Resort, where there are **hundreds of acres** and inviting paths to follow.

People pleasures include playing golf at the 27-hole Port Ludlow Golf Course or renting a boat from the marina and exploring the numerous inlets. The inn is situated on the Olympic Peninsula, and the entire northeast section of the **Olympic National Forest** it is available to hikers and their dogs. The best way to access it from Port Ludlow is to drive to Quilcene. Trailheads for hikes up **Mount Townsend** and **Mount Zion** are just outside of town, and plenty of other day hikes lie along the perimeter of this spectacular national forest. In the spring, the area is especially scenic as wildflowers are in full bloom.

The Bishop Victorian Guest Suites

714 Washington Street
Port Townsend, Washington 98368
(800) 824-4738, (360) 385-6122, Internet: http://www.waypt.com/bishop

Owners: *Joseph and Cindy Finnie*
Rooms: *14 suites*
Rates: *$69-139 (B&B), Children under 10 years of age are free*
Payment: *AE, MC, and VISA*
Dogs: *Welcome, with approval*
Children: *Welcome (cribs and cots are available, with prior notice)*
Open: *All year*

Port Townsend lies at the entrance to Puget Sound and has an appealing natural harbor. Residents, during the late 1800s, believed these characteristics to mean that Port Townsend would someday emerge as the Northwest's largest city. In anticipation of this potential growth, affluent people were drawn here, building elaborate Victorian homes and ornate public buildings along Water Street — thus creating an infrastructure that would support their future community. Unfortunately, the transcontinental railroad that was supposed to ensure the residents' prosperity never arrived, and the town became an isolated outpost. More recently, the city has enjoyed a resurgence after a portion of it was designated as a National Historic District.

Today, as visitors drive down Water Street, they will still see lovely brick buildings lining the waterfront. If they look up toward the bluffs, the eaves and turrets of the rambling Victorian homes come into view. The Bishop Victorian Guest Suites, formerly known as the Bishop Block Building, is a part of this history. Built in 1890 by William Bishop, this four-story brick building was designed as a warehouse and drayage facility.

In some ways The Bishop is still reminiscent of a bygone era, as small shops occupy the first floor of the building, and the guest rooms lie on the upper floors. We ascended the interior staircase, past authentic Victorian light fixtures and original art, and emerged into a broad space that was part hallway and part foyer. Here, we met one of the owners, Joseph Finnie, along with his manager's yellow lab, Artie. The dog wiggled out from behind the front desk, hoping for lots of TLC (and of course, getting it). Sated, he then wandered off in search of more attention elsewhere.

Joseph and his wife Cindy bought the suites in 1995 and are just completing a two-year renovation. The transformation from eclectic Victorian to a more sophisticated "West Country" Victorian has been achieved with fine furnishings, art, and fixtures from the period. The Finnies have even gone so far as to find authentic Victorian clothing, mount and frame the items, and then display them in many of the suites.

The suites are spacious, but each offer their own unique nooks and crannies. Some of them boast exposed brick walls, while others offer distant water views through oversized windows. We walked into one suite with a large living room and kitchen adjoining a cozy rear bedroom. In another, two large bedrooms connect to a small sitting room and kitchenette. Guests may request suites with fireplaces or bathrooms with soaking tubs.

The decor varies as well; some beds are covered in fluffy floral spreads, others in handmade quilts. The Victorian furnishings have been carefully selected to complement the historic feeling of the inn. Brass or carved oak headboards work well with the antique oak dressers and maple end tables. These pieces may not be museum quality, but they do add personality to each of the suites. The addition of live plants and dried flower arrangements creates a residential feeling in these chambers. Guests who want assurance that they will not be disturbed by street noise should request a suite to the rear of the building.

Each morning a light Continental repast is laid out in the foyer, where guests can select from juice, coffee, fresh fruit, and muffins. Most take this meal back to their suite. If they haven't already noticed the antique rosewood couches covered in green velvet that line the main hall, they will want to take a moment to admire them. Guests craving something a little more substantial may wish to stock their refrigerators with eggs, bacon, and other breakfast goodies, to add to this light fare.

Of course, morning is also the time when the dogs are ready for some exercise. We discovered that this is one of the best times to walk around Port Townsend, as the streets are quiet and it's mostly locals who are out and about. We found a wonderful bakery just a half block from the inn. It makes a variety of luscious breads and pastries and an excellent cup of cappucino.

Walks along **Water Street** and the harbor are easy because it is flat; however, anyone wanting more of a workout can ascend the steep hill behind the inn to **the bluff**. The water views from the top vie for attention with the quaint Victorian homes that line these residential streets. Another walking option is the **444-acre estate of Fort Worden**, which is only a mile outside of town. Visitors can take tours of the restored Victorian homes and barracks, and visit the Marine Science Center. Dogs are also welcome here and can romp across the open grassy areas and through the woods. Yet another option is **Marrowstone Island**. Although it is a 20-mile drive from Port Townsend, the 775 acres of forests and trails make this an fine choice for both canines and their human friends.

As a final note, the Finnies also own a property in Port Townsend called The Swan. Dogs are also welcome to stay here. This is a recent purchase for them, and although we were unable to review it, we still feel comfortable recommending these spacious apartments to anyone traveling with their canine companion.

Lake Quinault Lodge

P.O. Box 7
South Shore Road
Quinault, Washington 98575
(800) 562-6672 in WA, (360) 288-2571, Fax: (360) 288-2901
Internet: http://www.travel-in-wa.com/ADS/html/#quinault

Manager: Russell Steele
Rooms: 89 doubles, 3 suites
Rates: Doubles $99-140 (EP), Suites $195-210 (EP), Children
    under the age of 5 are free of charge, ages 5 and over are $10
Payment: AE, MC and VISA
Dogs: Welcome in the annex guest rooms with a $10 daily fee per pet
Children: Welcome (cribs, cots, and baby-sitters are available)
Open: All year

    Far from civilization, in territory still owned partly by the Quinault Indian Reservation, stands a classic cedar lodge that has proudly withstood the test of time. The Lake Quinault Lodge was built in 1926 through the combined efforts of Frank McNeil and a wealthy lumber man, Ralph Emerson. McNeil had spent his vacations in these spectacular rain forests of the Pacific Northwest and had fallen in love with them. He knew there would be others who would also cherish this majestic region. McNeil and Emerson applied to the U.S. Forest Service for a special permit enabling them to build on the shores of Lake Quinault. The lodge they designed was constructed in an incredible ten weeks, using the talents of many skilled craftsmen. Materials were hauled over 50 miles of dirt roads to the crews working 24-hours-a-day.

The expansive two-story, shingled lodge has also played host to many famous people over the years, including Franklin D. Roosevelt. In 1937, he was traveling through the region and was so impressed by its natural splendor that he felt moved to give it national park status in order to preserve its fragile beauty. Today's visitors will find that time has changed little in the Olympic National Forest, including the lodge.

The Lake Quinault Lodge has been beautifully maintained and much of its historic feeling is still intact. People tend to congregate in the lobby of this rambling structure, whose dozens of tiny paned windows overlook emerald-green lawns and the lapping waters of Lake Quinault. The lobby's open-beamed ceilings have been stenciled with Northwest Native American designs, while old newspaper clippings and Northwest Native American art hang from the walls, acting as reminders of its rich heritage. The day we arrived, the rain was falling steadily. (It frequently falls steadily, and anyone who doubts this should just check the totem pole outside that doubles as the rain gauge — it often shows rainfall well into the multi-foot range.) This did not seem to hamper anyone's good spirits on this day, as guests were gathered around the massive wood-burning fireplace, whiling away the hours reading or playing games. The turn-of-the-century wicker chairs looked as though they had held countless numbers of guests over the years. The warm and inviting atmosphere is equally appealing in the main dining room, known as much for its fine food and seafood specialties as it is for its scenic views. The lodge serves three excellent meals each day, but most noteworthy is dinner.

Lodge rooms have also remained relatively unchanged from the 1920s. Brass or white iron double and queen beds grace the creaky hardwood floors, along with comfortable couches and arm chairs. Old-fashioned floral wallpapers enliven these spaces. Bathrooms are a bit dated, but clean, and are outfitted with a few thoughtful amenities such as almond soaps, fragrant shampoos, and shower caps. Natural board walls add a warm, rustic quality. Those traveling with dogs are asked to stay in the equally historic one-story annex building, as each room has a separate outside entrance. The eight guest rooms have a cabin-like quality to them, especially with their paneled walls. As with the lodge rooms, these chambers are primarily equipped with brass beds and some wicker furnishings. On the other end of the lodging scale are the more contemporary lake-side guest rooms. These relatively new additions to the resort are housed in two, three-story buildings. They are decorated with pastel color schemes and are quite luxurious. (We suggest reserving these for friends or family who don't have Bowser in tow.)

An indoor heated swimming pool, Jacuzzi, and sauna are available for those who are not fond of lake swimming. There is also a game room with ping-pong, pool tables, and video games. Canoes and rowboats may be rented for fishing or exploring the lake. Fishing is one of the more popular pastimes at the lodge, and draws a fair number of guests each year. Anglers will find

Dolly Varden, rainbow, and cutthroat trout abundant in these waters. (Fishing licenses must be secured from the Quinault Indian Tribe.) Croquet, badminton, and horseshoes are also available on the grounds. Those interested in exploring the rain forest should know that nearly 200 inches of rain fall on it each year, creating incredibly an ecological environment that is unique in the United States. The hiking in these parts is as beautiful as it is wet.

The rangers at the National Forest Service station will be happy to offer suggestions for extensive day and overnight hikes or lead visitors on any of its numerous interpretive excursions. For those who don't already know it: dogs cannot even set a paw in the Olympic National Park. But the lodge is not in the national park; it is in the national forest. Dogs and their human friends are welcome to explore the **many trails near Lake Quinault**. One of the easiest and most spectacular hikes is around the lake. This seems like one big **nature trail**, with markers along the way describing what people and their dogs are seeing. Another slightly more aerobic option is just off the Lake Quinault Trail, and is known as the **Willaby Creek Trail**. It follows Willaby Creek for a bit, and, although it never climbs above the tree line, it does offer a closer look at some of the old growth rain forests for which this area is so famous.

Alexis Hotel

1007 First Avenue at Madison
Seattle, Washington 98104
(800) 426-7033, (206) 624-4844, Fax: (206) 621-9009

Manager: Michael DeFrino
Rooms: *109 doubles and suites*
Rates: *Doubles and Suites $195-380 (B&B); Children are free of charge when staying in rooms with their parents*
Payment: *AE, CB, DC, DSC, MC, and VISA*
Dogs: *Well-behaved dogs are welcome, but their human counter-parts must sign a damage waiver*
Children: *Welcome (cribs, cots, and baby-sitters are available)*
Open: *All year*

The ownership of the Alexis Hotel changed a few years ago, and it is now a part of the Kimpton group of fine hotels; however, it remains true to its original precept — a small, luxurious, service-intensive hotel. Set within the heart of Seattle's financial district, it is within easy walking distance of the famous Pike's Place Farmers' Market and Pioneer Square. The Alexis Hotel was built in 1901, but was then known as the Globe Building. Throughout the 1920s, it housed assorted specialty shops; in the 1930s it was renovated and became the Arlington Garage. Finally, in 1980, the structure was gutted so that only the exterior walls remained intact. The completed renovation — including the intricate moldings, rounded windows, and intimate alcoves — was so inspired that it won the Honor Award from the American Institute of Architects and was soon listed in the National Register of Historic Places.

We always look forward to visiting the Alexis, as it exudes a certain degree of European charm and sophistication. The lobby is intimate, with a few comfortable sitting areas separated from one another by potted plants and Oriental vases filled with flowers. Guests' privacy is highly respected, which is perhaps why the hotel attracts those who are interested in maintaining theirs. Bob Dylan, who visited with his bulldog, and Robert De Niro, who likes to travel with his canine entourage, are just two of the Alexis' more notable guests who enjoy bringing their canine companions.

Famous or not so famous, guests are often intrigued with this wonderful hotel because they can always find a room to suit their mood. Each formal space is individually decorated, with some spaces containing black-lacquered furniture set against deep rose-colored walls, while others emphasize natural woods and soothing earth tones. Guests may expect to find at least one antique, be it an armoire concealing a television, a nest of bedside tables, or a mahogany sideboard. When the Sultan of Brunei was visiting, he took over half the hotel and redid many of the rooms in rich, dark colors. Subsequent guests who stay in these spaces might feel as though they are, in some small way, privy to the royal treatment.

We did not stay in the Sultan's suite, but in another enormous space with boxed-beamed ceilings and floor-to-ceiling windows. Pinpoint lighting fell against the draperies, tapestry-covered couches, and antique armoire. The king bed was separated from the living room by a sliding Shoji screen. The next day, we peeked at some of the other rooms and ventured into one with a mahogany bed topped by a virtual mountain of oversized pillows. Another chamber was equally appealing, but not as much for the decor as for its corner location. Given the choice, we would request a corner room with windows facing the street. (The other option is a back alley — not as interesting, but it is quiet.) Another especially intriguing possibility is one of the six wood-burning fireplace suites. Regardless of room choice, guests will find their chamber appointed with well-stocked minibars containing complimentary sodas, tonics, and juices. The whirlpool baths are the focal point of the dramatic, black-tiled and marbled bathrooms that can be found in some of the suites. All guests enjoy the luxury of thick terry robes, cotton towels, sewing kits, shampoos, and an assortment of toiletries. Those who want to thoroughly indulge themselves can sample the full line of spa products available in each bedroom. In the evening, guests return to find turned-down beds and gold-wrapped chocolates placed on their down pillows.

A recent renovation has combined the seven-story Arlington Building (circa 1901) with the original hotel. The Arlington Building once contained all suites catering to families and long-term guests; however, the space has been converted to a combination of suites and standard rooms. Each accommodation is unique, although an overall Art Deco style prevails. Guests may request kitchens, dining rooms, living rooms, and either one or two bedrooms. Our favorites: those with fireplaces and balconies, the latter of which are privy to views of Elliott Bay.

Most guests, whether they stay in the suites or main hotel, eventually end up in the Bookstore — an intimate bar by night and an equally great place to start the morning. The excellent coffee and fresh fruit, coupled with a choice of croissants, muffins, and pastries is a surprisingly substantial breakfast. Some who might skip the morning meal may find themselves here in the evening, sipping on a drink and looking through the eclectic collection of books and magazines. Others are waiting for their table at one of the city's premier restaurants, The Painted Table.

We have always liked the physical layout of The Painted Table, with its regularly changing art display and impressive collection of designer plates. Evidently, the food did not always match the ambiance, but this has all changed recently with the addition of a new chef to whom Seattle seems to be responding favorably — Chef J. Tim Kelley. His appetizers are substantial enough to be meals in themselves. We suggest the organic beef tartar with arugula and horseradish oil, the lemon grass cured salmon, or the grilled five spice quail. Entrées range from the Mongolian barbecue loin of pork served with an egg noodle and scallion cake, pea vines, and Asian slaw; the seafood risotto brimming with mussels, tiger shrimp, and bay scallops; or the pan seared salmon with potato gnocchi, tarragon and corn sauté, and an herb salad. Desserts vary with the day, but two popular choices are the mocha silk mousse gâteau, with an espresso caramel sauce, and the frozen banana soufflé, with strawberry, chocolate, and mango sauces.

Those who want to work off their culinary indulgences can utilize either of the two sports clubs that are within walking distance of the hotel, or they can head out for a jog along the waterfront. Something more rejuvenating in mind? Perhaps a session in the steam room will provide the needed remedy.

Those who are fond of late night walks may wish to reconsider — we didn't feel especially safe wandering the streets at this time of the evening. During the day, though, there is the **waterfront to explore**, along with a small park near Pike's Place Farmers' Market. A short drive to northern Seattle brings visitors and their dogs to **Green Lake**. This is the area to see and be seen in. On a nice day, the city dwellers find this an easy place to come and walk, run, do in-line skating, and most importantly, walk their dogs. There is a **trail** that most walkers follow around the lake or through the trees. As with most popular spots, though, it is busiest in the summer months, but quite manageable during the off season.

Four Seasons Olympic Hotel

411 University Street
Seattle, Washington 98101
(800) 332-3442/U.S., (800) 821-8106/WA, (206) 621-1700
Fax: (206) 682-9633, Internet: http://www.fourseasonsregent.com

General Manager: Peter Martin
Rooms: 450 doubles and suites
Rates: Doubles $260-290 (EP), Suites $330-1,435 (EP), Children under 18 are free of charge
Payment: AE, CB, DC, MC, and VISA
Dogs: Welcome, but they must receive special permission if the dog weighs over 50 pounds
Children: Welcome (cribs, cots, and baby-sitter services are available)
Open: All year

The Olympic Hotel opened in 1924 to much fanfare. This elegant and sophisticated Italian Renaissance-style building was the first of its kind in the still provincial Pacific Northwest. As spacious and ornate as the hotel was, its wide open facade and inefficient use of space turned out to be a very inappropriate design for a hotel. Not only did it not appeal to the guests, but the hotel soon began to lose business and eventually fell into disrepair. In the late 1970s there was talk of demolishing the hotel. However, the residents of Seattle felt strongly that a building with such history and unique features should be saved and restored. The Four Seasons Ltd. and the partnership of Urban Investment and Development Company were granted a lease in 1980 and began renovating the structure.

The Olympic Hotel's 60 million dollar restoration was one of the largest privately financed, historic restorations ever undertaken in the United States. Detailed plans were drawn up and executed, with as much attention devoted to the comfort of future guests as to maintaining the exquisite details. The number of guest rooms was reduced from 756 to 450, giving each chamber a more spacious configuration. Fifty percent of these bedrooms are now alcove rooms, where French doors separate the sleeping areas from the sitting rooms. All these rooms combine old-world formality and elegance with modern-day comfort and a pleasing array of amenities.

The furnishings are reproductions of fine English antiques by Henredon and Baker furniture makers, and are coupled with richly textured fabrics and hand-woven carpets. Varying shades of chocolate brown, taupe, and cream colors combine for an elegant warmth. Beds are triple-sheeted and covered with thick comforters and masses of pillows. Everything a guest would expect lies within these luxurious spaces. If, perchance, it does not, it can often be readily secured. Armoires conceal the remote-control televisions and VCRs, along with the well-stocked minibars. A basket of gourmet goodies is set on top of an end table. In addition to a secondary telephone in the bathroom, there are hair dryers, make-up mirrors, scales, and terry cloth robes. As one would expect, the hotel prides itself on first-class service, whether guests need their shoes shined, clothes laundered, or special treats for their children or dogs. Doggie visitors receive a bottle of water, along with a bowl and gourmet dog biscuits. Children, on the other hand, may request special movies, videos and board games, all of which may be accompanied by cookies and milk.

The guest rooms are lovely, but it is the public areas that are especially noteworthy, as ceilings seem to soar overhead. Ornately-carved oak highlights the cavernous two-story main lobby; however, it is not all original. During the restoration, architects discovered that segments of oak were missing from the paneling. They ultimately found matching oak in England and imported it. Craftsmen spent hundreds of hours carving and treating the wood so it would match the original. The adjacent Garden Court is especially spectacular, mainly due to the expansive floor-to-ceiling Palladian windows. This is a veritable garden of immense, fresh flower arrangements and mature ficus trees illuminated with twinkling white lights — at night the effect is especially festive. Those who come here frequently do so for lunch or cocktails; however, high tea tends to draw its share of regulars as well.

The Georgian dining room not only sounds regal — it looks regal. Lustrous, paneled walls interspersed with Palladian windows and elaborately-carved moldings, crystal chandeliers, and potted palms set the overall elegant ambiance. This is an à la carte menu, with some guests opting to start with the oyster bisque and a warm wild rice pancake, lobster and roasted forest mushrooms in a morel sauce, or the Northwest oysters on the half shell. During our visit, the Georgian Room's signature entrées included the thick cut, smoked salmon with Washington apples and apple brandy sauce, and the veal tenderloin with morel mushrooms. We thought the braised duck with caramelized orange sauce, the mountain berry spiced game hen, and the venison pepper steak sounded equally tempting. Shuckers is the hotel's popular oyster bar, and is a terrific place to grab a quick bite to eat.

Guests in search of a little exercise will enjoy the well-conceived health club with its large pool and Jacuzzi set in a huge glass atrium. Just outside the glass structure are nicely landscaped sun decks. A nearby weight room contains rowing machines, bicycles, treadmills, Stairmasters, and a Nordic Track. Best of all, guests who forget their athletic gear need not worry — they have complimentary use of swimsuits, shorts, T-shirts, athletic shoes and even shampoos, conditioners, combs and brushes. Of course, all this will appease the human guests, but not necessarily their canine companions; however, doggie guests should remain patient — there are plenty of terrific walks we can suggest.

We love the location of the Four Seasons Olympic. It is set in the heart of the city's finest shopping and strolling district, and is less than a block from the theater. We felt comfortable walking throughout this portion of the city, both day and night, as there is always plenty going on and plenty of people around. There is even a pedestrian mall just a few blocks away that city dogs will enjoy. Others may prefer to take a stroll down to the waterfront, or simply window shop along the wide streets.

Those searching for a little green space, though, should probably jump in their car and head over to the **Washington Park Arboretum**, situated near the University of Washington. Once here, visitors and their dogs can follow the Waterfront Trail, which is a boardwalk crossing over the marshes. There is plenty to see in the way of native flora and fauna, not to mention waterfowl. Another great outing leads people and their dogs to **Seward Park** on Lake Washington, just south of Seattle. There are 280 acres for walking and exploring, including some forested acreage and picturesque shoreline beaches. Two other options within the metropolitan area are the **Cougar Mountain Regional Wild Land Park** and the **Tiger Mountain State Forest** — both accessible to people and their dogs.

Pensione Nichols

1923 First Avenue
Seattle, Washington 98101
(206) 441-7125

Innkeepers: *Lindsay and Nancy Nichols*
Rooms: *10 doubles, 2 suites*
Rates: *Doubles $85 (B&B), Suites $160 (EP)*
Payment: *AE, DSC, MC, and VISA*
Dogs: *Smaller dogs welcome, but negotiable*
Children: *Welcome*
Open: *All year*

We've stayed in pensione's all over Europe, because they are intimate, personal, and reasonably priced. The Pensione Nichols may lie on American shores, but it is more reminiscent of the European version. Moreover, it is ideally located in downtown Seattle, and within easy walking distance of Pike Place Market, the Kingdome, and the theater and shopping districts. Those familiar with the historic Smith Block building may know that the Pensione Nichols also shares this address; however, we had to search carefully before locating the tiny sign pointing us to the doorway.

We arrived a little early one afternoon, and had to wait a bit for someone to let us in. While this may have been a little inconvenient, we must admit, we liked the security aspect. Guests ascend two flights of stairs to reach the top floor of the pensione, where they will emerge into a bright foyer that serves as the reception area. Chloe, the 15-year-old resident dog, trotted up to say hello and then disappeared to the back of the pensione. Guests tend to gather in the foyer's small sitting area, or retreat, like Chloe, to the rear of the building. We followed Lindsay into an enormous living room with a wall of windows overlooking Elliott Bay. Some people had settled into the pair of gray sofas, deluged with late-day sunlight. Given the exposure, we knew just why the huge ficus tree in here was thriving. On the opposite side of the room, various mismatched, round wooden tables were set for the following morning's Continental breakfast.

The bedrooms are found mostly on the third floor, with a few spilling over onto the second floor. All are simply furnished, but offer all the necessities. We like the fact that unoccupied rooms are left open, so that newly arriving guests can peruse the room choices and pick the one that is most appropriate for them. The doors are propped open with whimsical little stone doorstops, in shapes ranging from a hedgehog to a cat and a dog. These rather boxy chambers are enlivened with pale yellow walls, which are brightened by the natural sunlight pouring in through the old-fashioned frosted skylights housed in the high ceilings. Simple, white cotton spreads cover the beds, while neatly folded comforters are placed at the foot. There is usually a chair or an antique oak bureau, with bath towels laid out on a rack. All these bedrooms share two bathrooms, and those who can overlook the shared WC will find them to be well appointed and quite expansive. Our favorite bathroom is sort of an Art Deco space with black and white tiles and a claw-foot tub. (There is also a separate shower.) Those who prefer real windows with views should request the largest rooms overlooking First Avenue. Travelers who would like to ensure a peaceful night's sleep might be more happy with a bedroom at the rear of the building.

Families with dogs will want to think about reserving one of the two suites on the second floor. These were completed only recently and offer far more space, amenities, and privacy than the others. We like the one facing Elliott Bay, although a fire escape ladder partially obscures the views. These chambers are long, narrow spaces, which guests enter from the back. We came upon a raised area, surrounded by a half-wall, that contained a queen bed and a sofa bed. Guests walk past the bedroom area and the full, modern kitchen to the living room. The only drawback to these spaces is that although they have one wall of windows, they do not have the benefit of the third-floor skylights — so they can be a little dark at times.

Pensione Nichols is a fine place for walking a dog during the day, but we would not have felt as comfortable wandering about during the wee hours of the night, as there are a couple of adult-oriented businesses in the area. The Pensione is centrally located, so that everything is just a short walk away (and we know your dog will enjoy the exercise). Just outside of Seattle, there are a number of interesting areas that might appeal to people and their dogs.

Washington

Carkeek Park offers a diversity of walking trails that meander throughout its 200 acres of forest and creeks. Just to the south are two more wonderful parks, known as **Washington** and **Seward Parks**. Both offer plenty of easy walks and an abundance of scenery.

The Beech Tree Manor

1405 Queen Anne Avenue North
Seattle, Washington 98109
(206) 281-7037, Fax: (206) 284-2350
Internet: http://www.uspan.com/sbba

Hostess: *Virginia Lucero*
Rooms: *1 single, 5 doubles*
Rates: *Single $59 (B&B), Doubles $69-89 (B&B), Suite $105-145 (B&B)*
Payment: *MC and VISA*
Dogs: *Welcome with notice and approval*
Children: *Over 5 years of age are welcome (roll-away beds are available)*
Open: *All year*

Take a lovely, turn-of-the-century Victorian home, furnish it with antiques and exquisite linens, and most importantly, find a hostess who is as delightful as Virginia Lucero, and herein lies the very essence of a truly inviting B&B. The Beech Tree Manor was built in 1903, and is named for the majestic copper beech tree that dominates the front of the house. There have been only two owners in all these years — Virginia and the original builder. He and his 14-year-old Irish bride built the home and then lived here until the 1970s. The house sat on the market for five years before Virginia discovered it, bought it, and renovated it. Today, it is one of many well-preserved historic homes in this attractive Queen Anne Hill neighborhood.

Virginia is a native of Seattle, although she also spent a number of years in Washington, D.C. Her home reflects these two periods of her life; formal antiques and contemporary Northwest art comfortably meld together. Apart from Virginia's collection of massive canvases of modern artwork, lining both the circular stairway and upstairs hall, the feeling of the Beech Tree Manor is reminiscent of an English country home. The original hand-carved moldings and embossed tin wall coverings are original. The beamed-ceiling living room is often the central gathering place. It runs the length of the house and is filled with a wonderful hodgepodge of chintzes covering the overstuffed couches, armchairs, and window seat. There are pillows everywhere, and still more fabric and lace framing the windows. Against the walls, Virginia displays her collection of pottery, which she hangs from decorative ribbons. Jake, the resident bulldog, can usually be found lounging in front of the massive beachstone fireplace. In the evening, guests often congregate here to enjoy a quiet moment or two while sipping a little sherry before the fire. This combination of warmth from the sherry and the fire is quite relaxing, but once guests head up to bed, they will discover one of the best features of this enchanting B&B.

The charming guest rooms all occupy the second floor, and evoke the same homey feeling as the downstairs public areas. Brass or ebony bedsteads are covered with extra fluffy down comforters. The softness of white antique sheets and pillow cases is a marked contrast to the floral and bold-striped chintzes on many of the duvets. The linens are unlike anything most people have ever slept on. Whether appliquéd or embroidered with delicate flowers, all are exquisite. Virginia used to sell these fine linens out of the B&B, but not longer does so. Most of the bathrooms are private, and although they lack the endearing character of the bedrooms, they do contain the necessities — ivory soaps, modern showers, and soft, fluffy towels. A few of the bedrooms connect with a bathroom containing a claw-footed tub. One of the most requested rooms is set to the rear of the house, and is quite romantic with its quarter-canopy bed and antique white linen coverlet. Virginia's most recent addition to the inn is a third floor attic suite set in the eaves. She has furnished it with antiques and decorated it with her fine linens. This lovely space is private, sleeps five, and is the only room to have a television.

The morning breakfast is a full meal that is served in the formal dining room, around an antique table set for twelve. Virginia makes everything from scratch, often including hard-to-find seasonal fruit in her fruit plates and homemade muffins and breads. Depending upon her whim and the number of guests she is cooking for, there is everything from quiche and chili eggs to pancakes and baked French toast with nuts, cinnamon, and fresh cream. Those who look forward to a great cup of morning coffee will thoroughly enjoy Virginia's variety of freshly-ground coffees.

After breakfast, some like to step onto the outdoor porch, set with wicker rockers, where they can read the morning newspaper or one of the B&B's many magazines and books. From here, guests will find the extensive flower gardens that line one side of the house. Set within the midst of the gardens is a small statue of a bulldog — appropriate, given Jake's prominent position in the household. We always enjoy taking our dogs for a morning stroll about Queen Anne Hill. **Two small parks** are located just a few blocks down from the B&B. From either vantage point, there are scenic views of downtown Seattle and the harbor. A still more interesting adventure is a hike through **Seattle's Discovery Park,** just north of the city. Dogs are welcome across the 500-acre expanse of trees, bluffs, and beaches. Lush with foliage and natural beauty, the park lies directly on Puget Sound and there is usually plenty of wildlife to distract everyone. For those who would like to investigate the array of diversions in the downtown area, there are trolleys and buses that can whisk both human and beast to Seattle's center in just a little over five minutes.

The Historic Sou'wester Lodge

P.O. Box 102
Beach Access Road (38th Place)
Seaview, Washington 98644
(360) 642-2542

Hosts: Len and Miriam Atkins
Rooms: *6 lodge rooms, 4 cottages, 8 trailers*
Rates: *Lodge Rooms $59-99 (EP), Cottages $75-85 (EP),*
  Trailers $35-87 (EP)
Payment: *VISA*
Dogs: *Welcome everywhere except for the main inn, but they cannot be*
  left unattended
Children: *Welcome (cribs, cots, and baby-sitters are available)*
Open: *All year*

The Long Beach Peninsula reputedly has the longest stretch of beach in the world, and at 28 miles long, we won't argue the point. We hope readers will believe us when we tell them that the peninsula also contains one of the more unique accommodations in the Northwest — the Historic Sou'wester Lodge. The name seems innocuous enough, and the location can't be beat, as it lies at the end of a beach access road and across from high, grass-covered sand dunes. As we drove up, we first noticed the barn-board red, rambling old lodge, dwarfed by a stand of pine trees. Off to one side were four small cottages painted to match the lodge. So far, nothing out of the ordinary. That is, until we happened to glance across the way to see the vintage collection of mobile homes — their domed silver exteriors festooned with murals. But we will get back to them a little later. To understand the Historic Sou'wester, it is important to know a little about its history — and, more importantly, to understand Miriam and Len.

The Westborough House, as the Historic Sou'wester was formerly known, was built in 1892 by Oregon Senator Henry Winslow Corbett, who used it as his family's country estate. Almost 100 years later — in 1980, to be exact — Miriam and Len discovered the neglected home and decided to buy it. At the time, they were also in the process of creating a new life for themselves. For over 15 years Len had assisted Bruno Bettelheim (the noted child psychologist) at the University of Chicago. He and Miriam wanted a change, though, and drove across country thinking they would open a center for troubled children in Southern California. Fortunately, they never reached California, stopping instead in Seaview. They liked what they found and thought this would be a wonderful place to settle, especially when they learned that the old Westborough House was for sale. After buying it, they repaired the roof, rewired and repainted the interior, and filled it with all their worldly possessions. In 1981, The Historic Sou'wester Lodge was ready for business.

Guests traveling with dogs can stay in either the cabins or the refurbished trailers, but will undoubtedly gravitate to the lodge, as this tends to be the social and cultural center for the place. We entered through the glassed-in, wraparound porch and found Len, an affable, gray-bearded gentleman with a wonderful South African accent. We chatted a bit in the expansive living room, which reminded us of a scholar's library, with its beamed ceilings, tongue and groove fir walls, and built-in bookshelves flanking the fireplace. Throughout this common area we discovered an intriguing collection of the Atkins' furniture and literature, which they have acquired during their world travels. A brass chandelier casts muted lighting across the worn Oriental carpet and hardwood floors. Other than a little refurbishing, so little has been done to the place since the Corbett era that it is easy to imagine what life at the lodge must have been like over 100 years ago. Just off the living room are the three downstairs guest rooms, each quite Spartan and simply decorated. These accommodations are part of the famous Bed & (MYOD) Breakfast, which, as Len jokingly explains, means "Make Your Own Damn Breakfast." The kitchen is just around the corner and is open for guests' use. The remaining lodge guest rooms are apartments, complete with kitchenettes, which are rented for longer periods of time.

Our focus, though, is on the cottages and trailers. The cottages are simply furnished in what Len describes as "Early Salvation Army" and offer such amenities as a kitchen, one or two bedrooms, a sitting room, and a bathroom.

Guests usually enter these quarters by way of the enclosed car park, which opens up into the 1950s-style kitchen. From here, the circular flow of the cottage brings guests to either a bedroom or sitting room, and then finally into the bathroom. The decorative touches consist of an assortment of Post Impressionist posters and postcards, which Miriam has placed about the rooms. Other than that, there is definitely nothing fancy, cute, or contrived about these accommodations — just clean and unpretentious guest cabins, with the pounding surf and smell of salt air drifting in through the windows. We took special notice of the tiny note in each kitchen that begins with *From your dog...* and continues by asking guests to please make a special effort to keep dog hair swept up, as it easily gets imbedded in furniture, beds, etc.

The second option for those traveling with Bowser is the Tch! Tch! RVs, which are set off to the other side of the lodge. The Atkins mockingly refer to Tch (the British equivalent of Tsk) as Trailer Classics Hodgepodge, jesting that Senator Henry Corbett and his "patrician *petit bourgeois* alliance" would surely have "perished at the thought of... having this motley, proletarian assortment of recreational vehicles" parked in their neighborhood, much less in their own backyard. In any case, the trailers are the original American classic, with true "Sears Roebuck/Montgomery Ward 1971 catalogue ambiance." They are, in fact, 1950's curved-chrome trailers that come fully furnished, complete with kitchens. Visitors can step inside to see an "Early Salvation Army" chic, with plenty of books, linens, and space. Some of the trailers are painted on the outside — similar to the many murals we now find on buildings from time to time. One sketch replicates a memorable scene from the movie *The African Queen*. Another trailer, which Len affectionately calls "The Disoriented Express," depicts a train chugging along the side of it. The ambiance is decidedly unique, but thoroughly appeals to the low-key type of guest who generally stays here.

What newcomers will soon discover, if they didn't suspect it already, is that the Long Beach Peninsula lends itself to **long strolls along the beach** and unhurried days. People come in the spring to dig for razor clams or fly their kite — kite flying has long been a passion among residents of these parts. The roads are also flat, making bicycling a natural diversion. The region is also renowned for other particularities, such as cranberry bogs, having one of the oldest lighthouses in the Pacific Northwest (the **Cape Disappointment Lighthouse**), and being the termination point of the Lewis and Clark expedition (the Fort Canby State Park). **Fort Canby**, by the way, offers all sorts of recreational diversions for people and their dogs. There are nature trails, spectacular walks along the rocky shoreline, and even a forest — all of which should provide enough exercise for human and beast. For those hoping to stay closer to home, there is a **secret path** along the beach that is perfect for walks with dogs. The exact location is not so secret, though, especially for those who follow the detailed map located on a wall in the entry.

A tired dog will happily sleep in the evening, giving his human friends the opportunity to steal over to the lodge for the Atkins' Fireside Evenings.

These are held in the living room, where, depending on the night, guests are treated to concerts, theatrical performances, or poetry readings; or they might participate in worldly discussions. Guests and their children (because "even infants should not be denied the opportunity for cultural enrichment") are encouraged to participate, bringing with them a valued and appreciated contribution to the overall atmosphere. Visitors from all backgrounds are thus provided with a wonderful opportunity to get to know each other and to share in the informal and fun discourse. The ambiance here is truly unique, and perfect for anyone who wants to be within steps of an expansive beach and who thinks the off-beat accommodations merely add to the experience. After years of playing host, Len issues this warning: his guests either love the place or detest it. We hope our description helps our readers to decide which category they fall into.

Groveland Cottage

4861 Sequim Dungeness Way
Sequim/Dungeness, Washington 98382
(800) 879-8859, (360) 683-3565, Fax: (360) 683-5181

Innkeeper: *Simone Nichols*
Rooms: *4 doubles, 1 cottage*
Rates: *Doubles $80-110 (B&B), Cottage $90*
Payment: *AE, DC, DSC, MC, and VISA*
Dogs: *Small dogs welcome in the "Secret Room"*
Children: *Not appropriate for children under the age of 12*
Open: *All year*

Sequim is one of those rare places on the Olympic Peninsula that does not get much rain. This area lies in the rain shadow of the Olympic Mountains — it is therefore a desirable destination for travelers who are tired of crossing their fingers hoping for a rain-free vacation. Fertile farmland seems to stretch for miles here, before sloping up into the foothills of the Olympics. But closer to the ocean, flat roads wend along bluffs and rural routes to all sorts of wonderful villages. One of these is Dungeness, home to the exquisite Dungeness National Wildlife Refuge. One of the lesser-known treasures in this area is Simone's Groveland Cottage, set just a half-mile from the beach and harbor.

Built at the turn of the century, the cottage was once a private home for a wealthy merchant and his family. Today, it reminds us of an English country cottage with its white picket fences, trellises, and arbors draped in roses and climbing vines. Surrounding this white clapboard and shingled house are vibrant perennial gardens, which were still in bloom when we visited, even though it was late in the season. This bucolic setting is even further enhanced by a creek that skirts the edge of the property — and by the canopy of fruit and shade trees filtering the sun in the backyard. The main house is connected to an old-fashioned general store, where sloping wood floors and unfinished walls provide plenty of character. Simone was in the process of closing the store permanently, though, so that she could finally implement what she had long been contemplating — converting it back into a Great Room. By the time guests visit again, this will be a formal space for weddings, chamber music, or simply relaxing before the substantial river rock fireplace.

The rest of the inn will remain the same — which should greatly please returning guests who are used to their well-appointed rooms and Simone's pampering. As we mentioned, the main inn is reminiscent of an English country B&B, and once inside, guests will discover that each corner is filled with an unusual antique, *object d' art*, or knickknack. We especially like the living room, with its wall of double-hung windows and its comfortable overstuffed sofas and chairs. With all the interesting collectibles in here, including china, contemporary art, and mountains of books and magazines, it is easy to overlook the lovely stained glass windows. The adjoining dining room, which overlooks the backyard, is the site for each morning's bountiful breakfast. This is quite a feast, beginning with bowls of fresh fruit and scones, accompanied by a baked egg dish or other delectables. The treats begin much earlier than this, though, as first thing each morning, a tray with coffee and a newspaper is brought to each guest's bedroom.

While there are four upstairs guest rooms in the inn, they are not really appropriate for people traveling with a dog. There is, however, a separate cottage known as the Secret Room. We found it by walking through the back of the general store and across a short path. The cottage would be our preferred space, with or without a dog, as guests staying out here enjoy the ultimate in privacy. The cottage is awash in various hues of purple, ranging from a pale lilac to a deep lavender. Naturally finished, paneled-wood walls are inset with small windows framed by lilac-hued cotton curtains. Guests sleep in a high brass bed, or may relax on the adjacent couch enlivened by a purple floral throw. Surprisingly, the best views of the backyard are garnered from the tiny windows in the kitchen. A Dutch door opens from here out into the yard — guests can open just the top and let the breezes drift through the cottage. Guests staying here also have a television with a VCR.

People stay here for a variety of reasons, but it is the birders who truly love this place. There are plenty of birds to see right on the property; however, the most popular spot from which to watch the assorted wildfowl is on the Dungeness Sand Spit. While dogs are not allowed on this particular adventure, there is a pleasant walk that appeals to canines along the **rural roads** leading to the Dungeness Harbor. Once at the harbor, we recommend stopping at The Three Crabs to check out its excellent menu. Slightly further afield, at the **Sequim Bay State Park**, leashed dogs are allowed to explore with their human friends. Another nearby option is the **Dungeness River Valley**, which is one of the few areas in the Olympic Mountains that allows hikers and their dogs. Another option is the **Gold Creek Trail**, which happens to be located right on the way to the Dungeness River Valley. If guests plan to be out and about for the better part of the day, they may wish to ask Simone to pack them a picnic lunch.

Juan de Fuca Cottages

182 Marine Drive
Sequim, Washington 98382
(800) 683-4432, (360) 683-4433

Innkeeper: *Sheila Ramus*
Rooms: *6 cottages*
Rates: *$100-105 (EP)*
Payment: *MC and VISA*
Dogs: *Depending upon the dog, they are welcome with notice*
Children: *Welcome*
Open: *All year*

The Juan de Fuca Cottages are a secret — and it seems that longtime guests and the innkeeper want to keep it that way. When we first called to get more information on the place, the innkeeper filled us in on the details only verbally, because the inn does not have a brochure or a rate sheet. This did not discourage us; rather, it made us all the more interested in investigating the clutch of cottages set on Dungeness Bay.

The Juan de Fuca Cottages, as it turns out, lie in a quiet residential neighborhood. The houses lining the road along the windswept bluff all look overlook the Juan de Fuca Strait, and the cottages are no exception. They are arranged in a semi-circle around a beautifully-manicured central lawn and glassed-in gazebo. These appealing, blue-shingled buildings are quite endearing, with their white gingerbread trim lining the eaves, their shutters with carved seahorse motifs, and their window boxes filled with flowers. Each is also fashioned with a tiny glassed-in porch, with just enough room for a pair of chairs and a side table. While the porch is privy to some exceptional views of the water, we decided to venture inside rather than linger on the porch.

We were surprised by the interior spaces, which exhibit far more character than we were expecting. The floors are fully carpeted, and the walls paneled in a honey-colored wood. Hues of blue and pink highlight the floral spreads covering the beds. One alcove holds a queen bed, while built-in cabinets form a storage space in which to slide the other bed when it is not being used. A small sitting area lies to the front of the cottage, in front of a plate glass window that overlooks the grounds and the ocean. To the rear is a fully-equipped modern kitchen, with such amenities as a microwave, full refrigerator, and dishwasher. An oak table and matching Windsor chairs fill the area separating the kitchen from the sitting room. The bathrooms are new as well, and are brightened by skylights set over the whirlpool tubs. Bottles of Nivea creme, bath gel, and soap are thoughtful extras we don't normally expect to find in housekeeping cottages. Families with up to two children would be comfortable in most of the cottages, although they are cozy. For families with more children, the two-bedroom cottage set off by itself to the rear of the property is ideal.

Regardless of how guests decide to accommodate their group, most are sure to relish the fact that they are well removed from the rest of civilization. Once we arrived at the Juan de Fuca Cottages, we indeed felt quite separate from the commercial world (strip malls, movie theaters, fast food restaurants), and frankly had little desire to go find it. Therefore, we recommend that guests bring their own food and simply plan to use these low-key accommodations as an ideal place to unwind. Some entertainment is available in the form of television and VCRs, and there are over 250 movies that guests may borrow. Each cottage also has a library of books, should travelers have forgotten their own. Best of all, if guests do not find a book to their liking, a neighbor probably has one more to their fancy.

As we mentioned, there is plenty of grass around the cottages, and when the wind blows, which is often, the glassed-in gazebo is a convenient shelter. **Walks along the bluffs** are also a delightful way to exercise dogs. Guests can follow the bluff road down the hill to **Cline Spit**, where many enjoy watching the sailboarders tackle the high winds. This is also a favorite spot for crabbing, and many of the locals are often busy pulling in their catch. Most days, it is easy to see all the way across the Juan de Fuca Strait to Vancouver Island. We were also able to look back toward the Dungeness National Wildlife Refuge. Unfortunately, dogs will have to stay at home or in the car for this latter outing. This six-mile strip of land is one of the longest natural sand spits in the United States. The walk along the spit is exceptional, and for those who pick the right time of day, it can feel as if they are hundreds of miles away from home.

The Salish Lodge

P.O. Box 1109
Snoqualmie Falls Road (Highway 202)
Snoqualmie, Washington 98065
(800) 826-6124, (425) 888-2556, Fax: (425) 888-2420
Internet: http://www.travel-in-com/CITIES/PS/snoqualmie/salish.html

General Manager: *Loy Helmley*
Rooms: *87 doubles, 4 suites*
Rates: *Doubles $165-295 (EP), Suites $500-575 (EP)*
Payment: *AE, CB, DC, DSC, MC, and VISA*
Dogs: *Welcome in the first-floor rooms, with a $50 non-refundable deposit*
Children: *Welcome (cribs, cots, and baby-sitters are available)*
Open: *All year*

There are plenty of waterfalls throughout the Pacific Northwest, but among the more famous (and therefore most visited) are the Snoqualimie Falls. We had to admit, the falls were spectacular as they dropped 268 feet to the river below. As one might imagine, the sound effects are also stupendous. Set at the top of these falls is the famous Salish Lodge which, if viewed from the bottom of the falls, appears to rise from the mist like a medieval fortress.

The architecture cleverly utilizes native woods, and stone that seems to meld with every rocky outcropping it touches. Because the lodge lies near a popular tourist destination, the gracious staff works especially hard to keep the curious public at bay. For the most part, it all works quite well, creating an interior oasis that appeals to those searching for a romantic or relaxing holiday experience. The falls can be deafening at times, but as we stepped into the interior a sense of calm settled upon us. We were again impressed with the abundant use of natural materials in evidence throughout the contemporary lodge, ranging from slate floors to finely hewn redwood beams. Where there isn't natural wood or rock, there is glass — either in the floor-to-ceiling windows or in the walls of tiny crank-out windows. Ficus trees and assorted plant life also help to create private areas where guests can sit before the fireplace and soak in the tranquil ambiance.

The Salish Lodge is reminiscent of a grand country manor, with guests feeling pampered and protected from the moment they venture inside. Hallways are accessed through locked doors; so only guests with keys are able to enter these private enclaves. We were interested primarily in the first-floor rooms, as this is where guests traveling with dogs are permitted to stay. There is a reason for this, as each of these spaces opens onto grass terraces accessed through sliding glass doors. From here, guests and their dogs step down to a path that circumnavigates the lodge. The bedrooms are huge, and resemble something out of a Ralph Lauren catalog — the masculine country version, that is. King beds appear immense when topped by fluffy down comforters and piles of oversized feather pillows. Hand-crafted furniture might include a classic, naturally-finished wicker chair, a streamlined cherry Shaker table, or an oak armoire concealing the television. Interesting lithographs and black and white photographs highlight the cream-colored walls, but the focal point is a slate fireplace that faces the bed. Amenities are equally well conceived, as a huge basket of gourmet goodies rests on one table and a refrigerator is stocked with champagne, wine, and sparkling water. Bathrooms are modern and outfitted with hair dryers, robes, and a full complement of toiletries. All contain Jacuzzi soaking tubs; in some bedrooms, these rest under frosted windows that slide open so that bathers can enjoy watching the crackling fire from their spa. There are only four suites, one of which occupies a corner of the first floor. For a truly special occasion, guests can reserve this incredible space. Most notable in here are the wall of hand-carved cherry cabinets, hiding an entertainment center, and the deep, cushioned window seats that meet in the corner of the room under two plate glass windows. The glass doors open to a patio that wraps around the suite to the separate bedroom. Both the bedroom and living room have wood burning fireplaces.

This is a hotel to which travelers come when they need to rejuvenate. The food wins rave reviews, as does the wine cellar — and guests may enjoy all of this within their rooms. However, at some point, even the most reclusive guests should make their way upstairs to either the Attic Lounge or the Salish Dining Room. We like the feeling of the Attic Lounge, whose ceiling follows the contours of the roof and gives this inviting space more interest. Guests can have a drink around one of the small tables, on the leather couches, or hidden away behind a half-wall. There is usually live music in the evenings; a few lucky ones can listen to this from a table overlooking the falls. One flight down is the equally appealing Salish Dining Room — an intimate space, which, unfortunately, has only a few tables that are privy to views of the falls. Amid this backdrop, dining patrons might select such appetizers as the smoked breast of squab with a cranberry bean stew and ginger plum compôte, the Napoleon of lobster and spinach with a light tarragon sauce, or the smoked tomato and bell pepper bisque. This could be followed by the rabbit with a porcini brioche, quail stuffed with smoked squab and a fig relish, or the pheasant stuffed with wild mushrooms. The Salish Lodge's weekend brunch has won many accolades over the years, and continues to draw guests and patrons from the Seattle area.

During the day, dogs and their human friends will find plenty to do here as well. They can walk the property, which consists of a path along the falls. There is also a **one-mile trail** that leads visitors and their dogs to the bottom of the falls. Those who have come to hike will enjoy the many opportunities available throughout the region. One of these begins in the **Tiger Mountain State Forest**, where miles of trails head off in all sorts of directions; several even climb to the top of Tiger Mountain. **Mount Si** is another good choice for hikers, as is the neighboring **Little Si**. One word of caution: Because these outdoor areas are all so close to the urban world, weekends usually draw large numbers of people. If planning a short trip, we suggest trying to visit on a Sunday and Monday, as the lodge will be quieter then, and so will the many attractions that draw visitors to the area.

Some people may want to visit the St. Michelle and Columbia wineries or to peruse the many local nurseries. One of the best is Carnation Farm, with more than 1,200 acres of gardens to peruse. At the end of the day, guests can return to the lodge and totally relax in the roof-top hot tub set amid flowers and gardens.

Cavanaugh's Inn at the Park

West 303 North River Drive
Spokane, Washington 99201
(800) THE-INNS, (509) 326-8000, Fax: (509) 325-7329

General Manager: *John Taffin*
Rooms: *240 doubles, 24 suites*
Rates: *Doubles $94-142 (EP), Suites $185-500 (EP)*
Payment: *AE, DC, DSC, MC, and VISA*
Dogs: *Welcome; they must be leashed in the public areas*
Children: *Welcome (cribs, cots, and baby-sitters are available)*
Open: *All year*

In 1974, Spokane received a great deal of notoriety as the host of the World's Fair. The fair served as the impetus for revitalizing the town, creating a river front park and developing a number of fine hotels. Today, some consider it to be the most livable city in the Pacific Northwest. The 100-acre Riverfront Park is still one of the more popular gathering places, with its gardens, turn-of-the-century carousel, and paths that are great for walking dogs. At the edge of the park is Cavanaugh's Inn at the Park that seems well connected to this natural setting.

What new arrivals will discover about this large city inn is that, true to its name, it does have great views of the Riverfront Park and the Spokane River. Moreover, the design of the inn is such that the natural beauty outside has also been incorporated into its lobby. This light and airy atrium, which is filled with gardens of fresh flowers, decorative shrubs, and full-size trees, is drenched in sunlight. Within this cavernous space is the Atrium Café and Deli, where breakfast and lunch are served amid these semi-tropical surroundings. Besides the Atrium Café, there is the sophisticated Windows of the Seasons restaurant, offering equally lovely views of the park and river. The twinkling lights of the chandeliers in here reflect off the highly polished marble and lustrous wood accents, making this a fine place for an intimate dinner. The menu is Continental, with entrées that include a mesquite-grilled salmon, coquilles St. Jacques, crab-and-shrimp veal roulade, Cajun blackened New York sirloin, and the pistachio stuffed pheasant breast.

Accommodations at the Inn on the Park have been recently updated with brighter colors and a more contemporary flair. The standard amenities are also present, including a television, telephone, individual heating and air-conditioning, and balconies overlooking the swimming pool and river area. A relatively new wing, which is geared primarily for business travelers, offers a higher level of luxury than most of the other chambers. The two- to four-bedroom suites, at the upper end of the price scale, often include such features as fireplaces, whirlpools, wet bars, and access to the rooftop pool and decks.

There are numerous recreational diversions at the Inn at the Park. Many will enjoy the fitness center, with its exercise room, whirlpool, sauna, and lap pool. There is also an indoor and outdoor swimming pool (or "lagoon"). The latter is built to resemble a grotto, with boulders stacked to support a water slide and form a waterfall. A nearby footbridge brings guests over to the Riverside Park, where there is a children's petting zoo, miniature golf, and the opera house (offering a number of children's programs during the year). Dogs would probably be a little more intrigued with the **Riverside State Park**, which boasts over 7,000 acres for exploration. The **Centennial Trail** also offers miles of trails, where visitors can even view petroglyphs along the river. The **Dishman Hills Natural** area is a preserve in Spokane Valley, which also has an intriguing trail network to explore. Outside of Spokane, there are two wilderness areas known as **Goose Butte** and the **Fishtrap Lake** area — both are good choices for day trips with dogs.

Spokane is a great destination for people and their dogs, because there are an abundance of outdoor diversions. This is not the sort of city where it is difficult to find green space; it seems to be everywhere — a fact appreciated by both dogs and their friends.

Circle H Holiday Ranch

810 Watt Canyon Road
Thorp, Washington 98946
(509) 964-2000

Hosts: *Betsy and Jamie Ogden*
Rooms: *5 cabins*
Rates: *$65-75/person, summer (MAP), $110/cabin — winter (B&B);*
Children under 2 are free, ages 3-12 are $30-35 (MAP)
Payment: *MC and VISA*
Dogs: *Welcome*
Children: *Welcome (baby-sitters are available)*
Open: *All year*

If the mention of Washington state conjures up only images of pine-studded, snow-capped mountains, deep blue waters surrounding lush islands, and plenty of rainfall, then we recommend venturing east over the Cascades into central Washington. Here, vivid blue skies, wide open spaces, and drier terrain predominate. A pleasant one-and-a-half-hour drive from Seattle leads visitors to the foothill ranch lands, where white fences and horses are more abundant than people. The Circle H Holiday Ranch is nestled into these foothills, overlooking the Kittitas Valley. A short jog off the highway and up a country road leads visitors to the Circle H. Our arrival was announced by the Ogdens' two friendly dogs, who reacquainted us with the place. The ranch itself is low-key and intimate, although the area around it is expansive — some 100,000 acres of the LT Murray Wildlife Recreation Area.

The ranch's busiest season is from Memorial Day through Labor Day, when extended families and their canine companions are in abundance. No wonder they like it — they get their own cabin, fabulous views, and a true taste of ranch living. While many choose this spot so they can spend their time riding, there are all sorts of other recreational outlets. The informal children's play area, along with horseshoes and tether ball, is always a popular diversion with the younger set. Hot summer days are usually spent near the tree-lined swimming pond. But it is the stables and lovable farm animals that are still the perennial favorites. Children often rise early to go off and help the ranch hands feed the horses. There are also ducks, goats, sheep, llamas, and a pig — a menagerie that reminded us of the cast of creatures from *Charlotte's Web*. A "baby-sitting" horse is gentle enough for the little ones to ride, or kids can create their own amusement by jumping in a haystack or two. Our only word of warning is to be sure that visiting dogs are kept under close supervision when they're busy checking out the barn animals, especially the ducks. This is about the only restriction we can think of, as for the most part, dogs have seemingly endless amounts of terrain to explore.

Besides bringing their own dog, many guests also BYOH (horse). The Ogdens have facilities to accommodate horses, and for a small fee, they also provide the feed and hay. Guests may also enjoy either a guided or unguided trail ride. The saddlebag lunch should keep most people happily sated until their return, when another ample repast awaits. The food is varied, with hearty steaks and barbecued chicken topping off the list of the most popular dishes, while hamburgers and hot dogs are two of the perennial favorites for the kids. The vegetables are simply prepared, but fresh — as is the bread. Guests might find an occasional casserole or lasagna slipping onto the menu as well. Kids of all ages will want to save room for dessert, which includes freshly-baked fruit pies or strawberry shortcake.

After dinner during the high season, there are sometimes square dances, campfires, or hayrides. During quieter times of year, guests might gravitate to the ranch house to watch a movie on the wide screen television before heading back to the cabin for the night. We prefer a trip to the sauna to work out any muscle strains from the day, then heading back to the cabin for some much-deserved sleep. A short walk from the ranch house leads to the cabins. These "rustic antique-filled cabin suites" originally housed the ranch hands, but are nicely refurbished with Betsy's collection of western memorabilia.

We liked the Lone Ranger and Tonto cabins, connected by a door that allows them to become one big suite. The bleached knotty pine walls, slatted ceilings, and painted floors provide the frame-work for an eclectic assortment of furnishings. Accents are bright red, whether in the curtains at the windows, the colorful carpets covering the floors, or the thickly woven wool blankets topping the bedsteads. After a day on the trails, the wonderful beds built with substantial logs and branches are a welcome sight. Small shelves placed over the windows hold western memorabilia, such as miniature totem poles and pictures of high mountain lakes set in rustic wood frames. The kitchen, complete with a microwave and a refrigerator, has a day bed set alongside it that gives guests additional room to spread out. We thought that hanging wooden fruit crates along the walls was a clever way to store china and glassware.

Another popular room combination is Dale Evans and Roy Rogers. Roy Rogers faces down the valley and has unobstructed views through the small paned windows. Guests who are looking for a good deal of privacy might consider staying in Gene Autry. Here, the sitting room is enhanced by a freestanding fireplace. The master bedroom has a colorful quilt on the bed, and there is a smaller room toward the rear fashioned with a day bed. This boasts one of the larger kitchens. Few people do much cooking in-season, though, as breakfast is delivered to each cabin the night before and only needs heating in the morning. Although Gene Autry is slightly more contemporary than the rest of the cabins, all are, thankfully, without modern distractions, such as televisions or telephones.

Few guests and their dogs find a need to leave the ranch or its immediate environs, as there are great hiking opportunities in the **L.T. Murray Wildlife**

Recreation Area. A short drive, though, just past the town of Cle Elum, leads to two good hiking trails that allow dogs. The first is the **West Fork of the Teanaway River,** which is reached off Route 903. Hikers and their dogs will discover a trail lined with ample river crossings and plenty of open space for enjoying the scenic vistas. The second option is the **Yellow Hill/Elbow Peak Trail,** located near the West Fork of the Teanaway River trailhead. Besides the lovely views of the Teanaway Valley, hikers will also find magnificent panoramas of Mount Rainier and its majestic neighbors.

Inn of the White Salmon

P.O. Box 1549
172 West Jewett
White Salmon, Washington 98672
(800) 972-5226, (509) 493-2335
E-mail: innkeeper@gorge.net, Internet: http://www.gorge.net/lodging/iws

Innkeepers: *Janet and Roger Holen*
Rooms: *11 doubles, 5 suites*
Rates: *Doubles $89 (B&B), Suites $99-115 (B&B)*
Payment: *AE, DSC, DC, MC, and VISA*
Dogs: *Welcome in specific rooms*
Children: *Welcome*
Open: *All year*

While Hood River, Oregon and its famous Columbia Gorge still draw plenty of sightseers and sail boarders, just across the river, its sister community of White Salmon does not enjoy the same notoriety. Sure, when the winds begin to blow, both sides of the river become launching points for sailboarders, who view this as one of the few nearly perfect Windsurfing spots in the United States. But when these winds dissipate, life becomes quiet here, more reminiscent of the days when the timber industry, not tourism, reigned.

White Salmon may not be as easily accessible as Hood River, but it exudes almost as much character. To get to White Salmon, visitors must pay a toll in Hood River and cross a narrow metal bridge that leads over to the hamlet of Bingen. There isn't much reason to stop in Bingen, and most just continue up the hill a mile or so to the village of White Salmon. Here, the storefronts are reminiscent of something out of the Swiss Alps. Though the plain brick facade of the inn (which dates back to 1937) is not very alluring, guests will be pleasantly pleased with what they find inside.

We stepped into the foyer and were greeted with the most divine smells emanating from somewhere deep in the inn. As if to tempt us, a glass jar filled with freshly baked peanut butter cookies beckoned interested raiders.

Meandering further into the inn, we expected the decor to resemble the rather bland exterior. Instead, we discovered a strong Victorian theme predominating, with a few antiques, marble-topped tables, and historic pictures lining the long, straight hallways. At the end of one hall, we found a charming parlor, where classical music was playing. This is a large space, dominated by an antique sideboard set in the midst of comfortable couches, armchairs, and still more Victorian antiques. There is a television in here, but guests are more likely to be reading from the inn's assortment of magazines and books, or playing one of the many board games. Although the views are not of the gorge, they are nonetheless endearing, with expanses of glass revealing a neatly planted hillside of grass and flowers. Guests step out through a pair of glass doors to find the ever popular hot tub. When not relaxing in these common areas, most head up to their comfortable bedrooms.

Once again, we were delightfully surprised. These spaces may not have intriguing nooks and crannies, but they more than make up for this with high ceilings and a scattering of antiques. Floral comforters cover the brass or carved wood, framed beds. The muted green and rose tones reflect the Victorian period, with old-fashioned lamps with fringed shades casting a subdued light. Area rugs dampen footsteps across the hardwood floors, and amenities include televisions, air conditioning, and private bathrooms. The corner rooms are some of the most popular chambers, as they offer a few more windows and a little additional space. After a good night's sleep, guests awaken to an aroma of baked breakfast breads that is so strong it permeates every corner of the inn.

Following one's nose is the easiest way to find the breakfast room. Guests dine at small tables covered with lovely white lace overlays and are served on old-fashioned china that reminded us of our trips to Germany's small guest houses. The food that follows is also more reminiscent of Europe than America, especially the pastries that almost defy description. Guests may start with a small bowl of fresh fruit and, perhaps, a French tart, chocolate raspberry cheesecake, baklava, or cinnamon roll. (This is only a sampling of the 20 or more pastries available each day.) The main courses are equally international, and include such options as a frittata, quiche, chile relleno, or Hungarian flauf. (Flauf consists of eggs baked with ham, Swiss cheese, scallions, and caraway.)

There are no excuses not to get a little exercise after a breakfast of this magnitude. It is almost imperative to walk, hike, stroll — anything to get the legs moving before giving in to the strong urge to retreat back to bed for a midmorning nap. Fortunately, there are plenty of things to do here, without leaving this side of the river. As one might imagine, our curiosity was piqued when we learned about the nearby **Dog Mountain**, just west of the Bingen. Here, there is a nice hike that begins at the Gorge and heads up to the summit, through mountain meadows and forests. Those who want to venture further north toward Trout Lake can have their pick of day hikes. Cool mornings are an ideal time to climb **Little Huckleberry Mountain**, where fabulous views can be enjoyed from the summit. Another dog-friendly option in the Trout Lake area is a hike up the **Snipes Mountain Trail** which wends along Gotchen Creek and through lava fields; the **Buck Creek Trail,** that parallels the White Salmon River; or the **Cold Springs Trail,** which offers incredible views of Mount Adams. For more details, visitors can check with the Mount Adams Ranger Station in Trout Lake. Of course, visitors and their dogs can also limit themselves to leisurely walks around White Salmon. Many of the steep hills here provide a good workout — as much as some may want when on vacation.

British Columbia

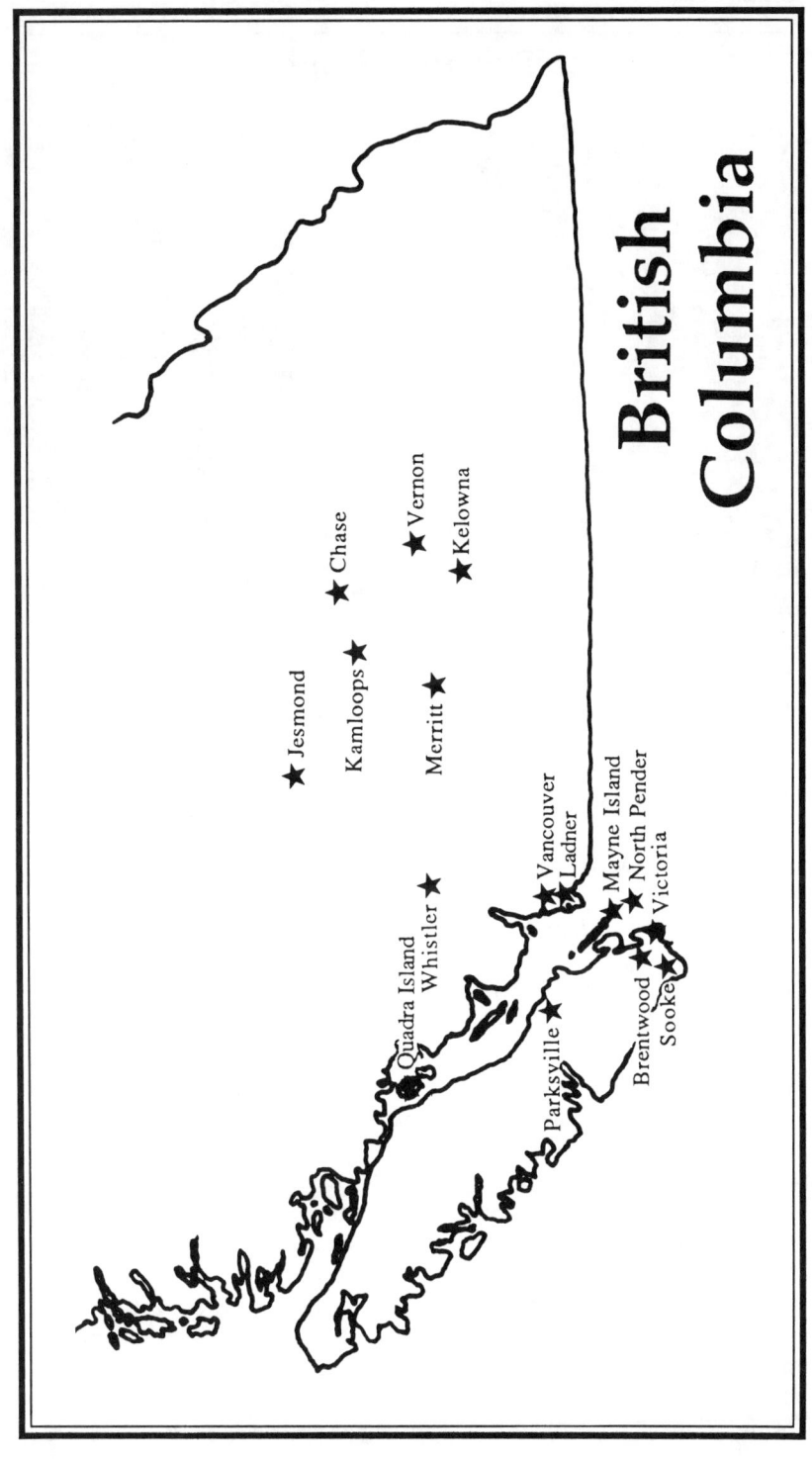

The Boathouse

746 Sea Drive
Brentwood Bay, B.C., Canada V8M 1B1
(250) 652-9370
Internet: http://www.monday.com/tourism

Hosts: *Harvey and Jean Merritt*
Rooms: *1 cottage*
Canadian Rates: *$130 (B&B)*
Payment: *MC and VISA*
Dogs: *Welcome with notice*
Children: *Not appropriate for children*
Open: *March 15 through September 30*

Brentwood Bay is famous for the Butchart Gardens and Butterfly World. While memories of flowers and butterflies might fade, guests' impressions of The Boathouse will undoubtedly remain firmly fixed in their minds. The Boathouse was built in 1927 as a summer cottage, but for the past eleven years the Merritts have used it as a waterside Bed and Breakfast. The sense of isolation here is complete, as guests walk down a steep hillside of stairs and pass through dense woods before emerging at the cottage and bathhouse. The cottage is set on pilings over the water, and once guests step inside, they begin to lose all sense of the land, focusing instead on the surrounding water and wildlife that thrives here.

We really liked the character of this place, with its red fir floors and white-washed board walls. Its fresh crisp feeling is accentuated by the sheer white tab curtains and the robin-egg blue cabinetry. Though this is only a one-room cottage, it actually feels quite spacious. Neatly displayed on the open shelves are wine glasses, china, and clay pots filled with coffee, sugar, etc. The cottage is also equipped with a toaster, tea kettle, coffee maker, and a barbecue. A refrigerator keeps things cool — especially the breakfasts, which are brought down the night before and placed in here so they will be ready for guests at whatever time they may decide to arise. After making a cup of coffee and spreading a little fresh blackberry jam on the homemade muffins, we were content to relax and enjoy the lovely vistas visible through the walls of windows. Freshly-squeezed orange juice and a fruit salad complete this repast, which may be taken at the small breakfast table set under a window or out on the porch.

If the day turns inclement, comfortable armchairs and a couch (which opens to a sofa bed) are just the place to play games, read a book, or stretch out for a nap. The adjacent bathhouse contains a private bathroom and shower. Even if the hour is late, guests often enjoy the short stroll to the bathhouse under moon and starlit skies. The early-morning hours are the best time to catch the harbor seals and otters playing on and around the rocks, or to watch the great blue herons and kingfishers swooping over the water in search of food. Bald eagles have also been spotted here. With the dock and a dinghy available for guests to use, it is fun to load up your dog and head out for a little **harbor tour**, following it up with an exploration of **the island** across from the Boathouse.

Many people like to row over to the world-famous Butchart Gardens (unfortunately, dogs are not permitted), thereby avoiding the usual traffic. Few can claim to arrive here by water, but guests staying at the Boathouse will have no problem doing so. These gardens lie on the Tod Inlet on what was formerly an old limestone quarry. The Butcharts built their home here at the turn of the century, and imported many of the exotic plants visitors will find here today. The gardens are spectacular, and there are always special programs, seminars, and other interesting horticultural events taking place here. In the summer months, Butchart Gardens puts on a fireworks' display which is visible from the Boathouse. Another favorite destination, especially for those looking for a peaceful picnic site, is the lovely **white shell beach**, situated just a little further down Tod Inlet.

The streets near the B&B are great for walking and are fairly quiet, as this is mostly a **residential area**. People love it here, and wax poetic about the serenity and calm that permeate the place. Many plan their trip around Butchart Gardens, but as the time passes, they are content to spend their vacation inside the cottage and out exploring the many inlets and eddies throughout the area. This is the place where, as Ralph Waldo Emerson put it, "A little warmth, a little food, and an immense quiet" go a long way.

Quaaout Lodge

P.O. Box 1215
Chase, B.C., Canada V0E 1M0
(800) 663-4303, (250) 679-3090, Fax: (250) 679-3039
Internet: http://www.travel.bc.ca/q/quaaout/

General Manager: *Brian Turnbull*
Rooms: *66 doubles, 6 suites*
Canadian Rates: *Doubles $79-103 (EP), Suites $150 (EP)*
Payment: *AE, DSC, MC, and VISA*
Dogs: *Welcome with a $5 fee*
Children: *Welcome; children under 16 are free of charge*
Open: *All year*

A Kekuli is the winter shelter for the Shuswap Indians. Although rarely used anymore, these round dwellings were constructed with a wood shell that was covered with cedar mats and then packed with soil for insulation. An opening at the top of the shell served two purposes — it allowed the smoke from the cook fire to escape, and also provided an additional entrance and egress. Another opening at ground level was typically used as an escape tunnel. Woven mats were used for just about everything, although the tribespeople did sleep on mattresses made of animal skins stuffed with cedar frawns, feathers, or bunches of grass.

The contemporary Quaaout Lodge's gently flowing lines are similar to those of a huge Kekuli. Although guests won't be sleeping on animal skin furs or cooking over a fire, they will be able to appreciate the history and beauty of this space. We did not enter this Kekuli from the roof, but through pairs of massive wooden doors. The first pair of doors was fashioned with a pair of hand-carved bear head handles, while the second set was outfitted with carved wolf head handles. This Kekuli's domed ceiling and central fireplace are authentic, but instead of mud-matted walls, guests will find plate glass windows revealing views of the woods and beyond to Little Lake Shuswap. An extension of the main Kekuli forms a glassed-in dining room, while another wing contains the guest bedrooms.

As we looked around, we noticed some guests were lounging about and enjoying hot chocolate before the fire, while others were out walking along the lake. Off to the edge of the property, there are a few teepees that guests may reserve in the summer months. Camping in teepees is a novel experience that our kids would love, but we rather preferred the bedrooms on this visit.

The guest room wing's exterior design resembles an accordion of sorts. The unusual jagged pattern allows each of the guest rooms to have a nice view of the lake. The decor consists of brightly-colored Shuswap patterns found on the quilted spreads and at curtains framing the windows. Most of the spaces have just enough room for the bedsteads, a small table with two chairs, and a long bureau with a television, a coffee maker, and some other goodies. Bathrooms are modern, tiled, and well appointed. The suites offer the best views and the most amenities. These chambers are exceptionally large and have king beds set in front of fireplaces and near Jacuzzi tubs. Light the candles, enjoy a soak, and then wrap up in a terry robe afterwards.

The food at the lodge's restaurant is excellent, and should appeal to most guests. Against the backdrop of the lake, patrons can peruse this seasonally changing menu. Some might opt to start with pasta tossed in a basil cream sauce; the rabbit and chicken ragoût with fiddlehead greens; or the platter of smoked and poached local fish. Entrées include honey glazed baby back ribs; pork loin with a cranberry honey jus; and an herb crusted salmon. Apple crisp, berry bannock with maple cream, and a chocolate mousse terrine served with a berry coulis are several of the dessert options.

Dogs love it at the Quaaout Lodge. The property has **jogging and hiking trails**, as well as plenty of grass. There is a sandy beach (almost a half-mile long) that children will love, along with a good-sized playground. We especially like the see-saw of carefully balanced logs. Horseshoes, volleyballs, and Frisbees can be secured from the front desk. There is an indoor exercise room; however, during the summer months most of the exercise equipment is brought out to an open-air gazebo overlooking the lake.

After an invigorating workout, many enjoy relaxing in the sauna or hot tub, or cooling off in the attractive indoor pool. The staff can advise on nearby cross-country and downhill skiing options, or arrange for canoe, sailboat, or houseboat rentals. Many come here in October to observe the famous sockeye salmon run in the nearby Adams River. People can walk along platforms and easily observe this impressive natural phenomenon. One of the best viewing points, according to the staff at the lodge, is from the **Roderick Haig-Brown Provincial Park**. When the salmon are not running, there are over 2,500 acres of trails for hiking with a dog. Another lake (slightly more isolated than Little Lake Shuswap) is **Adams Lake**, where leashed dogs are welcome.

Circle H Mountain Lodge

Summer: P.O. Box 7
Jesmond, Clinton, B.C., Canada V0K 1K0
Telephone/Fax: (250) 459-2565
Winter: *3086 Babich Street*
Abbotsford, B.C., Canada V2S 5H7
Telephone/Fax: (604) 850-1873, E-mail: circle_h@mindlink.bc.ca
Internet: http://www.monday.com/homepage/65_1.htm

Owners: *Mitch, Daphne, Kerry, and Trevor Henselwood*
Rooms: *5 doubles, 4 cabins*
Canadian Rates: *Daily—Adults $110 (AP), Children $87 (AP), Weekly—Adults $670 (AP), Children $515 (AP)*
Payment: *Personal checks*
Dogs: *Welcome in the cabins*
Children: *Most appropriate for children 6 years of age and older (baby-sitting is available)*
Open: *May through October*

    If horses, mountains, and wild open spaces spur your imagination, then head north to British Columbia's Cariboo region, where the Fraser River still steadily carves out portions of this magnificent terrain. Traveling along these isolated back roads, it doesn't take much to imagine what life here must have been like during the 1850s — a time when gold drew prospectors to this region. Soon after the discovery of gold, a north/south stagecoach route was established that started in Lilloet (at Mile 0) and worked its way north to Cariboo. Along the way, roadhouses were built to offer food, drink, and overnight accommodations to travelers. At the time, the roadhouses were commonly referred to by the mile marker they were located nearest to along the route. Today, visitors will still run across hamlets known simply as 70, 100, and 108 Mile Houses. Clinton was the site of one such "mile house," and still contains many of the historic buildings from the turn of the century.

    Unlike the desert climate further south, the area around Clinton and Jesmond is verdant and dotted with trees, ponds, and lakes. Settlers have built their ranches here, erected miles of fences, and set their horses out to graze amid the expansive pastures. Clinton is the last real town travelers come to before making the final 25-mile push up a dirt road leading to Jesmond. The Henselwoods warn first-time visitors to trust their directions, because usually, just when new arrivals think they are hopelessly lost, they come upon the Circle H Mountain Lodge. The effort is well worth it.

    The lodge is set in a high valley surrounded by beautiful limestone mountains, and the even more spectacular Mount Bowman. The lodge is nestled in the midst of it all, giving guests a sense of isolation that isn't easy to find these days. The friendly nature of the Henselwoods and casual feeling of the ranch have long drawn guests to the Circle H Mountain Lodge. Over 160 acres of green meadows, stands of mixed wood trees, and a creek surround the ranch, which consists of the old-fashioned log lodge, a guest wing, and four sleeping cabins. The entire ranch can accommodate only 16 guests at a time. Five bedrooms lie in the guest wing, which is fashioned with two shared bathrooms and a shower room. The bathroom facilities are also used by those staying in the rustic log cabins. Guests with dogs will reside in the cabins, which can accommodate from two to four people and are a perfectly pleasant place to bed down for the night.

Many come here to ride. The Henselwoods once leased their horses; however, they are now raising their own herd. They recently purchased enough horses to accommodate all of their guests. These horses, along with some newborn colts, are now theirs to train and care for year round. Two rides are offered each day — either a morning and an afternoon ride or a morning ride with a long midday break before the early-evening ride. Twice a week guests can also go out on the full-day ride, which consists of traversing the high country meadows and passing through the deep cool forests. The guides leading these rides bring people into some beautiful back country, where wild horses still run and exotic wildflowers grow in abundance.

When not riding, some take their dogs and head off on a fishing expedition or a leisurely canoe ride on **Kelly Lake. Hiking** through this country with a dog is just as appealing as horseback riding. Along the way the dogs might track down upland birds, deer, or moose, while their human friends search for wild strawberries, onions, and rose hips. As the day winds to a close, most look forward to their return to the ranch, perhaps to go for a swim in the pool or relax in the sauna before enjoying a home-cooked meal around the wood stove.

The ranch is situated at an altitude of over 5,000 feet, and something about the elevation and fresh air causes appetites to spiral out of control. (The fabulous food might also have something to do with it.) Daphne is in charge of these feasts, which are complemented with freshly-baked breads. All of the food is cooked in, or on, a huge wood stove. Guests settle down at the long dining room table, which is covered with an oil-skin cloth and lined with pitchers of wildflowers. Platters of cheese and bread, bowls filled with fresh fruit, and salads are all served family style. If a guest catches some trout, Daphne will prepare them for dinner. Daphne is British, and will sometimes present an old-fashioned English meal of roast beef, Yorkshire pudding, potatoes with mushroom gravy, and a strawberry trifle. Should guests like an alcoholic libation to accompany their dinner, they need to bring their own.The hosts also recommend bringing a few extra goodies for children, to satisfy any between-meal cravings.

After dinner, most like to hang out on the covered porch that runs the length of the lodge. This is the quiet time of the evening when the adults put up their boots, the children play, and dogs snooze — just another great day at the Circle H Mountain Lodge.

Lac Le Jeune Resort
Woody Life Village

650 Victoria Street
Kamloops, B.C., Canada V2C 2B4
(800) 561-5253, (250) 372-2722, Fax: (250) 374-9997

Owner: Derick McDonald
Rooms: Lac Le Jeune — 6 cabins, Woody Life — 30 cabins
Canadian Rates: Lac Le Jeune — $79-144 (EP),
	Woody Life — $95-135 (EP)
Payment: AE, DC, MC, and VISA
Dogs: Welcome in the cabins
Children: Welcome (cots and high chairs are available)
Open: April - October

Fish Lake is not exactly a name that inspires people to visit — unless, of course, they are avid fishermen. The name Lac Le Jeune, on the other hand, is far more intriguing. However, it still is not a natural destination for most people, unless they happen to be headed between Calgary and Vancouver via tour bus. We discovered this little known fact on the day we visited, as this tiny resort frequently books tour groups. When we arrived, though, it was absolutely deserted. This is the way it is most of the time, as the buses (usually two) generally arrive late in the day and depart early the next morning. This allows those who book independently of the tours to have the entire place to themselves for most of the day.

There are two distinct parts to the resort. Lac Le Jeune Resort has been around for more than 20 years. Just down the road lies its sister resort, the Woody Life, built in 1990. Given a choice, we prefer the old-fashioned look and feel of Lac Le Jeune, and especially its lovely lakeside setting. The main lodge and cabins are built of dark timbers, but inside they are a pleasing combination of contemporary decor and traditional design.

The cabins are set beyond the lodge, on a grassy knoll above the lake. We were pleasantly surprised by the cabins' interiors, which are fashioned with natural wood walls, contemporary furniture, and pretty peach and green floral fabrics. The dark green accents are carried through to the kitchenette's countertops as well. Guests have a small living room with a fireplace, and generally one or two bedrooms. Sofas and rocking chairs are comfortable places for passing the time inside, or guests can step outside to the small porch. The smell of the surrounding woods and views of the lake are most invigorating.

Guests are free to cook in their cabin kitchens, or they may dine in either one of the resort's restaurants. Both dining rooms offer good home cooking, topped off by a variety of fresh trout dishes. We prefer the intimate feeling at the Lac Le Jeune Resort's restaurant, as much for the big, old-fashioned stone fireplace as for the views of the lake through the plate glass windows. While the restaurant does not serve to the general public, the staff appreciates knowing ahead of time if cabin guests are planning on dining with them that evening.

Just down the road is the Woody Life Village, with its huge log chalets topped by light green-colored roofs. These chalets generally contain two sets of housekeeping accommodations, fashioned with queen beds, a living room space, modern kitchens, and private bathrooms. The decor is attractive, but simple, and the units are spotless. Although they are situated near the water, they don't have the same lake views as the cabins back at Lac Le Jeune. This is, however, an ideal spot for families who want to be close to the indoor swimming pool complex, which comes complete with a slide, a whirlpool, exercise and weight rooms, and saunas. There is even a fitness trail that wends through the property, for those who are looking for a fun outing that includes their canine cohort.

Guests staying at the Woody Life Village gather for meals in the main lodge, which is a larger version of the housekeeping chalets. The honey-colored log walls are exposed; in one corner is a stone fireplace. Although the place can get busy, the small, naturally finished oak tables surrounded by Windsor chairs give patrons a sense of intimacy. While this section of the resort is new, well established beds of flowers and newly planted trees will soon lend a sense of timelessness to the grounds.

As we mentioned, the days around here are mostly quiet — and perfect for relaxing. Dogs love to be walked along **the lake**, and there are plenty of hiking trails criss-crossing the region. Guests may also wish to take a stroll across the street to the primitive log store, where dinghies and canoes are rented.

Dogs are welcome to accompany their human friends on an exploration of the lake. This is an ideal spot to test out fly fishing skills, and it is well known for its good-sized fish. Lac Le Jeune is part of a provincial park that is only 60 acres but offers plenty of diversions in this small space — including an archeological site.

British Columbia

The Grand Okanagan

1310 Water Street
Kelowna, B.C., Canada V1Y 9P3
(800) 465-4651, (604) 763-4500, Fax: (604) 763-4565

General Manager: *Frank Faigauf*
Rooms: *150 doubles, 25 suites, 30 homes*
Canadian Rates: *Doubles $145-220 (EP), Suites $189-230(EP), Homes $265-325(EP)*
Payment: *AE, DC, JCB, MC, and VISA*
Dogs: *Welcome with a $100 refundable deposit*
Children: *Welcome (cribs, cots, and high chairs are available)*
Open: *All year*

An ancient legend still circulates along the shores of Okanagan Lake that a mythical monster, Ogopogo, lives somewhere in its depths. This whimsical sea serpent is depicted in a statue set along the lakefront in Kelowna. While the fables about Ogopogo date back centuries, The Grand Okanagan Resort does not.

This is a first-class resort, which combines a contemporary hotel with time-share vacation homes and condominiums to form an expansive enclave encompassing 25 acres of park land and beach. It is built in a Mediterranean style. (Although Kelowna is far from the sea, the area's temperate climate does lend itself to this form of architecture.) The designers kept the interior spaces light by incorporating two massive Palladian windows that mirror one another. We walked through one framing the hotel's main entrance, and after emerging into the cavernous tiled lobby, found another one overlooking the water side of the hotel. In the midst of the lobby is a massive statue of a black dolphin and its calf, which seem to be leaping from a huge fountain.

As we walked over to the main desk to inquire about the guest rooms, we stopped to greet a pair of terriers strolling with their owners. The main portion of the hotel is surrounded by three-story wings containing the more expansive two-bedroom suites. Most of the guest rooms in the adjacent buildings are preferable for those traveling with dogs, as they have easy outside access to the lakefront boardwalk. Unfortunately, many of these are also time-share units that can only be reserved 48-hours in advance. Anyone planning a last minute trip to Kelowna might want to check out this option.

All of the rooms are attractive, though, and are decorated in pale peach, ecru, and sea-foam green color schemes. Beds have thickly quilted floral spreads and dust ruffles that are coordinated with the full-length draperies and valances. Bleached woods in the contemporary furnishings lighten these spaces even more. Brass sconces and bedside table lamps provide crisp contrasts to the colorful paintings, potted plants, and decorative flower arrangements. The amenities are just what we would expect of a four-star hotel, with televisions concealed in small cabinets, direct-dial telephones, and modern bathrooms fashioned with an array of toiletries.

We especially liked the larger suites, as they offered a more varied list of amenities, and usually better water views. Some have tiled Jacuzzi tubs nestled into the corner of the rooms, fireplaces in separate living rooms, and even small kitchens. The two-bedroom suites are perfect for families traveling with a dog, as they are outfitted with a central living room, a kitchen, and a bedroom off to either side. All of these suites also have private patios or balconies. Those who do not require as much space, but enjoy many of the aforementioned luxuries may wish to inquire about the Grand Club rooms, where wet bars, bathrobes, newspapers, and a complimentary breakfast are *de rigeur*.

Water seems to be a reccurring theme at the Grand Okanagan, in evidence whether dining at Dolphins overlooking the lagoon, sitting in the lobby and listening to the water splash from the fountain, or relaxing in a guest room overlooking the lake or the swimming pool. The heated pool is very inviting, and is set in one of the hotel's courtyards overlooking the lake. Those who don't want to get their exercise by swimming laps can use the exercise room, equipped with free weights and an assortment of cardiovascular equipment, as well as baby-sitting services.

The hotel's intimate restaurant is Dolphins, where the views are as fine as the cuisine. Guests may wish to start with an appetizer of spicy prawns sautéed with tomatoes, lime, red chili, and garlic; oysters on the half shell; or the smoked yellowfin tuna. When we were there, entrées included the jasmine smoked duck breast with a mango purée; rack of lamb with garlic, rosemary, and Pommerey mustard; or the halibut poached in a Grand Marnier sauce. The Sunday brunch is as popular among guests as it is with locals. Children have their own mini-buffet table, while adults may sample from a lavish assortment of foods that include everything from a custom omelet station and a carving trolley to an extensive assortment of unique desserts. The stipend for young children is hard to beat — $1 for each year of the child's age.

While there is plenty of grass at the resort, the place most appropriate for walking dogs is along the boardwalk. Just next to the resort there is also an open, lawn that is great for exercising dogs. Guests and their canines can also walk into town along the water, and continue along the lake for miles. Unfortunately, the major waterfront park in town is off-limits to dogs, but there are plenty of other great walks and hikes to be enjoyed in the surrounding area. **Wild Horse Canyon** has a fun hike that can be reached by following Lake Shore Road 16 km to the south. A parking area is situated off to the right and the trail is just beyond it. The **Crawford Hiking Trails**, located off June Springs Road, are also quite popular. To reach them, travelers follow the Bellevue Creek Forest Service Road. Parking is available above Bellevue Creek Canyon. **Bear Creek Provincial Park** also has plenty of hiking trails that allow dogs. One of the best is found by following Highway 97 south to Westside Road, then turning onto Beach Creek Road. A vacation to the Okanagan Valley is not complete without visiting the wineries or golfing at some of the 39 regional courses. Hot-air ballooning, float plane adventures, boating on the area's lakes, and even tours of the apple farms and North America's largest alpaca farm should also be on guests' short list of things to do.

Idabel Lake Resort

S. 13E, C.2, R.R. #5
Kelowna, B.C., Canada V1X 4K4
(250) 765-9511

Owners: *Vivien and Paul Burridge and Lesley and Doug Johnson*
Rooms: *10 rooms, 6 cabins*
Canadian Rates: *Rooms: $105-195 (EP), Cabins $120 (EP)*
Payment: *MC and VISA*
Dogs: *Welcome in the cottages, but they must be leashed when on the grounds and the beach*
Children: *Welcome*
Open: *All year*

The Idabel Lake Resort is not one of those resorts guests just stumble on; even with directions it is not easy to locate. However, once we arrived, we knew it had been worth every twist and turn on the logging roads that led us here. The little resort is not in Kelowna — it's actually 55 km up in the mountains, past the turnoff to the Big White Ski Resort. A two-lane highway took us most of the way, before we turned off onto the logging roads. These wide, dirt highways are the domain of the logging companies and their massive rumbling trucks. People unfamiliar with these types of roads need to keep only two things in mind — stay to the right, and pay attention. The trucks seem to appear out of nowhere and take up the majority of the road. They are in radio contact with each other, though, so once they spot a visiting vehicle, they will often relay information about its whereabouts to other truckers heading in that direction.

The Idabel Lake Resort is set in a small mountainous valley right on the edge of the lake. There are some houses around the lake, but guests of the resort generally have the lake to themselves. The mile-and-a-half-long Idabel

Lake is unusual in that it is actually swimmable; most of the mountain lakes in this region contain leeches, making them less than desirable for humans or dogs. The resort is comprised of an old-fashioned main lodge, a few outbuildings, and the cabins. The main lodge is a rustic, dark wood edifice, with interiors naturally brightened by three walls of windows overlooking the water. As we climbed the stairs, we heard wind chimes blowing in the breeze. Sisters Vivien and Lesley have owned the resort with their husbands for the past six years. The sisters are from England, and have enchanting British accents. Best of all, they have brought an assortment of memorabilia from their homeland. Pictures of the English countryside and its cottages are displayed against one wall in the lodge, while the menu in their restaurant reflects some of Great Britain's more intriguing dishes.

The Idabel offers guests everything they could possibly desire in a tranquil mountain vacation. While some guests stay in the lodge rooms, we prefer the cabins that are nestled behind some boulders on a bluff overlooking the water. The unusual, rounded shape of the cabins' green roofs is modeled after the work of an architect by the name of Steiner, who designed his buildings to blend in with their natural surroundings. The interiors are far more common in appearance, with knotty pine walls, beamed ceilings, and an open floor plan that focuses on the lake views. These are minimally-furnished affairs, but relatively new; they were built less than ten years ago. The kitchens contain electric appliances and all the basics needed for preparing meals. A central living room is furnished with some chairs and a sofa bed, and upstairs is an open loft with two futon beds set upon platforms. It is also upstairs where guests can appreciate the rounded curves of the roof line. Navy blue floral cotton prints frame the windows and cover the futon cushions. Other than this decorative touch, the furnishings are fairly basic. What we, and most others, focus on are the nice views of the lake that are visible through a pair of picture windows and a Palladian window set above them.

While the cabins are a good place to gather at night, there is so much to do in the daytime that few spend much time indoors. The lake encompasses more than 10 acres, but guests tend to stay in the waters near the lodge. Here, they can swim from the 60-foot dock or take a dinghy out for some fishing. Children love this place, especially in the summer months, when they can play on the cleverly-designed adventure playgrounds or head out to the Jolly Roger pirate ship on the lake. The former consists of a small log cabin that serves as a playhouse, an 80-foot slide, and plenty of logs and things to climb upon. Mother Nature also supplies all sorts of big rocks — which make for equally fine climbing. More organized activities might include horseshoes, baseball, and volleyball.

The resort also has a reputation for its well-trained horses. The stables are within walking distance of the lodge. Guests can go out for an hour, for a dinner ride, or overnight adventure. Others may prefer to do their riding on mountain bikes — either their own or the resort's. There are miles of trails and roads throughout this region. Even in winter, the resort is a hub of activity,

British Columbia

with a lighted skating rink on the lake, miles of cross-country ski trails, and guided snowmobile rides. Although dogs are required to be leashed on the property, they have **unlimited trails** to explore, a **lake to swim in**, and more walks along **back country roads** than they could ever take advantage of during their stay.

If the weather is not cooperating on a particular day, then some guests enjoy heading indoors to the game room where there are table tennis and video games. The pool table is another popular outlet and is found in the lounge near the small restaurant. While the cottages have cooking facilities, we rather like the atmosphere in the dining room, with its dried flowers, small cluster of tables, and fabulous lake views. The menu is a hearty one, topped by an English favorite — cottage pie (a British version of shepherds pie). Guests may also dine on steak and kidney pie with a hint of rosemary and thyme; a chicken and mushroom pie; or beef bourguignonne. The garlic mushroom fettucini, beef stroganoff, and the seafood linguine are also perennial favorites.

We were very pleased to discover the Idabel Lake Resort. It is a special kind of lodge that offers personalized attention, a variety of diversions, and loads of character. Guests who stay here once are likely to find it to be one of those places that will easily become an annual tradition.

River Run Cottages

4551 River Road West
Ladner, B.C., Canada V4K 1R9
(604) 946-7778, Fax: (604) 940-1970
E-mail: riverrun@direct.ca
Internet: http://www.virtualcities.com/ons/bc/l/bcl6601.html

Hosts: *Bill and Janice Harkley or Terry and Deborah Millichamp*
Rooms: *5 cottages*
Canadian Rates: *$90-160 (B&B)*
Payment: *MC and VISA*
Dogs: *Welcome with notice*
Children: *Welcome*
Open: *All year*

The Harkley's found a passage in Mary Emmerling's *Cottages* that they feel aptly describes their four riverside cottages. "All cottages are small, but small size does not preclude richness of form. The cottage floor plan permits a generosity of movement, a minimum of doors and corridors, and a central space, with nooks around it for conversation, intimacy, meditation and contemplation of nature. All cottages are linked to their natural surroundings in ways that mere houses often are not." Life at River Run Cottages is about as close to Emmerling's ideal as most of us are likely to find.

A swing of the gate and guests enter a magical world of color, form, and texture. Multicolored flowers and greenery are found throughout, from the hanging baskets and window boxes to the decorative wine casks. Grape vines entwine a pergola overhead. A wooden walkway leads to each of the cottages, whether they are floating, set high on the river banks, or tucked somewhere in between. Regardless of one's ultimate choice, guests will be in for a treat.

Waterlily is an intriguing cottage that floats on a wooden platform. White exterior walls are merely the backdrop to the blazing red, pink, and yellow flowers overflowing from the planters. Off to the side, softer hues of color emanate from the cottage's stained glass windows. Once inside, a glowing union of lustrous teak, mahogany, and bird's eye maple combine in the fine cabinetry. Pale blue, lavender, and rose chintz fabric covers the thick cushions lining the built-in sofa. Guests who arrive at night will find that the lights have been turned on, soft music is playing, and a fire is ready to be lit in the wood stove. A kitchenette has a refrigerator, two burners, and glasses and china neatly lining the shelves. The queen-bedded loft is a cozy place to settle into for a night (or two, or three). In the morning, guests can walk out to their private deck containing captain's chairs and a table, drink their coffee, and watch the ducks paddle about and the birds soar overhead.

Another intimate space is the Net Loft, which is named for the fishermen who, years ago, mended their nets here. This two-level suite is connected by a spiral staircase. At the top of the stairs is the bedroom, with its four-poster log bed. Guests can settle in here, or perhaps on the huge white sofa in the living room, and enjoy the river views. There is a fresh look to this entire space, as terra cotta floors nicely combine with light oak and wicker accents. At night, this spacious abode becomes even cozier, when the fire is lit and the shades are drawn. French doors open to a private deck, complete with a Japanese soaking tub.

The Keepers Quarters is set out from the banks of the river, complete with a deck from which to enjoy the view. Guests walk through French doors onto hardwood floors that lead to a full kitchen, then beyond to a cozy sitting room, complete with an antique wood stove. Guests may relax on the sofa or in the chintz-covered armchair. Regardless of choice, the views are great. The separate bedroom contains a driftwood bed, and next to it is the tiled bathroom with a Jacuzzi for two.

The Northwest Room lies across the footbridge on dry land, but guests still have a sense of the river through the French doors or from the deck. The entire mood of this place is evocative of the Northwest, which caused us to want to hibernate in front of the crackling fire. We couldn't decide on the highlight in this space, as the massive four poster log bed and grotto-like shower both captured our imagination.

The River Room was built to accommodate all those potential guests the hosts were forced to turn away for lack of space. This studio is situated in a corner of the Harkley's house, and even shares their bathroom. Cranberry and hunter green colors lend a warmth to this cozy chamber, complete with a pull-out queen bed, wood burning fireplace, and views of the water through a greenhouse window. The dock is just outside the doors, and guests will find chairs and a hammock for lounging, as well as various water craft for launching.

All guests are welcome to borrow the rowboat, double kayak, or canoe. They may also use the cottage bicycles and ride the flat roads around Ladner. An easy 20-minute ride from River Run brings guests to the ferry that runs over to the Vancouver Island. Some may want to take their dog and a rowboat out to one of the small islands near the inn for a picnic.

Bill is a runner and jogs throughout the area. He is happy to have guests and their dogs tag along, as he shows them some of the more intriguing points of interest along the way. One of his favorites he has dubbed **Eagle Park**, because he once counted 30 eagles in the trees of this little oasis. (Another woman counted 80.) The eagles seem to come in at dusk, so this is the best time to head out to look for them. Other birds that are fun to watch are the cormorants, loons, swans, and ducks. Another popular outing is to take your dog for a leisurely **stroll along the dike** into Ladner.

There are a number of fine restaurants in the area for dinner, but diners shoud save a little room because the next morning's breakfast is an extravaganza. Breakfast menus are left in the cottages each evening. The fare varies with the day, but guests can always look forward to their "appetizer" of French press coffee, orange juice, and fresh fruit. Homemade baked goodies are presented just before the main portion of the meal arrives. On any given day this includes such options as Eggs Benedict with hollandaise and fresh chives, a fresh salmon and leek quiche, thick French toast with maple syrup, or Bill's famous River Run Eggs. The now not-so-secret recipe recently appeared in the cottages' newsletter. The trick is the homemade salsa, which smothers the two eggs on English muffins. If that isn't enough to start the day, then guests can also have some cereal, porridge, toast, or yogurt. Whether they take this hearty affair on the deck or in the privacy of the cottage, it is a meal not soon forgotten — and neither is a stay at the River Run Cottages.

Fernhill Lodge

C-4, R.R. 1
610 Fernhill Road
Mayne Island, B.C., Canada V0N 2J0
(250) 539-2544

Hosts: *Brian and Mary Crumblehulme*
Rooms: *7 doubles*
Canadian Rates: *$99-149 (B&B)*
Payment: *MC and VISA*
Dogs: *Welcome with approval*
Children: *Welcome; under the age of 5 are free of charge*
Open: *All year*

Mayne Island has a rich history that dates back to the mid-1800s. Miners from Vancouver Island, who were trying to head north to join the Fraser River Valley's gold rush, would come together on Mayne Island before attempting to row across the Georgia Strait. As a result, there are plenty of historic enclaves on the island. One of the most interesting is Miners' Bay. First-time visitors will find everything from intriguing antique buildings and a lovely old church to the town's original jail. This hamlet isn't just for history buffs, though, as there are an assortment of outdoor opportunities to take advantage of as well. Bennet Bay Beach is one of the more popular destinations for a leisurely outing, while Mount Parke might be a little more appealing for those who want to take their canines on a hiking adventure. Nearby Campbell Bay has a scenic trail that leads to a beautiful swimming beach and some sandstone caves that are fun to explore. Most visitors, however, come to Mayne Island to relax amid the quiet surroundings.

Fernhill Lodge is one of the more intriguing places to unwind. It is situated on five hilltop acres surrounded by manicured gardens and dense forests. Guests and their well-mannered dogs are welcome to explore this acreage, where arbutus trees and conifers create a veritable park-like setting. The grounds are somewhat reminiscent of traditional English gardens, where arbors are draped with vines, trellises are dripping with fragrant flowers, and benches are set in private hideaways. Those yearning for a place for quiet contemplation may wish to follow a path down to the cliff, where there is a bench that looks out over the water. Guests who visit during the summer months will be surrounded by the aromatic fragrances emanating from the rose and herb gardens. These gardens are well known to those in horticultural circles, but even novices can appreciate the lovely combination of texture and color. Brian uses many of the plants he grows in the array of authentic international dishes he prepares several nights a week. Guests who study the books in the Crumblehulme's library are certain to pick up on Brian and Mary's wide range of interests — especially history and food.

Brian has gathered a number of intriguing recipes from the Roman, Medieval, and Renaissance periods, which guests can enjoy by making dinner reservations in advance. The theme is usually set by the first person to make a reservation. If the above food categories are not of interest, then Brian can prepare one of his native West Coast or all-encompassing international meals. One of the more popular dishes from the Medieval era is the game hen tart sprinkled with fresh herbs. A favorite entrée from the Roman era is lamb marinated in a coriander wine sauce. One of the assistant chefs also prepares authentic Japanese meals on occasion.

Breakfast, on the other hand, usually begins with fresh juice, fruit muffins, and scones. This is often followed by light pancakes, herbed omelets, and other assorted dishes adorned with edible flowers. Eggs are provided by the lodge's "happy hens." When not eating, guests may relax in the sun out on one of the decks, or inside in the library. They can read, play a game of Medieval skittles, or perhaps the piano — this is the place to completely relax amid the tranquil surroundings.

With all this history floating around the place, guests might think they're staying in an antique house; however, it is a far more contemporary cottage with weathered shingles and paned windows. Each guest room has a private entrance, making the rooms especially desirable for traveling dogs. Each room also has its own motif. The guest room themes often feature furnishings or accent pieces from a particular period. The chambers include such decorative themes as Asian, Jacobean, French, Victorian, Moroccan, and Indian. Some might think the rooms are a little on the dark side, but we thought this an inherent part of their appeal. Even without knowing the specific theme of the room, guests usually recognize the general gist of the chamber.

All are filled with a delightful and eclectic mix of furnishings. The Asian is fashioned with traditional tatami mats, Japanese screens, and a low queen bedstead, while the Edwardian is furnished with a 17th-century, four-poster oak bed surrounded by a blue and white color scheme and assorted pewter knickknacks. A third chamber, the Moroccan, also has a four-poster bed, but it is surrounded by dark, ornately carved woods. All have private baths. The newer additions, East Indian and Moroccan, offer private decks and hot tubs.

The Crumblehulme's know Mayne Island very well and can recommend all sorts of activities for guests and their canines to investigate. There are interesting **coves** to explore and wonderful **hiking trails** that meander through dense forests. The wildlife on the island ranges from deer and raccoons to sea otter, seals, and king fishers. Bicycling is as popular as boating, and your hosts can suggest places to rent a kayak or canoe; or they can explain where to secure a sailboat or fishing charter to explore the surrounding waters. At the end of the day, though, most enjoy returning to Fernhill Lodge, where they can relax in the sauna out in the woods, soak in their private hot tub, or perhaps sip a cup of tea out on the deck.

Corbett Lake Country Inn

Box 327
Merritt, B.C., Canada V0K 2B0
(250) 378-4334

Innkeeper *Peter McVey*
Rooms: *3 doubles, 10 cabins*
Canadian Rates: *Doubles $55-75 per person (MAP), Cabins $47-89 per person (includes dinner)*
Payment: *Personal checks*
Dogs: *Welcome if leashed on the property*
Children: *Welcome; children under 9 years of age are half price*
Open: *May-October*

The Corbett Inn lies along a spectacular stretch of highway known as the Coquihalla, which traverses the high mountain plateaus between Peachland and Merritt. The inn is only three hours from Vancouver, yet it feels far more removed from civilization than that. These are the high, dry foothills of the Cascades, and it is here that the lodge rests on what was originally part of the Duke of Portland's ranch. Peter McVey now owns 305 of these acres, to which guests return to experience its unpretentious surroundings, superb fly fishing, and gourmet meals. Peter is from England, where he trained in the kitchens of the Lord Mayor of London. He brings his flair for food and his passion for fly fishing to the wilds of British Columbia.

We drove in from the Okanagan Valley, and were so busy admiring the scenery that we almost missed the lodge, which is set well off the road behind stands of pines and aspen trees. We first came across the gray cedar lodge, but could also spy the cedar-shingled cabins in the woods. The lodge is just as we imagined it — dark wood walls, hardwood floors worn with years of use, and rooms brimming with treasured fishing paraphernalia. Along the hall, leading to the dining room, delicate hand-tied flies are framed and displayed like miniature trophies. The dining room, appropriately enough, is the largest chamber in the lodge, with views of the forest and lake framed in two walls of windows. This room is reminiscent of an old-fashioned hunting lodge, with animal skins and antlers decorating its walls. In July and August, cabin guests are left to their own culinary devices, but during the remaining months of operation, dinner is included in the tariff. Guests will find it is worth every penny.

Peter serves a four-course meal each evening and there are no choices. Guests are treated to whatever is fresh and whatever inspires him. In this way, most feel less like *guests*, and more like personal friends of the innkeeper. A meal might begin with consommé or a rich soup, followed by a delicate smoked salmon or hearty Caesar salad. The entrée of the evening could range from rack of lamb or chateaubriand to beef Wellington or trout. The dessert might feature a fresh fruit cobbler, or Peter's specialty — cheesecake. The wine list is equally interesting, although it is fun to let Peter do the selecting.

During the day, guests are left to their own devices, although Peter is usually available to give some advice on the finer points of fly fishing. Anglers may fish in Corbett and Courtney lakes either from the shore or from a rowboat. The truly passionate fisherman can arrange to fly fish on two other private lakes located on the Douglas Lake Ranch. Peter has spent years restoring the natural balance of these two lakes and restocking them with trout. He even has his own stocking farm. Corbett Lake is also blessed with a small, deep water swimming area where people can take a dip on very hot summer days.

Like the lodge, the authentic, rustic feeling has been well preserved in the cabins. A couple of these are in the pine groves near the lake shore, but most are situated off the lake on a bluff overlooking the distant mountains. These gray cedar cabins look festive with their cherry red doors and window trim. Hardwood floors lining these informal interiors are sometimes brightened by an Oriental or braided rug, but in general, guests can expect an eclectic grouping of mismatched furniture and bedsteads. We liked the crisp red and white gingham curtains framing a kitchen window in one cabin, and the old-fashioned easy chair in another. Most of the cabins have some type of kitchen, a living room, a separate bedroom, and a private bath. Guests may sleep in a twin, fold-out, or a double bedstead, and a lucky few will get a fireplace. All of the cabins are as immaculate as they are appealing.

While dogs must be leashed around the cabins, some guests prefer heading off across **the bluff to let their dogs run**. The property has enough acreage to keep most dogs and their human friends happily occupied for hours, although guests shouldn't expect many deep forests. The trees are fairly spread out and the terrain rocky. Some of the more popular day trips include venturing south on 5A to the **Kentucky-Alleyne Provincial Park**, where there are wilderness areas, hiking trails, and an assortment of fishing and swimming options to investigate. Also south of the inn is **Allison Lake**, a park where people and dogs can spend time near the water or hiking around it.

Cliffside Inn

Box 50
North Pender Island, B.C., Canada V0N 2M0
(250) 629-6691

Innkeeper: *Penny Tomlin*
Rooms: *2 doubles, 2 suites, 1 cottage*
Canadian Rates: *Doubles $135-145 (B&B), Suites $145-185 (B&B),*
  Cottage $165 (B&B)
Payment: *MC and VISA*
Dogs: *Welcome in the Edgewater Cottage and in the Rosehip Room,*
  with approval
Children: *Not appropriate for children under 16 years of age*
Open: *All year*

North and South Pender Islands have the same climate as most of the other Gulf Islands — sub-Mediterranean. The "Penders," as they are often referred to, are joined by a bridge, so visitors can double their fun by exploring both islands. These islands have been called "the islands of hidden coves and beaches" and "the friendly islands." Most who stay here would agree that these are accurate descriptions. Not only can people and their dogs explore the hidden coves and walk along the picturesque paths, but they can also bicycle along the gently sloping hills. There are few towns here, and even fewer tourists — making these islands an ideal getaway for those seeking a little solitude.

Driving from the ferry to the Cliffside Inn, guests are likely to be tempted by the roadside vegetable stands and small art galleries; but these stops can be saved for later, as more surprises await at the inn. The Cliffside Inn is located on three secluded oceanfront acres, which have been in Penny's family for nearly a century.

More recently, Penny Tomlin created a private retreat for adults (and their well-mannered dogs). Guests can come for the exquisite breakfasts, distinctive rooms, old-fashioned pampering, or for the complete privacy. The lush landscape surrounding the inn is a mixture of huge shade trees, forests, and lawns framed by split rail fences. This is merely the backdrop, though, for the most impressive views are overlooking the channel and Mount Baker. Each room offers some view of the water; however, only two of these welcome dogs — so we will focus on these chambers.

Guests who stay in the Rosehip Room are treated to all the privileges of the inn. This private abode offers a wall of sliding glass doors that opens out to a patio and beyond to the gardens. Many also enjoy watching the birds and wildlife frolic — right from the brass bed, which is covered with a feather comforter. There is a private bathroom, but the adjacent fireside sitting room is shared. Those staying here are also treated to a gourmet breakfast in the solarium each morning. Many of the omelets, breads, and other delectable edibles are created with ingredients from Penny's extensive herb, vegetable, and berry gardens.

Edgewater Cottage offers a completely different vacation experience. This board and batten cedar house is set just 20 feet from the cliff's edge on a very private acre. It, too, is decorated in a casual country-style, but it is a little more rustic and lacks the ruffles and knickknacks that characterize some of the inn rooms. Penny has intermixed comfortable furnishings with some of the antiques from her family's home. Two bedrooms contain double beds, and in the living room there is an air-tight wood stove. Guests have a full kitchen, which is stocked with all the breakfast provisions they might need — and more. Eggs, fruit, ham, bread, croissants, and juice provide plenty of options for this morning meal. The television is a modern convenience, but we much preferred the expansive deck, which offers some of the finest water views on the property.

Most dogs are completely at home here, as there is plenty of acreage and privacy. Penny has a cute terrier-poodle mix who loves it when dogs come to visit. Penny tells us that her dog often gets bored exploring the B&B's three acres alone and welcomes a companion.

Descend the long staircase to the **sandstone beach**, where dogs and their friends can walk for awhile before reaching its end. Penny knows of other interesting outings as well; guests can just tell her approximately what they have in mind and she will come up with some great suggestions.

The **Prior Centennial Provincial Park** is on North Pender Island and is brimming with 40 acres of deep forests set below Lively Peak. Some prefer to meander about **Medicine Beach** on Bedwell Harbor. Over on South Pender, there is **Mount Norman**, and dogs and their owners are invited to hike up this peak, as well.

One of the best things about returning after a long day of exploring this region is the chance to soak a while in the hot tub, which is set on cliff-hanger deck. Even if guests have not left the premises all day, we recommend an evening visit out here, where the deep and dark starry nights are sure to make a lasting impression.

Tigh-Na-Mara

1095 East Island Highway
Parksville, B.C., Canada V9P 2E5
(800) 663-7373, (250) 248-2072, Fax: (250) 248-4140
E-mail: tnm@island.net Internet: http://www.island.net/~tnm/index.html

Managers: *Joe and Jackie Hirsch*
Rooms: *110 doubles, 37 cottages*
Canadian Rates: *Doubles $72-94 (EP), Cottages $109-160 (EP)*
Payment: *AE, DSC, MC, and VISA*
Dogs: *Welcome in the cottages, except during July and August*
Children: *Welcome for a $5 nightly fee (cribs, cots, high chairs, and baby-sitters are available)*
Open: *All year*

Warm water and soft sand beaches are not normally what people associate with British Columbia's coastline. Scenic and rugged — yes. Swimmable water — rarely. The Tigh-Na-Mara lies along Vancouver Island's longest stretch of sandy beach; a beach that also happens to come and go with the tide. When the tide is out, miles of sand flats extend out into the Strait of Georgia. In the summertime, the sun warms the exposed sand and it, in turn, warms the incoming water and makes it swimmable. As one might imagine, these ideal conditions draw a large summer crowd to the resort. Unfortunately, Bowser is not a preferred guest during this time of year, but that is probably for the best, as it would be just too chaotic for most canines. Our hosts are actually doing us a favor by restricting the dog-visiting season, since the ideal time to be here is after the crowds are gone and a sense of calm returns to the resort.

The Tigh-Na-Mara lies well off the main route, under a canopy of Douglas firs and arbutus trees. The log cabins and lodge are fixtures within this forest, and though the condominiums are new, they are tucked unobtrusively into the wooded shoreline. Guests traveling with their dogs may request cabins situated near the shore, the children's play areas, or along an edge of the resort. The one-bedroom cabins are just right for couples and their dogs, while families may want to reserve a two-bedroom unit. The log exteriors still look rather new; and the natural knotty-pine paneled walls make each cabin homey. Vaulted ceilings inset with skylights and plenty of paned windows let in a surprising amount of sunlight. Mauve and gray tones predominate, whether in the good quality carpet, sofas, or armchairs. A fieldstone fireplace warms the living room, dining area, and kitchen. Fully-stocked kitchens include coffee makers, along with a small supply of coffee and tea. Linens and towels are furnished, and even though these are housekeeping cottages, we were pleasantly surprised to find a nice complement of shampoos, soaps, and other toiletries. The separate bedrooms are just large enough to hold a twin or queen bed, which is covered with a simple cotton spread. The butcher block dining room table is large enough for everyone to have a sit-down meal together, although we thought it was equally fun to barbecue out on the grill and eat at the picnic table on the little patio. The cottages are very private, and maids will not even visit unless specifically asked.

Guests may also take any of their meals in the resort's fine restaurant. The chef, who is British, has cooked at restaurants all over the world. It is difficult to decide where to sit here, whether in front of the massive stone fireplace or out on a glassed-in porch. This restaurant is extremely popular, but guests who visit in the off-season will find reservations much more easily secured. The cuisine is Continental; the fall menu offered such appetizers as a pumpkin and hazelnut soup, steamed mussels, and a game pâté with a fall chutney. Main courses included the pheasant breast with a wild mushroom brandy sauce; the steamed halibut with pink peppercorns and a rosé butter; and a lemon pepper pasta with shrimp, salmon, scallops, and snapper.

After dinner, it is often nice to stretch our collective legs. This is the best time of day to head down to the shore for a leisurely evening stroll. This place is great for families, as there are two well-designed playgrounds set up in different parts of the resort. They offer substantial wooden jungle gyms, slides, and even trampolines. Children of all ages will find something appealing about these play areas. There is also a tennis court, swimming pool, spa, and exercise room. Nature trails wend throughout the resort, although most people and their dogs eventually find themselves on the beach or flats.

It was a gray day when we visited and the beach was quite deserted — just the way we like it. A stairway and path lead down to the wide swath of **pristine beach** with its gentle sandy shoreline — much of which is covered with knotty driftwood. The tide was out, and a few people were out walking on the flats with their dogs. Anyone who runs out of things to do here can set off to investigate any of the lovely provincial parks in the area. One of the best is **Englishman River Falls Provincial Park**, which has lush woods, plenty of water, and fine hiking trails that allow dogs. Another popular option, situated a short distance from the resort, is **Rathtrevor Provincial Park**. Dogs are welcome here, and there are plenty of beachside trails that turn into woodland trails. Swimming is also available.

April Point
Lodge and Fishing Resort

P.O. Box 1
Quadra Island, Campbell River, B.C., Canada V9W 4Z9
(250) 285-2222, Fax: (250) 285-2411, E-mail: aprilpoint@obevon.ark.com
Inernet: http://www.ohwy.com/bc/a/aprilpoi.htm

Innkeepers: The Peterson Family
Rooms: 37 rooms, suites, houses
Canadian Rates: Rooms $99-229 (EP), Suites $395 (EP), Houses $395 (EP)
Payment: AE, DC, MC, and VISA
Dogs: Welcome in select accommodations
Children: Welcome, children under 16 years of age are free of charge
Open: All year

If the words Tyee, Coho, and Chinook set your heart a racing, then we would like to recommend an exclusive vacation retreat. This is the consummate fisherman's ultimate destination, with a combination of rustic and well-appointed accommodations, a complete flotilla of Boston Whalers, and enough black labs to keep your dog in doggie heaven for years to come. We were greeted by Max, a handsome Black Labrador, along with Katie, Katie, and Katie, three of his black lab friends. Max and Katie are Eric's dogs — Eric is one of the owners of the place — the rest belong to longtime guests, and all happen to be named Katie.

We spent most of our time with Eric and his black labs. He is a gracious man, whose keen knowledge and love of Quadra Island stem back to his childhood. When he was a young boy, his father and mother moved the entire family here from San Francisco. When they first arrived at April Point, there were seven fishing shacks — and nothing else. As Eric describes it, first there were seven shacks, and then there were none; it seems the local anglers did not appreciate the rambunctious children who interrupted their solitude. Though it was not an easy life, it was an interesting one, with Eric's dad rowing the children to a neighboring cove for school each day.

The family is still a tight-knit team. Eric watches over the lodge, and is a food and wine connoisseur — which helps in developing an intriguing menu and extensive wine list. He also owns a farm on the south end of the island and spends a great deal of time there tending to his livestock and gardens. Eric's brother Warren handles corporate clients; when he is not doing that, he is often out in search of the ultimate fishing spot. On any given day, Warren, or one of the excellent guides, will know just where to go in search of fish.

Getting here by car requires a little tenacity, as most visitors need to take two ferries to get to the island. During the season, though, guests frequently arrive by seaplane or private boat. For anyone arriving by land, April Point is located down a narrow, twisting road that eventually ends at the point. Actually, this is not a natural point of land, but rather, a shellfish depository. For hundreds of years, the inhabitants would gather here and break open their oysters and shellfish, tossing the shells aside when they were done. Over the years, it built up to such a level that it formed a point of land; the point is now considered historic and cannot be altered beyond what the Petersons have done to it.

Guests will find a series of accommodations available to them and their dogs. Four cabins sit nestled in the woods overlooking Discovery Passage — these would be our first choices. Next to these abodes are the Passage View Rooms (#36-38). These are surprisingly modern inside, being attractively decorated with Northwest art and complemented by bright patterned spreads on the pairs of queen bedsteads. Modern bathrooms, some with Jacuzzi tubs, are as welcome a sight as the freestanding fireplaces. The remaining rooms are tucked into the rocky crags all around the resort, forming private enclaves. These include the laid back boathouse suites (#4-7), that are the most rustic accommodations, and are perched over the harbor. Each of these offers two bedrooms, a living room with a fireplace, and a private bathroom. What endears guests to the April Point Lodge, though, is not the rooms or the amenities, it is their feeling of oneness with the wilderness around them and the other guests. We felt like part of the lodge's extended family.

Whether admiring a bald eagle perched on a piling or looking out past the pool to the grass jetty — and beyond to Discovery Passage — the scenery is truly out of this world. We loved the "pool," which is simply a rocky indentation that fills up with water when the tide comes in. It also effectively separates the lodge from the rock and grass jetty. Out on this jetty, Eric often prepares authentic Pacific coast native feasts for his guests, using bentwood boxes. He steams the salmon, crabs, mussels, shrimp, and vegetables in these boxes, using skunk cabbage as the lining. Eric is now an expert, having gained his experience through the teachings of local anthropologists and writers who are familiar with these techniques. When not dining on the spit, guests eat in the lodge. The atmosphere in here is especially restful at night, with candlelight flickering off the wall of windows overlooking the water.

During the day, however, the focus is on fishing. April Point has some of the best guides available anywhere and they know these waters well. If there are salmon to catch, the guides will find them. During the season, there are fishing competitions and derbies. We loved listening to all the stories about the fish that did — or didn't — get away. Unfortunately, on the day we went out, the big one never materialized; however, we did pull in a couple of smaller salmon. After we came in off the water, Max, his entourage of Katies, and our guide's dog Shadow, were on hand to greet us. It was the day before Thanksgiving, and everyone was heading into the lodge to carve the pumpkins that would eventually be used for making April Point's famous pumpkin soup (served in the pumpkin shell, no less). Unfortunately, we could not stay for the festivities, and had to catch the next ferry off the island.

Dogs have a fine time here, and are treated like members of the family. This is a heavily wooded peninsula, with little to no car traffic, so guests and their canines should thoroughly enjoy quiet walks along the water. Quadra Island is huge, with mountains to climb and forests to explore. One good picnic spot is the **Rebecca Spit Provincial Park**, just off Heriot Bay Rd. Here, visitors can picnic, swim if they like, or simply explore the wooded spit with their dog. Three hiking trails that we can recommend lie in the middle of the island. One of these, the **Morte Lake Trail**, is a moderately difficult hike up to the lake. The **Chinese Mountain Trail** is adjacent to this and offers similar terrain. Just up the road, visitors will find the last of the three trails — the **Old Growth Trail** — via Nugedzi Lake. This is the most difficult of the bunch, and is perfect for energetic dogs and their human counterparts.

April Point is truly a family affair, with generations of people returning year after year. Eric told us of one fellow from Argentina who, at 86 years old, has made the annual pilgrimage back to April Point for years. He recently called Eric with the sad news that he might not be able to make it this year. Eric told us that he was thinking of flying down and bringing the man back up with him, so that this gentleman wouldn't miss a year. After spending a comparatively short amount of time at the April Point Lodge, it is easy to understand why this old-fashioned fishing resort has such a dedicated following.

Sooke Harbour House

1528 Whiffen Spit Road, R.R. 4
Sooke B.C. Canada V0S 1N0
(800) 889-9688, (250) 642-3421, Fax: (250) 642-6988
E-mail: shh@sookenet.com Internet: http://www.sookenet.com/shh/

Innkeepers: *Fredrica and Sinclair Philip*
Rooms: *13 doubles*
Canadian Rates: *$250-295 (breakfast and lunch included)*
Payment: *AE, MC, and VISA*
Dogs: *Welcome with a $20 fee (Canadian)*
Children: *Welcome (cribs, cots, and high chairs are available)*
Open: *All year*

Fifteen years ago, Fredrica and Sinclair Philip bought a small, white clapboard farmhouse overlooking the sea. They originally wanted to open a restaurant here, specializing in native island foods, but what they created was a little bit of paradise for anyone needing a total escape from reality. Fredrica tells us the inn is a work in progress, but as with all great artists, she and Sinclair are continually adjusting and fine tuning. It isn't really necessary though, as most visitors feel the Philips have already created their masterpiece.

Theirs is an oasis of sorts, protected by mature trees and plantings and surrounded by an incredible array of impressive flower, herb, and vegetable gardens. Some of these lie in raised beds, while others line the walks; everywhere one looks there is a delicious palate of color. This artful display is carried into the inn. Most of what is grown in the gardens is eaten — including the flowers. In many of the rooms guests will find lovely dried flowers hanging from the beams and fresh flowers filling decorative vases. Some of the guest rooms reflect their horticultural ties, including the Edible Blossom Room, The Herb Garden Room, and the Underwater Orchard.

Guests may reserve rooms in either the Old House or the New House. We stayed in the Blue Heron Room, which is fashioned with a wall of French doors and windows that reveal mesmerizing colors of the sea, mountains, and sky. From just about any angle, whether in the Jacuzzi soaking tub, in front of the fire, or on the deck, we could relax and still enjoy these lovely views. A wet bar is convenient, as is the small refrigerator containing coffee and other items for an early- morning treat. (Breakfast is delivered to the room a little later.) As with all of the other guest rooms, in here little personal touches appear; for example, a tiny wood box filled with treasures from the ocean, dried flower wreaths, or books on romance by the sea.

The Blue Heron may be one of the more luxurious spaces, but each room boasts a beauty all its own. Stark white walls make the vivid, sometimes impressionistic art all the more riveting. Bedsteads are covered with thick down comforters, soft linens, and layers of pillows. Guests may warm themselves under the down or by the fireplace, but more often, they are drawn to the oversized French doors that reveal views of the gardens and water. A small tray holds fruit, homemade cookies, and a decanter of port. Dogs are treated with equal consideration; a pair of dog bowls are set out on a mat, along with a blanket or bedding, should they be needed.

The intimate dining room has little alcoves and walls of windows, where climbing vines frame vistas of the Juan de Fuca Strait. This is a place for quiet contemplation — and fine food. Actually, it was food that originally drew the Philips to the inn. They wanted to start a restaurant that specialized in native ingredients. It turned out they couldn't always get what they needed, so they ended up growing most of the ingredients right on the premises. The preparation and presentation of the food is truly impressive.

In the afternoon, we walked by the back door of the kitchen and found, discreetly hidden from view by more lush plantings, a sort of outdoor kitchen, with breads left out on racks to cool. There are few steadfast recipes here, just a wish to combine the most interesting flavors to create the most appealing foods. Instead of selecting specific courses, we asked the chef to use his imagination. He created multiple courses that were as visually unforgettable as they were gastronomically memorable. Our salads arrived looking more like miniature flower arrangements — far too lovely to eat, but we managed. A lightly-smoked trout served with a baby red potato salad, golden tomatoes, and a smoked-apple horseradish sauce; herb-crusted oysters with a curry spice yogurt sauce; and grilled local prawns were fabulously presented. Entrées could have included sole stuffed with salmon, ginger, and Vietnamese coriander mousse on a bisque of Dungeness crab; halibut with a red and black currant, Japanese plum wine, and lemon thyme butter glaze; or a cracked Dungeness crab. Organic meats are also available, including the Malahat Farm veal short ribs with a wild mushroom, sun-dried tomato, roast garlic and rosemary sauce. The sauces add far more than taste — they are a visual backdrop for the artistic presentation. With each course, we sampled a different wine from British Columbia. Philip is a wine connoisseur, and had just returned from a buying trip to the Province's wineries. His passion for wine, especially for British Columbia wine, is contagious.

Afterwards, we sat on the huge sofa and enjoyed a sweet after-dinner wine before the fire. Most people do linger here after their meal, enjoying a little coffee and the overall ambiance. Others might go for a moonlight walk along the mile-long **Whiffen Spit**, just below the inn. This is also a wonderful place to stroll with your dog during the day. We found seals playing in the water and a bald eagle circling overhead, as well as plenty of intriguing waterfowl. Along the way, we met another Golden Retriever, three Collies, two Dachshunds, a Scottish Terrier, and a Cocker Spaniel — this is indeed doggie heaven. Those wanting a longer outing may wish to take the **Galloping Goose Trail** or pick up another mountain trail that parallels the water. Whatever recreational outlet guests choose, they will find that the attention the Philips give to their suites and their fine food is most impressive — as is their genuine desire to make their guests and their dogs completely comfortable in this enchanting inn by the sea.

Fossil Bay Resort

1603 West Coat Road, R.R. 2
Sooke, B.C., Canada V0S 1N0
(250) 646-2073, Fax: (250) 646-2121

Host: *Gerhard Wild*
Rooms: *6 cottages*
Canadian Rates: *$135-170 (EP)*
Payment: *MC and VISA*
Dogs: *Welcome in two cottages*
Children: *Not suitable for children, as the resort is close to cliffs*
Open: *All year*

The Fossil Bay Resort is one of the newer additions to Sooke's oceanside cottage resort community. Of the four that we mention, Fossil Bay is the westernmost, and consequently, has the feeling of being the most remote. When we asked some of the locals in Sooke about the Fossil Bay Resort, they just shook their heads in puzzlement, because they couldn't visualize where it was located. We found it, though, just five miles from the scenic Juan de Fuca Marine Trail — one of the better places to hike with a dog along this section of Vancouver Island.

Dense forests line the road up to Fossil Bay, and at various points a clearing reveals water views. As we neared the resort, it appeared that some clear cutting had occurred fairly recently. Whoever was responsible for it left just enough pine trees to conceal the resort from the road. We drove down a dirt lane toward the water, then turned into a little parking area across from the main lodge — a contemporary log house edged by woods. We could just make out the rooftops of the cottages set along the cliffs below.

We met Gerhard, who has owned the property for the past nine years. It wasn't until just recently, however, that he was able to build the cottages and open them to guests. The lodge and the cottages are quite separate, giving guests the feeling of privacy. We followed a path from the lodge down to the cottages that line the cliff, some 30 feet above the water. These contemporary clapboard buildings reveal little from the outside, but once inside, the light and airy interiors have almost a Caribbean feeling to them.

We stepped across terra cotta tiles to the center of the pale peach-colored room. To the rear is an alcove containing a king bed backed by a handsome oak headboard with wildflowers carved into it. A white cotton spread covers the bed, which is flanked by draped bedside tables. The room's lines are clean, the place is spotless, yet there is still plenty of character. We loved the small fireplace, with its decorative brickwork. Set on the mantel are knickknacks from the sea — intriguing shells, pieces of unusually shaped driftwood, or smooth stones. The only other collectibles are duck decoys and baskets of dried flowers. The bathrooms and kitchen are both outfitted with the same white, raised-panel cabinets and green Corian countertops. Guests will discover that they have just about everything they will need to create meals; they will just have to stock up in Sooke, as there are no stores for miles. This is a very romantic spot, which seems ideal for couples (and their dogs) who need to unwind. Whether lying in bed, sitting in front of the fire, or eating dinner by candlelight, guests can always look through the windows to the ocean. At times, the water seems close enough to touch, especially when rejuvenating in the hot tub on one's private deck. Those who cannot seem to relax without a television will find that each cottage has a remote controlled television and a VCR.

Hiking trails abound throughout Sooke. As we mentioned, the extensive **Juan de Fuca Marine Trail** is only five miles from the resort. By following the West Coast Road, visitors and their dogs will also find three oceanside provincial parks — **Whiffen Spit**, **French Beach**, and **Jordan River**. These places are as wonderful for walks along the beach as they are for serious hiking. Another outing that we enjoyed entailed walking a quarter mile through **China Beach's** rain forest before we emerged at a sandy beach. Those interested in heading further afield may wish to venture up the coast to Port Renfrew. From here, a gravel road leads to **Fairy Lake**, **Lizard Lake**, and **Lake Cowichan** — providing more than enough swimming and hiking adventures for a canine companion.

Ocean Wilderness

109 West Coast Rd., R.R. #2
Sooke, B.C., Canada V0S 1N0
(800) 323-2116, (250) 646-2116
E-mail: ocean@sookenet.com Internet: http://www.sookenet.com/ocean/

Innkeeper: *Marion Rolston*
Rooms: *9 doubles, 1 cottage*
Canadian Rates: *Doubles $85-175 (B&B), Cottage $225 (B&B)*
Payment: *MC and VISA*
Dogs: *Welcome with a $7 nightly fee*
Children: *Welcome (high chairs, cots, and baby-sitters are available)*
Open: *All year*

Rugged, mountainous beauty combines with a gently curving shoreline to make Vancouver Island's west coast memorable. Sooke lies along this stretch of coastline, with the urban charms of Victoria less than an hour away. It is easily accessible from Victoria, and even from Vancouver, yet Sooke feels remote. It would be silly to come all this way and not stay at an inn on the water, which is one of the many reasons we liked the Ocean Wilderness. It lies just steps from the beach amid five acres of old growth rain forest. Ocean Wilderness is a delightful Bed and Breakfast, and one with a good deal of pizzazz. The centerpiece is an authentic log cabin that was built in the 1930s by a local Norwegian logger. Surprisingly, Marion is only the second owner in all these years. During her tenure, she has made several changes to the property by building a guest wing (of rough hewn cedar, not logs) and a Japanese teahouse — and by clearing various paths across the property.

As guests enter the guest wing, they will find hardwood floors often covered with Oriental carpets or braided rugs. Marion's diverse antique collection, from the world over, also fills these spaces. She might have an antique side table from France, a settee from England, or an Oriental urn that serves as a lamp. Guests sleep in canopied beds with heavy down comforters, and can choose rooms with soaking tubs for two that also have unobstructed views of the ocean, mountains, and wilderness. Candlelight often flickers in these windows at night, setting a romantic tone for couples. The Mate's Room and Rainforest Room offer skylights for stargazing and forest views, while the Captain's Quarters and Pacific Panorama are fashioned with soaking tubs set in front of windows that overlook the Strait. Sheringham and Carmanah, on the other hand, lie on the first floor and guests staying here feel as though they are surrounded by dense woods. Wilderness, the only guest room located in the log house, is a little cozier than the others, and feels more rustic, primarily due to the log walls. Bathrooms are well appointed in all the rooms — including bathrobes. About a half-hour before breakfast, Marion, or one of her staff, will deliver coffee or tea on a silver tray decorated with flowers — a most civilized way to start the day. Afterwards, most enjoy taking their dogs for a walk about the property before heading over to the log house for breakfast. Ocean Wilderness works especially well for guests and their dogs, because every room but one has a private outside entrance.

The log house, too, is filled with Marion's Victorian antiques, especially in the dining room. A long table draped with a linen tablecloth is set up in front of a plate glass window. China, silver, and crystal, along with vases filled with fresh flowers, are the backdrop for the lavish repast to follow. The morning meal begins with homemade cinnamon rolls and melt-in-your-mouth biscuits that guests often smother with homemade jams and jellies. Farm fresh eggs are used for creating the various baked dishes that follow. Most are surprised to discover that the dining room isn't used only for breakfast. Marion has also used it for everything from putting on plays to hosting a clairvoyant. In the summer months, she has wonderful cookouts on the beach. On Thursdays and Sundays, guests come down to the shore to enjoy salmon, crab, prawns, halibut, shrimp, and clams, along with corn on the cob, cobblers, and other delectable edibles. As guests sip wine and sample the various wares, otters and seals often frolic just offshore. While dogs should probably forego the cookout, they will find there are plenty of other things in the area to make them leap for joy.

During the day, guests and their canines can follow the trail to the inn's beach and private cove. Just up the road, there are all sorts of hiking trails to take advantage of — one of the more popular is the ever growing **Juan de Fuca Marine Trail**. Almost all trails in the area offer varied terrain, as well as unparalleled views of the ocean and mountains.

At the end of the day, let your dog nap in the room while you navigate the stone path to the miniature Japanese teahouse for a soak in the private hot tub. There is also a wonderful massage therapist available, who will undoubtedly be able to massage away muscle fatigue or tension. Whether it be a rejuvenating massage or a therapeutic soak, we can think of no better way to end a day on the western shore of Vancouver Island.

Point-No-Point Resort

1505 West Coast Road, R.R. 2
Sooke, B.C., Canada V0S 1N0
(250) 646-2020

Managers: *Sharon and Stuart Soderberg*
Rooms: *20 cottages*
Canadian Rates: *$85-160 (B&B), Additional person $8*
Payment: *AE, MC, and VISA*
Dogs: *Welcome in cabins 3 and 4*
Children: *Welcome (cribs and high chairs are available)*
Open: *All year*

The Point-No-Point Resort has been *quietly* attracting visitors since 1952 — and no wonder; once people discover this place they want to keep it a secret. It lies just north of Sooke, along a mile of oceanfront. There are 40 acres surrounding the resort — a mixture of deep forest and shrubbery. Footpaths that weave along the craggy hillside and down 75 feet to the ocean make for fine nature walks with a canine companion. But many guests feel the most captivating feature is the serene, yet breathtaking, view. We could see the bay — and beyond to the Olympics — from just about anywhere on the property, whether from the hillside cabins or from the intimate restaurant.

The restaurant is nestled on the top of this craggy hillside and serves fine food. While we waited to be seated, we relaxed in comfortable couches and armchairs set in front of the fieldstone fireplace. Although it was late in the day, the glassed-in summer porch was filled with a number of people enjoying high tea. There are only six tables in here, but the lucky ones who garner a spot feel as though little is separating them from the ocean and wildlife. From this perch, patrons can often watch eagles soaring, or perhaps see a pod of grey whales making their way along the coast.

The restaurant serves all three meals, and each one is innovative. During our visit, lunch consisted of a creamy seafood chowder with cornbread, a warm salad of mixed greens topped with grilled scallops and a pesto vinaigrette, and an herbed fettucine with smoked chicken, mushrooms, and sun-dried cranberries in a white wine cream sauce. But it is the sunset dinners that are most memorable. Appetizers might include a seafood gratinée with scallops, prawns, and red onions in a fish velouté or the Thai spinach appetizer. The latter is a combination of onion, ginger, spinach, coconut, and peanuts baked in filo, then topped with blackberry coulis on a bed of spinach chiffonade. Some of the more popular entrées were the barbecued salmon, marinated and grilled to order, the pork tenderloin with an apricot-raisin glaze, or the breast of chicken stuffed with a ricotta cheese and mushroom duxelle.

After dinner, guests need only walk a short distance to get to their cabins. While there are cabins situated all over this craggy hillside, only two of them allow dogs. These are set into the woods, with dark wood exteriors that cause them to blend in with their surroundings. When we stepped inside it was so dark we could barely make out the shapes in the room. But as soon as we opened the draperies, the sunlight flooded in through the plate glass windows revealing log walls and ceilings. Guests will discover there is more than enough space, as there is a living room, a small bedroom, a kitchenette, and a private bathroom. Two day beds in the living room double as sofas, and are positioned to equally maximize the warmth from the fire and the views of the ocean. For the most part, these simply decorated and furnished chambers are enhanced with pretty quilts covering the beds and braided rugs topping the linoleum floors. Guests have linens, daily maid service, and even a little coffee maker in the kitchen. For a substantial breakfast, most prefer the restaurant's five-grain granola, fruit salad, pancakes, and assortment of omelets.

From this high perch, bird watchers frequently spot unusual winged creatures. The resort has even developed its own detailed list of birds that guests have seen over the years. We cannot claim any expertise in this field; however, we would be curious to know what a Rufous-sided Towhee, Red-Necked Grebe, Northern Phalarope, or Water Pipit all look like. Dogs would probably be far more interested in checking out the local hiking trails. The **Juan de Fuca Marine Trail** is in the process of being expanded, but in its present form, it still makes for a great oceanside outing with a canine companion. **The Galloping Goose Trail** is another fun hiking option, that also happens to be located in Sooke.

Best of all, there are dozens of pullouts along the road, and often paths that lead to **wilderness beaches**. One of the most beautiful (and underutilized) of these is the 146-acre **French Beach Provincial Park**. Here, visitors and their dogs can walk for miles along the rugged beach and look for treasures that have washed ashore, or just observe the river otters, sea lions, and bald eagles in their natural state. The second growth forest here is also pleasant for extensive walks, and the views of the Olympics are fabulous.

Four Seasons Hotel

791 West Georgia Street
Vancouver, B.C., Canada V6C 2T4
(800) 268-6282 (Canada), (800) 332-8442 (U.S.), (604) 689-9333,
Fax: (604) 684-4555, Internet: http://www.fourseasonsregent.com

General Manager: *Ruy Paes-Braga*
Rooms: *274 doubles, 111 suites*
Canadian Rates: *Doubles $285-335 (EP), Suites $335-900 (EP)*
Payment: *AE, DC, MC, and VISA*
Dogs: *Welcome, extensive doggie amenities are available*
Children: *Welcome — extensive children's amenities are available; children are free of charge when sharing a room with parents*
Open: *All year*

If people wanted to take their dog on a first-class trip through parts of western British Columbia, where both human and beast would be thoroughly pampered, it would be easy — all they'd have to do is start in Vancouver at the Four Seasons Hotel, then move on to the Ocean Pointe in Victoria, and finally to the Sooke Harbor House in Sooke. All three of these places know just how to cater to canines and their human friends, in royal style. There are plenty of fabulous hotels in Vancouver, but only one truly rolls out the red carpet for dogs — The Four Seasons Hotel.

This luxurious hotel is set behind an unassuming contemporary facade, but as we took the escalator up from street level, its elegant interiors began to unfold. Dark wood walls, subdued lighting, and impressive antiques give the lobby a warm, residential quality. In true Four Seasons tradition, huge vases filled with lavish flower arrangements are placed upon highly polished antique tables. The lobby is merely the centerpiece for the various restaurants and small gift shops encircling it. Two of the more notable restaurants are the intimate Chartwell restaurant, and the equally inviting Garden Terrace. While the former is fashioned with paneled walls and old-world sophistication, the terrace is a veritable rain forest of potted plants and ficus trees that thrive under natural light. In addition to the light and airy garden setting, this chamber is also bedecked with an exquisite handmade Inuit rug draped across one wall. Guests may relax here for cocktails, or sample the elaborate brunch that is served each Sunday.

British Columbia

The Four Seasons rises 28 floors above the city of Vancouver. As one might imagine, there is an ongoing renovation program in place to maintain the fresh and sophisticated look of both the common areas and the guest chambers. This building was once filled with apartments, and although it was converted to a hotel years ago, there is still a residential quality about the guest bedrooms. There are many types of rooms available to travelers and their canine companions. Some of the smaller rooms are outfitted with oversized writing desks and intimate sitting areas; the corner deluxe chambers are fashioned with separate sitting rooms and floor-to-ceiling windows; and the executive suites are furnished with mirrored French doors that can be closed to separate the bedroom from the spacious living room.

The color schemes also vary with the room, and while some have sophisticated black and white coordinated fabrics, others are festooned in equally lovely shades of russet or celadon green. Sitting rooms often contain overstuffed sofas and armchairs, as well as inlaid mahogany reproductions of English antiques. In many of the rooms, Chippendale chairs surround Queen Anne coffee tables, while drop leaf end tables are usually topped with Oriental vase lamps. Even the artwork is noteworthy, incorporating black and white sketches of the English countryside or a notable scene of the Northwest. The amenities, both human and doggie, are also extensive. Beds are covered in fine linen, and fluffy down comforters. Down pillows are also available, as are foam pillows for those who are allergic to feathers. Armoires contain well-stocked private bars and a televisions. VCRs are standard features in the suites. Bathrooms include hair dryers, scales, lighted mirrors, and trays filled with every convenience — including European soaps, conditioners, cotton balls and swabs, lotions, and bath gels. Telephones are found in the bathrooms, as well as in the sitting areas and bedrooms.

Dogs may not think much of the human amenities, but they will certainly appreciate the gourmet biscuits that await their arrival in the room (a recipe card for these biscuits is provided). These are placed in two handmade pottery bowls, alongside a large bottle of Evian water on a silver tray. Should Bowser require a few additional services, guests need only ask on his behalf. In addition to providing a special dog-oriented menu or a comfy dog bed, the staff will walk Bowser for guests who might be otherwise occupied at walking time.

While Bowser is dining on gourmet kibble, guests might want to slip downstairs to Chartwell. Dark, wood-paneled walls create a sense of warmth in this intimate space, enhanced only by the flickering fireplace. A hand-painted mural and other original works of art make this chamber seem more like a private dining room, rather than just another hotel restaurant. Guests dine at small linen-covered tables set with fine china and cobalt blue goblets. The service is impeccable, and patrons enjoy the feeling of being thoroughly pampered. Some might choose to start their meal with the smoked candied salmon loin, accented with a horseradish crème fraîche and onion and dill bannock; the Dungeness crab cake with dandelion and saffron aioli; or the charred lamb loin carpaccio with a sharp mustard and oregano sauce. The open-faced vegetarian lasagna was intriguing, with a smoked tomato oil and truffle pesto; as was the pheasant breast filled with homemade ricotta and grilled leeks. Patrons might also want to order the pepper seared beef tenderloin with a goat cheese crust, crispy elephant garlic, and a red wine sauce; the Maine lobster; the Pacific salmon; or the Fraser Valley vegetables baked in a delicate crust.

We would recommend limiting after-dinner walks with dogs to the immediate area and saving longer strolls for the daylight hours. The Four Seasons is in the center of Vancouver's financial and shopping districts, within easy walking distance of just about any attraction. The hotel is situated across the street from the Vancouver Art Gallery, just above the Pacific Centre Mall, which has more than 200 shops, restaurants, and clubs.

Dogs who feel comfortable in the city will very much enjoy Vancouver, as there are fine walks to the waterfront, the botanical gardens, and an assortment of lush city parks nearby the hotel. The general rule of thumb for dogs and parks is that they are welcome, provided they remain leashed. The **park** closest to the hotel is situated between **Nelson and Comox streets**. Those who are looking forward to a longer outing can visit the 1,200-acre **Stanley Park**, which is absolutely spectacular. One of our favorite strolls here is along the **Seawall Promenade**, which edges the circumference of this park. In downtown Vancouver, it is possible to find a number of other small green grassy areas, but these are generally off limits to dogs in the summer months.

After a long walk, your dog will undoubtedly be a little tired. During her nap, you may wish to visit the hotel's health club, where, in addition to a full complement of weights, rowing machines, and Lifecycles, there is an indoor whirlpool, a sauna, and a 60-foot-long pool, all of which should provide just the right combination of passive therapy to rejuvenate the entire body.

Hotel Vancouver

900 West Georgia Street
Vancouver, B.C., Canada V6C 2W6
(800) 441-1414, (604) 684-3131, Fax: (604) 662-1937
Internet: http://www.cphotels.ca

General Manager: *Michael Lambert*
Rooms: *550 doubles and suites*
Canadian Rates: *$175-3335 (EP)*
Payment: *AE, CB, DC, DSC, JCB, MC and VISA*
Dogs: *Welcome on the smoking floor; cannot be left alone in the room*
Children: *Welcome; under 18 are free of charge when sharing a room with parents*
Open: *Open*

The Hotel Vancouver looks like an old world palace, with its steeply-pitched copper roofs and magnificent sandstone facade rising high into the city's skyscape. It was built in 1939, but in a 16th-century style reminiscent of a French Renaissance château, complete with stone carvings of Greek mythological figures. Artisans were hired to create the intricate statues of native West Coast and Central Plains' chieftains, along with more Classical and Gothic subjects that still guard the facade today.

The history of the hotel is an interesting one, especially when considering that this particular Hotel Vancouver is the third hotel in a series to bear the same name. It all started in 1887, when the Canadian Pacific Railroad built a four-story, wooden hotel at this location. It was replaced in 1916 with a far grander hotel, but its beauty was short-lived, as the building fell into complete disarray within 20 years of its completion, and eventually had to be torn down. At this point, the Canadian National Railroad stepped in and began construction of the majestic hotel that we now know as the Hotel Vancouver. Surprisingly, the railroad ran out of money midway through the project. This hotel would have also gone by the wayside had it not been for the Canadian Pacific Railroad, which offered its financial support in 1937. By 1939 the hotel was completed. Ever since then, the Canadian Pacific Railroad has had a sporadic interest in the hotel. Finally, in 1987 it took over permanent management of it. The seemingly unending restoration process continues, but throughout it all, the historic beauty of the hotel survives. The lobby is the most recent project. Although we have not seen the final result, we hope the existing, prefabricated 1970s look will soon be replaced by a new decor more in keeping with the old-world style of the rest of the hotel.

The former lobby is just one example of renovations run amuck over the years. One person who saw the value in preserving the past, though, was Ethel Ferguson. She was a housekeeper who worked at the hotel for more than 20 years. In the 1960s, someone tried to eradicate the hotel's historic character in favor of bright lights and dizzying geometric patterns. Ethel had the chutzpah to take a large number of the antique furnishings and hide them. For 15 years she kept her secret, and when the management finally came to its senses and returned to an interior design more befitting that of this grand dame, she brought forward enough furniture from her secret stash to decorate 35 rooms. Those who want to take a look at some of these original pieces should ask for one of the 12th-floor guest rooms, which are decorated with many of these furnishings.

Each floor of bedrooms is different from the others. We saw a number of them and were impressed with their strong traditional English decor. Some are graced with lovely mahogany pieces, while others have a more contemporary twist that features slightly more brass and glass. Most are accented with ceiling moldings, original thick wood doors, and brass fixtures. Chintzes cover the quilted spreads and tailored dust ruffles, while coordinated draperies frame the double hung windows. Colors range from a pale blue with white and yellow accents to a burgundy coupled with subtle green hues.

The windows open, but unless guests are on the uppermost floors, they will want to keep them closed — it can be noisy.

Some of the thoughtful extras are down comforters, chocolates, vases of fresh flowers, and minibars set in armoires alongside cable televisions. Even the bathrooms have been beautifully refurbished, and all are stocked with an array of toiletries. Our favorite chambers are the corner rooms. We like them as much for their impressive views as for the abundance of sunshine that permeates them.

One of the newer additions to the hotel is the award-winning spa, located on the third floor. The huge atrium pool is surrounded by outdoor gardens filled with potted trees and flowers. The health club has everything guests could want, including a full complement of exercise equipment. The spa will loan Walkmans, or guests may watch television while they workout. During our visit, we also noticed plenty of people either heading out to or coming back from power walks and jogs with their dogs.

Those who are looking for a nearby outing will find a small **grassy park** just down the street from the hotel. Here they can visit anytime *except* for the summer months. To get to **Stanley Park**, guests walk down Georgia Street five or six blocks. Once in the park, it is great fun to follow the paths that lead through the forested setting. Just a block from the hotel is the trendy Robson Street with its many boutiques and sidewalk cafés. Some may want to stop for a cappuccino in one of these outdoor cafés. A winsome dog might be able to persuade her human companion to part with a few delectable treats. **Sunset Beach** is another option, situated on the other side of Vancouver. North Vancouver is just one bridge away, and visitors and their canines will discover even more outdoor diversions there. One of the more popular options is to head up **Grouse Mountain** by tram. At the top, there are great hiking trails, paved paths, and fabulous views looking back over to Vancouver.

After a busy day, guests will enjoy returning to the comfortable confines of the hotel, where they may enjoy a memorable meal. For years, the Vancouver Hotel's rooftop restaurant was the place for romantic dining and dancing. It rests on the 14th floor and anyone who has been here knows about the spectacular city views. The formal restaurant still attracts patrons who want a romantic dining experience with a view, but this intimate space has been somewhat modernized. The ambiance might not be the same as in the original, but guests can still dine on fine food. They might wish to start with an appetizer such as the lobster bisque, a warm seafood salad, or escargot. Dungeness crab meat crêpes, prime rib with Yorkshire pudding, and medallions of venison with grilled polenta and fall vegetables were a few of the selections that topped the fall menu. Guests come here for the views and fine cuisine; but they head downstairs to Griffins for unabashed fun.

The hotel's formal mascot is a griffin, and it has been incorporated into this convivial restaurant bearing the same name. This high-ceilinged chamber's walls are painted a lemon yellow, while black and white checked tiles and large square columns of mahogany provide decorative accents. The floor-to-ceiling windows allow plenty of natural light to permeate this space. We came for the buffet (as most people do). It had been highly recommended — and sure enough, it delivered. Children will love the kiddy buffet, where they are able make their own pancakes, pour their own cereal, and create their own ice cream concoctions. An array of sweet and colorful toppings and side dishes await the younger patrons on a side table. Festive plates, napkins, and plastic cutlery complete this delightful experience. This place is fun, for both children and adults. Now if only the management could devise a special eatery geared for dogs, then everyone would be able to enjoy this place.

Metropolitan Hotel Vancouver

645 Howe Street
Vancouver, B.C., Canada V6C 2Y9
(800) 667-2300, (604) 687-1122, Fax: (604) 689-7044
E-mail: reservations@metropolitan.com
Internet: http://metropolitan.com/vanc/metro

General Manager: Brian Young
Rooms: 197 doubles, 18 suites
Canadian Rates: Doubles $150-285 (EP), Suites $255-625 (EP)
Payment: AE, DC, MC, and VISA
Dogs: *Welcome with notice, but guests must sign a damage waiver*
Children: *Welcome (cribs, cots, and high chairs are available)*
Open: *All year*

We have always loved the boutique hotels in New York City, as they provide visitors (and, very often, their dogs) with a residential feeling. While Vancouver does not claim to be anything like New York City, it is a bustling place. At the end of the day, there is nothing better than walking into a small hotel like the Metropolitan, where guests instantly feel enveloped in the luxurious surroundings. The Metropolitan Hotel Vancouver was built in 1985 as a Mandarin Oriental Hotel, and it still reflects its Asian heritage (even though the Delta Hotel chain owned it from 1987 to 1995). A privately owned company out of Hong Kong bought the hotel in the fall of 1995 and reestablished the gracious traditions of the Mandarin.

On our first visit to the Metropolitan it was still a work in progress, with talk of establishing an elegant restaurant to match its exquisite five-star guest rooms. On our recent return to the hotel, their new restaurant, Diva, was already winning awards as the best new gourmet restaurant in Vancouver.

Diva is located on the first floor, just off the hotel's intimate lobby. Check-in is handled at the inconspicuous front desk, after which guests and their dogs are whisked to the upper levels. We followed gracefully curving hallways past charming alcoves to reach the bedrooms. These elegantly appointed spaces are accented with soothing taupe and cream color schemes, and although small, they are well designed. One illuminated nook might contain a small bronze statue, while another has a figure carved in stone.

When guests settle in for the night under their European duvets, they probably will not need to get up again — the lights, the stereo, and the television can all be controlled by pushing a few buttons on their bedside table's console. The marble bathrooms are filled with a full complement of Swiss botanical shampoos, soaps, and lotions. The terry robes are not found in the bathroom, though, but in the closets, where there is also a small iron and ironing board for touching up wrinkled garments. The bedrooms are totally soundproof; however, guests can open the sliding door to the tiny terrace and let the refreshing breezes drift in off the water. Guests who are here to work can use the writing desks, while those who have come for relaxation can sample some of the gourmet offerings in the fully stocked minibar.

For more elaborate offerings, there is Diva. The current chef was permanently "borrowed" from the Four Seasons Hotel. The menu is inspired, with patrons choosing from items such as a roasted garlic and white bean puree with morel mushroom sausage or the seared foie gras with a nectarine compote and port wine glaze. The main courses range from a bamboo-steamed salmon with wild grain pancakes and a lavender honey-brushed poussin with artichoke and sweet corn polenta to the rack of lamb with a crisp potato and vegetable Napoleon drizzled with calmata olive butter. Much of the menu is a la carte, and the price can be steep, but for a special treat we recommend splurging on a meal at Diva.

The hotel's health spa is one of the best in the city. Although not as elaborate as the one at the Pan Pacific, it is state-of-the-art and outfitted with every exercise machine imaginable, not to mention squash courts. The spa also offers an indoor swimming pool, whirlpools, saunas, and massage therapy. Guests can even watch television as they work out, which might help pass the time during particularly strenuous reps.

The Metropolitan Hotel Vancouver is conveniently located halfway between the waterfront and the shopping and financial districts. From here, guests can walk a few blocks up to the trendy Robson Street, or down to the waterfront area. Dogs may be included in all these outings, as there are **grassy areas** to enjoy along the way. There are also plenty of parks in Vancouver — 174, at last count. Those who want to venture a little further afield may wish to visit the **Mount Seymour Provincial Park**. This is a semi-wilderness park with incredible views looking out to the Gulf and San Juan Islands. Dogs and their friends can hike up Mount Seymour, or follow the easier **Flower Loop Trail** that is also in the same vicinity. Another option is the **Goldie Lake Loop Trail**. Guests can bring a picnic and enjoy the day in this picturesque setting, knowing that in the evening, they can return to the more urban adventures awaiting in the city.

Pan Pacific Hotel Vancouver

300-999 Canada Place
Vancouver, B.C., Canada V6C 3B5
(800) 663-1515 (Canada), (800) 937-1515 (US), (604) 662-8111,
Fax: (604) 662-3815, Internet: http://www.panpat.com

General Manager: *Susan Gomez*
Rooms: *467 doubles, 39 suites*
Canadian Rates: *Doubles $220-460 (EP), Suites $375-1,200 (EP)*
Payment: *AE, CB, DC, MC, and VISA*
Dogs: *Welcome — they've had all sizes*
Children: *Welcome (cribs, cots, high chairs, and baby-sitters available)*
Open: *All year*

The Pan Pacific Hotel seems more like a small city than a hotel; but then again, it needs to be big, since it sits atop Canada Place, which houses Vancouver's Convention Center. The complex was built in 1986 for the World's Fair, but it still attracts plenty of attention. From Burrard Inlet, the entire building appears to float on the water, with its five massive white sails appearing poised to pull the buildings away from the shore. Cruise ships tie up here before heading further north, and just about all visitors to Vancouver find their way to the hotel sometime during their stay.

Since the World's Fair, the Pan Pacific Hotel Vancouver continues to attract countless accolades, visiting dignitaries, and celebrities. Bill Clinton and Boris Yeltsin met here for their presidential summit in 1993. HRH, the Sultan of Brunei, stayed here, as did His Highness The Aga Khan IV. The parade of princesses and princes seems too great to mention here, but has included royalty from the Netherlands, Japan, Thailand, and Tongo. Guests over the years have spotted such celebrities as Sean Connery, Bob Hope, and George Burns, along with sports notables Wayne Gretzky and Stefan Edberg. Robert De Niro holed up here for months with his dogs, but was left pretty much to his own devices. Five diamonds have been awarded to the hotel, and the readers of Condé Nast's *Traveler* voted it one of the 25 best foreign hotels in the world. We wondered if the Canadian Pacific Vancouver could live up to all the positive press.

Anyone looking for intimacy and luxury had better steer clear of the Pan Pacific, but those looking for accessibility, fabulous water views, and the best athletic facilities in town should consider the Pan Pacific Hotel Vancouver. As visitors enter the building their eyes are immediately drawn upwards. The ceiling towers overhead some eight stories above the atrium. We rode up a series of escalators just to reach the main lobby. Once we arrived, the combination of falling water echoing off the marble floors and lush greenery made it seem like an indoor tropical rainforest. Natural light pours into the lobby through 40-foot-high windows that seem to wrap themselves around this chamber. Anyone who wants to watch the activity on the docked cruise ships below, or get a closer look at those massive sails, need only step out past these windows to the observation deck.

There is no need to worry about noisy children or dogs in the public areas, as this place is so big that no one would ever notice a dog's yip or a child's enthusiastic banter. The upper floors are carpeted and quieter, but do seem to stretch on forever. The bedrooms are well appointed and are decorated in subdued color schemes with an Asian twist. The bedspreads have a bamboo pattern that nicely complements the grass wallpaper. The furnishings are quite streamlined and constructed of lightly-stained wood. The bedrooms have all the usual amenities, such as clock radios, fully-stocked minibars, and remote controlled televisions with a full complement of movie channels. Marble bathrooms are fully outfitted with toiletries and other conveniences. Guests may request same-day laundry and valet, use of the safety deposit boxes, complimentary shoeshine, and baby-sitting services.

While the standard guest rooms are fine, they are not especially noteworthy, except for the views. From the upper levels, guests feel as though they are sitting in the crow's nest, with miles of unobstructed views. The suites are far more elaborate, and are designed for extended stays. Some of the most elaborate have private steam rooms, saunas, and whirlpools, along with kitchens and separate living rooms.

Some guests come to the Canadian Pacific Hotel and never have to leave, not even to exercise. The health club and spa attract professional and weekend athletes who come to play racquetball, squash, or paddle tennis; run on the indoor track; take aerobics classes — and then spend some time in the sauna, steam room, or with a massage therapist. Tanning salons make guests look healthy — even when the sun has been hidden for days. Just in case the sun does come out, the eighth-floor sun deck is available to those who want to take advantage of the 50-foot outdoor heated pool, the chaise lounges, and the Jacuzzi.

The hotel has restaurants to suit just about any palate and price level. For those in search of an elegant dining experience, the Five Sails is probably the best bet. Vancouver has an inordinate number of fine restaurants, and many of these are within easy walking distance of the hotel.

Dogs will enjoy cruising the docks around the property. There are also a series of **tiered terraces and fountains** just across from the hotel; these make a pleasant area for walks with canine critters. The expansive **Stanley Park** is also within walking distance. Guests can easily get their car out from the 750-car parking lot under the hotel — and head off on short adventures across the city's bridges to other notable parks. West Vancouver offers the **Cypress Provincial Park**, where the views of the Georgia Strait are inspiring. From the downtown area, it is only seven miles to the Lions Gate Bridge, which leads into the park. Once here, visitors can hike around the 7,000 acres of park land and wilderness. Two of the more intriguing trails here are the **Howe**

British Columbia

Sound Crest Trail and the **Baden-Powell Centennial '71 Trail**. The park's forests contain trees that are over 1,000 years old, as well as low-lying ferns, false azaleas, and heather. In the winter months, visitors and their canine cohorts may wish to bring their cross-country skiing paraphernalia along as well.

Waterfront Centre Hotel

900 Canada Place Way
Vancouver, B.C., Canada V6C 3L5
(800) 268-9411, (604) 691-1991, Fax: (604) 691-1999
Internet: http://www.cphotels.ca

General Manager: *Michael Kaile*
Rooms: *429 doubles, 26 suites*
Canadian Rates: *Doubles $215-335 (EP), Suites $465-1,700 (EP)*
Payment: *AE, CB, DSC, DC, JCB, MC, and VISA*
Dogs: *Welcome if "knee level or below" with a one-time fee of $25*
Children: *Welcome; under 18 are free of charge*
Open: *All year*

Vancouver is a spectacular city, especially when visitors can see the sun and clouds reflected off the deep blue water and the mountains looming off in the distance. The best place to capture this vivid panorama is down along the waterfront, as the views further up the hill are often obscured by tall buildings. There are not too many options in the noteworthy "waterfront hotel" category, but fortunately, one of the best of these welcomes guests with "knee-high" dogs. The Waterfront Centre Hotel is one of the newer additions to the group of luxury hotels owned by Canadian Pacific. Even from a distance this building is striking. It rises 23 stories in a crescent of blue reflective glass set against a white framework. Surrounding it are well-designed terraces and fountains edged by beautifully-tended flower gardens. This place is huge, yet once inside, the feeling is far more personal and private than initial impressions would lead one to believe.

A single wall of glass seems to wrap itself around the lobby, letting in an abundance of natural light that falls across the sandstone-colored marble floors. Deep, overstuffed sofas — the type people sink into and have difficulty climbing out of — create private sitting areas that are nestled behind towering columns. We were drawn, as most are, to what appears to be a massive antique map set against one wall. Upon closer inspection, we noticed this was really a contemporary piece of art, entitled *Voyage of Discovery*. This chart tracks George Vancouver's trip to the Northwest in 1790. We thought he would be quite surprised to see all of the changes to this once wild territory.

With most of the guest rooms providing stunning vistas, we had difficulty choosing from among the many available views, which included views of the harbor, views across the water toward Stanley Park, or over the cityscape. Others who are stumped by the array of vistas should keep in mind that nearly 300 guest rooms offer views of the water. Regardless of one's ultimate decision, all of the chambers are decorated in soft earth tones, ranging from pale peach and ivory to ecru and dove gray. As new arrivals enter their room, they will find music playing, quilted bedspreads turned down, and baskets of edibles, as well as trays of mints and bottled water — all waiting to refresh them. The entire effect is designed to be soothing, and it succeeds. At night, guests can open their windows and let the refreshing breezes drift in from the water. Of course, there are plenty of other amenities, such as minibars and remote controlled televisions set in the armoire, clock radios placed upon bedside tables, and bathrooms outfitted with just about every imaginable toiletry. In the morning, coffee is set out on each floor and interested guests may help themselves. Those who want to settle under a down duvet at night — and have the convenience of a continental breakfast in the morning — may wish to reserve the Concierge Level Rooms, where, in addition to breakfast, guests are also offered complimentary cocktails and *hors' d' oeuvres* in the evenings.

The hotel offers guests the use of a full-service health club, which is outfitted with a steam room, a whirlpool, workout equipment, and a masseuse. But it is the outdoor swimming pool, set on the a third-story roof deck, that usually gets the most attention. From the pool, we had a great view of the mountains, harbor, and city. The pool is on one end of the roof deck, while the remainder of the deck is comprised of a little park of shade trees and extensive herb gardens. The chef at Herons Restaurant, just downstairs, picks most of his herbs from these gardens and uses them to create his inspiring menu. The physical layout of Herons is equally eye-catching, with walls of glass, hand-crafted wrought iron, and an atrium setting — all of which are worth visiting on the basis of visual appeal alone. The restaurant specializes in food and wine indigenous to British Columbia, ranging from organic fruits and vegetables to local meats and game. The extensive wine list contains some of the best wines that British Columbia has to offer.

Dogs are generally more interested in getting out to explore some of the more verdant sections of the city. **Stanley Park** allows dogs on all the trails in the park, but they cannot go into the Children's Zoo. Another walk takes visitors and their dogs to **Brockton Point** and the lighthouse. Along the way, they will pass the Royal Vancouver Yacht Club and Hallelujah Point, where an extensive collection of totem poles is found. A car is needed to visit some of the other intriguing parks near Vancouver. We suggest crossing the Burrard Bridge. Once across, both human and beast will be able to roam freely at **Vanier Park**, the Vancouver Museum, the Planetarium, and the Maritime Museum. **Jericho Park** is another viable option; it is comprised of more than 125 acres of grass, trees, and gardens.

British Columbia

Laburnam Cottage

1388 Terrace Avenue
North Vancouver, B.C., Canada V7R 1B4
(604) 988-4877

Hostess: *Delphine Masterton*
Rooms: *4 doubles, 2 cottages*
Canadian Rates: *Doubles $155 (B&B), Cottages $200 (B&B)*
Payment: *MC and VISA*
Dogs: *Welcome with approval*
Children: *Welcome in the cottages*
Open: *Open*

The Laburnum Cottage is only 15 minutes from downtown Vancouver, but once here, guests might as well be in the English countryside. Don't misunderstand us; the Laburnum Cottage lies in a residential area with houses all around it, but somehow, Delphine Masterton has created a lovely enclave for her guests. We found this Tudor-style cottage at the bottom of a cobblestone driveway. Gardens aside, the house also resembles something out of England, with its leaded glass windows, dark wood trim, and multiple-peaked roof line that seems to ramble off in every direction. While it appears quite historic, we soon discovered that it wasn't built until the 1940s. The outside was so appealing, we could hardly wait to see the interior.

We rang the bell and Delphine answered. As we stepped into the sunny foyer, we could hear sounds of laughter coming from the kitchen. It was Thanksgiving and Delphine's family was visiting, yet she graciously welcomed us and invited us into her warm and cozy country kitchen. One of her daughters was chopping, another was pulling pies out of the immense Aga stove, and the rest of the famil was having a fine time chatting around the table. We were tempted to join them, until we caught sight of Delphine's gardens. It was fall, and even though the growing season was almost over, the gardens were still remarkable.

In fact, the gardens alone often attract many guests to the Laburnum Cottage, which resembles something out of a fine gardening coffee-table book. Narrow stone paths lead to all corners of the property, and eventually to a small footbridge that crosses a creek. Huge trees, including one fine old willow, create a canopy for the mix of shade-loving rhododendrons and azaleas. Roses were still blooming around the patio, offering the last bits of color visitors would see until springtime. This place must be spectacular in the height of the growing season, when bulbs are popping from the earth, delicate perennials are in full bloom, and dogwoods are flashing their pink and white flowers.

Set invitingly amid these gardens is our favorite chamber, the Summer House. This is a separate cottage, which seems as if it once could have been a large potting shed. Now it is a storybook cottage covered with wisteria, and an ideal place for a couple and their dog. The wood walls are painted out white, and little paned windows catch the sun as it pours in during the afternoon. A brass bed covered with a handmade quilt combines with antique wicker chairs and tables to set the overall decorative tone. Original watercolors provide a splash of color. The bathroom has recently been redone and now contains a luxurious soaking tub. Guests out here are totally self-sufficient, with a kitchenette, a small television, and a fireplace.

The rest of the bedrooms are in the main house and the adjacent cottage, just off the kitchen. All the bedrooms overlook these magnificent gardens; three are situated on the upper floors and one downstairs. The beds are made of brass and covered with soft cotton sheets and puffy down comforters. We felt surrounded at times by pale pinks and yellows reminiscent of a Monet watercolor. Lustrous hardwood floors are covered with Oriental rugs, while floral chintzes and silks line the armchairs and sofas and frame the windows. This traditional look is accentuated by the patina emanating from the English and French antiques. Delphine is a collector of things, and she displays her porcelains, china, and crystal throughout the house.

If the main house seems, for small children, like a disaster waiting to happen, guests should keep in mind that Delphine raised a large family here and has a keen appreciation for what it is like traveling with young ones. She recently completed a separate cottage suite; this is ideal for families and is located through the back door of the kitchen. We stepped out onto a little courtyard before entering an expansive suite. This space is fashioned with a master bedroom, along with a loft area for the children. They can bring their sleeping bags and have a fine time sleeping up here on comfy mats. Guests will also appreciate the full kitchen, stereo, and television, as well as the ambiance of a fireplace.

Regardless of room choice, all guests are treated to a full breakfast in the morning. Delphine creates fabulous meals, which most enjoy in the separate breakfast room overlooking the gardens. The terra cotta tiles on the floors, coupled with large windows, make this chamber seem almost like an atrium. Guests are treated to a full English breakfast with a continental twist, starting with fresh fruit, orange juice, and coffee or tea. Baskets of freshly baked scones, muffins, or cinnamon buns are set out for all to enjoy, while guests wait for, perhaps, blueberry or strawberry pancakes, French toast, crèpes, or omelets. Bacon and sausage also accompany this hearty repast.

Afterwards, your dog will be all too eager to take a walk. The neighborhood is quiet and there are plenty of streets that are ideal for leisurely strolls with a dog. It is also easy to access the seemingly unlimited number of hiking trails in North Vancouver. Within minutes, visitors can be on their way to walking up the steep mountain trails, crossing suspension bridges, or simply driving to a spot to enjoy the remarkable views. The **Capilano Suspension Bridge and Park** is a popular destination for visitors, although dogs might get a bit nervous on the suspension bridge; it stretches 450 feet across a canyon floor that is 220 feet below. Also within the park are a number of grassy areas and nature trails that dogs will enjoy investigating. **Lynn Canyon Park** has a number of trails, as well as a suspension bridge. (People are not charged a fee to walk across it.) Grouse Mountain has a gondola that can bring people and their canines up to the top of the mountain, where they can access trails along the **West Coast Mountain Range**. At the end of the day, though, most like to return to the Laburnum Cottage for a civilized cup of tea and scones amid the peaceful garden setting.

The Maria Rose B&B

8083 Aspen Road
Site 11, Comp. 156, R.R. #3
Vernon, B.C., Canada V1T 6L6
Telephone and Fax: (250) 549-4773

Innkeepers: *Ruth-Maria Cushing, Peter Filas*
Rooms: *4 doubles*
Canadian Rates: *$60-75 (B&B)*
Payment: *VISA*
Dogs: *Welcome, for a small fee*
Children: *Welcome*
Open: *All year*

Vernon lies at the northern end of the Okanagan Valley — a region known for everything from apples to emus. Farms dot the landscape beginning in Vernon and reaching as far south as Penticon. Throughout this valley, vintners, orchardists, and farmers grow grains, grapes, and even bananas; some specialize in raising emus, llamas, and bees. While the climate is temperate all year, a short trip up Silver Star Mountain will generally yield cold, dry mountain air and a good deal of snow. We visited in the fall, when the valley was still warm, but as we climbed the steep, winding switchbacks toward the mountain top, snow began to fall. The views along the way were magnificent, and as night fell, the lights of Vernon twinkled below.

Halfway up the mountain, the twinkling lights on a delicate hand-carved sign pointed us toward the Maria Rose B&B. Its lovely old-world name was matched only by our gracious hosts, Maria and Peter. Both are originally from Germany and are well versed in European hospitality. We felt as though we had stumbled upon an intimate European pensione, and had to keep reminding ourselves that we were still on North American soil. The personal touches abound, yet nothing is contrived.

When we arrived it was getting late and we were both exhausted. Thus, our hosts escorted us over to a converted garage called the Royal Coach House, where the B&B guest rooms are located. Maria told us that when she bought the property, this seemed like the ideal space to convert into bedrooms. As with most simple projects, this one had its share of complications; however, the end result seems to justify all their effort — four lovely guest chambers named King, Queen, Prince, and Princess. On this particular evening, we needed — and received — the royal treatment. Peter led us to the Princess Room, which is painted a pale pink with bright floral accents. He took the coverlet off the bed, fluffed the down comforter and pillows, and gave us a rejuvenating gel for the bath. He then left us to take a hot bath and sink into the soft cotton sheets.

A sense of solitude and utter quiet made for a wonderful night's sleep. By the next morning, we were ready to learn more about the B&B. Our room and the Prince's Room connect and also share a bathroom, making these an ideal choice for a family. Ours was the more feminine of the two spaces, with lots of lace and bright floral fabrics. A grouping of tiny pictures lined one wall, along with a heart-shaped wreath. A small, mirrored dressing table was adorned with a tray and two glasses, all of which were hand-painted with wildflowers. Even our pillowcases had delicate pink and blue flowers embroidered along the edges. The Prince's Room is fashioned in darker greens, but also has lace accents framing the windows. There is a double bed in here, along with a small sitting area. The entry to each bedroom is tiled, and brass hooks line the wall for hanging up one's outer garments. These spaces were so immaculate that we felt compelled to take off our shoes. The King's and Queen's Rooms are located on the first floor. Both have private bathrooms and small sitting areas. The King's Room is dominated by a king-size bed covered with a down comforter and a turquoise coverlet. Modern amenities include a television and small refrigerator. The Queen's Room is substantially larger than the Princess's Room, but utilizes the same basic color schemes. We liked the added touch of a little stuffed toy dog placed on each of the beds, as well as the little rose on our room key.

Both the main house and the guest house rest on seven forested acres. In the morning, the views to the valley are spectacular, if not dizzying. As we walked to the house, we noticed the resident cat happily snoozing on a rooftop. Breakfast is served in the main house, and guests generally enjoy this in the downstairs dining room. This cozy chamber is warmed by a wood stove. On this day, though, we were the only guests, and we enjoyed breakfast in the formal upstairs dining room off the kitchen. Maria is a collector, and displayed throughout her house is fine china, crystal, and silver. Everything about their home is European, including the breakfast. We started with strong coffee, coffee cake, and a light fruit salad. This was followed by delicate crêpes filled with homemade applesauce. During this hearty repast, we learned that Maria lived in Toronto for years before coming to Vernon. She traveled extensively with her dog throughout Canada, and frequently, south to Cape Cod. It was always difficult for her to find places to stay that welcomed dogs, which is why she and Peter decided to accept well-mannered pets at their B&B.

While there are plenty of things to do in the area, guests might find themselves content just to explore the property or read on the patio. Within easy driving distance, there is horseback riding, golf, swimming, boating, fishing and plenty of hiking and biking trails. The best place to take a dog is to the top of **Silver Star Mountain.** This is a part of the Silver Star Provincial Park. Up here, visitors and their canines can hike the area throughout the summer and fall, and in the winter, try a little skiing instead. At the end of the day, guests are usually ready to head back to the B&B for a therapeutic sauna. We would have liked to spend a long weekend here, but unfortunately had to move on the next day. As we were leaving, Maria gave us a little goodie bag for our journey, filled with all sorts of tasty treats.

Silver Lode Inn

P.O. Box 5
Silver Star Mountain Resort
Vernon, B.C., Canada VOE 1GO
(250) 549-5105, Fax: (250) 549-5101 (For reservations call collect)

Hosts: *Max Schlaepfer and Trudy Amstutz*
Rooms: *16 doubles, 6 suites*
Canadian Rates: *Doubles $68-146 (EP), Suites $114-183 (EP)*
Payment: *AE, MC, and VISA*
Dogs: *Welcome with a $10 nightly fee*
Children: *Welcome*
Open: *All year except for May*

The Silver Lode Inn is set on top of Silver Star Mountain. We knew this was the second largest ski resort in British Columbia; however, what we found at the top of the hill was unlike anything we had ever seen in a ski resort — outside of, perhaps, Vail, Colorado. Silver Star, like Vail, was built around a theme. The powers behind this area created a Victorian community that borders on being almost too cute, but stops just short of it. It would be difficult to tell what is renovated and what is original, but it is all colorful and looks authentic.

The Victorian theme village is the centerpiece, with an array of Victorian homes with vibrant facades lining the hills. The entire resort comprises a few square miles at the most, which makes it an ideal area for visitors and their canines to explore on foot. We had a fine time investigating the surrounding neighborhoods, and looking at the assortment of house styles, both large and small. Some are rambling Victorian-style ski houses, with porches, turrets, and decorative shingles. A few are painted hunter green with mustard yellow and burgundy highlights. Others are a slate blue with crimson red and green accents. Still other buildings resemble the Victorian row houses that line the hills in San Francisco. Their bright facades are especially spectacular when contrasted against the whiteness of the snow. Most of these houses are found in an area called The Knoll. Along with private residences, many of these dwellings are rented to skiers (and sometimes their dogs).

The highlight, though, is the town center, with its boardwalks and vibrant facades that consist of a few hotels and restaurants, a saloon, and an assortment of shops. Cars are left in outlying lots, and most visitors generally walk to the village from there. Set in the midst of it all is the Silver Lode Inn. Although it was built in 1986, the inn looks as though it was here long before the village grew up around it. The inn is known for its fine Swiss food. Although we were visiting during the off season, the restaurant was quite busy. We asked for a window table, then spent the better part of the evening dipping into the fondue, sipping wine, and watching the activity in the village below. Actually, the menu is far more extensive than just fondue. We were most intrigued with a few of the Swiss specialties, such as raclette, which is a crispy wedge of cheese accompanied by jacket potatoes, onions, gherkins, tomatoes, or mushrooms. More familiar dishes were the veal cordon bleu and the wiener schnitzel — both are light and delicious. All meals are served with vegetables and a choice of potatoes. Two of the more popular potato dishes are the roesti potatoes and the special Silver Lode potatoes. After dinner, we gravitated to the fireside lounge for a hot toddy before retiring. During the summer months, most guests love to sit out on the deck and enjoy their food amid planters overflowing with flowers.

While dogs are welcome in the guest rooms, they do need to steer clear of the dining room. They can do this by coming in through a separate entrance that connects directly into the guest room wing. The bedrooms lie off one long hallway and are just what we would expect of a ski lodge. They are perfectly functional, exceptionally clean, but a little on the Spartan side. We were told that they are going to be refurbished soon. For now, guests can expect to see pretty floral curtains at the windows that match the spread on the bed. Some opt for a room with either a queen bed and a sofa bed or perhaps a pair of adjoining rooms with a kitchenette. The kitchenettes are a good option, because they come with a small refrigerator, a sink, and a two-burner stove top that allows guests to create a few simple lunches and dinners. At the end of the hall, there is a private hot tub that guests are welcome to use.

In the winter, the emphasis is obviously on skiing, both downhill and cross-country. This place isn't huge, yet somehow there are 81 runs and 2,500 vertical feet packed onto the mountain. The inn also offers a High Altitude Training Center; this attracts members of the Canadian Ski Team, who like to train here. There is also plenty of après ski activity, with an old-fashioned saloon, along with a theatrical group known as the Silver Star Players. Just across from the inn, visitors will find Doc Willies, which is outfitted with a swimming pool and a Jacuzzi and spa for loosening up tired muscles at the end of the day. Within walking distance of the inn is Brewers Pond, for ice skating.

The summer months are not quite as busy, but they are an equally enticing time for mountain bikers and Rollerbladers, who come to test their mettle on these hills. The chair lift will transport people up the mountain; they can mountain bike back down again. Dogs can walk just about anywhere their human friends want to go, and there are plenty of **hiking trails** that lead through forests, near creeks, and into scenic valleys. It is fine to have a dog here and to ski as well. The mountain is so small that it is easy to ski for a couple of hours, come back to the inn for lunch, walk the dog, and then head back out again while the canine naps.

Dashwood Manor

One Cook Street
Victoria, B.C., Canada V8W 3W6
(250) 385-5517, E-mail: reservations@dashwoodmanor.com
Internet: http://www.dashwoodmanor.com

Hosts: *Derek Dashwood and Family*
Rooms: *14 suites*
Canadian Rates: *$115-285 (B&B), Weekly and monthly rates available*
Payment: *AE, MC, and VISA*
Dogs: *Welcome*
Children: *Welcome*
Open: *All year*

Dashwood Manor. The name alone conjures up images of aristocracy and great wealth. The story behind this Edwardian Tudor Revival home is not of the idle rich, but of a dedicated young man working to fulfill a dream. The house was built in 1912 in a neighborhood of other lavish homes that line a bluff overlooking the Strait of Juan de Fuca. Little expense was spared when building this manor, with slashed grain fir paneling in the main hallways and white oak paneling in the dining room. As with most houses of this era, the ornate plaster work was reserved for the public spaces; today's guests can still find some of it in the Windsor Oak or Oxford Grand suites.

Although the house changed hands a few times over the years, it was not until the building was converted from a private home to apartments that it really began to deteriorate. Derek Dashwood watched the property's decline and decided to purchase it in 1978. The price tag alone was daunting, but the work that needed to be done was even more so. It nearly bankrupted him, as the rent from the apartment dwellers could not even begin to cover the maintenance costs. Derek carefully planned the building's final restoration and converted the 8 apartments into 14 suites. In the winter months, they are occupied as long term rentals, with returning guests booking into the next century. During the other three months of the year, these suites are rented by the night or the week, opening their doors to guests and their vacationing dogs.

We followed the shoreline drive from Victoria's harbor to the manor. There are faster ways to get from there to here, but this was by far the most scenic. Along the way, we passed all sorts of people and their dogs walking along the sea wall that edges the ocean. At the far end of Beacon Hill Park, we found the Dashwood Manor. From the exterior, this is still an imposing structure, with its dark timber beams and multiple eaves rising up three stories. We suspected that all the rooms facing the ocean have remarkable views — and we were right.

Stepping through the front door is similar to entering a medieval manor. Dark, paneled walls line the foyer and the massive central staircase. Sunlight streams in through the six-foot-high stained glass window at the top of the landing, and down the stairwell into the foyer. The air was faintly scented by wood smoke drifting out from the stone fireplace. We spent some time admiring the engravings of the English countryside, along with the antique brass plates that lined the walls, before beginning our tour of the Dashwood Manor.

Guests with dogs might want to think about reserving one of the first-floor bedrooms, as these have the easiest access to the outdoors. The Oxford Grand suite offers fabulous views of the ocean, through a plate glass window inset with stained glass. This was the house's original parlor, a place where the men used to gather after dinner. In similar fashion, suite guests may come back here in the evenings and relax before the fire. An adjacent alcove, separated from the parlor by a wide arch, holds a queen bed and an antique bureau. The colors in this suite are a dusty pink, and the furnishings, while antique, are a bit on the worn side. Across the hall is the Windsor Oak Room, which has just as much character. The simple furnishings are surrounded by beamed ceilings, oak paneling, and a fireplace. The room overlooks Beacon Hill Park, and also has glimpses of the ocean.

The remaining suites are found upstairs, with the most newly renovated chamber situated on the second floor, and the most original located on the third floor. What the third floor rooms may lack in modern amenities, they more than make up for in unparalleled ocean views. The most recently refurbished suites have light oak reproduction furnishings, while the older rooms contain a combination of antiques and comfortably worn pieces. Cambridge is one of these newly restored spaces — in fact, it still smelled like freshly cut timber. It is a corner suite, with a tiled Jacuzzi tucked into one corner. Dark green colors combine with the natural wood paneling to create a garden room setting. When Derek described these second-floor suites, he also shared with us the names of some who once slept here. For instance, the light and festive Chelsea Room was Arthur Lineham's bedroom. (He commissioned the house). The Tudor Room is a bachelor suite today, but was once Miss Madigan's bedroom, the nanny to the Lineham's children. We liked the cozy feeling of the Tudor Room, with its plush, green carpet and brass bed tucked up against a half wall. Guests look through the large windows for indirect ocean views. Those staying in the third-floor suites see only the sea and sky. Camelot is one of these expansive suites, set up in the third floor's eaves. This space could use new carpeting; however, it is the most versatile suite, with a queen bed and two sofa beds. The best combination of views and luxury are found in the Somerset, as the remodeled bathroom is huge and contains a Jacuzzi. Guests also have a private balcony to sit on, where they can easily enjoy the sunset over the sea and mountains. Access to the third-floor chambers can be attained through an outside staircase, making them acceptable choices for those who are concerned about making too much noise walking their dogs late at night.

We were impressed with the thoughtful amenities in all the suites. The bathrooms, both new and old, have a full complement of Lord and Mayfair soaps and shampoos. Guests can be totally self-sufficient, as all suites have full kitchens that are stocked with everything they might need to create their own breakfasts. Eggs, bacon, bread, juice, and coffee are some of the basics, which can be supplemented with a few goodies from the local bakeries and food shops.

We really like the Dashwood Manor's location, and not just because of its views. It is easy to walk dogs here — we just stepped out the front door and across the street to the promenade that winds along the sea. The Manor is also right next door to **Beacon Hill Park**, a lovely place with all sorts of intriguing areas for a dog to investigate. There are 185 acres to visit, including formal gardens, ponds, and fountains, all intertwined with paths. A twenty-minute walk through the park puts visitors and their dogs in downtown Victoria. Since parking can be difficult, this is an ideal and energetic option. Another possible outing is to climb up **Moss Rock on Fairfield Hill** — or walk along **Dallas Road** back toward Victoria. Along the way, visitors are certain to meet all sorts of local dogs out enjoying the day as well.

Laurel Point Inn

680 Montreal Street
Victoria, B.C., Canada, V8V 1Z8
(800) 663-7667, (250) 386-8721, Fax: (250) 386-9547
Internet: http://www.islandnet.com/~cvprod/laurel.html

General Manager: *Spencer Villam*
Rooms: *200 doubles and suites*
Rates: *Doubles $125-185 (EP), Suites $140-650 (EP)*
Payment: *AE, ENR, MC, and VISA*
Dogs: *Welcome*
Children: *Welcome (cribs, cots, and high chairs are available)*
Open: *All year*

For pure convenience to downtown Victoria and its inner harbor, it is difficult to beat the Laurel Point Inn. Located on a six-acre point of land overlooking Victoria's inner harbor, this resort-style hotel is hard to miss. Its white facade and graduated levels are reminiscent of a cruise liner, particularly the hotel's newer South Wing, which was designed by world-renowned architect Arthur Erickson and completed in 1989. The main part of the resort began operations in 1979, which gave the grounds, the gardens, and reflecting pools time to mature into its current tableau of lush greenery and light.

As we walked through the Laurel Point Inn's public areas, we noticed the absence of important pieces of art and lavish furnishings. Yet the rather Spartan decor drew our eyes to the walls of glass opening onto the gardens, pools, and even a waterfall. One of our favorite spaces is the outdoor terrace, which overlooks a reflecting pond and extensive Japanese gardens. Other atrium spaces dotted with chairs invite guests to linger awhile.

The motif of the public areas is carried through to the guest bedrooms. The lines are clean and contemporary — "Asian minimalist" might be the best way to describe them. Light woods, neutral earth-tone color schemes, and contemporary furnishings meld with their surroundings. Once again, it is the views that are highlighted, often through floor-to-ceiling windows.

Although the guest rooms in the older North Wing were renovated recently, we recommend chambers in the South Wing. Most of these spaces offer unobstructed water views, especially in the suites. Even without the better vistas, we encourage an upgrade from a standard deluxe room to a junior suite — the true stars of the hotel. We particularly enjoyed the separate living and sleeping areas in the suites, which often are enhanced by shoji screens. The oversized marble bathrooms are fashioned with soaking tubs, glassed-in showers, telephones, televisions, and a host of toiletries. The small refrigerators in the suites are quite handy for cooling drinks or keeping any extra goodies for discerning canines.

British Columbia

Although there are plenty of fine restaurants in Victoria within easy walking distance of the hotel, it would be difficult to find better views than those of the Laurel Point Inn. The casual Cafe Laurel provides most meals. Patrons can choose between a bistro menu or slightly more intriguing fare. The oysters Victoria are dressed with brandy, garlic, and herbs and the native smoked salmon is served more simply with capers and lemon wedges. Intriguing entrées included the gingered prawns, roast duck with an orange sauce, and the lamb Santa Fe served on creamed garlic and roasted onions.

We applaud the Laurel Point Inn's attitude toward dogs — all sizes are welcome at this city hotel. Best of all, there are a number of things to do in and around the complex — consult with the **front desk** for a list of options. While the water might lure some dogs, please keep them on the walking paths that surround the inn. Take more extensive trips along the waterfront, or follow the sea-**wall** that runs past the inner harbor. A short walk in one direction leads to Victoria's beaches. Head off to one of Victoria's parks — Beacon Hill Park where visitors and their dogs have acres to explore, throw a Frisbee, or just relax in the sun.

Ocean Pointe Resort

On the Harbour at 45 Songhees Road
Victoria, B.C., Canada V9A 6T3
(800) 667-4OPR, (250) 360-2999, Fax: (250) 360-1041
E-Mail: ocean_pointe@pinc.com, Internet: http://www.opr.hotel.com

General Manager: *F. Ulrich "Rick" Stolle*
Rooms: *217 doubles, 33 suites*
Rates: *Doubles $120-220 (EP), Suites $170-400 (EP)*
Payment: *AE, CB, DC, JCB, MC and VISA*
Dogs: *Welcome with a $50 fee*
Children: *Welcome (cribs, cots, high chairs, and baby-sitters are available)*
Open: *All year*

Someone once said, "that if they built it no one would come." Yet the magnificent Ocean Pointe Resort continues to defy this prediction, despite its location across the Johnson Street Bridge in an area that was known more for its factories than for its residential qualities. Implementing their vision that this harbor-front site would be the perfect place for a luxury hotel, Kathryn and Rick Stolle opened the Ocean Pointe Resort in 1992. It is clearly here to stay, as everyone from the readers of Condé Naste to the staff at Consumer Reports touts the Ocean Pointe Resort as the place to stay in Victoria. We have to agree.

Victoria

The elegant resort attracts an upscale clientele seeking to escape life's pressures. The combination of a full-service spa, fine restaurants, and restful public areas and guest rooms combine to create the ultimate in luxury. As we drew closer, we saw that the "walls" offering the loveliest views of all — looking across to the Parliament Buildings (illuminated at night with twinkling lights) and Victoria's picturesque harbor — were actually glass. The architect who designed the resort sought to create a European look that maintained a warm, residential ambiance. From the exterior, the hotel resembles a contemporary chateau with sharply peaked roofs, arches, and even a few rotundas.

As we stepped inside, we felt comfortable amid the mix of wood, granite, and slate interspersed with an assortment of live plants and even a caged bird or two. The entire interior seems to flow, with few straight edges. A staircase curves up from the lobby; seating arrangements have a circular configuration; and walls seemingly meld into the windows. The Victorian Restaurant is the perfect example of this architecture, with three walls of glass surrounding patrons in a pavilion-like setting. The food here is some of the finest in Victoria, and highlights West Coast Canadian cuisine. During the summer months, many guests prefer the Boardwalk Restaurant, as it opens directly onto the paths that meander about the resort.

The guest bedrooms offer a similar mix of light woods, warm color schemes, and interesting nooks. The decor is contemporary with a European twist. Quilted spreads with dust ruffles sport handsome floral fabrics, while brass lamps, armoires, and writing desks fill the rest of these oversized chambers. The details are excellent, including lights in the closets that illuminate when opened, ample drawer space for long-term guests, and marble bathrooms with all the amenities. Televisions and minibars are tucked into the armoires, and other high-tech gadgetry such as fax lines and modems are concealed.

Those who want the top level in service should request the Executive Club Class, where they will discover that evening turn-down, coffee makers, in-room pressing, and irons and ironing boards are standard. Bathrooms in these upscale rooms also contain hair dryers, make-up mirrors, and thick cotton bathrobes. Executive Club Class guests receive a complimentary continental breakfast, parking, and free local telephone calls. All guests, though, regardless of room choice, will appreciate the staff-to-guest ratio — 150 staff for the 250 guest rooms and suites.

The on-site spa is a huge draw for many of the Ocean Pointe's patrons. One can choose to be pampered or tone muscles — or possibly a little of both. We particularly liked the unusual indoor swimming pool, which is equipped with a special ozone filter (rather than using chlorine) for cleaning and which opens directly onto the boardwalk. Tennis courts, a squash/racquetball court, and even a jogging path complete the extensive list of potential activities at the resort.

Although dogs would eschew most of these amenities, a stroll along the **walking trail** will surely peak any canine's interest. The trail begins just outside the resort and meanders along the shoreline. We also enjoyed the resort's easy access to green spaces and waterfront. For those who like a little adventure, we recommend a five-minute walk over the bridge to town, where there are a number of verdant spaces worth visiting. Beacon **Hill Park** is one of the more popular choices, with its forested trails around both **Beaver and Elk Lakes**. Visitors also might want to climb Moss **Rock on Fairfield Hill**. All in all, we found Victoria to be a very dog-friendly town with plenty of places to delight both people and their beasts.

Chateau Whistler Resort

4599 Chateau Blvd.
Whistler, B.C., Canada V0N 1B4
(800) 441-1414, (604) 938-8000, Fax: (604) 938-2020

General Manager: *David Roberts*
Rooms: *306 doubles, 36 suites*
Canadian Rates: *Doubles $125-335 (EP), Suites $400-1,100 (EP)*
Payment: *AE, CB, DC, DSC, JCB, MC, and VISA*
Dogs: *Welcome with a $20 nightly fee, and must be attended at all times*
Children: *Welcome (cribs, cots, high chairs, and baby-sitters are available)*
Open: *All year*

The Chateau Whistler was the first mountain resort chateau built in almost 100 years by Canadian Pacific Hotels and Resorts. This place is so extraordinary, that we wouldn't be surprised if it took another 100 years to create anything else comparable. The drive from Vancouver along the Sea to Sky Highway was, as usual, spectacular. Cliffs dropping thousands of feet to the ocean gave way to mountain valleys and snow-capped peaks. We so enjoyed the vistas, that it felt as though we arrived in Whistler before out journey had even gotten under way. The 12-story Chateau Whistler should stand out in this valley, but instead, it is nestled above the main village in the foothills of Blackcomb Mountain. The hotel was all we had imagined a great chateau to be — turrets, spires, and steeply sloping roofs set against this lush, mountainous landscape.

This feeling is carried through to the interior spaces as well, especially in the Great Hall, where even royalty would feel at home. The exposed beams of the vaulted ceilings rise 60 feet above the hall, while below a combination of stone pillars, slate floors, and pecan paneling surrounds the sumptuous sitting areas. Sophisticated French Provincial furnishings, both antiques and fine reproductions, form small sitting areas. Accents are provided by whimsical folk art, dried and fresh flowers, and woven baskets. At the end of the Great Hall, there is a glass wall that begins at floor level and rises to the peak of the ceiling. This chamber is an excellent spot for guests to settle in. Here, we were not only be privy to terrific views but also the cracking and popping fire in large stone hearth. Aprés ski activity is generally at its best, however, next door in the Mallard Bar. Walls of glass also make this an especially sunny space during the day, but at night it is transformed into an intimate chamber with flickering candlelight reflecting off the wall of glass. A huge stone fireplace, overstuffed chairs, and a warm drink seem like the perfect way to end a day on the slopes.

The resort sits up so high that all of the guest rooms, whether facing Blackcomb or overlooking the valley, have fantastic views. From the smallest to the most elaborate two-story suites, all the guest chambers are well appointed. Handmade quilts top down comforters and fine linens. The furnishings are substantial pieces, and reproduced to emulate fine antiques. Unusual carved headboards crown the beds, while long benches lie at their feet. Some rooms are furnished with armoires edged with carved wood that resembles rope. Baskets and an array of folk art are interspersed into these spaces as well, adding delightful decorative touches. In many rooms, quilts line the walls, while in others, an original watercolor or gilt framed botanical print are placed about the rooms. Each of these spacious chambers also has a residential quality to them, with potted plants and a full array of amenities. Some contain French doors that open to terraces, while the majority have walls of windows that simply provide panoramic views. Well-designed bathrooms offer a full complement of toiletries, along with terry robes, thick towels, and hair dryers. This luxurious setting is also an environmentally correct one, utilizing an extensive recycling program that includes blue bins in the bathrooms, donating unused toiletries to charity, and giving guests the option to go a day without fresh towels.

Wildflowers is the premier restaurant at the hotel, and executive chef Bernard Casavant is renowned for his fine cuisine. The adjoining dining rooms have walls of glass and are decorated in a French Provincial motif, with accents provided by Audubon prints, antiques, and lavish arrangements of fresh flowers. We enjoyed perusing the menu, as much for the innovative offerings as for the lovely watercolor wildflowers printed upon it. The seasonally changing dishes always feature local ingredients and the wine list includes an impressive array of British Columbia vintages. Some might choose to start with an appetizer such as the wild mushroom and ricotta turnover served with a grilled sweet pepper salad; a warm tomato and sundried olive tart with a balsamic essence and basil pesto; or a traditional Caesar salad topped with either baby shrimp, smoked salmon, or roasted garlic. Entrées on the fall menu included a barbecued duck breast with sundried cranberry crepes; a rack of lamb with a sweet mustard and a wild mint crust, or the Harvest buffet. On weekend nights, guests can come and sample a wide range of culinary treats, that include fresh seasonal salads, baked wild salmon, roast prime rib, harvest vegetables, and the best of all, the dessert buffet. The breakfast buffet is equally lavish.

Dogs and Whistler seem like natural extensions of one another. Canines can walk the **Valley Trail** that winds by the resort and throughout the valley. In the summer, people Rollerblade along this trail and in the winter it becomes a cross-country ski trail. We suggest taking Bowser on a hike to either **Joffre Lake**, **Rainbow Lake**, or **Singing Pass**. More leisurely outings are available in any of the area's **provincial parks**, near **Nairn Falls** or **Birkenhead Lake**. If this is a family trip, we can recommend a number of good hikes for children and dogs. Follow the **Lost Lake Trail**, which can be picked up in the village, for an easy day hike with young ones. The **Cheakamus Lake Trails** can be found off the Cheakamus Lake Road, just off Highway 99. Follow this trail to the **Singing Creek Trail**, which is a slightly more difficult route, that is probably better for older children. Everyone will enjoy a visit to the **Ancient Cedars** of Cougar Mountain. Drive up Cougar Mountain to **Showh Lake**. The short trail leads to a forest of ancient cedar trees that are so big a family would have to link hands just to surround one. Less dog-oriented options include skiing in the winter, and golf in the summer months on the resort's Robert Trent Jones course. Windsurfing, mountain biking, river rafting, and Rollerblading are also very popular diversions at Whistler. At the end of the day, when the muscles have had just about enough, we recommend investigating the fabulous spa at Chateau Whistler. This is, without a doubt, the place for some lavish pampering. The indoor/outdoor swimming pool is complemented by a soaking tub, hot tubs, saunas, steam rooms, and a weight room. The spa offers a full range of services, including massage therapy, herbs for detoxification, and facials. Now all they need to do is implement a comparable doggie program and we would almost feel a little less guilty for enjoying all these facilities as much as we do.

Listel Whistler Hotel

4121 Village Green
Whistler, B.C., Canada V0N 1B0
(800) 663-5472, (604) 932-1133, Fax: (604) 932-8383

Manager: Brian Ennis
Rooms: 100 doubles, 4 suites
Canadian Rates: $99-229 (B&B), Suites $155-395 (B&B)
Payment: AE, ENR, DC, DSC, JCB, MC, and VISA
Dogs: Welcome
Children: Welcome; under 16 years of age are free of charge when sharing a room with their parents
Open: All year

The Listel Whistler Hotel came as a complete surprise to us. We arrived in Whistler prepared to write about the Delta Hotel Whistler, but were drawn instead to this far more intimate hotel, which is also situated in the village. The Delta is an enormous and somewhat impersonal hotel that does in fact take dogs; however, we preferred the more reasonable rates and intimate character of the Listel Whistler Hotel.

The Listel Whistler is set in the village at the base of Whistler and Blackcomb mountains. Brightly colored international flags line the rooftop of this attractive, three-story building. The small lobby is as welcoming as its staff. After acquainting us with the hotel, they showed us a range of accommodations. We walked down wide hallways painted an appealing shade of salmon, lined with hunter green carpets. Prospective guests may choose between rooms facing the ski mountains or rooms looking over the valley. Regardless of choice, most should be pleased with these chambers, even though they are a little on the cozy side. We suggest requesting a king bedded room, as the standard rooms with two queen beds have just enough additional space for the bureau and a small table flanked by a pair of chairs. We liked the interesting eaves in the top-floor bedrooms, and the fact that the windows were designed to resemble the shape of the dormers.

Beds are covered with festive and contemporary Northwest native-patterned spreads. Chairs are constructed out of light woods with caned backs. Remote controlled televisions offer movie systems, and clock radios and direct dial telephones add to the list of standard amenities. Families will need two rooms, or they may request one of the larger suites. The most spacious of these is the Executive Suite, which has a king-bedded room separated from a fireplaced living room by a pair of French doors. The two couches in the living room fold out and a large table can easily accommodate the family's breakfast needs. The junior suite, on the other hand, is equipped with a bedroom with a good-sized sitting room. In the morning, a Continental breakfast is waiting downstairs, but guests who happen to wake up a little early can also take advantage of the coffee maker in the room to brew a cup of coffee. (Starbucks is in the village — for those who want to buy a package of gourmet coffee, or who would just prefer for someone else to make their morning coffee.) Guests can also store drinks and snacks, or cans of dog food, in the small refrigerators. Some will be pleased to know there is a valet and guest laundry.

These features are all typical of a larger property, but in a hotel of this size they are an unexpected pleasantry. We also enjoyed the outdoor, heated swimming pool, Jacuzzi, and saunas. Alpine and Nordic skiers will be happy to know that they may store their skis in a special area, so they don't have to worry about lugging them up to the rooms. Convenient underground parking is available to hotel guests, for a small fee. After skiing or a day spent hiking, guests tend to gravitate to the intimate Rodeo Bar. This is a welcoming space, where people hang out in front of the fire, along the intimate bar, or over by the dart boards. Parents would even feel comfortable relaxing in here with their children before heading around the corner for dinner. There are, of course, plenty of other great restaurants within walking distance of the Listel, but after a long day of exercise it is sometimes nice just to eat in.

O'Doul's is the café-style restaurant, which resembles something out of the Caribbean, with its festive green and peach wall treatment, tropical plants, and ceiling fans. Two walls of windows look out towards the golf course or up to the mountains. Some guests might start their meal with the West Coast seafood chowder, escargots Provençale, or the prawns St. Tropez. The latter are fried with cayenne and red peppers, then seasoned with white wine and lemon. The salads and pastas looked excellent; but then again, so did the fresh trout stuffed with Dungeness crab and the fisherman's stew of prawns, scallops, mussels, salmon, clams, and shrimp. Those with a hearty appetite can request the filet mignon with mushrooms and Bernaise sauce, the rack of lamb with a sweet vermouth sauce, or the delicious prime rib.

Dogs love it at Whistler. They have **mountains to climb** and **rivers to explore** in the immediate vicinity, and more **provincial parks** situated in the outlying area than they could visit in a year. The **Valley Trail** is a paved trail that starts at one end of the valley and encircles it. Fun day hikes can be taken to **Singing Pass-Russet Lake** and to **Rainbow Lake**. Another popular option that is a bit shorter and easier than most, leads dogs and their human counterparts to **Lost Lake Park**. With the onset of snow, many of these trails become **fine cross-country ski trails**. Guests can either cross-country or downhill ski in the morning, make a short trip back over to the hotel at lunch time, and pick up Bowser for a little impromptu **walk about the village**.

The Best of the Rest

B&B, Inns, Motels, and Hotels

California

AGOURA HILLS
- Radisson Hotel
  30100 Agoura Rd.
  (818) 707-1220

ALTURAS
- Best Western Trailside
  343 North Main St.
  (916) 233-4111

ANAHEIM
- Anaheim Hilton
  777 Convention Way
  (714) 750-4321
- Anaheim Inn at the Park
  1855 So. Harbor Blvd.
  (714) 750-1811
- Anaheim Marriott
  700 West Convention Way
  (714) 750-8000
- Best Western Stardust
  1057 West Ball Rd.
  (714) 772-2470
- Cavalier Inn
  11811 S. Harbor Blvd.
  (714) 750-1000
- Holiday Inn at the Park
  1221 S. Harbor Blvd.
  (714) 772-0900
- Quality Inn
  616 Convention Way
  (714) 750-3131
- Residence Inn
  1700 S. Clementine
  (714) 533-3555
- Station Inn
  989 W. Ball Rd.
  (714) 991-5500
- Travelodge at the Park
  1166 W. Katella Ave.
  (714) 774-7817

ANAHEIM HILLS
- Best Western
  5710 East La Palma Ave.
  (714) 779-0252

ANDERSON
- Anderson Valley Inn
  2861 McMurray Dr.
  (916) 365-2566

- Best Western Knight's Inn
  2688 Gateway Dr.
  (916) 365-2753

ANGELS CAMP
- Angels Inn Motel
  600 N. Main
  (209) 736-4242
- Gold Country Inn
  330 Murphys Grade Rd.
  (209) 736-4611

ANTIOCH
- Best Western
  3210 Delta Fair Blvd.
  (510) 778-2000
- Ramada Inn
  2436 Mahogany Way
  (510) 754-6600

APTOS
- Best Western Seacliff Inn
  7500 Old Dominion Ct.
  (408) 688-7300

ARCADIA
- Hampton Inn
  311 E. Huntington Dr.
  (818) 574-5600
- Residence Inn
  321 E. Huntington Dr.
  (818) 446-5824

ARCATA
- Best Western Arcata
  4827 Valley West Blvd.
  (707) 826-0313
- Comfort Inn
  4701 Valley West Blvd.
  (707) 826-2827
- North Coast Inn
  4975 Valley West Blvd.
  (707) 822-8888
- Quality Inn-Mad River
  3535 Janes Rd.
  (707) 822-0409
- Super 8
  4887 Valley West Blvd.
  (707) 822-8888

ARROYO GRANDE
Best Western Casa Grande
850 Oak Park Rd.
(805) 481-7398
ATASCADERO
Best Western Colony Inn
3600 El Camino Real
(805) 466-4449
AUBURN
Best Western Golden Key
13450 Lincoln Way
(916) 885-8611
Holiday Inn
120 Grass Valley Hwy
(916) 887-8787
BAKERSFIELD
Best Western Heritage Inn
253 Trask St
(805) 764-6268
Best Western Hill House
700 Truxtun Ave.
(805) 327-4064
California Inn
1030 Wible Rd
(805) 834-3377
La Quinta
3232 Riverside Dr.
(805) 325-7400
Lone Oak Inn
10614 Rosedale Hwy
(805) 589-6600
Quality Inn
1011 Oak St.
(805) 325-0772
Red Lion Inn
3100 Camino del Rio
(805) 327-7111
Residence Inn
4241 Chester Ln.
(805) 321-9800
BARSTOW
Super 8
170 Coolwater Lane
(760) 256-8443
BASS LAKE
Forks Resort
39150 Rte. 222
(209) 642-3737

BELMONT
Holiday Inn
1101 Shoreway Rd.
(415) 591-1471
BENICIA
Best Western Heritage Inn
1955 East 2nd St
(707) 746-0401
BIG BEAR
Eagle's Nest B&B
41675 Big Bear Blvd.
(909) 866-6465
Frontier Lodge
40472 Big Bear Blvd.
(909) 866-5888
Grey Squirrel Resort
Big Bear Blvd.
(909) 866-4335
Happy Bear Village
40154 Big Bear Blvd.
(909) 866-2415
Robinhood Inn
Lakeview Drive
(909) 866-8200
Thundercloud Resort
40598 Lakeview Drive
(909) 866-7594
Timber Haven Lodge
877 Tulip Lane
(909) 866-3568
Wildwood Resort
40210 Big Bear Blvd.
(909) 878-2178
Wishing Well Motel
540 Pine Knot Blvd.
(909) 866-3505
BIG PINE
Big Pine Motel
370 South Main
(760) 938-2282
BISHOP
Best Western Creekside
725 N. Main St.
(760) 872-3044
Best Western Holiday Spa
1025 North Main St.
(760) 873-3543
Bishop Inn
805 North Main St.
(760) 873-4284

California

Rodeway Inn
150 East Elm St.
(760) 873-3564
Sierra Foothills Motel
535 South Main St.
(760) 872-1386
Vagabond Inn
1030 North Main St
(760) 873-6351
BLYTHE
Best Western Sahara Motel
825 W. Hobson Way
(760) 922-7105
Best Western Tropics Motel
9274 East Hobson Way
(760) 922-5101
Comfort Inn
903 W. Hobson Way
(760) 922-4146
Hampton Inn
900 W. Hobson Way
(760) 922-9000
Holiday Inn
600 West Donion St
(760) 921-2300
BODEGA BAY
Bodega Coast Inn
521 Highway 1
(707) 875-2217
BOULDER CREEK
Town House Lodge
135 Main St
(760) 344-5120
BORREGO SPRINGS
La Casa del Zorro
3845 Yaqui Pass Rd.
(619) 767-5323
BRAWLEY
Townhouse Lodge
135 Main St.
(619) 344-5120
BREA
Woodfin Suites
3100 E. Imperial Hwy.
(714) 579-3200
BRIDGEPORT
Best Western Ruby Inn
333 Main St.
(760) 932-7241

Walker River Lodge
One Main St.
(760) 932-7021
BUELTON
Econo Lodge
630 Ave. of the Flags
(805) 688-0022
BUENA PARK
Colony Inn
7800 Crescent Ave.
(714) 527-2201
BURBANK
Burbank Airport Hilton
2500 Hollywood Way
(818) 843-6000
Holiday Inn
150 East Angeleno
(818) 841-4770
Ramada Inn Burbank Airport
2900 N. San Fernando Blvd.
(818) 843-5955
BURLINGAME
Days Inn-Airport
777 Airport Rd.
(415) 342-7772
Doubletree Hotel
835 Airport Blvd.
(415) 344-5500
Embassy Suites
150 Anza Blvd.
(415) 342-4600
Marriott-Airport
1800 Old Bayshore Hwy.
(415) 692-9100
Radisson Hotel-Airport
1177 Airport Blvd.
(415) 342-9200
Red Roof Inn
777 Airport Blvd.
(415) 342-7772
BURNEY
Shasta Pines Motel
37386 Main St
(916) 335-2201
BUTTONWILLOW
Good Nite Inn
20645 Tracy Road
(805) 764-5121
Super 8 Motel
20681 Tracy Road
(805) 764-5117

California

CALIPATRIA
  Calipatria Inn
    Route 111
    (760) 348-7348
CALISTOGA
  Mountain Home Ranch
    3400 Mountain Home Rd.
    (707) 942-6616
CAMBRIA
  Cambria Pines Lodge
    2905 Burton Dr.
    (805) 927-4200
  Cambria Shores Inn
    6276 Moonstone Beach Dr
    (805) 927-8644
  Mariners Inn
    6180 Moonstone Beach Dr.
    (805) 927-4624
CAMERON PARK
  Best Western Cameron Park
    3361 Coach Lane
    (916) 677-2203
CAMPBELL
  Residence Inn
    2761 S. Bascom Ave.
    (408) 559-1551
CANOGA PARK
  Warner Center Motor Inn
    7132 DeSoto Ave.
    (818) 346-5400
CAPITOLA
  Capitola Inn
    822 Bay Ave.
    (408) 462-3004
CARLSBAD
  Carlsbad/La Costa Travelodge
    760 Macademia Dr.
    (760) 438-2828
  Four Seasons Resort Aviara
    7100 Four Seasons Point
    (760) 931-6672 (open 7/97)
  Inns of America
    751 Raintree Dr.
    (760) 931-1185
CARMEL-BY-THE-SEA
  Carmel Country Inn
    3rd and Dolores
    (408) 625-3263

Carmel Garden Court
  Fourth and Torres
  (408) 624-6942
Carmel Mission Inn
  3665 Rio Rd.
  (408) 624-1841
Carmel Tradewinds Inn
  Mission and Third
  (408) 624-2776
Coachman's Inn
  San Carlos St.
  (4080 624-6421
Dolores Lodge
  Ocean Ave.
  (408) 625-3263
CARPINTERIA
  Best Western Carpinteria Inn
    4558 Carpinteria Ave.
    (805) 684-0473
CASTAIC
  Castaic Inn
    31411 Ridge Rt.
    (805) 257-0229
CASTRO VALLEY
  Castro Valley Travelodge
    2532 Castro Valley Blvd.
    (510) 538-9501
CATHEDRAL CITY
  Days Inn
    69-151 E. Palm Canyon Dr.
    (760) 324-5939
  Doubletree Resort
    67-967 Vista Chino
    (760) 322-7000
CERRITOS
  Sheraton Hotel
    12725 Center Court Dr
    (562) 809-1500
  Summerfield Suites
    21902 Lassen St.
    (562) 773-0707
CHATSWORTH
  Summerfield Suites
    21920 Lassen St
    (818) 773-0707
CHICO
  Holiday Inn of Chico
    685 Manzanita Ct.
    (916) 345-2491

CHULA VISTA
    Chula Vista Travelodge
        394 Broadway at G St.
        (619) 420-6600
    Good Nite Inn
        225 Bay Blvd.
        (619) 425-8200
    La Quinta
        150 Bonita Rd.
        (619) 691-1211
CITRUS HEIGHTS
    Olive Grove Suites
        6143 Auburn Blvd.
        (916) 725-0100
CLAREMONT
    Ramada Inn & Tennis Club
        840 S. Indian Hill Blvd.
        (909) 621-6559
CLEARLAKE OAKS
    Lake Point Lodge
        13440 East Route 20
        (707) 998-4350
COALINGA
    Big Country Inn
        25020 W. Dolores Ave.
        (209) 935-0866
COLOMA
    Golden Lotus
        1006 Lotus Rd.
        (916) 621-4562
COMMERCE
    Ramada Inn
        7272 Gage Ave.
        (562) 806-4777
    Wyndham Garden Hotel
        5757 Telegraph Rd.
        (213) 887-8100
CONCORD
    Holiday Inn
        1050 Burnett Ave.
        (510) 687-5500
    Sheraton Hotel
        45 John Glenn Dr.
        (510) 825-7700
CORNING
    Corning Olive Inn
        2165 Solano St.
        (916) 824-2468

    Days Inn
        3475 Hwy. 99 W.
        (916) 824-2000
    Shilo Inn
        3350 Sunrise Way
        (916) 824-2940
CORONA
    Dynasty Suites
        1805 West 6th St
        (909) 371-7185
CORONADO
    Le Meridien San Diego
        2000 2nd St.
        (619) 435-3000
COSTA MESA
    Best Western Newport Mesa
        2642 Newport Blvd.
        (714) 650-3020
    Comfort Inn
        2430 Newport Blvd.
        (714) 650-3020
    La Quinta
        1515 S. Coast Dr.
        (714) 957-5841
    Newport Bay Inn
        2070 Newport Blvd.
        (714) 631-6000
    Ramada Limited
        1680 Superior Ave.
        (714) 645-2221
    Red Lion Hotel
        3050 Bristol St.
        (714) 540-7000
    Residence Inn
        881 W. Baker St.
        (714) 241-8800
    Westin South Coast Hotel
        686 Anton Blvd.
        (714) 540-2500
    Wyndham Garden Hotel
        3350 Ave of the Arts
        (714) 751-5100
CRESCENT CITY
    Pacific Motor Hotel
        440 Hwy 101 North
        (707) 464-4141
    Super 8 Motel
        685 Route 101
        (707) 464-4111

California

CULVER CITY
  Red Lion Hotel-LA Airport
    6161 Centinela Blvd.
    (310) 649-1776
CYPRESS
  Woodfin Suites
    5905 Corporate Ave.
    (714) 828-4000
DANVILLE
  Danville Inn
    803 Camino Ramon
    (510) 838-8080
DAVIS
  Best Western University Lodge
    123 B Street
    (916) 756-7890
  University Inn B&B
    340 A Street
    (916) 756-8648
DEATH VALLEY
  Stove Pipe Wells Village
    Route 190
    (760) 786-2387
DELANO
  Comfort Inn
    2211 Girard St.
    (805) 725-1022
  Shilo Inn
    2231 Girard St.
    (805) 725-7551
DEL MAR
  Del Mar Hilton
    15575 Jimmy Durante Blvd.
    (619) 792-5200
  Del Mar Inn
    720 Camino Del Mar
    (619) 755-9765
DIXON
  Best Western Inn
    1345 Commercial Way
    (916) 678-1400
DOWNEY
  Embassy Suites
    8245 Firestone Blvd.
    (562) 861-1900
DUNNIGAN
  Best Western Inn
    Route I-5
    (916) 724-3471

  IMA Value Lodge
    Route I-5
    (916) 724-3333
DUNSMUIR
  Cave Springs
    4727 Dunsmuir Ave.
    (916) 235-2721
  Cedar Lodge Motel
    4201 Dunsmuir Ave.
    (916) 235-4331
  Dunsmuir Travelodge
    5400 Dunsmuir Ave.
    (916) 235-4395
EL CAJON
  Best Western
    1355 East Main St.
    (619) 440-7378
  Travelodge
    471 N. Magnolia Ave.
    (619) 447-3999
EL CENTRO
  Barbara Worth Golf Resort
    2050 Country Club Road
    (760) 356-2806
  Brunner's
    215 N. Imperial Ave.
    (760) 352-6431
  El Dorado Motel
    1464 Adams Ave.
    (760) 352-7333
  Ramada Inn
    1455 Ocotillo Dr.
    (760) 352-5152
  Vacation Inn
    2015 Cottonwood Circle
    (760) 352-9523
EL PORTAL
  Yosemite View Motel
    11136 Route 140
    (209) 379-2681
EL SEGUNDO
  Crown Sterling Suites-LAX
    1440 E. Imperial Ave.
    (310) 640-3600
  Embassy Suites
    1440 East Imprerial Ave.
    (310) 640-3600
  Summerfield Suites
    810 So. Douglas Ave.
    (310) 725-0100

California

Travelodge at LAX
1804 E. Sycamore
(310) 615-1073
ENCINITAS
Friendship Inn
410 N. Highway 101
(760) 436-4999
ESCONDIDO
Sheridan Inn
1341 N. Escondido Blvd.
(760) 743-8338
Super 8 Motel
528 West Washington
(760) 747-3711
EUREKA
Carson House Inn
1209 Fourth St.
(707) 443-1601
Red Lion Inn
1929 Fourth St.
(707) 445-0844
FAIRFIELD
Best Western Cordelia
4873 Central Pl.
(707) 864-2029
FALLBROOK
Best Western Franciscan Inn
1635 S. Mission Rd.
(760) 728-6174
La Estancia Inn
3135 S. Old Hwy.
(760) 723-2888
FORT BRAGG
Beachcomber Motel
1111 North Main St
(707) 964-2402
Cleone Lodge Inn
24600 North Hwy 1
(707) 964-2788
Mendocino Coast Reservations
1000 Main St.
(707) 937-5033
FORTUNA
Best Western Country Inn
1528 Kenmar Rd.
(707) 725-6822
Fortuna Motor Lodge
275 12th St
(707) 725-6993

Super 8 Motel
1805 Alamar Way
(707) 725-2888
Holiday Inn Express
1859 Alamar Way
(707) 725-5500
FOUNTAIN VALLEY
Residence Inn
9930 Slater Ave.
(714) 965-8000
FREMONT
Best Western Thunderbird
5400 Mowry Ave. East
(510) 792-4300
Residence Inn
5400 Farwell Pl.
(510) 794-5900
FRESNO
Best Western Tradewinds
2141 North Parkway Dr.
(209) 237-1881
Days Inn
1101 North Parkway Dr.
(209) 268-6211
Fresno Hilton
1055 Van Ness Ave.
(209) 485-9000
Holiday Inn
2233 Ventura St.
(209) 268-1000
La Quinta
2926 Tulare St.
(209) 442-1110
Super 8
1087 North Parkway Dr.
(209) 268-0741
FULLERTON
Fullerton Inn
2604 W. Orangethorpe Ave.
(714) 773-4900
Fullerton Marriott Hotel
2701 E. Nutwood
(714) 738-7800
GARBERVILLE
Best Western Humboldt House
701 Redwood Dr.
(707) 923-2771

California

Motel Garberville
948 Redwood Dr.
(707) 923-2422
Sherwood Forest Motel
814 Redwood Dr.
(707) 923-2721
GILROY
Leavesley Inn
8430 Murray Ave.
(408) 847-5500
Rodeway Inn
611 Leavesley Rd
(408) 847-0688
GLENDALE
Days Inn
600 North Pacific Ave.
(818) 956-0202
Red Lion
100 W. Glenoaks Rd.
(818) 956-5466
GRANT GROVE
Grant Grove Lodge
Route 180
(209) 235-2314
GRASS VALLEY
Alta Sierra Motel
11858 Tammy Way
(916) 273-9102
Best Western Gold Cntry. Inn
11972 Sutton Way
(916) 273-1393
Golden Chain Motel
Route 49
(916) 273-7279
GROVELAND
Yosemite West Gate Motel
7633 Route 120
(209) 962-5281
GROVER BEACH
Holiday Inn
775 Ocean Park Blvd.
(805) 481-4448
HALF MOON BAY
Ramada Ltd.
3020 No. Cabrillo Hwy.
(415) 726-9700
HANFORD
Irwin St. Inn
522 North Irwin
(209) 583-8000

HAYWARD
Best Western Inn-Hayward
360 West A St.
(510) 785-8700
Executive Inn-Hayward
20777 Hesperian Blvd.
(510) 732-6300
HEALDSBURG
Best Western Dry Creek Inn
198 Dry Creek Rd.
(707) 433-0300
HEMET
Best Western
2625 West Florida Ave.
(909) 925-6605
Hemet Inn
800 W. Florida Ave.
(909) 929-6366
Ramada Inn
3885 W. Florida Ave.
(909) 929-8900
Super 8 Motel
3510 W. Florida Ave.
(909) 658-2281
Travelodge
1201 W. Florida Ave.
(909) 766-1902
HESPERIA
Days Inn
14865 Bear Valley Rd
(760) 948-0600
HOLLYWOOD
Chateau Marmont Hotel
8221 Sunset Blvd.
(213) 656-1010
Holiday Inn-Hollywood
1755 N. Highland Ave.
(213) 462-7181
HOLTVILLE
Barbara Worth Country Club
2050 Country Club Dr.
(619) 356-2806
IDYLLWILD
Fireside Inn
54540 N. Circle Dr.
(909) 659-2966
IMPERIAL BEACH
Best Western Imperial Vly. Inn
1093 Airport Blvd.
(760) 355-4500

Hawaiian Gardens
1031 Imperial Beach Blvd.
(619) 429-5303

INDIO
Best Western Date Tree Hotel
81-909 Indio Blvd.
(760) 347-3421
Comfort Inn
43-505 Monroe St.
(760) 347-4044
Palm Shadow Inn
80-761 Hwy 111
(760) 347-3476
Royal Plaza Inn
82-347 Hwy 111
(760) 347-0911

LEBEC
Flying J Inn
42810 Frazier Mtn Park Rd.
(805) 248-2700

LEE VINING
Murphey's Motel
Route 395
(760) 647-6316

INGLEWOOD
Econo Lodge LAX
4123 W. Century Blvd.
(310) 672-7285
Hampton Inn-LAX
10300 La Cienega
(310) 337-1000
Motel 6
5101 West Century Blvd.
(310) 419-1234

IRVINE
Atrium Hotel
18700 MacArthur Blvd.
(714) 833-2770
Holiday Inn
17941 Von Karman Ave.
(714) 863-1999
Hyatt Regency
17900 Jamboree Rd.
(714) 975-1234
La Quinta
14972 San Canyon Ave.
(714) 551-0909
Marriott Hotel
18000 Von Karman Ave.
(714) 553-0100

Residence Inn
10 Morgan
(714) 380-3000

JACKSON
El Campo Casa Motel
12548 Kennedy Flat
(209) 223-0100
Jackson Holiday Lodge
850 N. California 49
(209) 223-0486

JAMESTOWN
Sonora Country Inn
18755 Chanbroullian Ln.
(209) 984-0315

JULIAN
Apple Tree Inn
4360 Route 78
(760) 765-0222

JUNE LAKE
June Lake Motel and Cabins
Route 158
(760) 648-6547
June Lake Villager
Route 158
(760) 648-7712

KING CITY
Courtesy Inn
4 Broadway Circle
(408) 385-4646

KINGSBURG
Swedish Inn
401 Conejo St
(209) 897-1022

LA JOLLA
Andrea Villa Inn
2402 Torrey Pines Rd.
(619) 459-3311
Colonial Inn
910 Prospect St.
(619) 454-2181
Holiday Inn
6705 La Jolla Blvd.
(619) 552-1234
La Jolla Marriott
4240 La Jolla Village Dr.
(619) 587-1414
La Jolla Palms Inn
6705 La Jolla Blvd.
(619) 454-7101

Residence Inn
8901 Gilman Dr.
(619) 587-1770
LAKE ARROWHEAD
Arrowhead Tree Top
Route 173
(909) 337-2311
Lake Arrowhead Resort
27984 Route 189
(909) 336-1511
LAKE ELSINORE
Lakeview Inn
31808 Casino Dr.
(909) 674-9694
LA MESA
Comfort Inn
8000 Parkway Dr.
(619) 698-7747
La Mesa Springs Hotel
4210 Spring St.
(619) 589-7288
LA MIRADA
Residence Inn
14419 Firestone Blvd.
(714) 523-2800
LAKEHEAD
Antler's Resort and Marina
Antlers Road
(916) 238-2553
O'Banion's Sugarloaf Cottages
19667 Lakeshore Dr.
(916) 238-2448
LANCASTER
Best Western Antelope Inn
44055 N. Sierra Hwy
(805) 948-4651
Desert Inn Motor Hotel
44219 North Sierra Hwy
(805) 942-8401
LA PALMA
La Quinta Inn
3 Centerpointe Dr.
(714) 670-1400
LEBEC
Flying J Inn
42810 Frazier Mtn Park Rd
(805) 248-2700
LEE VINING
Murphy's Motel
Route 395
(760) 647-6316

LEMOORE
Best Western Vineyard Inn
877 East D St.
(209) 924-1261
LINDSAY
Olive Tree Inn
390 North Route 65
(209) 562-5188
LIVERMORE
Residence Inn
1000 Airway Blvd.
(510) 373-1800
LODI
Best Western Royal Host Inn
710 So. Cherokee Lane
(209) 369-8484
Comfort Inn
118 North Cherokee Lane
(209) 367-4848
LOMPOC
Best Western Vandenberg Inn
940 E. Ocean Ave.
(805) 735-7731
Inn of Lompoc
1122 North H St.
(805) 735-7744
Quality Inn
1621 North H St.
(805) 735-8555
Tally Ho Motor Inn
1020 E. Ocean Ave.
(805) 735-6444
LONE PINE
Alabama Hills Inn
1920 S. Main St.
(760) 876-8700
Best Western Frontier Motel
1008 So. Main St.
(760) 876-5571
Dow Villa Motel
310 S. Main St.
(760) 876-5521
LONG BEACH
Clarion Hotel Edgewater
6400 E. Pacific Coast Hwy.
(562) 434-8451
Hilton at World Trade Center
Two World Trade Center
(562) 983-3400

California

Holiday Inn (Airport)
2640 Lakewood Blvd.
(562) 597-4401
Ramada Inn
5325 E. Pacific Coast Hwy.
(562) 597-1341
Seaport Marina
6400 E. Pacific Coast Hwy.
(562) 598-6028
Travelodge Resort and Marina
700 Queensway
(562) 435-7676
LOS ANGELES
Best Western - Mayfair
1256 West 7th St.
(213) 484-9789
Best Western Westwood
11250 Santa Monica Blvd.
(310) 478-1400
Beverly Hills Ritz Hotel
10300 Wilshire Blvd.
(310) 275-5575
Century Plaza
2025 Ave. of the Stars
(310) 277-2000
Continental Plaza LAX
9750 Airport Blvd.
(310) 645-4600
Embassy Suites-LAX
9801 Airport Rd.
(310) 215-1000
Holiday Inn-City Center
1020 S. Figueroa
(213) 748-1291
Holiday Inn - Downtown
750 Garland Ave.
(213) 628-5242
Hotel Intercontinental - LA
251 S. Olive St.
(213) 617-3300
Hotel Del Capri
10587 Wilshire Blvd.
(310) 474-3511
Hotel Sofitel
8555 Beverly Blvd.
(310) 278-5444
Los Angeles Hilton
930 Wilshire Blvd.
(213) 629-4321

Marriott-LAX
5855 W. Century Blvd.
(310) 641-5700
Sheraton Gateway
6101 West Century Blvd.
(310) 642-1111
Travelodge - LAX
5547 W. Century Blvd.
(310) 469-4000
Westin Bonaventure
404 S. Figueroa
(213) 624-1000
Westwood Marquis Hotel
930 Hilgard Ave.
(310) 208-8765
Wyndham Hotel
6225 West Century Blvd.
(310) 670-9000
LOS BANOS
Best Western John Jay Inn
301 W. Pacheco Blvd.
(209) 827-0954
LOS GATOS
Los Gatos Lodge
50 Saratoga Ave.
(408) 354-3300
Los Gatos Motor Inn
55 Saratoga Ave.
(408) 354-9191
Toll House Hotel
Santa Cruz Ave.
(408) 395-7070
MADERA
Best Western Madera Valley
317 North G St.
(209) 673-5164
MAMMOTH LAKES
Austria Hof Lodge
924 Canyon Blvd.
(760) 934-2764
Cinnamon Bear Inn
113 Center St
(760) 934-2873
Crystal Crag Lodge
307 Crystal Crag Dr.
(760) 934-2436
Econolodge Wildwood Inn
Route 203
(760) 934-6855

Mammoth High Country Inns
  6156 Minaret Rd.
  (760) 934-2416
Royal Pines Resort
  3814 View Point Rd.
  (760) 934-2306
Shilo Inn
  Route 203
  (760) 934-4500
MARINA DEL REY
Foghorn Hotel
  4140 Via Marina
  (310) 823-4626
Marina del Rey Hotel
  13534 Bali Way
  (310) 301-1000
Marina del Rey Marriott
  13480 Maxella Ave.
  (310) 822-8555
MANHATTAN BEACH
Residence Inn
  1700 No. Sepulveda Blvd.
  (310) 546-7627
MANTECA
Best Western Inn
  1415 E. Yosemite Ave.
  (209) 825-1415
MARIPOSA
Mariposa Lodge
  Route 140
  (209) 966-3607
Miners Inn
  Route 49
  (209) 742-7777
MARYSVILLE
The Vagabond Inn
  721 10th St
  (916) 742-8586
MENDOCINO
Blackberry Inn
  44951 Larkin Rd
  (707) 937-5281
Sears House
  44840 Main St.
  (707) 937-0866
MERCED
Best Western Sequoia Inn
  1213 V St.
  (209) 723-3711

Days Inn
  1199 Motel Dr.
  (209) 722-2726
Holiday Inn
  730 Motel Dr.
  (209) 380333
MILL VALLEY
Holiday Inn Express
  160 Shoreline Hwy.
  (415) 332-5700
MILLBRAE
Clarion Hotel
  401 E. Millbrae Ave.
  (415) 692-6363
Westin Hotel
  1 Old Bayshore Hwy.
  (415) 692-3500
MILPITAS
Beverly Heritage Hotel
  1820 Barber lane
  (408) 943-9080
Economy Inns of America
  270 So. Abbott Ave.
  (408) 946-8889
MIRANDA
Miranda Gardens Resort
  6766 Avenue of the Giants
  (707) 943-3011
MISSION HILLS
Best Western Mission Hills
  10621 Sepulveda Blvd.
  (818) 891-1771
Holiday Inn
  924 W. Huntington Dr.
  (818) 357-1900
MI-WUK VILLAGE
Mi-Wuk Motor Lodge
  Route 108
  (209) 586-3031
MODESTO
Best Western Town House
  909 16th St.
  (209) 524-7261
Red Lion Hotel
  1150 9th St.
  (209) 526-6000
MOJAVE
Scottish Inns
  16352 Sierra Hwy
  (805) 824-9317

California

MONROVIA
  Holiday Inn
    924 W. Huntington Dr.
    (818) 357-1900
  Wyndham Garden Hotel
    700 W. Huntington Dr.
    (818) 357-5211
MONTEREY
  Bay Park Hotel
    1425 Munras Ave.
    (408) 649-1020
  Cypress Gardens Motel
    1150 Munras Ave.
    (408) 373-2761
  El Adobe
    936 Munras Ave.
    (408) 372-5409
  Holiday Inn - Resort
    1000 Aguajito Rd.
    (408) 373-6141
  Hyatt Regency Monterey
    1 Old Golf Course Rd.
    (408) 372-1234
  Monterey Bay Lodge
    55 Camino Aquajito
    (408) 372-8057
  Monterey Beach Hotel
    2600 Sand Dunes Dr.
    (408) 394-3321
  Monterey Marriott
    350 Calle Principal
    (408) 649-4234
  Monterey Motor Lodge
    55 Camino Aguajito
    (408) 372-8057
  Munras Lodge
    1010 Munras Rd
    (408) 646-9696
  Way Station Inn
    1200 Olmstead Rd.
    (408) 372-2945
MONTEREY PARK
  Days Inn
    434 Potrero Grande Dr.
    (213) 728-8444
MORGAN HILL
  Best Western Country Inn
    16525 Condit Rd.
    (408) 779-0447

MORRO BAY
  Best Western El Rancho Motel
    2460 Main St.
    (805) 772-2212
  Best Western Tradewinds
    225 Beach St.
    (805) 772-7376
  Gold Coast
    670 Main St.
    (805) 772-7740
  Sundown Motel
    640 Main St.
    (805) 772-7381
  Sunset Travelodge
    1080 Market Ave.
    (805) 772-1259
MOUNTAIN VIEW
  Best Western Tropicana Lodge
    1720 El Camino Real
    (415) 961-0220
  Residence Inn
    1854 El Camino Real
    (415) 940-1300
MOUNT SHASTA
  Alpine Lodge Motel
    908 So. Mt. Shasta Blvd.
    (916) 926-3145
  Mountain Air Lodge
    1121 Mount Shasta Blvd.
    (916) 926-3411
  Pine Needles Motel
    1340 Mt. Shasta Blvd.
    (916) 926-4811
  Swiss Holiday Lodge
    2400 S. Mt. Shasta
    (916) 926-3446
  Tree House Best Western
    Mount Shasta Blvd.
    (916) 926-3101
NAPA
  Sheraton Inn Napa Valley
    3425 Solano Ave.
    (707) 253-7433
NATIONAL CITY
  Holiday Inn
    700 National City Blvd.
    (619) 474-2800
  Radisson Suites
    801 National City Blvd.
    (619) 474-2800

California

NEEDLES
   Best Western Colorado River
   2371 West Broadway
   (760) 326-4552
   Days Inn
   1111 Pashard St.
   (760) 326-5660
   Super 8
   1102 East Broadway
   (760) 326-4501
NEWPORT BEACH
   Hyatt Newpoerter
   1107 Jamboree Rd
   (714) 729-1234
   Marriott Suites
   500 Bayview Circle
   (714) 854-4500
NORTH HOLLYWOOD
   La Maida House
   11159 La Maida St.
   (818) 769-3857
OAKHURST
   Best Western Yosemite Hotel
   40530 Hwy 41
   (209) 683-2378
   Comfort Inn
   40489 Rte 41
   (209) 683-8282
   Ramada Inn
   48800 Royal Oaks Dr.
   (209) 658-5500
OAKLAND
   Clarion Suites Lake Merritt
   1800 Madison St.
   (510) 832-2300
   Hampton Inn
   8465 Enterprise Dr.
   (510) 632-8900
   Oakland Airport Hilton
   1 Hegenberger Rd.
   (510) 635-5000
OJAI
   Los Padres Inn
   1208 E. Ojai Ave.
   (805) 646-4365
   Oakridge Inn
   780 North Ventura Ave.
   (805) 649-4018

ONTARIO
   Country Suites by Carlson
   231 N. Vineyard Ave.
   (909) 983-8484
   Good Nite Inn
   1801 E. G St.
   (909) 983-3604
   Holiday Inn - Airport
   3400 Shelby St.
   (909) 466-9600
   Marriott Hotel
   2200 E. Holt Blvd.
   (909) 986-8811
   Red Lion Inn
   222 N. Vineyard
   (909) 983-0909
   Red Roof Inn
   1818 E. Holt Blvd.
   (909) 988-8466
   Residence Inn
   2025 E. D St.
   (909) 983-6788
ORANGE
   Hilton Suites
   400 N. State College Blvd.
   (714) 938-1111
   Residence Inn
   201 N. State College Blvd.
   (714) 978-7700
ORLAND
   Amber Light Inn
   828 Newville Rd.
   (916) 865-7655
   Orland Inn
   1052 South St.
   (916) 865-7632
OROVILLE
   Travelodge
   580 Oro Dam Blvd.
   (916) 533-7070
OXNARD
   Best Western Oxnard Inn
   1156 So. Oxnard Blvd.
   (805) 483-9581
   Oxnard Hilton
   600 Esplanade Dr.
   (805) 485-9666
   Radisson Suite Hotel
   2101 Vineyard Ave.
   (805) 988-0130

California

PACIFIC GROVE
Lighthouse Lodge Suites
1150-1249 Lighthouse Dr.
(408) 655-2111

PALMDALE
Holiday Inn
38630 5th St. West
(805) 947-8055

PALM DESERT
Casa Larrea Resort Motel
73-771 Larrea St.
(760) 568-0311
Desert Patch Inn
73758 Shadow Mountain
(760) 346-9161
Inn at Deep Canyon
74740 Abronia Trail
(760) 346-8061
Vacation Inn
74-715 Route 111
(760) 340-4441

PALM SPRINGS
Estrella Inn at Palm Springs
415 S. Belardo Rd.
(760) 320-4117
Hyatt Regency Suites
285 N. Palm Canyon Dr.
(760) 322-9000
Hilton Resort
400 E. Tahquitz Canyon Way
(760) 320-6868
Korakia Pensione
257 S. Patencio Rd.
(760) 320-0708
Palm Springs Riviera Resort
1600 N. Indian Canyon Dr.
(760) 327-8311
Place in the Sun
754 San Lorenzo Rd.
(760) 325-0254
Quality Inn
1269 Palm Canyon Dr.
(760)323-2775
Ramada Inn Resort
1800 E. Palm Canyon Dr.
(760) 323-1711
Wyndham Palm Springs
888 Tahquitz Canyon Way
(760) 322-6000

PALO ALTO
Holiday Inn-Palo Alto
625 El Camino Real
(415) 328-2800
Hyatt Rickeys
4219 El Camino Real
(415) 493-8000

PARADISE
Ponderosa Gardens Motel
7010 Skyway
(916) 872-9094

PASADENA
Hilton
150 S. Los Robles
(818) 577-1000
Holiday Inn
303 E. Cordova
(818) 449-4000
Holiday Inn
3321 E. Colorado Blvd.
(818) 796-9291
Vagabond Inn
1203 E. Colorado Blvd.
(818) 577-8873

PASO ROBLES
Travelodge Paso Robles
2701 Spring St.
(805) 238-0078

PETALUMA
Quality Inn
5100 Montero Way
(707) 664-1155

PICO RIVER
Travelodge
7222 Rosemead Blvd.
(562) 949-6648

PIONEER
Pioneer Inn
24144 Hwy. 88
(209) 295-3490

PISMO BEACH
The Cliffs at Shell Beach
2757 Shell Beach Rd.
(805) 773-5000
Oxford Suites Resort
651 Five Cities Dr.
(805) 773-3773
Shell Beach Motel
653 Shell Beach Rd.
(805) 773-4373

California

Spyglass Inn
2705 Spyglass Dr.
(805) 773-4855
PLACERVILLE
Best Western
6850 Green Leaf Dr.
(916) 622-9100
PLEASANT HILL
Residence Inn
700 Ellinwood Way
(510) 689-1010
PLEASANTON
Doubletree Club
5990 Stoneridge Mall Rd.
(510) 463-3330
Hilton Hotel
7050 Johnson Dr.
(510) 463-8000
Holiday Inn
11950 Dublin Canyon Rd.
(510) 847-6000
PLYMOUTH
Best Western Shenandoah
17674 Village Dr.
(209) 245-4491
POLLOCK PINES
Stagecoach Motor Inn
5940 Pony Express Tr.
(916) 644-2029
POMONA
Sheraton Suites
600 W. McKinley Ave.
(909) 622-2220
Shilo Inn
3200 Temple Ave.
(909) 598-0073
POWAY
Poway Country Inn
13845 Poway Rd.
(619) 748-6320
RAMONA
Ramona Valley Inn
416 Main St.
(760) 789-6433
RANCHO BERNARDO
Doubletree Carmel Highland
14455 Penasquitos Dr.
(619) 672-9100
La Quinta Inn
10185 Paseo Montril
(619) 484-8800

Radisson Suite Hotel
11520 W. Bernardo Ct.
(619) 451-6600
Rancho Bernardo Travelodge
16929 W. Bernardo Dr.
(619) 487-0445
Residence Inn
11002 Rancho Carmel Dr.
(619) 673-1900
RANCHO CORDOVA
Best Western Heritage Inn
11269 Point East Dr.
(916) 635-4040
Comfort Inn
3240 Mather Field Rd.
(916) 363-3344
Economy Inn
12249 Folsom Blvd.
(916) 351-1213
RANCHO MIRAGE
Westin Mission Hills
71-333 Dinah Shore Dr.
(619) 328-5955
RANCHO SANTA FE
Morgan Run Resort & Club
5690 Cancha de Golf
(619) 756-2471
RAVENDALE
Spanish Springs Ranch
Box 70
(800) 272-8282
RED BLUFF
Red Bluff Inn
30 Gilmore Rd.
(916) 529-2028
Super 8
203 Antelope Blvd.
(916) 527-8882
REDDING
Best Western
532 N. Market St.
(916) 241-6464
La Quinta
2180 Hilltop Dr.
(916) 221-8200
Oxford Suites
1967 Hilltop Dr.
(916) 221-0100

California

Park Terrace Inn
1900 Hilltop Dr.
(916) 221-7500
Red Lion
1830 Hilltop Dr.
(916) 221-8700
River Inn
1835 Park Marina Dr.
(916) 241-9500
Vagabond Inn
536 E. Cypress Ave.
(916) 223-1600
REDLANDS
Best Western Sandman Motel
1120 W. Colton Ave.
(909) 793-2001
REEDLEY
Edgewater Inn
1977 W. Manning Ave.
(209) 637-7777
REDWOOD CITY
Good Nite Inn
485 Veterans Blvd.
(415) 365-5500
Hotel Sofitel
223 Twin Dolphin Dr.
(415) 598-9000
RIALTO
Best Western Empire Inn
475 W. Valley Blvd.
(909) 877-0690
RIDGECREST
Econo Lodge
201 Inyokem Rd.
(760) 446-2551
El Rancho Motel
507 S. China Lake Blvd.
(760) 375-9731
Heritage Inn & Suites
1050 N. Norma
(760) 446-6543
RIVERSIDE
Dynasty Suites
3735 Iowa Ave.
(909) 369-8200
Hampton Inn
1590 University Ave.
(909) 683-6000

Travelodge La Sierra
11043 Magnolia Ave.
(909) 688-5000
ROCKLIN
First Choice Inn
4420 Rocklin Rd.
(916) 624-4500
ROHNERT PARK
Red Lion Hotel
1 Red Lion Dr.
(707) 584-5466
ROSAMOND
Devonshire Motel
2076 Rosamond Blvd.
(805) 256-3454
ROSEVILLE
Best Western Roseville Inn
220 Harding Blvd.
(916) 782-4434
SACRAMENTO
Best Western Expo Inn
1413 Howe Ave.
(916) 922-9833
Best Western Harbor Inn
1250 Halyard Dr.
(916) 371-2100
Beverly Garland Hotel
1780 Tribute Rd.
(916) 929-7900
Canterbury Inn
1900 Canterbury Rd.
(916) 927-0927
Clarion Hotel
700 16th St.
(916) 444-8000
Days Inn-Discovery Park
350 Bercut Dr.
(916) 442-6971
La Quinta Inn
4604 Madison Ave.
(916) 348-0900
Marriott Residence Inn
1530 Howe Ave.
(916) 920-9111
Radisson Hotel
500 Leisure Ln.
(916) 922-2020
Red Lion Hotel
2001 Point West Way
(916) 929-8855

California

Red Lion's Sacramento Inn
1401 Arden Way
(916) 922-8041
Sacramento Hilton Inn
2200 Harvard St.
(916) 922-4700
Vagabond Inn
909 3rd St.
(916) 446-1481
ST. HELENA
El Bonita Motel
195 Main St.
(707) 963-3216
SALINAS
Vagabond Inn
131 Kern St.
(408) 758-4693
SAN BERNARDINO
Best Western Sands
606 North H
(909) 889-8391
La Quinta Inn
205 E. Hospitality Ln.
(909) 888-7571
Sands Motel
606 No. H St.
(909) 889-8391
SAN CLEMENTE
Holiday Inn-San Clemente
111 S. Avenida de Estrella
(714) 361-3000
SAN DIEGO
Beach Haven Inn
4740 Mission Blvd.
(619) 272-3812
Best Western Hanalei Hotel
2270 Hotel Circle
(619) 297-1101
Best Western Seven Seas
411 South Hotel Circle
(619) 291-1300
Crown Point View Suites
4088 Crown Point Dr.
(619) 272-0676
Four Points Hotel, Sheraton
8110 Aero Dr.
(619) 277-8888
Good Nite Inn
4545 Waring Rd.
(619) 286-7000
Grosvenor Inn
810 Ash St.
(619) 233-8826
Handlery Hotel
950 Hotel Circle No.
(619) 298-0511
Holiday Inn on the Bay
1355 N. Harbor Dr.
(619) 232-3861
King's Inn
1333 Hotel Circle South
(619) 297-2231
Marriott San Diego Marina
333 West Harbor Dr.
(619) 234-1500
Pacific Shores Inn
4802 Mission Blvd.
(619) 483-6300
Radisson Harbor View
1646 Front St.
(619) 239-6800
Ramada Inn
5550 Kearny Mesa Rd.
(619) 278-0800
Red Lion Hotel
7450 Hazard Center Dr.
(619) 297-5466
Residence Inn Kearny Mesa
5400 Kearny Mesa Rd.
(619) 278-2100
San Diego Hilton & Tennis
1775 E. Mission Bay Dr.
(619) 276-4010
San Diego Marriott
8757 Rio San Diego Dr.
(619) 692-3800
San Diego Marriott Suites
701 A St.
(619) 696-9800
Super 8 Mission Bay
4540 Mission Bay Dr.
(619) 274-7888
Vagabond Inn
625 Hotel Circle South
(619) 297-1691
SAN FRANCISCO
Beresford Arms
121 7th St.
(415) 626-0200

California

Best Western Civic Center
364 9th St.
(415) 621-2826
Hotel Nikko
222 Mason St
(415) 394-1111
Hotel Juliana
590 Bush St.
(415) 392-2540
Laurel Motor Inn
444 Presidio Ave.
(415) 567-8467
La Quinta
20 Airport Blvd.
(415) 583-2223
Marriott - Fishermans Wharf
1250 Columbus Ave.
(415) 775-7555
Pacific Heights Inn
1555 Union St.
(415) 776-3310
Rodeway Inn by the Bay
1450 Lombard St.
(415) 673-3232
San Francisco Marriott
55 Fourth St.
(415) 896-1600
San Francisco Airport Hilton
Route 101
(415) 589-0770
Travelodge
1450 Lombard St.
(415) 673-0691
SAN JACINTO
Crown Motel
138 South Ramona Blvd.
(909) 654-7133
SAN JOSE
Airport Inn
1355 North 4th St
(408) 453-5340
Best Western San Jose Lodge
North First St.
(408) 453-7750
Crowne Plaza
282 Almaden Blvd.
(408) 998-0400
Doubletree Hotel
1350 North 1st St
(408) 453-6200
Hanford Hotel
1755 North 1st St
(408) 453-3133
Hilton Hotel
300 Almaden Blvd.
(408) 287-2100
Holiday Inn-Park Center Plaza
282 Almaden Blvd.
(408) 998-0400
Homewood Suites
10 West Trimble Rd.
(408) 428-9900
Hyatt Hotel
302 South Market
(408) 885-1234
Red Lion Hotel
2050 Gateway Pl.
(408) 453-4000
SAN JUAN BAUTISTA
San Juan Inn
410 Alameda
(408) 623-4380
SAN JUAN CAPISTRANO
Best Western Capistrano Inn
27174 Ortega Hwy.
(714) 493-5661
SAN LUIS OBISPO
Best Western Royal Oak
214 Madonna Rd.
(805) 544-4410
Best Western Somerset Manor
1895 Monterey St.
(805) 544-0973
Howard Johnson
1585 Calle Joaquin
(805) 544-5300
Olive Tree Inn
1000 Olive St.
(805) 544-2800
Sands Motel
1930 Monterey St
(805) 544-0500
San Luis Obispo Travelodge
1825 Monterey
(805) 543-5110

SAN MARCOS
Quails Inn at Lake San Marcos
1025 La Bonita
(760) 744-0120

SAN MATEO
Best Western Los Prados
2940 South Norfolk St.
(415) 341-3300
Holiday Inn-San Mateo
300 North Bayshore Blvd.
(415) 344-3219
Quality Hotel Airport South
101 W. Hillsdale Blvd.
(415) 341-0966
Residence Inn
2000 Winward Way
(415) 574-4700
Villa Hotel
101 West Hillsdale Blvd.
(415) 341-0966

SAN RAFAEL
Embassy Suites Hotel
101 McInnis Pkwy.
(415) 499-9222
Villa Inn
1600 Lincoln Ave.
(415) 456-4975
Wyndham Garden Hotel
1010 Northgate Dr.
(415) 479-9800

SAN RAMON
Marriott/Bishop Ranch
2600 Bishop Dr.
(510) 867-9200
Residence Inn
1071 Market Pl.
(510) 277-9292

SAN SIMEON
Best Western Courtesy Inn
9450 Castillo Dr.
(805) 927-4691
Cavalier Oceanfront Resort
9415 Hearst Dr.
(805) 927-4688
Silver Surf Motel
9390 Castillo Dr.
(805) 927-4661

SANTA ANA
Crown Sterling Suites
1325 East Dyer Rd.
(714) 241-3800
Motel 6
1717 East Dyer Rd.
(714) 261-1515

SANTA BARBARA
Holiday Inn
5650 Calle Real
(805) 964-6241
Motel 6
3505 State St.
(805) 687-5400
Ocean Palms Hotel
232 W. Cabrillo Blvd.
(805) 966-9133
Pacifica Suites
5490 Hollister Ave.
(805) 683-6722

SANTA CLARA
Days Inn
4200 Great American Pkwy.
(408) 980-1525
Econo Lodge Silicon Valley
2930 El Camino Real
(408) 241-3010
Marriott Hotel
2700 Mission College Blvd.
(408) 988-1500
Westin Hotel - Santa Clara
5101 Great American Pkwy.
(408) 986-0700

SANTA CLARITA
Hampton Inn
25259 Old Rd.
(805) 253-2400
Hilton Garden Inn
27710 Old Rd.
(805) 254-8800

SANTA CRUZ
Candlelite Inn
1101 Ocean St.
(408) 427-1616
Inn at Pasatiempo
555 Route 17
(408) 423-5000
Ocean Pacific Inn
120 Washington St.
(408) 457-1234

California

Pacific Inn
330 Ocean St.
(408) 425-3722
Travelodge Riviera
619 Riverside Ave.
(408) 423-9515
SAN DIMAS
Red Roof Inn
204 No. Village Ct.
(909) 599-2362
SANTA MARIA
Best Western Inn
1725 N. Broadway
(805) 922-5200
Comfort Inn
210 Nicholson Ave.
(805) 922-5891
Hunter's Inn
1514 S. Broadway
(805) 922-2123
Ramada Suites
2050 N. Preisker Ln.
(805) 928-6000
Rose Garden Inn
1007 E. Main St.
(805) 922-4505
SANTA MONICA
The Georgian
1415 Ocean Blvd.
(310) 395-9945
Holiday Inn
120 Colorado Blvd.
(310) 451-0676
Loews Santa Monica Beach Htl
1700 Ocean Ave.
(310) 458-6700
Pacific Shore Hotel
1819 Ocean Ave.
(310) 451-8711
SANTA NELLA
Best Western Andersen's Inn
12367 Hwy 33 South
(209) 826-5534
Holiday Inn Mission de Oro
13070 Hwy 33 South
(209) 826-4444
Ramada Inn
28976 West Plaza Dr.
(209) 826-4444

SANTA ROSA
Best Western Garden Inn
1500 Santa Rosa Ave.
(707) 546-4031
Best Western Hillside
2901 Fourth St.
(707) 546-9353
Hillside Inn
2901 4th St
(707) 546-9353
Holiday Inn
870 Hopper Ave.
(707) 545-9000
Los Robles Lodge
1985 Cleveland Ave.
(707) 545-6330
Santa Rosa Travelodge
1815 Santa Rosa Ave.
(707) 542-3472
SARATOGA
The Inn at Saratoga
20645 Fourth St
(408) 867-5020
SCOTTS BEACH
Best Western Inn
6020 Scotts Valley Dr.
(408) 438-6666
SEAL BEACH
Radisson Inn of Seal Beach
600 Marina Dr.
(562) 493-7501
SEASIDE
Day Breeze Inn
2049 Fremont Blvd.
(408) 899-7111
SIERRA CITY
Herrington's Sierra Pines
Route 49
(916) 862-1151
SIMI VALLEY
Radisson Simi Valley
999 Enchanted Way
(805) 583-2000
SMITH RIVER
Best Western Ship Ashore
Route 101
(707) 487-3141

California

SOLVANG
  Best Western
    1440 Mission Dr.
    (805) 688-2383
SONOMA
  Best Western Sonoma Valley
    550 Second St.
    (707) 938-9200
SONORA
  Aladdin Motor Inn
    14260 Mono Way
    (209) 533-4971
  Best Western Sonora Oaks
    19551 Hess Ave.
    (209) 533-4400
SOUTH LAKE TAHOE
  Adler Inn
    1072 Ski Run Blvd.
    (916) 544-4485
  Blue Jay Lodge
    4133 Cedar Ave.
    (916) 544-5232
  Days Inn
    968 Park Ave.
    (916) 541-4800
  La Baer Inn
    4133 Lake Tahoe Blvd.
    (916) 544-1239
  Lakepark Lodge
    4081 Cedar Ave.
    (916) 541-5004
  Lampliter Motel
    4143 Cedar Ave
    (916) 544-2936
  Super 8
    3600 Lake Tahoe Blvd.
    (916) 544-3476
  Tahoe Keys Resort
    599 Tahoe Keys Blvd.
    (916) 544-5397
  Tahoe Marina Inn
    930 Bal Bijou Rd.
    (916) 541-2180
  Tahoe Valley Motel
    2241 Lake Tahoe Blvd.
    (916) 541-0353
  Torchlite Inn
    965 Park Ave.
    (916) 541-2363

SPRING VALLEY
  Super 8 Motel
    9603 Campo Rd.
    (619) 589-1111
STATELINE
  Harrah's Hotel & Casino
    Casino Center
    (pets in hotel kennel)
    (702) 588-6611
STOCKTON
  Best Western Charter Way Inn
    550 West Charter Way
    (209) 948-0321
  Days Inn
    33 North Center St.
    (209) 948-6151
  Holiday Inn
    111 East March Lane
    (209) 474-3301
  La Quinta
    2710 West March Lane
    (209) 952-7800
SUNNYVALE
  Best Western Sunnyvale Inn
    940 Weddell Dr.
    (408) 734-3742
  Residence Inn
    750 Lakeway Dr.
    (408) 720-8893
  Vagabond Inn
    816 Ahwanee Ave.
    (408) 734-4607
SUSANVILLE
  Best Western Trailside
    2785 Main St.
    (916) 257-4123
  River Inn Motel
    1710 Main St.
    (916) 257-6051
  Super Budget Motel
    2975 Johnstonville Rd.
    (916) 257-2782
TEHACHAPI
  Best Western Mountain Inn
    416 W. Tehachapi Blvd.
    (805) 822-5591
  Tahachapi Summit Travelodge
    500 Steuber Rd.
    (805) 823-8000

California

TAHOE VISTA
   Tatami Cottage Resort
      7449 North Lake Blvd.
      (916) 546-3523
TEMECULA
   Comfort Inn
      27338 Jefferson Ave.
      (909) 699-5888
   Temecula Creek
      44501 Rainbow Canyon Rd
      (909) 694-1000
THREE RIVERS
   Best Western Holiday Lodge
      40105 Sierra Drive
      (209) 561-4119
   Lazy J Ranch Motel
      39625 Sierra Dr.
      (209) 561-4449
   The River Inn
      45176 Sierra Dr.
      (209) 561-4367
   Sequoia Village Inn
      45971 Sierra Dr.
      (209) 561-3652
   Sierra Lodge
      43175 Sierra Dr.
      (209) 561-3681
TIBURON
   Tiburon Lodge
      1651 Tiburon Blvd.
      (415) 435-3133
TORRANCE
   Residence Inn
      3701 Torrance Blvd.
      (310) 543-4566
   Summerfield Suites
      19901 Prairie Ave.
      (310) 371-8525
TRINIDAD
   Bishop Pine Lodge
      1481 Patricks Point Rd.
      (707) 677-3314
TRINITY CENTER
   Coffee Creek Ranch
      Box 4940K
      (916) 266-3343
TULARE
   Best Western Town & Country
      1051 North Blackstone
      (209) 688-7537

TURLOCK
   Best Western Orchard Inn
      5025 N. Golden State Blvd.
      (209) 667-2827
   Comfort Inn-Turlock
      200 West Glenwood Ave.
      (209) 668-3400
TWENTY NINE PINES
   Circle C Motel
      6340 El Rey Ave.
      (760) 367-7615
UKIAH
   Days Inn
      950 North State Rd.
      (707) 462-7584
   Western Traveler Motel
      693 S. Orchard Ave.
      (707) 468-9167
VACAVILLE
   Best Western Heritage Inn
      1420 East Monte Vista Ave.
      (707) 448-8453
VALENCIA
   Hilton Garden Inn (at Six Flags)
      27710 The Old Rd.
      (805) 254-8800
VALLEJO
   Holiday Inn
      1000 Fairgrounds Dr.
      (707) 644-1220
   Ramada Inn
      1000 Admiral Callaghan
      (707) 643-2700
   Windmill Inn at Marine World
      1596 Fairgrounds Dr.
      (707) 554-9655
VENTURA
   La Quinta
      5818 Valentine Rd.
      (805) 658-6200
   Vagabond Inn
      756 E. Thompson Blvd.
      (805) 648-5371
VICTORVILLE
   Holiday Inn
      15494 Palmdale Rd.
      (760) 245-6565
   Red Roof Inn
      13409 Mariposa Rd.
      (760) 241-1577

California

VISALIA
    Best Western Visalia Inn
    623 Main St.
    (209) 732-4561
    Holiday Inn Plaza Park
    9000 W. Airport Dr.
    (209) 651-5000

VISTA
    La Quinta Inn
    630 Sycamore Ave.
    (760) 727-8180

VOLCANO
    St. George Hotel
    Box 9
    (209) 296-4458

WALNUT CREEK
    Embassy Suites Hotel
    1345 Treat Blvd.
    (510) 934-2500
    Holiday Inn
    2730 North Main St
    (510) 932-3332
    Walnut Creek Motor Lodge
    1960 North Main St.
    (510) 932-2811

WATSONVILLE
    Best Western Inn
    740 Freedom Blvd.
    (408) 724-3367

WEST HOLLYWOOD
    Le Montrose Suite Hotel
    900 Hammond St.
    (310) 855-1115
    Le Parc
    733 N. West Knoll Dr.
    (310) 855-8888
    Mondrian Hotel
    8440 Sunset Blvd.
    (213) 650-8999
    Summerfield Suites
    1000 Westmount Dr.
    (310) 657-7400
    Wyndham Bel Age Hotel
    1020 N. San Vincente Blvd.
    (310) 854-1111

WEAVERVILLE
    49er Motel
    718 Main St.
    (916) 623-4937
    Weaverville Victorian Inn
    1709 Main St.
    (916) 623-4432

WEED
    Sis-Q-Inn Motel
    1825 Shastina Dr.
    (916) 938-4194

WILLIAMS
    Granzella's Inn
    391 6th St
    (916) 473-3310
    Woodcrest Inn
    400 C Street
    (916) 473-2381

WILLOWS
    Best Western Golden Pheasant
    249 N. Humboldt Ave.
    (916) 934-4603

WOODLAND HILLS
    Vagabond Inn
    20175 Ventrua Blvd.
    (818) 347-8080

YOSEMITE
    The Redwoods
    8038 Chilnualna Falls Rd.
    (209) 375-6666

YREKA
    Best Western Miner's Inn
    122 E. Miner St.
    (916) 842-4355
    Wayside Inn
    1235 So. Main St.
    (916) 842-4412

YUBA CITY
    Motel Orleans
    730 Palora Ave.
    (916) 674-1592
    Vada's Motel
    545 Colusa Ave.
    (916) 671-1151

YUCCA VALLEY
    Oasis of Eden Inn
    56377 Twentynine Palms
    (916) 473-2381

Oregon

ALBANY
   Best Western Pony Soldier
      315 Airport Rd. SE
      (541) 928-6322
   Comfort Inn
      251 Airport Rd. SE
      (541) 928-0921
   Holiday Inn Express
      1100 Price Rd.
      (541) 928-5050

ASHLAND
   Ashland Village Inn B&B
      639 N. Main St.
      (541) 482-9171
   Best Western Bard's Inn
      132 North Main St
      (541) 482-0049
   Best Western Heritage Inn
      434 Valley View Rd
      (541) 482-6932
   Quality Inn Flagship
      2520 Ashland St
      (541) 488-2330
   Rodeway Inn
      1193 Siskiyou Blvd.
      (541) 482-2641
   Windmill's Ashland Hills Inn
      2525 Ashland St
      (541) 482-8310

ASTORIA
   Bayshore Motor Inn
      555 Hamburg St
      (503) 325-2205
   Crest Motel
      5366 Leif Erickson Dr
      (503) 325-3141
   Red Lion Inn
      400 Industry St
      (503) 325-7373

BAKER CITY
   Quality Inn
      810 Campbell
      (541) 523-2242

BANDON
   Caprice Motel
      Route 101
      (541) 347-4494
   Inn at Face Rock Resort
      3225 Bandon-By-The-Sea
      (800) 638-3092

BEAVERTON
   Greenwood Inn
      10700 SW Allen Blvd.
      (503) 643-7444

BEND
   Best Western Entrada
      19221 Century Dr
      (541) 382-4080
   Best Western Woodstone
      721 NE 3rd
      (541) 382-1515
   Comfort Inn
      61200 S Route 97
      (541) 388-2227
   Hampton Inn
      15 NE Butler Market Rd
      (541) 388-4114
   Red Lion Inn (North)
      1415 NE 3rd St
      (541) 382-7011
   Red Lion Inn (South)
      849 NE 3rd St.
      (541) 382-8384
   Shilo Inn
      3105 O B Riley Rd
      (541) 389-9600
   Sleep Inn of Bend
      600 NE Bellevue
      (541) 330-0050

BOARDMAN
   Nuggett Inn
      Hwy 84 & Boardman Rd
      (541) 481-2375

BROOKINGS
   Best Western Beachfront Inn
      Lower Harbor Rd
      (541) 469-7779

Harbor Inn Motel
15991 Rte 101
(541) 469-3194
Pacific Sunset Motel
1144 Chetco
(541) 469-2141
BURNS
Best Western Ponderosa
577 W. Monroe
(541) 573-2047
Royal Inn
999 Oregon Ave.
(541) 573-5295
CAMP SHERMAN
Cold Springs Resort
Cold Springs Resort Lane
(541) 595-6271
CANNON BEACH
Best Western
Ocean Front
(503) 436-2274
Ecola Creek Lodge
208 5th St.
(503) 436-1566
Surfsand Resort
Gower St.
(503) 436-2274
Tolvana Inn
3400 S. Hemlock
(503) 436-2211
CASCADE LOCKS
Best Western Columbia River
735 WaNaPa
(541) 374-8777
CLACKAMAS
Clackamas Inn
16010 SE 82nd St.
(503) 650-5340
Cypress Inn
9040 SE Adams
(503) 655-0062
COOS BAY
Best Western Holiday
411 N. Bayshore
(541) 269-5111
Edgewater Inn
275 E. Johnson
(541) 267-0423

Red Lion Inn
1313 N. Bayshore
(541) 267-4141
COQUILLE
Myrtle Lane Motel
787 N. Central Blvd.
(541) 396-2102
CORVALLIS
Harrison House B&B
2310 NW Harrison
(541) 752-6248
Shanico Inn
1113 NW 9th Ave.
(541) 754-7474
COTTAGE GROVE
Best Western Village Green
725 Row River Rd.
(541) 942-2491
Comfort Inn
845 Gateway Blvd.
(541) 942-9747
Holiday Inn Express
1601 Gateway Blvd.
(541) 942-1000
CRESCENT
Woodsman Country Lodge
Route 97
(541) 433-2710
EUGENE
Best Western Greentree
1759 Franklin Blvd.
(541) 485-2727
Best Western New Oregon
1655 Franklin Blvd.
(541) 683-3669
Eugene Hilton
66 E 6th St.
(541) 342-2000
Ramada Inn
225 Coburg Rd.
(541) 342-5181
Red Lion Inn
205 Coburg Rd.
(541) 342-5201
The Valley River Inn
1000 Valley River Way
(541) 687-0123

FLORENCE
Money Saver Motel
170 Hwy 101
(541) 997-7131
Ocean Breeze Motel
85165 Highway 101
(541) 997-2642
Park Motel
85034 Hwy 101
(541) 997-2634

GEARHEART
Gearheart by the Sea
1157 N. Marion
(503) 738-8331

GOLD BEACH
Best Western Beachcomber
1250 S. Hwy 101
(541) 247-6691
Inn at Gold Beach
29171 S. Ellensburg Ave
(541) 247-6606
Ireland's Rustic Cottages
29330 S. Ellensburg Ave.
(541) 247-7718

GRANTS PASS
Best Western Grants Pass
111 NE Agness
(541) 476-1117
Best Western at the Rogue
8959 Rogue River Hwy
(541) 582-2200
Holiday Inn Express
105 NE Agness
(541)471-6144
Motel Orleans
1889 NE 6th St.
(541) 479-8301
Motel 6
1800 NE 7th St.
(541) 474-1331
Redwood Motel
815 NE 6th St.
(541) 476-0878
Riverside Inn
971 SE 6th St
(541) 476-6873
River's Reach B&B
4025 Williams Hwy
(541) 474-4411

GRESHAM
Holiday Inn Express
2323 NE 181 St
(503) 492-4000

HOOD RIVER
Best Western Hood River
1108 E. Marina Way
(541) 386-2200
Vagabond Lodge
4070 Westcliff Dr
(541) 386-2992

JACKSONVILLE
Stage Lodge
830 N. 5th St
(541) 899-3953

JOHN DAY
Best Western
315 W. Main St
(541) 575-1700
Dreamers Lodge
144 N. Canyon
(541) 575-0526

HARBOR
Chart House
15833 Pedroili
(541) 465-3867

HILLSBORO
Best Western Hallmark
3500 NE Cornell Rd
(503) 648-3500
Residence Inn
18855 NW Tanasbourne
(503) 531-3200

KLAMATH FALLS
Best Western Klamath
4061 South 6th St
(541) 882-1200
Oregon Motel 8
5225 Route 97
(541) 883-3431
Red Lion Inn
3612 S. 6th St
(541) 882-8864
Shilo Suites Hotel
2500 Almond St.
(541) 885-7980

LA GRANDE
Best Western Pony Soldier
2612 Island Ave
(541) 963-7195

LAKE OSWEGO
Best Western Sherwood
15700 SW Upper Boones
(503) 620-2980
Crowne Plaza
14811 Kruse Oaks Blvd
(503) 624-8400

LAKEVIEW
Best Western
414 N. G St
(541) 947-2194

LINCOLN CITY
Best Western Lincoln Sands
535 NW Inlet
(541) 994-4227
Coho Inn
1635 NW Harbor
(541) 994-3684
Dock of the Bay Motel
116 SW 51st St
(541) 996-3549
Holiday Inn Express
1091 SE 1st St
(541) 996-4400

LONG CREEK
Long Creek Lodge
171 W. Main St
(541) 421-9212

MADRAS
Best Western Rama
12 SW 4th
(541) 475-6141
Sonny's Motel
1539 Rte 97
(541) 475-7217

MEDFORD
Best Western Medford Inn
1015 S. Riverside
(541) 773-8266
Best Western Pony Soldier Inn
2340 Crater Lake Hwy
(541) 779-2011
Holiday Inn
2300 Crater Lake Hwy
(541) 779-2623
Horizon Motor Inn
1154 E. Barnett Rd.
(541) 779-5085
Pear Tree Motel
3730 Fern Valley
(541) 535-4445
Red Lion Inn
200 N. Riverside
(541) 779-5811
Reston Hotel
2300 Crater Lake Hwy.
(541) 779-3141
Windmill Inn
1950 Biddle Rd.
(541) 779-0050

MOUNT HOOD
Mount Hood Inn
87450 E. Gov. Camp Loop
(541) 272-3205
Red Lion Inn
3612 So. 6th St.
(541) 882-8864

MYRTLE POINT
Myrtle Trees Motel
1010 8th St.
(541) 572-5811

NEWBURG
Shilo Inn
501 Sitka Ave.
503) 537-0303

NEWPORT
Best Western Hallmark Resort
744 SW Elizabeth St.
(541) 265-8853
Shilo Inn-Oceanside
536 SW Elizabeth St.
(541) 265-7701
Val-U-Inn
531 SW Fall St.
(541) 265-6203
Whaler Motel
155 SW Elizabeth St.
(541) 265-9261

OAKRIDGE
Best Western Oakridge Inn
47433 Rte 58
(541) 782-2212

ONTARIO
Best Western
251 Goodfellow St.
(541) 889-2600

Oregon

Holiday Inn
 1249 Tapadera Ave.
 (541) 889-8621
Super 8 Motel
 266 Goodfellow St.
 (541) 889-8282
OREGON CITY
 Val-U Inn
  1900 Clackamette Dr.
  (503) 655-7141
PENDLETON
 Chaparral Motel
  620 SW Tutillla
  (541) 276-8654
 Red Lion Inn
  304 SE Nye Ave.
  (541) 276-6111
 Super 8 Motel
  601 SE Nye Ave.
  (541) 276-8881
 Wildhorse Resort
  72779 Route 331
  (541) 278-2274
PORTLAND
 Best Western Inn
  420 NE Holladay
  (503) 233-6331
 Best Western Heritage
  4319 NW Yeon
  (503) 497-9044
 Best Western Inn at Meadows
  1215 N Hayden Meadows Dr.
  (503) 286-9600
 Clarion Hotel (Airport)
  6233 NE 78th
  (503) 251-2000
 Comfort Inn
  431 NE Multnomah
  (503) 233-7933
 Days Inn
  1414 SW 6th Ave.
  (503) 221-1611
 Delta Inn
  9930 N. Whitaker
  (503) 289-1800
 Fifth Avenue Suites
  521 SW 5th
  (800) 711-2971

Hotel Vintage Plaza
 422 SW Broadway
 (503) 228-1212
Howard Johnsons (Airport)
 7101 NE 82nd Ave
 (503) 255-6722
Imperial Hotel
 400 SW Broadway
 (503) 228-7221
Marriott Hotel
 1401 SW Front Ave
 (503) 226-7600
Oxford Suites
 12226 N. Jantzen Dr
 (503) 283-3030
Red Lion Hotel
 310 SW Lincoln
 (503) 221-0450
Oxford Suites
 12226 N. Jantzen Dr
 (503) 283-3030
Quality Inn (Airport)
 8247 NE Sandy Blvd
 (503) 254-4111
Red Lion Hotel Columbia Rvr.
 1401 N. Hayden Dr
 (503) 283-2111
Red Lion Inn-Jantzen Beach
 909 N. Hayden Island Dr.
 (503) 283-4466
Residence Inn
 1710 NE Multnomah
 (503) 288-1400
Riverside Inn
 50 SW Morrison
 (503) 221-0711
PORT ORFORD
 Econo Lodge
  544 6th St.
  (541) 332-3040
REDMOND
 Redmond Inn
  1545 Hwy 97
  (541) 548-1091
REEDSPORT
 Anchor Bay Inn
  1821 Rte 101
  (541) 271-2149

Oregon

Best Western Salbasgeon
1400 Rte 101
(541) 271-4831
Salbasgeon Inn of Umpqua
45209 Rte 38
(541) 271-2025
ROCKAWAY BEACH
Silver Sands Motel
215 S. Pacific
(503) 355-2206
Tradewinds Motel
523 N. Pacific Ave
(503) 355-2112
ROSEBURG
Best Western Garden Villa
760 Garden Valley Blvd
(541) 672-1601
Holiday Inn Express
375 W. Harvard Blvd
(541) 673-7517
ROGUE RIVER
Best Western Inn
8959 Rogue River Hwy
(541) 582-2200
Howard Johnson
978 NE Stephen
(541) 673-5082
Windmill Inn of Roseburg
1450 NW Mulholland Dr
(541) 673-0901
ST. HELENS
Best Western Oak Meadows
585 S. Columbia River Hwy
(503) 397-3000
SALEM
Phoenix Inn
4370 Comercial SE
(503) 588-9220
Quality Inn
3301 Market St SE
(503) 370-7888
SEASIDE
Aloha Inn
441 2nd Ave
(503) 738-9581
Best Western Oceanside
414 N. Prom
(503) 738-3334

Comfort Inn Boardwalk
545 Broadway
(503) 738-3011
SISTERS
Best Western Ponderosa Lodge
505 W Rte 20
(541) 549-1234
Comfort Inn
540 Route 20 W
(541) 549-7829
SPRINGFIELD
Motel Orleans
3315 Gateway Rd
(541) 746-1314
Red Lion Inn/Eugene
3280 Gateway Rd
(541) 726-8181
Rodeway Inn
3480 Hutton St
(541) 746-8471
Village Inn Motel
1875 Mohawk Blvd
(541) 747-4546
SUTHERLIN
Pennywise Motel
150 Myrtle St
(541) 459-1424
THE DALLES
Best Western Tapadera
112 W. 2nd
(541) 296-9107
Days Inn
2500 W. 6th
(541) 296-1191
Lone Pine Motel
351 Lone Pine Rd
(541) 298-2800
Quality Inn
2114 W. 6th
(541) 298-5161
Shilo Inn
3223 Bret Clodfelter Way
(541) 298-5502
TIGARD
Best Western Inn Chateau
17993 Lower Boones Ferry
(541) 620-2030
Embassy Suites
9000 SW Washington Sq.
(541) 644-4000

Oregon

Shilo Inn
10830 SW Greenburg Rd
(503) 620-4320
TILLAMOOK
Shilo
2515 N. Main St
(503) 842-7971
Western Royal Inn
1125 N. Main St
(503) 842-8844
Whiskey Creek B&B
7500 Whiskey Creek Rd.
(503) 842-2408
TROUTDALE
Phoenix Inn
477 NW Phoenix Dr
(541) 669-6500
TUALATIN
Sweetbriar Inn
7125 SW Nyberg Rd
(503) 692-5800
WARRENTON
Shilo Inn
1609 E. Harbor Dr
(541) 861-2181

WILSONVILLE
Holiday Inn
25425 SW Boones Ferry Rd
(541) 682-2211
WINCHESTER BAY
Winchester Bay Rodeway Inn
390 Broadway
(541) 271-4871
WOODBURN
Comfort Inn
120 NE Amey Rd.
(503) 982-1727
Holiday Inn Express
2887 Newburg Hwy
(503) 982-6515
YACHATS
The Adobe Motel
1555 Hwy 101
(541) 547-3141
Fireside Motel
1881 Hwy 101
(541) 547-3636
Holiday Inn Motel
5933 Hwy 101
(541) 547-3120

Washington

ABERDEEN
    Olympic Inn
        616 W. Heron St
        (360) 533-4200
    Red Lion Inn
        521 W. Wishkah
        (360) 532-5210

ANACORTES INN
    Anacortes Inn
        3006 Commercial Ave
        (360) 293-3153
    Fidalgo Country Inn
        1250 Rte 20
        (360) 293-3494
    Islands Inn
        3401 Commercial Ave
        (360) 293-4644

ARLINGTON INN
    Arlington Motor Inn
        2214 Route 530
        (360) 652-9595

AUBURN
    Best Western Pony Soldier Inn
        1521 D St NE
        (253) 939-5950
    Nendels Inn Auburn
        102 15th St NE
        (253) 833-8007
    Val-U Inn
        9 14th Ave NW
        (253) 735-9600

BELFAIR
    Belfair Motel
        Route 3
        (206) 275-4485

BELLEVUE
    Best Western Bellevue Inn
        11211 Main St
        (425) 455-5240
    Red Lion Inn Bellevue Center
        818 112th Ave. NE
        (425) 455-1515
    Residence Inn
        14455 29th Ave. NE
        (425) 882-1222
    West Coast Bellevue Hotel
        625 - 116th Ave NE
        (425) 455-9444

BELLINGHAM
    Best Western Lakeway
        714 Lakeway Dr
        (360) 671-1011
    Days Inn
        125 E. Kellog Rd
        (360) 671-6200
    Lions Inn Motel
        2419 Elm St
        (360) 733-2330
    Motel 6
        3701 Byron
        (360) 671-4494
    Quality Inn
        100 E. Kellogg Rd
        (360) 647-8000
    Rodeway Inn
        3710 Meridian St
        (360) 738-6000
    Travelodge
        101 N. Samish Way
        (360) 733-8280
    Val-U Inn
        805 Lakeway Dr
        (360) 671-9600

BOTHELL
    Residence Inn
        11920 NE 195th St
        (206) 485-3030

BREMERTON
    Dunes Motel
        3400 11th St
        (360) 377-0093
    Flagship Inn
        4320 Kitsap Way
        (360) 479-6566
    Midway Inn
        2909 Wheaton Way
        (360) 479-2909
    Oyster Bay Inn
        4412 Kitsap Way
        (360) 377-5510

Quality Inn
    4303 Kitsap Way
    (360) 405-1111
BUCKLEY
    Mountain View Inn
    Route 410
    (360) 829-1100
CASTLE ROCK
    Timberland Motor Inn
    1271 Mt. St. Helens Way
    (360) 274-6002
CENTRALIA
    Days Inn
    702 Harrison
    (360) 736-2875
    Ferryman's Inn
    1003 Eckerson Rd
    (360) 330-2094
    Motel 6
    1310 Belmont Ave
    (360) 330-2057
    Peppertree West Motor Inn
    1208 Alder St
    (360) 736-1124
CHEHALIS
    Mendels Inn
    122 Interstate Ave.
    (360) 748-0101
    Relax Inn
    550 SW Parkland Dr
    (360) 748-8608
CHENEY
    Willow Springs Motel
    5 B St
    (509) 235-5138
CHEWELAH
    Nordlig Motel
    101 W. Grant St
    (509) 935-6704
CLE ELUM
    Cedars Motel
    1001 East 1st St
    (509) 674-5535
    Stewart Lodge
    805 W. First St
    (509) 674-4548
    Timber Lodge Motel
    301 W. First St
    (509) 674-5966

COULEE DAM
    Coulee House Motel
    110 Roosevelt Way
    (509) 633-1101
COUPEVILLE
    Coupeville Inn
    200 Coveland St.
    (206) 678-6668
DAYTON
    Weinhard Hotel
    235 E. Main St
    (509) 382-4032
EAST WENATCHEE
    Fours Seasons Inn
    11 W. Grant Rd
    (509) 884-6611
EDMONDS
    Edmonds Harbor Inn
    130 W. Dayton St
    (425) 771-5021
    K & E Motor Inn
    23921 Route 99
    (425) 778-2181
ELLENSBURG
    Best Western Inn
    1700 Canyon Rd
    (509) 925-9801
    I-90 Motel
    1390 Dollar Way
    (509) 925-9844
    Nites Inn
    1200 S. Ruby
    (509) 962-9600
EVERETT
    Cypress Inn
    12619 - 4th Ave West
    (425) 347-9099
    Days Inn
    1122 N. Broadway
    (425) 252-8000
    Travelodge, Everett
    3030 Broadway
    (425) 259-6141
    Holiday Inn
    101 128th St SE
    (425) 745-2555
    Ramada Inn
    9602 19th Ave SE
    (425) 337-9090

Welcome Motor Inn
1205 N Broadway
(425) 252-4000
FEDERAL WAY
Best Western Inn
31611 20th Ave S
(253) 941-6000
FIFE
Best Western Inn
5700 Pacific Hwy E
(253) 922-0080
Econo Lodge
3518 Pacific Hwy E
(253) 922-0550
Royal Coachman Inn
5805 Pacific Hwy E
(253) 922-2500
FORKS
Forks Motel
351 Forks Ave
(360) 374-6243
Miller Tree B&B
654 E Division
(360) 374-6806
FREELAND
Harbour Inn Motel
1606 Main St
(360) 331-6900
GOLDENDALE
Ponderosa Motel
775 E. Broadway St
(509) 773-5842
HOQUIAM
Westwood Inn
910 Simpson Ave
(360) 532-8161
GREEN ACRES
Alpine Motel
18815 E. Cataldo
(509) 928-2700
HOQUIAM
Westwood Inn
910 Simpson Ave
(360) 532-8161
ISSAQUAH
Motel 6
1885 15th Pl. NW
(425) 392-8405

KELSO
Best Western Inn
310 Long Ave
(360) 425-9660
Motel 6
106 Minor Rd
(360) 425-3229
Red Lion Inn
510 Kelso Dr
(360) 636-4400
KENNEWICK
Cavanaugh's at Columbia Cntr
1101 N. Columbia Center
(509) 783-0611
Clearwater Inn
5616 W Clearwater Ave
(509) 735-2242
Comfort Inn
7801 W. Quinault
(509) 783-8396
Holiday Inn Express
4220 W. 27th Pl
(509) 736-2236
Kennewick Silver Cloud
7901 W. Quinault Ave
(509) 735-6100
Shaniko Suites
321 N. Johnson St.
(509) 735-6385
Tapadera Inn
300 N. Ely St
(509) 783-6191
KENT
Best Western Pony Soldier
1233 N. Central
(425) 852-7224
Days Inn Seattle-Kent
1711 Meeker St W
(425) 854-1950
Val U Inn
22420 84th Ave., South
(425) 872-5525
KIRKLAND
Best Western
12223 Northeast 116th
(425) 822-2300
La Quinta
10530 Northeast Northup
(425) 828-6585

Washington

LA CONNER
  The Heron in La Conner B&B
  117 Maple Ave.
  (360) 466-4626
LACEY
  Days Inn
  120 College St
  (360) 493-1991
LAKEWOOD
  Best Western Lakewood
  615 Motor Ave SW
  (253) 584-2212
LANGLEY
  Island Tyme B&B
  4940 Bayview R
  (360) 221-5078
LEAVENWORTH
  Bayern On the River
  1505 Alpen
  (509) 548-5875
  Bosch Garten
  9846 Dye Rd
  (509) 548-6900
  Der Ritterhof Motor Inn
  190 Route 2
  (509) 548-5845
  Evergreen Inn
  1117 Front St
  (509) 548-5515
  Obertal Motor Inn
  922 Commercial St.
  (509) 548-5204
  River's Edge Motel
  8401 Route 2
  (509) 548-7612
  Tyrolean Ritz
  633 Front St
  (509) 548-5455
LONG BEACH
  Anchorage Motor Court
  2209 N Blvd
  (360) 642-2351
  Nendel's Edgewater Inn
  409 10th St. SW
  (360) 642-2311
  Our Place at the Beach
  1309 South Blvd.
  (360) 642-3793

  Shaman Motel
  115 3rd St. SW
  (360) 642-3714
LONGVIEW
  Holiday Inn Express
  723 7th Ave.
  (360) 414-1000
  Hudson Manor Motel
  1616 Hudson St
  (360) 425-1100
  The Townhouse
  744 Washington Way
  (360) 423-1100
LYNDEN
  Windmill Inn Motel
  8022 Guide Meridien
  (360) 354-3424
LYNNWOOD
  Best Western Landmark
  4300 200th St. S.W.
  (425) 775-7447
  Residence Inn
  18200 Alderwood Mall
  (206) 771-1100
  Silver Cloud Lynnwood
  19332 36th Ave W
  (425) 775-7600
MARYSVILLE
  The Village Motor Inn
  235 Beech St.
  (360) 659-0005
MOCLIPS
  High Tide Ocean Beach Resort
  4890 Railroad Ave.
  (360) 276-4142
MONROE
  Best Western Baron
  19233 Route 2
  (360) 794-3111
MORTON
  Seasons Motel
  200 Westlake
  (360) 496-6835
MOSES LAKE
  Best Western Halmark
  3000 Marina Dr.
  (509) 765-9211
  Holiday Inn Express
  1745 East Kittleson
  (509) 766-2000

Washington

Shilo Inn
1819 East Kittleson
(509) 765-9317
Travelodge Moses Lake
316 S Pioneer Way
(509) 765-8631

MOUNT VERNON
Best Western College Way
300 West College Way
(360) 424-4287
Best Western Cotton Tree
2300 Market
(360) 428-5678
Days Inn
2009 Riverside Dr
(360) 424-4141
Mount Vernon Travelodge
1910 Freeway Dr.
(360) 428-7020

OAK HARBOR
Auld Holland Inn
5861 North Rte. 20
(360) 675-2288
Acorn Motor Inn
Route 20
(360) 675-6646
Best Western Harbor
Route 20
(360) 679-4567

OCEAN SHORES
Discovery Inn
1031 Discovery Ave., SE
(360) 289-3371
Grey Gull
651 Ocean Shores Blvd SW
(360) 289-3381
Polynesian Condominiums
615 Ocean Shores Blvd
(360) 289-3361
Shilo Inn Family Resort
707 Ocean Shores Blvd NW
(360) 289-4600

OKANOGAN
Ponderosa Motor Lodge
1034 S 2nd Ave
(509) 422-0400

OLYMPIA
Best Western Aladdin
900 Capitol Way
(360) 352-7200

Deep Lake Resort
12405 Tilley Road South
(360) 352-7388
Holiday Inn
2300 S Evergreen Pk
(360) 943-4000

OMAK
Omak Inn
912 Koala Dr
(509) 826-3822

OROVILLE
Red Apple Inn
1815 Main St.
(509) 476-3694

PACKWOOD
Crest Trail Lodge
12729 Hwy 12
(360) 494-4944
Mountain View Motel
13163 Hwy 12
(360) 494-5555
Woodland Motel
11890 Rte 12
(360) 494-6766

PASCO
King City Truck Stop
2100 E. Hillsboro Rd.
(509) 547-3475
Red Lion Inn
2525 N. 20th Ave.
(509) 547-0701
Vineyard Inn
1800 W. Lewis St
(509) 547-0791

PORT ANGELES
Flagstone Motel
415 E. First St
(360) 457-9494
Red Lion Bayshore Inn
221 North Lincoln St.
(360) 452-9215
Uptown Motel
101 E. 2nd St
(360) 457-9434

PORT TOWNSEND
Annapurna Inn
538 Adams St.
(360) 385-2909
Harborside Inn
330 Benedict St.
(360) 385-7509

Palace Hotel
1004 Water St
(360) 385-0773
Port Townsend Inn
2020 Washington St
(360) 385-2211
Water Street Hotel
635 Water St
(360) 385-5467
POULSBO
Poulsbo Inn
18680 Rte. 305
(360) 779-3921
PROSSER
Best Western
225 Meriot Dr.
(509) 786-7977
PULLMAN
American Travel Inn
515 S. Grand
(509) 334-3500
Holiday Inn Express
1190 Bishop Blvd.
(509) 334-4437
Quality Inn Paradise Creek
1050 Bishop Blvd.
(509) 332-0500
PURDY
Westwynd Motel
6703 144 St. NW
(800) 468-9963
PUYALLUP
Northwest Motor Inn
1409 South Meridian
(206) 841-2600
QUINCY
Traditional Inns
500 SW F St
(509) 787-3525
RAYMOND
Maunu's Mountcastle Motel
524 Third St.
(360) 942-5571
REDMOND
Silver Cloud Redmond
15304 NE 21st St
(425) 746-8200

RENTON
Nendel's Inn
3700 E. Valley Rd.
(425) 251-9591
Silver Cloud at Renton
1850 Maple Valley Hwy.
(425) 226-7600
RICHLAND
Bali Hi Motel
1201 George Washington
(509) 943-3101
Columbia Center Dunes
1751 Fowler Ave.
(509) 783-8181
Nendels Inn
615 Jadwin Ave
(509) 943-4611
Red Lion Inn - Hanford House
802 George Washington
(509) 946-7611
Shilo Inn
50 Comstock St.
(509) 946-4661
Vagabond Inn
515 George Washington
(509) 946-6117
RITZVILLE
Best Western Heritage
1405 Smitty's Blvd.
(509) 659-1007
Colwell Motor Inn
501 West First Ave
(509) 659-1620
The Portico
502 South Adams
(509) 659-0800
SAN JUAN ISLANDS
Inn at Friday Harbor Suites
680 Spring St.
(360) 378-3031
SEATAC
Airport Plaza Hotel
18601 International Blvd.
(206) 433-0400
Best Western Executel
20717 International Blvd.
(206) 878-3300
Econo Lodge
19225 International Blvd.
(206) 824-1350

Red Lion
  18740 International Blvd.
  (206) 246-8600
Seattle Airport Hilton
  17629 International Blvd.
  (206) 244-4800
Seattle Marriott
  3201 South 176th St.
  (206) 241-2000

SEATTLE
Aurora Seafair Inn
  9100 Aurora N
  (206) 522-3754
Best Western Executive Inn
  200 Taylor Ave North
  (206) 448-9444
Days Inn Town Center
  2205 7th Ave
  (206) 448-3434
Emerald Inn
  8512 Aurora Ave
  (206) 522-5000
Executive Residence
  2400 Elliott
  (206) 329-8000
Quality Inn
  2224 8th Ave
  (206) 624-6820
Ramada Inn, Northgate
  2140 N. Northgate
  (206) 365-0700
Residence Inn
  800 Fairview Ave North
  (206) 624-6000
Stouffer Madison Hotel
  515 Madison St
  (206) 583-0300
Travelodge Space Needle
  200 6th Ave.
  (206) 441-7878
Vagabond Space Needle
  325 Aurora N
  (206) 441-0400
Westin Hotel
  1900 5th Ave
  (206) 728-1000

SEDRO-WOOLLEY
Three Rivers Inn
  210 Ball St
  (360) 855-2626

SEQUIM
Best Western Sequim Bay Lodge
  268522 Rte 101
  (360) 683-0691
Econo Lodge
  810 E. Washington St
  (360) 683-7113
Great House Motel
  740 E. Washington
  (360) 683-7272
Red Ranch Inn
  830 W. Washington
  (360) 683-4195
Sundowner Motel
  364 W. Washington St.
  (360) 683-5532

SHELTON
Shelton Inn
  628 Railroad Ave
  (360) 426-4468
Super 8
  2943 Northview Circle
  (360) 426-1654

SILVERDALE
Cimarron Motel
  9734 NW Silverdale
  (360) 692-7777

SKYKOMISH
Skyriver Inn
  333 E. River Dr
  (360) 677-2261

SNOHOMISH
The Countryman
  119 Cedar Ave.
  (360) 568-9622

SNOQUALMIE PASS
Summit Inn at Snoqualmie Pass
  Route 906
  (425) 434-6300

SOAP LAKE
Notaras Lodge
  236 E. Main St
  (509) 246-0462

SPOKANE
Apple Tree Inn
  9508 N. Division St.
  (509) 466-3020
Best Western Northpointe
  9601 N. Newport Hwy.
  (509) 468-4201

Best Western Thunderbird
120 W Third Ave
(509) 747-2011

Best Western Tradewinds
3033 N. Division
(509) 326-5500

Cavanaugh's Fourth Ave.
110 E. Fourth Ave.
(509) 838-6101

Cavanaugh's River Inn
700 North Division St
(509) 326-5577

Comfort Inn
6309 E Broadway
(509) 535-7185

Days Inn
1919 N. Hutchinson
(509) 926-5399

Quality Inn
8923 E. Mission St.
(509) 928-5218

Ramada Inn
Spokane Intrnl. Airport
(509) 838-5211

Red Lion Hotel Spokane Center
322 N. Spokane Fall Court
(509) 455-9600

Red Lion Spokane Valley
1100 N. Sullivan Rd
(509) 924-9000

Rodeway Inn Center
827 W. First Ave
(509) 838-8271

Shilo Inn
923 E Third Ave
(509) 535-9000

Sierra Hotel Spokane
4212 West Sunset Rd
(509) 747-2021

Suntree Inn
211 S. Division St
(509) 838-6630

Super 8
2020 Argonne Rd
(509) 838-4888

Super 8 West
11102 Westbow Blvd
(509) 838-8800

Valu Inn/Nendels
1420 W. Second Ave
(509) 838-2026

SULTAN
Dutch Cup Motel
918 Main St
(360) 793-2215

SUNNYSIDE
Sunnyside Travelodge
408 Yakima Valley Hwy
(509) 837-7878

TACOMA
Best Western Tacoma
8726 S. Hosmer St
(253) 535-2880

Days Inn
6802 Tacoma Mall Blvd
(253) 475-5900

La Quinta Inn
1425 E 27th St
(253) 383-0146

Sheraton Hotel
1320 Broadway Plaza
(253) 572-3200

Shilo Inn
7414 Hosmer St
(253) 475-4020

Tacoma Travelodge
8820 S. Hosmer
(253) 539-1153

TONASKET
Red Apple Inn
Route 97
(509) 486-2119

TOPPENISH
Toppenish Inn Motel
515 S. Elm St
(509) 865-7444

TUKWILA
Best Western South
15901 W. Valley Rd
(206) 226-1812

Doubletree Suites Seattle
16500 Southcenter Pkwy
(206) 575-8220

Doubletree Inn Southcenter
205 Strander Blvd
(206) 246-8220

Hampton Inn
  7200 S 156th St
  (206) 228-5800
Homewood Suites
  6955 Southcenter Pkwy
  (206) 762-0300
Marriott Residence Inn
  16201 W. Valley Hwy
  (206) 226-5500

TUMWATER
  Best Western Tumwater
    5188 Capitol Blvd.
    (360) 956-1235
  Westcoast Tyee Hotel
    500 Tyee Dr.
    (360) 352-0511

TWISP
  Idle-A-While Motel
    505 N. Rte 20
    (509) 997-3222
  Alderbrook Resort
    E. 7101 Rte 106
    (509) 898-2200

UNION GAP
  Quality Inn
    12 E. Valley Mall Blvd.
    (509) 248-6924

VANCOUVER
  Best Western
    7901 NE 6th Ave.
    (360) 574-2151
  Quality Inn
    7001 NE Rte 99
    (360) 696-0516
  Red Lion Inn
    100 Columbia St
    (360) 694-8341
  Residence Inn
    8005 NE Parkway Dr
    (360) 253-4800
  Shilo Inn
    401 E. 13th St
    (360) 696-0411
  Shilo Inn
    13206 Rte 99
    (360) 573-0511

VASHON
  Swallows Nest Cottages
    6030 SW 248th St.
    (206) 463-2646

WALLA WALLA
  Best Western Walla Walla Suites
    7 East Oak St
    (509) 525-4700
  Comfort Inn
    520 N 2nd Ave
    (509) 525-2522
  Pony Soldier Motor Inn
    325 E. Main St
    (509) 529-4360
  Whitman Motor Inn
    107 N. 2nd St
    (509) 525-2200

WASHOUGAL
  Econo Lodge
    544 - 6th St
    (360) 835-8591

WENATCHEE
  Avenue Motel
    720 N. Wenatchee
    (509) 663-7161
  Best Western Inn
    1905 N. Wenatchee
    (509) 664-6565
  Holiday Lodge
    610 N. Wenatchee
    (509) 663-8167
  Orchard Inn
    1401 N. Miller St
    (509) 662-3443
  Red Lion
    1225 N. Wenatchee
    (509) 663-0711
  Vagabond Inn
    700 N. Wenatchee
    (509) 663-8133
  Westcoast Wenatchee Hotel
    201 N. Wenatchee
    (509) 662-1234

WINTHROP
  Cascade Inn
    960 Rte 20
    (509) 996-3100
  Riverun Inn
    27 Rader Rd
    (509) 996-2173
  The Virginian Resort
    808 N. Cascade Hwy
    (509) 996-2535

Winthrop Resort
950 Rte 20
(509) 996-2217
Wolfridge Resort
412 Wolf Creek Rd
(509) 996-2828
WOODLAND
Lewis River Inn
110 Lewis River Rd
(360) 225-6257
Scandia Motel
1123 Hoffman St
(360) 225-8006
Woodlander Inn
1500 Atlantic St
(360) 225-6548

YAKIMA
Cavanaugh's at Yakima Center
607 E. Yakima
(509) 248-5900
Holiday Inn Yakima
9 North Ninth St
(509) 452-6511
Red Lion Inn
818 N. First St
(509) 453-0391
Red Lion Inn-Yakima Valley
1507 N. First St
(509) 248-7850
Vagabond Inn
510 North First St
(509) 457-6155

British Columbia

ABBOTSFORD
  Holiday Inn Express
    2073 Clearbrook Rd.
    (604) 859-6211
  Quality Inn
    1881 Sumas Way
    (604) 853-1141
BARRIERE
  Mountain Spring Motel
    253 Yellowhead Hwy
    (250) 672-0090
BLACK CREEK
  Country Comfort B&B
    8214 Island Hwy.
    (250) 337-5273
BLIND BAY
  Birch Lane B&B
    Box 18
    (250) 675-4970
BLUE RIVER
  Mike Wiegele Heli Ski Village
    Hartwood St.
    (250) 673-8381
BOSWELL
  Mountain Shores Resort
    Route 3A
    (250) 223-8258
  401 Motor Inn
    2950 Boundry Rd.
    (250) 438-3451
  Lake City Motor Inn
    5415 Loughheed Hwy
    (250) 294-7545
BURNABY
  401 Motor Inn
    2950 Boundry Rd.
    (604) 438-3451
  Lake City Motor Inn
    5415 Lougheed Hwy
    (604) 294-5331
  Stay n Save Motor Inn
    3777 Henning Dr.
    (604) 473-5000

BURNS LAKE
  Burns Lake Motor Inn
    Route 16 E
    (250) 692-7545
CACHE CREEK
  Bonaparte Motel
    1395 Rte 97
    (250) 457-9693
  Tumbleweed Motel
    Hwy 97
    (604) 457-6522
CAMPBELL RIVER
  Anchor Inn
    261 Island Hwy.
    (250) 286-1131
  Austrian Chalet Resort
    462 S. Island Hwy.
    (250) 923-4231
  Best Western Austrian Chalet
    462 S. Island Hwy
    (250) 923-4231
  Campbell River Lodge
    1760 Island Hwy
    (250) 287-7446
CHASE
  Chase Country Motel
    576 Coburn St
    (250) 679-3333
CHEMAINUS
  Fuller Lake Motel
    9300 Trans Canada Hwy
    (250) 246-3282
CHETWYND
  Stagecoach Inn
    5413 South Access Rd.
    (250) 788-9666
CHILLIWACK
  Best Western Rainbow Country
    43971 Industrial Way
    (604) 795-3828
  Chilliwack Travelodge
    45466 Yale Rd.
    (604) 792-4240

British Columbia

Comfort Inn
45405 Luckakuck Way
(604) 858-0636
Hazelgreen B&B
4080 Steward Rd.
(604) 823-2496
Holiday Inn
45920 First Ave.
(604) 795-4788

CLEARWATER
Jasper Way Inn
57 E. Old Thompson Rd.
(250) 674-3345
Mountainview B&B
290 Murtle Cres.
(250) 674-2499
Wells Gray Inn
5 Village Rd.
(250) 674-2214

CLOWHOM
Clowhom Lake
Box 2720
(250) 226-4044

COURTENAY
Arbutus Hotel
275 8th St.
(250) 334-3121
Coast Westerly Hotel
1590 Cliffe Ave.
(250) 338-7741
Collingwood Inn
1675 Cliffe Ave.
(250) 338-1464
Forest Glen B&B
5760 Sea Terrace Rd.
(250) 334-4374
Quality Inn Kingfisher
4330 S. Island Hwy.
(250) 338-1323
Travelodge Courtenay
2605 S. Island Hwy.
(250) 334-4491

COWICHAN BAY
Kilpahlas Beach Resort
1681 Botwood Ln
(250) 748-6222

CRANBROOK
Inn of the South
803 Cranbrook St.
(250) 489-4301

Model A Inn
1908 Cranbrook St.
(250) 489-4600

CRESTON
City Centre Motel
220 15th Ave N.
(250) 428-2257
Downtowner Motor Inn
1218 Canyon St.
(250) 428-2238
Heighs House Antiques B&B
306 10th Ave. N
(250) 426-9905
Sunset Motel
2705 Canyon St.
(250) 428-2229

DAWSON CREEK
Trail Inn
1748 Alaska Ave.
(250) 782-8595

DELTA
Best Western Tsawwassen
1665 56th St.
(604) 943-8221
Delta Town and Country
6005 Hwy 17
(604) 946-4404
Our House Enterprises
4837 44A Ave.
(604) 946-2628

DUNCAN
Best Western Cowichan Valley
6474 Trans-Canada Hwy
(250) 748-2722
Falcon Nest Motel
5867 Trans-Canada Hwy.
(250) 748-8818
Silver Bridge Inn
140 Trans-Canada Hwy.
(250) 748-4311

FANNY BAY
Gull Cottage B&B
6634 Island Hwy S.
(888) 288-2144

FERNIE
Cedar Lodge Motel
101 7th Ave.
(250) 423-4622

Park Place Lodge
742 Hwy 3
(250) 423-6871

FIELD

Kicking Horse Lodge
100 Centre St.
(250) 343-6303

FORT NELSON

Coachouse Inn
4711 50th Ave. S.
(250) 774-3911

GALIANO ISLAND

Casa de Edrie Holloway
107 Cain Rd.
(888) 539-2581

GIBSONS

Casita B&B
744 Hillcrest
(604) 886-0686

Cedars Inn
895 Sunshine Coast Hwy
(604) 886-3008

GOLDEN

Golden Gate Motel
Trans-Canada Hwy
(250) 344-2252

Golden Rim Motor Inn
1416 Golden View Rd.
(250) 344-2216

Prestige Inn
1049 Trans-Canada Hwy
(250) 344-7990

GRAND FORKS

Western Traveler
1591 Central Ave
(250) 442-5566

HARRISON HOT SPRINGS

Harrison Hot Springs Hotel
On the Lake
(604) 796-2244

HOPE

Alpine Motel
505 Old Hope/Princeton Way
(604) 869-9931

Best Continental Motel
860 Fraser Ave
(604) 869-9726

Evergreen B&B
1208 Ryder St., Box 11
(604) 869-9918

Inn-Towne Motel
510 Trans-Canada Hwy
(604) 869-7276

Maple Leaf Motor Inn
377 Old Hope/Princeton Way
(604) 869-7101

Park Motel
832 4th Ave.
(604) 869-5891

Quality Inn
350 Old Hope/Princeton Way
(604) 869-9951

Swiss Chalets
456 Trans-Canada Hwy
(604) 869-9020

INVERMERE

Best Western Invermere
1310 7th Ave
(250) 34-9246

ISKUT

Red Goat Lodge
Hwy 37
(250) 234-3261

KALEDEN

Eden House B&B
104 Arlayne Rd.
(250) 497-8362

KAMLOOPS

Courtesy Inn Motel
1773 Trans-Canada Hwy.
(250) 372-8533

Days Inn
1285 Trans-Canada Hwy.
(250) 374-5911

Hospitality Inn
500 W. Columbia St.
(250) 374-4164

Kamloops Super 8
1521 Hugh Allen Dr.
(250) 374-8688

Kamloops Travelodge
430 Columbia St.
(250) 372-8202

Kings Motor Inn
1775 E. Trans-Canada Hwy
(250) 372-2800

Panorama Inn
610 W. Columbia St.
(250) 374-1515

British Columbia

Roche Lake Resort
Hwy 5A S.
(250) 828-2007
Stay n Save Motor Inn
1325 Columbia St
(250) 374-8877
Thompson Hotel
650 Victoria St.
(250) 374-1999
KELOWNA
Abbott Villa Motor Inn
1627 Abbott St.
(250) 763-7771
Big White Motor Lodge
1891 Parkinson Way
(250) 860-3982
Oasis Motor Inn
1884 Gordon Dr
(250) 763-5396
Siesta Motor Inn
3152 Lakeshore Rd
(250) 763-5013
Stay n Save Motor Inn
1140 Harvey Ave
(250) 762-8222
Prestige Inn Park Lake
1675 Abbott St.
(604) 860-7900
Town and Country
2629 Rte 97
(250) 860-7121
View to Remember B&B
1090 Trevor Dr.
(250) 769-4028
LADYSMITH
The Loyalist B&B
10890 Chemainus Rd.
(250) 245-2590
Secret Garden B&B
3511 Paulson Rd.
(250) 245-3578
LANGELEY
Country Style B&B
20324 49A Ave.
(604) 530-6647
Westward Inn
19650 Fraser Hwy
(604) 534-9238

LANTZVILLE
Ocean View B&B
7171 Dickinson Rd.
(250) 245-3578
MALAHAT
Malahat Bungalows Motel
Malahat Dr.
(604) 478-3011
MANNING PARK
Manning Park Resort
Hwy 3
(604) 840-8822
MAPLE RIDGE
Best Western Maple Ridge
21735 Lougheed Hwy
(604) 463-5111
Travelodge Maple Ridge
21650 Lougheed Hwy
(604) 467-1511
MCBRIDE
North Country Lodge
Route 16
(250) 569-0001
MERRITT
Merritt Motor Inn
3561 Vought St.
(250) 378-9422
Merritt Travelodge
3581 Vought St.
(250) 378-8830
NAKSUP
The Selkirk Inn
210 West 6th.
(250) 265-3666
NANAIMO
Beach Drive B&B
1011 Beach Dr.
(250) 753-9140
Best Western Northgate
6450 Metral Dr.
(250) 390-2222
Harbourview Days Inn
809 Island Hwy. S.
(250) 754-8171
Jingle Pot B&B
4321 Jingle Pot Rd.
(250) 758-5149
Travelodge
505 N. Terminal Ave.
(250) 754-6355

British Columbia

NARAMATA
Village Motel
244 Robinson Dr
(250) 496-5535
100 MILE HOUSE
Red Coach Inn
170 Cariboo Hwy.
(250) 395-2266
OLIVER
Southwind Inn
Route 97
(250) 498-3442
OSOYOOS
Bella Villa Resort Motel
6904 64A Ave. E
(250) 495-6751
Mont Kobau Motor Inn
Hwy 97
(250) 495-7322
Sahara Courtyard Inn
6204 67th St
(250) 495-7211
PARKSVILLE
Holiday Inn Express
424 W. Island Hwy
(250) 248-2232
Sand Dollar B&B
261 Pioneer Cres.
(250) 954-0200
PAUL LAKE
Sevinth Heaven B&B
7001 Paul Lake Rd.
(250) 573-7533
PENDER ISLAND
Corbett House Heritage
4309 Corbett Rd.
(250) 629-6305
PENTICTON
Bel-Air Motel
2670 Shaka Lake Rd.
(250) 492-6111
Clarion Lakeside Resort
21 Lakeshore Dr.
(250) 493-8221
Golden Sands Resort
1028 Lakeshore Dr.
(250) 492-3600
Ramada Courtyard Inn
1050 Eckhardt Ave. W.
(250) 492-8926

Spanish Villa Resort
890 Lakeshore Dr
(250) 492-2922
Waterfront Inn
3688 Parkview St.
(250) 492-8228
PORT ALBERNI
Alberni Inn
3805 Redford St.
(250) 723-9405
Timberlodge
Port Alberni Rd. South
(250) 723-9415
Village Motel
4151 Redford St.
(250) 723-8133
PORT HARDY
The Old House B&B
8735 Hastings St.
(250) 949-8372
PORT MCNEIL
Ev's Bunkhouse on the Beach
2250 Beach Dr.
(250) 956-4993
PRINCE GEORGE
Connaught Motor Inn
1550 Victoria St.
(250) 562-4441
Ramada Hotel Downtown
444 George St.
(250) 563-0055
PRINCE RUPERT
Aleeda Motel
900 Third Ave
(250) 627-1367
Coast Prince Rupert Hotel
118 Sixth St.
(250) 624-6711
Crest Motor Hotel
222 First Ave. W.
(250) 224-6771
QUALICUM BEACH
Blue Willow B&B
524 Quatna Rd.
(250) 752-9052
Old Dutch Inn (by the sea)
2690 Island Hwy W.
(250) 752-6914

British Columbia

QUESNEL
  Talisman Inn
    753 Front St
    (250) 992-7247
RADIUM HOT SPRINGS
  Cedar Motel
    7593 Main St. W.
    (250) 347-9463
  The Chalet
    5063 Madsen Rd.
    (250) 347-9305
  Lido Motel
    4876 McKay St.
    (250) 347-9533
  Sunset Motel
    4883 McKay St.
    (250) 347-9863
REVELSTOKE
  Alpine Lane B&B
    487 Alpine Lane
    (250) 837-6106
  Best Western Wayside Inn
    1901 LaForme Blvd.
    (250) 837-6161
  Regent Inn
    112 Victoria Rd.
    (250) 837-2107
  Wintergreen Inn B&B
    312 Kootenay St.
    (800) 216-2008
RICHMOND
  Best Western Richmond
    7551 Westminster Hwy
    (604) 273-7878
  Delta Pacific Resort
    10251 St. Edward's Dr.
    (604) 278-9611
  Delta Vancouver Airport
    3500 Cessna Dr.
    (604) 278-1241
  Radisson President Hotel
    8181 Cambie Rd.
    (604) 276-8181
  Stay n Save Motor Inn
    10551 St. Edwards Dr.
    (604) 273-3311
  Travelodge-Vancouver Airport
    3071 St. Edwards
    (604) 278-5155

SAANICHTON
  Super 8
    2477 Mount Newton
    (250) 652-6888
SALMON ARM
  Coast Shuswap Inn
    Trans-Canada Hwy.
    (250) 832-7081
  Super 8
    2901 10th Ave
    (250) 832-8812
  Travelodge
    2401 Trans-Canada Hwy.
    (250) 832-9721
SAVONA
  Lakeside Country Inn
    1001 Savona Access Rd.
    (250) 373-2528
SIDNEY
  Best Western Emerald Isle
    2306 Beacon Ave.
    (250) 656-4441
  Cedarwood Motel
    Lochside Dr.
    (250) 656-5551
  Ease-mate
    11435 Hawthorne Pl.
    (250) 655-0600
  Hotel Sidney Waterfront
    2537 Beacon Ave.
    (250) 656-1131
  Log House
    1510 Sylvan Pl.
    (250) 656-4421
  Mandeville Tudor Cottage
    1064 Landsend Rd.
    (250) 655-1587
  Pine Needle Place
    9314 Lochside Dr.
    (250) 656-2095
  Quality Inn Waddling Dog
    2476 Mt. Newton Rd.
    (250) 652-1146
  Travelodge-Victoria Airport
    2280 Beacon Ave.
    (250) 656-1176
SMITHERS
  Aspen Motor Inn
    4628 Yellowhead Hwy
    (250) 847-4551

SOOKE
Blackfish B&B
2440 Blackfish Rd.
(250) 642-6842
SOINTULA
Donovan B&B
20 Lands End Rd.
(250) 973-6030
SUMMERLAND
Eagle's Bluff B&B
RR 1, Site 31F, Comp 18
(250) 494-7357
Summerland Motel
2107 Tait St.
(250) 494-4444
SURREY
Ramada Limited
19225 Hwy. 10
(604) 576-8388
Surrey Inn at Skytrain
9860 King George Hwy
(604) 588-9511
TATLA LAKE
Chilko Lake Resort
Off Route 20
(250) 481-1135
TERRACE
Coast Inn of the West
4620 Lakesle Rd.
(250) 638-8141
TOFINO
Clayoquot Retreat B&B
120 Arnett St.
(250) 725-3305
Wickaninnish Inn
4 Osprey Ln.
(250) 725-3100
TSAWWASSEN
Southland House
1160 Boundry Bay
(604) 943-1846
UCLUELET
Spring Cove B&B
963 Peninsula Rd.
(250) 726-2955
VALEMOUNT
Chalet Continental
1450 Fifth Ave.
(250) 566-9787

VAN ANDA
Bunkhouse B&B
Box 62
(604) 483-1157
VANCOUVER
Best Western Chateau Granville
1100 Granville St.
(604) 669-7070
Bosman's Motor Hotel
1060 Howe St.
(604) 682-3171
Canyon Court Motel
1748 Capilano Rd.
(604) 988-3181
Coast Vancouver Airport
1041 SW Marine Dr
(604) 263-1555
French Quarter B&B
2051 W. 19th Ave.
(604) 737-0973
Georgian Court Hotel
773 Beatty St.
(604) 682-555
Holiday Inn Hotel/Suites
1110 Howe St.
(604) 684-2151
Holiday Inn/Vancouver Center
711 W. Broadway
(604) 879-0511
Lion's Gate Travelodge
2060 Marine Dr.
(604) 985-5311
Quality Hotel-Downtown
1335 Howe St.
(604) 682-0229
Quality Inn - Airport
725 SE Marine Dr.
(604) 321-6611
Sylvia Historic Hotel
1154 Gilford St.
(604) 681-9321
Vancouver Renaissance
1133 Hastings St.
(604) 689-9211
Westin Bayshore
1601 Georgia St.
(604) 682-3377

VERNON
Best Western Vernon Lodge
3914 32nd St.
(250) 545-3385
Prestige Inn
4411 32nd St.
(250) 558-5991
Schell Motel
2810 35th St.
(250) 545-1351
Vernon Travelodge
3000 28th St.
(250) 545-2161

VICTORIA
Admiral Motel
257 Belleville St.
(250) 388-6267
Carriage House B&B
596 Toronto St.
(250) 384-7437
Executive House Hotel
777 Douglas St.
(250) 388-5111
Gate Inn B&B
(250) 744-8757
Harbor Towers
Oswego St.
(250) 385-2405
Oxford Castle Inn
133 Gorge Rd. E.
(250) 388-6431
Robin Hood Motel
136 Gorge Rd.
(250) 388-4302
Ryan's B&B
224 Superior St.
(250) 389-0012
Shamrock Motel
675 Superior St.
(250) 385-8768

Stay n Save Motel
3233 Maple St.
(250) 475-7500
Tally Ho Motor Inn
3020 Douglas St.
(250) 386-6141

WASA LAKE
Wasa Lakeside B&B
Spruce Rd.
(888) 422-3636

WHISTLER
Delta Whistler Resort
4050 Whistler Dr.
(604) 932-1962
Edgewater Lodge
8841 Hwy 99
(604) 932-0688
Tantalus Resort Condominium
4200 Whistler Way
(604) 932-4146
Whistler Fairways Hotel
4005 Whistler Way
(604) 932-2522

WHITE DOCK
Crescent Green B&B
3467 141st St.
(604) 538-2935

WILLIAMS LAKE
Drummond Lodge Motel
1405 Cariboo Hwy
(250) 392-5334
Williams Lake Super 8
1712 Broadway Ave
(250) 398-8884

YELLOWPOINT
Inn of the Sea Resort
3600 Yellowpoint Rd.
(250) 245-2211

Chain Hotels/Motels
Web Sites/800 Numbers

Best Western: (800) 528-1234
http://www.bestwestern.com/
Budgetel Inns: (800) 4-BUDGET
http://www.budgetel.com/
Comfort Inns: (800) 228-5150
http://www.hotelchoice.com/
Courtyard: (800) 321-2211
http://www.marriott.com/courtyard/
Canadian Pacific: (800) 441-1414
http://www.cphotels.ca/
Clarion: (800) 252-7466
http://www.hotelchoice.com/
Days Inn: (800) DAYS INN
http://www.daysinn.com/
Delta: (800) 268-1133
http://www.DeltaHotels.com/
Doubletree: (800) 222-TREE
http://www.doubletreehotels.com/
Econo Lodge: (800) 553-2666
http://www.EconoLodge.com/
Embassy Suites: (800) 362-2779
http://www.embassy-suites.com/
Fairfield Inn: (800) 228-2800
http://www.marriott.com/fairfieldinn/
Four Seasons: (800) 332-3442
http://www.fourseasons.com/
Guest Quarters: (800) 424-2900
http://www.doubletreehotels.com/
Hampton Inns: (800) HAMPTON
http://www.hamptoninn.com/
Hawthorne Suites: (800) 527-1133
http://www.hyatt.com/
Hilton Hotels: (800) HILTONS
http://www.hilton.com/
Holiday Inn: (800) HOLIDAY
http://www.holidayinn.com/
Homewood Suites: (800) 225-5466
http://www.homewoodsuites.com/
Howard Johnson: (800) 446-4656
http://www.hojo.com/
Hyatt Corp: (800) 233-1234
http://www.hyatt.com/

La Quinta: (800) 531-5900
http://www.travelweb.com/
TravelWeb/lq/common/laquinta.html
Loews: (800) 445-6937
http://loewshotels.com/
Marriott Hotels: (800) 228-9290
http://www.marriott.com/
Motel 6: (800) 466-8356
Quality Inns: (800) 228-5151
http://www.hotelchoice.com/
Radisson Hotels: (800) 333-3333
https://www.radisson.com/
Ramada Inns: (800) 2-RAMADA
http://www.ramada.com/
Red Lion: (800) RED-LION
http://www.doubletreehotels.com
Red Roof Inns: (800) 843-7663
http://www.redroof.com/
Residence Inn: (800) 331-3131
http://www.marriott.com/residenceinn/
Ritz-Carlton: (800) 241-3333
http://www.marriott.com/ritzcarlton/
Rodeway: (800) 228-2000
http://www.rodeway.com/
Sheraton Hotels: (800) 325-3535
http://www.sheraton.com/
Shilo Inn: (800) 222-2244
http://www.shiloinns.com/
Shoney's Inns: (800) 222-2222
http://www.shoneysinn.com/
Sleep Inn: (800) 753-3746
http://www.hotelchoice.com
Super 8: (800) 800-8000
http://www.super8motels.com/
Travelodge: (800) 578-7878
http://www.travelweb.com/
Westin: (800) 228-3000
http://www.westin.com/
Wyndham: (800) WYNDHAM
http://www.wyndham.com/

Regulations for California's State Forests/Parks

Dogs older than four months must have a certificate stating they have been vaccinated against rabies within the last year. For more information, please telephone the California State Park Service at (916) 653-6995. You may also call the California Division of Tourism at (800) 462-2543. California's State Park regulations **permit** leashed dogs in the following areas:

Anderson Marsch State Park
Andrew Molera State Park
Annadel State Park
Anthony Chabot Regional Park
Anza Borrego Desert State Park
Armstrong Redwoods State Park
Auburn State Park
Austin Creek State Park
Benbow Lake State Park
Bethany Reservoir State Park
Big Basin Redwoods State Park
Big Lagoon Park
Brannan Island State Park
Butano State Park
Calaveras Big Trees State Park
Castaic Lake State Park
Castle Crags State Park
Caswell Memorial State Park
Cayucos Beach
Clear Lake State Park
Columbia State Historic Park
Colusa-Sacramento River State Park
Contra Loma Park
Cow Mountain Park
Cuyamaca Rancho State Park
D.L. Bliss State Park
Del Norte Coast Redwoods State Park
Del Valle Park
Doran Park
Eagle Lake Park
Freemont Peak State Park
George J. Hatfield State Park
Golden Gate Park
Golden Gate Recreational Area
Griffith Park
Grizzly Creek Redwoods State Park
Gualala Point Park
Hendy Woods State Park
Henry Cowell Redwood State Park
Henry W. Coe State Park
Humboldt Lagoons State Park
Jedediah Smith Redwoods State Park
Lake Berryessa
Lake Casitas
Lake Elsinore State Park
Lake Nacimiento
Lake Perris State Park
Loch Lomand Park
Los Baños Creek Reservoir State Park
MacKerricher State Park
Malakoff Diggins State Park
Manresa Beach State Park
Martinez Shoreline Park
McArthur-Burney Falls State Park
McConnell State Park
Millerton Lake State Park
Mission Bay Park
Morro Strand Beach State Park
Mt. San Jacinto Wilderness State Park
Napa Valley State Park
Palomar Mountain State Park
Patrick's Point State Park
Plumas-Eureka State Parks
Point Mugu State Park
Point Pinole Shoreline
Portola State ParkPrarie Creek
Redwoods State Park
Pyramid Lake State Park
Richardson Cove State Park
Russian Gulch State Park
San Bernardino Recreation Area
San Leandro Bay Shoreline
Santa Monica Mountains
Senator Wash Reservoir
Shadow Cliffs Park
Smith River Recreation Area
South Yuba River State Park
Spring Lake
Squaw Lake
Sunol Wilderness
Temescal Park
Vasona Park
Whiskeytown-Shasta/Trinity
Will Roger's State Historic Park

Regulations for California's National Parks and Forests

All of the National Parks and Forests listed below allow dogs on the trails and in the wilderness areas. They may be on or off leash, but if they are off leash they must be under voice control at all times. For further information please call the National Park Service at (415) 556-0560 or the National Forest Service at (415) 705-2874.

Angeles National Forest
Cleveland National Forest
Death Valley National Monument
Devil's Postpile National Monument
East Mojave Park National
 Conservation Area
Eldorado National Forest
Inyo National Forest
King Range National
 Conservation Area
Klamath National Forest
Lake Tahoe Basin Management Unit
Lassen National Forest
Lassen Volcanic National Park
Los Padres National Forest

Mendocino National Forest
Mondoc National Forest
Plumas National Forest
Redwood National Park
San Bernardino National Forest
Sequoia and Kings Canyon
 National Park
Sequoia National Forest
Shasta-Trinity National Forest
Sierra National Forest
Six Rivers National Forest
Stanislaus National Forest
Tahoe National Forest
Toiyabe National Forest

Regulations for Oregon's State and National Parks and Forests

Dogs are allowed in the Crater Lake National Park, as well as in the Hells Canyon and Oregon Dunes Recreation Areas. They are allowed in all of Oregon's national forests and areas run by the Army Corps of Engineers. For further information about Oregon's national forests please call the national forest service at 503-326-2877. For further information about Oregon's state parks and recreation areas please call 503-378-6305. They are also allowed in most of Oregon's state parks. The following state parks and lakes **do not allow** dogs:

Ainsworth
Bastendorff Beach
Beachside
Benson
Beverly Beach
Cape Arago

Cape Blanco
Cape Kiwanda
Casey
Emigrant Springs
Pioneer Park
William M. Tugman

Regulations for Washington's State and National Parks and Forests

Dogs are **not allowed** in any of Washington's national parks, recreation areas, or lands run by the Army Corps of Engineers. (The only exceptions are the Coulee Dam and the Olympic National Forest where leashed dogs are allowed.) They are allowed in most of Washington's state parks. The following state parks and lakes **do not allow** dogs:

Cascade
Chief Looking Glasss
Columbia
Connelly
Entiat
Lake Gillette
Lake Sacajawea
Lighthouse Marine
Mayfield Lake County Park
McNary Loch and Dam
Montlake Park
Moses Lake R.V. Park
Phil Simon Park
Point Defiance Park
Samish Park
Semiahmoo County Park
Silver Lake County Park
Skamokawa Vista Park
Sunny Beach PointThornton A.
Sullivan Park
Washington Park

For further information on Washington's national parks and forests please call 206-220-7450. For more information on Washington's state parks and recreation areas please call 360-753-2027.

Washington State Ferries: Animals are not allowed in terminals, above the car decks, or on the passenger ferries unless they are in a container.

Regulations for British Columbia's National and Provincial Parks

U.S. and Canadian Regulations for Transporting Dogs Across the Border

Dogs and cats from the United States, more than three months of age, must be accompanied by a certificate signed by a licensed veterinarian of Canada or the U.S. certifying that the animal has been vaccinated against rabies during the preceding 36 months. The certificate must have a description of the animal and date of vaccination. For further information contact: Agriculture Canada, 620 Royal Avenue, New Westminster, BC V3L 5A8 (604) 666-8750

British Columbia's National and Provincial Parks

Dogs are allowed in virtually all of British Columbia's national and provincial parks. The following is a list of the provincial parks where dogs **are not allowed**. (While this list might seem extensive, keep in mind that British Columbia has over 20 million acres of land set aside for parks. Of the 380 provincial parks, only 26 of these prohibit dogs.) They are as follows:

Andrews Bay
Bowron Lake
Bull Canyon
Canyon Hot Springs
Creston Valley
Dioisio Point
Emory Creek
Eskers
Fairmont Hot Springs
Garibaldi
Grohman Narrows
Harrison Hot Springs
Kalamalka Lake
Kawkawa Lake
Kickininee
Kootenay Lake
Monkman
Nakusp Hot Springs
Nairn Falls
Niskonlith Lake
Okanagan Falls
Okanagan Mountain
One Island Lake
Stake-McConnell Lakes
Sunnybrae
Whytecliff Park
Wistaria

British Columbia Ferries: BC Ferries will transport your pet free of charge. Pets must remain in your vehicle or be kept on leashes on the vehicle decks as they are not allowed above the car decks.

Helpful Telephone Numbers

American Animal Hospital Association .... (303) 986-2800
American Humane Association .... (800) 227-4645
A.S.P.C.A .... (212) 876-7700
Assistance Dogs International .... (303) 234-9512
Guide Dog Foundation for the Blind .... (800) 548-4337
Humane Society for the U.S. .... (202) 452-1100
National Animal Poison Control Center .... (800) 548-2423
Pet Loss Support Hot line .... (916) 752-4200
Pet Finders .... (800) 666-5678
Tattoo -A-Pet International .... (800) TATTOOS

Index

Albatross B&B 243
Alexis Hotel 281
Andril Fireplace Cottages 114
April Point 331
Beech Tree Manor, The 288
Benson, The 219
Berry Patch Cottage 121
Bird and Hat B&B 227
Bishop Victorian Guest Suites 277
Boathouse, The 308
Campton Place Hotel 140
Carriage House, The 79
Casa Del Mar Inn 161
Casa Laguna Inn 81
Checkers Hotel 87
Circle H Mountain Lodge 312
Clear Creek Farm 204
Cliffside Inn 327
Clift, The 142
Columbia Gorge Hotel 208
Coos Bay Manor 194
Corbett Lake Country Inn 325
Cozy Hollow Lodge 10
Cypress Inn 18
Dancing Coyote Beach 62
Dashwood Manor 358
Edgewater Cottages 231
Eureka Inn, The 43
Fernhill Lodge 323
Fess Parker's Red Lion Resort 166
Flying M Ranch 259
Fossil Bay Resort 335
Four Seasons Biltmore
   (Santa Barbara) 163
Four Seasons Hotel
   (Los Angeles) 89
Four Seasons Hotel
   (Newport Beach) 105
Four Seasons Hotel
   (Vancouver) 341
Four Seasons Olympic Hotel
   (Seattle) 284
Friday Harbor House 258
Grand Okanagan, The 316
Green Spring Box R Ranch, The 188
Greenwood Pier Inn 38

Groveland Cottage 293
Groveland Hotel, The 51
Hallmark Resort 191
Harvest Inn 169
Heritage Inn B&B 157
Hideaway Motel 216
Highlands Inn 20
Historic Sou'western Lodge 290
Holiday Harbor 108
Homestead, The 98
Hood River Hotel 211
Horton Grand Hotel, The 131
Hotel Bel-Air 92
Hotel Charlotte, The 53
Hotel Nikko Beverly Hills 8
Hotel Vancouver 343
Howard Creek Ranch 177
Idabel Lake Resort 318
Inn at Arch Park 199
Inn at Harris Ranch 31
Inn at Ludlow Bay 275
Inn at Rancho Santa Fe, The 128
Inn at the Opera 152
Inn San Francisco, The 144
Isis Oasis 47
Jacksonville Inn 213
Jasmine Cottage-Gray's Retreat 122
Jenner Inn & Cottages 70
Jot's Resort 202
Juan de Fuca Cottages 295
Kalaloch Lodge 254
La Conner Country Inn 264
La Quinta Resort and Club 76
La Valencia Hotel 74
Laburnam Lodge 352
Lac Le Jeune Resort 314
Lake Creek Lodge 225
Lake Crescent Lodge 272
Lake Quinault Lodge 279
Laurel Point 361
Lawrence Welk Resort 41
Lincoln Green Inn-Vagabond
   House Inn 26
Lodge at Pebble Beach, The 117
Loews Coronado Bay Resort 33
Logs Resort, The 249

Madrona Manor 57
Mallory Hotel 221
Manka's Inverness Lodge 63
Mansions Hotel, The 146
Maria Rose B&B, The 354
Mary May Inn, The 159
Meadow Lark Country Inn 14
Mendocino Village Cottages 96
Metropolitan Hotel Vancouver 346
Moby Dick Hotel and
    Oyster Farm 266
National Hotel, The 68
Newport Beach Marriott 103
Norfolk Woods Inn 173
North Beach Inn 251
Ocean Pointe 362
Ocean View House 167
Ocean Wilderness 337
Odell Lake Lodge 197
Ojai Manor Hotel 112
Ojai Valley Inn 110
Old Welches Inn 233
Pan Pacific Hotel Vancouver 348
Pan Pacific Hotel, The 148
Pensione Nichols 286
Pensione San Francisco 150
Pine Valley Lodge 206
Pink Mansion, The 16
Point Reyes Cottages 65
Point-No-Point Resort 339
Puget View Guest House 269
Purple House, The 247
Quaaout Lodge 310
Quail Lodge 24
Quiet Cannon Lodgings 193
Railroad Park Resort 35
Rancho Bernardo Inn 135
Rancho Las Palmas Resort 124
Rancho Valencia Resort 126
Regent Beverly Wilshire, The 6
Ripple Creek Cabins 175
River Run Cottages 320
Riverplace Hotel 222
Riverside, The 189
S.S. Seafoam Lodge 85
Salish Lodge, The 297
Salishan Lodge 200
San Diego Princess Resort 133
San Ysidro Ranch 99

Sandpiper Beach Resort, The 271
See Vue, The 235
Shamrock Lodgettes 237
Sheep Dung Estates 179
Shore Acres Lodge 12
Silver Lode Inn 356
Sooke Harbour House 333
Sorensen's 60
South Fork Moorage 252
Stanford Inn by the Sea, The 94
Starfish Point 217
Stillwater Cove Ranch 72
Sunset House B&B 22
Sunset House B&B 25
Swan-Levine House 49
Tenaya Lodge 47
Thirty-Nine Cypress 119
Tigh-Na-Mara 329
Trinity Alps Resort 83
Tucker House 262
U.S. Grant 137
Vagabond House and
    Lincoln Green Inn 26
Valley Lodge 29
Victorian B&B, The 245
Victorian Inn 102
Vintage Inn 182
Waterfront Centre Hotel 350
Wayfarer Resort, The 229
Wayside Inn 28
Weaver's Inn 45
Webber Place, The 184
Westin St. Francis, The 155
Westwinds Inn and
    Harmony Cottage 256
Wharfside B&B 260
Wine Country Victorian Inn 171
Zaballa House, The 55

Ordering Information

We distribute our books through Ingram, Baker and Taylor, Koen, and Book People. If you are unable to find the *On the Road Again with Man's Best Friend* regional travel guides through these sources or at your local bookstore, please contact the publisher, Dawbert Press, Inc.

Telephone: (800) 93-DAWBERT
Fax: (617) 934-2945
E-Mail: dawbert@thecia.net

On the Road Again with Man's Best Friend - New England
ISBN#: 0-933603-03-7
$17.95

On the Road Again with Man's Best Friend - Mid-Atlantic
ISBN#: 0-933603-08-8
$17.95

On the Road Again with Man's Best Friend - Southeast
ISBN#: 0-933603-06-1
$17.95

On the Road Again with Man's Best Friend - Southwest
ISBN#: 0-933603-05-3
$17.95

On the Road Again with Man's Best Friend - California, Oregon Washington, and British Columbia
ISBN#: 0-933603-04-5
$19.95

On the Road Again with Man's Best Friend - The Best of the United States (release date 11/97)
ISBN#: 0-933603-09-6
$19.95

Look for the Rocky Mountain, Midwest, and the Southern editions in the future!